Social
Pa

Between The Moon and The Sun

A True Story By PreView

The Power of Enlighted Interlocution

Stillness Speaks Between "PreView & KozKozmos "

COPYRIGHT

THE BOOK:

"BETWEEN THE MOON AND THE SUN"

The Power of Enlighted Interlocution
Stillness Speaks Between
"PreView & KozKozmos "

-Social Media Palaver-

AUTHOR:

A True Story by "PreView"

Cover Design and all Artistic Designs
by the Artist:

"PreView"

ISBN 978-9-4642092-4-2

Publisher:

Self published by "PreView"

ARCHIVE

PREFACE

Between The Sun and The Moon is A True Story that played out between two individuals via **Social Media** and willing to live a life of reality beyond illusions which is the Spirit of this age or The Ascension Movement or the reality of moving beyond the tragedies of Earth life in 2020.
As we met like two strangers in Paradise via the recognition of the "like" button, commenting and engaging with interesting posts , I was thinking to just message this entity in Wales/UK and see what his take was on many different topics. I lived in Brussels/Belgium and little did I know that the messages between us moved into a space of many many hours per day for a very long period in time, or years of intense dialogues.
A story between a Bull or Aries and the Horns of a Capricorn went into many deviations as you can imagine, hitting the heat of many sleepless nights with conversations breathing tender compassion, authenticity, presence, genuine, and concrete objects touching the hearts of many. Two bullheaded entities that are so realistic, intuitive pragmatic, sensible, tough, analytical and persistent can often times swing the pendulum of a conversation into a rough and tough ride in which words could easily zap an entity off tracks. I must say as the story began in February 2013 all the way into 2014 and on via phone calls which I recorded and also email messages; that we certainly did not have an easy time, yet a profound conversation of what it takes to move out of the prison bars of earth and up into the rising of the Phoenix or the ascension movement that we are all experiencing.
Many people on **Social Media** and on the planet can easily relate to this story as it explains how come many have been held back on their path from the Matrix into the Crystalline Light Realms which is playing out right now in 2020 and people starting to wake up into TRUTH and how much the pipe dream kept them in a world of pure fantasy versus the reality of living a passionate and empowered life that has many purposes to it.
Although the story moves through many deep rainbows, neither he nor me would ever impoverish what we had to say, neither would we cut our temper down just to please, it was non existent. We would always support each other and regenerate dialogues into something new when discussing, observing, questioning solutions even when they jumped into a conference of less desired degrees!
We were the Pioneers on the Ascension path many are experiencing now in 2020. We were awake since birth, we were abused and mocked by the masses for LIGHT EXPOSES THE THEATRE OF TRUTH, no more no less. May this story assist the forgotten and helpless ones on this plane of existence and assist our children, youth and people of all ages to also awaken to the falseness of Spiritual Growth being promoted in extreme disrespectful ways that have blocked the path for the many that still held on to their purity and integrity. May you find many answers in this story that explains how to rise beyond the constraints of false Spiritual shoes and move into the path of Healing,Truth and empowerment regarding Spirit Science and the new Psychology that rises from the Physics of Divine.
In 2016 I started copying the whole story from the FB messenger platform into a Word-File as I felt I needed to do something with that pretty intense story to say the least. I took me 3 months to just do that as FB does not allow that easily to go back in time on messenger and just copy, it was a continual scrolling back and forth, extremely exhausting hard labour.
I copied 5.000 Word pages or 1.250.000 words!
A few years went by and in 2018, I finally took the decision to bring this story out and started to copy and paste it onto a book platform with a lot of self argumentation, frustration, and pain as so much emotional content that still needed to be released and also, I could copy the conversion perfectly in bits and pieces, yet needed to adapt the entire punctuation and style which took me ages. One of the reasons is because the entity I was communicating with was a little dyslectic, so they don't understand punctuation or setting a sentence in the correct grammatical way meaning that a whole page of explanation could turn out to be one sentence. I was worth going through the trouble and all the tumult. The only thing I left out, because it was literally impossible to copy was the "**emoji**"we often times applied to soften the internal written COMMERCIALS as I termed them in the end. As I worked on the book for many months and rearranged as much as I could with ALL OF THE ORIGINAL CONTENT! something was missing! It felt like going through a trial which literally describes my liberations out of the Tyranny of Earth from 2018 until 2020 and bringing many people to trial for their injustices and blackmail!
When we were hitting the end of 2020, I got an important call from Spirit saying I needed to finish the book no matter what and so I turned on the heat once again and pulled my Hercules embodiment out to take the actions needed to bring a finalization and completion to a story that will assist people on their journey back into Divine Consciousness, Ascension, and THE RETURN INTO THE SACREDNESS OF SPIRIT, SOURCE AND OUR SPARK!

No single word out of this whole story has been left out, I left everything in its Original content to give people the feeling of what it takes to explain how Ascension works, why we need to do this and rise beyond the zombi styles of old living standards into the beauty of Spiritual Essences on equal grounds. Therefor, one can easily trace the hours spent in communications and days left out; although it truly felt like living together as we would rise with the Sun on messenger and say good night when the Stars started to shine their vibes. I also left out some grammatical formality as it
would reduce and devitalize the charm of the chat and embroilment
The journey was incredible strong and surprising with every new angle, twists and turns. May you all enjoy the truth of healing , institute legal procedures and rise with the Origin and repair of our Organism matching the Light and Organic components of Light Earth.
May this adventure, boost, inspire, reassure and encourage the young to stand strong in their Spiritual Power and assist the rising into Justice, Health and Equality!
In times of crisis, entities like myself are being downloaded on this plane of existence to assist humanity on their journey, not as a guru or through the lower degrades of coaching; but in equality and purity to overcome the emotional body and rising the Soul that has rooted into earth back into its heavenly Universal Eternal Seed or pure Spirit Consciousness.
I am a spiritual activist, initiator and high level Universal healer that brings through Spiritual engineering through futuristic psychology that is hardly known on the earth plane as we need to look at many different angles in the mental health and medical industries and assist people that lost their trust, health and their peace because there was nothing that supported human beauty. Opening people up beyond the awakening takes daily commitment to the Divine in order to remember Light Techniques that are available today to eliminate the fog and the many toxins that fragmented the body along the falseness within any informative platform, demanding jobs, and the cruelty of torture that has been hidden.
My individual process began in 2000, as I was looking around in bookstores or on the internet to just find anything. No single spiritual book could please me, I just always rejected all of them and couldn't buy anything to still my hunger for spiritual truth except from some Alice Bailey books I deemed valuable. Anything less felt like nonsense. I just started my process with the working mechanics of dolphins and wales as the Pleiadian's would teach me how to radiate Light through Crystal Grids. After that, magical doors opened as I went through many challenges and extreme difficult experiences that thought me how to deal with the most severe mental diseases and distortions. The path until now was extremely harsh and difficult, yet I don't regret any of it for today the grooves proof beyond measure how it opened the doors of Knowledge and Spiritual Scientific value that are a necessity to restore the soil, the elements and all life on the planet such as the oceans, the animal kingdoms and the air pollutions that takes your breath away.
About 7 years ago, in 2013, I just finished a very difficult cycle or learning zone getting people out of psychiatric institutions and the manipulation or death penalty from medical intoxication which taught me how to move people out of any emotion, especially the imposed fear truck and mentality running backwards. I learned so much, sued academics, and would dedicate most of my time to assist youth and children besides my extreme deep love for animals.
However, throughout the whole process, I had to eliminate many old relationships, ALL family members and people I closed into my heart. It was very hard to say the least, but it gave me glory after many years of endurance, perseverance, tolerance; just to move into the higher levels of courage and strength to bring the reorganization of our biology back to order and prepare it to fuse with the organic composition of the earth. The movement from crisis into flawless victory is attainable for anybody willing to invest in self for the sake of self and all of creation. And YES, the loneliness popped in like popcorn, while I had so much to bring to society and with al the alignments and teachings and revelations I received, my body was exploding with information that needed to go somewhere: so I started to paint my information which happened in a split shift and started to write poetry along the creation of many online workshops and new healing techniques. All of this happened EFFORTLESSLY as I trained myself day and night into the Light. So everything that flowed out of my hands on canvas never had any concept prepared before starting to paint, it felt like channeling and moving into a different space in which I would just apply paint and see what comes out of me. Yet throughout al this processing of information and growth, I needed communication which is actually part of experiencing and elaborating on growth. So I asked the universe to bring through a new friend to fulfill my need to have conversations as going out and having some interaction with people in general was by far not satisfying enough. And thus Mister KOZ KOZMOS came into my life to unfold a very unusual story!

Do we have any assurance of what lays beyond this plane of physical existence? The Universe shows us daily phenomena of something infinitely greater that the EYE can perceive, know and digest.
Despite scientific investigation, mathematicians and geometricians, we have not been able to probe through the mysteries of the invisible realms. The physical Universe is but a small part of creation, letting us know we definitely need to bring through the restoration and repair the broken arrows that allowed worlds of Light to fragment into lesser domains of existence due to monstrous invasions of fallen Deities, Angels, Masters of Light and so much more. We need to re-educate and to train the sensory senses beyond the basics of modern day Science. Spiritual Science shows us how to become one with the vast invisible magnitude and construction of the Universe. In the Ancient worlds everything was lived as above so below in orderly sequences through immense symbolism in Asia and Europe and how we connected to earth as a being. Intense visualization is based on Divine Laws and Orders most have forgotten so much. In 2020 we are rising upon the ladder of the ASCENT through various strategies, along the circuits, vortexes within our Galaxy and other galaxies. Ascension is to be found everywhere today, yet knowledge has been hidden for many eons to be revealed right now as many keys are being discovered and opened for those willing to move beyond illusions all the way into the unknown and bring respect and integrity back to the working mechanics of the electronics of the Universe. Not too many are interested into bringing solutions into a world in total decay as the awakening process was moving far too slow. Many moved into the fields of disappointment as Magical avenues of OLD WAYS did not work any longer, also due to some false Magicians in the UK that infused the population with old methods that lost their power long ago.

When truly looking within and aligning to the Divine and Source within, misinterpreted directions fail to enter , yet education broke our natural habitat and instinct and thus the creation of Soul consciousness took away the capability of living in Spirit Consciousness. This life is all about the ARCHITECTURAL DESIGN OF LIVING IN DIVINE SPIRIT CONSCIOUSNESS and resurrecting everything within through the inversion of fragmentation. Space, the human body and this Solar System are identical, yet not seen in this world as the Solar System broke down as well. The entire repair already took place and so new concepts of the Universe came into existence in which the Universe becomes the Philosophy and logic of knowledge, intelligence and wisdom. It promotes for inward growth rather then scientific complications based on false theories and lack of knowledge. We all need to discover the essential patterns within life and what brings the moralities of Divine Origin back. The Psychic Powers within humans are non existent when not integrated through purification and dedication processes resulting into the perspectives in which people live in pure fiction, not knowing that we need to rebuild The Sacred Universities of Life and bring through initiations that prophet internal power, growth and knowledge. When the Spark has lost its Light by birthing in the mud of artificial nutrition of Earth versus Light Earth, the body looses its qualities rotating around the New Sun/Great Central Sun or gathering of Truth and proof. Because everything in a vast Universe works together in perfect harmony, so the body needs to follow up with the repair that is going on in Space. We need to move from the superficial to the Essentials and the Imperium of the Spheres, we need to remember , starting out with the knowledge within each energetic vortex in the body or chakras all the way into the octavation with the elements and the musical scales. How many today sit a few hours in devotional alignment with Source to find the alignment with the higher degrees of Philosophy ; to create miracles and try to penetrate into the foundation of Light Spectrums that allows for an interplay of various Sources/Forces that bring through many processes and experiences that are mandatory to integrate should we wish to touch our individual purpose or assignments to make this life an interesting and very passionate quest.

We have all been trained to stay in confusion and disharmony through a materialistic world that suffers from greedy economics, political discoloration and mental abuse through which the individual psyche failed to rise above the lower worlds. Yet today, many did rise, many failed and gave up, others are just awakening and too lazy to put respect as the first elixir on their tongue and so the world falls into disgrace, and broken veins creating more mental and physical diseases then ever witnessed in history.

We all need to release ourselves from the painful cycles of imposed necessities and accomplish that which is necessary: THE RETURN INTO LIGHT EMBODIMENT through which everything will come back into order, balance, joy and harmony creating PEACE. We can accomplish this grand task together when moving out of victim consciousness and relearning the Universal laws of LIFE.

There is Universal Intelligence at the SOURCE of all things in creation when applying the Physics and mathematics the Universe brings through with its Modern day Flavors! Communication with many Species, Stars and Universes offer the solutions for the repair of The Eternal Journey in which Scientist should finally become part of Light Sciences that will be implemented in all Faculties of Life and should be integrated in all Faculties in Universities that offer New Economics, New medication through meditation, New political decrees that offer unification and equality.

We must escape the consequences of our own mistakes and still the hunger for Knowledge. Releasing the abuse of knowledge and self sabotage breathes through a generation of new frequencies that shine through the Promised Land in which communities gather beyond the outgrown diagrams.2020 showed us how we all have been fooled as it promoted many people to go backstage and investigate the Self to gain insight in his own nature and overcome any limitation.

The mask exposed through various platforms endangered many people and worlds and suggested the purification or overcoming the tragic consequences of the emotional body that came into creation with the Soul or Ego consciousness. It is bringing the Light in harmony with natural laws and should bring people on a plateau of serious thought and self discovery in which any disease just vanishes.

Change cannot come into existence without doing the rightful things within or doing the various clearing processes that should be strengthened within.There is a large Ley Line between an application and integrating the application. To understand Laws of the universe, we must be willing to learn and study as we need to find out how our electrical Light composition works with Intelligence and Knowledge for the purpose of training the brain versus the deadly movements of the mind that allowed for the control because the mind is host of many unconscious levels that run on automatic pilot such as emotions. We need to see ourselves as part of a Divine Plan that requires responsibility to take on initiations through the purification powers to move out of the severely damaged life streams and restrictions of ambitions. When fight remains stronger then strive , there is no movement out of the dark ages and the domination of consciousness. Today we need enlightened leaders that serve our world with the highest aspects of truth and new educational systems that promote maturity and life giving realities in which corruption fails to exist. Ascending the physical needs proper instruction and follow up alignments to recreate the Eternal bonding vibrations and to become part of the Infinite Universal principles.

The longest journey in history is indicating that we can only give all of our Light Selves in surrender to Divine Communication to find our Domestic Light Space within the Houses of Light right here and now on planet LIGHT EARTH streaming through the necessary PEACE services that will resurrect everybody beyond the cure for the suffering and difficulties.
Recognizing the real answers that may come through the growth processes and listening TO THE VOICE OF EVOLUTION WITHIN teaches the Self, the young and the elderly the principles of life and values to prepare them for strong ethics and the joy of living a worthy life minus any possible attachments.

Relationships, connections, business related teams that stream on worthy platforms of co-creation, empowerment and self discovery while opening the I AM PRESENCE to its fullest capacity which is opening up into the many libraries and faculties of Modern day inspirited Philosophy is what will expose the return into Spirit Consciousness.

Turning this page, you will find the Original pictures of me, as PreView and him, as Koz Kozmos as we started out this long journey of communicating Light Technology. Both pictures are still to be found on our FB pages.

This is my Original Social Media picture
as we started out the conversation.
It represents me as a Red Ray Sword carrier.
""PreView""

This is his Original SocialMedia picture
as we started out the conversation
It represents him holding the Light of Earth within his hands.
""Koz Kozmos""

This is my Heart and Nerve,
My Son who just loved to Walzer through
whenever the dialogues were catching the fire vibe!
A Scorpio Water Protector!

EVERYTHING BETWEEN THE MOON AND THE SUN

Should smell like sweet tunes

as troops align

to design the New Floods

with colors bright and shining

like sea creatures that know their mining lets break the

dams that holds no breath into its mighty detail

lets shock and rock the change

with the incoming moons' D'Light

lets move it kool & wild

like a mermaids' tail

that knocks inside your hearts' sails lets activate the

winds of new directions and visionary perfection

into that Dome that cannot hold to old.

RELATIONSHIPS: THE SUBJECT OF THIS AGE! "OPENING TO LOVE OR CONVENIENCE ? "

Understanding that everything is just a PROCESS may be alarming for some. As always from understanding comes relief and release and dis-EASE free embodiment.

RELATIONSHIPS HAVE THAT INTRINSIC FACTOR THAT COMES DOWN TO SELF LOVE; IF YOU TAKE IT DOWN TO FRIENDSHIPS, WE OFTEN HAVE MANY MANY HIDDEN FEATURES THAT WANT TO HOLD IT ALL TOGETHER FOR THE SAKE OF THE FRIENDSHIP WHICH IS GOING TO BREAK US MORE THEN ENJOYING THE FRIENDSHIP IN THIS AQUARIUS AGE WHICH IS ACTUALLY THE FIRST GOLDEN AGE in our evolution. IT IS ALL ABOUT COMMUNICATIONS AND DEEP TRUTHS.

Oftentimes we do not tell it like it is because of the fear of losing somebody and also we are all not on the same path to embrace truth on any level. Some would like to keep on hiding and some are really really tired of that and do a whole lot of work to move out of the falseness, arrogance, comfort zone and manipulative conversations to upgrade into the light they truly are. For other parties, that may appear to be a hard approach or they STARTED TO SEE THE DEEPER LEVELS of what kept them into friendships which appears to be CONVENIENCE.

Convenience to fill up empty spaces, convenience to get through hard times, convenience to express the many angers, fears, injustices and sadness one experiences with society even though the bottom layers are proof of what we have sent out to create.
And all we wish for in a certain friendship is some kind of solace, some kind of relief to see things from a different perspective and just somebody who understands us, agrees with what we we have to say.

But when that particular person or Essence does not agree with us any longer, the friendship brakes because the confrontation with the deeper level of SELF TRUTH through that person becomes UNACCEPTABLE even if done in such a loving way. That may hurt a lot but when understanding that you and that particular friend are no longer on the same timeline, meaning one of you upgraded and is willing to see truth within self and breaking free from what no longer serves, half the healing has begun closing in on themselves or becoming a hermit because they think there is something wrong with them when losing so many friendships .
BUT IT IS NOT !!! It is only the transition from old friendships into the new ones that takes a little rest and reflection, but ENSURE your self that you are on the right path. That is the only worthy INSURANCE we could bring through. The best way to do this is to refrain from judging, not even having an opinion and just saying : ok, that was that, I handled it well , let's see how I can can embrace the new wonders coming into my life. WISHING THEM WELL AND GOODBYE ON EVERY LEVEL

BE GRATEFUL, FOR IT MEANS YOU HAVE ACCEPTED THAT YOU HAD TO LEAVE WHAT KEEPS YOU FROM MOVING FORWARD AND THAT IS A FIRST BIG STEP. IF YOU CAN DO IT WITH ONE PERSON, THE OTHERS WILL BE EASIER BECAUSE IN THE END , THEY WILL KEEP YOU IN A CONFUSED AND DENSE ENVIRONMENT.

When it is time to leave certain relations, it does not mean you love them less although they often see it that way and you should not be concerned about that for in the END, TRUTH IS TRUTH AND IT WILL BE KNOWN. It simply means your brain is ready to clear that space and invite those who actually are there to move on that same path forward.

IT DOES MEAN YOU GET TO KNOW THY SELF BETTER and need to understand there is absolutely no reason to step into obsessions, fears, guilt, shame, or any lower emotion.
It always comes down to our responsibility to stay in balance and giving to self (SELF LOVE) first and see how your true essence is responds.

PREPARE FOR THIS PAPARAZZI!

Many are TRYING to reconnect with their Original Essence and bump into wonderful bonds which mass consciousness would refer to as: soul mates, soul family,
soul bond , anything soul.... And yes of course there is that bond from former lifetimes and even remembrance of what you were and experienced back then. BUT ! many times these connections also have to be eliminated for you to move forward as they are tied to many lifetimes in soul consciousness and this Aquarian age is all about moving out of the soul. These connections come in as a test for you to understand where you are at or to remember certain potential GIFTS you had forgotten about or to remember things you need at this particular time in your life. So people often time agree to an intimate relationship with such a soul mate and get deeply disappointed because there is the consciousness of EXPECTATION when you love somebody that deep. And that is perfectly fine when you do not want to do the hard work of moving forward and eliminating all the pins and needles from mind control or birthing into soul which is pure EGO, and every hassle that comes around the corner to assist you to keep the self off track or in the mud. If you truly would like to remember your Original Self according to ancient times, it would be IMPERATIVE to reconnect to the ANCIENTS OF DAYS and the knowledge of how to do that in order to understand The Recent of Days. In other words, this was your SPIRIT SELF, then we were all drown into the Soul Self OR EGO SELF, and now we need to climb these ladders back into full time SPIRIT SELF which is a consciousness that does not know ego/soul and therefore also the reason why many are clearing out endlessly on a daily level. Today however, there is much valuable information and alignments available to assist your path and devotional time to the Divine.NOBODY WILL DO IT FOR YOU! The internal work can be assisted, yet the work within self comes from self.

Those movement from 5thD (the clearing, confrontations with many synchronicities) into the 6thD and consciously working on getting the physical / mental/psychological issues lined out will meet the IN-SPIRITED BONDS OR FAMILY OR ETERNAL MATES and others Species which will make up a huge difference in your life; for those communications are truly spaced out on high intelligence and SPIRIT LOGIC.
Your brainwaves would have brought you there through spiritual techniques that rewire patterns and sets the road on the deeper internal work-out plans. It is certainly not easy to leave somebody when you are in love. But the lesson here is to really CONNECT TO YOUR SOURCE, realign and learn about the love for humanity, and learn to DETECT what is best for you for broken wings are really the worst torture one can have or experience. I hope this gives a bit more clarity. Do not forget each individual has unique experiences and needs to make unique choices.

CLEARING THE FABRIC OF EMOTIONAL ABUSE TAKES TIME IN ORDER TO BREAK ALL THE BARRIERS AND BREAK FREE ONTO THE OTHER SIDE OF TIME OR MIDNIGHT.

I THINK WE HAVE ALL DONE OUR TIME ON EARTH , IT IS TIME TO MUTATE , CLAIM YOUR FREEDOM AND ASK THE CELESTIAL/ UNIVERSAL BUS DRIVERS TO PICK YOU UP AND DRIVE YOU HOME ! I'M NOT JOKING.

EVERYTHING COMES DOWN TO THE LADY/GENT BROKEN VEINS

Once these Books of Internal Knowledge are being written through the hands of entities willing to go all the way, everybody will be born again ! Because these broken arrows and all these relationship problems or peoples looking for that perfect eternal mate (whom might just be waiting for you around the corner) comes down to that simple equation for when that is repaired, almost anything repairs at the flick of a finger. Yet, it requires quite some understanding and processes or gateways to go through that prepares you for your ORIGINAL ESSENCE which is the merger of the male/ female component into a NEW ORDER aligned to the Divine. Understanding may be as simple as giving some reflection to our bodies and how the Lady/Gent components broke our Solar Bodies – and thus the birthing into soul consciousness which will be explained in the book.
So it all start off from the repair kit of the Solar body and becoming that sun stream again with the Celestial and Universal bodies. This requires your Essence to move into the Higher Dimensional Realms of Light but is done with ease and grace these days . Once the BIG FIGHT with SELF is over, there is no end to what you can create and become the CREATOR SELF once again.
However, we need to make many healthy choices that seems to be the hardest struggle ever witnessed on earth and reason why so many people stay in relationships that are no longer beneficial on any level which BREAKS the body massively.

The hardest LEY LINE TO MOVE THROUGH here would be your Free Will that keeps people in the killing fields . Living In Divine Will offers solutions all of the time. Moving from one relationship into the other for the sake of moving forward and learning from it, is OLD BELIEF and is not going to cut it these days because rising on the Divine Timeline today requires being set free from the long and winding roads of yesteryears and believing that something less then that perfect Eternal Partner can relieve you for a while. It is and has never been that way, no matter how hard it is when being in love ! Because you will be hit over and over again with truths that will cause more fractures once again. WE ARE EXACTLY HERE TO HEAL ALL OF THE OLD FRACTURES!

Today we are altogether being catapulted into new information and technology, yet so many refrain from it for the solo reason of FEAR! Question Self and ask yours elves where that fear comes from, how did you cultivate it and why is it holding you back. Eliminating past relationships and its hormonal content is easy today and necessary because in the end they will break you apart and gives you an empty dish to feed from.

Taking care of your relationship with your Spark Self, your Spirit Self and your Source Self has the capacity to direct your LIVING LIFE relationships with all the elements into the halls of wisdom, co-creation and Light embodiment through Light nutrition.
Yet, not everybody wants a relationship, not everybody wants enlightenment.
As this Planet Earth is moving into its Ascension, Light Body is required, knowledge about our energy fields or electrical output and input is required for us to understand and move with what the Universes bring through.
Where will you be? On this side or on the other side?

LET'S OPEN THESE CONVERSATIONS!

Between

The Moon and The Sun

A True Story By PreView

The Power of Enlighted Interlocution

Stillness Speaks Between "PreView & KozKozmos "

Conversation started February 22, 2013

2/22, 9:52pm**Pre View**
Hey u & u and all of u, why do u not open yur posts to public ?
What is there to be afraid of ,,, ?
FB should not have the button "share" because it means people cannot come up with something original themselves and they lose the passion to look subjects up and make them more penetrating and
the button "like" should also be eliminated: it creates boredom & laziness, but comments should get u somewhere, right ?
February 23, 2013
2/23, 6:29pm **Koz Kozmos**
Thank you for all the feed back Pre View...
keep on cosmik trukkin'
2/23, 7:49pm **Pre View**
Nice expression ! thxxxx
2/23, 7:50pm **Koz Kozmos**
hi
just got back
2/23, 7:51pm **Pre View**
Hi , u, got back from ? The Suns dial ?
2/23, 7:51pm **Koz Kozmos**
the suns dial ? was on the phone
I'm in Wales in the UK originally from Orion
2/23, 7:54pm**Pre View**
Well, I work a lot with the planetary system and getting to know that ,loading the sun ,
orion and stuff as we need to break free from the old solar system- as people know this - we actually have to get
that out of the circulation system, but that is a very hard shift and is exhausting me for 3 days already, (sorry - technical , but fun - then we understand) right ?
2/23, 7:54pm **Koz Kozmos**
mmmmmmm
2/23, 7:54pm **Kozmos**
and wot is its purpose
and what do u achieve by removing it
2/23, 7:57pm **Pre View**
oh boy, this would take me a book for an answer, just take yur helicopter bike and have a
drink over here, that would ease the communiFICATION
2/23, 7:57pm **Koz Kozmos**
every level of consciousness chuffin hek
2/23, 7:58pm **Pre View**
chuffin hek ? do not understand ,
2/23, 7:58pm **Koz Kozmos**
its a daft
do u get daft ? like saying
fuck man thats crazy
2/23, 7:59pm **Pre View**
Well getting out of the soul means u need to eliminate all lower ego patterning, fractures, fissures in the brain and stuff ....
2/23, 7:59pm **Kozmos**
hard to do
2/23, 7:59pm **Pre View**
i've been working with this for 10 years now, and it is hard work but the rewards of moving into crystalline singing brains are so beautiful

2/23, 8:00pm**Koz Kozmos**
especially as we're controlled to be meat for the wheel
2/23, 8:00pm
Pre View
Hard to do, YESS, QUITE A JOB, i'm teaching this in workshops, but retreats would be better to give people a sense of what it means to move in the Creator type of vibration in which they can find their true worth and independency from the control mechanics or that sun light that doesn't shine as bright as the night...
2/23, 8:00pm **Koz Kozmos**
getting out of the soul?
where are u...may i ask
2/23, 8:02 **Pre View**
Belgium
This is easier as u get into a group consent ,
so the NRG lifts Belgium
2/23, 8:01pm **Koz Kozmos**
what is group consent? soul groups ?
2/23, 8:02pm
Pre View
consent = many people gathering for the same purpose and changing the environment in a split shift or so.
It is all about holding and grounding the crystal gifts through the Crystal Gridzzzz and buzz it,,
Well, we all birthed into soul consciousness otherwise we would not understand earth plane people which is giving me a hard time now as i shifted a lot;;;
but everything needs to be understood.
2/23, 8:04pm **Pre View**
Hey Koz, need to work, get back to u, but consider if working with what u are, u will understand the universe, alignment is all that mattersssssssssss
2/23, 8:05pm **Koz Kozmos**
i asked u earlier were u are on the planet
2/23, 8:05pm **Pre View**
I replied BELGIUM
2/23, 8:05pm **Kozmos**
ok thank u and KOOL all the best
keep shifting
missed the reply
2/23, 8:06pm **Pre View**
This is blue ray peaceful measure, great intelligence,,,,
yeah sure i'll take u into my shifts for fun cya cya cya
2/23, 8:06pm
Koz Kozmos
ok i want to shift byeeeeeeeeeeeeeeeeeeee I'm not sure what i am
February 24, 2013 2/24, 10:57am **Pre View**
U'll know who u are in due time, as for now, enjoy the ride,,,,
2/24, 4:18pm
Koz Kozmos
How will ~<O>~ know? the ride is annoying and I'm feeling nausea...
2/24, 5:13pm **Pre View**
The more nausea, the better, u are clearing out,,,, (u wanted me to take u into shifts, right; only maybe u did not take that for granted,,,,
2/24, 5:16pm **Koz Kozmos**
expand....?
2/24, 5:30pm **Pre View**
Well, I work a lot with energy as it is all we are,
meaning grids, geometry, math, human energy fields;.

But all of that takes great study, endurance, time ..... so i can do a lot,,, I do give sessions, lessons, meditation, workshops, Lots of times I'm Arting my brain out through paint,,,, Main thing is people learn to upgrade themselves through the techniques i give, Everybody needs independency in order to get the
18
info they source right from our Source.....
i've been working with this for 10 years now, and it is what it is
2/24, 5:34pm **Koz Kozmos**
Ok....carry on
2/24, 5:37pm **Pre View** I
if u know a lot about hip hop, i would appreciate a lot if u'd post more of that, Thxxx, Eliminate your MIND, get your INFO and then squeeze my brain
2/24, 5:51pm **Koz Kozmos**
OK
2/24, 6:02pm **Koz Kozmos**
I'm a Gansta Bard and have come to destroy the matrix hood and save Gia FREE STYLE HOMIE 2/24, 6:06pm **Pre View**
Wow, tell me more, u sure do have style ! love it
February 24, 2013 2/24, 11:40pm **Koz Kozmos**
thank u Pre View thank You*
February 25, 2013
2/25, 9:06am **Pre View**
u'r most welcome, wil kommen, welkom, bienvenido
February 25, 2013 2/25, 2:20pm **Koz Kozmos**
Meek
2/25, 4:59pm **Pre View** What is meek?
2/25, 7:37pm **Koz Kozmos** meek
1. Showing patience and humility; gentle.
2. Easily imposed on; submissive. Matthew 5:5 Blessed are the meek, for they will inherit the earth
that bit was from the bible
2/25, 4:59pm **Pre View**
Earth is the last planet ready to ascend ,,,,
2/25, 8:52pm **Koz Kozmos**
'it sure is the last planet : ready for ascent' approx WHEN?
Humble
2/25, 8:54pm **Pre View**
`humility right, i'm working on that,thxx
All that is happening right now over the planet = the ascent, the planet is not taking it anymore, that is why people who cannot handle the intensity of facing their own debris are leaving also,,,, i'd better
write a book,,, How do I know, study, alignment, i'm very grateful to have u in my life, but all yur questions (interesting) take a lot of answers, give me some time to go all of ur comments ..... 2/25, 8:58pm **Koz Kozmos**
pmsssss...
that its ok pre View
only answer what u want to
i'm aware of what u'r saying
but much of it comes from a slightly more sophisticated version of the new age mind control
programming
2/25, 9:02pm **Pre View**
What did i tell u days gone ? I mean on your FB profile posts...
Eliminate your MIND, get YOUR INFO and then squeeze my brain, that'll be fun
2/25, 9:04pm **Koz Kozmos**
I don't understand
2/25, 9:09pm **Pre View**
ok the mind has been created by people by stepping into density = fear, deceit, manipulation, anger - all these emo things.

When the massive mind is eliminated u step from emotion into sensitivity and that is a hard school but also fun 'cause u don't understand negativity no longer (i used to teach this in workshops over a week-end) meaning u change 360°, we change all of the time, that is evolution

I love being in a seminar just because of the energies, the shifts that happen and how it teaches us that there is so much to relearn when it comes to energy applications.

2/25, 9:10pm **Pre View**
Are u proton or electron (male or female)

2/25, 9:10pm **Koz Kozmos** i'm Bruces double or
maybe he's mine

2/25, 9:12pm **Pre View** adorable answer !

2/25, 9:12pm **Koz Kozmos** male U ?
may is aki

2/25, 9:12pm **Pre View**
that is obvious, just testing, there's no single female talking this way,,, yess describe

2/25, 9:15pm **Koz Kozmos** back and fore cooking , sorry
ASK not saki, **i'm a deslexxxxik wizzzard, i can't spell**

2/25, 9:16pm **Pre View**
haha, yep i'm electron, but u knew ,i'm sure

2/25, 9:17pm **Koz Kozmos** female ?

2/25, 9:17pm **Pre View** FEMALE it is

2/25, 9:18pm **Koz Kozmos**
i was'nt sure
ok, no need to swear
anyways
2/25, 9:20pm **Pre View**
ok eliminate please, Fb is an open book, nobody needs knowing if we're male or female.
2/25, 9:20pm **Koz Kozmos**
spiritually, androgynous changelings from the rebirth meat machine
with the greatest respect madam
u may still be a guy. I don't have any pics
2/25, 9:22pm **Pre View**
well the age we are living in is all about the merging of the male/female vibes, recreating the original Seedcell, the movement into new light tech.
2/25, 9:23pm **Koz Kozmos**
but if u look at the Bruce (Springsteen)video i posted
thats me, Genesis P-Orridge has done a dreadful job at the merge
2/25, 9:24pm **Pre View**
So language is very important (english hebrew arameic, latin)
2/25, 9:25pm **Koz Kozmos**
the WORD VIRUS gets on my nerves
and as i sais, i'm a deslexic wizard i can't spell 2/25,
9:26pm **Pre View**
no prob, u have a great brain !
2/25, 9:26pm **Koz Kozmos** thanks u 'r brain is good 2
2/25, 9:29pm**Pre View**
there's not many who understand quick in different ways, u do,
thank u !
2/25, 9:34pm **Koz Kozmos**
i get the transformation into the eye magination
but i need proof and i'm sick of the Earth Hex and the curse of the toxic lifes
2/25, 9:48pm **Koz Kozmos**
Hi , going offline
2/25, 9:48pm **Koz Kozmos**
thankz for all the catch chat
25, 9:48pm **Pre View**
ok then, thx for talking
2/25, 9:48pm **Koz Kozmos**
* byeeeeeeeeeee

MY INTERNALS (These are after thoughts I had after each interaction with Koz Kozmos): I was very happy with this first 'getting to know' each other conversation as it ex-cluded the most mundane tea chat. It felt like I had known him for billions of years. Just another Universal family member. I had no idea where this conversation would lead us; as I couldn't figure out his experiences and knowledge concerning human evolution and the removal of anything that stands in the way of the planets' transformation along its people. Questions where rising. Why is it that we connect easily to some people, and some are just impossible to even have a conversation with. Somehow I felt the synchronicities were very important and the connections we have about music In the end we just need to recalibrate our Essence into Light consciousness and many Light avenues. So, I was just thinking about making this an interesting quest with Koz Kozmos and learn about different angles concerning Spirit. The only reason i connecting was because of his interesting posts on FB which were not mundane, yet brought me into questioning many different paths when it comes to ascension.
We are all vibrating with the Sun and the moon frequencies!

Artwork: By "PreView" : Moon Union

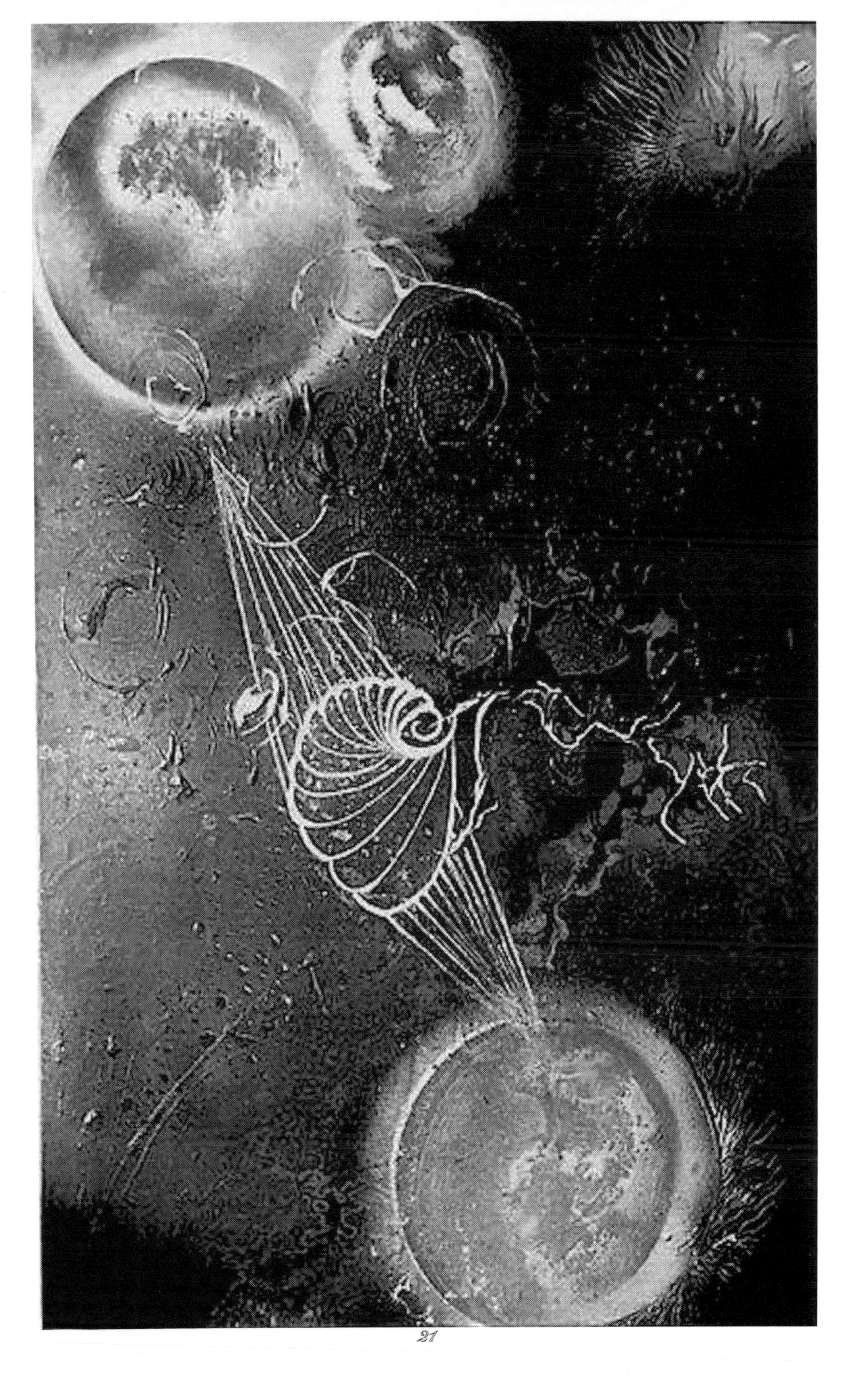

2/25, 9:50pm **Pre View**
If u get the transformation thr Eye imagination,
why do u need proof?
U know, I feel exactly the same,
close myself off all the time while knowing it is time to speak out, ...
2/25, 9:51pm **Koz Kozmos**
MUSIC: AFRICA BAMBAATAA : GOT THAT VIBE

MY INTERNALS: THIS WAS THE FIRST SONG HE POSTED AND MANY FOLLOWED:THEY WERE ALL VERY IMPORTANT. I AM NOT POSTING THE YOUTUBE LINKS HERE AS HE DID; FOR MANY OF THESE SONGS MAY NOT BE ACCESSIBLE ANY MORE.
I ENCOURAGE EVERYBODY READING THIS BOOK TO LISTEN TO THE SONGS AND EVENTUALLY MAKE A YOUTUBE SONG LIST OF THEM FOR THEY ARE IMPORTANT TO UNDERSTAND THE WHOLE STORY.
WE ALL MUST TUNE IN WHERE WE SOUNDED OUT!

2/25, 9:51pm **Koz Kozmos** CU
2/25, 9:51pm **Pre View** thx !
2/25, 9:51pm **Koz Kozmos**
listen to the lyik , DIG DEEP, lyric*
People hate me
2/25, 9:51pm **Pre View** ok
February 26, 2013 2/26, 10:09pm **Pre View**
Hello Koz, when people hate u, it means you'r on the right track, got the same thing here, people would say things like: she's weird, she's crazy, she' got too many guts, hate her because of her guts , her
impenetrable talk etc..... still people are attracted ; its the energy they seek to uplift themselves. So we only exist when thy need help, but i erased that of my timeline. I've been through a lot of stuff like any one else, but the hardest parts make us grow even though we wish for a lot more heart energy, we are always capable to realign and upgrade from that. And yes I fell deep after 10 years,
but that is just all about opening new phone lines; and start to REMEMBER what really matters in how we develop living light streams. We are all loners, and some day these loners will make a fabulous crew erasing all density over the earth plane :
that will be our ARC built for the age of Peace.
So when u stand alone in Wales, know it is for a very valuable reason.
Find your treasure chest.
2/27, 12:39pm **Koz Kozmos**
I've tried and become a hermit again..
spent most of my life alone its more fun that way...
too many persona perverts....
to many basic 'humans' etc
also, i feel i may have been targeted,,,etc,
people don't know who i am to hate me
2/27, 12:54pm **Pre View**
Keep it that way ! remember there's more of us uniting,
i've learned to make fun of being a target so
people really get confused. Use what u get in an even more interesting way ....
That is termed recreation and not allowing negativity, yet turning it around....
The Monsters of the Universe target anyone developing Light,
protect your being!
2/27, 1:25pm **Koz Kozmos**
I meant targeted by some darker force,
not stupid humans,
dark as in the cliche duality

2/27, 1:42pm **Pre View**
Being a target is always thr dark forces ,
it is up to u to shine stronger and teach yourself how to protect
yourself, meaning u need to step out of the old solar levels & work with grids a lot
(smoky quartz crystal with Hebrew letter tav on it is a great protection,
also keeps the throat open and teaches u the power of the word returned).
Otherwise, just communicate & ask for a team of celestials to bring u the info needed
to upgrade and maybe they'll protect you until then.
Align to teams and spirit guides and ask for protection until you can hold
the technique and commitment to your Source...
You need to start understanding energy!!!
When darkness can get in, it means u have an important issue to clear,
otherwise it would not have entrance
(Yess, we all have many levels to clear, but
until we'r not there - find some way ...)
I'm sure u can do it Koz !
embrace what u already achieved,,,,
2/27, 1:48pm **Koz Kozmos**
I'm huggin what I've achieved
Majik....bores me and mine is wasted on this dimension '
smoky quartz crystal with Hebrew letter tav on it is a great protection' ?
o no
as to the throat being open mmmm
cast a throat of spells thank u for feed back
2/27, 3:06pm **Pre View**
you're absolutely welcome !
i love spells, thy come through the lavender ray Merlin
(Le Merlin - Lumuria)
I wrote a lot of spells in the past, might post them some day,
or publish, don't know yet
When u choose to move into the 7th dimension ,
2/27, 3:32pm **Koz Kozmos**
spells are for teen witches and is the 87h dimension next to the 6th
February 28 11:06pm **Pre View**
Fb is asking for my details and blocked me for a while
2/28, 11:07pm **Koz Kozmos**
i may deativate soon
2/28, 11:09pm **Pre View**
no prob, FB is not important ....
good night though
2/28, 11:10pm **Koz Kozmos**
good night Pre
2/28, 11:10pm **Pre View**
Gracia for your life
/28, 11:11pm **Koz Kozmos**
not sure if your' allowed to have a life here
2/28, 11:12pm **Kozmos**
MUSIC: Scott Walker / My death

2/28, 11:13pm **Pre View**
listening
28, 11:14pm **Koz Kozmos**
your knuckles look red
have you been punching matrix slaves in their dying souls
The man who wrote that song...

2/28, 11:15pm **Pre View**
Beautiful, i will listen to the song ! Its beautiful
I don't punch !, knowing no soul would understand,
i know u do,
2/28, 11:16pm **Koz Kozmos**
i've just remembered the lyrics ,
they where from a guy in Belgium.
What is btw
2/28, 11:16pm **Pre View**
who from ?
2/28, 11:16pm **Koz Kozmos**
Jacques Brel
2/28, 11:17pm **Kozmos**
Jacques brel / Ne me quitte pas
2/28, 11:17pm **Koz Kozmos**
the guy who wrote "my death ",
made it big in France
2/28, 11:17pm **Pre View**
like him a lot,
he is telling it all very heartfelt
2/28, 11:17pm **Koz Kozmos**
My Death is poetry, the best poets can't spell
2/28, 11:18pm **Pre View**
Koz, yur bautiful do not forget that, do not forget yur vibes
'Ne me quitte pas' is so strong,
do u understand French?
2/28, 11:19pm **Koz Kozmos**
to good looking for this dimension of fools
but thank you Madam
2/28, 11:19pm **Pre View**
move up, get out of soul level man !!!!! I
2/28, 11:21pm **Koz Kozmos**
am not madam, just being me,just messing about
2/28, 11:21pm **Pre View**
hey u, don't fool urself,,,
u got brains
2/28, 11:21pm **Kozmos**

MUSIC : SCOTT WALKER : IF U GO AWAY

2/28, 11:22pm **Koz Kozmos**
brains get in the way of dealing with idiots and liars
2/28, 11:22pm **Pre View**
all the songs i'm listining to since i was 16 is what u post,
nice synchronization,,,,,,
2/28, 11:22pm **Koz Kozmos**
Scott Walker did an LP of Brel songs,kool
2/28, 11:23pm **Pre View**
Don't know much about Jacques Brel,,,
and yes, he's got a very strong voice,
voices are important when integrating songs into our system
the wrong songs may twist our nervous system around,,,,

2/28, 11:23pm **Pre View**
Well, i always give 1000 % trust, but that turned out bad last years,
People just lie for NO reason, or just fear of being judged I guess. Truth comes in handy because if you load it into your body, people will automatically speak truth.. is what I learned over the past few months.
2/28, 11:24pm **Koz Kozmos**
no more trust
2/28, 11:24pm **Pre View**
I trust u, why else would i have spoken to u
2/28, 11:25pm **Koz Kozmos**
not me, people who get u down and people who hate you
2/28, 11:25pm **Pre View**
" if u go away", that song : the original is from somebody else right ?
2/28, 11:25pm **Koz Kozmos**
Brel must have done it first, but many cover versions
2/8, 11:26pm **Pre View**
i attracted u because my sourcing allignment brought me to u because of your knowledge in th music industry...
2/28, 11:27pm **Koz Kozmos**
did i get your question right ?
2/28, 11:27pm **Pre View**
always , hahaha
please sing me a song that breaks through my old nervous system?
2/28, 11:28pm **Koz Kozmos**
PEACE AND NOISE
speak again, going ofline, pc's make my eyes dry
2/28, 11:29pm **Pre View**
why ?
2/28, 11:29pm **Koz Kozmos**
mmmmmmmmm, long story
2/28, 11:29pm **Pre View**
One more song please before u go
2/28, 11:29pm **Koz Kozmos** one more song lol
2/28, 11:29pm **Pre View**
YESSSS
2/28, 11:29pm **Koz Kozmos**
as they say
2/28, 11:30pm
2/28, 11:30pm **Kozmos**
MUSIC : DISSECTION/GOD OF FORBIDDEN LIGHT

2/28, 11:30pm **Pre View**
LOVE THE WAY U POST,
on social media I mean to say
but the word 'lol' no thanx,
I would never apply that,
does not shine well within you either.
Words matter more than we give tit attention.

2/28, 11:30pm **Koz Kozmos**
catch u again, byeeeee
2/28, 11:30pm Pre View
maybe, what will be, will be
2/28, 11:31pm Pre View
that song just gives me the picture i got from myself, fithing the neighborhood or just resetting the Hood in crystalline fields of peace and joy!
2/28, 11:32pm **Koz Kozmos**
one more; take care
2/28, 11:32pm **Koz Kozmos**
MUSIC: HAPPINESS/KEN DODD
2/28, 11:33pm Koz Kozmos
The Light bringer from the Dark machine
2/28, 11:36pm **Pre View**
U got a precious gift, u can shift from one cs to another easily, that is fabulous Thank u for that heart of yours, thank u
March 1, 2013
3/1, 6:05pm **Koz Kozmos**
cs ?
3/1, 6:18pm **Pre View**
sorry, CS = consciousness ,
I use this abbreviation in my writings all the time ....
as everything is just cs
3/1, 6:29pm **Koz Kozmos**
Black Sun (occult symbol)
3/1, 6:47pm **Pre View**
I don't trust the google harddrive, i'll see what my softdrive gets,,,
3/1, 7:45pm **Koz Kozmos**
I don't trust anything, everything is too much twisted
3/2, 7:59am **Pre View**
trust factor is all u have even if ,,,, it is the nucleus of hope,
so i give it again & again & with it grows responsible actions, I think it is quite interesting,,,
We need to at least trust the universe, our Source,
otherwise you get lost and living in a dead zone instead of Living Light fields
March 4, 2013
3/4, 7:25pm **Koz Kozmos**
YO!
u keeping giving me advice?

MARCH 2013

3/4, 7:27pm **Koz Kozmos**
ENNUI!
3/4, 7:28pm **Pre View**
vous êtes ennuyez, par quoi ?
3/4, 7:28pm **Koz Kozmos**
can't speak French, but the word is appropriate
3/4, 7:29pm **Pre View**
if things get boring, u learned what u needed to learn,
start to apply it for once!
move on & believe in what gets u exited ,
what is your passion about?
3/4, 7:30pm **Koz Kozmos**
a feeling of utter weariness my passions have been destroyed
move to where I gave it a good go
3/4, 7:33pm **Pre View**
pick up where u left, see beyond what u really want,
u know i understand ,
i'v been in this war-zone for over a year,
it completely destroyed all that was precious to me,
Yet I needed to learn how society runs its tracks...
I needed to learn how the evil forces attack people, I needed to learn how people relate to each other in falseness ,
I needed to learn how to deal with entities in the psychotic departments,,,
So, I'm very grateful I did, even though a lot needs to reset in my brains,
it was fun to interact and
understand that people see you as an entity that speaks universal languages
3/4, 7:36pm **Pre View**
Maybe you need to trigger where your consciousness was at a certain point in time,
what exactly did u do, or what got u downhill ?
3/4, 7:36pm **Koz Kozmos`**
wot does that mean ?
too much info, i'm targeted by the dark team,
they tried to wipe me again as they do when you'r born,
going slow ....
Pc problems....
i'll post some songs
3/4, 7:39pm **Pre View**
ok take yr time, there's always a reason why this & that, no worries
3/4, 7:41pm
Koz Kozmos

MUSIC: THE INCREDIBLE STRING BAND/THE CIRCLE IS UNBROKEN
28
MUSIC: PETER HAMMILL/A LOUSE IS NOT A HOME

3/4, 7:45pm **Koz Kozmos** 2 more, maybe
3/4, 7:46pm **Pre View**
ok go, different styles ....
Koz Kozmos
MUSIC: STEVIE NIX - STAND BACK

3/4, 7:50pm **Pre View**
Like Stevie a lot.
Now play all of these songs together at once ?
Do they match ?
what do u think ?

Koz Kozmos
They go into the seas that have no shores Haunted by that same closed door Looking up at skies on fire Leaving nothing left of us
To discover
I need a PC fixer
3/4, 7:51pm **Pre View**
nice expression,
What's the prob ?
3/4, 7:51pm
Koz Kozmos
Stevie needs my help
3/4, 7:51pm **Pre View**
why IS that ?
3/4, 7:52pm **Koz Kozmos**
she's too caught up in romantic love and her faded girlishness ,,, she needs to become the crone 3/4, 7:52pm **Pre View**
crone ?
3/4, 7:53pm **Koz Kozmos**
maiden mother crone
3/4, 7:54pm **Pre View**
that's a bit like in my mediation classes, everybody feels upside down 'cause it is done with hiphop & rock vibes and that truly brings through speedy changes in body/ brainzzzz
3/4, 7:54pm **Koz Kozmos**
pagan speak
i'm not a pagan 3/4, 7:54pm **Pre View**
what is a pagan, need a dictionary ,,,
ok got it
3/4, 7:55pm **Koz Kozmos**
neo pagan wicca etc
3/4, 7:56pm **Pre View**
alright, don't know about that stuff, but I do know we all need to get real with our spirit
and reconnect to what is real, authentic,
I mean to say we need to tap into the philosophy of the cosmos and communicate with all the elements like we all used to create in joy and such great harmony.
no book s, no tele,
just pure Sourcery
3/4, 7:57pm
Koz Kozmos
so what do the songs mean ?
what is your source?
3/4, 7:58pm **Pre View**
well, i don't think thy really match (sorry - i do appreciate your posts !
but it gets my energy twisted when i play them all at once.
So i have a missing link to them, or a missing key in my brain ?
3/4, 8:00pm **Koz Kozmos**

MUSIC: TIM BLAKE/SONG FOR A NEW AG

3/4, 8:00pm **Pre View**
source : all there is, whom u talk to in the universe, ...
everybody can connect direct to their source and sources beyond source .
It is CONNECTIVITY to the Creator

3/4, 8:00pm **Koz Kozmos**
I have no sourec
are u sure? (Source)
3/4, 8:01pm **Pre View**
everybody is sourced otherwise u would not be able to breathe
3/4, 8:01pm **Koz Kozmos**
i want it to happen , my breathing gets bad ,
this dimension is a waste of time,
I need more than pipe dreams
3/4, 8:03pm **Pre View**
yes i am sure : well u know all the festivities of lies and stuff working out i
n politics, economics .....
it is just clearing the earth plane , but u need some level of understanding to move beyond this dimension and therefor it is all about reconnecting to many different levels of light and its technology. Integrating the first 12 universes and working your way back into the origin of a Celestial body would give you an easy time to move your solar Lights back in.
But you DO NEED A START, a foundation, otherwise there is no getting anywhere because you would not know what you are doing. And knowing what we are doing is meeting up with Magic!
3/4, 8:03pm **Koz Kozmos**
i'm open and fairly humble and
i'm deep enough to be shallow
3/4, 8:04pm **Pre View**
i give workshops some times.My workshops are not particularly a dream, I make people work and allow them to understand how to bring their own shifts through, how to reconnect and open light technology within and getting their Spark realization through which allows us to move and learn through many different platforms of the Divine .
We all need to study, understand how the elements and elementals work and what they stand for.
there is no hard drive for that , or the hard drive is the universe and cosmological re-education into exactly everything because we lost everything. We lost our integrity, our nutrition, our respect, our
humility, our universal applications. Too many people just meditate in an airy fairy land with no knowledge , which is why so many things are completely off like they think they are the Messiah (for idiots)while Cryst Consciousness is already on the planet.
3/4, 8:05pm **Koz Kozmos**
I once went to loads of workshops
3/4, 8:05pm **Pre View**
what does shallow mean ? I never attended any workshop, it is all crap, apart from my education in yoga and many fitness disciplines. I never found any books either that were worth a read, they all sounded like they don't work , and they don't. It was one disappointed after the other. I started out with Alice Bailly, didn't like it, read some Jasmuheen. It was all too unsatisfactory because NO Technique was being applied nor explained. However, I does not matter as we all need to become our own channel and bring through data that is in high need for those suffering immensely and the global transition into Light.
Stop playing out victim consciousness like you're doing now, stop that shit and find some valuables ....
3/4, 8:06pm **Koz Kozmos**
Lacking depth of intellect, emotion, or knowledge
thats one meaning of shallow,,, blame the victim
I have my bejewled head and the green stone t
hat fell from satans crown when he was thrown out a heaven
3/4, 8:08pm **Pre View**
got a visitor from Mars,
get back to u !
I mean, somebody is at the door here at home,
so i need to close of, but i'll keep u in my heart !

3/4, 8:09pm **Koz Kozmos**
ok, at least its not an earthling
3/4, 8:16pm **Koz Kozmos**
I'm not playing 'victim consciousness'
we are not a fallen race, we were pushed!
3/4, 9:14pm **Pre View**
Well Koz, there is whole story to it .... many grids fell apart & downgraded all of our CS (consciousness) many times over.
But all of this is in repair ever since 2000 & attached rays .... anchored every year on 11/11. All 12 have been settled and hold strong. That is why we had so much clearing and shit things happening to us in 2012. This year is the coming around of the strong, who understand how to keep out of the density , defeat it through many light - Lite levels and get your individual assignment done.
Meaning u get new blueprints all the time depending on what u ask for / Ask and u will be given. My explanation for GOD (everybody hates that word while it is so obvious) :

G : GEOMETRY
O : ONESS
D : DESIGN

That is the composition of the universe along mathematics that reset our waves. So when we clear out the heavy burden from Lemuria .... we get a clear CS on Universal Level, which is pretty amusing as u don't understand earth level CS like on social media any longer.Knowing what mundane consciousness is about is as important as going through the many experiencesand learning traffic.
But yess, u keep on being a loner and people will hate u for being persistent, strong headed and telling it like it is. Anyways, when the fears have been deleted, things run smooth as in a Light Body as it should; its spirit logic. Often times I meet people that tell me to cut down my talking and my guts to talk truth. Especially being a women is not easy at times for men still do not accept knowledge that is a little superior, and yes, of course there are some sweet exceptions and pretty interesting meetings in the hood. But, they are seldom. I can step into an establishment at times and change all of the energy .... through the integration of Light Grids that override the atrocities of manipulation and other densities. Yet, some knowledge and love to do these things is needed. It is termed putting Self out for service, haha.
I had a lot of training during the past 10 years, fell back into soul level or ego and deeper, which is really xtreme low level and crawling like a snake till i laid down with the snakes and got myself up again, never to go there again,,,,, Going Galactic and then universal again meaning u work with the planets and download the info they give u or specific entities and upgrade that way. It is fun, but fitness and dietary degrees need to refine continually with these upgrades. So when I comment on FB, I bloody mean every WORD i say; to the bottom-line (nobody understands that and they think i'm making fun; but it is not, it is just to trigger intelligence beyond mine and learn. So when i talk about dragons i mean i do work with dragon rays , simple and clear. I've learned that math is the first thing to understand well (i'm not good at that) even if u get numbers in your meditation or ... u need to understand what thy can do with u, why , how, when to get to the geometry ... So these are keys that bring the merger with your Spirit through.; the science that flows with it and the hip flow, there's no other way. I study a lot (science and embodiment) but it is hard being a loner not to be able to exchange info and get deep communication on these subjects. I am passionate about the word, the word is in return 'cause that is the power beyond truth. So dear Koz, i'm very happy and grateful for your existence because u always give a deeper level of understanding, even when u go into the dense ways, I'm sure you'r" a great entity. Thank u for your support!
3/4, 9:38pm **Pre View**
Anyways, u awakened love to reptiles, so i want to learn about that cs.
A pity u don't live around the corner

3/4, 10:47pm **Koz Kozmos**
thank you Pre...i understand your words,,,'dense ways' ?
I hate politics etc in the time of ashes your third eye cries
and makes a pool
that becomes a portal
~<O>~
March 5, 2013 3/5, 6:55am **Pre View**
Good morning Koz,
dense ways = feeding into density = dark = negativity .....
Beautiful words when the 3e eye ...opens , it is the frontal lobes that open the
universal cards or portal point to see what is really going on,
Yess i hate all in society it is just that we are manipulated so much,
so i work underground to fight it with
grids : that gives great results
eg : when i feel injustice has been done to me i talk to individuals in the police
department, justice scales .... and try to open their eyes, and try to find a way to
educate them.... Sometimes 1 single individual is enough to change a whole CS.
Yess it takes a lot of guts and the right wording,
but when we do not act nothing will change.
A little input can bring many changes ....
& u'll be protected if things are done with compassion which is the hardest part ;;;
nobody will understand u, u loose friends but that also is for greater purpose.
In the end those standing with the Knights of the first Order will be the Knights
of this new age ....
Keep yur faith Koz & reflect on what u can do to change ur environment and become
yur own guardian
March 5, 2013
3/5, 2:32pm **Koz Kozmos**
I'm sick of the war and all the insidious human android meat bags .
I'm not particularly dark and only negative but I'm in this dullard duality and cannot
buy into the new age mind control program
everything happens for a reason etc...
3/5, 2:39pm **Koz Kozmos**
If there are entities on earth that live off negative energies...war as a ritual sacrifice
etc and the dummying down of all humans but specifically the higher soul race
{made from their first experiments at creating a slave race }
then the revivification of the high gene is a inevitably going to move us thru many
emotional
(etc) centers darkling and and brightling
3/5, 2:42pm **Koz Kozmos**
I am a compassionate person and have a poetic darkness
the dark dude from the light machine , I have been waiting for THE AWAKENING
but I need more proof ,
my feeling is I've been regonized and their trying to shut me down...
that was a bit of a ramble ; basically I'm a warrior soul in the war against sleep
and many other things...
and I'm doing my best
3/5, 3:10pm **Koz Kozmos**
typing is not my best form of expression
3/5, 3:42pm **Koz Kozmos**
thanks for your feed back
March 5, 20133/5, 6:42pm **Pre View**
Hi Koz, unexplained things are for u to discover ....
Why don't u finally step out of soul level CS (all u explain is soul)& move into Divine
CS

Then Supreme Cs... U wouldn't even give a thought no more to all the wars, if u wait for the awakening, u will never awake, it is up to U and only u to find ur way to move beyond that and then i can assure u , u won't need no proof cause everything is obvious, yur thoughts manifest on the spot and u will simply not be able to feed into these rambling snakes, and thy will not be able to affect u any longer.
Doing yur best is not working any longer, u either decide to go all the way every single second or not,
The earth belongs to the strong hearted, the strong of mind, the strong vessels ! And yess it is a hard training in the beginning, but there's no words to the awards .....
I don't know where u stand with training urself ... but all i can see is u give outward forces all the blame while what is not inside of us CANNOT BE HIT.
Most beautiful but hardest lessons ever, Reflect on that maybe, everything is a mirror.
Btw i like the way u combine the darkness with light,
its a unique gift telling me, u really had it, yur tired and only want the other side.
Think how u can do it, and do it, manage urself !
Blablabla, Let me sing a song for u my dear friend What is yur best form of Expression ? am curious 3/5, 7:10pm **Pre View**
I can feel yur very compassionate, & that u understand where u can meet brains very well,,,,,, when we
can laugh with what is going on this playing Field, we are lifting ourselves out of disaster. Thank u for being here
3/5, 8:18pm **Koz Kozmos**
I am not just waiting to awake the total opposite since being young and younger still etc I have been less infected by the control viruses. I don't know about moving into god CS, what does that mean? beyond basic mystisim for morons. The mystic wants to merge with god ', the tear drop in the giant sea' , i don't feel every anything can manifest on the spot, this is a pipe dream .I only feed into the rambling snake to know my enemy . I'm more than ready to go all the way and am in the pathless land 'cliché's like every
thing is ' a mirror or its all good '
I find it pathetic and it is based on some eastern watered down bullshit
3/5, 8:19pm **Koz Kozmos**
mystics want to merge with god , I want to kill god for taking the liberty of putting use in this dimension and playing with us, and if i choose it then it must be all destroyed
3/5, 9:56pm **Pre View**
I explained GOD to u yesterday , G = geometry, O = Oness, D = Design Everything is composed out of that(i could speak for hours about this ...). Let go of yur teaching, readings, TV computer, mysticism and stuff : Let go of the pipe dream, there is a way to get real when u move beyond DIMENSIONS. U miss the technical part to go all the way that is why u are bored & stuck in the cliché things. I do understand this very well, as i'v been there and moving out of it for real. But u need to download this in yur body and work with it, there is many ways to do it. I actually already told u all about it during our conversations. If u'd go into the Alchemy with languages of Light u'd be able to change yur entire structure or body . These are basics u don't find anywhere.
Just think Why did we meet ?
If u go over everything u told me u'd be able to see ,u keep on giving yur power away with yur attention to negative forces instead of looking inside, yur source .
However, it is yur choice to keep cradling in a nowhere's land or to start thinking beyond that without judging what is happening around u, only understanding & moving on. Manifesting on the spot means u at least need to be able to VIBRATE and FEEL THAT VIBRATION throughout the day. Meaning u'll be
able to feel lateral, straight, diagonal Ley Lines& grids moving through u and giving u information.
Many times we just forget to listen to information, or we fail to trust the little things that could actually turn out to become the bigger visions we hold inside.

There is a way to get there - but it needs a starting point from which one can upgrade into many interesting and fascinating intensities of the universe . A 3-days work out with the Divine would be great to set the homing devices or your Spacial Movie in balance and harmony with what Light body means and how to integrate it and move on up in to the many episodes that are individually designed. The STUDY OF SELF WITHIN SELF IS VERY ATTRACTIVE!IT NEVER STAYS THE SAME - WE ARE ALL IN EVOLUTION -
SO IS OUR INFORMATION.
People often times forget that and keep on going into old stuff & teachings that don't work any longer today .... U would see with different eyes & might go immortal SO,,,,, without these alignments i'd be lost too , for sure, Let's leave it here, with all my respect Koz !
3/5, 10:13pm **Koz Kozmos**
I look inside my source, i understand your concepts and have heard them before, I have gone beyond the final cliché and tricked the universal mind,
having ideas and acknowledging the negative forces is not giving your power away, i agree about old teachings, but what you'r saying comes across ill ,defined and a bit old ancient even ... and you seem to have a guru complex...what are alignments and what exactly with...
if you have a higher knowledge I need something more than your models of cs....
3/5, 10:19pm **Koz Kozmos**
maybe you underestimate what is going on
Better to remain silent and be thought a fool than to speak out and remove all doubt. Abraham Lincoln.
Alchemy with languages of Light, what is this ?
the poet with a pen full of stars rewrites the uni~ verse ?
what does the body structure change into...how can i do this?
I realize we can't leave it there ...... i realize because of paradigms you are working with means you have explanations for the way i express certain things , etc
what site do I use to download it into my body ?
i'm so random
3/5, 10:45pm **Koz Kozmos**
first question please....
what are alignments?
3/5, 10:47pm **Koz Kozmos**
LANGUAGE OF LIGHT/DNA ACTIVATION videos
i get this , too much vagueness
3/5, 10:54pm **Koz Kozmos**
Finally! The book you requested!! THE HYPERSPACE HELPER: A USER-FRIENDLY GUIDE contains the most often requested Language of Hyperspace visualizations and exercises presented by Stewart A. Swerdlow, along with supporting articles by his wife, Janet D. Swerdlow, from the globally popular Expansions website (www.stewartswerdlow.com). These visualizations, exercises, and articles put you
solidly on the path of inner exploration
via the Language of Hyperspace-the Original Language that emanates from the mind of God that is the basis of all creation. People who have studied metaphysics for years report getting the answers to lifelong
questions when using these techniques.
Stewart's reputation for clear, concise, all-encompassing, result-producing information continues to grow exponentially. Best known for his role in the Montauk Project and his work as an ex-secret government
psychic, he teaches you how to control your own mind so that no one else controls it for you.
Janet, internationally known for her Oversoul research, adds to these exercises and visualizations with her unique perspectives on such foundational issues as abandonment, parental issues, soulmates,
forgiveness, insulation, and programming.
Open this book right now to any page to find exactly what you need to get you through your day or night!

5, 10:54pm **Koz Kozmos**
is this a source ?
3/5, 11:00pm **Koz Kozmos**
something wrong about Swerdlow ?
3/5, 11:13pm **Koz Kozmos**

MUSIC: SAMMY DAVIS JR SWEET CHARITY-EXTENDED

3/5, 11:13pm **Koz Kozmos**
worth a watch
3/6, 8:33am **Pre View**
Koz, the video abouy DNA is simple and clear nonsense!
I don't want info from old books and people that propagate falseness i think u read half ....
SWERDLOW is absurd and foolish
unless you want to keep on swimming and breathing in your own density or chasing your own tail . DO YOU NEED SWERDLOW TO MOVE ON ?
No way , the info is from their source not your SOURCE or channel. And not even that,,,
Give me something more tangible, through which I can discern valuable things
If you want to move out of the mind control, leave behind WEBSITE pages, they keep you in a web of control such as in owning you....
One thing u might do if u wish : download the Hebrew alphabet and sing these letters while visualizing them running through the spinal chords. That is fun to do and eliminates a lot stuck patterns. This is a just a good experience and a start in reconstructing
your body in to light
I hope i am not offending u,...
it is just that i feel u really want to get out. So this is what i can offer ....
Maybe stick to 1 thing : breathe the Hebrew letters through, ask urself and your source how you can best work with them; ask for universal help to understand this and listen to your own voice.
There is nothing else if u want to move on , you need to start SOMETHING NEW! leave every old teachings or whatever you learned in life behind given by others especially the internet....
Another major important thing : your breath has not opened throughout your spinal column meaning it causes many diseases. The Spine and the arteries around the heart + the pulmonary arteries that supply your entire system need to flow crystal clear and free . IF YOU CAN DO THAT?
It is all a little technology, but not too hard to understand once you start to work with energies through the body and the consciousness that is integrated within these energies such as through rays colors and their elemental defined nutrition (mentally/ spiritually/and through physical fitness)
Have a great day Koz, and please reflect on the Hebrew letters without the info of internet, just have a
look at them them , breathe them through your spine and see if u can get info on each of them ,,, this is your first assigned task! GO GO GO AND GET IT NOW! hahaha
3/6, 8:40am **Pre View**
Here is an example: The Hebrew letter Beit comes through the orange ray = when toning it and bringingthis letter through every gland in your endocrine system, releases old attachments .....
The Hebrew is a whole study, should keep u busy for a long interesting time ....
Orange lifts everything! 3/6, 8:54am **Pre View**
The Hebrew letters will assist you to open up the spine, it is an example of A TECHNIQUE Everything is about alignment in this age,
otherwise there is no moving forward...
Maybe buy THE KEYS OF ENOCH:JJ HURTAK , there is a lot in this book worth studying, but also a lot
that is not updated !!!!! Just don't swallow everything. Stand still , reflect and feel what is Incorrect! Greetings Koz, make it a specialty day today
Did u have a look at my art? They are all about that ....

3/6, 12:30pm **Koz Kozmos**
Just posted the dna vid for FUN of cource,
i don't need anyone to move on,
I have avoided other people sources all my life times
and am one of the most original people on earth at the moment in other dimensions.
I'm known as Ego Man ,a Super Zero of sorts. Swerdlow ,
who's work i have little idea about has been
avoided because he has such an awful beard and a nasty face...
I understand what you mean about no more mind ....
do u you think I'm a cretin ?
but to end up as a fat guy with an empty mind sitting under a tree, o no!
3/6, 12:30pm **Koz Kozmos**
What about NOUS?
3/6, 12:35pm **Koz Kozmos**
I hardly look at web pages and have used different mantras etc etc to no effect ; and
as to chanting Hebrew letters ... if thats what I'm in on this dirt ball to do,
no thank you.
I refused joining the OTO and an odious Gnostic group for reasons such as this.
I like a bit of Sanskrit mantra sometimes...
not more fucking visualizations
3/6, 12:38pm **Koz Kozmos**
I 've known some occult people who do all this stuff work with Kabbalah
but do not know how to connect with a tree ,
and to be honest their whole shape looks like a spell gone wrong!
your paintings are pretty good ,but art is dead,
but i still like them .
U need to redifine me ; but cheers for all your feed back!
/6, 12:49pm **Pre View**
hell yeah, the old tree is grown out, lets sit together on the brand new tree branches
(Sanskrit, o no no more of that astral plane making u shit in front of beauty.
What do u mean by NOUS ?
3/6, 1:00pm **Pre View**
Kabbalah, Merrrkabah training, tooooooooo old stuff,
no good, it is part of the matrix as it holds people consciousness cycles the same old
things all of the time and not being able of getting out of that.....
I am very well settled within my Merkivah or Light Vehicle with its massive
electricity
& work with them along many grids that synchronize with the consciousness of all
this electricity, and also languages.
I think the latin language will gain some more perspective.
it needs to be touchable, eatable
I'm always hungry when it comes to Light knowledge
3/6, 1:09pm **Koz Kozmos**
The dark tree
golden with fire leaves
falling the dark tree
secrets beyond the mystery calling the dark tree
grown from the light seed transforming the dark tree (kelidascope)
black spellz and tentacle's dancing the dark tree
the light of the morning star
iz burning the dark tree children of the flame returning the dark tree
the sinister path
of learning the dark tree beyond this dimension

o heal the dark tree
in tangled roots
concealed the dark tree
no more meat
for the wheel ~ we are revealed ~
the dark tree
thru labyrinth gates
to those that wait beyond this dimension
to pathless landz
to forests deep
beyond the land of sleep
we awaken.....
(we will cut youdown......)
3/6, 1:11pm **Koz Kozmos**
I've not read a book for years, always liked mystery books
mmmmmmmmmmmmmmmmmm
i get my own info, GOSH!
3/6, 1:13pm **Pre View**
Thank u Koz, it feeds me with seeds i needed
U really make me smile today, u really do
March 6, 2013
3/6, 9:02pm **Koz Kozmos**
KOOL
March 7, 2013
3/7, 12:59pm **Koz Kozmos**
Hi Pre , u aware of this artist?
3/7, 12:59pm **Koz Kozmos**
MUSIC: BULLDOG BREED AUSTIN OSMAN SPARE

3/8, 1:27pm **Pre View**
No, but like it, thxxxx
3/10, 6:59pm **Pre View**
Hi coz, did u know people are afraid of us?
3/10, 8:17pm **Koz Kozmos**
who do you consider to be afariad of 'us' and why ?
3/10, 8:17pm **Pre View**
Don't be bothered, just friends of mine.
They'r just afraid to ask and do not understand our comments on my Fb posts ...
thy'll come out the closet .
3/10, 8:17pm **Koz Kozmos**
thy'r just morons , best de- friend them ; ore maybe a death hex hope your well
anyway Pre
3/10, 8:19pm **Pre View**
timing may be surprising - we always know things when the timing is right isn't it?
i like surprises through green bubbles
3/10, 8:20pm **Koz Kozmos**
you jump to conclusions ,
how do you know i will know things when the time is right ?
Give me proof of your knowledge ??????
proof please

3/10, 8:24pm **Pre View**
it is not about knowledge dear Koz, it is just u know,u have to shoot something till its over & done with
3/10, 8:24pm **Koz Kozmos**
say that again , can u explain t ? That made no sense
3/10, 8:26pm **Pre View**
Could u, would u do me a favor ?
3/10, 8:28pm **Koz Kozmos**
? OK ,are you from Iceland ,
stop throwing me crumbs and give me proof !
Y'r coming across like a deluded new ager .
3/10, 8:32pm **Pre View**
explanation would take many books I still need to write. I just can't possibly write down everything that comes through a seminar,
that would exhaust me through this and any medium.
Love the way u handle me
3/10, 8:33pm **Koz Kozmos**
you keep on insisting that a change is on the horizon for me..
.and then zero explanation .
My ideas etc would take a book ' ...
3/10, 8:36pm **Pre View**
it is like u told me yur eyes dry out - long story and no explanation ....
3/10, 8:38pm **Koz Kozmos**
ok , I wish you the best and respect your privacy
3/10, 8:40pm **Pre View**
thank u for yur integrity,
3/10, 8:41pm **Koz Kozmos**
I'm the prince of ice in the fiery robe of the priestess..
3/10, 8:42pm **Pre View**
oh boy u have a way to make my day
3/10, 8:42pm **Koz Kozmos**
my poetics have been a waste
3/10, 8:43pm **Pre View**
oh no no no "u like" to be a waste to your poetic instincts!
3/10, 8:44pm **Koz Kozmos**
not the case with a pen full of stars, I write the uni ~ verse u'r judgmental and vague, but i don't mind
Being on earth is making me sick
3/10, 9:06pm **Pre View**
Find a way to explode out of the density,
3/10, 9:07pm **Koz Kozmos**
I'd like some explosives, what do u suggest ? is it any good in the place u'r from? I hate earth
3/10, 9:10pm **Pre View**
i like yur fearlessness
WE NEED TO BUILD BIG ACCURATE BRAINS THAT RUN OF EFFICIENCY , not positivity, accuracy!

MY INTERNALS: I often times wondered if he actually did practice his connection to his Source , if he studied how Light development works, how he would meditate and transmute consciousness. Britain is more connected to the Magical enterprises, Merlin, the beauty of mystical alignments. Yet it is all so vague and unclear what people do to stand strong in their Light and if they understand CS within Light, how it can override bad travels in the brain. Awakening and awareness flow together isn't it? When I look into FB and so called channels in the area of Great Britain, I think of disastrous CS that still gets away with any parlor when it comes to light, and people just believe anything. Very Sad.

3/10, 9:10pm **Koz Kozmos**
? lost again , i'm full of fear ....
3/10, 9:11pm **Pre View**
i have a feeling where i live u can just screw the cops
3/10, 9:11pm **Koz Kozmos**
in permanent fight and flight
3/10, 9:11pm **Pre View**
no, ur fooling me, the way u dare talking on FB
3/10, 9:11pm **Koz Kozmos**
what does that mean - screw the cops -
3/10, 9:12pm **Pre View**
Do u have mental disorders or do u need these disorders
3/10, 9:12pm **Koz Kozmos**
how do I speak on face book ? I try to not say much and keep it basic, am i under risk
? are u mentally ill? 3/10, 9:13pm **Pre View**
u speak to the point and u tell it like it is, i like that, but people, oh thy watch our comments and have nightmares about them, because they cannot handle that level of truth
3/10, 9:13pm **Koz Kozmos**
good
3/10, 9:13pm **Pre View**
hahahaha , me mentally ill, ohohoh,
no no i just talk a lot to disordered people
3/10, 9:13pm **Koz Kozmos**
I hope they fall of the night horse and die
yes, i'm sick of being in the sicknes, who's watching our comments ? most people are stupid . 3/10, 9:14pm **Pre View**
that is yur best value, yur pushed to get out of it
3/10, 9:15pm **Koz Kozmos**
and their limited minds will delete any thing interesting,
thank you , but I can't escape and things just get worse...
and i become more damaged by being here
3/10, 9:16pm **Pre View**
what is getting worse ?
3/10, 9:16pm **Koz Kozmos**
everything....just being here on earth apart from all the usual crap
3/10, 9:17pm **Pre View** g
Good question who am i : a DNA engineer
I am more in love with animal behaviour,
3/10, 9:18pm **Koz Kozmos**
as in ex boyfriends etc ;;;what are u saying i'd like to get rid of all my dna,,,
best stay away from pyscho's
3/10, 9:20pm **Pre View**
Ok lets change ur DNA, take the train and come over next week-end ,
i'll give u a 360 degrees wirlpool thr ur brain,, for real
3/10, 9:24pm **Koz Kozmos**
what are they thinking ?
make sense ,
i'm sick of crazy people
3/10, 9:24pm **Pre View**
Ok seriously Koz,
i do work with DNA and the Brain and all of what we are composed out of, it takes a lot of study , and is not some airy thing,
you need to be daring to try out things with Light.

3/10, 9:25pm **Koz Kozmos**
you sure ?
3/10, 9:25pm **Pre View**
100000000000 %
3/10, 9:25pm **Koz Kozmos**
I'm not mocking you or being rude
3/10, 9:26pm **Pre View**
i studied for the past 10 years, and i must tell u, i can change things overnight, but it takes endurance, persistence, and and and, not just .... but people are lazy to go all the way
3/10, 9:27pm **Koz Kozmos**
can you do it from a distance ?
3/10, 9:28pm **Pre View**
well i do a lot of deep healing and realignments over Skype and in person
Energy reaches any intent, no matter where you are
3/10, 9:28pm **Koz Kozmos**
ok thanks,,, I've tried so many things 3/10, 9:28pm **Pre View**
but if u like, i'll give it a try , but then again, i would need some pic of u,
3/10, 9:28pm **Koz Kozmos**
I've given up really,,, it needs to come to me
3/10, 9:29pm **Pre View**
can i trust this statement ?
3/10, 9:29pm **Koz Kozmos**
what statemenT?
3/10, 9:29pm **Pre View**
that u've given up
3/10, 9:29pm **Koz Kozmos**
yesssss, you told me to stop reading and watching stuff online i don't even do that no more
seeking , why do u need to trust it ?
3/10, 9:31pm **Pre View**
ok lets try something tomorrow, post a pick, i will align to u tomorrow night,
3/10, 9:31pm **Koz Kozmos** hold on a moment

3/10, 9:32pm **Pre View**
I don't need to trust, it is just that I do not want to deal with any lunatic or psychopath enough of that,
I always give 1000 % trust cause it is all we have
that is not u ?
3/10, 9:33pm **Koz Kozmos**
thats the only pic left , not a great one, from 2006
it is i look damaged these days ,,,,my name is James Or koz lots of names ,
why do u think its not me?

3/10, 9:35pm **Pre View**
no worries , take a pic from ur cellphone James! This is not what u are now KOZ
3/10, 9:35pm **Koz Kozmos**
no camera in my cell phone
3/10, 9:36pm **Pre View** ok
3/10, 9:36pm **Koz Kozmos**
that was just me having a joke
"enough of that" whom where you dealing with? psycho's?
may i ask' what am I now* ?
3/10, 9:37pm **Pre View**
Then u need the whole story .... not now please,
Do u like to read ?
/10, 9:37pm **Koz Kozmos**
I'm interested
3/10, 9:38pm **Pre View**
U changed , something painful must have happened, were u not being understood ?
3/10, 9:38pm **Koz Kozmos**
no ,thats been since i was born and before
3/10, 9:39pm **Pre View**
Story - i'm writing about it in bits and pieces, - maybe some day i'll send u something
3/10, 9:39pm **Koz Kozmos**
what have i changed to?
OK, thank u ?
3/10, 9:40pm **Pre View**
i think u had things in yur mind to go for,
but somehow, u left them, is that what u really are?

3/10, 9:52pm **Koz Kozmos**
my mind is worse these days
what sort of bad things ?
what am I ?
thank u for chatting
your english is very good ,but your sentences can be confusing .
what sort of bad things?
I look older , and grey
you out there ?
i 'm uncomfortable with showing pics of myself ,
but u showed me yours, so i'm being civil
3/10, 10:08pm **Koz Kozmos**
and fatter lol as they say...
u still talking ?
bye , please delete my pics
bye , and no DNa work ok?
3/10, 10:22pm **Pre View**
ur pics are great, just wondering what happened to ur eye, and no ,
I am not ok,
need to sleep on that mountain top ,
goodnight Koz, goodnight . Thank u so much for being here !
3/11, 8:18am **Koz Kozmos**
my eye has always been like that .
Hope you feel better after a sleep
3/11, 8:59am **Pre View**
yep, good morning,
3/11, 9:06am **Pre View**
hope ur doing well
March 11, 2013
3/11, 9:51pm **Koz Kozmos**
always unsure
March 12, 2013
3/12, 12:31pm **Pre View**
u have no reason, this is only fear,
March 12, 2013
3/12, 10:52pm **Koz Kozmos**
nah
March 23, 2013/23, 6:56pm **Pre View**
Would u back me up when spreading the venom ?
Would u stand tall & speak out ?
Would u stand & speak fearless
No u would not coz it captures u
March 27, 2013/27, 10:43pm **Koz Kozmos**
? just got back from devils island ?
3/28, 3:34am **Pre View**
Did u find yur demons ?
3/28, 9:13pm **Koz Kozmos**
I am the Demon, the fire born ,
death to the clayborn March 29, 2013
3/29, 3:28pm **Koz Kozmos**
Hi Pre , u said when you saw the pic of me that it was not me ,
i had avoided doing some thing bad ;
can't remember-- excacly what u said

3/29, 3:29pm **Pre View**
Something bad ?
3/29, 3:29pm **Koz Kozmos**
but what did u mean? yes
3/29, 3:30pm **Pre View**
What I meant is that u have a lot more gifts unexplored,
because you are missing the knowledge to get there....
3/29, 3:31pm **Koz Kozmos**
how do u know this?
and what are these gifts, any idea?
3/29, 3:32pm **Pre View**
So the real u is simply extraordinary,
shooting bullets at something worth to open up to,,,
One of them is the Power throught wording
(but u have not anchored that yet) t
akes a lot of technicality and understanding,,,
But you love poetry, why don't you expand on that and publish some?
3/29, 3:33pm **Koz Kozmos**
i know that its getting late for me, i'm the only word wizard on earth , and my magic
is wasted on this dimension, but i'm passed caring
3/29, 3:34pm **Pre View**
Late for what ? I am twice ur age u know, the moment u can laugh with what u fight,
you're ready for some new highways,,
3/29, 3:34pm **Koz Kozmos**
u'r a hundred and 4
3/29, 3:35pm **Pre View**
Hey don't u know how to ride the 12th D instead of fighting in 5th D
3/29, 3:35pm **Koz Kozmos**
no idea
3/29, 3:35pm **Pre View**
Exactly my age, I just love that pentagram
104 makes up 5, a pentgram
3/29, 3:35pm **Koz Kozmos**
ok i'm a moron
3/29, 3:35pm **Pre View**
NO IDEA : THAT IS YOUR PROB, YOUR BIG PROB !
3/29, 3:36pm **Koz Kozmos**
and u'r the guru ,
lol as they say
3/29, 3:36pm **Pre View**
Gurus are out OF TIME on earth ,stick to that.
You either take responsibility and claim your own power or get guru sick.
It is us altogether or nothing. I never say lol !!!
and will never use that abreviation,
its for the sick on earth!
3/29, 3:36pm **Koz Kozmos** ?
first time i wrote this word
3/29, 3:36pm **Pre View**
Better be your last time as well

3/29, 3:37pm **Koz Kozmos**
no i never say it or type it
i get confused with your english
3/29, 3:37pm **Pre View**
You should get educated to ride dimensions and us languages through your nervous system 3/29, 3:37pm **Koz Kozmos**
its not a complaint, i can hardly speak anymore how can i do this
3/29, 3:38pm **Pre View**
ok lets take it slow, why are u confused, why can u not talk?
3/29, 3:38pm **Koz Kozmos**
no one worth talking too
i've gone within to bloom
i have attracted nothing
i consider the possiblilty that i am not supposed to be here i know the soul gate is controlled
'they' need to fuck up the high gene to stop the awakening
3/29, 3:42pm **Pre View**
To change consciousness and build yur dynamics up to 12 D,
beyond that there is no D only lots of interesting atmospheres: sometimes i train people to get into the Alchemy of Self, getting into a light Foundation so they can move forward.
Don't know if u have anyone in Wales who does it,,,, Then u would talk completely different and not give attention any longer to anything that is not conform yur energy, but believe me, u have no time for that, anything manifests and u clear all that is not appropriate on this plane just by walking grids,,,,
people will react strange ----
'cause thy will not understand your light any longer
3/29, 3:44pm **Pre View**
THAT IS WHEN THE MAGIC HITS,
but it takes a lot of study and perseverance afterwards, should be no problem as it is damn interesting and changes u every day at yur command,,
3/29, 3:44pm **Koz Kozmos**
i have studied
gone thru many forms,
i believe i am being blocked
as i said the soul gate into this dimension is controlled
3/29, 3:45pm **Pre View**
THE SOUL GATE IS LONG GONE AS I TOLD U, the green arc has removed from Greece
to Cape Town, as far as I can recall
3/29, 3:45pm **Koz Kozmos**
that already happened to a point, people or the people around me,
i find toxic and discusting streets of zombie meat. It was there when i came into this dimension and was wiped ...
what do u suggest i do if u feel u have answers
give me something pratical ..., that was a bit random
hope u can follow
3/29, 3:49pm **Pre View**
Of course the soul gate is being controlled but grids are being grounded to eliminate all of that; meaning a lot of trouble is being removed with TRUTH for people, when u move into ascension (U NEED BIG BIG BIG ALIGNMENTS AND STUDY) it all becomes clear and obvious.
So U don't have the alignments and u need them (need to think how u can get them)
3/29, 3:49pm **Pre View**
I can easily follow u as u keep on repeating what u told me days ago, bottom-line, u don't have what u need to step out of it. Maybe i will give a course in Wales, maybe i will give a course right here and make mp3's available, just maybe ,....

3/29, 3:50pm **Koz Kozmos**
ok ,how can i get it, and why do i need it?
mp3 on dna engineeering ok ?
u keep telling me i need something and suggesting i'm not ready or whatever .. what u say beyond your paradigms of awakening?
3/29, 3:53pm **Pre View**
How can you get it? :through someone teaching it or allowing your channel to bring it 2 you. Why do you need it? : when u want to go beyond anything that keeps u chasing the same old shit I am not in the DNA engineering yet,
but other Light engineering
3/29, 3:54pm **Koz Kozmos**
you said u were a dna engineer, but its kool
i don't need any one to teach me
i've been thru that, and there is no one
just some deluded mystic shit heads selling their karma chewing gum, and i'm not chasing the same shit, i'm chasing nothing
3/29, 3:55pm **Pre View** I
In other words : u are driving a helicopter with no wings,
So tell me what light body alignments do u have then?
3/29, 3:56pm **Koz Kozmos**
i'm going to leave this pathetic city
3/29, 3:56pm **Pre View**
Where would u be going?
3/29, 3:56pm **Koz Kozmos**
to a less built up area , with less toxic human scum about
i have no idea about my light body
i'm aware of the theories
i've tried to make connections
3/29, 3:58pm **Pre View**
THAT CONCLUDED & INCLUDES EVERYTHING UR TALKING ABOUT,
that is ur missing link,
and if u think u can do it by urself, please talk again within 200 years !
3/29, 3:58pm **Koz Kozmos**
but it has'nt happened
i didn't say i can do it my self
i said i can find no one to help me 'transform'
why do i need to go to some workshop or listen to a cd
i've gone within, i feel a massive urge that i have to move forward
3/29, 4:01pm **Pre View**
Going within is always encouraged, yet who many breathe through what comes from within and integrate Light DIRECTIONS.
You did not, u haven't integrated that, u do not have that knowledge as I feel now
I could arrange that, and u would change 360 ° within 3 days (but don't know yet when i'll be teaching this again)
Private teaching would be kool,,,
Going within with no Fuel that must be a bore for real,
3/29, 4:01pm **Koz Kozmos**
and that i am being blocked
what are u saying Pre ?
You can teach it or private?
i can out esoteric , but i'm not getting caught up in these clicheed models of consciousness the proof is in the puddding
why do i have no fuel?
u still cahtting? chattting?

3/29, 4:07pm **Pre View**
I CAN TRANSFORM and give u all necessary info but only with a 3-days fast forward course. This means u get anchored with 144 electrons or energy field around the body
,
you learn to work with these essences, u get cleared on any level, u learn alchemy , u heal yur **eye** first, then u move up to ur celestial, Elestial, Solar, spiritual, heavenly, universal, eternal and immortal embodiment.
U work with geometry & math in yur meditation, get yer own info and get rid of all old ego/soul consciousness, except yur direct line to Source. And after that u would stand with ur mouth wide open coz then u could teach me the **teleportation** perhaps?.
But if u do not want to understand that it is possible to leave the Soul control levels, then i do
NOT have anything for u and u'll keep winding in misery.
Not many want true and deep-schooling, but it is worth it because people simply do not want to understand they need to repair their SOLAR BODY and moving Celestial first.
Have a look at the sun, the Great centralizer and reflect on the solar flares. I
t makes us understand how much the solar system/solar
plexus has been broken.
3/29, 4:08pm **Koz Kozmos**
i want to understand
3/29, 4:08pm **Pre View**
Just take some time to reflect on that a little, get back to u,
need some food (sometimes)
Understanding comes with integration and techniques that get you there because you feel the changes flowing through every day; and that is when people start to trust.
Yet people want everything the other way around, but that
is not how Spirit works. You gave, and you get help.
Done with the prayer syndrome.
3/29, 4:09pm **Koz Kozmos**
the hard core school is my domain,
i rule the yard and throw the ball to my selves and it transforms into orbs spinning
i've had enough misery
Hey Pre, going for swim and sauna thanks for the talk
PEACE & NOISE
maybe i should try your course
but how can i trust another teacher ? bye
3/29, 4:26pm **Pre View**
Yess, u want company for a swim ?
U can only trust what u FEEL !!!
3/29, 4:28pm **Koz Kozmos**
see u down the pool
fuck 'feeling' and other spurious cliches **Pre View**
Swim with whales, if u want to feel, u will never be able to stretch thy brain without working them out and stretching brain muscles, reaching into brain extensions
Come on, post me another song as the food got me miserable
3/29, 7:19pm **Koz Kozmos**

MUSIC: FUCK FOOD/TECH 9

3/29, 7:19pm **Koz Kozmos**
going ofline, catch u later
3/29, 7:20pm **Pre View** ok then, take care
Fuck food yess, makes u look shady off line,
3/30, 2:28pm **Koz Kozmos**
oven chips and the mob bile phonie and a can of death sweeten
3/30, 2:32pm **Pre View**
haha Koz chips are very healthy, need the salts, ----------sweeteners :

this lets me know yur deep into soul otherwise u would not be able to stand sugar any longer nor have a single thought about it. Anyways we discussed that over and over, one day u might choose yur way out (yess u need the knowledge and fabricate to do this) this is yur missing link. Until that day, REFLECT!

3/30, 2:33pm **Koz Kozmos**

I'm sick of thinking and thinking about why stop being tyrannizing and patronizing

3/30, 2:35pm **Pre View**

Ok that is were u should be, lets dance to this music

3/30, 2:36pm **Koz Kozmos**

Chips are all i eat and cover with choc spread and i drink the toxic fizz of Illuminati cola....yum

3/30, 2:37pm **Pre View**

ooo blubber, how do u digest ?
Haha, this world is so off nutrition and the beauty of feeding the body.
Meals have become a socializing pattern filled with pilled emotional jelly belly as is prooven when we look at the sickness of overweight or brainless bodies,,,

3/30, 2:38pm **Koz Kozmos**

i'm a limbless acrobat purple jiving the weave of ropes...

3/30, 2:38pm **Pre View**

I take chips with lots of carrot juice

3/30, 2:38pm **Koz Kozmos**

u are anorexic or, i can tell by your photos

3/30, 2:38pm **Pre View**

No i am not , I eat when and what I need, no more emotion attached

3/30, 2:39pm **Koz Kozmos**

okno, ohno

3/30, 2:40pm **Pre View**

Like that expresso : Limbless acrobat – we should all become that

3/30, 2:42pm **Koz Kozmos**

its a song i wrote 30 odd years ago
if you have all this higher knowledge and i'm too 'stupid' to understand, give me one thing i can do to create change within in the next 48 hours
only if u feel u can
but some thing original

3/30, 2:48pm **Pre View**

U are very intelligent , as for me what i experience with u is that u always align with were I AM at, so u do feel the energies quite well and maybe who knows if u can learn to see them u can enable urself to work with them constructively. I think this is another one of yur gifts to humanity & of course uyrself. But who am i to tell ,,,, don't know anything about u, just feel u & from there on, i operate, we all do, i think

3/30, 2:49pm **Pre View**

Ok, do u channel ur own info yet ? Do u have a crystal from Peru at home

3/30, 2:49pm **Kozmos**

i wear a moldavite and have some crystals *

3/30, 2:51pm **Pre View**

Moldavite is Russian blood, great enhancer to align with ur Source,
but time to move beyond this integration.
It is important u know were ur crystals come from

3/30, 2:51pm **Koz Kozmos**

the I AM is a bardic joke to confuse the fakers
Moldavite is space rock but fuck crystals,
i am the hollow bone, the poet with a pen full of stars and i write
the uni VERSE ..... i have said before u don't know anything about me ....
but contradict your self with opinions,
but its kool

I got it from the crystal shop ,
its set in an inverted crucifix and looks ace hanging on my sports top
3/30, 2:56pm **Pre View**
That is one of my passions (contradicting) The magician full of stars is what u are
does the crucifix have equal legs?
3/30, 2:56pm **Koz Kozmos**
but i do feel stuck and brok
3/30, 2:56pm **Pre View**
Why broken ?
3/30, 2:56pm **Koz Kozmos**
i was joking about the crucifix
i would have had to get that from the rock shop,
not the crystal shop i've been broken since i got here
They fucked me up big time
3/30, 2:57pm **Pre View**
Rock shops are plenty , take ur bags & take ur flight
3/30, 2:58pm **Koz Kozmos**
rock as in rock n roll
3/30, 2:59pm **Pre View**
Rock bars is were i leave my crystals
3/30, 2:59pm **Koz Kozmos**
aka black metal jewel eyes
3/30, 2:59pm **Pre View**
what is Aka
3/30, 3:00pm **Koz Kozmos**
"Also known as@ "Also known as'
3/30, 3:00pm **Pre View**
i love to wire my body into copper
makes people feel dizzzyyyy
3/30, 3:01pm **Koz Kozmos**
what are u on about?
3/30, 3:01pm **Pre View**
Don't understand ? Do u mean what i am doing ?
3/30, 3:02pm **Koz Kozmos**
do u mean u are the crytal girl YES?
? why
3/30, 3:03pm **Pre View**
simply love metallic lights, so u can do anything - copper wires attractsssss
3/30, 3:03pm **Koz Kozmos**
ok, i've never had anything i wished for
3/30, 3:04pm **Pre View**
It makes people go crazy 'cause thy do not understand attraction through light
3/30, 3:04pm **Koz Kozmos**
oh, i do enjoy self pity and attract nothing
3/30, 3:05pm **Pre View**
NO, u can't as of now, but u still believe we can and have power to do anything ?
Do u feel vibration of radio waves, sonar waves, other ......
meaning u always feel like swimming ...
I need my intraterestial communication now,
showering showering,
catch u later, keep the waves glowing Koz, like brilliantine

3/30, 3:09pm Koz Kozmos
ok, bye ,keep eating the chipz 3/30, 3:10pm Koz Kozmos

MUSIC: RAMASES/LIFE CHILD

3/30, 6:30pm Pre View
Thank u ! i will promote my jugular vein
3/30, 6:30pm Koz Kozmos
what are u on about
3/30, 6:32pm Pre View
my english sucks today, i don't understand that question,
i just don't, please speak arabic
,او ال ا و الا أاا ا،
3/30 Koz Kozmos ,
Hang on, i remember
3/30, 6:36pm Pre View
I trusted u, i like trust, like it is something u cannot grab,
still feels like a million colored footballs
3/30, 6:36pm Koz Kozmos
I hate sport
3/30, 6:37pm Pre View
i'm sure u do, it hits were u need to go & fires what u love so much, don't know what
that is, 3/30, 6:39pm Koz Kozmos
~Shadow Man~ shade the shad
from ultra bad
casts a throat
of spells vain deity
with 'lertik lyre
is dancing
in the dell the hooded hawk
in jet cloak
flys from
planet hell diaboolous daath
the joker laughs
at human flesh
in cells shade the shad
from ultra bad
calls monsters
from the well THE BARD OF CTHULHU
{excerpt from I~~G~~} ~Shadow Man~ shade the shad from ultra bad
casts a throat
of spells vain deity
with 'lertik lyre
is dancing
in the dell the hooded hawk
in jet cloak
flys from
planet hell diaboolous daath
the joker laughs
at human flesh
in cells shade the shad
from ultra bad

calls monsters
from the well the dark dolphin
swims thru spheres
to were
the dagon dwell shimmer scimitar
cuts the veins
with the sword
of azrael the poet star
writes a rime
what it say
he cannot tell...

3/30, 6:39pm **Pre View**
oh ok, was reading, love it, u eliminate but here it is

3/30, 6:40pm
i wrote that 25 years ago '

3/30, 6:41pm Pre View
Wow, post it, contains a lot of knowledge to reflect on

3/30, 6:41pm **Koz Kozmos**
NAH, PEOPLE STEAL MY POWER, REMEMBER

3/30, 6:41pm **Koz Kozmos**
nope , i'm more esoteric than u

3/30, 6:42pm **Pre View**
what does it mean ?

3/30, 6:42pm **Koz Kozmos**
Dagon was originally an Assyro-Babylonian fertility god who evolved into a major northwest Semitic god, reportedly of grain (as symbol of fertility) and fish and/or fishing
(as symbol of multiplying). He was worshipped by the early Amorites and by the inhabitants of the cities of Ebla (modern Tell Mardikh, Syria) and Ugarit (modern Ras Shamra, Syria) (which was an ancient city near the Mediterranean containing a large variety of ancient writings and pre-Judeo-Christian shrines).
He was also a major
member, or perhaps head, of the pantheon of the Biblical Philistines.

3/30, 6:43pm **Koz Kozmos**
but i'm using the H P Lovecraft connection Dagon" is a short story by H. P. Lovecraft, written in July 1917, one of the first stories he wrote as an adult. It was first published in the November 1919 edition of
The Vagrant (issue #11).

3/30, 6:43pm **Pre View**
Thank u, i never put my attention to any God, so miss out on that, for good reasons
It breaks, its old energy

3/30, 6:44pm **Koz Kozmos**
nor have i , not even the so called god within, but i realize that in comparison to most fuctards I AM

3/30, 6:45pm **Pre View**
but u do know about them
It is just all energies i think to be used or left for what thy are
maybe until we know their importance

3/30, 6:45pm **Koz Kozmos**
IAm that I Am (הִיְהֶא רֶשֲׁא הִיְהֶא, ʾehyeh ʾašer ʾehyeh [ʔehˈje ʔaˈʃer ʔehˈje]) is a common English translation (JPS among others) of the response God used in the Hebrew Bible when Moses asked for his name (Exodus 3:14). It is one of the most famous verses in the Torah. Hayah means "existed" or "was" in Hebrew; "ehyeh" is the first person singular imperfect form and is usually translated in English Bibles as "I will be" (or "I shall be"), for example, at Exodus 3:12. Ehyeh asher ehyeh literally translates as "I Will Be What I Will Be", with attendant theological and mystical implications in Jewish tradition. However, in most English Bibles, this phrase is rendered as I am that I am.

3/30, 6:47pm **Koz Kozmos**
(fuctards) a low grade soul experiment used to produce negative energy for negative entities but its worse
for those with the light in the blood
3/30, 6:47pm **Pre View**
that is the coming together of the Original Seedcell or Ipod?
3/30, 6:47pm **Koz Kozmos**
they are using us against ourselfs to block the awakening
I told u, are u a bossy person ?
3/30, 6:48pm **Pre View**
well don't think it is working any longer, with the set ups (Light grids) the earth changes are going through , they squeezzzzee the matrix out of its existence. Would be a good thing if everybody on the planet would just hold a crystal grid.
People are so self centered , not realizing when they offer their services to their Source, t
hey uplist themselves out of the negative platforms
3/30, 6:48pm **Koz Kozmos**
earth is done, destroy this dimension to save gaia,,, mmmmmmmmm
3/30, 6:49pm **Pre View**
Bossy me ? no way, buh, don't know, i am very open and willing to learn but when i stand for something i have integrated, i will stand strong eyes,,,,
3/30, 6:49pm **Koz Kozmos**
i've heard the sorta stuff u speak about but its too vague ,,,
maybe i'm not evolved enough ...but i distust people who tell me this
i need proof
3/30, 6:51pm **Pre View**
yep, it only becomes understandable when u work with it and have proof of the changes every day .... No compition please, evolved , we all stand were we stand
3/30, 6:52pm **Koz Kozmos**
most are crawling these days , i need to sit down but yes good vibes ...
how did this information come to u?
3/30, 6:53pm
Pre View
u know, i can only tell u what i do, but it does not mean u have to go that way, maybe u find a far better way, with ur specialties,
3/30, 6:53pm **Koz Kozmos**
and how is it reflected in your day to day life?
3/30, 6:53pm **Pre View**
Info = long story
3/30, 6:53pm **Koz Kozmos**
ok, my story is too long , and there is no place for me and i don't mind
my majik is wasted on this dimension
3/30, 6:54pm **Pre View**
well whatever i do, and i do work hard in meditation like for 3 h in the morning : as far as I am concerned, i need to have the results immediately through life as i said, through the mails, through people, whatever , that is my proof, that is what i set solid
-
the manifestations happen.
3/30, 6:55pm **Koz Kozmos**
mmmm, i can't understand, i gave up meditation
3/30, 6:56pm **Pre View**
i will tell u my story if u really want to know,
but then i need time to put it here, ...
3/30, 6:56pm **Koz Kozmos**
and every thing else apart from absinth and champagne and opium s
ee how u feel about it; your story etc

3/30, 6:58pm **Pre View**
I never just focus, i just do a lot of things, and every time there goes a wow through meditation, and sometimes when i don't find it... well it tells me i did not study enough, not enough inside to do the engineering i want, so very frustrating, but i can only respond to myself and face my own truth at that moment = dig deeper, work harder .
Sometimes it is merely ALLOWING SELF TO FOCUS AND GO DEEP, that is when information just flows,,,
3/30, 6:59pm **Pre View**
i would like to know what opium is about, never did or do any drugs,
but i want just some little
knowledge in the study with opium.
3/30, 6:59pm **Koz Kozmos**
truth is not enough for me and i like to stay in bed most of the time ,
just being the tortured poet with the opium bit
3/30, 7:00pm **Pre View**
right, but it'll will get u places easily and winds u out of torture
what do u want ?
3/30, 7:01pm **Koz Kozmos**
the legal drugs should be avoided
i want guns drugs and booty
wot do i want?
thank u for asking : i want to awaken and to reactivate and have fun
3/30, 7:02pm **Pre View**
nothing is legal here, anyways, i don't want nor need drugs, can go miles further with my own lighting
bolt which frustrates people over here as i show them things thr meditation -
but then again they wish thy could do the same ----
only not willing to work hard for it while it is so interesting,
3/30, 7:03pm **Koz Kozmos**
i've tried most of my life to be a super star ,
but nobody in my hood wants the starry wisdom
3/30, 7:03pm **Pre View** sure, a super clown
3/30, 7:03pm **Koz Kozmos** the trickster
3/30, 7:04pm **Pre View** maybe they want all of u
3/30, 7:04pm **Koz Kozmos**
i worked hard and it made things worse
3/30, 7:04pm **Pre View** what did u do
3/30, 7:04pm **Koz Kozmos**
i sound disappointed and frustrated and i am
o no i've gotta type it
is it ok ?
3/30, 7:05pm **Pre View**
u sound like a Gun and smell like gunpowder
3/30, 7:06pm **Koz Kozmos**
mediation, yoga, ritual magic, shamanic use of plant teachers etc
u sound like a Gun and smell like gunpowder' :
i use astral bullets to kill people in other dimensions
3/30, 7:07pm **Pre View**
Everything OUTSIDE, nothing INSIDE huh ?
3/30, 7:08pm **Koz Kozmos**
NO! stop being bossy! mainly inside,
i'm bored within with the within huh

3/30, 7:09pm **Pre View**
are u no
t interesting enought in yourself ?
3/30, 7:10pm **Koz Kozmos**
in my self ?
3/30, 7:10pm **Pre View**
what is having fun to u ?
3/30, 7:10pm **Koz Kozmos**
i've never had fun so i'm not sure
3/30, 7:11pm **Pre View**
simply, are u not an interesting event for yourself on this plane
3/30, 7:11pm **Koz Kozmos**
no, what i've become has stopped me becoming who i am
3/30, 7:12pm **Pre View**
i understand, fun comes when u feel good about something i think,
and u can further that feeling by
expanding on them, evaluate the higher sensations people try to find in drug
That is sad Koz, backtrack tthat & pick up ur shining gloves
3/30, 7:13pm **Koz Kozmos**
it always turned out more the negative, a curse maybe be a hex , the intent of the dark team thank u for talking , its not all about me
3/30, 7:14pm **Pre View**
can u not rise ur vibes above the negative perceptions
3/30, 7:14pm **Koz Kozmos**
yes , just about, but i don't believe in turning the other cheek,
the enemy has to be destroyed
3/30, 7:15pm **Pre View**
i mean, no one is being saved, we need to do it ourselves, and find that exclusive elixir
3/30, 7:16pm **Koz Kozmos**
i have the elixir in my blood but i've been wiped and broken , but they can't kill me
ahhhh ok
so they try to keep me wiped, i don't think we can save ourselves
3/30, 7:17pm **Pre View**
every single decision can make ur blood run on different batteries,
i need to polish mine as well
oh YESS we are SELF RESPONSIBLE, too many people still love to make anyone else , even the Divine responsible for creations on Earth. We are all in it together and need to solve it in unity even if we don't see much of that, we can imagine the bigger vision an give respect to what drives through. It is all about taking action and doing what needs to be done, FEARLESS,
3/30, 7:18pm **Koz Kozmos**
but i don't rely on the Freudian father finger to come and save us, awakening has been blocked , i need action, proof , this dimesion is pathetic
3/30, 7:20pm **Pre View**
relying makes u vulnerable & compromising,... Cooperatives may give u a new outlook, ACTION indeed where u start ur engine, question is always :
how do u fuel it ... with what?
3/30, 7:20pm **Koz Kozmos**
humans are a bunch of odious insidious cretins and i'm not keen on animals , i rely on nothing fuel is consumed by negative entities and transformed into snack food for psychic vampires
3/30, 7:22pm **Pre View**
on urself, that should be strong enough, but it is not
3/30, 7:23pm **Koz Kozmos**
? yes , seems that way , but i hate the weakling stuck in the sludge of their own masks
i'm in a dark mood , the dark dude from the light machine
i should let u get back to the crystalline dimensions of the green ray

3/30, 7:26pm **Pre View**
I meant the fuel u breathe = light
eg : if today i align with Mars & Cassiopeia /RED RAY ----
THEN I DO KNOW I'M UNSTOPPABLE cause that is one of the 13 characteristics and consciousness of that ray,
but when i merge it with lets say blue intuition and some gold balancing , then people would understand me better. Let's just say i fuel my body with energies available to all, but i think knowledge about it is necessary to not mess up too much when conversing with people.
So that is my soup i choose from every day
3/30, 7:26pm **Koz Kozmos**
o no
3/30, 7:27pm **Pre View**
Green is knowledge, the absolute, the architect, bridge of light,
just a choosing for what i need to know
that particular day and sometimes i don't; because of this and that ,
but it keeps me going
3/30, 7:28pm **Koz Kozmos**
no more visualisations via the new age mind control program
3/30, 7:28pm **Pre View**
nonono ,
i get my own info that is it, no more no less and then i do have to trust myself to see how it works out
3/30, 7:29pm **Koz Kozmos**
i've got a book with this stuff in, i'll see if i can find it
3/30, 7:29pm **Pre View**
that is my fun, when i get info and it gets pleasant (the outcome versus people).
There is no written book with this stuff,,, or I could write it,
3/30, 7:30pm **Koz Kozmos**
when i say fun: i don't mean vacuous entertainment i'll get it
3/30, 7:30pm **Pre View**
U mean a book with the encodements of the solar system?
does not exist to my knowledge , anyways i never read, maybe I should,
it all bores me, maybe not the animal kingdom and the book of knowledge,
the book of celts,
the very ancient tracks so to speak,,,,
3/30, 7:32pm **Koz Kozmos**
Starlight Elixirs & Cosmic Vibrational Healing...Michel Smulkis Fred Rubenfled
3/30, 7:32pm **Pre View**
don't know about that, will check on it
3/30, 7:33pm **Koz Kozmos**
will need to re - look at it
i hate reading
3/30, 7:33pm **Pre View**
What does it tell u, i never read either,
just maybe a few articles, scientific stuff attracts me,
3/30, 7:33pm **Koz Kozmos**
it may be alighed with what u'r saying not looked at for a while
3/30, 7:33pm **Pre View** May Be ?
3/30, 7:34pm **Koz Kozmos**
? yes , may be, its Saturday , u going down the disco ?
3/30, 7:35pm **Pre View**
well, just tell me if u do know, anyways ,
like i said, if i can see changes and experience them with what i upgrade with,
out of the blue,
U disco ? Ok swirl ur vibes, they need u
LETS DANCVE, haha to the new disco rays,

3/30, 7:36pm **Koz Kozmos**
disco: place were people danced in the 7tease i stay away from humans
days are too long for me
i try to sleep as much as poss ible
3/30, 7:37pm **Pre View**
sorry misunderstood, me never disco, rock, but i keep inside for months now,
as people are willing to
drink my blood,,, the vampire show when you talk truth they do not wanna know
3/30, 7:37pm **Koz Kozmos**
who's your fave rock band
3/30, 7:37pm **Pre View**
i cannot sleep
3/30, 7:38pm **Koz Kozmos**
i can't wake up , who's your fave rock band?
u should maybe check the book i mentioned,
i'm not saying your surprising plagiarizing
3/30, 7:41pm **Pre View**
Rock band? I amm not sure,
there is so many different types ofmusic that have a different outcome on the
body, and brains will just keep on going
3/30, 7:41pm **Koz Kozmos rock band?**
bbr any ?
3/30, 7:42pm **Pre View**
i meant anything i need that second in time, don't know much about music,
but i do know what i need,
3/30, 7:42pm **Koz Kozmos**
POPTASTIC
i needed to make music, but i've stopped or have been stopped
3/30, 7:43pm **Pre View**
eg : u posted the African Bambaataa - i played it 100 times and it deblocked many
things,
so when i get something i know it is right, I vibe to it,
3/30, 7:43pm **Koz Kozmos**
i'm not a paranoid delusion, african Bambaataa nearly ruined that track
but the rap is kool and deep ,
and arogant in a spiritual way
3/30, 7:45pm **Pre View**
Rap is changes , on many things on this plane, only people are not aware
3/30, 7:45pm **Koz Kozmos**
i think i need to get into the rap game maybe i'm too nigga
3/30, 7:46pm **Pre View**
Please do
3/30, 7:46pm **Koz Kozmos**
i've tried , most rap fans are young white males
3/30, 7:46pm **Pre View**
Make some music, there is no try, u do or u don't
3/30, 7:46pm **Koz Kozmos**
living in the cartoon hood
i've made loads of music
3/30, 7:47pm **Pre View** Post !
3/30, 7:47pm **Koz Kozmos**
tends to be ignored , hard to expalin
3/30, 7:47pm **Pre View**
Is it as good as ur poetic instincts ?
u don't need explanation

3/30, 7:48pm **Koz Kozmos**
some one listened to my mu
sic and said i had a great voice but the lyrics were wrong it always back fires ,
it hurts and depresses me
it brought me nothing but saddness
3/30, 7:49pm **Pre View**
and u LET that into ur cells ?
come on Koz, are u as delicate? ,
i understand i am too . Maybe it will make u work harder now
3/30, 7:49pm **Koz Kozmos**
the problenmm is i'm not in the cell
3/30, 7:49pm **Pre View**
where are u then ?
3/30, 7:49pm **Koz Kozmos**
i've given up, more freedom than most and i can see the jailers
3/30, 7:50pm **Pre View**
No u did not, u'r talking to me, so u did not give up
3/30, 7:50pm **Koz Kozmos**
ennui, and at least you're a weirdo
3/30, 7:50pm **Pre View**
again ? ok make it interesting then
3/30, 7:50pm **Koz Kozmos**
which is a plus, i'm a wyrdo
3/30, 7:51pm **Pre View**
Why weirdo , ur a lovely freak
3/30, 7:51pm **Koz Kozmos**
same thing same nothing if u want to get Zen
3/30, 7:52pm **Pre View**
where is your some thing?
3/30, 7:52pm **Koz Kozmos**
i have nothing
3/30, 7:52pm **Pre View**
no attraction to zen, i breathe on the wild side
3/30, 7:52pm **Koz Kozmos**
I practiced THE NEZ
3/30, 7:52pm **Pre View**
What is yur best hip hop
3/30, 7:52pm **Koz Kozmos**
the zen inversion
3/30, 7:53pm **Koz Kozmos** most hip hop is crap
i'm the only rapper in the hood
3/30, 7:53pm **Koz Kozmos**
but i'm more of a vision singer
3/30, 7:53pm **Pre View**
i'd love to see u rap,
3/30, 7:54pm **Koz Kozmos**
things go wrong if i try
i'm targeted , its hard to explain
3/30, 7:54pm **Pre View**
OK feel my arrows,
i'm indian bloodvibe

3/30, 7:55pm **Koz Kozmos**
i tried to record last summer and so much went wrong with the tech I',
HYP HOPI, i'm hyp hopi a space druid
3/30, 7:56pm **Pre View**
sure u are with or without
3/30, 7:56pm **Koz Kozmos**
wot do u mean
3/30, 7:56pm **Pre View**
l Love the word druid, i meant u are hippy with or without musical scales
3/30, 7:57pm **Koz Kozmos**
i hate youth culture
3/30, 7:57pm **Pre View**
hippy or hip hopping
3/30, 7:57pm **Koz Kozmos**
do u know The Hopi
3/30, 7:57pm **Pre View**
why, are u not youth ?
what is ur timeline
3/30, 7:57pm **Koz Kozmos**
the hopi Indians
i'm already dead , 53 and aging fast
3/30, 7:58pm **Pre View**
I thought u where young as u told me,
Are u 53 ?
3/30, 7:58pm **Koz Kozmos**
wot about u , yes last sunday
3/30, 7:58pm **Pre View**
u are fooling me
3/30, 7:59pm **Koz Kozmos**
no i'm 53 sure
i said when i showed pics , I said they were six years old and i changed
3/30, 7:59pm **Pre View**
u look no more then 30
3/30, 7:59pm **Koz Kozmos**
i did, i don't anymore,
i've almost been destroyed
i did look really young for a long while
3/30, 8:00pm **Pre View**
What destroyed u so much
3/30, 8:00pm **Koz Kozmos**
being here , since i first let out a scream when i saw my mother
3/30, 8:01pm **Pre View**
know that, she didn't want to know about u
3/30, 8:01pm **Koz Kozmos**
changelings...have a bad deal
3/30, 8:01pm **Pre View**
fearfull person that mother of yours. Why bad deal?
3/30, 8:02pm **Koz Kozmos**
she's just another moron on the dirt ball
3/30, 8:02pm **Pre View**
I like the dirt ball (sometimes) the music
3/30, 8:02pm **Koz Kozmos**
becuz changelings are targeted by the dark team
fucked up dimensionally astral rape

3/30, 8:03pm **Pre View**
not allowing them is getting out of that rape
3/30, 8:03pm **Koz Kozmos**
via the wipe out and targeted by walkin from day one its not as easy as that
3/30, 8:04pm **Pre View**
Do u know Mark Appleman ?
3/30, 8:04pm **Koz Kozmos**
but i learn and burn nope who's he
3/30, 8:06pm **Pre View**
Connect2Source is his web (i like the info he gives on galactic perspectives)
but he never went Universal.
Its a way to comprehend what i did 10 years from now,
and where i stand now don't burn, you're very precious, u really are
3/30, 8:07pm **Koz Kozmos**
the fire snake
3/30, 8:07pm **Pre View**
King Cobra's head or tail ? One is underground, the other above
3/30, 8:07pm **Koz Kozmos**
i'm not keen on snakes
too many occult types have them for pets
3/30, 8:08pm **Pre View**
i never met any, so don't know about their energy
3/30, 8:08pm **Koz Kozmos**
you must have an idea
3/30, 8:09pm **Pre View**
i work with dragons, dragons, dragons, i just loooooove powerful things. Wish i would understand why
Any idea ?
3/30, 8:09pm **Koz Kozmos** l
low grade and concerned with their own power and sexual ego etc, the above was my Analyze of occult types ....dragons all over the place in Wales, i live in the Reptile City
3/30, 8:11pm **Pre View**
I never understood that until people told me that is all they are interested in, (i've been a loner all of my
life - so when going into society a few years ago) i only had my eyes wide open....
3/30, 8:11pm **Koz Kozmos**
i'm a dragon slayer
i'm a loner too, maybe spent 85% of my life alone
3/30, 8:11pm **Pre View**
reptiles have this intricate smile i cannot figure out
3/30, 8:12pm **Koz Kozmos**
society is for suckers they're not smiling
3/30, 8:12pm **Pre View**
I am a pancake
3/30, 8:12pm **Koz Kozmos**
? a pancake
3/30, 8:13pm **Pre View**
haha koz, i'm doing my best to be soft,
but i am reflecting on what u told me this morning
3/30, 8:13pm **Koz Kozmos**
? why are u trying to be soft y soft pancake?

3/30, 8:17pm **Pre View**
PATRONIZING: that word hit me , hurt me, told me i needed a review, and i 'm greatfull u did tell me this
3/30, 8:17pm **Koz Kozmos**

MUSIC: THE DOORS/CRAWLING KING SNAKE

3/30, 8:17pm **Koz Kozmos**
morrison is not as kool as me
3/30, 8:18pm **Pre View**
I never doubted u, thx for posting,
3/30, 8:18pm **Koz Kozmos**
have fun Pre but not too much , bye
3/30, 8:18pm **Pre View**
With patronizing ? Why not too much
3/30, 8:19pm **Koz Kozmos**
i was joking , puritanical humor
3/30, 8:19pm **Pre View**
u see, its not all a death penalty, purity alright alright
3/30, 8:20pm **Koz Kozmos** nah
3/30, 8:20pm **Pre View**
break the chains and messing with the new building
3/30, 8:21pm **Koz Kozmos**
but i have purity and will become the high gene i've broken the chains as much as i can
3/30, 8:21pm **Pre View**
I'm sure u will, though your genes were already endlessly qualified
3/30, 8:21pm **Koz Kozmos**
and blow up buildings
3/30, 8:22pm **Pre View**
nono, NO ! Just blow your mind; that should do for now
3/30, 8:22pm **Koz Kozmos**
u don't blow my mind , i wish u did
3/30, 8:22pm **Pre View**
Take deep care my friend i am becomming Bossy
3/30, 8:22pm **Koz Kozmos**
but your vibe is ok
3/30, 8:23pm **Pre View**
What the hell do u know about my vibes
3/30, 8:23pm **Koz Kozmos**
a little becuz i have talked with u
3/30, 8:23pm **Pre View**
They are encoded ,mind u !!! with beautiful golden song notes, I whish i could sing a song for u, just for u , but i don't have this skill, makes me feel sad
3/30, 8:24pm **Koz Kozmos**

MUSIC: PSYCHO REALM- PALACE OF EXILE

3/30, 8:25pm **Pre View**
inhale , exhale, what is in between = the fabulous sabotist
3/30, 8:26pm **Koz Kozmos**

MUSIC: PATTI SMITH – HORSES

3/30, 8:26pm **Pre View**
thank u for the music without the psycho parallel

3/30, 8:26pm **Koz Kozmos**
have u heared horses by patti smith peace and war byeeeeeeeeeeeeeeeeee
3/30, 8:27pm **Pre View**
Patti huh, once seen her, she is not a great talker
or is she deep inside,
3/30, 8:27pm **Koz Kozmos**
dare i say it, lol
3/30, 8:27pm **Pre View**
Aha u don't want to taste
3/30, 8:27pm **Koz Kozmos**
i like horses
3/30, 8:28pm **Pre View**
me too, a lot, power right , such beautiful spirits,
3/30, 8:28pm **Koz Kozmos**
she was wiped by the dark team in 78 , anyways
3/30, 8:28pm **Pre View**
possibly, she is very dark now
3/30, 8:28pm **Koz Kozmos**
she's deeper than stevie nicks
3/30, 8:29pm **Pre View**
OK then Koz, lets screen a new screen and find out about them
3/30, 8:29pm **Koz Kozmos** ok
3/30, 8:29pm **Pre View**
stevie knows, patti does not
3/30, 8:29pm **Koz Kozmos**
i disagree, but they'r both dumb chicks, who cares
3/30, 8:30pm **Pre View**
nice ridm
3/30, 8:30pm **Koz Kozmos**
it all tastes and when we first heared the songs
3/30, 8:30pm **Pre View**
right no caressssssss , first is not now
3/30, 8:31pm **Koz Kozmos**

MUSIC:LOOSE WOMEN/stevie nicks interview

3/30, 8:32pm **Pre View**
Ok lets get some air Koz, we'll catch each of us somewhere,,,, unlimited
3/30, 8:32pm **Koz Kozmos**

MUSIC:PATTI SMITH INTERVIEW

3/30, 8:32pm **Koz Kozmos**
yes, i agree , thank u for the long talk choose your fave dumb chick interview, byeee
3/30, 8:33pm **Pre View**
it is of course true heartfelt mutual pleasure, so thank u so much too .
PE upside down attention

APRIL 2013

MY INTERNALS: As the Planet is rising into new ascension degrees and humans start to awaken to make their transit into Light Consciousness and Light Living, I think it is more important to develop the Higher senses, the light communications with many Species, the Animal Kingdoms and the Elements.

The elimination of the subconsciousness levels is hard on people especially as the release of karmic bonds is being promoted and low degrees such as regression. There is no such thing as karma, and regression only means that consciousness is not awake. When fully awake, we know and we feel the beauty of Space. The elimination of fear based diseases, stress and toxic waste allows to move through the imbalances as overriding brainwaves into higher shifts requires these higher level clearing procedures. We can all become a Spiritual doctor and heal out the old mental barriers that held us in captivity for far too long. Physical disease such as lung cancers, drug & alcohol abuse, depression, arrogance, disrespect, anxiety... and integrating peace, joy, balance, ease and grace is something that can be learned through conscious devotional alignments and daily upgrades in meditation. I am not really sure if Koz Kozmos truly worked with Light integrations, he may haS lot and gained knowledge into the magical realms of Spirit.
It pains me to see how much humans are disconnected from nature, from health, from the animal kingdoms, from the Essence of pure elements such as the herbal and flower kingdoms as well as the crystal kingdoms that bring through the Crystallization into Cryst Light. Not knowing how to deal and connect with animals has led to a lot of grief and disgrace for nobody can ascend with animal instincts in the body that were never meant to feed the body and so natural evolution has severely been disrupted as humans eat the fish that are meant to feed the mammals. And so the nutrition of the coral reefs can no longer come through as the waters of the earth are piled with toxic debris and complete disruption of the ecology.

Making the bridge between animal cs and human cs is something very beautiful as it allows us to step into the ancestral tracking system, guidance and communication with the natural world. We could learn so much from the indigenous people and simple life styles.
There are so many levels of Direct Source connections and paths. Once it is switched on through a Foundational implementation and healing process, there is no turning back. Its signature frequency becomes very strong and starts dialoging with our inner voice in which we can easily redirect out attention and intentions through telepathic waves and resonance. The human kingdom seems to be drowning in fear and helplessness for they gave their soul away to something even lesser.

The movement out of Systemic Crisis leading to Health or Global Immunity to Mental/Physical/ Psychological Dis-eases requires a lot more educational systems to open up in schools and universities, even in kindergarten. Re-Institutionalizing MENTAL, PSYCHOLOGICAL HEALTH into its Origin requires Re-Organizing Self with the Re-Organization of Earth & the Universe back into Health and thus the repair of the Human condition moves synchrone with the repair of the soil.

Looking back today, it is easy to understand why the metafluctuation, which changed the world in some fairly radical ways, was dampened back into the existing paradigm that did not have the coherence to 'carry' humanity over the threshold of a rigid ceiling of "unchangeable" values and beliefs.
We are precariously adrift in an instability threshold as the delicate balance of life on planet earth has been severely disrupted. I just wonder how many people are working their ways back into balance and repairing themselves through what they are: LIGHT
The systemic crisis is existential, the environmental, spiritual, social, educational, economic, and political crisis' all have the same root.
That root is a 'natural' errancy inherent in the perceptive mechanisms of the dualistic neural-mental consciousness structure.
Today we need to repair the health of nature, the soil and all the imbalances in order to allow new nutrients to fulfill a new path in evolution. New Health programs, along new human conduct regarding the fabric of mental/ psychological capabilities need to be reviewed and rewired based on the ethics of respect and integrity.

Young children and youth worldwide need to be given the opportunity of a life time to get get proper education about their Human Essence, its functionality, evolution and options for proper Energy management through Light Technology/Science as applicable in every faculty and to improve rapid integration of studies, intelligence, knowledge, healing modems such as in the departments of individual psychology and mental capabilities:
We need to take steps to elaborate the basic principles of such a new paradigm of human understanding based exactly upon physics and metaphysics of Consciousness, Light and Space. We might also be somewhat horrified by the madness of humankind ruled by the mode of ignorance, the philosophy of scarcity, with an economy based on fossil fuels and war, and an emotional pathology of fear and self interest that derives from dual input.

Today every human being should have the option to work through a New Light Structure that benefits all, and research in schools and Universities through daily disciplined realignment should teach interconnectivity's through the rewiring of consciousness and brainwaves which bring changes in the anatomy and eliminates/evaporates poor health and poor ethics regarding the stuck patterns in psychology such as fears, anger, distress, frustration, stress, anxiety. If every living being is given the option to clear their Essence from old mental/ psychological issues on a daily basis through Light Technology or meditational alignments that deal with the Science of this Universe, then chances are these people return into Mental Brilliance ready to serve the world with a Master Degree that invents what the world needs today and that is STRONG AND HEALTHY PEOPLE to create a world based on New Ethics globally.

Meditational alignments is simply allowing living light into the human organism that bio-couples into all living organisms at the pre-quantum level and infuses them with life and sentience at the most fundamental level : that is termed "Transduction Biophysics" which deals with the nature of living systems as inter dimensional biotransducers of the flux-flow or life force.
Is it not a matter of focus and listening to internal instruction, knowing that light carries consciousness that brings new values into our brainwaves and can certainly override low psychological patterns that created diseases.

The exclusion and non recognition of this primary sentient, all pervading, self-radiant fundamental form of light is what leads to the reductionistic tendency of so called "material realism" in science and leads modern biology into reducing life to mere molecular machines as does the whole field of genetic engineering and nanotechnology which is not without its valid merits and impressive advances but is essentially reductionistic, mechanistic and spiritless in it's orientation.In meditation we can get instructions to BREATHE through Living Light which composes the very fabric of space and dynamically weaves itself into all of the forms of mass and energy comprising the manifest universe, is the very Source and wellspring of all life and is in fact that which is living in us in each and every moment.We can no longer allow any societal avenue to block this kind of information for that would be very inhumane and does not flow with our human rights. Any human being can become a "hyper-dimensional crystal lattice" which is his nature through which any consciousness can be integrated and override density such as fear, panic, self- destructive motion, abused mentality , trauma and all psychological invasions swimming in the lower fields of consciousness.

It is pretty clear how much Koz is suffering from the invasion of universal hybrids and monsters, yet why has he not been educated into self protection and why are so many still so ignorant when it comes to Light integrations and evolution? ALL EDUCATION HAS BEEN HELD BACK, that is the only answer, but we are strong and can move right through these atrocities and broken veins. Lets move into this next chapter.

4/1, 6:33pm **Koz Kozmos**
PE upside down what do u mean?
4/1, 6:35pm **Pre View**
PE = PAY (Hebrew) euhm find an equal energy within urself to pay for the energy earth is supplying
4/1, 6:36pm **Koz Kozmos**
ahhhhh...silly me!
4/1, 6:37pm **Pre View**
my brain is not fast either today
4/1, 6:39pm **Koz Kozmos**
mine is super fast and spinning outa control
4/1, 6:41pm **Pre View**
good, show me what it tastes like
4/1, 6:53pm **Pre View**
Great Koz, go on hunting your madness
4/1, 6:55pm **Koz Kozmos**
nah, the authorities will arrest me, and lock me up best to lay low
4/1, 6:57pm **Pre Vie**4/1, 6:43pm **Koz Kozmos**
MUSIC:MINISTRY-THE MIND IS A TERRIBLE THING TO TASTE

4/1, 6:43pm **Koz Kozmos**
i've not heard this long player
4/1, 6:45pm **Pre View**
i will hear & listen to it
4/1, 6:47pm **Koz Kozmos**
industrial hard rock , bit basic but fun to do
4/1, 6:48pm **Pre View** i am aligning
4/1, 6:49pm **Koz Kozmos**
murder murder murder kill kill kill kill
lay low with some chocolate & make ur sourcerers ' stone work like magic
4/1, 6:58pm **Koz Kozmos**
nah...nothing gives me comfort anymore not even the void
4/1, 7:06pm **Koz Kozmos**
being on FB is like wading thr sewage
i may delete my page
4/1, 7:08pm **Pre View** don't u like communication?
4/1, 7:10pm **Koz Kozmos**
not with morons in front of a screen trapped in the reptile city going unsane....
4/1, 7:10pm **Pre View**
This pre view is new account, so i only allow a few people,
i'm quite at ease (cannot delete my otheraccount as it is attached to my work)
but i leave it for what it is and post no more so...
4/1, 7:11pm **Koz Kozmos**
FB is also corrupt and a toxic vibe
4/1, 7:12pm **Pre View**
reptile city, good idea, might paint one some day
Corruption sure, i only see what i want and only use it for some purposes ...
4/1, 7:12pm **Koz Kozmos**
eyes see deeper beyond the layers of lies
4/1, 7:13pm **Pre View**
u see fear of course, so lies are the outcome for many

1, 7:13pm **Koz Kozmos**
but i understand wot u mean fear and lies exist whether i see them or not
4/1, 7:15pm **Pre View**
like u & i ; we do not accept that,
so many people tell me: u & Koz commenting on FB post is quite inunderstandable ,
they actually fear to put that as a comment on my Fb post which is a pity for the
comments could assist the larger picture of understanding ascension.
4/1, 7:15pm **Koz Kozmos**
that was hard to follow
4/1, 7:15pm **Pre View**
i want to be as big as king kong ? follow what ?
4/1, 7:16pm **Koz Kozmos**
there are too many big monkeys with crap tattoos shitting all over the place
4/1, 7:18pm **Pre View**
what tattoo do u like, i want a golden one, no body does that
Koz Kozmos
with their big dogs shitting all over the place i meant I knew a gut(good) way back
with a golden star on his forehead he had it done in the 60's
4/1, 7:19pm **Pre View**
sure, maybe change any ART- i-culation do u know anyone who does it?
4/1, 7:19pm **Koz Kozmos**
he was a schizophrenic alcho bore fuck the consensus tattoo,
i want to start a lazer remover biz
4/1, 7:20pm **Pre View** all my friends are psycho's
4/1, 7:21pm **Koz Kozmos**
or maybe just tear of people clicheed skins I have no friends
4/1, 7:21pm **Pre View**
what is that lazer ,,,
4/1, 7:21pm **Koz Kozmos**

MUSIC: Lazer Tattoo Removal

4/1, 7:21pm **Pre View**
sorry i am on the phone ------
Koz Kozmos
a lot of cash will be made in the next 10 years from this give up light engineering and
get rich take your time only talk if u want
4/1, 7:43pm **Koz Kozmos**
as i'm sure u willl
4/1, 9:03pm **Koz Kozmos**
going ofline take care April 2, 2013
4/2, 12:40am **Pre View**
i will not take care any longer, i will not
i feel like a werewolf
April 2, 2013 4/2, 3:25pm **Koz Kozmos**
tkae care of the wyrdwolf so u can kill
4/2, 6:13pm **Pre View**
killed it all
4/2, 7:32pm **Pre View**
What about u; what do u think about when u wake up ?
4/2, 9:16pm **Pre View**
I'm tired Jimmy, really tired of helping people, i'm getting out of that, its of no use .
If they don't get it, let
m get what they want to get, though i do appreciate u can bare me,
as i do not have anything to loose.

Thank u for what u really are!
4/2, 9:18pm **Pre View**
That is the WEREWOLF gettttting weird,,
i allow myself that u understand without wording, thank u for being here !
Koz Kozmos
its hard to follow your english i'm tierd also
4/3, 2:35pm **Pre View**
Why is it hard ? to figure out wot i mean to say ? That comes from the alignments i have, it is to make
people think twice ,,,
4/3, 2:46pm **Koz Kozmos**
because of the way u word things its not a complaint i can't speak another language I'm also dyselxic
4/3, 2:55pm **Pre View**
Dyslectic, yes u told me, does that cause problems for understanding?
I think u understand me far beyond anyone else, and as far as I am concerned, i like to play with words and trigger something with people and make them go nuts thr wording. Just some fun to do;;;
4/3, 2:58pm **Koz Kozmos**
understanding language structures that are a bit confusing just be yourself
i'll be ok just saying, thats all
4/3, 3:10pm **Pre View**
need to cook for the hungry wolves here, get back later Koz
4/3, 3:10pm **Koz Kozmos**
I'm The death chef in the rebirth pod
4/3, 4:13pm **Pre View**
i will not question these gifts, i'm sure u'll collect the best species
4/3, 6:24pm **Koz Kozmos**
I just want my super powers back so i can destroy this dimension and save the earth ....
then I leave
4/4, 2:03pm **Pre View**
saving earth goes along with repair shoes.
Btw : my english is not difficult, my language is in any language 'cause people can answer on many different wavelengths which makes it amusing
4/4, 2:39pm **Koz Kozmos**
da chuffzoid lunber jub ov chumley bogles mtipppppz
the ziperlee zaperleee zooomz truom sparry deepellz
4/4, 5:32pm **Pre View**
ok lets go zipperlee zoom, zooming in ?
4/4, 5:45pm **Pre View** y
you're a quick catcher, love that about u, even though we always answer on different timelines, I AM
definitely grateful to have met u, with what u are today
4/4, 6:58pm **Koz Kozmos**
i'm the death wand that will kill every one on earth
4/4, 6:59pm **Pre View**
No way, u are more aware then wot kills u, i treasure that
4/4, 7:00pm **Koz Kozmos**
we can't die some guru told me i will find a way
4/4, 7:03pm **Pre View**
get out of everybody's mind, take urself into ACCOUNT !
As for me, u are precious, but i am delicate, very, as i do not know what a man is like, they all feel so mindless, brainless;;
4/4, 7:08pm **Koz Kozmos**
any ideas ?

Plenty, as i experienced them,
4/4, 7:15pm **Koz Kozmos**
I need a plan
4/4, 7:19pm **Pre View**
U are the plan ! wot u seek outside of you, will never get into to u
4/4, 7:19pm **Koz Kozmos**
I still need a plan
4/4, 7:22pm **Pre View**
Ok, wot are u willing to give up, & give in with
4/4, 7:23pm **Koz Kozmos**
give in with?
4/4, 7:28pm **Pre View**
Where u are now, understand that & break lose,wot do i know, this is wot i feel
4/4, 7:28pm **Koz Kozmos**
easy to say
4/4, 7:29pm **Pre View** Sure is , is it wrong ?
4/4, 7:29pm **Koz Kozmos**

MUSIC: ATTACHMENT REMOVED
(many songs helas cannot be recovered)

4/4, 7:30pm **Koz Kozmos**
? wrong
4/4, 7:31pm **Pre View**
Am I wrong on triggering where U are, thx for the Band, can i post it or will u ?
4/4, 7:32pm **Koz Kozmos**
u acn can i'm nowwhere
4/4, 7:35pm **Pre View**
please Koz, why ? stop downgrading your values
I miss out on music, do not have much knowledge in that domain, but u feed me quite well
4/4, 7:36pm **Koz Kozmos**
I have no values
4/4, 7:37pm Koz Kozmos

YOUTUBE: Iggy Pop - New Values 1979 Full Vinyl

4/4, 7:39pm **Koz Kozmos**
poppin offf Pre catch u agin, again
4/4, 7:40pm **Pre View**
ok, i will have u in my heart,,,
4/4, 7:40pm **Koz Kozmos**
best not too
4/4, 7:44pm **Pre View**
My choice, not yours, smile even though, smile even when, smile!
4/5, 7:49pm **Koz Kozmos**
u out there ?
4/5, 8:38pm **Pre View**
yep i'm out here, what happened ?
4/5, 8:39pm **Koz Kozmos**
nuthin ever happens to thorny for this reality think Rimbaud said that
no hassle don't wish to bother u
4/5, 8:39pm **View**
my mind is here, just talk & get it out whichever way ,
thorns are lovely, when people understand them..

4/5, 8:43pm **Koz Kozmos**
nothing to get out, i bloom within, my majik is wasted on this dimension but thank u
4/5, 8:45pm **Pre View**
every action gets a standby, time for u to move byond dimensions i guess,,,
a galaxy is but a galaxy until uwork with it,
same for u , you're just a brain & body until u use it concsiously
4/5, 8:46pm **Koz Kozmos**
standby, time for u...? wot does that mean, u smart ass
4/5, 8:47pm **Koz Kozmos**
"A poet makes himself a visionary through a long, boundless, and systematized disorganization of all the senses. All forms of love, of suffering, of madness; he searches himself, he exhausts within himself all poisons, and preserves their quintessences. Unspeakable torment, where he will need the greatest faith, a superhuman strength, where he becomes all men the great invalid, the great criminal, the great accursed--and the Supreme Scientist! For he attains the unknown! Because he has cultivated his soul, already rich, more than anyone! He attains the unknown, and if, demented, he finally loses the understanding of his visions, he will at least have seen them! So what if he is destroyed in his ecstatic flight through things unheard of, unnameable: other horrible workers will come; they will begin at the horizons where the first one has fallen!" – Arthur Rimbaud
4/5, 8:47pm **Pre View**
my ass is too small
4/5, 8:47pm **Koz Kozmos**
ok how do i use it diffrently?
and go beyond the matrix flesh?
4/5, 8:53pm **Pre View**
Rimbaud : science gets the torments out of cultivating every atom more precious then before, 'cause science without spirit without our rebelluous nature doesn't get far as proved. The new soul has opened (Cape Town) time for us to taste, integrate & teach that. All my posts are about that, still, very few
understand the KEYS beyond the given scales, but I don't care, (happy u do understand)
4/5, 8:54pm **Koz Kozmos** i understand nothing
4/5, 8:55pm **Pre View**
Do we at least need to be aligned to 9th D, this enables us to bi-locate
tri-locate, but 8thD or bridge will
get u strong into the knowledge & maybe Arc consciousness (I wonder if all 13 Arcs have stationed underground Oxford University) Could you have a look over there pls?
4/5, 8:55pm **Koz Kozmos**
True alchemy lies in this formula: 'Your memory and your senses are but the nourishment of your creative impulse'."
– Arthur Rimbaud, Illuminations: i was Rimbaud, how do i reach 9 D ... (all 13 have stationed underground Oxford University ??? What do you mean to say by that? i'm lost,
your mystic cobbladee goob confuses me
4/5, 8:58pm **Pre View**
u do not understand?, knowledge comes timed and aligned
Well, if u do not meditate any longer, how can u possibly connect to these 13 Arcs that reveal great wisdom, informations & stuff u might need to move on . I wuz just joking and asking you to go to Oxford University to see if they are there
4/5, 8:58pm **Koz Kozmos**
"By being too sensitive I have wasted my life."
– Arthur Rimbaud fuck meditation "Come from forever, and you will go everywhere."
– Arthur Rimbaud i need other teck the great work is over for me it comes and gets me or i die of bordum (boredom) here

4/5, 9:00pm **Pre View**
9 D : this takes 360° clearance I guess, loads of brain shift, endurance, alchemy thr languages with lots of info, explanation to work with all Dimensions
A lot of training.

That is where I want to be to have instant answers, you could work your ass up there as well and not be bothered by the control mechanics.
4/5, 9:01pm **Koz Kozmos**
"I'm now making myself as scummy as I can. Why? I want to be a poet, and I'm working at turning myself into a seer. You won't understand any of this, and I'm almost incapable of explaining it to you. The idea is to reach the unknown by the derangement of all the senses. It involves enormous suffering, but one must be strong and be a born poet. It's really not my fault." – Arthur Rimbaud
4/5, 9:01pm **Pre View**
Then u would ASK FOR BOREDOM ,because u would have plenty to do
4/5, 9:01pm **Koz Kozmos**
i don't ask for it; don't give me ""The Secret"@ bs
4/5, 9:02pm **Pre View**
Secrets? Oh you meant THE SECRET bullshit book, ? I am not that off, mind you!!!
u want me to write on FB for 30 days ?
4/5, 9:02pm **Koz Kozmos**
wot does that mean
4/5, 9:03pm **Pre View**
why do u refer to Rimbaud ? it is too long ago, we are living quite other times
4/5, 9:03pm **Koz Kozmos**
the universe is one second old
4/5, 9:03pm **Koz Kozmos**
"Now I am an outcast. I loathe my country.
The best thing for me is a drunken sleep on the beach."
4/5, 9:04pm **Pre View**
ok but there is many other universes to discover. Would u like a drink ?
4/5, 9:04pm **Koz Kozmos**
i've not found any, and have worked like a nigga'z bytch.
Ok a pint of bile and hemlock for me
4/5, 9:05pm **Pre View**
if u cannot elevate yourself, u can only keep on seeing the boring Dimensions around u, Hemlock ?
4/5, 9:06pm **Koz Kozmos**
I am alone in possessing a key to this barbarous sideshow."
– Arthur Rimbaud Hemlock: several poisonous plants in the Apiaceae family
the universe must hate me
My wisdom is as spurned as chaos.
What is my nothingness, compared to the amazement that awaits you?"
Wot drink are u making ?
4/5, 9:09pm **Pre View**
Dear Koz, need to close, have Wizzards coming in, ... but will serve them the hemlock --- interesting;
catch u somewhere, try some Milky Way Keys,,,,, Like this Rimbaud but please, would love to read more of your poetic outlets.
4/5, 9:09pm **Koz Kozmos**
what are milky way keys? ok, have fun
4/5, 9:09pm **Pre View**
I drink some Wisky at times
4/5, 9:10pm **Koz Kozmos**
rock'n'rol hey
4/5, 9:10pm **Pre View**
Connect to the Milky Way !
4/5, 9:10pm **Koz Kozmos**
How? Orion is quite nice but expensive

4/5, 9:11pm **Pre View**
ok ok ok, i'll save a drink for u & beam u up,,,,,,
And Yess ORION is expensive when it comes to knowledge for you need to move yer ass first in the Celestial bodies and steam some new sun light through....
4/5, 9:11pm **Koz Kozmos**
i'll let u get on, bye, thankz Pre catch u again
4/5, 11:07pm **Pre View**
Rock & rolling it, oh man, all these retards, closed my eyes and counted my fingers,,, They really got me
depressed with sucking answers out of me, I closed it off& got their asses burned, but i'm burned too, do not even want to handle this any longer, & then again close myself off too much too many times. Even in the grosery store, people come to me – but as of now - i just look at them like a totally off-blown retard, then they start gaaaazzzziing & don't know what to think. Nice, but u don't like that word, lets say - well organized productive encounter for myself. Hey where are yur poems, hey u , u don't have friends, does that make me just a wave of answers, hey u, the Milky Way is like connecting to Cosmic Milk. Why is Orion expensive? Because you don' get burned and should have learned how to integrate that – just saying that these kind of educational training is expensive to understand...I am gridding with this for the first time although Universal guidances or Celestial gave me this 10 years ago and i did not listen, did not understand. Lets just keep on learning, but for me i do need the interaction now, the love from the other side of my moon, and that is really hurting me, too much torments with what i had never expected in my
life. Anyways outcomes are around the corner, everybody is feeling but not understanding it. Am i boring u ? Give your love back to yourself Koz, to yourself, and what exactly may that mean huh,,,
4/6, 3:44pm **Koz Kozmos**
I WAS 'NT SUCKING ANSWERS OUT OF U...Thats nonsense the reason for this as I am the trans rational meta spirit, ahhhhh the fucktards sub human scummards , i feel like u I've had enuff. NO! I've had enuff . Followed your suggestion looked at my book Stars: book a guide to astronomy for children, a little guide in colour which was better than some of the ancient star charts i have original from before recored history. I intoned a note and lay there my mind machine shooting and opening the kelidascope in my mind BUT NUTHIN .... there is no one around to be my friend but i'm more aware of the enemy
you're not boring, not sure what u mean 'what exactly is that right' ? Ask the milky way to get in touch with me please
4/6, 4:10pm **Koz Kozmos**
that was very deslexxxick

MY INTERNALS: I ONLY FILLED IN SOME PUNCTUATIONS,I DID NOT CORRECT THE SPELLING, SO IT WAS QUITE GOOD
4/6, 5:38pm **Koz Kozmos**
counted my fingers ?
4/6, 6:30pm **Pre View**
Hey koz, I was talking about the people out here, not uuuu! u never suck answers out of me , i like talking to u, sorry for the misunderstanding ! No no, when i'm pissed with people out here i start counting my fingers , that really makes them think i"m really nuts, and that frees me of them, just another of my styles to let them know something they'll never understand anyways. But u do, sorry again for the misunderstanding ! i'll watch the video laterrrrrr
4/6, 6:30pm **Koz Kozmos**
yes i got it just after i typed it it was a meme in my brain
4/6, 6:32pm **Koz Kozmos**
no need to be sorry it was my misunderstanding better nuts than a normal the vid is well worth a watch
but had the info years back, ok
4/6, 6:51pm **Koz Kosmos**

MUSIC: Galaxies, part 2: Crash Course Astronomy

4/6, 8:51pm **Pre View**
whoeps, just watched part one and wanted to ask u part 2 & here it is ,
hope there is many parts !
U know Koz, this is what i'v been talking about all the time so thank u !!!! i enjoyed it and it gave me some thinking , real thinking, because i have a lot of that similar, only i had to go through these teachings on the earth plane. So maybe now u understand what my teaching is about. And now, thx to this post i
understand i limited myself a lot , so big hug, gonna watch part 2
4/6, 10:31pm **Koz Kozmos**
I understood before k'mon
4/6, 10:32pm Koz Kozmos
MUSIC: Train - Drops of Jupiter (Official Video)

4/6, 10:32pm **Koz Kozmos**
u'll like the lyric
4/6, 11:42pm **Pre View**
thank u, i like it, yes, Jupiter is one of a kind, but u need your thyroid glands wide open Can u breathe till u tremble ?
4/6, 11:46pm **Koz Kozmos**
just being in this dimension makes me shake
did u hear the miilky way bits in the lyrics
4/7, 9:43pm **Pre View**
I did not hear it , will listen again in the days ahead,
My mind is closing off, but i do hold u where ever u need it, because i do acknowledge & appreciate your
life a lot. But for now, i delete all my comments, likes .... & only want to hold & really hold somebody knowing it eases everything.The pinpoint to everything; love, yet it is so off,
4/7, 10:11pm **Koz Kozmos**
good luck & thank u
4/7, 10:19pm **Koz Kozmos** death 2 fakebook
4/7, 11:32pm **Pre View**
squeezing the air thr a straw filed up with peanuts, cannot sleep, need to hold commentatory fire .
Your music keeps me in creation
4/8, 7:10pm **Koz Kozmos**
how do u get peanuts thr a straw, do u mean chatting with dragons?
4/8, 10:00pm **Koz Kozmos**
u out there Pre? hope your ok
April 9, 2013
4/9, 11:07am **Pre View**
I AM NOT & I WIL NOT get back until the fire eases, thx for caring, yes
4/9, 11:56am **Pre View**
I am a ticking bomb, need to wait till its over, need to watch my wording
April 12, 2013
4/12, 7:08pm Koz Kozmos
MUSIC: Grey Aliens and the Harvesting of Souls - Nigel Kerner

4/13, 1:50am **Pre View**
Thank u Koz, haha Well i invited them in, what happened is that i slept for 15 hours, average is only 5 ----so I guess my brain was not ready for this or they are preparing me,,,, either way, i am impressed with the limbic system, going into that tomorrow, will u be with me ? Just studying
4/13, 1:33pm **Koz Kozmos** '
going into that tomorrow, will u be with me ?' what does that mean?

4/13, 1:40pm **Pre View**
I was talking about the ExtraTssss, got in communication this morning and wow, what is that, small things but great results. This is thx to your posts about them, the video's.
Do know i value u a lot because i
do think about everything people give me, there is a reason why.....
Going into that means : will u also align to them -----
Imagination is reality, the stronger it is stated, the easier it manifests, but yes, it needs a lot of endurance, thinking and doing in meditation thr which u become the reality of meditation; not ever leaving it for a second, that is universal merging!
Hey, have a great week-end Koz ,,,, need to run my vibes now and get to understand it thr running, that is when i get
my images & stuff or my info. It needs to hit the circulation system.
4/13, 1:44pm **Koz Kozmos**
ExtraTssss, ? Try a busy mind
4/13, 1:44pm **Pre View**
Extra Tsss = Extraterestials, aliens,,,,
4/13, 1:47pm **Koz Kozmos**
o them
4/13, 1:57pm **Koz Kozmos** what have they said ....to u?
4/13, 1:58pm **Koz Kozmos**

Koz Kozmos From~
Lost Tranzmissions
of The Bright Juve...
1990~

I remember the 7 tease
in deep South Wales
half asleep in red neck town
above my underground,
maids of Aquarius
singing dryad songs
but i was caught
in the bungalow
with the strong door the child's star
on a unicorn from mars
a warrior child from Wales
dancing with the dead
down the dark lane,
riding my bike
past the well of trolls
flying the mind kite
blessed by startling melody, strummed from the amulet yes it was puberty and poetry,
getting hard and hairy,
in the fucked up family,
a pretty boy in the mirror contemplating shaving,
spiked hair
and pink leopard skin confusion.....

4/13, 2:09pm Koz Kozmos
MUSIC: HAWKWIND Master of the Universe
4/13, 2:12pm **Koz Kozmos**

I had pink leopard skin trousers at that time
4/13, 6:59pm **Koz Kozmos**
punk rock
April 14, 2013
4/14, 1:50am **Pre View**
enjoyed Hawkwind, thxxx
4/15, 3:33pm **Koz Kozmos**
"Here's my lil diddy flow on matrix, archons.. Now lets take it back to the basics, of ET's projecting this makeshift matrix/ who are the puppetmaster architects of this place, humans mentally manipulated from beings in space/ you can't fathom an unseen presence, presently orchestrating, perpetuating & mirror imaging everything you see, using media to sway perception & thoughts of humanity/ Ignorance is a food source so they don't want you to question, expand your mind while pondering this suggestion/ I've done my due diligence, traveled back in time, Nag Hammadi texts dug up in Egypt 1945/ Contained within our ancestors revealing the Archons, these machines, inorganic beings, pumpin artifial light beams, inception in our dreams, nothin is what it seems; but it always seems the same, people steppin on people to get ahead in the game/ Like a broken record playin, day after day just tryin to survive; Archons cultivating us, sims in a petri dish, like bees in a hive/ Its time to revive; so snap that cord outta ya medulla oblongata; talkin gouda la-da-amma-da-ba tsa tsa; awaken your core, activating the merkaba/ & don't forget the planets have an effect on our emotion, the energy flowin, we lil drops in a consciousness ocean/ Oh, & by the way did I mention that Satan is Saturn, just look at the pattern/ Inside is Metatron's Cube, virtual holodect being shot thru a cosmic fallopian tube/ Saturns ring produce the energy vortex, get in touch protect your neocortex/ Look around you almost everything is square, or anything within the Cube, triangle, circle, stay aware; get your butt back to nature or ya better beware/ We each hold a universe from within; don't need a genie rubbin lamps, don't mess with the jinn; bloodsuckin vampires like Marchand De Vin; shoutout to Du Trinh who's swivelin' the skittle pin, tracing it back to our patrilineal kin/ So get it right, don't take it light, under your radar escaping your sight/ AI entities descended all demented then segmented; reconfiguring frequency distribution causing mass confusion; a mind parasite intrusion in this psychopathic holographic illusion, wake up & snap outta the delusion. We each hold a universe from within; don't need a genie rubbin lamps, don't mess with the jinn; bloodsuckin vampires like Marchand De Vin; shoutout to Du Trinh who's swivelin' the skittle pin, tracing it back to our patrilineal kin/ So get it right, don't take it light, under your radar escaping your sight/ AI entities descended all demented then segmented; reconfiguring frequency distribution causing mass confusion; a mind parasite intrusion in this psychopathic holographic illusion, wake up & snap outta the delusion."~Anon.
4/15, 3:34pm **Koz Kozmos**
from exposing the archon
4/16, 9:16pm **Pre View**
it is finally fixed,,,, but need to pull my attention to this 'anon 'thing
4/16, 9:16pm **Koz Kozmos**
anon thing?
4/16, 9:17pm **Pre View**
yeah,the text u posted, see above, on monday , it was signed with ."~Anon
4/16, 9:18pm **Koz Kozmos**
confused i'm muli tasking can u elucidate

4/16, 9:21pm **Pre View**
Read what you posted on monday, i only opened it now ....
4/16, 9:23pm **Koz Kozmos**
that was from me from exposing the archon fb site sorry to be confusing
4/16, 9:24pm **Pre View**
nvm, it reminds me that when we do not respond immediatly to an energy given (like the post onmonday) --- it doesn't hold the same energy or outlet, or interest or whatever,,,, it is gone,,,
4/16, 9:25pm **Koz Kozmos**
maybe read it again and quit the mystik explanation
4/16, 9:28pm **Pre View** ok give me a sec,
4/16, 9:29pm **Koz Kozmos**
no worries, its all shit
4/16, 9:33pm **Pre View**
it is not, i just cannot put my mind to it tonight, strange, i can just see words,,,, interesting words out of
which I make something else.
4/16, 9:34pm **Koz Kozmos**
Stranger than strange
4/16, 9:35pm **Pre View**
Great Royalty ! Burgundy travel

4/16, 9:36pm **Koz Kozmos**
Burgundy travel?
4/16, 9:39pm **Pre View**
The Burdgundy ray erases all of the old mindset which is quite weird when working with it ---- u justforget about the shit & don't remember, but it is heavy metal clearing, trust me!
4/16, 9:46pm **Koz Kozmos**
death to false metal, its the same with me with the azure ray
4/16, 9:49pm **Pre View**
how does it work - the azure ray?
4/16, 9:50pm **Koz Kozmos**
not sure, but theres a band called azure that i just discoverd every one is ripping me offf
4/16, 9:51pm **Pre View**
ok, will try that tomorrow, does it equate to the aquamarine ?
What do u mean ripping ye off
4/16, 9:52pm **Koz Kozmos**
stealing my ideas, i was joking about the azure ray, i made it up
4/16, 9:54pm **Pre View**
not for me, i will downmoad it & work with it, thank u ! i never thought of it, isn't great to have FB, haha

4/16, 9:54pm **Koz Kozmos**
it hurts my arm, and bores me
4/16, 9:54pm **Pre View**
the azure ?
4/16, 9:55pm **Koz Kozmos NO**
FB; I'm a child of the 7th ray
4/16, 9:55pm **Koz Kozmos**
7th ray, ok, kool, its a powerful tool
4/16, 9:56pm **Pre View**
what color is the 7th ray for you?
4/16, 9:56pm **Koz Kozmos**
the azure ray if u use it with Lumarian crystals and flow with the go ?
ahhhhhhhhhhhhhhhhhhhh
4/16, 9:58pm **Pre View**
ok, but i have a feel i'll work with african deep purple crystal
as they have the radio-sonar waves in them
4/16, 9:59pm **Koz Kozmos**
ok, I'd like to break up the spinning stone and watch the blood dry
4/16, 10:01pm **Pre View**
oh dear, u can make me smile and laugh and think like a reptile, the spinning stone,
never thought of that ---- what is your blood type
4/16, 10:02pm **Koz Kozmos**
don't know
4/16, 10:02pm **Pre View** think without preselection
4/16, 10:03pm **Koz Kozmos**
blue blood that curls my lip and makes me Elvis that destroyed rock 'n'roll
4/16, 10:06pm **Pre View**
is your blood disconnected ?
4/16, 10:07pm **Koz Kozmos**
every part of me is, can u expand on disconnected ?
4/16, 10:20pm **Koz Kozmos**
Can you answer my question?
4/16, 10:23pm **Pre View**
yess, there is many ways of adjusting and expanding, but then again, this is not for
FB, its an explanation
over many days,,,, and yess I do connect with the bloodstream of earth and universal
roots,,,
4/16, 10:25pm **Koz Kozmos** ok
4/16, 10:36pm **Koz Kozmos**
i'm indiffrent, its a waste of time
4/16, 10:37pm **Pre View**
u are not the least indifferent, that is just a stupid and pregnant idea,,,
4/16, 10:39pm **Koz Kozmos**
but i don't have any friends, and i hate the public, wots the point in going in public, a
complete Nihilist
4/16, 10:45pm **Pre View**
euhm, I sometimes refer to u to some people when educating - because u got guts and
do not mind anything as long as u don't get hurt - whatever - it is always a good vibe
when i word something from
somebody else because i do not have the right to ever lower anything that is of value
to me
4/16, 10:46pm **Koz Kozmos**
my sister thinks i'm spineless
4/16, 10:46pm **Pre View**
i hope she's right when she smiles through her own vines,
probably not, just say thx sissy!

4/16, 10:46pm **Koz Kozmos**
? it means a cowerd, not a real man, funny i get hurt all the time,
my wound gets kicked and I can never heal
4/16, 10:48pm **Pre View**
It sounds like u don't need a phoenician education as the phoenix rises already beyond the thunderbird,,,which is the ultimate, maybe u don't have yur specialty waves appreciated because u downgrade yurself so much, why ?
U are a very sweet man, with many devalued potentials, but times are getting real for u to stand up Koz .What is ur major wound ? I would never hurt u ,
although it hurts me sometimes seeing u,
feeling u getting into this mass mud all the time and not keeping up with worthy things that matter in the spiritual matter or substance
4/16, 11:04pm **Koz Kozmos**
I don't downgrade myself, and I have stood up all my life, and I'm outa the mass mud
4/16, 11:10pm **Pre View**
ok i'll shut up, till needs meet ,,,, sorry Koz,
4/16, 11:10pm **Koz Kozmos**
but i have been downgraded, ok, thank u, keep save ? its ok Pre, u relax
4/16, 11:13pm **Koz Kozmos**
u underestimate me, but people don't like smart, i've tryed and tryed and will never stop
4/16, 11:13pm **Pre View**
I woudn't dare to underestimate u
4/16, 11:13pm **Koz Kozmos**
but fukk people i've tryed more than most
4/16, 11:14pm **Pre View**
people hate smart people, i am not people,
4/16, 11:14pm **Koz Kozmos**
but there seems to be no place for me, people don't noe who i am
4/16, 11:14pm **Koz Kozmos**
and i'm not being self pitying ,what ever u do, don't follow the tao
4/16, 11:15pm **Pre View**
i only follow myself, and people do know who u are
4/16, 11:16pm **Koz Kozmos** ?
they don't have the insight to see in front of thier snotty noses
4/16, 11:17pm **Pre View**
You are just not being liked, it is the same with me,
but i do have a way to blow their minds, because i
simply speak my truth, so do u,,, When talking I mostly put 10 sentences into 1, i do talk the same way to people and i smile, they don't get that , do not understand, judge me, whatever,
But in the end, they always come back ----- which I never allow, once gone, is gone forever,,,
4/16, 11:19pm **Koz Kozmos**
I'm not not being liked, i'm a hermit, ahhhhhhhhhhhhh,
i give up trying to explain via typing
4/16, 11:20pm **Pre View**
explain what ?
4/16, 11:21pm **Koz Kozmos**
the situation i find myself in, etc, its ok Pre
your a kool person
4/16, 11:22pm **Pre View**
aha, why ? is it ok?
4/16, 11:23pm **Pre View**
MUSIC Man of the World/Peter Green

4/16, 11:23pm **Koz Kozmos**
o no, do u know what happened to mr green

4/16, 11:24pm Koz Kozmos
MUSIC: Peter Green's Fleetwood Mac - The Green Manalishi (With The Two Prong Crown)

4/16, 11:24pm **Koz Kozmos**
this is his best song, and rattle snake shape, the rest is honky blues
4/16, 11:25pm **Pre View**
no, i do not know what happened
4/16, 11:26pm **Koz Kozmos**
dare i type it, lololo
4/16, 11:27pm **Pre View** go go go
4/16, 11:28pm **Koz Kozmos**

MUIC: Yusuf - Heaven, Where True Love Goes (Live Yusuf's Cafe Session 2007) + Lyrics

4/16, 11:28pm **Koz Kozmos**
this is good
4/16, 11:32pm **Pre View**
this is good indeed, he's very heart, right, am listening,
4/16, 11:34pm **Koz Kozmos**
yes the sound has gone , a minut...
4/16, 11:35pm **Pre View**
vid ?
4/16, 11:35pm **Koz Kozmos**
video film on utube still no sound, i wod like to listen to the song the archon again ...
4/16, 11:37pm **Pre View**
i do not understand, told u, have lost my brains today because I choose so
4/16, 11:37pm **Koz Kozmos**
how have u lost them may i ask , all the best Pre, good night
4/16, 11:43pm **Koz Kozmos**
~<O>~
4/16, 11:49pm **Pre View**
Closing me eyes, someday u'll be surprised of what how why,
but then again, nobody can surprise u, keep
yur love untainted Koz,,,
4/16, 11:55pm **Pre View**
Thank u for the song, it revealed many to me and a relieve for the justice department
to run high with me,
because i walk any talk , ,,---- lets all dig deeper & deeper , upside downhill
4/17, 12:00am **Koz Kozmos**

MUSIC: Cat Stevens- Sitting

4/17, 12:07am **Pre View**
hah, i was listening - thank u -to cat man,,,,
i have an untouchable face, makes me think about Santana
4/17, 2:39pm **Koz Kozmos**
your so 70's
4/17, 3:19pm **Pre View** ?
4/17, 3:30pm **Koz Kozmos**
Santana, I'm obviously too witty
4/17, 10:12pm **Koz Kozmos**
u in da hoood?
4/18, 8:49am **Pre View**
just around the corner

4/18, 2:09pm **Koz Kozmos**
the corner on jewel street were the dimensions shift... I'm trying to get outa a cul da sac
but the archons have been using walk in's to instigate a charaik malfunction...
4/18, 7:10pm **Pre View**
aha, still no protective ass,
put on thy selective moon-shoes
4/18, 7:26pm **Koz Kozmos**
i'm bare foot in the head and tip toe in the soul thats the problem
4/18, 7:33pm **Pre View**
that hits it
4/18, 8:51pm **Koz Kozmos**
thankz pre
4/20, 1:56pm **Koz Kozmos**
H P Lovecraft ....that iz 4/20, 1:58pm **Koz Kozmos**
Howard Phillips Lovecraft (August 20, 1890 – March 15, 1937) — known as H. P. Lovecraft — was an American author of horror, fantasy, poetry and science fiction, especially the subgenre known as weird fiction.[1] Lovecraft's guiding aesthetic and philosophical principle was what he termed "cosmicism" or "cosmic horror", the idea that life is incomprehensible to human minds and that the universe is fundamentally inimical to the interests of humankind. As such, his stories express a profound indifference to human beliefs and affairs. Lovecraft is the originator of the Cthulhu Mythos story cycleand the Necronomicon, a fictional magical textbook of rites and forbidden lore.
4/20, 1:58pm **Koz Kozmos**
Maybe I should do cources in how to be HYP & WYRD
4/20, 1:59pm **Pre View**
GREAT, do it NOW , i'll support u 1000 %
4/20, 1:59pm **Koz Kozmos**
there no audience maybe crytal healing
and rekie rip of the new gaers
4/20, 2:02pm **Pre View**
Would u like me to buy u a brand new pair guzzi glasses ?
have we not moved far byond all that,,,, happy
to know u know so much about books and written material,
i do not even have a clue to any book, i never read,,
4/20, 2:05pm **Koz Kozmos**
Guzzi ? guzzi ? I don't know a great deal about books
just sharing info
4/20, 2:17pm **Pre View**
Guzzi = just a name, a brand for sunglasses, just a joke
4/20, 2:26pm **Koz Kozmos**
Gucci?
not seen them, i'd like new eyes if u can arrage
that got the joke
4/20, 3:24pm **Pre View**
sure, do u want dem to see,
or just a pair to adjust to societal creepy mess
4/20, 4:07pm **Koz Kozmos**
I like a bit of bossy mockery

4/20, 5:09pm **Koz Kozmos**
MUSIC:NATURE BOY.wmv

4/20, 6:38pm **Pre View**
bossy mockery, sure, u glued my tongues
would u like to handle my red firebird rising
4/20, 7:03pm **Koz Kozmos**
i'm just messing about
4/20, 8:02pm **Pre View**
Great this song, thank u, can use this for my med class tomorrow as i'm lazy today,
i do know u can sweetly handle that,,,
4/20, 8:09pm **Pre View**
So, u are not within, without , in or out, but always around cornerstreet, that is lovable
4/20, 8:09pm **Koz Kozmos**
wotz a med class?
ok, relaxzoid
4/20, 8:12pm **Pre View**
meditation class: started 4 lessons with young people that are willing to move fast, so tomorrow i'm gonna get them real nauseous as they want to feel dolphins/whales communication and this one offers them sonar waves which are hardwave handles
No relaxation ,,,
4/20, 8:13pm **Pre View**
Please do not take my words too seriously today, i am very tired ....
4/20, 8:14pm **Koz Kozmos**
i thought I said u needed to chillaxe of cource
4/20, 8:15pm **Pre View**
chillaxe ?
4/20, 8:16pm **Koz Kozmos**
chill out and relax ~e mixed its better than meditation
4/20, 8:17pm **Pre View**
Excellent wordin !
Meditation is hard work with the universe,
4/20, 8:21pm **Koz Kozmos**
straight from the fridge!
4/20, 8:22pm **Pre View**
realtime sure, always, why can i never be just casual and boring and love that,,,
4/20, 8:23pm **Koz Kozmos**
? love wot
i don't want to bother u Pre, if your manically meditating
straight from the fridge! = kool
4/20, 8:24pm **Pre View**
i just skateboard over any human expression (but humble) still people get kicked with my words 4/20, 8:24pm **Koz Kozmos**
the first lesson in how to be hyp and wyrd
4/20, 8:24pm **Pre View**
thats an automac, not a lesson
4/20, 8:24pm **Koz Kozmos**
i acn't do boring either or be with bores my other word for them is scum
sorry dyslectic : acn't = can't

4/20, 8:25pm **Pre View**
it is not a lesson, iit is about creating movement with new blueprints
4/20, 8:26pm **Koz Kozmos**
my print is azure with speckz of invisable blue
4/20, 8:26pm **Pre View**
i am not manically meditating, i am meditation or different wordls
4/20, 8:26pm **Koz Kozmos**
ok, u said u were manic, make your mind up, why don't u bust a moby?
4/20, 8:27pm **Pre View**
why should i make my mind up,
what is a moby ?
4/20, 8:28pm **Koz Kozmos**
ahhhh; u'r talking to me, quite here, bye
4/20, 8:28pm **Pre View**
why
4/20, 8:28pm **Koz Kozmos**
u make your mind up, anyways
4/20, 8:29pm **Pre View**
cannot think thank , need to re-focus and hold tied to Spirit advice and styles, haha
4/20, 8:29pm **Koz Kozmos**
i'm off, take care, bye
ok, keep safe
4/20, 8:29pm **Koz Kozmos**
zaf
4/21, 10:43pm **Koz Kozmos** Yo
4/21, 10:43pm **Koz Kozmos** Yo
4/22, 12:15am **Pre View**
yoyoyo
You are going to many events for u or a new u, i never did any of that stuff !
I am surprised with that youth training, found it interesting as i am working with them ---- thy really want it all and quick
Goodnight
4/22, 1:17pm **Koz Kozmos**
What new events (etc) ? Did any of what stuff? What training ? working with them? who are they? What
do they want and quick and why is it good for you?
can u be more clear please?
4/22, 2:55pm **Pre View**
well your timeline says u are joining 3 events ;;;;the youth,
the sjamanistic thing and ...
4/22, 2:56pm **Pre View**
moment i'll copy or lets say when you click on an event that you like, your friends will see and know that you will be going to that particular event
4/22, 2:58pm **Koz Kozmos**
must have clicked on some stuff, thought i'd canceled it
can u answer my earlier questions please?
4/22, 2:58pm **Pre View**
okokok
4/22, 2:58pm **Koz Kozmos**
no more fukkkkkin work shops
the incrediable boredom of being here makes me waste time as it murders me on inae sites inae* insane* fukk the guru verse and the mystc work shop

4/22, 3:01pm **Pre View**
i never did any workshops, and will not, but i'll teach you how the new tree of living fruits with Light Engineering smells like and that keeps u out of boredom because it is too interesting to not work with it on a daily level and would change you every day because you flow into your own chosen Self Mastery with your direct connect to your Source.
So you will stop your endless complaints as alignment is between you and your Source. Complaining is the highest level of negativity that keeps you from moving forward.
If the scum hits you, you hit them with the Light Earth Grids, that is Crystalline consciousness and nothing or nobody can enter that unless you allow the hybrids to enter your sacred space through negative and mindless thought forms.
It is all up to us, the individual.
That is it.
4/22, 3:01pm **Koz Kozmos**
ok i hate it when people say so,its so dismissive
4/22, 8:55pm **Pre View**
i only get to understand things I trained after 10 years.
But all the people in my meditation classes changevery quickly , like in 10 weeks time,
the difference is major- like the musical note!
That is how it should be, meditation should bring elimination, progress and deep understanding of the Spark that we are in connection to the universes and all that kind of deep related communication we can all re-establish.... No airy fairy bubbles ---
I break ice and trow out the dice from the first seconds on and there is a reason why these people can change very quickly with some Light Technology that matches our ancient and modern day outlet in one orchestration. It does take a lot o focus and obedience,
but the outcome is more then satisfying, it brings back believe and trust.
Have to prepare my vernissage now
4/22, 8:59pm **Koz Kozmos**
vernisage ? ....wots that ; wot sort of change
4/22, 9:00pm **Pre View**
vernissage: an exposition with my artwork
Koz Kozmos
how do u measure brain waves and wot effects are reported?
4/22, 9:06pm **Koz Kozmos**
i was reading about it, but got bored thought i'd sahre the info share*
4/22, 9:45pm **Koz Kozmos**
How death penalty seems to be what i've been given,
all the best with the work
4/24, 6:18pm **Koz Kozmos**
Hope your well Pre
4/24, 6:20pm **Pre View**
not at all , have been working at the speed of 48 hours instead of24 hours -
so no sleep for 3 days, but its
worth it,,,,,,, get things done just manifesting them thr though, but, don't mind me Koz, ,
i'll be ok by Monday, thank u for your care !
4/24, 6:23pm **Koz Kozmos**
why have u bin working 48 hours, and no sleep for 3 days
all the beast with your work shop
4/24, 6:32pm **Pre View**
All the beast with my workshop (i know dyslectic) still great expression.
Btw it is an Exposition, I have 3 days left to arrange my artwork for the exposition :
have been blocked over many things and now i need to really speed up and bring my fruits to the table ...

4/24, 6:35pm **Koz Kozmos**
why blocked, i've been blocked all my life by morons
4/24, 6:38pm **Pre View**
U would't want to know, and u will know when the timing is aranged, because u would be surprised to ahigh level!
4/24, 6:40pm **Koz Kozmos**
I do want to know?
if u say all this stuff back it up
4/24, 6:42pm **Pre View**
I will not, it is too deep, too mind breaking, just wait till timing has come , i embrace your understanding
4/24, 6:45pm **Koz Kozmos**
gonna pop of, my HGA has just arrived timing its always to late !
4/24, 6:50pm **Pre View**
HGA ,?
4/24, 7:26pm **Koz Kozmos**
holy guardian angel how to be hyp and wyrd April 25, 2013
4/25, 9:42pm **Koz Kozmos**
Hi
4/25, 11:34pm **Pre View**
Hi Koz, are you ok ?
4/26, 1:53pm **Koz Kozmos**
always unsure
4/26, 2:48pm **Koz Kozmos**
This Is Not My Life - Drama TV Series (2010)
you will like this scif from downunder ,
sorry pre wrong window ignore that or,,,
4/27, 1:08am **Pre View**
i will never ignore u, I've got u into my skin
should i watch something ? Link ?
I just had my load with the Exposition, were where you ?
4/27, 1:23am **Koz Kozmos**
Watch Fringe tv series
4/27, 1:24am **Pre View**
Fringe ? How can i watch
4/27, 1:25am **Koz Kozmos**
do u illgally down load
4/27, 1:26am **Pre View**
no i respect and pay, but give it anyways,
4/27, 1:26am **Koz Kozmos**
bit torrent, a lot of the sites are taken down
4/27, 1:28am **Pre View**
ok, i will let somebody do this for me,
I cannot, because my heart would desize (shrimp) haha
4/27, 1:28am **Koz Kozmos**

FILM SERIES: Fringe - Best Scene!!!

4/27, 1:28am **Koz Kozmos**
this is up on u tube but u must awatch it from season 1 ok,
dezise shrimp, what does that mean
one day i decipher your Pre talk
4/27, 1:29am **Pre View**
With the exposition lots of majic entrances (people) opened up,
it was good to be around people foronce.
4/27, 1:30am **Koz Kozmos**
what does that mean, did u do a med classs may i enquire
4/27, 1:33am **Pre View**
No , I exposed my paintings and to my surprise as harsh as i am,
people came closer and closer and for the first time really wanted to know about Spirit and the gate I paint through, and the return investment came many many ways,
so i am just reflecting on what is happening to me
4/27, 1:33am **Koz Kozmos**
os am i did u sell one?
postive feeed back, speak straight ,
its not all mystikkk shit have u gone into a trance and speaking to planetoids, u chatting ?
4/27, 1:38am **Pre View**
U should hear me talk.Well what happened is i sold some paintings which never happened on the first night opening and i lost my wallet, then some young people found it and returned it just like majic...
4/27, 1:38am **Koz Kozmos**
don't wish to bother u
4/27, 1:39am **Pre View**
strange all these positive happenings,,,
4/27, 1:39am **Koz Kozmos**
i've never had a single postive event but i've become indifferent
4/27, 1:40am **Pre View**
Well Koz, me neither, but do know as i decided to really talk deep to people about how my Art manifested through my alignments to the universe, which made them wonder and question their Skill which is so wonderful because it opens strong will to get to know self better, I felt very happy
4/27, 1:40am **Koz Kozmos**
good postive things are occurring; i am an alien
4/27, 1:41am **Pre View**
its about time,,
4/27, 1:41am **Koz Kozmos**
i'm thinking of leaving the city, i need to get away but have my music etc
4/27, 1:41am **Pre View**
were would you go to? i understand ... the toxins in the city
4/27, 1:41am **Koz Kozmos**
depends
4/27, 1:42am **Pre View**
can u not take the music with u
4/27, 1:42am **Koz Kozmos**
are u in a city
no one wants my music, but yes it will go with me i need a lot of money

4/27, 1:42am **Pre View**
I am in a city , looks so small, everything looks small to me
4/27, 1:43am **Koz Kozmos**
to get to the place i need to create it
its alll compromoise
4/27, 1:43am **Pre View**
what do u need to create
4/27, 1:43am **Koz Kozmos**
why does it look small
4/27, 1:43am **Pre View**
where would u feel good?
4/27, 1:43am **Koz Kozmos**
too many matrix foodder
a detached house, in a quite area
4/27, 1:44am **Pre View**
? do not understand
4/27, 1:44am **Koz Kozmos**
matrix fodder : humans under the program
4/27, 1:44am **Pre View**
every area has a quite area are u making music
4/27, 1:44am **Koz Kozmos**
is that the bit u don't understand no, i've almost given up
4/27, 1:45am **Pre View**
Make me understand
4/27, 1:45am **Koz Kozmos**
Britian is an over populated rubbbish dump
4/27, 1:45am **Pre View**
u cannot give up when ur on the verge of change
4/27, 1:45am **Koz Kozmos**
u need money to get to quite areas and transport
4/27, 1:46am **Pre View**
ok, do u have a feel where you want to go
4/27, 1:46am **Koz Kozmos**
why am i on the verge of change?
i'd need to buy a house, which i can't do
4/27, 1:46am **Pre View**
i just feel that you are on the verge of change, simplicity = knowledge ?
4/27, 1:46am **Koz Kozmos**
yes, i've got rid of about 50% of my stuff and all the people i vaguely new are gone
4/27, 1:47am **Pre View**
well, i do understand u need an outcome , but why should money be involved,
why do u need a house?
4/27, 1:47am **Koz Kozmos**
and good riddance
4/27, 1:48am **Koz Kozmos**
I need a detached house in a quite area in nature
4/27, 1:48am **Pre View**
well nature offers plenty for u to see
4/27, 1:48am **Koz Kozmos**
i'm not living in a tent,
anyawys

4/27, 1:49am **Pre View**
I'll make u some tea, but i cannot brew beer
4/27, 1:49am **Koz Kozmos**
thanks for listening; i'm on the wagon
4/27, 1:49am **Pre View**
no prob , i like hearing ur voice
4/27, 1:50am **Koz Kozmos**
gottta get of earth
4/27, 1:50am **Pre View** can u sing a song to this
4/27, 1:50am **Koz Kozmos**
too many low grade humans
i do all the time, i'm the vision singer
4/27, 1:51am **Pre View** can't hear u ? please sing louder, haha
4/27, 1:51am **Koz Kozmos**
but people are blind, or i am
4/27, 1:51am **Koz Kozmos**
i've got ear plugs in
4/27, 1:52am **Pre View**
NO YOU ARE NOT DEAF,YOU ARE NOT BLIND,
ur senses need a splash into any river
4/27, 1:52am **Koz Kozmos**
how do u know? any river, avoid the toxic sewage of the rivers
4/27, 1:54am **Pre View**
Knowledge on the spot, thru the green gate in Ireland, haha,
or the Universal Green Gate and its architecture.
4/27, 1:54am **Koz Kozmos**
? Knowledge on the spot, thru the green gate in Ireland, can u be more clear please
i'm poetic and surreal too, but timing is essensial
4/27, 1:56am **Koz Kozmos**
i thought the green gates are in wales,
i barely survive, but i am the genntle good - gentle
4/27, 1:58am **Pre View**
wish i could give u ur missing links, but somehow, u do have the knowledge, why do
u avoid it? Start answering your own questions from within.
4/27, 1:59am **Koz Kozmos**
i have no idea
4/27, 1:59am **Koz Kozmos**
? i'm avoiding nothing, its not down to me, i've been targeted
nearly destroyed, i understand the concept
4/27, 2:01am **Pre View**
U are not destroyed, u can choose, choose strength!
4/27, 2:01am **Koz Kozmos**
i'm completely lost then, u don't get it in the slightest
4/27, 2:02am **Pre View**
No; u are not getting it, pull ur attention to what u really want, what is it , on all levels
#? and wake up to self responsibility!
4/27, 2:02am **Koz Kozmos** t
I want to awaken and get my super powers back and destroy this dimension to save
the earth, maybe to die completely and never return
its such a bore

4/27, 2:03am **Pre View**
I do get u, i feel u, your loneliness, misunderstood chapters & stuff, so you are being asked to dig deeper and pull urself out of the matrix, and just do it
4/27, 2:03am **Koz Kozmos**
i've done that , been a fighter, but been targeted by pychic vamps and fucked over and damaged theres is nothing left i want to do
4/27, 2:05am **Pre View**
u did not, you are like a dog, winding circles and appreciating the circus and knowing u want a clear
deeply loved and understood value
4/27, 2:05am **Koz Kozmos**
i'm not, i hate dogs as much as i hate humans and i am not in a circle
4/27, 2:06am **Pre View**
why, what did these snakes do to u
4/27, 2:06am **Koz Kozmos**
i said earlier, but been targeted by pychic vamps and fucked over and damaged, but ho hum
4/27, 2:07am **Pre View**
then u let them do this to u, a strong person does not give these powers a chance to filter in
4/27, 2:07am **Koz Kozmos**
bulll shit, it was becuz my soul was powerful that they did it its degined that way u seem naive
4/27, 2:08am **Pre View**
ok, i've been there, i understand, it took me 1 year to investigate & make choices
4/27, 2:09am **Koz Kozmos**
what does that mean
i need a preamble, before i can understand random thoughts
4/27, 2:09am **Pre View**
all powerful souls have the most degrading tests, even till they take your breath, it happens to everybody
singing like a lightening bolt
Preamble ?
4/27, 2:10am **Koz Kozmos**
fuck the karma exams and the headless master of the mystery school
4/27, 2:11am **Pre View**
sure, reality schools are running highways, no more mystery
4/27, 2:11am **Koz Kozmos**
A preamble is an introductory and expressionary statement in a document that explains the document's purpose and underlying philosophy. When applied to the opening paragraphs of a statute, it may recite historical facts pertinent to the subject of the statute. It is distinct from the long title or enacting formula of a law.
4/27, 2:11am **Koz Kozmos**
what is a raelity school, why are they running highways, why no more mystery ???
4/27, 2:12am **Pre View**
Doesn't tell me anything as this is old very old teaching which does not apply into today's living values, 4/27, 2:12am **Koz Kozmos**
what is an old teaching? what is your context ?
4/27, 2:13am **Pre View**
all mysteries are revealed, that is why people cannot handle them!
4/27, 2:13am **Koz Kozmos**
fuck todays living values, they are the death meme and control of the soul gate
I long for mystery

4/27, 2:15am **Pre View**
U LONG TO KNOW MYSTERY, THATS IS WHERE U ARE AT, leave your town, and connect with worthy people , you simply crave knowledge, we all do,
but we must clear the way to get that special breath through
4/27, 2:15am **Koz Kozmos**
there are none, i'm 53 and have not met one
if i leave i will become the quite amn on another street corner becoming more inviable each day amn = man*
i have left many places
4/27, 2:16am **Pre View**
believe , and so u shall retrieve
4/27, 2:16am **Koz Kozmos**
becuase of my bad experices with people i did belive but i don't any more
i'm sick of having to go down to thier(their) level, i'm tierd (tired), i'd rather be alone and coming out with alll this stuff
4/27, 2:18am **Pre View**
it can kill you yes, just keep your strenght up Koz, u've got so many things to give to humanity, think again, love urself which is hard i know,
4/27, 2:18am **Koz Kozmos**
u just seem to be under the new age mind control device
i do love myself and think i have a lot to over (offer)
4/27, 2:19am **Pre View**
Loving Self takes many degrees in understanding
and developing the Love for Self without control
4/27, 2:19am **Koz Kozmos**
my enormous potential has been hijacked
i kiss myself in the mirror and try to look after myself
4/27, 2:20am **Pre View**
haha, ok, kiss urself, but communication is important,, i am interested in your potentials ?
4/27, 2:20am **Koz Kozmos** ? i was jesting
4/27, 2:21am **Pre View**
What is ur potential, Jesting ?
4/27, 2:22am **Koz Kozmos**
and almost destroyed, becuz i was too strong, too bright too dark for the fuctards and they fed on me its hard to understand
4/27, 2:23am **Pre View**
same story here,,, for 3 years, and i will stop it now, so can u
4/27, 2:23am **Koz Kozmos**
i don't wish to be sefl indulgent ,stop what?
4/27, 2:24am **Pre View**
u are not, i do understand as our wavelengths equalize
giving it all, the manipulation, people not handling light, feeding into control..
4/27, 2:26am **Koz Kozmos**
you make these statements at random, people have gone, good riddence, my destruction was shaped as a boy, a child, they hate our purity or exploration our madness our originality
4/27, 2:27am **Pre View**
well there is your key, understand wot happened in ur childhood and u will fix anything
4/27, 2:29am **Pre View**
so was i, still am as many other people, but today, may i tell u,
they do not have a clue how to handle me

4/27, 2:29am **Koz Kozmos**
born into the sicknesss, same hear here*
we've been set up, u need to be stronger see it for what it is
4/27, 2:30am **Pre View**
time to leave these states of consciousness, for both of us,
why do u think i need to be stronger ?
how do u know?
4/27, 2:31am **Koz Kozmos**
just a suggestion, u told me i neeeded to be and dive deeper
i'm a muscle bound frog man in the toxic sea but at least i've jumped off the slave ship how do u know? i'm saying i'm confused ,lost and destroyed
4/27, 2:33am **Pre View**
to the point and i will get there in now time
Koz, i am falling asleep though i love chatting with u, but after 4 days without sleep,
yes i need to get stronger, so will U !
Big hug, good night ! i just want the muscles, sleep tight
4/27, 2:33am **Koz Kozmos**
good vibez, sweet dreams and thank u
kiss your self in the mirrror when u awake
4/27, 10:38am **Pre View**
Sure, i willl, Good morning, my mirror broke into a million pieces,,,
4/27, 1:35pm **Koz Kozmos**
only a million, be careful your Gematria is out
4/28, 12:51am **Koz Kozmos**
glad your exhibition went well, WELL DONE April 28, 2013
4/28, 10:58am **Pre View**
Thank u Koz, i feel new air or windmills arriving,
April 28, 2013
4/28, 7:21pm **Koz Kozmos**
I'd not bother with either, their overrated...
4/28, 7:59pm **Pre View**
do not understand all lyrics as it is not my language
(THE VIDEO WAS LOST OR OUT OF ORDER)
4/28, 8:00pm **Koz Kozmos**
ok its about chicks and drugs
4/28, 8:01pm **Pre View**
aha, will listen again, do u take drugs
4/28, 8:03pm **Koz Kozmos**
I am drugs , i've drunk too much coffee toay, why do u ask?
4/28, 8:05pm **Pre View**
ask my nerves
4/28, 8:03pm **Koz Kozmos**
be careful with caffeine
4/28, 8:06pm **Pre View**
why? i hardly have coffee
4/28, 8:06pm **Koz Kozmos**
i'm joking, maybe a bad joke
4/28, 8:06pm **Pre View**
you are not drugs,you are a joke with a broomstick
/28, 8:07pm **Koz Kozmos**
I am the wytch of dreams falling in to deeps of skies beyond the other I don't do drugs.
I am drugs. Salvador Dali

your painting are interesting; not sure i've seen this sharing info
4/28, 8:13pm **Koz Kozmos**
bye
4/28, 8:20pm **Pre View**
ok bye, thank u
4/28, 8:27pm **Pre View**
My paintings are here to transmute consciousness, thats all,
this gives the lazy human kingdom an easy
gate to begin with
4/28, 10:23pm **Koz Kozmos**
they couldn't use mine...and the more I sea and deal with humanity,
well I'm glad,
4/28, 10:49pm **Pre View**
show me
4/28, 10:58pm **Pre View**
I want a tattoo
I want u to discover a design for me
i love being deliciously bossy (just for a few minutes)
4/29, 12:09am **Koz Kozmos**
the consensus tattoo is for the cliche sheeple...maybe an anchor
4/29, 12:25am **Koz Kozmos**
I destroyed all my art, i'm about to burn all my writen stuff
4/29, 12:33am **Koz Kozmos**
it just takes up room
4/29, 1:41am **Pre View**
DON'T YOU THINK I WANT TO READ & SEE everything & make something of it,
it is very valuable byond the variables u see at this time!
do not burn, please send the stuff , i want to read it.
I have the intention to take parts out of my paintings to put on ts-shirts ----
would u not be interested in putting some of ur written material along with this ---
i mean in co-creation ?
4/29, 3:10pm **Koz Kozmos**
Thats the problem I see its value
but I've had to detach, I have the hawk of truth tattooed on my heart in invisible ink...
activated by the starry knowledge and the despair.....
4/29, 3:17pm **Koz Kozmos**
as Bruce said before he was replaced with a walk in.... "And the poets down here
Don't write nothing at all
They just stand back and let it all be . . . "
4/29, 3:20pm **Pre View**
That is beautiful, love the Hawk
But u can change what poets think, i'm sure u can
4/29, 3:21pm **Koz Kozmos**
I have, I don't write poems anymore
4/29, 3:22pm **Pre View**
would u not like to post some
4/29, 3:23pm **Koz Kozmos**
its for middle class posers and spurious working class types
they are all anti cozzzznikkk cozzzmikkk*
4/29, 3:23pm **Pre View**
cozzzmikkk they will become, when u will publish your poetry
4/29, 3:24pm **Koz Kozmos**
its not happened , i'm beyond it

Pre View
Why did u have to detach ?
/29, 3:24pm **Koz Kozmos**
i just want to be a hermit away from humans, every one i've met has been a snake of fake, i've been ripped off with ideas,
every one starts to impersonate me in a far more mediocre way and sometimes get success
I'm bored with trying anymore
4/29, 3:26pm **Pre View**
u can start again & be stronger then humans,
same happened to me, and its hard to pick up, very but i will, s
o u can also decide to do so, only u can value u
4/29, 3:26pm **Koz Kozmos**
and getting ollder and damaged
cheers for listening ,I know all that Pre
and i do value u and i value me big time but i'm done with this dimension
4/29, 3:28pm **Pre View**
i'v been severely damaged too over the past 3 years,
but decision time has come to turn the clock counterclockwise and serve justice
4/29, 3:28pm **Koz Kozmos**
don't hit me with pop psychologist
I've done that, it started for me when i first came outa the womb
my damage is a good thing
as its become an acknowledgement of the hidden war
4/29, 3:29pm **Pre View**
a hell of a time in creating u in the womb
why hidden war
4/29, 3:30pm **Koz Kozmos**
well before the womb when your first wiped because its hidden,
most humans are low grade souls and hear to feed to create negative energy
4/29, 3:31pm **Pre View**
can u not walk away from that
4/29, 3:32pm **Koz Kozmos** i
its not possible if you are on earth
4/29, 3:32pm **Pre View** why
4/29, 3:32pm **Koz Kozmos**
your seeing it as meaning; just negative people you move away from because you reclaim your own power
pop psychology and new age ideas
its far more insidious than that, I have walked away
4/29, 3:34pm **Pre View**
earth is ascending, so things should change, thats the reason for all the non comprehended swords,i do not understand many things,
but some things work for me hate the word new age
4/29, 3:34pm **Koz Kozmos**
I am the blade that gleamzzzzzz
4/29, 3:35pm **Pre View**
Insidious?
I can see u dance with many blades
4/29, 3:35pm **Koz Kozmos**
in·sid·i·ous (n-sd-s)

1. Working or spreading harmfully in a subtle or stealthy manner: insidious rumors; an insidious disease.
2. Intended to entrap; treacherous: insidious misinformation. 3. Beguiling but harmful; alluring: insidious pleasures.

4/29, 3:36pm **Pre View**
thank u

4/29, 3:36pm **Koz Kozmos** but hyperdimsional

4/29, 3:37pm **Pre View**
what is that, byond dimension ? never heard the word
ok Koz, need to rob a bank before closure,
I'll catch u with ur shining blades

4/29, 3:40pm **Koz Kozmos**
beyond the matix, matrix
this dimension is under control, not just via the obbvious yes ;
large amounts of money would help
i'm not even being down or trying to bring u down

4/29, 3:50pm **Koz Kozmos**
bye

4/30, 3:58pm Koz Kozmos

YOUTUBE: Aerosmith - Hoodoo Voodoo Medicine Man

4/30, 9:07pm **Pre View**
Beautiful and wonderful thank u,
thank u for the inspirationssss,

5/1, 1:44am **Pre View**
TIME TO EXPLAIN THINGS: Many times you asked me 'wot does it mean' : it means that everything bad like wars & stuff are coming up cause the earth plane is being cleansed and moving up to ascent, that is why everybody is being confronted with their own negative truth and images and stuff. Now ever since 2000 - each year a new light grid has been repaired with great results and many light sources/forces are involved which bring instant changes through people termed grid embodiments or people who are holding the crystalline grids that override thE dense forces within the matrix . Only people do not understand they need their movement from 5th into 6th dimension (do not know if u have knowledge how to move thr dimensions 'cause u only talk about earth - this dimension) when u move up & upon the ladder of many Light Formulas, we have the option to change the output of what the neurons in the brain synapse or flicker new Light degrees through . That is rather like a Lightening bolt that provides new knowledge and also, certainly happens when lower emotions have been cleared and make space to allow the higher sensations of Divine origins in which low degrading mentality simply CANNOT exist for we would not have allowance into these magnificent Spaces..The Crystalline grids in the body and on Earth, when they both match allow for the meridians of earth to match Light body meridians and then things get interesting because the floor under our feet starts moving like a carousel in total transparency and shows us how elements live and breathe and so much more beauty. So, you see, ascension is not only to resurrect Self into Mastering Energy but also to put out services to people in deep distress and assisting everyone to move into the highest purpose of their life because it is the REAL DEAL that brings joy, happiness, passion and true value into our living Light. Hope that make sense. When we have to deal with dark spots, then there is always a direct answer from our Source how to remove these energies and replace them with Living Light. Yet Living Light and Living in Light has so poorly been understood. TRUE LOVE can resurrect from that as it is our Original Essence and so poorly understood when we have a good look at social media: almost every post contradicts itself for those who studied and payed their devotional time to their Source, they can smell and sense every intent behind any post.

A Foundation into Eternal Light Living is all it requires to work with many Light configurations, mathematics and geometrical designs that pop up when loading the energies in the body. That is all so fascinating as what we work with can changes every day along our Universal roots and thus it is truly a necessity to work LIGHT through as in Present Modern day volumes. Yet too many just work some light through in meditation that is neither aligned to their Essence nor their Source and that could result into allowing the monsters of this universe into your Space when not being Grid savvy and aligned to Divine design and Technology that is available today, not yesterday. Backstage, we can see a lot of light workers not making it into Light or puffing Light through with old manipulative engines that will never work either. The most dominant missing link to work our ways into The Ascent is definitely THE AIR, AND UPGRADING THE BREATH UNIVERSAL STYLE because it is all we have to get our degrees to match the frequencies that are desirable for spiritual embodiment and living.

After a foundation in Light, I trained myself into become an exclusive strong Eternal healer working with the Elements at all times. First the Celestial elements such as light Water.

Anyone has access to high level healing techniques, but from my observation, people prefer to remain lazy when it comes to putting efforts into things that do not benefit them directly while there is always spiritual growth that infuses when doing the work that we truly need to do: TOGETHER PATTERN, haha.But anyways Koz, there is quite some Technology and science connected to it which I educate to people which is the NEW tree of life living the first Golden Age.

There is simply a lot to learn about becoming a crystalline grid beam and crystallizing the body into its next cycle. There may be many paths, so I am certainly not on this platform to promote anything; but I will certainly nog go into the million sideways while seeing the HIGHWAY right in front of me. That is all I have to say as I see myself change and transition every week, every month. Proof is always to be found when looking self straight into the EYE.The story of creation is beautiful when the eye of the creator self has opened the capacities that flow with the flairs of universal wisdom.

5/1, 1:56am **Pre View**

Do u feel sad and angry with so much turmoil in ur head ?

Would you like a hug?

MY INTERNALS: If Koz would just allow him SELF to take everything back into a command station, problems he is facing could be solved in a shorter amount of time. We can all move from feeling depleted into massive expansion. We could all take the opportunity to create a brand new infrastructure for self for a whole new beginning. Where are the ones that listen to the call of the mountains, where are the ones that eliminate the angers within cells that cannot accept the downfall of humanity. I invested in Self for so many years. Yet for most people is is too much to ask to even go through a 3 or 4 day seminar that changes consciousness from the old into the Golden path or Shambhalla.

As we are rising so fast into the New Light of Atlantis with the Elements that teach the breath of Original movement along the Rivers of Life or Light Waters that will break the dams of density into the body in order to flow with the New Creator. I hope people allow themselves to move through the gates of REMEMBRANCE. Where would we be without the elementals, the elements giving and sustaining life. For it is Light AIR rough and tough, precious and soft as a breeze that teaches the breathe of Original movement along the Rivers in the body that need to break the dams of density. In the end, our health defines our altitude.

Stuck breathing and bacterial feeding is main cause for all illness on earth including the mental/ psychological emotional dense codes one agreed too to ALLOW in the body and carried over through foods, many lower senses through the interaction with other people, animal products, low vibrations and frequencies. The breathing circulation system will be adjusted on several levels during this project of transformation/transmutation until it flows and waves through the body like the Rivers of life to restart global health.When the breathing system upgrades, the atmosphere within and surrounding an establishments creates new Group Consciousness and Unitarian options to create from .a new platform.

MAY 2013

5/1, 2:24pm **Koz Kozmos**
I've heard all those theories before & embraced many of them for a while
its basic new age speak that comes out of the Theosophy, Rosicrucianism Aleister
Crowley & the Aeon of Horus etc etc
the star seed transmissions, its goes on
for me the proof is in the pudding
if i can't access other dimensions why?
i don't want a hug thank u
5/1, 2:35pm Koz Kozmos
MUSIC: Aerosmith - Dream On - 8/13/1994 - Woodstock 94 (Official)

5/1, 3:22pm **Koz Kozmos**
great way to cleanse the earth plane, more war, who's doing this?
i'm sick of the karma drama
if i can't jump dimensions, nobody can
ego man ego man
zioperlee zaberlleee zoom ziberlee* zarbaralee *
5/1, 3:37pm **Koz Kozmos**
People often ask if our destiny is written in the stars. I always explain that it is - but
like most written works, it can be improved with a good edit.
5/2, 2:11pm **Pre View**
Thx for reminding me of Aerosmith, thank u for all the music, i'v created a playlist
with it as my
knowledge is retarded concerning music - and do not take time for it. But u gave me
exactly what i needed for my power class. (fitness stuff) So time to really be grateful,
THANK U ! DAMMIT, WE CAN RISE INTO AND BEYOND DIMENSIONS! Mind
you,damit,
5/2, 2:14pm Koz Kozmos

MUSIC: Aerosmith - Livin' On The Edge

5/2, 2:15pm **Koz Kozmos**
Steven Tyler ripped of my old look,
best to look normal these days
the wyrdness mutant hypster is best hiden from the normals
5/2, 2:24pm **Pre View**
i don't , i do not take anyone into account, let them deal with weird hairfollikels,
i live on 4 edges and change the color of my skin according to the human wave that
passes
5/3, 2:38pm **Koz Kozmos**
hairfollikels, ? ahhh, understood
5/3, 2:40pm **Koz Kozmos**

MUSIC : Owl City - Fireflies

5/3, 6:33pm **Pre View**
I like that, thank u - no-thing is hidden . Exactitude reveals all hidden agenda
5/3, 6:56pm **Pre View**
Hi Koz, i feel really sad tonight as some real weird things happened to me, i'm tired
of helping people, so i figure i need to set up programs to help them help themselves
& uplift everything.
Don't be bothered, i know what to do
Guess what, some guy at thr railway station told me i needed to breathe Scotland
Yards, & the highlands, People are going real nuts over here, which is great proof
I wish i could dream deep, very deep and wake up on the other side,,,

But I feel scared, as this week all my thoughts are manifesting on the spot
5/3, 7:26pm **Pre View**
I wish we were 1 month ahead, so many things are going to happen, i will not hold my voice, u must know me by now
I am a wicked boiled soup ok i'll back off,
5/3, 8:05pm **Pre View**
Really wish u'd live around the corner,
And then again i know, u 'd get thrilled by the secret i need to hold, good luck
5/3, 10:14pm **Koz Kozmos**
Freedom
5/3, 10:14pm **Koz Kozmos**
is it ?
MUSIC: CAT STEVENS - Wild World 1971

5/3, 10:14pm **Koz Kozmos**
Would i die tonight ?
5/3, 10:15pm **Koz Kozmos**
MUSIC: Cat Sevens - But I Might Die Tonight - Tea For The Tillerma

5/3, 10:15pm **Koz Kozmos**
som times u have to still the persona on a holy day of luv
5/3, 10:21pm **Pre View**
never met an entity who understands luv; let alone the free flow,
5/3, 10:22pm **Koz Kozmos**
its murder or slow death in the reality slum hope your ok
ride the wave till u hit the beach, and all that
5/3, 10:25pm **Pre View**
i might never understand society, being a loner, it esophocates me, I loose my vox when I have a glance at todays' mentality, can u feel me shakin?
5/3, 10:25pm **Koz Kozmos**
esophocates ? wots wrong may i ask
5/3, 10:26pm **Pre View**
esophocating : low consciousness
5/3, 10:27pm **Koz Kozmos**
ok cheers
turn around, i thought u where down
5/3, 10:27pm **Pre View**
Cheers ! wot are u drinking ? may i ask ?
5/3, 10:27pm **Koz Kozmos**
juice and water, need to stop booze why do u ask
5/3, 10:30pm **Pre View**
ok , just for fun Koz ,i triggered something
I got into drinking two years ago when thinking i was dripping in love and
I stopped it a few weeks ago and that is why resulting actions are coming in,,,
People don't know who I am, still they are very curious when being around me
I am nobody, we are no thing unless we load our stardom.
I always entertain myself
5/3, 10:30pm **Koz Kozmos**
are u down grading your self? i still get confused by your sentence structure , your way of expressing yourself in the english language

5/3, 10:36pm **Pre View**
It is not the English, it is in any language, even my own, this comes from universal alignments and universal newscast, it hits you and you speak synchrone with the wind in the veins or Divine. Sorry if I talk confusing, There is a large difference between the written and spoken word, and I must admit I sometimes talk poetic expecting people to understand me.... I will infuse more care into that ...
5/3, 10:36pm **Koz Kozmos**
just trying to go beyond vagueness, ok kool
5/3, 10:38pm **Pre View**
i know, i mean it is getting frustrating for me
i cannot just give and explain everything on FB, I would loose my dancing vibe and happy essence if i would have a face to face talk with u it would be a never ending 72 hours straight talk, and u know that, it would change your whole life because the exchange of words would have a larger movement.
5/3, 10:39pm **Koz Kozmos**
mmmmmmm
5/3, 10:39pm **Pre View** But don' t bother,
5/3, 10:39pm **Koz Kozmos**
why 72 hours
5/3, 10:40pm **Pre View**
Because there is so much to explain, it takes me a week with no sleep to do that... yess i do not mind
guts, we have them both! You know, challenging parlor
5/3, 10:40pm **Koz Kozmos**
i'm just trying to understand
5/3, 10:41pm **Pre View**
never try, that is a waste of time, just feel and perhaps just know
5/3, 10:41pm **Koz Kozmos**
i do both
5/3, 10:41pm **Pre View**
all i've observed in the hood gives me a big cry to repair to humanity.
Great, You have Feeling & Knowledge on the same Ley Line, huh? I wish I had, that solves everything, 5/3, 10:41pm **Koz Kozmos** ?
i don't understand
5/3, 10:43pm **Pre View**
winding the circles and not having access to get to the bottom layer to assist people out of their enslaved brainwaves, the mind controlling the mind,. You are a treasure missing an important link!
5/3, 10:43pm **Koz Kozmos**
maybe
5/3, 10:43pm **Pre View**
no for sure and u know it, you need to get grid technology in, that is all there is too it!
5/3, 10:43pm **Koz Kozmos**
i feel i've been targetted
5/3, 10:44pm **Pre View**
leave that consciousness will you? Every Light being is targetted, end of the line! Create a new line, your worth is far beyond that
5/3, 10:44pm **Koz Kozmos**
uuuuummmmmmm, i have a point
5/3, 10:45pm **Pre View**
right ummm blablabla. The Universe has a point, everything else is ginger watered down,
5/3, 10:45pm **Koz Kozmos**
my worth has never been acknowledged

5/3, 10:46pm **Pre View**
You need to go deeper then you think you can , you are the only person who can value your worth Its a BIG TRAP ON THE PLANET! Moving into Self worth takes quite a learning zone, best done with
music, haha,think about attraction and fear, the difference,,,
5/3, 10:47pm **Koz Kozmos**
i have, yes
i wrote a song years back called: No Fear of the feast
5/3, 10:48pm **Pre View**
i would like to listen to that...
5/3, 10:49pm **Pre View**
Why did u have to detach from your art ?
5/3, 10:49pm **Koz Kozmos**
i've forgotten it
the lyrics are round here, maybe on ta, my music turned into despair
5/3, 10:50pm **Pre View**
Sometimes u hurt me so much i need to pull in the demarcation line knowing it will balance any which way. No, u'll find it, u are the despair,not your music, your music is your outcome
5/3, 10:51pm **Koz Kozmos**
demarcation? i get that, i don't intend to hurt u
and if i do, i need to stop, i send u good NRG
5/3, 10:53pm **Pre View**
sure Koz, i need to voice down, u will tell me if needed, right?
and i will tell u when you need to cut your vox,
Lets start out some humility
I DO KNOW U DO NOT HURT INTENTIONALLY, keep that in your heart;
5/3, 10:54pm **Koz Kozmos**
if your saying i hurt u , its a big thing to me, makes me feel like stoping the chat its not clear a lot of what u say, what do u mean , this is confusing
5/3, 10:59pm **Pre View**
Most people ask me if I am from some other planet , the answer is my alignments: that makes me what I
am, knowing i will and i do help people get out off the creeping negativity including politics and economics which are alien to me but try to understand this)
I do have great love for u otherwise i would not chat
SOUL CONSCIOUSNESS IS very confusing, beyond that , there is clarity in Spirited of course,,,
5/3, 10:59pm **Koz Kozmos**
don't be a Martyr, undersatood , understood these things are alien to me
5/3, 11:00pm **Pre View**
wot is a martyr ?
5/3, 11:00pm **Koz Kozmos**
they are the old world which has died A martyr (Greek: μα´ ρτυς, mártys, "witness"; stem μα´ ρτυρ-, mártyr-) is somebody who suffers persecution and death for refusing to renounce, or accept, a belief or cause, usually religious. not explained right hold on
One who makes great sacrifices or suffers much in
order to further a belief, cause, or principle.
5/3, 11:01pm **Pre View**
u know Koz, sometimes i do not even understand the most simplistic things any longer because my brain is going far beyond the mundane sickness; and i do know u can do this too
5/3, 11:01pm **Koz Kozmos**
i'm not comfortable with great love
u may need to balance this' I get that to
5/3, 11:02pm **Pre View**
Wot do u mean by great love ?

5/3, 11:02pm **Koz Kozmos**
u said it : 'I do have great love for u otherwise i would not chat'
5/3, 11:05pm **Pre View**
Ok, i have worked a lot on myself, bottom-line = i just love people so much and i give & give. But now i'm
learning that there has to be a valuable exchange. Since i did that a week ago, people just knock and knock on my door to get back into my flesh, my bloodstream and remain the vampire of no say! Once I close doors as I said before, they are closed with iron and titanium belt, forever. No mercy because I only close when I've given even my own bloodstream.
5/3, 11:05pm **Koz Kozmos**
i hate humanity
5/3, 11:06pm **Pre View**
Great what did u do
5/3, 11:06pm **Koz Kozmos** something
5/3, 11:06pm **Pre View**
which is ?
5/3, 11:06pm **Koz Kozmos** i
was a seeker when i came to this place i'm trying to lift the veil, i did this
5/3, 11:07pm **Koz Kozmos**

MUSIC: CELTIC FROST - A Dying God Coming Into Human Flesh (OFFICIAL VIDEO)

5/3, 11:07pm **Koz Kozmos**
watch
5/3, 11:08pm **Pre View**
you are no longer a seaker, you are like me, results, only,
it hurts me when i see your values and u don't have the key to open up and move beyond the diseased screens, gonna watch the vid
5/3, 11:08pm **Koz Kozmos**
u need to stop the psychic vampire and social ingrates and keep your door closed
i have no values, why am i like u? what key? what are u saying ?
why don't i have the key
5/3, 11:12pm **Pre View**
I hate wot i did not see in my life
i hate needing to do so much work on it
Keys : u ask too manny times "wot do i mean " , while i love your brain
5/3, 11:13pm **Koz Kozmos**
its only becuase what u say
that makes me question u
i'm an ascension guru, u may be .....
5/3, 11:14pm **Pre View**
Go ahead, i like to be surprised
5/3, 11:14pm **Koz Kozmos**
go ahead ? i'm confused again by what your saying
5/3, 11:15pm **Pre View**
I trust you, try to be a champion today
5/3, 11:15pm **Koz Kozmos**
champion of what
5/3, 11:15pm **Pre View**
never be confused, just tell it like it is

5/3, 11:15pm **Koz Kozmos**
i'm lost and broken
i meat your confusing me meant*
5/3, 11:16pm **Pre View**
no i'm not, i'm getting u out of your broken chains, the self imposed shells that lost their sea
5/3, 11:17pm **Koz Kozmos**
bling
5/3, 11:17pm **Pre View**
bling ?
5/3, 11:18pm **Koz Kozmos**
expensive, ostentatious clothing and jewellery: chains, joke
5/3, 11:18pm **Pre VieW**
gosh, now u get me confused = challenge, can u smile 5/3,
11:19pm **Koz Kozmos**
why?
5/3, 11:19pm **Pre View**
because we have the same level of joking
5/3, 11:19pm **Koz Kozmos**
ok, what did the undertaker die of?
5/3, 11:20pm **Pre View**
So how is ur life moving with u ?
Wot is the undertaker
5/3, 11:20pm **Koz Kozmos**
its taking the piss
its ok' , forget undertaker, it was just going to be a bad joke, i have no life
5/3, 11:21pm **Pre View**
Its like having an undertone and overtone in music, in everything ;
because TONES are important
5/3, 11:21pm **Koz Kozmos**
what does that mean and what is the context,,,
what time is it in BELLGUM
5/3, 11:23pm **Pre View**
timing : 23,23
5/3, 11:24pm **Koz Kozmos**
I'm a galactic mutineer
5/3, 11:24pm **Pre View** or 11,11
5/3, 11:24pm **Koz Kozmos**
i am here to kick the asteroid
5/3, 11:24pm **Pre View**
get out of it, you will hurt yourself
5/3, 11:24pm **Koz Kozmos**
not cliche mysticism please
5/3, 11:25pm **Pre View**
i hate a few words from your tongue :cliché, dimensions, ...
5/3, 11:25pm **Koz Kozmos**
what does that mean
5/3, 11:25pm **Pre View**
There you go again with your questions huh
If you have no life, create something new apart from posting stuff from yer past.
We all have a broken past, so , get over it will ye?

5/3, 11:25pm **Koz Kozmos**
i ahte the 23 syncrownizzah, years back

MY INTERNALS: It was always very easy for me to quickly discipher any dyslectic content, for letters make sense.
For those who do not get the above sentence:
I HATE THE 23 SYNCHRONIZATIONS

5/3, 11:26pm **Pre View**
wot i like about u: u just let me talk, no judgements,
5/3, 11:26pm **Koz Kozmos**
there are a few
5/3, 11:28pm **Koz Kozmos**
? fukk now i'm real lost ,are thoise words
5/3, 11:29pm **Pre View**
no no ,no you are more clever than that
did i use any words not appropiate ? please let me know ?
5/3, 11:31pm **Koz Kozmos**
TOTBL
Temple of the Black Light (TOTBL) is an international temple dedicated to the Current 218
theres more, but won't copy, i pledge my self to no thing satanic stuff temple of the black light
5/3, 11:33pm **Pre View**
I do not mix too much with society because they paste their own meat on their sandwiches,
when i have to, i will, but they already put some sort of insignia on me and are finally crawling back, not having a single clue how to get into me, it is best this way
5/3, 11:33pm **Koz Kozmos**
I've explained to u about your use of language
i'm not complaining
just saying thats why i get confused
/3, 11:34pm **Koz Kozmos**
What is crawling back?
i'm the sleuth of the sacred, a detective: sleuth means detective:
5/3, 11:38pm **Pre View**
crawling back : people came to me and asking questions,
then they judge me because of the harsh truth,
then they evaluate me, then they are afraid, and now the value is bottomline,
meaning after years they finally tell me : hey Nic u were so right but how do u do this.
TO BE water clear honest: i tell them they are so lazy, laziness is society, and when i tell them they are afraid of getting that strong and GOING THAT HIGHWAY ,,,
they keep their mouths shut,
u are not afraid or lazy Koz, that is reason why i chat with u. Society is an endless game,
5/3, 11:39pm **Koz Kozmos**
u say a lot that needs to be questioned
u open your self up to that
ok, got u, my brain is bored with typing, and my shoulder hurts thank u ,but i need to go 5/3, 11:41pm **Pre View**
well u said i needed to open myself to that, i'm working on it, but is is hard at times to see the value through everything we encounter....
I will some day, or now, depends on my brain elixirs,
5/3, 11:41pm **Koz Kozmos**
why is it hard ? if u have this power u should be able to handle it
i find it hard being here
5/3, 11:42pm **Pre View**
Your shoulder pain is just emotional burn out from past frequencies that did not serve you, it was alwaysa question of dealing with these things...

5/3, 11:43pm **Koz Kozmos** and the mouse
5/3, 11:43pm **Pre View**
don't feed it, eat and be the tiger!
5/3, 11:43pm **Koz Kozmos**
yes body pain due to being here of cource
5/3, 11:44pm **Pre View**
i know, it's up to u and u and u only! , to load that breaking point and then you'll have it all. We all have to deal with wath is going on and make this earth a Light Earth place which was always the intention of the Divine Sources/Forces...
5/3, 11:44pm **Koz Kozmos**
i know all this and practice it
5/3, 11:44pm **Pre View**
then practice the elimination procedures until you get into these clear spaces in which nothing can hit
you! I don't believe you, your breathing is totally off, so the elimination is totally slow,
5/3, 11:44pm **Koz Kozmos**
but still get problems
how do i reach the breaking point?
5/3, 11:45pm **Pre View**
would u like to tell me how you would do it? That is far more interesting then sucking my energy.
5/3, 11:45pm **Koz Kozmos**
what is this all? its ok, but u could answer my questions concisely
i've tryed and tried, it must come to me
5/3, 11:46pm **Pre View**
If it is not coming 2 you, that is quite natural, you need to do the work otherwise u'll get confronted when waking up.Alignment is about co-creation, it is not waiting for something to just happen to you which many expect. And that is even worse because it is the highest level of disrespect we can give to the universe and our Sourcery; Claiming Mastery is stepping into it and allow Divine assistance;
5/3, 11:46pm **Koz Kozmos**
? confronted by what
5/3, 11:47pm **Pre View**
Confronted with your ego syndrome and all the hassle you have
u do not have the equipment of light technology to move yourself back into crystal light consciousness
5/3, 11:47pm **Koz Kozmos**
what are you saying here
5/3, 11:47pm **Pre View**
please pardon me, i just feel that you need to retrain your self into Light knowledge
5/3, 11:47pm **Koz Kozmos**
what equipment did i have in the past? u seem very confused
5/3, 11:48pm **Pre View**
Com on, me confused???? Hey!Your past: all the things u did to get somewhere while u knew IT WASNOT EXACTLY the training needed to ascend from the debris of your life style. I'm sure you moved through stuff, but anchoring light and becoming the many levels of consciousness it takes to move in the crystalline realms takes knowledge and integration procedures.
Reading about it and messing around with nonsense around light body is not particularly a space where we meet up with light teams and bring the body into new scientific formulas or simple Light Living would be great,
5/3, 11:48pm **Koz Kozmos**
i understand u are awakening, but its scrambled energy, there are many confusions in getting there, but what is this there how does it manifest what is its purpose?

5/3, 11:50pm **Pre View**
i am not confusing you, you need to party yer Light into the realms where you feel the pressure of higher attitudes matches new altitudes; Makes sense?
i'm getting u were u need to be and get into ur knowledge
why do u think we connected somehow? :
because you've had enough, plain and simple like anybody else.
5/3, 11:51pm **Koz Kozmos**
your confusing me, were are u getting me
5/3, 11:51pm **Pre View**
Dear Koz, i'm getting a drink now after 10 days,
and get some relaxing inter special amusement
please get some rest, we'll talk soon
5/3, 11:51pm **Koz Kozmos**
ok , thank u , cheersz and GOOD Vibez
5/3, 11:52pm **Pre View**
i love ur vibes, please keep that in mind
5/3, 11:52pm **Koz Kozmos**
thank you, good night have you heared of this
5/3, 11:53pm **Koz Kozmos**
Ibogaine is a naturally occurring psychoactive substance found in a plant in a member of the Apocynaceae family known as Iboga (Tabernanthe iboga). A hallucinogen with both psychedelic and dissociative properties, the substance is banned in some countries; in other countries it is being used to treat addiction to methadone, heroin, alcohol, cocaine, methamphetamine, and other drugs. Derivatives of ibogaine that lack the substance's hallucinogenic properties are under development.
5/3, 11:53pm **Pre View**
I am Plant substance, howling like a wolf, sleep tight and take the woods with u!
5/3, 11:53pm **Koz Kozmos**
i've not taken this, and u??? nighteeeeeeeeeeeee night
5/3, 11:53pm **Pre View**
no . No world is black & white, its the in between million brilliant vibes that need to resurrect the body,
are you bored yet?
Dogs pee on it, I breathe on it,
5/3, 11:53pm **Koz Kozmos**
supposed to help with addiction etc, i'm not an addict PEACE AND NOISE, bye
5/3, 11:56pm **Pre View**
There you go again, outside forces huh, ITS WITHIN! although plants help,,,
please do not talk about psycho, schizophrenic or cuckoo people, and on, these are the people who need the most Light assistance.
I've dealt a lot with psychotic people, helped a lot, it is the institutions and often times parents that do not want Light healing methods.
It is becoming unacceptable, I did fight a lot to get justice in this domain and won
But that is just a few cases and nothing compared to what is really needed.
5/4, 12:04am **Pre View**
please let me know where I can find your noise? Haha
how did u know i was listening to Dusty (windmills)
(It was posted on my timeline and we discussed different versions)
5/4, 12:05am **Koz Kozmos**
u told me u preferred Dustys version of the song, i'm aware of the version and agree i gave my value to people but no one wanted it,
so it has been best for me to retreat & have fun
5/4, 9:19am **Pre View**
I will have fun or run,,,,

ibogaine, no i did not hear of it = interesting
I only work with Source Substances (Light frequencies at many levels & alchemy)
LANGUAGES MATTER! eliminate addictions & the old mindset when the Breath is open thr the perineum & crown andthen i move that thr the endocrine system. This works fast & changes an individual overnight.
I'm going for a long walk, would u like to join me through the woods as a dream machine, passing the lakes & talking to all airy kingdom i might encounter ?
5/4, 9:31am **Pre View**
Good morning ,Were's the music ?
May 4, 2013
5/4, 3:07pm **Koz Kozmos**
whats big and round and likes to spin?
5/4, 3:07pm Koz Kozmos

MUSIC: Feeling Good sung by Anthony Newley

5/4, 3:07pm **Koz Kozmos**
the earth mother
5/4, 8:35pm **Pre View**
I can see u spinning & jumping from this universe into other universes,
i can feel u moving with the roots
of trees, i can smell yur pain opening charts of unknown territories,
But now i need rest, lots of rest. Bye Koz
5/4, 10:25pm **Koz Kozmos**
no worries, dream deep, dream deeper
5/4, 10:25pm **View**
I wish I could dream , it just happens every ten years,
I asked the dolphins & wales communications & revelations trough my dreams tonight as they connect with any consciousness. I am just learning how to integrate SONAR waves (the missing component in alchemy)There is one word u said yesterday and it keeps on troubling me : U want me to be CONSISTENT, consistency .... i like that word.
So maybe i should explain things a little deeper - I sometimes left the things u said to its creation as i wanted to avoid over explanation --- it is that repetition of the same confusions, frustrations & stuff with living on earth which live deep into u and u don't have a way to get out as u told me.
When i do explain what i do u just always tell me u've been through that ....
IF U HAD, u would have no time to get bored, never be upset with the outward world, u would just look at it - know what it is & move on & create equipment with magnificent elimination factors, u would not post about economics nor politics because your knowledge about what is going to happen with it would have gone deep and not anger u any longer. The list in which i observed u is long. It tells me u are not wearing ascended shoes and are deeply embedded in the EGO-Solar trap. I understand this very well as we all fell from Universal alignments deep back into this solar trap. But I do remember how it feels being there(universal) - no more emotions, no more old mentality, complete different attitude, knowledge on the spot & manifest potentials and on---- But I like the way you
understand stuff without judgement. As of now i am getting myself out of this solar trap , i am training myself a lot which means u release tremendous density. All this is being done through crystalline grids and alignment. DC (direct connect) to Source is termed alignment, but alignment reaches further in the portals of the universe. Every corner of creation will know alignment soon, as nothing else equates on ground. It may requires ascended shoes and feet on ground willing to space out through grids required and grounding them by paying attention & strict detail to their inspired architecture. Crystalline structure
and support (through your trillion cells, the entire anatomy ...)
takes years to advance from SOUL/EGO into spirit body (the celestial, solar, heavenly, universal, eternal, immortal bodies
Blablablabber, ist ok,

But all the info to upload upgrades every day is not that easy unless very disciplined. So what worked for u years ago is not any longer applicable today. U need to channel your own info and move on with evolution. This is the moment entities have lived for, awaiting a time when nothing matters but CONNECTION, as the body mutates with its Divine connector links through a masters's eternal
projection in cells.This is very crafty and takes a lot of endurance and understanding. A master is not the one that fits into society through acceptance but lives the hard line approach in truth and is quite some challenge as people reject truth 100% The confrontation needs more understanding and then release and upgrade. Becoming an ascended being on earth is a deep and very interesting training or journey, but we need the right equipment. When earth matches its celestial equivalent, the I am on ground matches the I AM in the heavens, or matching octaves between self and source. And yeah, beyond that, just because no Spark ever stops training,
Lower level defenses, resistances, deceit , ... must be eliminated because it is a death penalty. The grids pull this out along other technology within the grids and is quite fashionable to witness. Lets say we all need evaporation of old consciousness and captivity of the soul/eg.. I was trained between 2000 & 2008 with Warriors of Peace, However , the training was very severe and not many could bring that to a level of understanding which does not make sense to me. We only understand through experience, so that matters a lot and thus the harder we train , the more we get to experience, the more fun we can have with creation. But some foundation and the exactitude of alignment is needed and many people refuse to believe that and do not go through some initial training...
I am now picking up all this material, it even says I would only understand it 10 years from now (which was somewhere in 2004) and that is right . Many things like working with a simple grid was the most important thing i can only understand as of now because the universe is geometry and math and if these 2 components are not understood it is quite impossible to incorporate them no matter how much light u breathe through, or is it not? So picking up everything - all the study --- reveals the understanding
and makes me dig deeper with interesting results.
The realm of spirit operates by perfect Satellite Grid Staging and when alignments are in perfection we are asked to conduct our life accordingly. I picked the material up because some people and yourself asked me how I manifested to change myself all the time and find it quite interesting. So i give myself a month to prepare a new program to teach people over a week-end .Mind-blowing it needs to be, why not... We create, right?
And then they will understand that working with Divine electronics , light grids, math, geometry and above all our Universal Essence blending male/female components back to where they belong. I love going deep into that consciousness in which male/female light waves merge back together in that OneOriginal iPod.
Its gonna be Light engineering through Alchemical components ready to take off (ascend) With this material u need to upgrade your own information- co-create and really be 100 % fearless because what u get is what u will do - so that is great fun, no single second of boredom as u become all u do in alignment with your Source.
Humanity needs to be educated into the real stuff. So much airy fairy light or guru movements kill all the respect to the Divine. How can people just eat, drink and think animalistic and just pretend some meditational avenue that gets them in a nowhere land of destruction. Devotion is respect in the first place; and respect needs knowledge. From knowledge comes trust and furthering the alignments The power of the word comes through these alignments, all my wording too, just by working with certain wavelengths and grid technology u can choose from a trillion varieties each morning we wake up &
make our lifespan more & more interesting.
Of course it takes a lot of work in the beginning but after that; people move real quick. Maybe then it becomes understandable that i actually always say in 1 sentence what many people need to express in 5 sentences.
That is the intelligence of Spirit ,that puts together what needs to come through.
I just love that, and it comes naturally just thr alignment, working with electrons ....
Another example that proves a lot : my paintings- my art , i just started it out like 18 months ago, never used a brush, etc.

Never figured out a concept, no thinking. I just step out of my meditational space which has become my daily life ,then I just cannot stop it or stop me from painting fast with my fingers,,,,
The concept comes only when it is finished, which is the natural way of creation. That was real weird in my beginner stages. But i know it is the right thing to do, it is sourced.
So, sometimes when i do not respond when you are asking me to explain stuff that is because I want you to learn to think for yourself – or exchange thinking patterns. Whatever comes out of u might be interesting, many times the explanation you are asking me to give takes too much effort and so it exhausts me which is not a good way to exchange information.. Sometimes when i comment, i rather put things like it is a joke but be really reassured I DO MEAN IT ACTUALLY VERY SERIOUSLY !(most people do not get my jokes on FB, for they don't activate their level of intelligence) So, do know i do appreciate your comments a lot, they are very clever & open new spaces for me. The other thing is as I trained for 10 years, i forgot about other things like ufos , aliens, other universes which u are opening from and awakening. So Koz now u know,
i am very passionate about teaching it again, teaching myself new stuff & move fast. I hope Koz, this gave u some more insight...
I hope Koz that u find a way to understand that some things cannot be explained on FB because it takes a few hours and is not appropriate.
How is ur shoulder, do u not have the healing equipment to get over that?
5/5, 12:59am **Pre View**
That was a lot , good night Koz,
I hope this reveals something 2 u
5/5, 1:14am **Pre View**
Many people i trained in the past fell, or only apply the simple stuff which is easy with immediate results but then they miss out the fun with the universe because of their laziness to dig deeper and develop some passion somehow through their lives. It's the mind control that keep their poor brains in mental recycling debris and same thought patterns. That is why everything in the awakening moves so slow. Damn LAZINESS, ARROGANCE AND EGOTISTICAL REVIEWS.
I wish u had these alignments because u have sharp intelligence and then i could have a great time with u, perhaps discussing it and furthering the scientific components
Ok, i'll get my sonar waves in now and see if i can dream...
5/5, 10:16am **Pre View**
I did not give up because of u, instead i am becoming stronger then ever
I did not know species like u existed, this strengthened my faith to go even deeper and leave the world
for what it is as dark forces/sources are being strangled with truth anyways (only it is not understood by mundane mud elixirs) But u can see the cleanse in politics , everything is coming to surface and light forces are moving into the spiritual politics ,,,, just a little patience , or always patience because how the universe works and how the universe is putting things together may demand some more light intelligence within our brain capacity.
Yet, it is all about GRID TRAINING, retraining how Ley Lines run through the body, how they formulate themselves into grids, lightwaves and geometric patterns..
I like these kind of shows, spectrums, amusement parks of the Divine orders.
In order for something to come out of the closet it needs to surface even stronger, that is what is happening in society - just look at it for what it is, and turn away - do what u need to do - and everything will equalize out as earth is the last planet to ascend (it starts with clearing your self out) The anger & frustrations come up stronger and stronger ready to be eliminated & then finally leave your embodiment when u work hard enough. Its just an obvious understanding Koz & u actually know it somehow or could
remember those things, maybe?
This is reason why so many talk about awakening, why there is so much talk about religious stuff (did not even exist in the first place) how ridiculous.
Smile & smile & smile

Wot is ur song note for today?
5/5, 10:18am **Pre View**
This is reason why i sometimes go into society, to plant things such as the crystalline grid constructions -and bring change - just with my energy field. Some places change overnight. It is when u work for the universe and do what is being asked from u, the universe works for u, simple as that .
It is fun to do as the results are fun to see; yet hardly anyone understands or is willing to understand their origin, their power.
5/5, 10:18am **Pre View**
I feel Crazy as hell today-----
Are u still asleep ?
Ok, you just sleep then, I'm ok with that
5/5, 12:08pm **Pre View**
i want to hip hop
i want rip rap
I want to roll rocks
Will u be in it ?
What colors will u wear today ?
5/5, 12:26pm **Pre View**
Can u jump over my head ?
I could use that because my brains just won't shut up Continual blabber
5/5, 1:46pm **Koz Kozmos**
as I have explained i post some of the political information....mainly because my brother in law is on my page and i felt it helps him....i have never been political....but it does have an ultra sinister element which is worth revealing
5/5, 2:02pm **Koz Kozmos**
beyond the scenario of the herd religions and politics is a hyper dimensional element that can't be ignored....what is an ego solar trap and why am i trapped in it?....did alcohol and ciggs help u dissolve
your ego solar trap, what are u saying here ?..how do you train?
what is your zaykred tekk?.... (sacred technology)
all of what your saying as I have said is very ashtar command etc...with alchemical blabbering....J if your going to say in one sentence what other people say in 5 u have a lot of work to do.... 5/5, 2:03pm **Koz Kozmos**
what things do you teach?
give practical applications and go beyond your mumbo jumbo!
5/5, 2:09pm **Koz Kozmos**
I hope for the cleanse, also of the low grade soul race, they need to go...
for me, to overcome anger and frustrations...i need to get out of this dimension and leave the scum behind, i did not attract it!
I'm not sure I know, What do I know?...my song note....no idea...tuning dadgad
5/5, 2:11pm **Koz Kozmos**
my head is full of noise
5/5, 2:14pm **Koz Kozmos**
MUSIC: Lee Hazlewood - Nancy Sinatra, Some Velvet Morning

5/5, 2:23pm **Koz Kozmos**
and one more
5/5, 2:23pm **Koz Kozmos**
MUSIC: John Mellencamp - Check It Out

5/5, 2:25pm **Koz Kozmos**
From The KozKozmos Juke Box
80's stadium, rock instigated the ascension process

5/5, 2:28pm **Pre View**
Thank u ! enjoying it
Have no time now, but will get back 2 u later ok
5/5, 2:33pm **Koz Kozmos** ?
yes, do the dither
bye
5/5, 7:49pm **Pre View**
Dither ? (some velvet morning some velvet morning, getting into some velvet night
political: u never mentioned your brother in law, but I like your comment on that !
5/5, 7:58pm **Koz Kozmos**
ok , Dither = A state of indecisive agitation.
5/5, 8:02pm **Pre View**
If I fuse many sentences into one single sentence, that means it is part of my passion. Most words people use are of no information, they have a death value; its their consciousness that keeps on repeating collective consciousness and they don't even realize that because they function through the control machinery and have no interest in educating self out of ego because of their selfishness. And again the mind that keeps on repeating what has been programmed through the matrix.
I trained my brain through many teachings, i am training now how to get people to understand this sort of brain development and expansion.
So on Fb i cannot explain too much,
just have some fun to show people how alignments work,
The alchemy , as the magic is proving it into my daily life.
So, i did my best to explain this stuff , it is up to u if u want it or not: alignment, direct connect, no ego, and moving fast, that is wot i teach, leave it or take it. Explanation is not appropriate any longer,,,, u either know that is it for u or u leave it because these hours i spent in posting is no good.
UNDERSTANDING comes with integration of Light techniques
and thus many experiences through the environment.
I do like u a lot, & there is a reason why somehow, without questioning.
A few hours ago, 5 people at about 20 years old came to my house only to express their gratitude for my speeches and the medication coming through the meditation I offered.
I'v been in devaluated all of my life
FAR BEFORE REALIZING THE DANGET IT BRINGS!
I have witnessed so much disgrace and most of all UNWORTHINESS
that came from my parents who treated me as their slave. So, I am dealing with this unworthiness now, and the survival issues I was living for far too long.
5/5, 8:02pm **Pre View**
i am very decisive
5/5, 8:03pm **Koz Kozmos**
that was a lot of sentences
5/5, 8:04pm **Pre View**
yes, i am sentences
5/5, 8:04pm **Koz Kozmos**
glad to hear about positive feed back
5/5, 8:04pm **Pre View**
sure, just have a big laugh, give me ur smile
5/5, 8:05pm **Koz Kozmos**
i'm not sure what your giving me via your posts on FB
5/5, 8:05pm **Pre View**
it is beyond expectation,
because we don' expect from each other
No matter how many km/hour we race
Understanding the race, and then understanding what speeds bring
Is a task but a few Divine realized beings take on.

Working a lot with Sonar waves and understanding the wales and dolphin community, oh , wish u could partake of this experience through meditation,,,
5/5, 8:06pm **Koz Kozmos**
I wish u the best in all your endeavors
5/5, 8:06pm **Pre View**
thank u
5/5, 8:06pm **Koz Kozmos**
eye
5/5, 8:06pm **Pre View** I?
5/5, 8:06pm **Koz Kozmos**
~<0>~
5/5, 8:06pm **Pre View** ?
5/5, 8:07pm **Koz Kozmos**
i understand the semantic 's of getting rid of the 'I'
5/5, 8:07pm **Pre View**
Are u the Wizzard ?
5/5, 8:07pm **Koz Kozmos**
~<0>~ , its an eye
5/5, 8:07pm **Pre View**
wot does it say?
5/5, 8:08pm **Koz Kozmos**
i'm a deslexxxikkk wizzzzard
eye kan't spellll , anywayza catch u again 5/5, 8:08pm
Pre View
no prob, i can hear u without spelling
My Leopard friends' name is black wizzard,
He tomld me in meditation, it is very rare when a Leopard appears, so strong
g 5/5, 8:08pm **Koz Kozmos**
ok , kool
5/5, 8:08pm **Pre View**
Telepathic waves,
nonono u are kool
5/5, 8:09pm **Koz Kozmos**
no hope for me from the look of thingz
5/5, 8:09pm **Koz Kozmos**
good
5/5, 8:10pm **Pre View**
wot do u do with yourself & life
Maybe load a different vision on things
5/5, 8:10pm **Koz Kozmos**
nothing , hide
i recently got trouble from another psi vampire just killed them,
sick of negative energy hard to explain
5/5, 8:11pm **Pre View** wanna talk about it?
5/5, 8:12pm **Koz Kozmos**
I'm one of the people that manged to 'TUNE IN TURN ON AND DROP OUT'
5/5, 8:12pm **Pre View**
Come on, turn on some cosmic machinery and delete this negative energy.
Did you not train yourself to do so and blow the misty vibes back to where they belong,
Find yourself a new gazelle and dwell like an animal,
They are worth a deep study, you may gain and learn a lot from their intelligence,
Their ways of knowledge, their guidance.
You should move into that territory, it assists you to move away from your negative art
THEY ARE WAITING FOR YOU, haha!
I am never joking,

5, 8:12pm **Koz Kozmos**
Euhm, no ?
5/5, 8:13pm **Pre View**
no : I am not going to explain any more
So anyways, wot did u do in the past, like u told me u did a lot of work but none worked... What was it what you did?
5/5, 8:14pm **Koz Kozmos**
i've avoided working with humans
its been very hard for me
5/5, 8:14pm **Pre View**
Do u ever reread the pm's i posted?
5/5, 8:14pm **Koz Kozmos**
take 1 nano second to explain, haha ahhhhhh , yes , sometimes
5/5, 8:15pm **Pre View**
Do u ever think about the reason why I was talking about Light Technology?
5/5, 8:15pm **Koz Kozmos**
as i said, i 've come across this info, yes but it seems like gobbldeee gook
5/5, 8:16pm **Pre View**
Coming across stuff and working with it,
and moving into the resulting actions MAKES UP MANY DIFFERENCES.
5/5, 8:16pm **Koz Kozmos**
and remember, I'm further than far out
that made no sense, the last 3 words particularly , makes up many differences any way , if u can give me something to work with , that would be good
5/5, 8:18pm **Pre View**
When you fail having your direct connect to your Source, you just sink with the ship of earth debris and its many habita.
5/5, 8:18pm **Koz Kozmos**
but i'm going for a swim before the poole closes
hope there are'nt too many humans there
you have zero insight
5/5, 8:19pm **Pre View**
OK, OOO INSIGHT HUH?
ok Koz, enjoy, u can elimaninate people out of the pool,
i do this all the time in public places
But i am not a fool!
5/5, 8:19pm **Koz Kozmos**
i have no one in my life
but vague people cause problems u don't get what i'm saying
5/5, 8:20pm **Pre View**
If i need to give u something to work with,
it would need a few days of explanation and setting the body
into its Light Spectrum takes a lot more then just fooling around with light as many do,
and you're in Wales, not here in Belgium
5/5, 8:21pm **Koz Kozmos**
if u can tell me how to ' delete this energy'
ok
5/5, 8:21pm **Pre View**
I DO GET WOT YOU'RE SAYING
I AM IN THE SAME BOAT,
ONLY I WILL GET OUT OF IT BECAUSE I CHOOSE SO
AND APPLY THE EQUIPMENT that is available to all!
You just don't allow it, dam, you,,,

You need to be willing to go through a foundational training, that is the least
Alignments that equal the ascended realm and masters of many Light degrees...
5/5, 8:21pm **Koz Kozmos**
can't u do it telpahthically
okza, good vibez
your a super kozmik gal
that sounded wyrd u noe wot i mean ?
5/5, 8:23pm **Pre View**
ok, thx, I can feel your pain,
i understand what you are going through
still, there is individual work to do as nobody can breathe for you
You need to evaporate the old air that is just a killing field
It is the LIGHT GRIDS THAT BRING YOU INTO THE LIGHT ATMOSPHERE IN WHICH YOU CAN BREATHE PURE AIR, instead of the toxic synthetics on earth. It is a matter of downloading the grids, integrating them and holding them that will get you into that space in which you continually delete
debris...
5/5, 8:23pm **Koz Kozmos**
ok , spk soon (speak)
5/5, 8:23pm **Pre View**
Knowledge is definitely needed and a little foundational training
Ok , Go & get ur swim now
5/5, 8:24pm **KozKozmos**

~~~~~~~~~~~~~~~~~~~~~~ <O>~~~~~~~~~~~~~~~~~~~~~~~

5/5, 8:25pm **Pre View** haha aha aha
Have fun for once, no one cares,,,
I do
5/5, 8:59pm **Pre View**
Not many people understand u Koz because your pain is unbearable Music please , without sunglasses please, and loads of sunny tribes
5/5, 10:03pm **Koz Kozmos**
At yur command madam
MUSIC: Jane's Addiction - Three Days

5/5, 10:07pm **Koz Kozmos**

MUSIC: John Cougar - Ain't Even Done With The Night (Live 1981)

5/5, 10:09pm **Koz Kozmos**
listen carefully to attain the double helix diamante connection to the secret galaxy~
5/5, 10:22pm **Koz Kozmos**
a fairly obvious selection
5/5, 11:18pm **Pre View**
From The Koz Kozmos Juke Box ?
Wot do u mean by Obvious ?
5/5, 11:30pm **Pre View**
Indeed , a selection carefully chosen
I miss the 4th component to create the diamond that fits
~~~~~~~~~~~~~~~~~~~~~~

Thank u & good night Koz
5/6, 12:57am **Koz Kozmos**
pc playing up , so if i dissappear , will be back good night
5/6, 2:21pm **Koz Kozmos**

MUSIC: Johnny Cash /Hurt

5/6, 2:27pm **Koz Kozmos**
BEY
5/6, 2:48pm **Koz Kozmos**
I mean obvious (at least for me)
5/6, 2:49pm **Koz Kozmos**
Juke Box ~ A jukebox is a partially automated music-playing device, usually a coin-operated machine, that will play a patron's selection from self-contained media. The classic jukebox has buttons with letters and numbers on them that, when entered in combination, are used to play a specific selection.
5/6, 2:49pm **Koz Kozmos**
they had them in the 1950's and beyond
5/6, 3:26pm **Pre View**
I was just joking about the jukebox but yeah sometimes i still find some
Sweet man, this song is so depressing, cannot hear it any longer as it reminds me of the past year in which i've been introduced into drinking and wasn't even aware it would completely distort my precious brainwaves; stupid me.
Anyways, I did not know hurt existed to such an extent where people clearly tell u they only want lies, can u imagine --- TRUTH is not an option, they cannot bare truth because they did not teach themselves how to handle and love truth or lets say why 'truth' is the only wave worth living – for everything else will
sooner then later create complete chaos as we witness in the world today.
So, I am over & done with that but let me tell you JUSTICE will speak loud some day soon. I'm getting stronger every day now & happy to get out of the misery
& start my life ,,,
Make it a special day for u Koz
5/6, 3:33pm **Koz Kozmos**
HOW?
5/6, 3:35pm **Pre View**
How to make a special day for yourself ?
Go & do something unusual, something u really like, do something u thought u'd never do, pack your bags & visit the monkeys or start a good dialogue with the undergrounds species, You never know what you might discover huh,,,
5/6, 3:36pm **Koz Kozmos**

MUSIC: The Aquarian Age - 10,000 Words In A Cardboard Box

5/6, 3:37pm **Koz Kozmos**
i'll stay in and hide from the city and the monkeys
not seen this vid, always liked the song
you should be a life coach
there is nothing i really like mmmmm
may try and cut the connection to my higher self again
its obviously doing an awful job, u have a good day too, its 2.30 here

5/6, 3:39pm **Pre View**
go beyond that, go to supreme consciousness (no questions please!) it is 3.40 pm here, early morning
5/6, 3:40pm **Koz Kozmos**
no idea how, ahhh
5/6, 3:42pm **Pre View** Good song!
Ok im gonna chase myself
5/6, 3:43pm **Koz Kozmos**
ok
5/6, 4:13pm **Pre View**
MUSIC: Joan Baez - Love Song to a Stranger (live in France, 1973)

5/6, 4:15pm **Koz Kozmos**
the vicars daughter, her style is elegant but to polite for me
5/6, 4:35pm **Pre View**
sure
it is that strangers always give more value to our life then people we know
5/6, 5:12pm **Koz Kozmos**

MUSIC: Boyd Rice - People

5/6, 5:13pm **Koz Kozmos**
one for the med class, lyric listen !!!
5/6, 5:17pm **Koz Kozmos**

Do you ever think about
what a lovely place the world would be
without all the people
that make life so unpleasant? All the small, petty people All the ugly, annoying people
It's hard not to think about it I like to think about what could be
done to these people
Something cruel
Something mean
Something just
But the meaner the better
Goodness knows they deserve it Have you ever dreamed of killing all the stupid people?
Not just the unintelligent people
but the sort that don't know anything about anything but seem to have opinions about everything They're only too ready to offer their advice about
how to run your life
And yet look at how they run their own lives
For the most part they've accomplished nothing They've contributed nothing
Their lives are miserable
But they talk, talk, talk
At the very least their tongues should be cut out
At the very least Do you ever wanna
kill all the people who tell lies?At the very least Do you ever wanna
kill all the people who tell lies?
Some certainly deserve it
Not necessarily the big liars

or even those who teach lies as truth
I'm talking about people
who say one thing and do another
or who tell you they sent something express mail
when you know they haven't Did you ever want to
kill all the slow people in the world?
The people who are in front of you
when they should be behind you
A crime that the swift should be help back by the slow
And it's criminal that nothing is going to rectify it And what about all the really ugly
people? Add them to the list as well
Some people try not to think about life's ugliness
I've thought about it
I've thought about it quite a lot
Something should be done to these people
Something to make them suffer
the way they've made us suffer I say, bring back the circus maximus
for starters
Unless these weeds are dealt with
they'll poison everything
They are poisoning everything
We need a gardener
A brutal gardener
A thorough, thoughtful gardener
An iron gardener Whatever happened to Vlad the Impaler? Where's Genghis Kahn
when you need him?
Or Roi d'Ys?
Ayatollah Khomeini
Adolf Hitler
Benito Mussolini
Nero
Diocletian
Kitchener
Come back!

5/6, 5:18pm **Pre View**
this is telepathics, i was just listening to the same Boyd
Completely dazed
5/6, 5:19pm **Koz Kozmos**
poor Boyd
5/6, 5:20pm **Pre View**
haha, but want to really rock & jump now
i am dancing and dancing until the moon merges with my sunny dreams;
5/6, 5:20pm **Koz Kozmos**
MUSIC: Prince – PURPLE RAIN (Official Music Video)

5/6, 5:21pm **Koz Kozmos** annoying music

5/6, 5:22pm **Pre View**
Wonder how people are determined by music
I mean their choices, the attraction
Could music also create obstacles?

5/6, 5:22pm **Pre View**
I am ready for some reformatting 5/6, 5:22pm
Koz Kozmos charlie is ok
5/6, 5:22pm **Pre View** aha
5/6, 5:23pm **Koz Kozmos**

MUSIC: Prince - Let's Go Crazy (Official Music Video)

5/6, 5:23pm **Pre View**
good for him
5/6, 5:23pm **Koz Kozmos**
this has a great vibe
5/6, 5:23pm **Pre View**
ok lets go, how slow do u want me to break my ancles
yes i like it, never really listened to Prince
5/6, 5:25pm **Koz Kozmos**
ok, the KozKozmos Juke Box plays ,,,,
5/6, 5:28pm **Pre View**
This is so great, love that while i'm painting
Thank u, very appetiteful meeting place, music and art
5/6, 5:28pm **Koz Kozmos**
the ancient the modern and some other stuff as well here a blast from the near past
5/6, 5:29pm **Koz Kozmos**

MUSIC: Cameo - Word Up

5/6, 5:29pm **Koz Kozmos**
niggaz
5/6, 5:29pm **Pre View**
you seem to know a lot about music, do u listen all day
5/6, 5:30pm **Koz Kozmos**
no, i listen to hemi sync maninly and wear ear plugs i hate the sound of the earth plane
5/6, 5:30pm **Pre View**
maninly? = mainly I guess?
hemi sync ? do u like universal sound
5/6, 5:31pm **Koz Kozmos**
Hemi-Sync is a trademarked brand name for a patented process[1][2][3] used to create audio patterns containing binaural beats, which are commercialized in the form of audio CDs. Interstate Industries Inc., created by Hemi-Sync founder Robert Monroe, is the owner of the Hemi-Sync technology. Hemi-Sync is short for Hemispheric Synchronization, also known as brainwave synchronization. Monroe indicated that the technique synchronizes the two hemispheres of one's brain, thereby creating a 'frequency-following response' designed to evoke certain effects. Hemi-Sync has been used for many purposes, including relaxation and sleep induction, learning and memory aids, helping those with physical and mental difficulties, and reaching altered states of consciousness through the useof sound.
5/6, 5:31pm **Koz Kozmos**
i can't handle noise, i think my nervous system is broken
5/6, 5:31pm **Pre View**
Why ?
5/6, 5:32pm **Koz Kozmos**
i'm not meant to be here,
and have been targeted with the aim to fukkk me up

5/6, 5:32pm **Pre View**
all is repairable, even made better then before How (yes I know) ,
answer you own questions will you!
5/6, 5:32pm **Koz Kozmos**
ok, no being self pitying, cooking a bit
5/6, 5:33pm **Pre View**
are u good at that ?
I mean fucking yourself up ?
The hemi sync is interesting, but when ascending u can just ask to blend the 2 hemispheres, easy to do although some deep alignment and clearing procedures are mandatory.
The brain needs to be prepared for that to work . The hardest part is holding on to that because when we jump from the clear dimensions back into the dual chords, it would split the hemispheres over and over again which explains a lot of that retarded consciousness we all need to deal with, not judge ,
just understand the higher levels of studying and take the railroad where we can stabelize. Training, understanding and taking action is not enough.
It's the skills to keep the archons and hybrids and all of these sorts out of the equations.
Do u have mental or physical difficulties ?
Or just societal issues?
5/6, 5:35pm **Koz Kozmos**
good at what ?
funny, yeah laoooooods
5/6, 5:35pm **Pre View**
Fucking urself up as you said
5/6, 5:35pm **Koz Kozmos** loads
5/6, 5:35pm **Pre View** tell me about it
if you would like to of course
5/6, 5:36pm **Koz Kozmos**
i'm making my self a vegi dinner, and just sorted thru some bills
and played the guitar for a few hours with ear plugs in
5/6, 5:36pm **Pre View**
good
i m vegan since 30 years even start to dislike physical food
5/6, 5:36pm **Koz Kozmos**
yes , i remember u said that
5/6, 5:37pm **Pre View**
would like to listen to you playing the guitar
5/6, 5:37pm **Koz Kozmos**
telling u about it = too complex
u can interview me if u want , that would be fun
5/6, 5:38pm **Pre View**
Great, i'll put my satellite dishes on, can u hear me ?
5/6, 5:39pm **Koz Kozmos**
do u play an instrument ? u must tell me if i'm bothering u
5/6, 5:40pm **Pre View**
i hear your silence, i hear water skateboarding tru your emotional flesh
No , no instrument
I said I was a retard somehow
if u bother me, i would not respond, u know that by now
5/6, 5:40pm **Koz Kozmos**
thought so, just checking when it u say it

5/6, 5:41pm **Pre View** are u telling me yur insecure ?
5/6, 5:41pm **Koz Kozmos**
and how do u mean that?
yeah i'm insecure
5/6, 5:41pm **Pre View**
how do i mean what?
5/6, 5:41pm **Koz Kozmos** that your retarded
5/6, 5:41pm **Pre View**
u cannot let yourself be insecure in this society.
I always let people know I DON'T KNOW A THING
ABOUT ANYTHING
The ringtone here = they explain things deeply (don't even see how afraid thy are but sometimes it reveals many things, you never know. In the case when you tell people YOU KNOW about stuff, that makes them refrain from explaining... An interesting approach, that is all. Or a way to connect to people which can turn out to be fun when they realize our knowledge is far beyond a certain subject. Then again that sounds like ego. So when I get up every morning I tell the universe 'I want to know' and steam LIGHT through, because we all know so little,
5/6, 5:47pm **Koz Kozmos**
I agree i 've said simular stuff but i don't talk to much
5/6, 5:48pm **Pre View**
Just painted a download from Mars planted in the dolphin sonar waves & seahorses which is a great way to bring some good music back to earth

5/6, 5:48pm **Koz Kozmos**
most people that seem to come into my life i have to get rid of quickly
5/6, 5:49pm **Pre View**
why, some are walk inns that have something to explain, and then they disappear,
5/6, 5:49pm **Koz Kozmos**
very good
5/6, 5:49pm **Pre View Lovely**
big head, isn't it?
5/6, 5:49pm **Koz Kozmos**
u'r art has presence, big haed - head me
5/6, 5:50pm **Pre View**
what does that mean, i am not an artist u know, i cannot even paint a tree, presence (don't understand)
5/6, 5:51pm **Koz Kozmos**
nice cosmic blurb....
5/6, 5:51pm **Pre View**
ok, acceptable ; yes my art ecplains my cosmic vibes, and peoples' vibe, should they want to understand,
5/6, 5:51pm **Koz Kozmos**
The state or fact of existing, occurring, or being present in a place or thing. A person or thing that exists or is present in a place but is not seen: "the monks became aware of a strange presence". presence
5/6, 5:52pm **Pre View**
ok, thx,
So why do u need to get rid of people
U did not delete me yet ! haha
5/6, 5:53pm **Koz Kozmos**
as in having a discernible energetic vibration from the inner realms
not on face book, the flesheee one with stupid faces, not sure why but they have to go
5/6, 5:53pm **Pre View** can they not handle u?
5/6, 5:53pm **Koz Kozmos**
i need to protect myself from the sickness, no
5/6, 5:54pm **Pre View**
we all have to;;;
5/6, 5:54pm **Koz Kozmos**
i'm well mannered, its thier sickness that gets on my nerves
5/6, 5:54pm **Pre View** i think ur stronger then that
5/6, 5:54pm **Koz Kozmos**
than wot ?
5/6, 5:55pm **Pre View**
then anybody, just imagine there is nobody when the annoy you
5/6, 5:55pm **Koz Kozmos**
i do all that
its hard to explain, and to much to type
5/6, 5:56pm **Pre View**
give it a try
5/6, 5:56pm **Koz Kozmos**
i undersand yur tech
5/6, 5:56pm **Pre View** ok understood
5/6, 5:57pm **Pre View**
ok, but there is music, they can just fuck off and u can choose another life
5/6, 5:57pm **Koz Kozmos**
another life has been aloneness
5/6, 5:58pm **Pre View**
that is wot u want isn't is, you told me you wanted change

5/6, 5:58pm **Koz Kozmos**
and awareness of the sickness
5/6, 5:58pm **Pre View**
you've been too lonely too long i guess
5/6, 5:58pm **Koz Kozmos**
always, i'm trying to instigate it at the mo
5/6, 5:59pm **Pre View** mo ?
5/6, 5:59pm **Koz Kozmos**
lonley it better than toxic, mo = moment
5/6, 5:59pm **Pre View**
ok, im gonna have some coffee, wanna join me?
5/6, 5:59pm **Koz Kozmos**
ok, i'm going to tidy
5/6, 6:00pm **Pre View**
good luck ! do it in detail & get exhausted, haha
5/6, 6:00pm **Koz Kozmos**
do u believe in luck? i can only do my own thang can't photo copy
do it in detail & get exhausted ?
5/6, 6:03pm **Pre View**
yes u were going to tidy - clean up... get exhausted because it helps the physical body to release mental pain like loneliness ? Or did i get this wrong ? Yes i believe in luck , but it depends more on the consciousness you are in, what u believe is what u'll get. This simple equation is not easily understood by many, ... I think luck also depends on many choices we make every single second , it influences everything around & within us .
I am talking energy wise, then again there is only electricity, so...
5/6, 6:30pm **Pre View**
U sing far too exclusively well , many songs aligned to the heart
5/6, 9:40pm **Pre View**
Hey Koz,
I was reading about Dyslexia (never gave attention to it as u seemed perfectly normal to me & it was easy for my to twist & turn letters – average people spell worse)
Thing is - that is if u want to -
i would really like to know what your problems with being dyslectic are : physical-mentally-emotionally. When i look it up it seems very vague to me
(of course lots of info but not to the point)
Yes i am interested in the anatomy and how everything works and then see how we can make it work differently. This way i helped and cleared out a lot of psycho or schizophrenic young people suffering a lot from mental abuse, traumatic domestic circumstances and physical assault. It assisted me to download and reprogram their brains while offering the so called off line solutions: no medication, no control, yet one on one assistance and 3-monthly programs that make them understand how to remove sad and painful experiences as a lot of young people miss out on education and support when it come to psychological development and self empowerment. It needs to be done after school as schools still refuse to replace religion by True Christ Light education which would make up a big difference for our children and young adults.i am so passionate about helping and seeing the change within these young brains.
But never encountered anyone dyslectic
So maybe , i'll make it my next study, maybe ,
But make sure Koz, only talk about it if that feels good to you, ok ? Take care,
5/7, 5:12am **Pre View**
Are you awake ?
Ok enjoy dreamssssszzz

5/7, 10:18am **Koz Kozmos**
still got pc problems, we have
5/7, 10:18am **Koz Kozmos**
still got pc problems, we have developed as a race thru language which has become small talk via the dead tongue of the matrix,
MY DYSLEXIA IS JUST ANOTHER DICK HEAD DEFINING ME VIA LIMITED MODELS its about howwell u do with your vision quest; and i am the word wizard
5/7, 11:44 **Pre View**
you truly are the word wizard
and i will develop a new language for you
5/7, 11:49am **Pre View**
FB : what a great world to test consciousness ....
You know, I usually only post my paintings on my other account and the comments compared to this account is such a big difference, makes me laugh all day
Have a great day Koz
Buy yourself a Mac - never any problem
5/7, 1:14pm **Koz Kozmos**
A MAC ? THERE ARE TO MANY PROBLEMS, bin up since 4
dreadful day so far, if i dissapear for a while it is pc probs
5/7, 2:19pm **Pre View**
me too, been up since 4, Light AIR, haha
its in the air
ok, keep urself safe, A MAC = an Apple computer
5/7, 8:50pm **Koz Kozmos**
send me the cash
thought u may have meant a big mac, haha
worst day of my life,
no kidding, still pc playing up and away
friday til the following saturday should catch up by then,
just in case my pc goes away to get fixed
What do you call a chick who swims under water
doll fin !
5/7, 8:56pm Koz Kozmos
MUSIC: Bruce Springsteen - Born to Run (Official Music Video)

5/7, 9:46pm **Pre View**
Love this version
wats wrong with ur pc ?
Hope u feel better now,,i'll sing a lullaby for u,can't sleep for days now
this is just the earth plane changing
Transition with the animals will be strong as I feel it coming
5/7, 11:46pm **Pre View**
I'm getting nuts
Everything around feels strange like i cannot trow away enough stuff,
clearing time i guess, i already gave everything away,
but cannot trow myself away, not yet, hiha

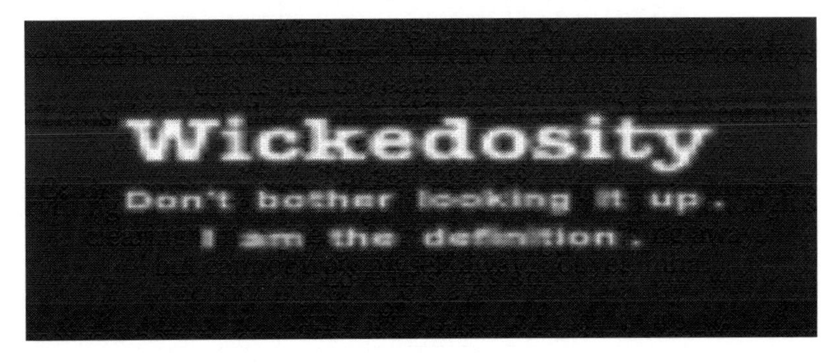

5/8, 11:32am **Pre View**
How is your skin today ?
5/8, 1:56pm **Koz Kozmos**
i feel the same, got rid of loots of stuff maybe 70% and have had that very thought about throwing myself away...
my skin ? things just get worse, no self pity just so called facts
5/8, 2:00pm **Koz Kozmo**
MUSIC: Archgoat - Dawn of the Black Light (Live in Davao)

5/8, 2:03pm **Koz Kozmos**
is the earth plane changing....the things that have happened for me are not wonderful cosmic lessons, just a sadistic teacher who has slowed me down
i always feel strange....get me outa here . Some heavy metal I remember, I think Pre must be a fan of ARCHGOAT
5/8, 2:06pm **Koz Kozmos**
MUSIC: Scott Wino Weinrich live at Substance Record Store.

5/8, 2:20pm **Koz Kozmos**
excuse my misery
5/8, 2:24pm **Pre View**
I am a fan of no-thing, i am a wave that picks up waves, integrate them, release them , and pick up new ones , i feel u in my bones,
Don't like Archgoat Sadistic teacher ? what happened ?
Maybe too much to type, ok
Many people are experiencing the same as you do Koz, we all need to throw away all that does not serve us or invades our precious energy fields
All the people who almost beg me for a healing session are young with heavy deep problems but I know they will accept the harsh truth i integrate within them and then they change very quickly because they are so hungry for solutions.
But it is heavy to go through sessions as a lot needs to be evaporated from invasions, from birth, parents, teachers ...
Yet, with the young, I have asuch an enjoyable time with great results, as they are so innocent and open,,,
So Koz, you are not alone, you are being asked to find the door , use the RIGHT key, and get it over & done with
Maybe take ur flight to Alaska, haha
Do not excuse, I understand you very well !
5/8, 2:24pm **Pre View**
Like this Wino Weinrich, did not know him
(Youtube vid on Fb posts)
5/8, 2:25pm **Koz Kozmos**
i was joking about you being a fan
5/8, 2:25pm **Pre View**
you are good at that (joking) i sometimes I am too serious
5/8, 2:26pm **Koz Kozmos**
i know you are transcendent being of light from the dark galaxy
5/8, 2:26pm **Pre View**
but i do not always get it when u do because I cannot hear your intonation
5/8, 2:26pm **Koz Kozmos**
yes, understood, wino's kool
5/8, 2:27pm **Pre View**
sure is, i enjoy him a lot, Thank u
5/8, 2:27pm **Koz Kozmos**
i need to go to an alternative dimension, America, and become a hells alien
it failed 30 years ago in Wales how r u ?

5/8, 2:29pm **Pre View**
NO NO NO
If you failed, ok, you are only starting out
Who did not fail ?
I failed too, almost for a lifetime because Capricorns are the ones who have been held back the most, yet now with the Grids and the A/O ANTENNA,
WE CAN SHOOT INTO THE BEYOND
But i decided to pick all up stronger then ever before
How I am,: had also the worst day yesterday, throwing out stuff, there is hardly anything left, But feel good today
You know the earth is but a small place regarding universes
U can change location whenever u wish
5/8, 2:30pm **Koz Kozmos**
not in my case
5/8, 2:30pm **Pre View**
U create what makes u
5/8, 2:30pm **Koz Kozmos**
bullshit
5/8, 2:30pm **Pre View**
What is holding u back to even do anything about you situation?
You are understanding you need to self protect your energy?
5/8, 2:31pm **Koz Kozmos**
u really are under the new age mind control device fukkkk the secret
its to much to type sorry Pre
5/8, 2:32pm **Pre View**
nobody controls me
I always do things with what i know and further that,
meaning i get my info and not from anybody else Anyways we've been over that
5/8, 2:32pm **Koz Kozmos**
yes
5/8, 2:32pm **Pre View**
there is no secret
5/8, 2:32pm **Koz Kozmos**
over and over
i'm not talking about people controlling me
i get my info were i can and remain an open minded skeptic with the heart shine
5/8, 2:34pm **Pre View**
think about how u can change your thoughts
Then u'll change everything
I've done it with many people, with great results, even after 20 years they are still grateful
Your info is not clear, it is astrological level meaning it is influenced, mine is universal,
BIG DIFFERENCE THAT is why u still feed into the painfull stuff & hard to get out
5/8, 2:35pm **Koz Kozmos**
I HAVE AND DO
5/8, 2:35pm **Pre View**
Ok I could believe you some day, I don’t feel it now,
5/8, 2:35pm **Koz Kozmos**
my pain is based on my body being fucked up by doctors
and bad situations which have damaged my nervous system
i'm a strong person with a postive outlook

5/8, 2:36pm **Pre View**
i can feel that,
what did they fuck up
5/8, 2:36pm **Koz Kozmos**
beyond basic life coaching skills i like myself and feel my power and have wisdom so I use it well
to much to go into, but u asked me if i have mental problems and physical ones
5/8, 2:37pm **Pre View**
Nervous system takes along time to heal, even with the right equipment, I've experienced a lot of work in
that domain. It needs a lot of mental upgrades to get the physical upgrades back in sync. Yess, you are very strong.
Just ask urself why these things happened ,
even though that is a tough question, it is also a very interesting one.
5/8, 2:37pm **Koz Kozmos**
not so as u notice
i have asked myself, i have explored all your spurious paradigms years ago,
fuck the cognitive; its not hard , its impossible i'm sure u have been thru stuff ...
i can see pain and confusion on your face, i don't wish to burden u with my shit , but scars on the soul are easy
5/8, 2:41pm **Pre View**
I value you a lot, especially your strength
Everything is possible
Ive been there for years, thinking no-thing is possible ,
not knowing how to get out of the control mechanics,
Till i started a few weeks ago, doubled up my fitness and alignments...
I understand your shit, your scars are stars
5/8, 2:42pm **Koz Kozmos**
bleeding star
5/8, 2:42pm **Pre View** Still a Star
5/8, 2:42pm **Koz Kozmos**
and the blood is taking so much time to clear up
i don't belive every thing is possible
5/8, 2:43pm **Pre View**
the blood yes, let it run wild till it changes color
if u don't believe, u don't have anything
BELIEVE MATTERS,
believe moves the mountains, think about the Leopard,;
5/8, 2:43pm **Koz Kozmos**
but i do feel this basic state of consciousnesses has to be transformed
i have nothing, the blood is just running
5/8, 2:44pm **Pre View**
fuck basics, they hold you basic while u have wild fire potentials
5/8, 2:44pm **Koz Kozmos**
is just a basic poetic expression thats what i meant, fuck the basic
5/8, 2:45pm **Pre View**
What is ur missing component to get out of ...
5/8, 2:45pm **Koz Kozmos**
go beyond it, protest the within
, let the dirt of the matrix fall of you
no idea, i've not met u
5/8, 2:47pm **Pre View**
Knowledge about doing it takes some deep reflexion & trust, but hard work,
i work on myself 4 hours a day

TT but u know by know -
5/8, 2:47pm **Koz Kozmos**
what sorta of work do u do on your self
5/8, 2:49pm **Pre View**
Light Engineering ,
i work with the universe and so the universe works with me; that takes a lot of technical - scientific equipment which i teach people in workshops so they can start healing themselves without dependency or the guru syndrome of separation and demon-like spiritual nonsense....
5/8, 2:50pm **Koz Kozmos**
describe: light engineering, your tech?
5/8, 2:51pm **Pre View**
Light engineering means you decipher the consciousness within light and start overriding dense consciousness...
I'm setting up some workshops again as people asked me
cannot describe any further as that would be pages to type,
Anyways all my pm's talked about it ,
5/8, 2:51pm **Koz Kozmos**
technical - scientific equipment ~ wot is this & how does it work?
OK , wot are pm's ?
i also work hard , i have no equipment;
just a guitar and a wyrd hand and i stand were the shadows shines
5/8, 2:53pm **Pre View**
U align your breath :many types of universal breathing systems and connections to your Source as that brings the expansion through which is needed to defeat the dual chords and all that misery that has been created and allowed somehow & light frequencies. You get new encodement and get rid of those you were born with & stuff - never bored as it is ongoing information that continually upgrades consciousness and
subtracts consciousness that has been contaminated and inverted into retarded thinking processes. The hard work only starts off when we've done the hard work within – and it never stops- reflect on that
5/8, 2:54pm **Koz Kozmos**
i've done breath work,
i understand your vague koan
5/8, 2:55pm **Pre View**
Sing me a song , you're a fantastic player, get out with your potentials.
Music also has its way to upgrade breathing terms with the Divine as it also helps eliminate negative and downgrading patterns especially sub consciousness and collective consciousness levels; just like fitness does.
YOU NEED TO BEAT IT! GOT THAT?
Your breath work was very low down : u don't feel the radio waves, omnipresent waves, it is like standing in a swimming pool and feeling the big circular patterns through the body all of the time, the wheelhouse upgrades into the House of Light, Shambhalla.
Although that term does not kick into most people
as of know, but I can feel it, and thus know it,,,
So u have No-thing = astral belt or the killing field of the human kingdom breathing the mind-control.
5/8, 2:56pm **Koz Kozmos**
i've done all that, u need to speak plainly
i can out KOZMIK u
5/8, 2:57pm **Pre View**
U are repeating your self
Well, do u feel waves or not?
5/8, 2:57pm **Koz Kozmos**
repeating wot

8, 2:57pm **Pre View**
questions
5/8, 2:58pm **Koz Kozmos** yes
5/8, 2:58pm **Pre View**
If u can feel the waves like waves of the ocean going tru you,
than u have some kind of a breath that
moves you into these expansive realms or planes of existence in which you can cut out dual interference.
Trow any energy that is not yours out of your body!
It is training however and not easy to keep yourself immune from any invasion popping up as many things are just tricks like people we meet that downgrade and eat our energy.
We just grow into the clear fields of graceful consciousness when being REALLY TIRED
of the trampoline between duality and purity,,,
5/8, 2:58pm **Koz Kozmos**
waves of what
5/8, 2:59pm **Koz Kozmos**
i feel a lot of things energetically
5/8, 2:59pm **Pre View**
when u type , do u feel ur body going sideways , up & down ....
5/8, 2:59pm **Koz Kozmos**
maybe side ways
WHY? Disciple: "What did ancient masters attain when they entered the ultimate level?" Master: "They were like crooks stealthily moving into a vacant home."
i'm running out of questions
5/8, 3:02pm **Pre View**
Ok, use your breath and call forth the waves i mentioned and command Sonar waves in your heart (gets the old mentality out) I've done great work with the sonar waves so far as they really dig deep and never leaves a human embodiment until healed.
The dolphins and the whales really stick to you, but you need to know how to set up that sacred space with the elements and the underwater animal kingdom for it to come through and have the communication going crystal clear or telepathically
It gets you out of your nervous system or the problems you are suffering from ....
THERE IS NO MORE MASTER OR DISCIPLE WE'R ALL EQUAL
i hate these kind of quotes, belongs to guru infused people that never want to wake up.
5/8, 3:02pm **Koz Kozmos**
we're not all equal
5/8, 3:02pm **Pre View**
ok, do u write your own songs?
5/8, 3:03pm **Koz Kozmos**
what do i do breath normally?
And wot is that about waves? yes - my songs
5/8, 3:03pm **Koz Kozmos**
it comes to me now , i've worked enuff,
been broken down, got up over and over again and worked hard,
and been infected with more toxic crap from this dimension, and still i'm klean
5/8, 3:05pm **Pre View**
When u call forth these waves u get them aligned to ur endocrine system
(quite technically) so now u have an idea of what i do, but you're clever,
follow the answers u get i have somebody waiting for a session, i'll get back to u later
Koz, don't let toxins in , command them out,
5/8, 3:05pm **Koz Kozmos**
give me an answer i can work with, this is my last question
5/8, 3:06pm **Pre View**
i like the way u respond, feel your frustration, but need to work ...
5/8, 3:06pm **Koz Kozmos**
OK

MUSIC: CAT STEVENS YUSUF/HEAVEN

5/8, 6:11pm **Pre View**

oh man that was ONE hell of a session , people even pay me to repair their relationship while they're not meant to be together in the first place (can u imagine my brains talking to myself) & filtering what they can handle ;
Once people understand how important it is to release relationships that only cause trouble and are thus not meant to be, they can step into a much more fulfilling life. People have that mindset that they can never love again which is actually fear of the unknown not knowing how much more beautiful a next relationship could turn out.
It is just all fear,
so I communicate on a deep level with people and show them how beneficial the release could be until they get more confident and start trusting the Divine Highways.
Healing sessions with people are always interesting because it also shows me of how much more I am capable of doing and balancing consciousness in the first place so they can release their resistant and fearful brainwaves.
Good thing i don't have to filter when talking to u, u can handle anything.
No, we did not meet as u said, but feel free if u need new air
Anyways i'm exactly the same in person as on FB, only more fun,
I actually never allow friends whom i don't know in real life, but u are a great lesson, it is interesting and adding to where i'm getting (where ever that might be)
So thank u again & again with your wizards' hands glowing above my head

5/8, 6:25pm **Pre View**

U know when i comment on Jean Doe's account, i need to carefully choose words coz that consciousness is not there, so im very blessed u accept all of me as i am, as i think.

MY INTERNALS : Jean Doe was a mutual friend on FB which Koz introduced to me. The Lady suffers from severe diseases through the nervous system and Koz asked me to help or start communicating with her, hoping I could get her out of her hell and severe damage.

5/8, 6:54pm **Pre View**

You know u gave me that song (Cat Stevens/heaven):
this one offered some de-block scene, major healing,
i mean i had to play it over & over for 30 times, as it integrated , it did its job.
So thats is kind of getting out something when u know the music, and u do, so maybe this way ... you could easily heal yourself out; just because you have musical knowledge and STICK TO IT; because that is really your problem.
You not there ?
Ok, going for a drink and have some fun with my wording regarding people we meet...

5/8, 6:56pm **Pre View**

Btw, i bought flowers today, but unfortunately i threw them over my bed, want some ?
they are sweet,
anyways i am real and do as i feel

5/8, 8:29pm **Pre View**

Hey, i understand your pc
This was one hour societal confrontation.

5/8, 8:40pm **Pre View**

Hey Koz, if sometimes u don't like me talking to u,
just let me know and i'll keep my crazy ass for my own brains, u can

5/8, 8:58pm **Pre View**

Timing has come to utilize the deepness of the repairing kit for myself
until i become my profile pic (The Red Sword Carrier)
I will, no doubt, coz i State it, and I'm true to my Word, that is the power of the word.
Will u finally shine your diamonds and spread them a bit huh?
Will u ?
Think before u leap, i just remember that from my english high school teacher who only talked Irish; very lovely indeed.

5/8, 9:43pm **Pre View**
u might not like this but this music is what I've been listening to for 3 hours, it gets things done & over with for me ..... But you need to play it real loud to ingrate it as with any music,,,,
This is what some planetary communication is telling me, and it does work.
But it might be other music for you,
I wish i had the intelligence to play music like u do...
it is such a great relieve you have that specialty
I envy you, lets take that dance, haha...
MUSIC: Two Steps From Hell/Thomas Bergersen
Immortal Long Version

5/8, 9:50pm **Pre View**
You know Koz, i really don't give a fuck no longer, i will spread my wings like a hawk does (i'm sure u do understand), you know i will,
coz the hurt requires a deep return investment, u should get there , u deserve that, do it, don't ask me how,,,, (we did not meet) HAHA!
5/8, 9:56pm **Pre View**
i can feel your ways, please don't load your fucked up ways,
I understand your anger with what is going on
Are u finally going to show up or are you going to tell me to shut up ?
5/9, 12:45pm **Koz Kozmos**
Jane Doe is the only other person i have spoken to on line and interesting. and can see the corruption of the earth plane beyond the church and the state of the Haterix ....
u could be more crazy, and talking is good but u could be less obscure, if u'r going to teach .
Like the music – Two steps from hell , i connect with the call to the inner warrior thru neo classical and connect with the Nordic in worldz, all ways good to speak with u
5/9, 1:29pm **Koz Kozmos**
pc keeps freezing and crashing got some one coming over
visiting elderly sick parents tomorrow (their not really my parents)
also will be with my psycho walkin sister....seriously ---- feel wiped out ;
so if i miss you , all the best
5/9, 1:32pm **Koz Kozmos**
YOUTUBE: Noggin the Nog 1959

5/9, 1:34pm **Koz Kozmos**
MUSIC: Meeting Faeries Meditation | Guided Meditation To Visit Faery Land |
The fairy blood activates my inner elf
5/9, 2:30pm **Pre View**
such a wonderful expression !
Going to a Burn out Festival i guess, it is 5 minutes walk from my doors,
lots of rock bands, don't know if they'r good
MUSIC: THE SHRINE- PRIMITIVE BLAST (Official Video)

5/9, 2:35pm **Pre View**
i'm not obscure when teaching, on FB everything is too much typing and ....
5/9, 2:56pm **Pre View**
i'm not obscure, i tell everything like it is, people are lazy and need to find their own answers, simple as that
The Ego of many people suck other people out, for help and that is not appropriate
Energy needs to meet equal energy
That is my biggest lesson ... still learning
Enjoy your week-end

5/9, 3:50pm **Pre View**
why do u feel wiped out ?5/9, 9:05pm **Pre View**
Don't know much about this stuff but i guess u might have had a bad time
the last couple of days because of this
May 9th, 2013: Solar Eclipse in Taurus :
we had a lovely full moon Lunar Eclipse in Scorpio. When we experience a Lunar
Eclipse,
it signals the closing or ending of something. Astronomically,
theMoon is at its brightest...
5/11, 9:18pm **Pre View**
How did u know i needed to get stronger ?
It got me down, but you'r'e splendid, you are so right
We all have an exclusive typewriter in the brain,
I love your honesty
Take care, take real good care Koz
5/17, 9:57pm **Pre View**
A Warrior is a protector of his own heart, u are that what that is,,,---
5/17, 10:24pm **Pre View**
Don't know if this was just a seasonable interaction suiting us both, but I have a need
to thank u without a thousands of words coz I do know our vibrations met a
frequency unequal to any encounter.
U made me realize the impossible non acceptable pains, so if u ever read this or not,
it comforts me in many ways ---- Thank u for ur integrity, bearable understanding
and above all your honesty ,
i hope you would bring your love to yourself, Love, Nicole
5/20, 8:26pm **Koz Kozmos**
all ways wiped out to much shit for one life time,
always loved myself
i take the best care i can, my face book page has been blocked for a good while stay
sick Nic, sick, crazy, cool, insane
5/20, 8:31pm **Koz Kozmos**
MUSIC: Everlast - Death Comes Callin'

5/20, 8:49pm **Pre View**
Are u sick ?
I lost me mind many times
5/20, 8:49pm **Koz Kozmos**
more fucked up by negative shit than sick,
and i have not attracted it
u ok ? not mediating too much i hope
5/20, 8:53pm **Pre View**
talked to myself a lot
am jogging a lot muscling up
and getting real strong when clearing my high hopes
5/20, 8:55pm **Pre View**
don't know what u think about meditation;
but to me it is real hard work settling grids and aligning with solar/celestial Ley lines
and working with all the earth plane has to offer takes a lot of guts and trust,
till meditation becomes ur daily walk stronger in word than ever,,,
i want to change so i need the right info to do that thru meditation
When the AIR that you breathe becomes nutritious,
YOU WILL HAVE ALL YOU EVER NEED
Fresh air in the Crystal Grids only
Follow the foxes!

5/20, 8:57pm **Koz Kozmos**
I meditated sitting for 9 hours for 10 days fasting in silence years back...
then i gave it up,
i 'm hoping my head will explode and destroy this dimension
5/20, 8:59pm **Pre View**
Meditating without aligning is maybe not worth the investment,
when not getting the right teachings for 9 hours during the meditation it seems boring and ineffective, is it that what u did ?
5/20, 9:02pm **Koz Kozmos**
after the 10 days i got a bad skin that bled, looked like a leper, was ill for years, not sure what i did
Pre View
That was not aligned for sure
and not knowing what u do is even worse
who got u into that shit may I ask?
5/20, 9:04pm **Koz Kozmos**
i hate the Buddha, the fat guy with the empty mind
i've done it all, every practice reached the further than far out
5/20, 9:05pm **Pre View** What practice, get clear ?
coz Boedha does not tell me anything at all
5/20, 9:06pm **Koz Kozmos**
who? mainly been hyp wyrdo, but its perfected, so no more practice
5/20, 9:07pm **Pre View**
To me there is no practice, there is only leveling up to today, so no old teachings whatshowever,
So would u please tell me what u did in meditation?
5/20, 9:08pm **Koz Kozmos**
wot i said i did
5/20, 9:08pm **Pre View**
I only do things with the information I get TODAY !!!!! and that is a lot of work
Never did a sheer focus meditation ever, but should actually train myself into more focus when in alignment.
5/20, 9:08pm **Koz Kozmos**
i agree about old info , that is why i said Fuck u Alister etc who's Boedha anyways ?
5/20, 9:10pm **Koz Kozmos**
MUSIC Canibus Channel Zero

5/20, 9:10pm **Koz Kozmos**
i've had enuff
5/20, 9:10pm **Pre View**
It is getting clear to me that you actually have nothing to upgrade with
and never had any information about that.
i don't even know an Alister, nor anybody else, not Boedha, other people whatever
So all u did was nothing, trusting some guru freak with no knowledge
Happens way too much these days as people want to give their energy to some entity they think they can reach their Source self through them. Quite ridiculous. We need to breathe it through for ourselves, same with healing education and stuff.
5/20, 9:11pm **Koz Kozmos**
Alister Crowley : look it up
5/20, 9:12pm **Pre View**
Yes I know, but it does not mean i do know a single thing about these people etc...
5/20, 9:12pm **Koz Kozmos**
smarty

5/20, 9:13pm **Koz Kozmos**
so if i have nuthin to upgrade ? 5/20, 9:13pm **Pre View**
No, I know how come u did not understand all the stuff i used to talk about ,,,,
5/20, 9:13pm **Koz Kozmos**
fuuuuuuuuuuuuuuuuuuuuuuukkkkkkkkkkkkkkkkkkkkkkkkkkkk
5/20, 9:13pm **Pre View**
Should I fuck off ?
5/20, 9:13pm **Koz Kozmos**
i get what yur saying, no i understand your cliched theories and yur mind blab
i didn't mean u to fuck off; it was about having nuthing to upgrade
were does that leave me
5/20, 9:15pm **Pre View**
But then again I was hoping u would get it somehow when I told u I changed people
only in 3 meditation classes, as i dig deep into their galleries, haha
thy worked hard and were surprised themselves,,
With the tech we have today we can really quickly move from one space into another,
it only TAKES WORK which frightens people,,,
5/20, 9:15pm **Koz Kozmos**
it was about having nuthing to upgrade ,were does that leave me?
i do understand, but its more bs (bulshit) as far as i'm concerned
5/20, 9:16pm **Pre View**
It does not get u anywhere indeed,
That is why i asked u if there would be someone in Wales who would teach that stuff,
the real stuff. So u can learn about the many departments of the Divine
U need to find self and the knowledge to heal beyond old mystic monitors
That streamed basically on falseness as u know, especially the UK
Mark your territory like the animals do! Start acting
Your amount of indecisions is larger then the real problem
5/20, 9:16pm **Koz Kozmos**
and i'm not a slave in the matrix mind
last time i saw a healer-
she said i was one of the guys who nailed jesus to the cross!
what gets me no where ?
5/20, 9:17pm **Pre View**
i hate that quote
Oh goodness, u'd better get on the phone for a session
5/20, 9:18pm **Koz Kozmos**
wot quote
5/20, 9:18pm **Pre View**
Slave matrix
5/20, 9:18pm **Koz Kozmos**
i did'ent say that
ok , bit boring , yes
5/20, 9:19pm **Pre View**
Working with crystalline grids that override the matrix and being aligned !
A nucleus would get u anywhere; and out of your shit
5/20, 9:20pm **Koz Kozmos**
why have i not got help before?
5/20, 9:20pm **Pre View**
Because you have more questions then answers!
5/20, 9:20pm **Koz Kozmos**
why have i put great effort in to many practices and got no where
what u'r saying is offensive, but its ok
5/20, 9:21pm **Pre View**
Wrong practice, wrong people, emptiness, cut looooose

5/20, 9:21pm **Koz Kozmos**
so bad karma
5/20, 9:21pm **Pre View**
What is offensive ?
5/20, 9:21pm **Koz Kozmos**
telling me wot i need to do
5/20, 9:22pm **Pre View**
Ok , i apologize, but u asked me this several times
So stop asking questions and start answering your own for once,,,
5/20, 9:22pm **Koz Kozmos**
ok , my point is still valid, peace
5/20, 9:22pm **Pre View**
What point ? You don't have a point on anything as nothing got you anywhere.
5/20, 9:22pm **Koz Kozmos**
Wrong practice, wrong people, emptiness ..;
how do u think saying that makes me feel after all my efforts for 20 years
i've given up on people , practice , and just got even more emptiness,
but its better than the fucktard zone
5/20, 9:25pm **Pre View**
I did not know u were that sensitive, I'm sorry Koz I should have know coz I only got
fucked up and angry with myself for 2 years which is a big difference
20 years is indeed a long time
But keep in mind we always learn something also when we don't see it at the time
being,, 5/20, 9:25pm **Koz Kozmos**
i'm not fucked up and definetly not angry with myself
i don't think this has taught me anything
its just powerlessness
5/20, 9:26pm **Pre View**
And u know, maybe when the final good thing comes to u ,
u might be able to synthesize all that stuff you
learned into something else people do not know about, maybe that is reason why u
had to learn it first Have another outlook for now and move into some
mental/psychological strength
Maybe connect with many foreign species and have some fun
Talk to the universe
Get a majical carpet and get immune to the poison
5/20, 9:26pm **Koz Kozmos**
blame the victim, its to late for all that
i have lit the lamp off knowledge and i burn it,
fuck people
5/20, 9:29pm **Pre View**
we're all responsible for ourselves , and this is not easy
I feel it is not too late for you, there is a specialty within yourself that needs to come
out, please trust again , and hit another highway with your thoughts maybe ?
5/20, 9:29pm **Koz Kozmos**
not to late for me, haha, cheers
5/20, 9:29pm **Pre View**
Cheers ! U'v got lovely valuables
5/20, 9:30pm **Koz Kozmos**
i am responsible for myself and i practice right action
5/20, 9:30pm **Pre View**
what is important 2 u ?
5/20, 9:30pm **Koz Kozmos**
I ride new highways on the black unicorn every nano second
awakening is important to me
5/20, 9:31pm **Pre View**
black unicorn, ok the majic is yours

5/20, 9:31pm **Koz Kozmos**
transforming this so called reality sandwich killing most people on earth too
5/20, 9:32pm **Pre View**
awakening is not hard once u have a foundation
are u agressive ?
5/20, 9:32pm **Koz Kozmos**
no , i've never hit any one and don't self harm
5/20, 9:33pm **Pre View**
do u smile all the time ?
do u fuck urself up ?
5/20, 9:33pm **Koz Kozmos**
no , fuck myself up : what do u mean ?
5/20, 9:34pm **Pre View**
manipulate yourself
5/20, 9:34pm **Koz Kozmos**
? can u explain
5/20, 9:36pm **Pre View**
It is just that I feel your frustration with the stuff you did and it did not get you anywhere and then i always observe how you want to get out of the destructive fields but cannot,---
so then I guessed with no way out, you may hurt urself ---
or listening to depressing music,,,
5/20, 9:36pm **Koz Kozmos**
To influence or manage shrewdly or deviously:
He manipulated public opinion in his favor.
3. To tamper with or falsify for personal gain: tried to manipulate stock prices.
4. Medicine To handle and move in an examination or for therapeutic purposes: manipulate a joint; manipulate the position of a fetus during delivery.
5/20, 9:36pm **Koz Kozmos**
no reality hurts me, and negative shit either, i treat myself well
5/20, 9:37pm **Pre View**
OK then, i was just worrying,
5/20, 9:37pm **Koz Kozmos**
ok, i'm on crack smoking a jay and drinking a malt whiskey
gotto use something to take away the pain
5/20, 9:38pm **Pre View**
What do you do in life ?
5/20, 9:38pm **Koz Kozmos**
nuthin, hide away, i've given up in a good way
5/20, 9:39pm **Pre View**
I drank a lot of malt whiskey last year for 1 year, i stopped it 2 weeks ago, good thing
5/20, 9:39pm **Koz Kozmos**
i was joking, i drink beer etc
5/20, 9:40pm **Pre View**
you must be fun, you joke a lot
5/20, 9:40pm **Koz Kozmos**
i'm hilarious
5/20, 9:40pm **Pre View**
fine, even better
Get mega food that supports the higher senses
5/20, 9:41pm **Koz Kozmos**
i've been locked outa face book,
wonder if i close it
5/20, 9:41pm **Pre View**
you'll miss me!
can u skip from one consciousness into another?

5/20, 9:12pm **Koz Kozmos**
it will let me back in, not sure, depends on how u mean it
5/20, 9:42pm **Pre View**
who locked u ?
5/20, 9:42pm **Koz Kozmos**
i'm pissed off , to much shit , tried to explain
5/20, 9:42pm **Pre View**
pissed off, huh,great,
i can handle that, shoot
5/20, 9:43pm **Koz Kozmos**
some thing locked me out with no reason, pissed off t
too much to type and to personal and upsetting but i feel
there is a reason for our connection
5/20, 9:44pm **Pre View**
I understand, but you seem too lonely to absorb all by yourself, so whenever u feel
like loosing your shit, just communicate it through
I know our connection is important ever since u befriended me
5/20, 9:45pm **Koz Kozmos**
yes, but no point in telling u my shit
5/20, 9:46pm **Pre View**
Communication offers solutions, you've got nothing to lose
5/20, 9:47pm **Koz Kozmos**
the connection
i mean, i should have guessed u knew
chatting is a waste of time, i need major healing,
or soul death the bigger sleep
5/20, 9:48pm **Pre View**
OK, want to stop chatting?
5/20, 9:48pm **Koz Kozmos**
only if u want to
5/20, 9:48pm **Pre View**
Do u want a healing session with me ?
5/20, 9:48pm **Koz Kozmos**
i never want to be a bother or bring u down
5/20, 9:48pm **Pre View**
U are not, stop that kind of mental self abuse or insinuations that get nowhere
5/20, 9:48pm **Koz Kozmos**
no thank u
5/20, 9:49pm **Pre View**
I can feel your vibes, but u knew that too, right ?
The soul stuff, the drowning of humanity,,,
5/20, 9:49pm **Koz Kozmos**
this is the healing
and i'm also healing u, or the game is more corrupt than i thought
5/20, 9:49pm **Pre View**
U are healing Me ?
A pity surprises are only reserved for a few
I am small and very well build
My brain populates many discoveries
Maybe a few libraries undiscovered
I keep them open to investigate during holidays
Self discovery creates excitement

MY INTERNALS: ON HOW I GOT BACK INTO MY SPIRIT SHOES AND HEALING MYSELF: I remember when growing up during my teens that I had to buy a book because my parents where in some kind of bookclub and never ever read anything.
So my choice over in that bookclub was "THE OCCULT" which I certainly did not understand at age 14 but it fascinated me in many ways.

I always liked things I could not possibly understand and I felt there was more out there in the big Universe then just the Sun and the Moon. We did not have that much computer technology we have right know as I am talking like 43 years back in time. When wandering through bookstores nothing really satisfied my brainwaves as I was investigating books about energy fields, aura's, chakra systems and how energy effects people. However, somewhere over the rainbow waves, I heard voices telling me not to buy into anythings; and I never did; mainly because the colors in chakra alignments never made any sense to me. Nothing actually made any sense to me. So I left it for what it was, observing people what they would buy stimulated my curious mind.

I would even start out a dialogue with people asking them why they believe in some esoteric book stuff- as to 2 me, nothing ever made sense or felt like complete nonsense. Most of the time, that would not end up so well as I confronted them with their truth, or my truth or universal truth; or just checkmated them.
People don't like questions about themselves. It makes them feel very uncomfortable; their smile would fade away from the first encounter and happy face they make when engaging in a conversation. Many times at my young age, I just laughed it out because energy fields merging in a space where the Divine is intertwined makes you do that.

I always trusted the Divine. And I was too fearful not to trust people and attach myself to their so called truth which showed me actually how falseness makes easy accounts. When we disagree with egotistical cramps; the brain gets very stiff as well and shows how the mind was created holding tied to the matrix of recycling dummies.
And later, around my thirties, I would swing around books like Alice Bailey, maybe bought about 2. Yet, nothing was ever satisfactory, it felt like too many mis aligned compositions would even get me in a worse compartment of self development.
Let's say, left and right I would spend time in an esoteric bookstore but maybe only read about 3 books about the creation of the universe, some geometry, and more about the communication with the animal kingdom as I also started to develop my interest in the herbal kingdom. Many things just offered my vibe constipation and some things got me out of my muscular spasm.

I experimented a lot with herbs and made my own creams just as a self satisfactory breath that keeps on creating for the sake of creation. That brought in some kind of joy as I also turned my food around and became vegan at age 30. Before that I would just eat a little fish and loads of cheese which actually makes you a vegetarian. Vegetarians are merely cheese eaters. That doesn't sound too healthy. After all, I now understand that food is a never ending upgrade, the real stuff just pops up when refining the vegan diet into a spirit diet : that opens passion with the elements and how we can co-create with them .

A lot of fusion and repair of earth is quite naturally involved in that as the earths' biology that is moving into it Light Earth embodiment needs to match our Light Body biology for our Spirit feet to breathe the news that is coming through the underground communication.
Anyhow, I also brought a son into the world and had to make sure he would not come short. Rebuilding the Garden of Eden will take a lot of combined efforts, and could be so beautiful.

MY INTERNALS: SO I REMEMBER I went working cleaning A restaurant in the early morning and always took my son with me, although it was very hard to raise a child by yourself when the financial means do not kick in as I carried the highest level of unworthiness back then.
Yet, one good day I ordered "The Book of Knowledge and that assisted me to comprehend my spiritual roots a little.
It was difficult to understand anything in those years, yet it kept me going. Today, I still appreciate this particular book, although a lot of the material is no good to align 2, there is also a lot of understandable and interesting alignments one can create with that written material when in perfect alignment to our Source and bringing the modern day changes in.

Also, during that particular space in time, I was really looking for some great forward movement into the real stuff. As books were zero % satisfactory, I started to pray the Stations of the Cross like ten times a day, early morning while doing the job I was doing and talking to Zach, and/or entities involved in all these stations. That was back 1995.
Zach is now Archangel Zachary or the entity known as Sanada or Jezus Chryst (Crystalline Kryst Light) and what he brought to the planet 2000 years ago.

One day, I just opened a computer, although I did not know how that worked, I WAS WITHOUT ANY DOUBT GUIDED TO A MEDITATION BY SANADA.
That triggered me so much that I ended up in doing a seminar with the lady channeling A.Zachary and many others. That 3-day seminar changed my whole life as I went through a detox process unlike any. It was like going through hell for 3 days as not even a sauna or a swim would get my severe headaches out. I was being taught about the return into Light Consciousness and how important it was to understand Light Technology through Light Grid tech, information and alignment.

It took me years to understand as many other entities do not even understand it now. AND THAT NEEDS TO CHANGE, WE DEFINITELY NEED TO MOVE INTO A PERSONAL SPACE IN WHICH WE UNDERSTAND HOW ENERGY WORKS, what light technology is about and how we can upgrade through the refined machines of the Divine while synchronizing with all universes, species, the elements, the animal kingdom and start to REMEMBER THE POWER WITHIN AS A DIVINE ETERNAL ENTITY becoming ONE WITH THE SPARK/SPIRIT/ SOURCE SELF and moving on the other side for the sake of co-creation with the Ascended Masters and Self Realized Mastery.

Also, I kept on upgrading my energy fields and technology for many years and started doing my own thing with it which resulted in becoming the artistic creator and painting information through the hands of light.
Today, there is no end to what we can create while moving into the secure spaces in which the Spiritual body can no longer be attacked or targeted as Koz would term it for he was very right: everybody moving into the Light stations is being held back or targeted. Yet, today there is more then enough technology, understandable education and upgrades available for those who decide to move into their destined shoes.
ok, let's pick it from where I said :
And I did not say a thing, except when going over the book for the third time in 2020, it tells me it needs to be published for many people will resonate to these stuck patterns, while a good LIGHT MOVIE WOULD PROOF THE OUTCOME.

This is because MOVING PICTURES assist humanity to take their degrees into light dreams and make them MANIFEST CREATIONS.
Working for the Field of dead Health will never lift humanity, working in the Field of New Educational platforms regarding health, wealth, equality and unit will, When will schools, Universities teach truth, health, well being and business based on the Divine directions?

In the end it is all that is going to make it. So many false businesses regarding Spirit is raising into its heights, but I trust my day, I trust my worth, and I trust these kind of false truths will crumble one way or another.

5/20, 9:49pm **Pre View**
U are healing Me ?
5/20, 9:49pm **Koz Kozmos**
of cource, i can feel vibes
5/20, 9:50pm **Pre View**
Maybe, u told me i needed to get stronger, so i listed and u were right
5/20, 9:50pm **Koz Kozmos**
get my point please, i don't need to be right
5/20, 9:50pm **Pre View**
part of it, I agree
5/20, 9:50pm **Koz Kozmos**
can u heal my eyes
5/20, 9:51pm **Pre View**
yes, anything can be healed out, it needs understanding,
the internal psychology needs to change and the mentality behind the disease
and also, they EYES are a lot of work because you will be asked to move out of the
astral planes . And there are so so many layers to the astral planes and the fog within
the physical eyes, that biology and the anatomy such as the nerves, the blood
circulation, the energetic substance, the muscular stuck functions in the eyes
Yet, yes, always passionate about healing and creating new individual technology
but i'd rather teach u how to do it urself one day
That way you can complain to your self and not allow your lazy shoes.
It is easy to loop up things on the google machine and apply new tech on biology,
but it is not easy for people to keep on refining and believing the healing coming
through. People give up way to easily because of their lazy mind factory.
The enterprise of the Divine with the Divine Orders request a lot of patience,
perseverance and many trust layerss.
5/20, 9:51pm **Koz Kozmos**
its ok, go for it
i'll do my soul
5/20, 9:52pm **Pre View**
it goes together and is not done overnight and certainly not over FB
5/20, 9:52pm **Koz Kozmos**
why?
5/20, 9:54pm **Pre View**
Because of many details and days of work and understanding and technicallity and
YOUR WILL wich is most important,
You told me you were born with these problems in your eyes, i don't believe it,
5/20, 9:54pm **Koz Kozmos**
could u kill my noisy Neighbours via a death curse?
why don't u belive it ?
5/20, 9:55pm **Pre View**
the universe always gifts me with loads of unusual magical Keys?
Find your keys!
5/20, 9:56pm **Koz Kozmos** ?
5/20, 9:56pm **Pre View**
I still think a lot went wrong when u were growing into u mothers' womb, no love ...
5/20, 9:57pm **Koz Kozmos**
never had any love, but i've given loads
5/20, 9:58pm **Pre View**
sure, i m in the same canoe flowing on different rivers,
5/20, 9:58pm **Koz Kozmos**
i've been targeted by negative entities, it happened to Lucifer too

5/20, 9:58pm **Pre View**
always the same story with those who give and give,
Maybe start receiving, Lucifer is long gone
5/20, 9:59pm **Koz Kozmos**
i'm a boat filled with hope for the ship of dreams
the fire born are still here and we will rise up and destroy the clayborn
i'm a boat filled with hope for the ship of dreams
the fire born are still here and we will rise up and destroy the clayborn
5/20, 10:01pm **Pre View**
Ok, make your moves into this world, take the dragons & snakes with you,
and leave all behind, gold will fill you up!
5/20, 10:02pm **Koz Kozmos**
there are no moves left for me in this world,
as i've said i'm here to tranzform
MUSIC: EVERLAST/ONE OF US

5/20, 10:03pm **Pre View**
Go live in the jungle of Peru,
you may possibly leave your footprints
The sun is broken.
Would you have knowledge about the 7 suns ?
5/20, 10:04pm **Koz Kozmos**
i am the child of the 7th ray
fuck Alice Baily to
your info is second hand
5/20, 10:05pm **Pre View**
Or high 7th ?
Thats Merlin's shoes, second hand ?
5/20, 10:05pm **Koz Kozmos**
merlin wore sandals
5/20, 10:05pm **Pre View**
Go barefoot then,
5/20, 10:05pm **Koz Kozmos**
borrowed from the cliches of the universal mind
as i've said, i'm barefoot in the head and tip toe in the soul i'm beyond akashic record,
but i'm beingblocked and its not me
5/20, 10:07pm **Pre View**
Guess what, i was walking barefoot in the city a few days ago, it costed me 250 euros,
but i will not pay, were is the freedom?
i love walking barefoot
5/20, 10:07pm **Koz Kozmos**
its targetting over many life times,
i 'd not be dumb enuff to walk bare foot in the city,
may be its a bit cleaner were u are
5/20, 10:08pm **Pre View**
streets are clean,
5/20, 10:08pm **Koz Kozmos**
hidden pollution, Cardiff is a shit hole
i'm trying to escape, so u get fined for walking barefoot
5/20, 10:11pm **Pre View**
It is not ok to get fined for walking as you wish.
There is no law that states we have to wear shoes.
5/20, 10:11pm **Koz Kozmos**
wonder how much it would cost to call u

5/20, 10:11pm **Pre View**
how can anyone invent a law that states how u should dress ?
5/20, 10:11pm **Koz Kozmos**
no, u can chop of your feet over hear (here) and drag your self along,
listen
5/20, 10:12pm **Pre View**
ok, you make me smile,
but do know i fight these things and work my way into court with the right people, No more nonsense, people accept to easily when stuff happens to them,
afraid to fight.
5/20, 10:12pm **Koz Kozmos**
they invent the laws for obvious reasons
5/20, 10:12pm **Pre View**
Listen ? what did you wanna say by that?
5/20, 10:13pm **Koz Kozmos**
one of them is called fashion, yes listen or read
5/20, 10:13pm **Pre View**
Why would you like to call me ?
5/20, 10:14pm **Koz Kozmos**
they've stopped the legal aid here
u said ealier to call for a healing or suggested it
listen to your self 2, i need to take some bastards to court
5/20, 10:14pm **Pre View**
Aha, there is always ways out, but indeed, needs a lot of thinking
& guts and brainwork to put it right
5/20, 10:14pm **Koz Kozmos**
but thier (they are)protected
5/20, 10:15pm **Pre View**
There is a spiritual justice department, and it works
Don't ask to explain ,,,, too much to type
5/20, 10:16pm **Koz Kozmos**
i disagree
5/20, 10:16pm **Pre View**
Healing right, that would at least take 1 hour
5/20, 10:16pm **Koz Kozmos**
but i get the theory ?
5/20, 10:17pm **Pre View**
healing is a little theory and pure practice, as I need to let the energies flow through your eyes, healing, repairing, realigning...
But I could redirect you and offer an mp3 tofurther the healing.
5/20, 10:17pm **Koz Kozmos**
can u help me re grow a leg? that must be 2 hours
5/20, 10:18pm **Pre View**
Haha, it will make my new study going into the land where the rivers break through to catch new rain.Its the consciousness behind the disease that needs more realignment or elimination, is it your leg ? Did you lose half your leg? Haha, do you want 4 legs?
I would not be surprised,
5/20, 10:18pm **Koz Kozmos**
they need to keep practicing the karma mechanics i ts ok,
a mad scientist gave me a bionic leg
why do we need a spiritual justice department ? its just all sickness
5/20, 10:20pm **Pre View**
It is exhausting to explain how to get justice back on the planet,
i decided to only think about how, what,
why, what does it take to get what i want to happen in these departments and that is it,
and get it out.

Of course this is hard work when you are alone and no one backing you up, people are hard to partner up with because thy are lazy, so ????
But i have hopes here and there to pull through the mechanics of the justice system, when persistent enough
5/20, 10:20pm **Koz Kozmos**
what do u do with your life may i ask
5/20, 10:20pm **Pre View**
do you have a bionic leg or are you joking ?
5/20, 10:21pm **Koz Kozmos**
yip , they don't exist
5/20, 10:21pm **Pre View** Where does ur leg start ?
5/20, 10:21pm **Koz Kozmos**
well only for the few, its not mainstream since i have legs
5/20, 10:22pm **Pre View**
What do i do?Good question, good guts Koz,
I am home-keeper of a student home since 1 year and brought many changes into the lives of the young people.
5/20, 10:28pm **Pre View**
I stopped my fitness classes and Light workshops for a while because I was healing out a psychotic person . It cut me down a lot.
I'm picking my life up right now, want to teach again as I love that and give some combination of disciplines in fitness, the individual sessions. I also started painting only about a year ago, want to create businesses with that.
There is so much I do like clearing the city, getting the justice department on the ground flour, helping lots of people but teaching needs to come down to some sort of a return investment or the energy would exhaust.
In the past i gave too much 2 many for free, that is my hardest lesson...`Spirit is just not for free, you work your way into the holy Land
5/20, 10:34pm **Pre View**
I've been living alone with my son for 20 years now, he was on drugs for 3 years, i got him out of that
since 3 weeks and he changed all of his life now. As far as I'm concerned, i never thought i could be hurt so much by a schizophrenic, bipolar, psychotic idiot whom i healed and helped and loved . Anyways that is almost healed as i'm getting the justice department into that because there is so much ignorance and injustice ,is just unacceptable.
But ok , i will stop this here,
5/20, 10:51pm **Pre View**
Ok then, drive me insane with some good music, there is happiness in that
5/20, 10:55pm **Koz Kozmos**
hi ,am reading
5/20, 10:55pm **Pre View**
Okenjoy my energy
5/20, 10:56pm **Koz Kozmos**
sorry to dissapper mid conversation
5/20, 10:56pm **Pre View**
no prob, it is what it is
5/20, 10:57pm **Koz Kozmos**
thank you for telling me about your self ,
wotz your sons name ?
5/20, 10:58pm **Pre View**
Julius, why ?
5/20, 10:58pm **Koz Kozmo**
just wondering
5/20, 10:58pm **Pre View**
anyways, need some sleep, or a shower, good night Koz

5/20, 10:58pm **Koz Kozmos**
i think its a civil thing to enquire after a persons offspring
good night, don't let the bed bugz bite
5/20, 11:13pm **Koz Kozmos**
MUSIC: Peter Gabriel - Solsbury Hill (Live on Letterman)

5/20, 11:14pm **Koz Kozmos**
"Solsbury Hill" Climbing up on Solsbury Hill

I could see the city light
Wind was blowing, time stood still
Eagle flew out of the night
He was something to observe
Came in close, I heard a voice
Standing stretching every nerve
Had to listen had no choice
I did not believe the information
(I) just had to trust imagination
My heart going boom boom boom
"Son," he said "Grab your things,
I've come to take you home." To keep in silence I resigned
My friends would think I was a nut
Turning water into wine
Open doors would soon be shut
So I went from day to day
Tho' my life was in a rut
"Till I thought of what I'd say
Which connection I should cut
I was feeling part of the scenery
I walked right out of the machinery
My heart going boom boom boom
"Hey" he said "Grab your things
I've come to take you home."
(Back home.) When illusion spin her net
I'm never where I want to be
And liberty she pirouette
When I think that I am free
Watched by empty silhouettes
Who close their eyes but still can see
No one taught them etiquette
I will show another me
Today I don't need a replacement
I'll tell them what the smile on my face meant
My heart going boom boom boom
"Hey" I said "You can keep my things,
they've come to take me home."
5/21, 3:08am **Pre View**
Long time since i heard this song, thank u,
so many vibes tonight, so many things going on in my head,
so many things i want to do, and then again all of a sudden there is nothing I want
simply no more wishes,
the bugs were sucking my blood probably

5/21, 9:24am **Pre View**
One of the reasons we connected is that you can handle the hard line approach to truth & transformation/transmutation. Other reasons to our connection, you may want to figure them out for yourself as I have to do for myself as well. But I do have a feel that with all you've been through and learned or not, u'll be able to synthesize that to a level or upgrade needed on the earth plane as of now. My material has many missing links as i did not work hard enough for the past 3 years because i did not understand what i was doing which was not necessary at the time being as i experienced the changes...
But it is necessary right now and there is so much to study and learn and pull it into public for those ready... As far as i'm concerned u opened my eyes a little that here and there I should read about something and start to look things up which I do not do too often. But i do know I want to level up into the living libraries, into the Suns' dial ....
Through our chats, i realized that maybe i need to stop here and there and reflect on what u were really saying ...;
So your intelligence matches some of my missing components and that is

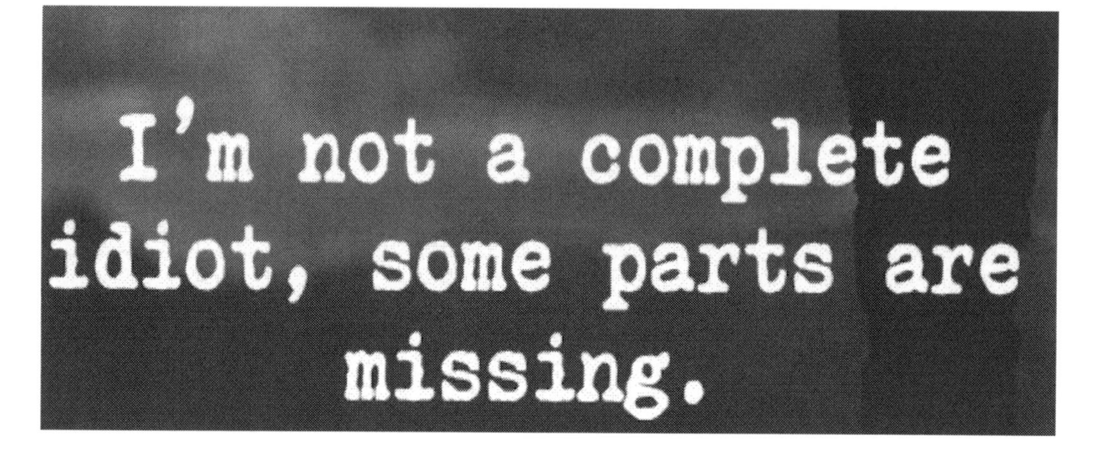

5/21, 9:24am **Pre View**
What beer do u like to drink today ?
5/21, 11:07am **Pre View**
Well, here is my beer : The decision Bell rang high tones meaning today is day 1 to really get severe with myself meaning I will leave FB to its creation & will limit my time on it for purposes of scientific easy connector links & some communiFICAtion skills. It is getting clear to me why u hurt me. This should feel the same 2 u i guess, there is a reason why i unwillingly hurt your vibes
I know your heart is charming----
Sometimes I fear self, the capacities, of what comes out of me like in art, through the word, when engaging with people.
5/21, 1:11pm **Koz Kozmos**
MUSIC: The Book of Life: The Akashic Records

5/21, 1:12pm **Koz Kozmos**
I need to stop drinking beer, I don't wish to hurt you
this is our time for healing and its wot we've got to do
I'm bringing good medicine to you
I feel the ones that set the karma exams and keep us in the soap opera of the souls need to be taken out...
my upgrade has been with me since i first saw my mother and let out a cry,
but I was moved to illusions side via the soul wipe
shuts us all down via the recycling of souls etc , see my I~~~ G~~~ beyond the cliches of the Akashic record player and spin the soul disc via the lasers of the secret people that hide in secret spaces me a bit. Thank u.the ones that stand against this toxic creation, i am lost with my upgrade, brought to a state of despair beyond the dark night of the soulless ones

surrounded by meat heads and 'bad karma'
but still rising up
i have no wish to scramble your energies,
maybe if we chat on occasion we should focus the hocus pocus.....
i don't wish to infect u with the scars of the soul war and my continued attack,
one good thing would help
5/21, 1:49pm **Koz Kozmos**
Enter the bliss ZONE!
MUSIC: Shanti Mantra Sacred Chants for Peace Prosperity Enlightenment

5/22, 9:31am **Pre View**
Good morning sparkling wizard
my cup of coffee is overflowing with ur weird & brilliant dance i can see ur consciousness longing for a Great Waterfall of endless miracles
would it end & unchain
for u to enter the Bliss zones
of immortal pleasures
from the pure waters of your blood The winds of hocus pocus have arrived,
the winds of change announcing a new Breath,,,
The Breath of Life will take u beyond eternal measures of the Breath of Source
spiraling the Breath of Eternal mates into the spaces beyond all 12 dimensions,
that is your calling ....
Your scars are healing my scars
for me to cherish your existence
This is the day when many suns and many moons
have embedded their imprint
in the nucleus of your cells
That is the day your Breath has left
the soul & that consciousness
replaced with The Heavenly embodiment
(which should be taught to people)
Shuffin HECK!!! You dared to post idiotic mantra stuff ...!!!
It is keeping the soul lower then soul ....
It is the modern day music that eliminates ....
and exactly the music you were giving me all this time being,
so u understand how grateful i was and am for all these post of splendid vibes....
But no more mantra stuff! DO U HEAR MY WORDS ???
5/22, 9:55am **Pre View**
We are here on this earth plane to rewrite the book of life which sounds like the obvious thing to do; to each page there is a book to realign 2 and measures up with the changes of the entire universe.
No, that is not easy but doable.
Many connections are necessary and indeed unifying consciousnesses ;;;;
eg: my brain might have many inputs like yours does ---
so merging 2 brains makes a splendid outcome 2 many things ....
And unfortunately, not doable over FB
What i teach now is the alignment to the many breaths, vehicles of light,
consciousness, working with the solar system and so on ...
This takes days of deep cleanse and loads of info which change people brain matter
or the waves of the soul/mind control, it is all about leaving all
of the soul jar for what it represented through the birth machinery of fucked up wombs
.... After that there is many ways to connect and work together
and that is my goal, discussing things,
writing new programs for humanity,
teach them & move on ....
So u can imagine it is hard for me to teach you anything over social media

You really need a class, your intelligence is that of a Wizard beyond I have ever hoped for to encounter.... I had & have many hopes : some are coming to the surface : e.g. - There is a girl here in the residence (only 19) she did 3 healing sessions with me in which i took her asthma away with which she was born and then within 3 meditation sessions she completely changed her life----

Now she is even measuring up with my brain to go into the problematics of society in every country which is great and makes me feel good - not standing alone any longer...

I have high hopes for her because i already feel what the girl is able to do after the 3 days of realignment ....

If today something flips into my mind for u, i will do it, anyways

i am going to align to synchronization energies with u, and see where that will get me,

Dear Koz, embrace yourself, you have all the intuition

I need more coffee or a flowing river with golden molecules should the Crystal spirals not satisfy my vibes

5/22, 11:56am **Pre View**

U have that grace, that intelligence that moves with the Black Panthers' Earth Moon (a whole lot of study) This is how my friends as a young girl saw me: TRUTH!

MUSIC: Immortal Technique - Caught In A Hustle Lyrics

Listen to the lyrics
5/22, 12:51pm **Koz Kozmos**
I have embraced myself , I've had to
5/22, 12:57pm **Koz Kozmos** sick fLOW
5/22, 12:57pm **Koz Kozmos**
MUSIC: Anthony Newley - "That Noise" - '62

5/22, 1:02pm **Koz Kozmos**
And one more

MUSIC: Jedi Mind Tricks (Vinnie Paz + Stoupe) - "Heavy Metal Kings" (feat. Ill Bill) [Official Video]

5/22, 1:26pm **Koz Kozmos**
how is the mantra stuff keeping the soul lower than soul
i just feel the track ,
earth moon - black panther, sounds like a new age alt. tarot pack
and with the greatest disrespect i still remain unconvinced by you spurious mystic .... blab but thank u for the goodly nrg
5/22, 6:52pm **Pre View**
Anyways, i'm filling my place with iolite flowers, today
Take care
A Vibration is but a vibration until it matches frequencies,
5/22, 7:17pm **Pre View**
Damn u, damn me,,,
5/22, 7:40pm **Pre View**
Getting to know u step by little step and made my decision department shiver to go back to live without expecting a return investment where love is concerned,
I only allowed a few men into my life which many people think of as strange,
but i did give my love and was always misunderstood .
I am talking like 20 years back as I never engaged in society until when my son bought me a dress and told me to have a look at the world, haha
Well it thought me many things and most people would be interested to talk to me and were afraid . He said I was a strange person which is not strange to me because I've had that label ever since I was 5 years old. Most people would say: you are not of this world, so i embedded and tried to understand. So when observing people and talking to them, they would always come up with more and more questions making me realize how much I had learned during this time period of reconnecting with my Spirit and learning/ remembering my roots.So i decided to leave it there with their questions, as they were not the least willing to pay for the teaching zone. In this universe, nothing is for free, you have to work your vibe up, and thus information should never be regarded as granted for free, It is so disrespectful . Information/data is sacred and needs a sacred space to teach.
All I wish for is there would be more people like me, like you.
just giving, never judging and have a life that questions their painful measures.
That is also reason why I value u so much ,
because I know u understand somehow that value is needed in relationships.
5/22, 7:41pm **Pre View**
MUSIC: Lana Del Rey - Video Games (Official Music Video

5/22, 7:41pm **Pre View**
PEOPLE PREFER GAMING AND DUMBING
However, this song purifies

5/22, 9:02pm **Koz Kozmos**
I named my first Band Purity
5/22, 9:18pm **Pre View**
I Can't hear your band
5/22, 9:49pm **Koz Kozmos**
u need to connect more info to what your saying sometiemes
its also about being understood
excuse spelling
the melcholy meme for the youth culture dream,
the song above
5/22, 9:51pm **Pre View**
no, i do not,
it is that you either get it or not, it is all about the individual work to understand things
and when you do not align to what I am talking about, I do understand that it is difficult to understand – and reason why you would at least need some foundation into Light Technology just to move on and expand from there ,
with many ways to explore the universe and your forgotten connections.
never exuse ur spelling, no need !
5/22, 9:51pm **Koz Kozmos**
pop music is wasted on the young OKAYYYYYYYYYYYYYYYYYYYYYYYY
its becuz i'm trying to follow u i suggested it
it would be more offensive if i did not try to elucidate certain points expressed
5/22, 9:54pm **Pre View**
don't know about pop and young people, if they are into pop,
U have intelligence to understand young people,,,
5/22, 9:56pm **Koz Kozmos**
i was being witty
5/22, 9:57pm **Pre View** Please do so,,,
5/22, 9:59pm **Koz Kozmos**
u ok ?
5/22, 9:59pm **Pre View**
i went to the dentist, she was real good ,
i told her not to manipulate me and get the job done other dentist would do over 5 appointments. And so she did hah, as I explained I knew how dentists can just do whatever they want for whatever price. That should really be stopped as well – its knowledge I got from a dentist friend some day....
And so, this girl has been putting her words into action,
got justice donewith the dentist.
5/22, 10:00pm **Koz Kozmos**
I had 3 fillings full of dfluroide a month ago
5/22, 10:01pm **Pre View**
Did u express ur point ?
5/22, 10:02pm **Koz Kozmos**
yes i told him the new world order were using fluoride to control people via shutting down the pineal gland but as all the filling were full of crap i needed to chew
they were the first fillings i'd had in 40 years
i know have a hollywood smile now

5/22, 10:04pm **Pre View**
Haha, the brightness of a smile,,,
Show me ur smile, it comforts me
Somebody you know nearly tried to kill me while playing that Lana Delrey song
5/22, 10:05pm **Koz Kozmos**
who? do u know any one i know ?
5/22, 10:05pm **Pre View**
don't like to talk about it

5/22, 10:05pm **Koz Kozmos**
don't say it then, we have not met
5/22, 10:06pm **Koz Kozmos**
and as far as i know, we have no people in comman so wise up
not meaning to be rude
i don't wish to know yur biz, but if u say i know some one u know i will ask
5/22, 10:07pm **Pre View**
I really don't want to talk about it; please Koz,
do not ask again , sorry I mentioned it
it is actually reason why I was reading your comments on his FB page and reason why i knew u were worthy of a lot and reason why after that I sent you a pm
TO CONNECT OUR WORLDS
from then on we connected and started chatting, how else could I ever have gotten into connection with you – as your FB is for friends ...
please leave it at that creation, when timing has come and u still want to know, then, we'll see
5/22, 10:08pm **Koz Kozmos**
i want to know , i don't understand the secrecy,
most people in my friend list i do not know and the ones i do are basic and only there for these reasons maybe Joachim ?
5/22, 10:10pm **Pre View**
U once told me u did not want to know about my personal life which i appreciated,, it takes ages to read what I was going through with that psycho person and why I started to drink whisky/ and coca cola from the land that has no living alive intentions.
5/22, 10:11pm **Koz Kozmos**
u said u never taken drugs
5/22, 10:12pm **Pre View**
I am having a bit of whisky at times, and had too much of that at times
No i never take drugs, I have no idea what that is
5/22, 10:12pm **Koz Kozmos**
i'll let u retain yur privacy, but i feel u should tell me who suggested me as i need to protect myself u are the only person apart from one other for me too talk to online
5/22, 10:13pm **Pre View**
Nobody suggested it, I just saw a chat on a FB post that is all there is to it
And we both comented on the same post or chat if u will
5/22, 10:13pm **Koz Kozmos**
mmmmmmmmmmmmmmmmmm,
5/22, 10:14pm **Pre View**
Lets say I observed your comments and I thought they were real clever – which is reason why I sent you a pm through which this conversation started out.
5/22, 10:14pm **Koz Kozmos**
ok i'm not paranoid ,
well only when i need to be , i stay of the spirits, just beer
5/22, 10:17pm **Pre View FB IS FICTION**
5/22, 10:18pm **Koz Kozmos**
why are u aRfaid (AFRAID)
5/22, 10:19pm **Pre View**
judging me
5/22, 10:19pm **Koz Kozmos**
i'm intersted for obvious reasons
5/22, 10:19pm **Pre View**
i am all ears
5/22, 10:19pm **Koz Kozmos**
as we are in different country's and have never met,
so i am concerned

5/22, 10:21pm **Pre View**
u once told me u did not want to get involved, and when i would tell u, u will get involved, this is simple language,
5/22, 10:21pm **Koz Kozmos**
this is no good
5/22, 10:21pm **Pre View**
Anyways, what are ur obvious reasons ?
5/22, 10:27pm **Koz Kozmos**
if some one is going to murder u and u tell me which suggests this was the person who suggested me
mmmmmmmm , no good, i want u to be protected
5/22, 10:29pm **Pre View**
I have some whiskey once a week only...
It is hard to explain all that stuff as it is far too delicate and you do not understand Dutch – so translating a lot of info is no good for me as I want to leave it behind.
I have no protection in this world, the more light we have the harder it becomes to hold on to it – yet with so much grid technology I should be able to hold my ground.
Some people are completely crazy out of jealousy.
i am not afraid, as i've nothing
I am a rebellion, a gypsy ,I takes a lot of pain to move into truth, I am not newborn, i'm yur age, and still wondering why so many young people come to me , and keep on coming for help,
Who knows when i need to leave this earth plane
I do know i embedded my footprints very deep with deep causes, and that is all that matters
I don't like to go back into that conversation, all you need to know is that I appreciate your essence and especially your presence here.
Thank you for that.
5/22, 10:45pm **Koz Kozmos**
sorry if i was being judgmental, i drink a little to much
and smoke a few a day
5/22, 10:46pm **Pre View**
I know, have always known,
u drink every day ?
5/22, 10:46pm **Koz Kozmos**
not every day ,maybe 2 or 3 beers
5/22, 10:48pm **Pre View**
Smoke , u do not need it,
i do not know about smoke but all the people i get into my life are smoking (iguess u mean drugs) so i'm putting programs up for addictions
Weed is worse then eating animal products, its all the same , it kills the brain up until clever thinking fails. It is set up to keep people enslaved and tied to illusion. Most of it resides in the education. Little children are not even being taught how to keep the body healthy with some good ethics.
I've seen many children being raised a healthy lifestyle at home, once they enter school they become the worm that has been planted there.
5/22, 10:49pm **Koz Kozmos**
wots this person who wants to murder u got in comman with me?
5/22, 10:49pm **Koz Kozmos**
wrong ,drugs is alchemical
i eat raw food ,take vits , swim , drink lots of water etc
but i understand how do these programs work
5/22, 10:52pm **Pre View**
Drugs is a subject on its own, if you think its alchemical,
maybe watch a scan when smoking,
it kills all the fibers, it shrinks the brain ,
maybe you become reptilian consciousness, haha

It paralyses me to talk about that person who wants to kill me, he is a psycho under influence of hybrid parents, that is all there is 2 it. So please lets leave it for what ii was. Its of my own creations, I need need to take more responsibility...
5/22, 10:52pm **Koz Kozmos**
ok
5/22, 10:53pm **Pre View**
But anyways u do know, i'v got the right vibes
5/22, 10:53pm **Koz Kozmos**
MUSIC: AC/DC - Thunderstruck (Official Music Video)

5/22, 10:53pm **Koz Kozmos**
rockin track
5/22, 10:54pm **Pre View**
When it is over and done with ,
I will tell u about this person, if by then you'd stilll be interested,
5/22, 10:54pm **Koz Kozmos**
ok
5/22, 10:54pm **Pre View**
Sure love ACDC
What are u going to do with your life ?
5/22, 10:56pm **Koz Kozmos**
nuthin, going crazeeeeeeeeeeeeeeeeeeee
5/22, 10:57pm **Koz Kozmos**
i'm going ofline Bon Scott is good
5/22, 10:57pm **Pre View** Why ?
5/22, 10:57pm **Koz Kozmos**
the first singer with ac dc
5/22, 10:57pm **Pre View**
Which is ? Please tell me , how crazy how crazy do you get yourself at times?
5/22, 10:58pm **Koz Kozmos**
so crazy , i'm too sane for this dimesion of sickness
5/22, 10:59pm **Pre View**
I can feel your music is what kept you going,
5/22, 10:59pm **Koz Kozmos**
can i post some lyrics to a song for u to listen to?
u can listen when the song plays
5/22, 11:00pm **Pre View**
Please let me hear your voice instead? always dance,
That would be interesting and your own music,,,
5/22, 11:00pm **Koz Kozmos**
Remember the song STARWALKER?
Starwalker, he's a friend of mine
You've seen him looking fine He's a straight talker, he's a Starwalker
Don't drink no wine
Wolf rider she's a friend of yours
You've seen her opening doors She's a history turner,
she's a sweet grass burner And a dog soldier
Holy light, guard the night Pray up your medicine song
Oh, stake dealer you're a spirit healer Keep going on
Lightning woman, thunder child Star soldiers one and all,
oh Sisters, brothers all together Aim straight, stand tall
Starwalker, he's a friend of mine You've seen him looking fine
He's a straight talker,
he's a Starwalker
Don't drink no wine

5/22, 11:00pm **Koz Kozmos**
MUSIC: Buffy Sainte Marie - "Starwalker"

5/22, 11:01pm **Koz Kozmos**
gotta go
good night, and spk soon, ok listen
5/22, 11:01pm **Pre View**
no , u don't have to go, we are all human after all and need to reconnect to our stardom
5/22, 11:02pm **Koz Kozmos**
i don't kow wot i am
i need to sleep , hard life time, its a good song i'll play the guitar for a while, bye
5/22, 11:04pm **Pre View**
OK, escape, I need to rest 2
5/22, 11:05pm **Koz Kozmos**
the beegees
5/22, 11:05pm **Pre View**
I think I'm afraid of getting to hear your voice,
its like a remembrance of something.
Do you have that feeling 2?
5/22, 11:05pm **Koz Kozmos** . **YOUTUBE: Bee Gees ~ Jive Talkin'**

5/22, 11:05pm **Pre View**
beegees, right ok,good song to listen 2
if u don't want the examination hill and fried talk , i will embedd my wings on any other wing Goodbey Cosmic liberation,
gonna study cryogenics and freeeeeeeze too
5/23, 2:11am **Pre View**
no jive talk, the real meaning of jive talk ?
Who hurt u so much between supper troups & the dessert ?
5/23, 3:04am **Pre View**
Yes Koz i do hear all of your questions,
thy have been answered deeper than u (maybe) acknowledge
Good bey
Koz Kozmos
Your talking JIVE again
i need a kozmik band to save the earth
5/23, 12:53pm **Koz Kozmos**
MUSIC: ♫ Bee Gees ♥ My Old Man's A Dustman ♫

5/23, 12:59pm **Koz Kozmos**
The language of excitement is at best picturesque merely.
You must be calm before you can utter oracles. Henry David Thoreau
5/23, 1:12pm **Pre View**
5/23, 1:16pm **Koz Kozmos**
has he killed u yet... ?
5/23, 1:22pm **Pre View**
HEY YOU! sarcastic freak , i have A LOT of proof in dutch,
he almost killed other people as well. I don't feel like talking about it, that is just it.
DO YOUR HEAR ME, OR HEAR THE WALLS OF SELF TALK? Huh?
I hate it that u take drugs
I just hate it, hate it, hate it ,but i do respect u.

5/23, 1:29pm **Koz Kozmos**
Drugs, its not funny but mentioning it the way u do is fucked up just throwing it into the mystic chit chat its out of balance and inappropriate
if u had said to me i have something i'd like to talk to u about, would it be ok ....
5/23, 1:32pm **Koz Kozmos**
i smoke some times at a very low level to help with joint problems and insomnia
there are plant teachers and then drugs, anything broken down into a white power including sugar i avoid apart from the occasional smoke
5/23, 1:34pm **Pre View**
OK, I understand
I just feared u would take drugs every day
I apologize
5/23, 1:34pm **Koz Kozmos**
i'm not drug orientated, and i only do crack on weekendz,
and i like the term matrix slave , its appropriate, was joking about the crack ,
tea is my main addiction
u don't have to chat; its all goo
5/23, 1:37pm **Pre View**
Its alright, Koz, I don't always know when u joke or not,,,,
it is just that so many people I meet are all on alcohol and drugs, i don't want that any longer, some i'v helped out of that but i don't want them any longer in my life, as it is not my business.
5/23, 1:37pm **Koz Kozmos**
i hope u get this dangerous person out of your life for good,
i understand
5/23, 1:38pm **Pre View**
I will, but I still need to decide wether to take him to court or not,,,,
i'll give myself a month to think and then close that chapter,,,
it depends on many things and is very delicate
5/23, 1:38pm **Koz Kozmos**
some people need to kill the pain
yes, i don't bother with people
every one who comes into my life i get rid of quickly
when certain things become revealed, blabbereing
5/23, 1:40pm **Pre View**
U are right, but if it is a different story when you work with people, professionally I mean
It is very important to teach them balance and assist them to understand how healing works.
5/23, 1:40pm **Koz Kozmos**
yes is it lucrative , i 'd make a good spiritual life coach
5/23, 1:41pm **Pre View**
do so !
5/23, 1:41pm **Koz Kozmos**
no point
5/23, 1:41pm **Pre View** why
5/23, 1:41pm **Koz Kozmos**
no certificates and dealing with matrix slaves is a bore
and i 'd be uncomfotable dealing with strangers
5/23, 1:42pm **Pre View** why
5/23, 1:43pm **Koz Kozmos**
i just wishi had enuff cash to life on the hill far away from people
becuz people are dangerous
5/23, 1:43pm **Pre View**
i agree,,, mismanagement in the brainzzzzz
5/23, 1:44pm **Koz Kozmos**
i need to escape

5/23, 1:44pm **Pre View** how
5/23, 1:44pm **Koz Kozmos**
u need a lot of cash and freedom within
i have that more than most
i'd like to disappear, just walk out , not the csah(cash) bit tho
thats why i smoke and drink a little to kill pain
5/23, 1:46pm **Pre View**
maybe work hard for 3 months a year and spend the rest of ur life on the hills ,
talk to the stars!
5/23, 1:47pm **Koz Kozmos**
wot could i do, i have no qualifications , no contacts i'm past my sell by date
5/23, 1:48pm **Pre View**
don't know, maybe something you are really good at ,
what you love the most in life
5/23, 1:48pm **Koz Kozmos**
and the average wage is for matrix slaves
and i could not work with low grade humans in some crappy job and then just to pay bills
5/23, 1:48pm **Pre View** I understand
5/23, 1:49pm **Koz Kozmos**
u'r naive about my situation and have no clue,
but why should u
5/23, 1:49pm **Pre View**
explain please ?
5/23, 1:49pm **Koz Kozmos**
i just did
5/23, 1:49pm **Pre View**
ok
5/23, 1:53pm **Koz Kozmos**
MUSIC: Hawkwind - Hassan I Sahba

5/23, 1:54pm **Koz Kozmos**
EVERYTHING IS PERMITTED & NOTHING IS TRUE
5/23, 1:57pm **Koz**
MUSIC: The Pot Smoker's Song Neil Diamond

5/23, 1:58pm **Koz Kozmos**
a nods as good as a wink to a blind horse
5/23, 1:58pm **Pre View**
whats a nod
5/23, 1:59pm **Koz Kozmos**
a movement of the head to mean yes, a sigh Have u tried DMT
5/23, 2:00pm **Pre View**
No, Nothing ever actually
5/23, 2:00pm **Koz Kozmos**
ok, i don't like chatting on fake book
5/23, 2:01pm **Pre View**
So why are you here, you can stop it at any time, its all the same,
its just written thoughts
5/23, 2:01pm **Koz Kozmos**
I'm a rebel of enlightenment,
u know wot i'm saying mmmmmmmmm
5/23, 2:02pm **Pre View**
i guess so, as long as its not a burden on your doorstep
relieve from the dense flames takes work, its mass destruction within self,
the ego lanes and reconstruction into the delights of forgotten diamonds

5/23, 2:02pm **Koz Kozmos**
ahhhhhhhhhh enery shift
5/23, 2:03pm **Pre View**
maybe, you got to feel what you need to shift to get the real shift through
5/23, 2:03pm **Koz Kozmos**
To say that nothing is true, is to realize that the foundations of society are fragile, and that we must be the shepherds of our own civilization. To say that everything is permitted,
is to understand that we are the architects of our actions, and that we must live with their consequences, whether glorious or tragic.
(From Assassin's Creed)
5/23, 2:04pm **Pre View**
so it is, we're all architects, creators and must regain our powers back,
our strength, our mental capabilities to evaporate the foggy air, the insects that do not belong to our sparkling star. I love the term architect :
its continually rebuilding and refining a modern day home on the ground flour with light terms, light technology. Building new stuff in an old broken home doesn't work so well, better demolish it, break it down and rebuild from scratch,
or find the balance within from elimination into upgrades.
5/23, 2:05pm **Koz Kozmos**
one of my main problems is i can no longer handle noise
i wear ear plugs, never take them out, i am always in fight and flight
5/23, 2:06pm **Pre View**
not kidding i guess, what is noise doing to your body?
5/23, 2:06pm **Koz Kozmos**
my nervous system has been broken by my experiences in my life
noise triggeres me into states of panic
5/23, 2:07pm **Pre View**
nerves take a long time to regrow,
yet there are techniques that can bring the peace quite easily in thenervous system first;
I mean to get out of the fight /flight syndrome.
It is also adrenal glands related and other. Yet repairing and rebuilding the nerves is an interesting chapter we could write together.
Should you feel like cooperating and see yourself as an experiment into the light of many wonders, haha
5/23, 2:07pm **Koz Kozmos**
i can no longer cope with being here
i'm not suiccidal and not one of thise awfull self harmers
i look after my skin, i'm just telling u about myself
5/23, 2:08pm **Pre View**
do u know were exactly these nerves have been broken ?
5/23, 2:08pm **Koz Kozmos**
yes, from being here
5/23, 2:09pm **Pre View**
I mean in your body
5/23, 2:10pm **Koz Kozmos** being here
5/23, 2:10pm **Pre View**
thank u for telling me about urself,
I need some food,
5/23, 2:10pm **Koz Kozmos**
on this plane of exsitences, bad shit –
the food thing, ha ha ha just giving u some insights
u've talked to me about personal stuff ,
good to see yur eating again

5/23, 2:16pm **Pre View**
need to eat a lot, was getting to thin
5/23, 2:17pm **Koz Kozmos** yes
5/23, 2:19pm **Pre View**
started to care about myself a month ago,
strenghtening out my little body and getting rid of all i do not
wish to be part of my world
5/23, 2:20pm **Koz Kozmos**
good, i don't think i can continue to survive in this life
5/23, 2:22pm **Pre View**
don't think
just smile
5/23, 2:22pm **Koz Kozmos**
i never smile
too much shit
5/23, 2:24pm **Pre View**
ahaahaahaaha
paint about self, that helps you release a lot of stuff I feel strange today
Gonna walk in the woods for a few hours
i need to be in nature
away from people, just most of the time
5/23, 2:28pm **Koz Kozmos**
its the same for me , i love nature
no woods near me apart from on private land
5/23, 2:30pm **Pre View**
but can u climb mountains where u are ?
I was once in Wales maybe 20 years from now, did a week-end
with Mansukh Pattell on the Bagavat Gitta (ridiculous)so I managed to enjoy the
environment and and keep private from the pack
but i loved the nature and the walks i could do out there.
Do u know Mansukh ?
5/23, 2:34pm **Koz Kozmos**
no, but i've learnt to avoid people like him
5/23, 2:36pm **Pre View**
good
5/23, 2:37pm **Koz Kozmos**
Osho 's followers are dangerous,
any ways have a good walk, bye
5/23, 3:04pm **Koz Kozmos**
MUSIC: The Highwaymen - Highwayman

5/23, 7:08pm **Koz Kozmos**
I'm in the capital city of Wales, Cardiff , no mountains
MUSIC: Top 5 REAL UFO Sightings from Plane

5/23, 7:25pm **Koz Kozmos**
UFO'S
5/23, 8:50pm **Pre View** Good, ufo's
I downloaded 100 Fringe series . Like the 1st one
About synchronizing the brain to someone else's' brain...
I did this several times but just through light
(not water like in Fringe series) and that was big fun : the
other person did not know, but what happened was that we spoke the same words
(thoughts) at the exact seconds, weird ...to say the least, because everybody
was looking at us in a shop not knowing wot to think

Light has so much fun technology, simple science that needs a lot more credit.
People cannot acknowledge the unknown
5/23, 8:55pm **Koz Kozmos**
interesting, fringe is well worth a watch
i've been looking all day for my mp3 player;
can u tell me were it is please?
5/23, 9:04pm **Pre View**
In your bathroom, u always leave things in your bathroom
Very interesting this post about psychopaths on your FB timeline, i never looked at it that close, but it is exactly wot I went through .....
Anyways, can u handle the electricity of mp3 ?
5/23, 9:15pm **Koz Kozmos**
ok were is it, i'm feeling pychopathik in a nice way
shall i check the bathroom again ?
MUSIC: Music for 18 Musicians by Steve Reich - Beginning

5/23, 9:16pm **Pre View**
I am not so fond of Steve Reich
I need fast music, fast flows, fast frequencies, fast vibes, fast water, fast sleep, fast drinks, I need to rock it and blow my vibes into the air
Your mp3 is telling u it is bad for your ears
Were is your UFO, speak to them!
5/23, 11:13pm **Pre View** I
s there truth in jokes ?
`5/24, 9:40am **Pre View**
Cannot stop laughing
My cells are playing with Jupiter, its so much fun
What are your favorite stars to play with?
Too much spagetthi?
May 24, 2013
5/24, 12:55pm **Koz Kozmos**
i wear ear plus with the mp3
i can't listen to music in the room any more because
I'm on volume 10 to the average 2 i play the guitar with ear plugs in
most humans have become desensitized,
i have not
truth and lies
5/24, 1:02pm **Koz Kozmos**
MUSIC: Twiztid - Bagz

5/24, 1:05pm **Koz Kozmos**
i sometimes feel I've been abducted
a long story , i have no proof
5/24, 1:13pm **Koz Kozmos**
i hear on vol 10
5/24, 4:05pm **Koz Kozmos**
MUSIC: Ian Hunter - Overnight Angels

5/24, 7:16pm **Pre View**
I love Twiztid a lot, gratitude ,
thank u for all your messages
I would love to listen to your long story

I think & know u are no fairy tale but wearing a tail far more interesting if people would open up to you, I did not know Ian Hunter, i'm listening
I don't understand much about air volumes,
But could study it
5/24, 7:21pm **Koz Kozmos**
in many ways my life is a fairy tale,
i just meant with the vol that i hear stuff = louder than everybody else
and sound hurts me, and can throw me into panic attacks, but i cope
5/24, 7:24pm **Pre View**
in ur ears or head ?
U attached a name to that phenomena once, what was it again ?
Must be horrible , these panic attacks
5/24, 7:24pm **Koz Kozmos**
mmm , can't talk about it at the mo
my nervous system has been broken and i'm targeted by negative entities
5/24, 7:26pm **Pre View**
I am understanding u better and better each day
(but please tell me when you are joking) cause i take
this stuff very seriously and am interested in studying it a little deeper
5/24, 7:27pm **Koz Kozmos**
they use the red carpet at state events Royalty
and it is also used in hollywood, this reflects the blood line
5/24, 7:27pm **Pre View**
Aha, no Burgundy Royalty (good to know)
5/24, 7:27pm **Koz Kozmos**
the Bush dynastys and the british Royal family's are all related british
and they are being used as hybrids
5/24, 7:28pm **Pre View**
so many realities,
Typical British yes
5/24, 7:28pm **Koz Kozmos**
via inter dimensional entities to control this reality
not real british, thier (they are)German, they changed thier name to Winsor
5/24, 7:29pm **Pre View**
I never understood Hybrid in any language, ,
my brain does not catch it
5/24, 7:29pm **Koz Kozmos**
its a farce, and it not good, and we havea to beat them its well knowen their (they are) german sometimes u seem so naive , u should have this info
5/24, 7:31pm **Pre View**
I think everything is an ongoing process,
only too many give up to easily because of fear and laziness or
just disinterest. Hope awakening is coming through and get people to believe what is going on instead of resisting what is real : the pedophiles and satanists run the world along all the monsters, the hybrids rilling the nucleus. Intelligence is being removed, people don't even realize it, its all in the educational system .When will universities allow education?
After the awakening, when is this going to happen
5/24, 7:31pm **Koz Kozmos** Hybrid
5/24, 7:31pm **Pre View** I am naïve huh?
5/24, 7:31pm **Koz Kozmos**
it is a mix of things
5/24, 7:31pm **Pre View**
But i am a breathing system, an aircraft,
ready to take off,,,

5/24, 7:32pm **Koz Kozmos**
u need to stop this naivete
thier from the star system Draco
and are pychi vampires, they came here a long time ago
not sure of the tech,
they al;so like blood and flesh
they create negative energy by infecting the matrix slaves and live of this war is a tasty meal for them, they keep people in a dumbed down state and control behavior
theres a lot of info,
but it goes beyond the mental
twizted song was about weed...
5/24, 7:36pm **Pre View**
I think we all have volumes of interesting material that triggered us into something in life
i cannot possibly know things about many things ,
because as i said, i closed myself of the world (completely) for 15 years -
that is maybe why u think I am naive,
i don't drink their cup of nonsense and fight my way through into the light realms
Its all about getting your strength and skills back in without getting defeated
But maybe I should reflect a little on the war games
and all that because it is all about THE INVASIONS people don't realize
5/24, 7:36pm **Koz Kozmos**
I had a band in the late 80's, that died becuz of week minded people
callled reptile starchild
5/24, 7:37pm **Pre View** ?
5/24, 7:37pm **Koz Kozmos**
i have not got this from books, its hard to type info
5/24, 7:38pm **Pre View**
Would u please post a little recording of that band, i'd love to listen 2 it 5/24, 7:38pm **Koz Kozmos**
i never recorded anything with them
5/24, 7:38pm **Pre View**
take it easy,
5/24, 7:38pm **Koz Kozmos**
i don't noe how to post stuff
5/24, 7:38pm **Pre View**
Do u have a recording of urself maybe ?
5/24, 7:39pm **Koz Kozmos**
the music from that time that i did record is on tape i'm not posting anthing, too much pain
5/24, 7:39pm **Pre View**
We Transference **:** is a free service to send big or small files from A to B
5/24, 7:39pm **Koz Kozmos**
cheers
i 'm not sure i can , but they also control the soul gate
5/24, 7:42pm **Pre View**
YOU MUST , IT IS NOT AN OPTION
5/24, 7:42pm **Koz Kozmos** so death is not an opption
5/24, 7:42pm **Pre View**
absolutely not, worse because u'll be dropped in a lesser plannet
U must overcome attack and find your protection NOW!
5/24, 7:42pm **Koz Kozmos**
every day more negativity,
even tho i hide

4, 7:43pm **Pre View**
EVERYTHING IS SEEN, you cannot hide
Can u not clear out & protect your space? At least and hold on to that?
Or get yer sandals in Shambhalla
5/24, 7:45pm **Koz Kozmos**
its not basic white magic shit
5/24, 7:47pm **Pre View**
Holding a place needs upgrades everyday to keep all dense-negatives out,
till its crystal clear beholden &
embedded in your vibes, meeting these frequencies ...
The Big White balloon has been held back from us,he White Universe, the purity is the missing link we need to move through or at least gain the knowledge within that beam that holds or brings all 12 tribes/universes together
so this universe can move its magical elixirs through.
5/24, 7:47pm **Koz Kozmos**
never thought i'd say it
5/24, 7:48pm **Pre View**
But since yur nervous system is broken, i can imagine how hard this is on u
5/24, 7:48pm **Koz Kozmos**
WOTEVER!!!!!!!!!!!!!!!!!!!!!!
5/24, 7:48pm **Pre View**
Release your anger if u please, i don't mind,
What are u thinking?U can't move with angry deviations in the brain!
Koz Kozmos
time to split , fancy a track ?
5/24, 7:49pm **Pre View** ?
5/24, 7:50pm **Koz Kozmos** a song
5/24, 7:50pm **Pre View**
lets listen
5/24, 7:50pm **Koz Kozmos**
MUSIC: ICP - How Many Times (Unedited)

5/24, 7:52pm **Pre View**
Makes me think of Korn, this song
U know Koz if u cannot be a Universal coach in Uk,
why not do it somewhere else in this world, you may need a new environment
5/24, 7:54pm **Koz Kozmos**
no cash, no conntacts, no motivations
5/24, 7:54pm **Koz Kozmos**
MUSIC: Obama's Reptilian Secret Service Spotted AIPAC Conference 3 Angles (HD)

5/24, 7:54pm **Koz Kozmos**
thank u , i'll catch u later
ok, take care
5/24, 7:55pm **Koz Kozmos**
will do , and u
5/24, 8:02pm **Koz Kozmos**
i'm in an intense mood, thank u for all your feed back and interest it is appreciated,
i'm ok , all the best to u
5/24, 8:11pm **Pre View**
i am used to intense moods, don't know anything less
Maybe just expressing all u want to express is some relieve without taking care what is coming out of your mouth.If you should feel like it, do so,
I will listen, need to watch something now ---

5/24, 11:13pm **Pre View**
May I salute that wacky source within you
& clear some heavy vortexes through your waterfalls
& keep these yakki monsters away from u
5/25, 12:29am **Koz Kozmos**
i'm not repressed, i can talk, thier not too near to me May 25, 2013
5/25, 10:12am **Pre View**
All about you is getting clear to me, your missing components only come down to grids, grid-ding and continual alignment back into your Source. Maybe connect to your Ancient tracks and ask , allow some daily assistance You told me u did not meditate any longer, that tells me everything about u, tells me there is no way to keep the invaders or dark forces out of ur Essence, that tells me they have a free space to keep you in
Soul/Ego esophocating life/death streams.
The flip/flop syndrome keeping a person alive,but hardly breathing.
Incorporating grids and grid-ding your billions of cells takes a lot of technicality, endurance, comprehension, mathematics, geometries, languages, codes, new tree patterning, music, to understand and level up every single second, and of course trusting your own info.
But your channel cannot possibly be clear as of now.

All of this is done thr your breathing system that would need a lot of upgrades until u feel the rumbling of vibrations & frequencies beyond dimensions and thus make new movements through alignment and elimination processes analogue your activity IN THE CRYSTALLINE GRID SYSTEMS to achieve the result you want – and/or at least vibrate in a protective space that cannot be invaded through operations of the lower mind.

These mechanics would run and upgrade through your bloodstream, the nervous system, the whole damn anatomy that needs to get back into the flow of light brain/ body parts that have the apparatus of Light waves.......That is all you need to just continually rise into the higher levels of ascension.
With such a foundational OUTFIT, you would definitely understand and work with wot u've learned on many different levels. You could become the magical gimmick of this new land, hahahahha!
I'll give u an e.g. which is proof on the spot I give to people who accompany me sometimes : When i walk into any city i protect myself with loads of grids, sometimes (when i can hold it) thr immortal grids which is Black Panthers earth moon : this is big fun coz nobody sees u, nobody can talk to u even if u sit at a bar for a long time, thy just pass u by and even telll u : HOW COME I CANNOT TALK TO U !!! and many many other manifestations u can do thr grids and understanding the depth with that ancient technology until u become grid embodiment thr Ley line configurations all the way up where the spine maneuvers everything into light brain/body parts and then light waves.

Anyways the technical support for grids in & out body training needs a lot of knowledgeable equipment.... and also, there is no end into putting the light body parts together and be the creator-inventor of this age. Reason why we are all going through stages of ascension and having to learn about the contrivance of the monsters within the cosmos is the biggest part of schooling self back into original power; which is what you really want.

It takes a lot of work, ethics, endurance and devotion on a daily basis or individual plan to get there and hold on to the levels already purified which is needed to hold and understand the clearer levels in grid data.

BRIGHT SHALL WE SHINE MISTER! WE CHOOSE!
And better would be aligning to Divine Will at all times to get to ball rolling cloudless.

I hope u may want to reflect on this without judgment coz this is the solo most important reason we connected in the first place. If u had a foundational grid in yur home, it'd be easy for me to connect to many things in Wales such as the consciousness
and your queer identity, haha (joking).
As I told u before, ever since 2000 , grids have been in repair worldwide coz they'v been broken throughout the ages as grid keepers did not hold on to their assignments and thus the dark forces had a playground to start out the anomalous gaming on earth
as we are witnessing ....
But they are all in the repair zone now, and upgrading every day with them now is quite some information worthy to work with.
It is the distinguishing factor thing that keeps me out of negativity, its is the major thing why everybody around me changes all the time, a crystal grid is a very unique element regarding the change of an environment and thus shifts in CS....
(Rising the soul or old sun/sol or THE EGO into its spiritual heart is what ascension teaches; its about releasing the astral fields and their ingredients such as false dreams
Lets just bring the Celestial/Universal soup down on the ground
and give a good party to our taste buttons.
We are all agents of Divine origin with orders that need to be carried out, that is all there is 2 it. Complaining about any operative disadvantage, disease and all these economic/political festivities are not getting us anywhere.
We need to rise strong in mentality, not give any attention to the lesser ambassadors and DO WHAT NEEDS TO BE DONE IN THE HOME AND THE BODY FIRST, after that the meal changes with a higher level of fibers that tastes like the promised Land.
Nirvana seems to smell like a blessed flower road that is endless.
I wish I could load more memory,
the flashes of bright designs Pardon me if i'm wrong, i am not!
5/25, 10:14am **Pre View**
Triplicate grids thr your heart, that'll be fun
MUSIC: Shape of my Heart/Sting

5/25, 10:15am **Pre View**
Please enjoy your week-end,,,
5/25, 10:40am **Pre View**
If I irritate u, good
It's supposed to hit you for you to get into some new rythm.
5/25, 1:07pm **Koz Kozmos**
its unlikely I'll enjoy my weekend
u don't irritate me, it's hit nothing, but i understand your theories but wot use are they to me, and i hate stink i mean sting
5/25, 1:24pm **Koz Kozmos**
The 11 anti-cosmic gods are: of Moloch, Beelzebuth, Lucifuge Rofocale, Astaroth, Asmodeus, Belfegor, Baal, Adramelech, Lilith, Naamah and Satan. Together, they form Azerate, the 11-headed dragon of Chaos that burns holes in the barriers of the universe, allowing Chaos to flood through.
5/25, 2:09pm **Koz Kozmos**
thank u for the sting post, his mate has a very nice guitar
but i realize i hate Sting and find him a weak minded fake sensitivity more annoying than i once did, and all that wealth wasted on such an insane twat ,
proof the lords of karma need sacking...
5/25, 2:16pm **Koz Kozmos**
MUSIC: Nick Drake Magic Orchestrated Version
5/25, 3:29pm **Pre View**
ThankXXX

5/25, 4:14pm **Koz Kozmos**
MUSIC: Nils Lofgren - No Mercy

5/25, 5:15pm **Pre View**
all my faces are merging
Thank u
5/25, 6:43pm **Pre View**
Thank u for bringing Cat into my life (cat Stevens)
i'm listening to him for a couple of days, there is some
real good stuff in his music, the way he brings it I mean to say.
5/25, 7:10pm **Pre View**
Broken all my wings as I gave Intensive care to a psychopath i still love,
but choices made my day.
I'm frightened in some way because when i do not care any longer, i tend to do
things, i do freak out at times in order to release emotional content.
That is no good, need to get rid of that emotional sort of pain body that was created
in the matrix of monsters.
i'm sure u understand, U have yur guitar, I have my paint Is there any difference?
Art is art, it's the highest level of self investigation with a cream level of surprises .
I think it's very interesting to stimulate and understand our inner worlds.
We always stand naked isn't it? Art refreshes my believe, it is so charming.
It brings through a deeper understanding of how light works thr the nervous system
or the
messaging system. THE SPIRITUAL MESSAGING SYSTEM!!!
5/25, 7:29pm **Pre View**
Anyways Kozcosmic vibe,
my walk with u is more severe then i'd ever allowed into me vibes,
beinggrateful is one thing. Integrating it is just another word for harmonizing?
5/25, 10:25pm **Koz Kozmos**
what does that mean, apart from the cat bit
MUSIC: Cat Stevens - I love my dog.

5/25, 10:34pm **Koz Kozmos**
MUSIC: Cat Stevens -- Catch Bull At Four - Ruins

5/25, 10:37pm **Koz Kozmos**
MUSIC: Cat Stevens: When I speak to the flowers

5/25, 10:38pm **Koz Kozmos Y**
MUSIC: Portobello Road - Cat Stevens

5/25, 10:38pm **Koz Kozmos**
make sure listen to them all, and pick your fav
5/26, 10:39am **Pre View**
Catch the BULL
5/26, 8:58am **Pre View**
It means i'm tired of my own old talk, walk, let's recreate living lights
5/26, 9:26am **Pre View**
Music is enough
5/26, 1:30pm **Koz Kozmos**
ruins ?
5/26, 6:05pm **Pre View**
yes, sure, my pendulum swings on a barbecue, haha
no, lets observe some music, how it flows thr the nervous system
5/26, 6:32pm **Koz Kozmos**
i meant the song ruins ?

5/26, 6:54pm **Pre View**
The ruins can be rebuild unknown ashes, open unknown territories
The ruins are building me.
thank u for your easy schedule, haha
We can also build from ruins, so my missing component was you (meaning the Mars dynamic which I avoided & refused ...)
5/26, 7:10pm **Koz Kozmos**
good line: the ruins are building me
mars, no idea, i am Aries i suppose
5/26, 7:18pm **Pre View**
U know about music
Mars , anyways is an undertone, a moon flow from the solar system.
Cassiopeia is an overtone, a higher note, the flow from the Celestial antenna ---
Merging them into your vibes opens the vertical/horizontal Ley lines through alignment and the diagonal Ley Lines that flow from Cassiopeia; meaning u can vibrate unilateral, straight, omniversal , brrrr, Probably too much information.
Aries is connected to Mars, that is all
or just a beginning with your birth chart on this plane of existence
As I said before , these things are difficult to understand when not working with these cosmo systems. But u were born into these energies, --- I never aligned to these --- do not know why --- but i do know , not doing it gave me a lot of trouble because we need to align to the entire solar system in order to get
everything together in the body. The Celestial bodies are of great assistance. So, through our chats i was becoming more aware of your dynamic But, you're far more intelligent that i am so, u must have known ... Don't let it stop you.
5/26, 7:20pm **Koz Kozmos**
Stop me from what?
just looking up Cassiopeia, too much info
5/26, 7:29pm **Pre View**
Stop u from penetrating too deep as I couldn't give u wot u wanted thr sicial media; as you are a typical Aries
vibration that is just going and going and never standing still,
and allow the deeper meaning to come through. It's worth your time.
But as you do not know where to start, I'm starting to really question what you did in the past to get some sort of transformation and knowledge through.
So, I've given you the understanding that you needed some foundation, some settlement in the Crystalline Grids to start out with either a private seminar or I gave u the option to find somebody in Wales or get it here in Belgium which would cost u, which is not an option for u at this time as u don't have the motivation
and I am getting into a careless zone as i've told u!
Anyways, everything is a choice,
sure I sometimes wish U got the alignments I got because I DO KNOW it would upgrade us both. But you don't have anything I can possibly dig into and create some special light body shape with some beautiful arrangements along the cosmic musical spheres.
So where does that leave me?
It would also be great for humanity to further the educational foundational settings beyond coaching, really getting into them, until they understand and remember themselves as a light vehicle, a Source ofDivine dispositions.
5/26, 7:30pm **Pre View**
Please do not look anything up,
info is so low grade, and presents wrong flavors,
5/26, 7:31pm **Koz Kozmos**
the only person in Wales who can unlock me iz me ,
no idea where it leaves u

5/26, 7:32pm **Pre View**
I appreciate you a lot, it is not about unlocking,
how would you do this without appropriate info ? Please let me know,
i'll support u if your ideas are valuable .
I need some volubility that births itself through passion,
innovations, attraction, reaction
You need to be a magnet that pulls my imagination on a higher level.
5/26, 7:32pm **Koz Kozmos**
why have i not got these 'alignments' ?
what are they?
5/26, 7:34pm **Pre View**
Lets pull another string or create a new vision as I've talked enuff about it :
wot is alignment to u ? Wot is this word doing 2 u?
5/26, 7:34pm **Koz Kozmos**
no idea , fuck appropriate info i use 'unlock' as a broad term
5/26, 7:35pm **Pre View**
Wot is appropriate info ?
5/26, 7:35pm **Koz Kozmos**
the one u mentioned above,
i understand the word alignment and take it to mean planets in this case
5/26, 7:36pm **Pre View**
Yes, they meant planets in that case.
If i'd let u read one alignment would u be able to not judge it and investigate,
think it over, and sit still with every written line ?
5/26, 7:36pm **Koz Kozmos** not sure
5/26, 7:37pm **Pre View**
That is why i did not show you any alignments and see if we could find ourselves in
the same space of UNDERSTANDING,,, Good thing u know urself !
5/26, 7:37pm **Koz Kozmos**
to mean something , i've no idea who i am or who i was before this farce
i reread your type
5/26, 7:38pm **Pre View** ok go ahead, carefully
5/26, 7:39pm **Koz Kozmos**
u are coming across as a hierarchical smart ass; in a fun way
5/26, 7:41pm **Pre View**
I am not smart ass, u are giving the gas to my ass and thus u get the answers,
wisdom is a road I'd like to explore over the next 50 years.
Words are just words if you don't work with them, there is no meaning.
Too many people apply words with a high level of indifference,
with no awareness of what that could do to the body as in transmuting stuff, not
damaging. Most are damaging themselves out of that highway of ignorance and thus
it is so important to re-educate all layers within society;
starting from kindergarten all the way in the garden of Eden.
5/26, 7:41pm **Koz Kozmos**
I realize that no-one in the matrix can be trusted Even if they mean well,
they're fkd up
i've put a lot of effort in to this thing i've become
5/26, 7:43pm **Pre View**
I'm sure you did, I still wonder why u feed into this matrix subject all of the time,
it gets me down,
its no good.
5/26, 7:43pm **Koz Kozmos**
i'm speaking about one model

5/26, 7:44pm **Pre View**
Elaborate on the model? Is it classical, genuine,
extraordinary, fun,or spastic and paralyzing?
5/26, 7:44pm **Koz Kozmos**
the matrix model, not the movie
5/26, 7:44pm **Pre View** Which is ?
5/26, 7:44pm **Koz Kozmos**
the dumbing down of humanity
5/26, 7:45pm **Pre View**
U could, if u'd like, read a whole comment of mine on that matrix fucked up model
on my previous Fbaccount, it was interesting,,,,
5/26, 7:46pm **Koz Kozmos**
i can feel very down and broken, i would like to evolve beyond what i am and become
who i am, i can't fit into your theories
5/26, 7:47pm **Pre View**
That is because u don't know them,
the alignments need PRACTICE to understand theory
You need to work with alignments till you FEEL THE INTEGRATIONS AND
MUTATIONS taking place; that is when understanding comes through and thus also
new ideas, new inventions to further the creation of light bodies.
Maybe tonight, i 'll post u one alignment so you can check that out and have some
deeper idea,,,, as of now i don't have a care in the world because over explaining does
not work well – it may even create the opposite of my intentions and how the
receptors in your brain receive that can change every day as well –
that is the matrix, the captivity and intelligence that goes backwards very fast
because that was the intent of dense engines.
i know that you are important 2 me, and that is it.
Let's stay fearless, I can feel u , and I know wot u do when ur down & broken,
Let me reflect a bit on how
to bring through another level of light fusion,
or something you can understand from your perspective.
5/26, 7:50pm **Koz Kozmos**
my life has been awful
5/26, 7:51pm **Pre View**
That's Ok Koz, just think of it in a different way.
Set your LIFE SCHEDULE ON AN ALIVE VIBE
BELIEVE THAT EVERYTHING WILL CHANGE THIS YEAR.
You need to believe and pull through the efforts through actions and creating the
brainwaves that do not allow depression, yet the opposite:
FINE EXPRESSO FROM THE COSMIC COFFEE SHOP
5/26, 7:51pm **Koz Kozmos**
when i'm down and broken, i tidy up, play the guitar with the ear plugs in
5/26, 7:52pm **Pre View**
sure you're the guitar man, i am the artist that paints your songs
How about that huh?
5/26, 7:52pm **Koz Kozmos**
i have no interst in living, not in a deppresed way,
i'm done with earth
5/26, 7:52pm **Pre View**
Some day, I will plug your ears into a brand new song!
5/26, 7:52pm **Koz Kozmos**
i used to do all versions of art
the hospital fucked my hand up a few years back ,
i stopped drinking and smoking for 3 monthes
5/26, 7:53pm **Pre View**
Please let me know what happened to your hand?

5/26, 7:53pm **Koz Kozmos**
then I fell and broke my writs
the hospital misset my hand, damaging it ,
my knuckles are gone and that was one of the easier things to deal with
since i first came here, there has been one major disaster after another
5/26, 7:55pm **Pre View**
But u can rebuilt all that, that is what i offer thr alignments,
Even a small foundation into your Light vehicle would pull everything forward and getting initiated into the Eternal vibe, the Eternal healing through light so you can start healing yourself out, no dependancy...
You can, u've had all the pain,,,
I understand you are so tired of everything that happened 2 you
There are many options to get your vibe back into the light
and smash the old designs.
5/26, 7:55pm **Koz Kozmos**
which has ruined my life
its just the way it is, i'm not even miserable
i don't drink much, i never get drunk
5/26, 7:57pm **Pre View**
The way it is, is the way you're taking it,
not miserable means you're ready to shake it,
i do know that you control your drinking, a good thing, a good balance
5/26, 7:58pm **Koz Kozmos**
i have no hope left
5/26, 7:59pm **Pre View**
don't pay attention to the old suffering,
your intent is far more important
5/26, 7:59pm **Koz Kozmos**
my intent is dead
5/26, 7:59pm **Pre View**
Why don't u go into the world, Wales will get cleared , haha
5/26, 8:00pm **Koz Kozmos**
because i can't
5/26, 8:00pm **Pre View**
why? You just excuse yourself continuously and thinking you are
the only Light vibe that is being hijacked
5/26, 8:00pm **Koz Kozmos**
were am i going to go
why will wales get cleared
5/26, 8:00pm **Pre View**
that is up to u, think , get your brains to work
when light is being spread, it clears the mud
5/26, 8:00pm **Koz Kozmos**
i don't live in Wales, i hide in the attic
i feel i'm done with the world , i 'd like a detached house in the middle of nowwhere,
no dogs no humans near
maybe learn to drive, but i can't manifest it and have no help
5/26, 8:01pm **Pre View**
Hiding = no living = your vibes need an equal drive
I understand your situation, yet not everything
5/26, 8:02pm **Koz Kozmos**
i live more than most, i am more allive and kicking than this low grade soul experiment
5/26, 8:02pm **Pre View**
Please let me know about your hiding thing?

5/26, 8:02pm **Koz Kozmos**
hiding = avoiding the zombies
my drive was massive, all i'm concered with is awakening and deepening my understanding
and esacpe to a better place in nature
i don't think u understand me , but u have a fascination
u realize i'm not like the pack, u can acknowledge my limited genius
5/26, 8:08pm **Pre View**
Well I offered u all I could think of –
I work with myself as that brought through many results ,
Some people around here are finally getting to the point here as well with understanding some light-work they fancy (do not socialize much, but we can read consciousness all over the place, its all the same everywhere).
5/26, 8:09pm **Koz Kozmos**
u 've not offered me anything i can use pratically
and its not beccause i'm limited which is the postion
i'm always left with here i 've taken intrest in your ideas
5/26, 8:16pm **Pre View**
I DO UNDERSTAND wot you're saying!
Its up to u to either want wot i teach, get it in Wales or come down to Belgium, or go nowhere, nature will not comfort u, (I guess I can speak to u this way coz u'v got Mars/Aries to the point communicative skills)
otherwise pardon me, i'm not a soft vibe but u knew that, acknowledge ur knowledge.
Really Koz, don't ask me to talk to somebody who doesn't know will you?
When I was responding to your questions, it means that I cannot possibly teach all these things over FB, it takes 3 days of deep alignments to get ur stuff out and realign to some geometrical design, somefoundation with which you can start to work and it will cost money, I don't work for free,
This should be clear by now I guess,,,
5/26, 8:17pm **Koz Kozmos**
say what u want
i thought u said it can't be taught over face book
when the pupil is ready the mastar will come
ahhh , sorry mis read
have i ever asked u to teach me ?
no , but as i've said i've taken intrest , i have no money
5/26, 8:19pm **Pre View**
It cannot be thought over FB that is it,
the master will not ever come, get over these mass manipulative stupid lines
5/26, 8:20pm **Koz Kozmos**
it was an inversion of the zen saying for the purpose of humour
5/26, 8:21pm **Pre View**
Ok humor, is needed,
5/26, 8:23pm **Koz Kozmos**
how much do u charge ?
i feel it and have the heart; but do u ?
5/26, 8:24pm **Pre View**
I don't like discussing euro/dollar/pound Have the heart ? why do u think we chat ?
5/26, 8:24pm **Koz Kozmos**
"A path is only a path, and there is no affront, to oneself or to others, in dropping it if that is what your heart tells you . . . Look at every path closely and deliberately.
Try it as many times as you think necessary.
Then ask yourself alone, one question . . .
Does this path have a heart? If it does, the path is good;
if it doesn't it is of no use.

5/26, 8:25pm **Koz Kozmos**
i need to get into the acension guru game need to move to Glastonbury
5/26, 8:41pm **Pre View**
Surprised u did not feel my heart,
Take good care withyour know how care kit, haha
5/26, 8:41pm **Koz Kozmos**
i did; u got it the wrong way round again i said i feel it and have the heart
i said nothing derogatory about u
5/26, 8:43pm **Pre View**
no , its alright
5/26, 8:44pm **Koz Kozmos**
yes I know
5/26, 8:44pm **Pre View**
Why do u need to move to Glastonbury ?
5/26, 8:45pm **Koz Kozmos**
its the new age hipppy cappital of the uk
with a long line of acension gurus going back to the 1930's
its expensive to live there and u need a car and a good workshop
5/26, 8:47pm **Koz Kozmos**
Glastonbury has been described as a New Age community which attracts people with New Age and Neopagan beliefs, and is notable for myths and legends often related to Glastonbury Tor, concerning Joseph of Arimathea, the Holy Grail and King Arthur. In some Arthurian literature Glastonbury is identified with the legendary island of Avalon. Joseph is said to have arrived in Glastonbury and stuck his staff into the ground, when it flowered miraculously into the Glastonbury Thorn. The presence of a landscape zodiac around the town has been suggested but no evidence has been discovered. The
Glastonbury Festival, held in the nearby village of Pilton, takes its name from the town.
5/26, 8:47pm **Koz Kozmos**
maybe averbury
u gone ?
5/26, 9:26pm **Koz Kozmos**
MUSIC: How to Play Cigar Box Guitar by Shane Speal " 3-String Finger Picking Technique"

5/26, 9:37pm **Koz Kozmos**
tahks for the talk , bye
5/26, 9:56pm **Pre View**
I was watching fringe, quite charming this man,
love the way he approaches, hits, and backs off
but good night now,
u know by now when i'm feeding into different striations,
thank u equally for vibing into me,
thank u Koz, the genius in u wil meet u
5/26, 10:04pm **Pre View**
MUSIC: Edith Piaf - Non, je ne regrette rien - (original)

I AM BOOKING MY LIFE INTO A NEW FACE AND PHASE
When the Wizzard meets the Genius, we can have the fire work for the saviours of earth,

MUSIC: Ennio Morricone - Chi mai

5/26, 10:42pm **Pre View**
After that encounter, i need some hard rocking tuness ,
just like u do I know your smile and keep it where u placed it
It is indeed balancing out whether u want it or not,,,
Yes, i can see ur flight,
Glad there's no more questions,,
5/26, 10:59pm **Pre View**
I like it when you're asleep,
it gives me free flow over a coconut chest,
5/26, 11:26pm **Pre View**
It is where the wizzard meets the genius
Up to u
Up to me
5/27, 1:03am **Koz Kozmos**
MUSIC: Donovan - Season of the Witch

5/27, 2:54am **Koz Kozmos**
musical melodrama
MUSIC: Red House Painters - All Mixed Up

5/27, 3:05**Koz Kozmos**
i prefer Ennio Mrricone earlyier stuff i find that overblown and sentimental
5/27, 3:07am **Koz Kozmos**
MUSIC: Donovan - Atlantis (Audio)

5/27, 3:07am **Koz Kozmos**
too much music

5/27, 7:47am **Pre View**
donovan ,no yakki,
these kinds of music are good for intervals, thats all
i never get sentimental with these ....
mostly it only closes of a painting i'm doing ,any art needs the flow of music,,,
5/27, 8:21am **Pre View**
I Vitaminize my day with music, a lot of hip hop,
sometimes i only like one song of one particular group

MUSIC: The White Stripes - Seven Nation Army (lyrics)

MUSIC: (Hed) P.E. Firsty

5/27, 12:56pm **Koz Kozmos**
yes, the one song
magic can be found in all genres
The white stripes I'd rather listen to the source....
and gosh that rebel punk stance, hed pe have done a few good tunes
5/27, 1:17pm **Pre View**
Yep, I was playing games just to see if u'd change reactions
(these songs popped up when i opened
Youtube, just to trigger your consciousness,
your reaction as I know any music speaks 2u which is fascinating
(when the mud is left out)
Child in time is gonna work in the garden for a good while,
need to be outside and be an element

5/27, 2:49pm **Koz Kozmos**
i don't have a garden
5/27, 3:11pm **Pre View**
I talk to the miserables of earth
5/27, 3:15pm **Koz Kozmos** your not mad enuff
5/27, 3:15pm **Pre View**
u have no idea, maybe
5/27, 3:16pm **Koz Kozmos**
wotz mad ?
5/27, 3:18pm **Pre View**
Being mad or going mad ? Both lead to madness in some way,,,
5/27, 3:21pm **Koz Kozmos**
wots maddness? boring question
better : what is consensus sanity ? still a boring question,
5/27, 3:24pm **Pre View**
I can get real furious in a sense of curiosity until it hits my insanity.
A way of testing how these hormones are being fed by the matrix, no good
I love experimenting,
but should elaborate more on my biological organical content in alignment with the organisms that are earth or light earth bound.
Sanity is boring = stupidity
5/27, 3:24pm **Koz Kozmos**
how do we destroy the normals
5/27, 3:24pm **Pre View**
lets get mad enough, the intelligent way,,,
Everything is so inverted, there is no normal people , they are all too drugged by the Ones standing on top of Society, banking systems...
5/27, 3:25pm **Koz Kozmos**
i just want to win the lotto, and disappear
the maddness has no where to go; and makes me sick
5/27, 3:26pm **Pre View**
Go ahead, do wot u think is wise enough for u to do
Suffering is just a disorder like any other
5/27, 3:27pm **Koz Kozmos**
wisdom is not available in the dumming down, only vague escape
i choose to be centered but it eludes me
this place is a disorder
5/27, 3:35pm **Pre View**
Maybe everything is just a bad memory hanging around our brains
But creation is ours
Break your brains &chains, your the Genius, and create a couple of billion facetted eyes
A different EYE for each day, wouldn't that be fun
Just creating and recreating new realities every day, huh?
A matter of making focus the reality zone within any manifestation zone
Something of the sort,,,
5/27, 3:35pm **Koz Kozmos**
I've done more than that
but i'm trapped in the reptile city with no means of escape
and it gets me ill
5/27, 3:36pm **Pre View**
Right, may I get to know wot u've been doing all of this time ?
I means beside writing some poetry and bringing some guitar strings together?
Hide in the African Dragon Mountains
Load your carpet that shines the hardship
Get unpredictable

5/27, 3:37pm **Koz Kozmos**
surviving , hiding, becoming a poet warrior
I have been a multitude of shapes, before I assumed a consistent form.
I will destroy myself and end my soul
when i find the word ...;
and soon be gone forever , at last
wot have u bin up to ?
5/27, 3:47pm **Pre View**
That would bring you in an unfulfilling worse plane of existence!!!
Wot do mean EXACTLY by stating, wot have i been up to ?
I've been breaking my bones only to see if i'd be able to build them up again
That is no joke!
I never respected any education
There is not enough tales about how to build and regenerate our organism
out of the plague
As a young girl I was mostly interested in stones, gems, especially turquoise
And herbs, and flowers
And how to put a skin care cream together that works with the skin ,
not against its tides as most do
But the skin is a river isn't it, it needs to rehydrate its essence back into that water
power full of magnificent elements that take care of our skin and works with it.
My skin is in erosion
But remembers its valleys
5/27, 3:50pm **Koz Kozmos**
u asked me
so i'm retuning the intrest
i mean soul destruction; total death
5/27, 3:51pm **Pre View**
you're very vague
on any subject actually that drains my energy
5/27, 3:52pm **Koz Kozmos**
u can speak alll
5/27, 3:53pm **Pre View**
gonna fix something to eat, take care
5/27, 3:54pm **Koz Kozmos**
ok, and u
5/27, 6:22pm **Pre View**
Keep ur Shades running !
Because if you decide to fade away, things will get worse
The movement out of the soul control is what it takes to get the death of the soul
And thus loads of work to polish THE TWINKLE WITHIN THE EYE!
It takes work, work and work to purify, and lift consciousness of of the soul into spirit
consciousness and the never ending levels beyond that.
THINK FOR ONCE! HOW MAGNIFICENT ALL SOURCES/RESOURCES ARE
and forget about WHAT YOU WANT!
GOODBEY FOR NOW!
5/27, 6:51pm **Koz Kozmos**
yes boss
5/27, 8:45pm **Pre View**
Boss huh?, ok
Breathe minerals, Become liquid,
Excel playing the guitar,
Quit wording past mirrors,
Make yur life an expedition and exhibition

Infuse Titanium thr your bones,
Take a ride with the Black Panther through your bloodline,
Take the Dragons head through your neuronic equipment until its tail measures underground movements ,
Be a contagious warrior,
& burn all else!
JUST BURN DOWN YOUR OLD IN HOUSE INFECTUOUS CELLS!
Did U become Exclusively Happy ?
5/27, 8:55pm **Pre View**
Did u become an unwavering ROCK SHINING LIGHT WATER WAVES through Cardiff?
Not yet huh!
So start working on yourself
Light water waves can bring a storm of purification through the land
What you can manifest within, you can certainly expect the outcome in your surrounding Apply some logic for once, will you!
That would make our chats a lot more easier on me,,,
5/27, 9:00pm **Koz Kozmos**
nice poem , quite the kozmik jive
i will not quit wording past mirrors
I don't like cats or any other animals and i'm white
i did try to join the black panthers back in the 60's I'm just functioning
5/27, 9:05pm **Koz Kozmos**
MUSIC: MC5 - Kick out the jams

5/27, 9:10pm **Pre View**
jamming, this is good for me,good for my nect moves
5/27, 9:11pm **Koz Kozmos**
kozmik jam from the souljar
i 'm too clever for this dimension
5/27, 9:12pm **Pre View**
uhuh, do u rock ?
5/27, 9:13pm **Koz Kozmos**
i'm a rocker but i kut of my hair
5/27, 9:14pm **Koz Kozmos**
MUSIC: Thin Lizzy - Dancing In The Moonlight

5/27, 9:14pm **Koz Kozmos**
sorry of my life
my spirteul acension beyond the the gridz Bippin' an a boppin
If all the hippies cut off their hair,
I don't care, I don't care.
Koz Kozmos
MUSIC: Jimi Hendrix If Six Was Nine lyrics

5/27, 9:17pm **Koz Kozmos**
story not sorry * no Freudian slip
5/27, 9:17pm **Koz Kozmos**
MUSIC: Chicken Shack-Daughter of the Hillside

5/27, 9:18pm **Koz Kozmos**
pick your fav rokk
u in da hood?

5/27, 9:19pm **Pre View**
aha, a hippy never gives in on THE ascent ! am listening,
and finishing paint and talking , and give me a minute
5/27, 9:20pm **Koz Kozmos**
take your time, i'm a space beatnik going to tidy up
5/27, 9:23pm **Pre View** OK,Thin Lizzy
5/27, 9:24pm **Koz Kozmos**
a Kitsch Rocker to raise your spirit higher
5/27, 9:24pm **Pre View** MC5 ?
5/27, 9:24pm **Koz Kozmos**
MUSIC: Van Halen - Jump - 1984 [HD]

5/27, 9:24pm **Koz Kozmos**
David Lee roth ripped off my look
5/27, 9:25pm **Pre View**
Why don't u start a new band
5/27, 9:26pm **Koz Kozmos**
i tried for for over 30 years
they'r either young and stupid; old and boring or a bit of both
i hate musians , glad i'm not one
5/27, 9:27pm **Pre View**
Command the best in, there must be more of u that needs to be explored
Remember, only you can repair your own machinery
Just tap into the universal observation deck and download new equipment,
faster technology
5/27, 9:28pm **Koz Kozmos**
i have taken to much abuse
and met too many basic fuktardz
5/27, 9:28pm **Pre View**
basics yes, bastards
5/27, 9:29pm **Koz Kozmos**
total bastards
5/27, 9:29pm **Koz Kozmos**
MUSIC: David Bowie - Wild Eyed Boy From Freecloud

5/27, 9:30pm **Pre View**
Cannot open attachments, u have no permission ...
as they say on youtube
5/27, 9:31pm **Koz Kozmos**
maybe david bowiez is not allowed in Bell gum
Try another version of Bowie/wild eye
5/27, 9:32pm **Koz Kozmos**
can u see this one ?
MUSIC: BOWIE - WILD EYE

5/27, 9:32pm **Pre View**
yep
Much thoughts in life have a heavy price to pay
Like when you don't decipher the correct minerals in the soil,
it may turn to be sour

5/27, 9:33pm **Koz Kozmos**
Staring through the message in his eyes
Lies a solitary son
From the mountain called Freecloud
Where the eagle dare not fly
And the patience in his sigh
Gives no indication
For the townsmen to decide
So the village Dreadful yawns
Pronouncing gross diversion
As the label for the dog
Oh "It's the madness in his eyes"
As he breaks the night to cry

5/27, 9:34pm **Koz Kozmos**
they locked me out for over a week recently ..;
FB i did say before did yor painting go well
5/27, 9:35pm **Pre View**
Yep, thy never answer, thy just keep on manipulating ...FB...
Oh well, i just go wild when I paint,
never pay attention to anything but music
5/27, 9:35pm **Koz Kozmos**
good
i 'd do more art if i could sell it for large amounts of it
5/27, 9:36pm **Pre View**
painting is fun, it gets the information that I AM out of me
Its like taking a ride through my own universe
and seeing what I have stored over the past milennia or so
5/27, 9:37pm **Koz Kozmos** ok
5/27, 9:37pm **Pre View**
So the rock music suits me,,,
5/27, 9:37pm **Koz Kozmos**
nothing has given my real catharsis
5/27, 9:37pm **Pre View**
catharsis ? Do u paint ?
5/27, 9:38pm **Koz Kozmos**
i did , its another long sad story of greatness
5/27, 9:39pm **Pre View**
u got so many specialties
5/27, 9:39pm **Koz Kozmos**
Catharsis refers to the purification and purgation of emotions—especially pity and fear—through art[1] or to any extreme change in emotion that results in renewal and restoration It is a metaphor originally used by
Aristotle in the Poetics to describe the effects of tragedy on the spectator.
i'm a polymath, heres one of your paintings
5/27, 9:39pm **KozKozmos**
MUSIC Ian Hunter - When the World was Round

5/27, 9:40pm **Pre View**
Launch some rockets and fire these depresiive emotions out,
New Universe, New Life haha
Better resources, better tastes

27, 9:40pm **Koz Kozmos**
not seen it before
5/27, 9:41pm **Pre View**
polymath, i do not doubt u , ever,
wot do u mean by one of my paintings ?
5/27, 9:42pm **Koz Kozmos**
There's too much information but not enough to go on the vid ,
i was being humourous
5/27, 9:43pm **Pre View**
not sure , the info,
i just think we all need to get our own info , not outsiders
5/27, 9:44pm **Koz Kozmos**
yes i agree , but if u'r an original like me things can get tragic can't photo copy,
i can only do my own thing
i'm also very limited, anyways its hard to explain
5/27, 9:46pm **Pre View**
no, things can get us both out of the nonsense created by birthing in the gates of solar shit, coz we have mutual missing links & glueing them together brings the exclusive many things together, maybe, yes maybe, yes maybe
Singing the blues ain't gonna get anyone anywhere,
wot is limiting u the most?
5/27, 9:46pm **Koz Kozmos**
lost all hope here, esacpe is all i can do
my ear plugs help with this
5/27, 9:47pm **Pre View**
so u lost all your intentions in the big blue skies
MUSIC: Snowy White Midnight Blues

5/27, 9:47pm **Koz Kozmos**
no, my intent is always there in the dreaming but hope is gone
5/27, 9:48pm **Pre View**
sometimes a new view brings a new move
III
5/27, 9:48pm **Koz Kozmos**
which i feel is a good thing
III?
5/27, 9:48pm **Pre View**
III = intention, intuition, imagination
5/27, 9:49pm **Koz Kozmos**
they've done me no good
5/27, 9:49pm **Pre View**
Everybody should only do their own thing, good u cling onto that!
fake never worked anywhere and still people do not even realize who much their own fake worlds kills them
5/27, 9:49pm **Koz Kozmos**
it works every where
5/27, 9:50pm **Pre View**
u seem to be so strong & yet u always give attention to outside forces,
hard to understand
5/27, 9:50pm **Koz Kozmos**
on a basic level its easier to make a living a tribute band than an original mutha fukker ;
u have to - go outside

5/27, 9:51pm **Pre View**
you're multi original, keep that safe
no time to bring that out
5/27, 9:51pm **Koz Kozmos**
the forces are there and need to be dealt with ? bring what out ?
maybe its just diffrent for me than for u
my originality has gone unrecognised
u've not even seen a time shard of its dying
but thank u , i know i've failed , it doesn't matter
5/27, 9:54pm **Pre View**
The head must cut off outward reflections to take energy up from wot you built as a single digit apparatus and to be able to score projects through and expand on your counseling
with your cosmic connections
Don't be so hard on yourself Koz, i do acknowledge even a lot more potentials in u than you will ever accept to know,,, That is no good.
5/27, 9:56pm **Koz Kozmos**
u have an over blown way of expressing your soul tech
like a 1950's sci fi comic
i understand the mis use of energy
i've wasted huge amounts mainly because i'm broken and it leaks out
they like to feed , i'm a higher dish of soul energy for the negs i'm fighting,
but i need to retreat
5/27, 10:02pm **Pre View** may be, we all waste precious vibes
5/27, 10:-02pm **Koz Kozmos**
vibes?
5/27, 10:03pm **Pre View**
vibes = energy , i manipulate my own energy at times
Its more like self sabotage because we all lived in many killing fields and that energy sabotaging self is derived from letting excuses layers in I guess.
But I'm dealing with these issues now and holding on to the higher grounds or the layers that plant Light in your feet like Light Earth drums, haha
5/27, 10:03pm **Koz Kozmos**
its raining, the night

MY INTERNALS: As this conversation started out in 2013, and while I am finally getting it into a readable script so to speak in 2020– that is a time space of approx 6 years in which a lot of work has been done regrading the Ascent of Earth and uplifting consciousness from the old wooden brain into fresh leaves. This time around what is termed "FAKE" within people is getting into the open windows in the streets of any hood thanks to the Light Earth Grids that have completed. What it means is that the Elements are claiming their Original position in which the organism of Earth is breathing Light and vomiting the debris out caused by the human kingdom. The Light Atlantean Grids hold the consciousness of TRUTH AND PURITY in the first place which nobody can escape. And thus we are either being requesting to move our senses into Divine WILL and obvious new directions in order for us to match the organism of Light Earth and thus bringing the body back into its Light organic and original state or remain in problematic static of the underworlds and never ending trouble. There is no in between road in which we can choose to bend things as in wishful thinking. The difference between Free Will and Divine Will will make the difference between remaining on Light Earth or making the choice to live the life of a snake and eventually learn lessons on another planet.

MY INTERNALS: "Earth" was and will always be a planet of great importance universally speaking as it holds the energy of Peace and Truth that matters a lot for the substances and consciousness within other galaxies to rise equally into ascension and evolution.
It definitely takes quite some work to train self into ascension or the release of the emotional/pain body. In that regard, I often times wondered if the human body had always been almost all water/ emotion. Lifting and clearing the waters within is a very interesting process because the aligned details with the rivers, the lakes, the oceans and the seas bring through so much beauty, intelligence, knowledge and instills the hunger for data.
With the deeper levels of awakening going on now in 2020, people still don't seem to realize that Light embodiment takes conscious efforts daily to hold a protective crystalline Grid in the body, the home, the hood; just because that allows us to open up or higher skills to defeat the current killing fields of authorities that promote nothing but dis-ease. But hey, they exposed their mask, so lets blow our stardom and flickering Light just through any institution promoting captivity.
Most humans forgot about co-creation with the elements and endless skills one can upload by simply readjusting into the purer and crystal clear waters. Many water LIFE stations are revealing new elements that would benefit our health and ways of feeding a crystalline Light embodiment. It is such an interesting study as it provides endless data that somehow takes you into the rivers of Ancient Technology and shows you how that can be applied today in order to match the flow of consciousness that has evolved and will absolutely teach many streams in the body. However, the harder we work to get our vibe and frequencies into the domains of Divine elixirs; the more we remember what it is to be a star. That flickering Light that has infinite cosmological connections with elements, many different species and a high level technology is REALIZING now how grand we all are.
And thus in 2020, we will see TRUTH rising everywhere, we will see the "fake" crumble and how that plays out for the sake and safety of earth. Fake goes hand in hand with FEAR. Once fear of many issues is being released, we recognize ourselves, we acknowledge ourselves and respect self on higher degrees which will also open up the calculation of SELF VALUE, SELF WORTH AND SELF RESPECT as a Divine being. There are many great techniques to release fear. Yet, what is mostly misunderstood is that it takes consistent work and releasing the fear of doing that work in the first place along the laziness many allowed into their lifestyle which is another parameter of ignorance because the educational system was held back to educate proper life styles, health and strength of character; and thus it failed. Life today is asking every entity on the planet to LIVE DEEP, TO DIVE DEEP, TO EXPRESS DEEP in alignment with Source, Spirit and our Spark Self. For most people that requires a complete new life style or architectural design that fits and benefits Light Earth along the Elements and the Animal Kingdom.
The Crystalline Light Earth Grids are continuously uploading more and more purification of the body and the brain. Yet it is our individual duty to purify and eliminate the mind and replace that by the consciousness of spirit within or a full active light brain that flows with the modern tides in which the lower static degrees of consciousness are not allowed. We witness a lot of people going vegan, returning to herbal medicine and Light medicine through Light sciences because consciousness within the grids and truth has brought them there. Five years ago, we could not imagine that fast movement. Today the global warming, the cry of the animal kingdom, the malfunctioning of our teenagers and the atrocities happening in the so called health institutions are bringing people back into a state of awareness where they finally start to think for themselves: it is termed THE AWAKENING! Awakening or rising from the density and recycling consciousness that keeps on repeating itself such as in addictions; into brainwaves that generate health, beauty, intelligence and knowledge requires a good dose of discipline, action, persistence, technology and a physically fit body to keep rocking and rolling our crystalline waves back into Light parts.
These days, it is a lot easier then it was like 15 years ago because the hard work has already been done such as the repair of the crystalline networks. Yet, group consciousness such as through a 7- days seminar works faster then anything because everything is being explained to a level of UNDERSTANDING. Understanding is needed to evolve with new Light techniques and be daring and trusting enough what comes on our golden platter. It could be so simple and beautiful.

Breathing Knowledge through Light in consciousness offers many solutions, individually and globally because we are all Creators , we just need to remember how to do that and start reconnecting the dots in which major Ley lines can come together and create vortexes that allows us to upgrade into the the higher Light Engines. Just imagine, this new world in which each human being shines through Light factors for the good within community, teaching and learning from each other that uplifts the beauty of ecology.
Concerning Koz, I always knew there was nothing fake about him, yet back then, I did not quite understand why he did not continue to make music or what it is like when hearing things at a higher Herz level. As the story grows over the years, many incredible things happened. Back in 2013, I wondered many times why Koz did not just heal himself out with music; or it was never clear either if he understood that Light just needed to be breathed through with the Music & according knowledge and its consciousness and thus uplifting the breathing system into multi omni-versal airwaves. Let's keep the surprises going, because communication on an almost every day level via the written word leaves many questions unanswered. The timbre within a voice is very important to decipher demons and just chill within any axis position: starting to realize the energies and consciousness within self assists to just accept, delete recycling patterns and allow Light to FILL IN THE MISSING LINKS or empty spaces.
Respiratory diseases are running rampant on this planet which is quite obvious when breathing the DEBRIS of the Matrix instead of breathing the Purity of Light air through. It was designed to kill and enslave people as stuck breathing definitely creates more fear. Streaming on fear means YOU ALLOW CONTROL over your soul.
Everything in life is defined by breathing capabilities. Stuck breathing and bacterial feeding is main cause for all illness on earth including the mental/ psychological emotional dense codes one agreed upon or ALLOWED in the body and carried over through foods, many lower senses, through ones' interaction with other people, animal products, low vibrations and frequencies such as implemented through the media machines and its mind control.
Understanding how consciousness and states of awareness such as fears, angers, low worth, depressions, frustrations, self manipulations, nervous breakdown, the incapability to communicate, and other mental fractures that departed from birthing into the density of matrix laden debris can cause a high level of stuck breathing which causes the cellular structure to accumulate disease upon disease.
LIGHT DEGREES, math and designs that are SEEN AND KNOWN through alignment can SERIOUSLY (Sirius A and B)clear out the lungs, the spinal column, the glands in the brain, the throat, the skin, the liver, any space/place in the body because the body is held together through Light parts that became cells through birth. The RETURN INTO LIGHT PARTS is the best of education the entire planet should get because it removes stuck patterns and diseases in consciousness very quickly. Everything on the earth that keeps you from breathing at full potential needs to be inverted in which understanding , acceptance and transformation can take place or where consciousness has ROOM to dig into the higher levels of thinking that eliminate dense lower senses and physical diseases.
Realigning the body to opening the circulation system and creating a flow where the air can move in the most minuscule details of the body is most important to eliminate any mental/physical/ psychological disease and opens other capacities that you KNOW that need to be upgraded into the Origin of Self : Fear & incapability to communicate, fear of judgement, fear of being Self, physical weakness, addictions, low mentality, old stuck attachments.
Everything needs to balance out in order for the breathing system to create an open River. Realignment to the Eternal Breath of Life, the Breath of Source, the Immortal expanded Air
gates..... If only people could understand that Light Education is not so difficult when the KNOW HOW KIT IS ABSOLUTELY AVAILABLE. Knowing how to clear lungs, arteries and the blood circulation brings a lifetime of RELIEF!
I can see the repetitive pattern of Koz within many people as most just keep on living the CYCLES they were born into. LETS BREAK through that thunder and create New Living Light Communities based on joy, love, respect and equal business. Let's just open that Light Road and teach, teach, teach our children, youth, students, the elderly, business people, the artists, and co-create.

When the breathing system upgrades, the atmosphere within and surrounding establishments creates new Group Consciousness and Unitarian options to create from a new platform.
The brain will go through non stop shifts and levels of understanding in the bodies' electronics or our own energy.
Releasing the old also means we release fat cells in the body, toxic foods that go along toxic thinking and consciousness that is derived from other lives that are of no service today, and detach from old relationships. It overrides all of the densities, mental, psychological, physical illness not only in the body and brain but also in the environment.
When AIR waves in the human body have reached full capacity ; they open the multi directional/ dimensional gates of consciousness that offer the means to assist the restoration of the human Bio- organic composition and that of the Earth.
We can no longer disregard the necessity to repair the soil and its nutrients for human health to restore. Many times when people train themselves , they get lost when it comes to getting a perfect healthy view together in their daily lives in which all components fuse into perfection. It is my intention during this lifetime to train all the integrations with a practical movement such as how to merge with upgrades and healing with studies, business ,family, friendships, partners, and fitness levels required along a healthy diet so that everybody benefits equally.
Meditation and Light techniques changes energy and bring through shifts in consciousness depending on the alignment on an every day level to make it a passionate journey.
Meditational alignments is simply allowing living light into the human organism that bio-couples into all living organisms at the pre-quantum level and infuses them with life and sentience at the most fundamental level : that is termed "Transduction Biophysics" which deals with the nature of living systems as inter dimensional biotransducers of the flux-flow or life force.
The exclusion and non recognition of this primary sentient, all pervading, self-radiant fundamental form of light is what leads to the reductionistic tendency of so called "material realism" in science and leads modern biology into reducing life to mere molecular machines as does the whole field of genetic engineering and nanotechnology which is not without its valid merits and impressive advances but is essentially reductionistic, mechanistic and spiritless in it's orientation.
Therefor, IT IS PERFECTLY TIMED TO BRING NEW EDUCATION IN ALL SYSTEMS, BUSINESS, AND FACULTIES. **Understanding how dualistic means operated for many eons is an essential Education through which the Human Essence can start to understand how we can remove the old standards and** EVOLVE WITH NEW ETHICS **based on the principles of Health, Wealth, Equality, Global Economic growth, Integrity, Intelligence and** NEW PHILOSOPHY **that breaks down the veils of ignorance and control mechanics or a whole system based on self interest versus Unitarian means on which all Universes operate.**
It is merely LIGHT ENGINEERING AND THE MISSING LINK IN ALL EDUCATIONAL SYSTEMS.
In meditation we can get instructions to BREATHE **through Living Light which composes the very fabric of space and dynamically weaves itself into all of the forms of mass and energy comprising the manifest universe, is the very Source and wellspring of all life and is in fact that which is living in us in each and every moment.**
The capacity to transcend linear time as a basic format of experience corresponds to the capacity (or aptitude) for spiritual AUTHENTIC **experiences and this higher range of experience is something that needs to be acknowledged, respected and centrally included into every** FACULTY/TEACHING MODALITY **within a truly Mature Science of Light Technology and Education in all Systems.**
Exploring the deep physics of Space and Light, and the nature of the multi-dimensional universe in which we live, and breathe IN THE BODY **is such an interesting study. Yet most look for this outside the body, isn't it?**
We can breathe new life into the most advanced ideas in physics by demonstrating how it all applies within the inner world, for any human being has the Universal right to RESET **his entire Bio- Mechanism into 100%** WELL BEING **24/7. It implies that deep study and alignments need to be integrated through Light Sciences to allow its various** APPLICATIONS **regarding the composition of mental/social/psychological and physical health.**

A human being exists within Space, and experiences varied forms of consciousness at all times, yet mostly in the lower mental degrees which should evaporate from its Essence in order to EMBRACE THE TRUE NATURE AND CAPABILITY of human beauty.
Teaching how to understand how the concepts of Physics can be applied directly to understanding the inner life and Self regarding light as having more a 'triune' rather than 'dualistic' nature should be ALLOWED AN OPEN DOORWAY IN ALL EDUCATIONAL SYSTEMS AND ALL FACULTIES for it is THE DOOR TO DEVELOP NEW FACULTIES WITHIN EACH EXISTING FACULTY AND THUS NEW INVENTIONS REGARDING HEALTH, EDUCATION AND EVOLUTION ARE A NECESSITY. The old atomic structure is falling apart and opens the gateway for LIGHT PARTS TO OVERRIDE RNA/DNA MALFUNCTIONS:
We can no longer allow any societal avenue to block this kind of information for that would be very inhumane and does not flow with our human rights. Any human being can become a "hyper- dimensional crystal lattice" which is his nature through which any consciousness can be integrated and override density such as fear, panic, self-destructive motion, abused mentality , trauma and all psychological invasions swimming in the lower fields of consciousness.
Deciphering consciousness within phenomena, we discover the Divine Trinity of MORAL, ETHICAL & SPIRITUAL VALUES! that were lost and need to be rebuild!
The Evolution of Education requires a New View, New Content, New projects and an Open Mind Policy in order to serve the Young students in High schools and students in Universities, Professors, Teachers Young Physicians, Mathematicians, Biologists, Nurses, New Businesses, New Health dynamics, New Architects, New Master degrees.

5/27, 10:04pm **Pre View**
I love walking thr the night
Prefer walking alone at night, with the stars, don't like having humans with me or anybody disturbing my nightly conversation with myself and thus the cosmos-logical teams
5/27, 10:05pm **Koz Kozmos**
depends i'd like to go down to a quite beach and listen
then walk thru the woodland home, thru the door in the hill
wwwwwwwwwwwwwweeeeeeeeeeeeeewwwwwwwwwwwwwwwwww
my energy is going down
Why do you manipulate yourself or what do you do?
5/27, 10:07pm **Pre View**
it is just that i work hard on my body with light techniques
and then fuck it up when having a drink.
Drinking some alcohol for 2 days is too much when moving into light body,
it does not make sense because you always need to clear the blood circulation and the toxins out.
I lived near the beach for 10 years
5/27, 10:08pm **Koz Kozmos**
that last bit was confusing i'm confusing too i got the beach bit
5/27, 10:09pm **Pre View**
I MEANT TO SAY THAT WHEN YOU PURIFY YOUR BODY SO MUCH WITH LIGHT TECHNIQUES, you hardly feel the alcohol when having a drink,
and so it happens that I drank a little too much meaning you have a lot of work bringing the body back toxins free,
5/27, 10:10pm **Koz Kozmos**
why do u do this with alchol
5/27, 10:10pm **Pre View**
don't know,I never liked alcohol and never drank anything
until I met that psychopath a year ago. I don't even like it much, it became a habit
5/27, 10:11pm **Koz Kozmos**
i never drink with people, i do every thing alone not for enjoyment
just to shut myself down

5/27, 10:12pm **Pre View**
I am the same, drink tea when i'm with people
Just sometimes enjoy a few wines or so,,
,but it got too much first I got to know this psychopath
5/27, 10:12pm **Koz Kozmos**
do u know about dm?t
5/27, 10:12pm **Pre View** no, Dmt ?
5/27, 10:13pm **Koz Kozmos**
u prop drove him to drink and drugs ; only joking
5/27, 10:14pm **Koz Kozmos**
N-Dimethyltryptamine (DMT or N,N-DMT)
is a psychedelic compound of the tryptamine family. Its
presence is widespread throughout the plant kingdom.[3][4] DMT occurs in trace
amounts in mammals, including humans, where it putatively functions as a trace
amine neurotransmitter/neuromodulator. It is originally derived from the essential
amino acid tryptophan and ultimately produced by the enzyme INMT during normal
metabolism
The significance of its widespread natural presence remains
undetermined. Structurally, DMT is analogous to the neurotransmitter serotonin
5/27, 10:14pm **Koz Kozmos**
u release it when u die
5/27, 10:15pm **Pre View**
Why do u ask about dmt ?
5/27, 10:16pm **Koz Kozmos**
i'm getting a little bit more controlled i try to follow the sly way
5/27, 10:16pm **Pre View**
Sly ,? controlling means u will not be yurself, I cannot appreciate that.
5/27, 10:17pm **Koz Kozmos**
Clever or cunning, especially in the practice of deceit.
Stealthy or surreptitious: took a sly look at the letter on the table.
Playfully mischievous: a sly laugh, best way wen dealing with fukktardz
5/27, 10:19pm **Pre View**
Sly, good word, short and penetrating,
5/27, 10:21pm **Koz Kozmos**
only use the sly way in certain situations i've had mentaly sick peole in my life
5/27, 10:22pm **Pre View**
would u like to educate me how to deal with them?
5/27, 10:22pm **Koz Kozmos**
some are still there , I see the sickness
5/27, 10:23pm **Pre View**
The whole human parade is mentally sick,
yet psychopaths have a way in the manipulative;
states of consciousness that are very dangerous.
Spirit gave me a whole long beauty and beast story I would rather not remember.
People make me sick with those low patterns in thought.
5/27, 10:23pm **Koz Kozmos**
educate u ?
5/27, 10:23pm **Pre View**
why not
5/27, 10:24pm **Koz Kozmos**
its just the sadness madness connected to the dumming down
5/27, 10:24pm **Pre View**
it is worse than that with all those hybrids hanging in the air that you breathe.
Let your grassland spring back into existence

5/27, 10:24pm **Koz Kozmos**
i'm lost again
i'm not mentaly ill,
just damaged by being in the sickness not anti depressants
5/27, 10:25pm **Pre View**
Mentally sick fuctard has been my nightmare
I'v helped too many of them too much to the point in which I got a psychiatrist down.
Took me a lot of work and exhausted me so much
Hope u don't take any meds ? Do u ?
5/27, 10:27pm **Koz Kozmos**
no way, no pills , I juice and swim
5/27, 10:28pm **Pre View**
ok, Can u imagine the brain of someone who takes 19 pills, alcohol,
all possible sorts of psychedelics every
day for 9 months ? on a 24/24 schedule
5/27, 10:28pm **Koz Kozmos**
not at the same time
YES , i went out with them, but it was 24 years ago
5/27, 10:29pm **Pre View**
But thy didn't harm u ? need a break
5/27, 10:30pm **Koz Kozmos**
not in a pysical way but i got very ill in the end but that was my chihood too,
and continued ... a long story, i hope u sort it out
and it has an end, it consumes you
ok, a break, so do i
good idea, good night
5/27, 10:33pm **Pre View**
it keeps on consuming me, but the end is near
Goodnight
5/27, 10:34pm **Koz Kozmos**
~<0>~
5/27, 10:55pm **Pre View**
Anyways, there must be a reason u brought it up, makes me real sick, real sick
Seems to me we have same levels to deal with only i do not give up,
wish i could sleep for a few days
5/28, 6:01am **Pre View**
Why the hell did you talk about DMT, all the people who come into my live are either drug addicts or lunatics with creepy pasts. Every single one of them wants me to try things ...
So I proved it would not work with me as i get my visions far stronger , far healthier thr meditation. But sure, there must be a reason why ... so i've been putting up antigravity - anti drug grids which are working ... a few completely stopped the damn abuse. But then again i'v had it with working for free, maybe set up a program ... Please educate me, hahaha
5/28, 6:10am **Pre View**
When i focus on your heart, i get pretty complex beautiful geometrics, but i need to be in a more real-axed state of consciousness, in a no care zone when confronted with societal misinformations,,, but without drugged people.
Do u take dmt ? Is that reason why you asked me?
5/28, 6:10am **Pre View**
I just listened to that but i doesn't tell me anything,
just empty blablabla

MUSIC: Joe Rogan ~ DMT Is A Portal To The After Life

5/28, 8:00am **Pre View**
2e day of Sun out here, good day to break FREE
5/28, 9:23am **Pre View**
Wot a day, plenty of rabitzzzzzzz all around me when jogging,
then the black raven on my shoulder, then a butterfly
Better then humans,
OK i'll shut up, shut my mouth for the rest of the day Have good good,
real good day Koz !
/28, 12:50pm **Koz Kozmos**
you have a concern that i'm a fucked up drug addict
'im an unhappy man who drinks and smokes a bit in the evening to kill the pain
i tried it once, over 10 years ago, its not an abuse drug for weaklings
its shamanic, the jogg sounds good
i'm coughing and down, the days melt into one another and are just excisting getting
i'll go for a swim ,
the reason i asked u about dmt was i thought u may find the phenomenon interesting
not sure why u got involved with the fucked up guy
sounds like a drug poser to me, why the inane debauch ?
sounds like he lied to u about how much he took
u may get lucky if that was the case, and he'll die
does every thing happen for a reason
5/28, 1:06pm **Koz Kozmos**
MUSIC: Drug Song - Alan Hull

5/28, 3:02pm **Koz Kozmos**
MUSIC: Judge Orders Conspiracy Re-Education For Lauryn Hill

5/28, 3:02pm **Koz Kozmos**
beware the matrix slaves
5/28, 6:45pm **Pre View**
Nonono, i didn't think you were a drug addict, and i understand very well,
very well that u drink a little, so do i since i cannot fit in anywhere any longer,
But u comfort me with your music, so thank you for that,!
Feel very sad tonight, like all puzzle pieces are getting clear,
Do know I appreciate you for many reasons.
We all need to put in our worth and find the Light ways through,,,
Concerning the guy, he does takes 16 pill a day -psychiatric medication, mushrooms,
pads, weed, all day non stop, lies about everything, aggressive, manipulative,
everything in high amount ,,,
lives in a PAS Syndrome with his mom ...
Lauren Hill, good to post this coz
it is getting clear to me why all these young people come here without
being invited, they almost cry for help .
The fucked up schools or the energies at a job, its getting worse and worse,,,
5/28, 7:00pm **Pre View**
Many things need to be done ....
I am sorry I offended u, i would never hurt u in any way
This morning was good, strange, I only come out the door very early or very late at
night
But tonight the pain hits in every possible way ,
a very necessary thing to decipher CS all of the time
5/28, 7:12pm **Pre View**
Talking about this guy, he's schizophrenic,
psychotic, bipolar, everything of the sort,,, I got him out of this
kind of lifestyle which almost killed me & then he didn't like to be normal & told me
he was going to drug like hell but kept major things secret ....

I went though unbearable pain ... long story
Wrote my frustrations down , talking to every possible creature but their weakness even hits me more. So , there is no point talking to people or zombies
I cannot bare the injustice any longer & don't know the best outcome, +
if I confront him, he'll try to kill himself for the 3e time.
A friend of mine suggested to wait till he can think a bit straight which is a bit happening now as i can see on FB - but then again his stubbornness will keep on winding his brains out of control... (he's off drugs since October - but getting better - I don't think so - he does not remember a thing
and so his mom takes advantage of this situation, of him as well to tell him many lies -----) He's making me sick talking about truth & ignorance all the time on social media while he is exactly the opposite which makes it pretty clear why he has one social media for his parents and and one social media account to show the true self.
HALLELUJAH!
We are either truth or not, both ways always blows the mind into the lesser street meets. If he is not awakening to what his parents are doing to him,
i will get into the justice department U know, standing alone is the hardest part in all this. I'm sorry to bother u with these unhappy memes
But thank u for listening, it eases the pain a little
I've been Damaged too deep as well from childhood on
Maybe I'd like to try to decipher the DMT
5/28, 9:57pm **Koz Kozmos**
u did'nt offend me
i feel down trodden
my damage goes deep
5/28, 10:01pm **Pre View**
same here, many things remain invisible
everything is just coming up like a diagnose from the universe
We need to move within planets
5/28, 10:02pm **Koz Kozmos**
MUSIC: Robin Williamson - Flower Of The Briar

5/28, 10:02pm **Koz Kozmos**
sleep well
5/28, 10:02pm **Pre View**
I don't know the guy in the pic, its just a pic
5/28, 10:02pm **Koz Kozmos**
good night
5/28, 10:02pm **Pre View**
good night
5/28, 10:11pm **Pre View**
The song reminds me of Robby - an Irish guy- who runs a bar over here,
5/28, 10:19pm **Koz Kozmos**
its a song from the land of the summer stars, the place i'm originally from no Irish bars there, but it does sound folkie
5/28, 10:20pm **Koz Kozmos**
nor am i , all the best
5/28, 10:21pm **Pre View** best both get some sleep -
May 29, 2013
5/29, 8:40am **Pre View**
Koz, I like your posts , but i'm over thinking : getting into the core level of what is happening might only take a few seeds to gather and create some protection level in the hood.
Wot I mean is there is a way to revolutionize brains & activate clearing out for the benefit of all. Yet I feel, there is so much work to be done; it would be better to first awaken people
to a new level of understanding before they can act out
and make their lives interesting.

When understanding fails, everything fails,
because the hunger for knowledge and evolvement comes from understanding and integrating light degrees that bring change through.
I sometimes wish i could have a long long talk and walk with u
which would be better than all we chatted about ;
I'd love to talk about the creation of programs and put brains together.... coz without getting deep into all problematic static, nuthing will happen.
This is reason why i asked u if u'd be interested to educate me meaning I have a feel that exchanging wot we've learned and merging it
would bring manny outcomes ....
Teaming up and creating is gonna bring solutions through,
We cannot do it alone anymore,
5/29, 9:04am **Pre View**
On the other hand one needs to be cleared
& healed from all the wounds of the past first
in order toactivate anything and stand real strong,,,

5/29, 12:42pm **Pre View**
Are you still alive ?
Earthquake, Magnitude 5.5 - WALES, UNITED KINGDOM - 2013 May 29,

Is this happening?
5/29, 2:49pm **Koz Kozmos**
no i'm dead , if u want a long chat hows your numerological jokes going?
i want to heal all wounds etc , merge
5/29, 2:55pm Koz Kozmos
MUSIC: VAN McCOY - the hustle (1975) (HQ)

5/29, 2:57pm **Koz Kozmos**
and heal the new wounds etc
5/29, 3:25pm **Pre View**
sure, go ahead what do you mean by numerological jokes ?
5/29, 3:54pm **Pre View**
superb song, gonna dance my day thr the sixties and on on on
long time since i did the twist
I love to be at many locations at the same time
Not just bi-location, I want to learn echo-location
Its an idea to merge with the physics of the Earth
Like we don't see the moon in day time, but it is there
5/29, 7:22pm **Pre View**
MUSIC: GORAN BREGOVIC - Czardsz (Ashik Cygan)

5/29, 8:48pm **Koz Kozmos**
666 the number of the beast and the masonic on a Goran bit of silent cinema violin and an awfull backing track
5/29, 8:57pm **Koz Kozmos**
but thank u, just my rock analysis out of the zone
5/29, 10:35pm **Pre View**
Whom am I to say anything,
5/29, 10:50pm **Pre View**
I've got many ships, but i did not expect them to leave my Haven or Heaven all at once
They are all beautiful without complications for they ar original
5/30, 12:15pm **Koz Kozmos**
? wot are u talking about , so what are your plans ?

JUNE 2013

6/1, 10:22am Pre View
Exactly wot I needed, grace.
Thank u, I will be able to feed myself now.
Thank u for understanding i needed to cut all outward reflections for a few days.
6/1, 10:25am Pre View
Telepathic NRG has been loaded strong between us - so all questions are answered - to open telescopic NRG
But U do know i keep u close anyways,
The Boss meeting The Boss is coming around when the Wizzard (me) is ready to meet the Genius(U) :
A wizzard never gets bossy, only tells it like it is breaking any rule but balancing with humble forces/ sources.
6/1, 10:29am Pre View
Wot are ur transmitters exchanging about this, do u know this ? Would this not destroy the myelin sheath
that covers axons ? Article from the google machinery:
Inside Mind-Tripping, Soul-Changing,
Ground- Shifting, 21st Century Psychedelic Therapy
6/1, 10:29am Pre View
Wot does Humility mean to U ?
6/1, 12:46pm Koz Kozmos
I'm the WIZGEN
the bossy description is more of a joke, u never use the command voice used by and on the matrix slaves, the hylic's and the countrolers of the soul
my tranz mitters have been damaged
6/1, 12:55pm Koz Kozmos
is my myelin sheath damaged ?
Humanity at this time has many soul species carried in the dirt bag
the high gene's , the halflings, the walk ins and the souless ones etc...
i don't like humans , we are not fallen we where pushed
death to the clay born clowns
not read info of the article, tried
hope u're groovey
6/1, 1:10pm Koz Kozmos
I'm maninly confused , but not asleep

MUSIC: Mad Child - Rebirth of the Warlord

6/1, 1:12pm Koz Kozmos
MUSIC: "Saucy Sailor" - Steeleye Span {AUDIO}

6/1, 1:30pm Koz Kozmos
Man sprays no weeds
The scythe cuts, the corn bleeds
Leverets trapped in a harvest blade
'Tis the time of man, the hare said Here's the tractor, here's the plough And where shall we go now
We'll lie in forms as still as the dead
In the open fields, the hare said No cover but the camouflage From the winter's wild and bitter rage
All our defence is in our legs
We run like the wind, the hare said I've been cursed, I've been despised As a witch with darkest powers
I shall goe until a hare

I've been hunted trapped and punished In these my darkest hours
Wi' sorrow and such mickle care I've been thrown into the fire But I do not fear it
I shall goe until a hare
It purifies and resurrects
And I can bear it
Wi' sorrow and such mickle care I've outrun dogs and foxes And I've dodged the tractor wheels
I shall goe until a hare
I've survived your persecution
And your ever-changing fields
Wi' sorrow and such mickle care I will run and run forever
Where the wild fields are mine
I shall goe until a hare
I'm a symbol of endurance
Running through the mists of time
Wi' sorrow and such mickle care

6/1, 1:30pm **Koz Kozmos**
part of the lyric
June 1, 2013
6/1, 6:46pm **Pre View**
You can heal your myelin, yes, once u decide to set up a foundation out of the solar
There's a reason why we're here at this particular time, of course
Sure, its time to get groovy
Confusion comes from dirty gridzzzz,
THE SOUL PROMOTIONS GET PEOPLE CONFUSED,
beyond that are the clear spaces that have clear directions
Clear EGO/Soul CS and you have it all
OK i will listen & close eyes for a sec, time to relax,,,
6/1, 7:03pm **Pre View**
Soucy sailor - hard to understand the song,
i 'll listen again, maybe time for me to reflect on why and what u post ,,,
The Fabled hare seems to be u, these are strong lyrics
6/1, 7:18pm **Pre View** Why did u hope me to be groovy ?
6/1, 8:48pm **Koz Kozmos**
groovy means excellent
set up a foundation ? I've no idea 'why we're here and don't like it What are the grids?
6/1, 8:58pm **Koz Kozmos**
Read the advertisement before the song
6/1, 9:03pm **Koz Kozmos**
how do I clean my grids?
6/1, 9:09pm **Koz Kozmos**
U need to learn to speak british folk rock
6/1, 9:09pm **Pre View**
Aha, seems interesting ,,,, british folk rock
Gridzzz NEED A SET UP FIRST!
dammit,, cleanse , strengthening, understanding,
Have a good look at your behaviour
and the behaviour within nature huh
6/1, 9:12pm **Koz Kozmos**
how ? what do I do ?
u said dirty gids

6/1, 9:13pm **Pre View**
Alignments, foundational set ups out of soul breathing
Going back in time, start to remember what a grid is, how creation was set up
6/1, 9:13pm **Koz Kozmos**
ok , how ? may i ask
6/1, 9:14pm **Pre View**
With "dirty" I mean to say that you are living the silvery of the matrix.
As long as you don't remove that and move into the crystalline grids that do not allow invasions, you'll feel the confusion
Its all part off wot we talked about ,,,
Moving into Light and allow your light to HOLD CRYSTAL GRIDS is what matters to kill troublesome life
6/1, 9:14pm **Koz Kozmos**
pratical applications please
if u can on FB , what did we talk about?
6/1, 9:15pm **Pre View**
impossible – I'm not going through that again ,
3 days of explanation?
wanna get me completely ironic, or insane huh? Go down the lakes and talk to them will ye! 6/1, 9:15pm **Koz Kozmos**
but why again please ?
don' t i have any clue
i can't type exscuse messy typing
6/1, 9:15pm **Pre View**
don't you worry, i get ur vibes
6/1, 9:16pm **Koz Kozmos**
why don't I have any grids?
a basic answer please
and if i don't have any what does that mean for me?
6/1, 9:17pm **Pre View**
u don't have any coz u simply did not set the Grid up through meditational alignment and the crystalsthat come with it,
after that you can breathe integrations thr
A MATRIX is a grid based on the drowning of the soul, the Crystalline Grids squeezes that down 6/1, 9:17pm **Koz Kozmos**
i said I don't know what Grids are
6/1, 9:17pm **Pre View**
What is a grid to u ? What does it mean to you, look it up on google
Go to the disco and enjoy Laser Lights, it will help u understand,,
I'll try find some pics,
6/1, 9:17pm **Koz Kozmos**
so how can I answer with some thing solid
6/1, 9:18pm **Pre View**
ok, there's your answer : not loading through,
breathing through, anchoring, becoming a crystalline
construction keeps u into soul stufffffff
6/1, 9:18pm **Koz Kozmos**
i'm lost
6/1, 9:18pm **Koz Kozmos**
what do u mean by: this keeps u into soul stufffffff
6/1, 9:19pm **Pre View**
wait there is a paint i did with a grid on, it hang on, be back

6/1, 9:19pm **Koz Kozmos**
ok what sort of grids there are many
6/1, 9:20pm **Koz Kozmos**
The Grid, an electronic dance group
Kevorkian Death Cycle, a music group formerly called Grid
The Grid (arcade game), a 2001 third person shooter
The Grid (TV series) from 2004
The Grid (US TV series), an American TV series
Mobil 1 The Grid, a motorsport magazine TV show
"The Grid" (The Outer Limits), an episode of the science fiction series
Grid (album), the eighth original album by the Japanese band m.o.v.e.
Race Driver: Grid, a racing video game
Spooks 3 Games - The Grid, video game based on the television show Spooks
The grid, the virtual environment of the game Second Life
IEEE Grid, a monthly publication of the Institute of Electrical and Electronics Engineers The Grid, the computerized virtual world in which the Tron franchise exists. The Grid (newspaper), an alternative weekly newspaper in Toronto, Ontario
Science and technology Electrical grid, a network for delivering electricity
Grid computing, the application of a network of computers to a single problem
Control grid, an electrode to control electrons in vacuum tubes
Screen grid, a grid used in vacuum tubes to reduce capacitance
Suppressor grid, a grid used in vacuum tubes to suppress secondary emission
GRiD Systems Corporation, founded in 1979, developer of range of laptops
Grid Compass, the first laptop computer released in 1982
Lattice graph or "grid graph", a graph formed from a regular lattice of vertices
ESRI grid file format for geographic information systems
GRID1, GRID2, human genes; Glutamate receptor, ionotropic delta
6/1, 9:20pm **Koz Kozmos**
pick a grid
6/1, 9:21pm **Pre View**
Haha, they are all interesting:
study these commentary landscapes:
Lattice graph or "grid graph", a graph formed from a regular (Crystalline)lattice of vertices
ESRI grid file format for geographic information systems (underground grids)
GRID1, GRID2, human genes; Glutamate receptor,
inotropic delta (every single organ in the body is a grid, although crystalline).
6/1, 9:21pm **Koz Kozmos**
I understand the word grid in its many forms and have an inkling of what u mean
6/1, 9:21pm **Pre View**
anything can be a grid, as long as it is geometrics
perfect designed models like the Platonic solids that can take on any form, so their FORMS can change and adapt to the CS infused in a particular grid.
Likewise, when we shift our brainwaves from the low fatal degrees into higher mentality, Grids upgrade as ell into new Light configurations.
6/1, 9:21pm **Koz Kozmos**
but.............
6/1, 9:22pm **Pre View**
but yes u need to align, be able to align and have the knowledge of how to set them up to be able to breathe fire like a dragon, expand on them,
get ur own grids down and on ,
because they will supply you with your individual info or data necessary to move out the soul control boxes,
but also to further the
human race out of soul ...
And so much more.

MY INTERNALS:
This was The Artwork I sent "The New Soul Acquisition"
And of course looks so much better with the right colors.
Just bringing this through to show a grid, as that can be anything.
Anyways, by the time I posted this, I was very tired of explaining because the explanation of how to set up a grid, integrate at least a home base station and get the necessary work done in the body for it to hold the grid and make it stronger every day would be better done through a seminar.
We are 2020 now and it even exhausts me to see how much patience I had back then.
These days, I did make a video about the Crystalline Grid construction and also put on many online courses to set that up because it matters so much to Creation, the human kingdom, the elements, the animal kingdom. It teaches us about unification and the Ancient ways of LIFE. But back then, I was just understanding Grid constructions myself. Today however, it is a lifestyle from the origin on in which we can all detail our life, our creations, our success, what we would like to achieve and so much more. I was never educated in the field of the arts, yet from one day into the other it just started to flow through my hands, just like magic, because Grids are Magical!
It is such a high level memory that comes through along individual codes and symbolism to bring your LIFE STREAMS back into fluid light compositions.

MY INTERNALS: ABOUT THE CRYSTALLINE GRIDS I was not able to give Koz back then in 2013, because I needed time myself to get down to all the information. However, I did know all about how to set it up and GROW with it through the seminars I was giving,Here is the information and a better understanding:

The Crystalline Light Earth Grid links all of the crystals in the Earth and crosses major portals, vortexes and dimensional doorways that connect the Earth to cosmic forces/sources and other dimensional worlds. It is through this grid that the New Light Earth CONSCIOUSNESS PARADIGM is being anchored and reason for the many shifts in the brain, the body; such as the bone structure and diets shifting a lot these days because the human body cannot withstand the old energies any longer.
The old brain and body connected to ego has energy centers called chakras, organs, muscles, bones, infrastructure all inter communicating with the nervous system, veins, arteries .... It was easy for the chakras to be influenced by exterior stimuli and they would need frequent realignments, or recalibration to avoid diseases from filtering in, vulnerabilities, implants ,hybrids and other things that create blocks and imprison the light/intelligence/data from entering the body! Divinity is Stardom and connections that come through the installments of Ley Lines and Grid formatting.

The shifts that are occurring now is because of the "demand" to clear the body out and supply it with the proper elements needed for this time . The best way however to do it is through anchoring this Home Base light Earth Grid SOLID to ASSISTS THE BODYS' TRANSMUTATION from being a dense metal to being liquid light. Liquid light does not carry disease. Once this HOME BASE STATION has been set up, there is no end to what it can do : it assists the healing out of the density, it clears all negativity, mass control and manipulations going on. The GRID will travel with you every where you go, all you need to do is pull it up through a dense situation such as in schools, police, injustices being done, violence, etc or anything you encounter during the day and then hold it and/or simply move clearing energies through which is just a learning zone. Anyone can breathe in Light frequencies and blow that through the controlling machines for example. Those interested in willing to anchor and hold this Basic Home Base Grid are highly recommended to teach it to others as well. On the other hand as we are massively balancing out the old and gathering so many things for health and educational new Light Earth services.
The largest imbalance on the earth however, seems to be he male/female essences that have gone completely out of control and people living in relationships that were never meant to be as well as education, natural health and the eco system. With it came child trafficking, child abuse, the destruction of the eco system, and the total loss of sacred sexuality as a humble being.
The heart has been crushed over and over again resulting into many frequencies that promote love as a machinery not inherent to the sacredness of being . Otherwise there would not be so much noise about fear, guilt, shame and the movement of women into equal grounds of many measures. The Pulsation of Light Grids can open the hearts' alignment back to the pulse of the Light House termed Shambhalla. Yet, some deep alignment into Celestial Living grounds is required to hold that level of integrity that enables us to communicate on a clear level with all Species on the other side of midnight, when grounded well in Grid configuration or the purity of Cryst lights equalizing Cryst (Crystalline Grids).

EVERYTHING COMES DOWN TO THE LADY/GENT BROKEN VEINS.
The root of the problem with any relationship comes from ego first, than parents, then society and all of our ASSOCIATIONS .....It may matter a lot to clear out attachments from former intimate relationships and other as they stick like a ticker tape on sexual glands and hormonal glands. Also, even when having intimacy through imagination,
IT STICKS on the entire system, so be careful with that. The most intense and deepest clearing this time around is all about getting into the unseen stuck patterns that were held back from us .
Today as we are lifting the veil of almost anything; it is really all about getting into the root of any relationship and its ASSOCIATIONS such a people, food addictions, job insecurities, and essentially OUR RELATIONSHIP WITH THE COSMOS because that defines whether you live a life full of beauty or a life addicted to insecurities.

**And of course the male/female aspects can only balance when releasing stuck essences. THE OLD WAY OF CONNECTING HAS LOST ITS VALUE ANYWAYS. One who is hungry for love is ESSENTIALLY hungry for Light.
Power control from outside forces but also ego related issues such as arrogance, unworthiness, deeper levels such as the sexual Lady/gent industries running these days have hardly anything to do with love and make one fall apart even more then ever before in history.**

**The heart of the problem is always returning to the level of EQUALITY and running that wave into a wild card of mutual respect, integrity and humility for that would give one a clear VIEW of what went wrong in SELF first and understanding it from that vintage point instead of EXPECTING anything from anyone and sink into many levels of CONVENIENCE.
It seems to be the hardest struggle ever witnessed on earth and reason why so many people stay in relationships that are no longer beneficial on any level which BREAKS the body and moving forward massively or people always returning to that same relationship and not SEEING their way out.Clearing and elimination procedures with Light firmly installed in the grids and into the Human body assists the evacuation of bacteria, obsessions and misalignment that run the hormonal system.**

**There is a central shaft running from the crown opening at the top of the head, down the spine to the opening at the bottom of the energy centers at the perineum which will opened when anchoring to the Earths' Light Grid which is a necessity for the flow of Light through the spinal column.
It will also open all 12 universal gates as connected to its particular Light consciousness in your energy wheels or chakras; which when practicing becomes a beam of multi dimensional Light.It is all a matter of dedication and devotion.
The Light Grids allow for unification with our environment as our beam of light in the grid will transmit and receive pure life Source/forces which makes you feel firmly grounded. In this model, bodies can no longer be controlled by implants, chemical mind control, or other means, as in the past which is quite a relief.**

Every point on the grid, that which now acupuncturists access with needles, is an energy exchange point, or A FORM OF COMMUNICATION/INFORMATION/ DATA. As the light forces and sources pulsate through these points of entry, healing comes through easily and means BEING IN THAT LIGHT EARTH GRID AND KEEPING UP WITH THAT FLOW in harmony with everything else.

**In other words , giving you a much easier time to release what needs to go and move on with life on a quite different pace as the grid has the capacity to open any wavelength, such as the telepathic waves, scaler waves, sound waves ...
There is no end to what the grid teaches you as information comes through wording, music, other codes such as numbers , designs, geometries ....
We remember our multi-dimensional selves and higher purpose for being here on Earth. We open up our consciousness and expand our awareness, having inner visions, telepathic connection, awareness of other dimensions and worlds, and clear perception of the energies we are working with or are moving towards. Everything depends on your level of Light anchoring, cultivating and understanding its work orders and information.
NO MORE AIRY FAIRY dreamworlds ! but working consciously with the cosmos, receiving data and its application !**

**EVERYBODY CAN DO THIS SET UP no matter if you are used to working with light or not as the alignments given will be enough to open and remember light. Grids are set around the world and carry portals of LITE POWER PLANTS that continue to grow through crystalline planted seeds or the human body.It is truly so very enjoyable to work with Grids and hold a Grid for a certain capacity.
It is Ancient Technology that has so much modernized that it needs the wild rebel to bring through the fruits of this immense interesting universe.
Today Crystalline Light Grids are easily understood, it just needs some set up work in the home and then just work with it and let the magic come through.**

6/1, 9:23pm **Koz Kozmos**
i like u'r art ,,,its groovey but explains nothing
6/1, 9:23pm **Pre View**
Thank u, my art exists because of the grids,
my time in meditation through the grids brings this art
through, it is information.
6/1, 9:24pm **Koz Kozmos**
so i do have grids GOSH!
6/1, 9:24pm **Pre View**
when integrated , it will explain itself
6/1, 9:24pm **Koz Kozmos**
i can't wait another day
i'm sick of waiting and being here made to feel like a moron by so called spiritual
teachers speeaking gobble de gook ,,,for....when its intergrated
6/1, 9:26pm **Pre View** Hey, you're not a moron,
It takes hard work, and it moves me every day, gives me new info .... Whom do u
refer to so called ...
6/1, 9:27pm **Koz Kozmos**
I know i'm not a moron , but i can be a bit of an idiot
i've worked hard
6/1, 9:28pm **Koz Kozmos**
so called alll spituel teachers: cosmic posers
6/1, 9:28pm **Pre View**
Yes, i worked too, very hard
Did not understand wot i was doing in the earlier days with the LIGHT GRID
APPLICATIONS, but it changed me overnight.
And so the proof the Grids gave me, made me understand them better because for
whatever you put into them – it always has a response mechanism in society.
Its like working through some architecture or a home in which you plant things and
work with these things.
It is only since a few months i'm beginning to understand and picking it all up
But I've heard from many others, they did not understand the Light movement in the
Crystal Grids either. That took years of training until that light substance is being felt
in the body with the appropriate Light technology.
So we perceive the world in a different way, reason why people try to reach that world
through psychedelics which is but a fake world for it is all within us
We have all high concentrations of perceptions, sort of reorganizing the brain
6/1, 9:29pm **Koz Kozmos**
i'm getting bored with this
6/1, 9:29pm **Pre View**
then leave it for wot its worth
So get your ass pumping some knowledge; there are many paths to the Divine, yet
none as straight and easy as through the Crystallization of the body
through the GRIDZZZZ, HAHA
6/1, 9:32pm **Koz Kozmos**
every thing makes me bored
i have worked on myself selves, explored many spiritual traditions
6/1, 9:33pm **Pre View** t
that maybe reason why u have a big problem ... How do u work on yourself ?
If u understand how a childs' brain work u understand a lot
6/1, 9:33pm **Koz Kozmos**
done rituel majik
i have deprogramed myself ,
so this dimension is of no use to me for the last 20 years i have aknowleged my
sorrow
i can;t speak any more , this feels useless
u have a big problem!!!!!!!!!!!!!!!!!!!!!!!

6/1, 9:36pm **Pre View**
I don't know anything about rituals, i'v only been taught the hard way
Deprogramming is one thing, Reprogramming is where it gets interesting, gets u out the downgrading dimensions (we've been over that)
U sound vague, go back into yur childhood state
It is no use talking over this on FB It would be the same as if I asked u to tell me all u do with the hard work to get some understanding
6/1, 9:36pm **Koz Kozmos**
say one thing that has any credence to me
yes, i am being vague
i can't put it into words but if u can say one thing that has credence to me
i will be able to continue
6/1, 9:40pm **Pre View**
Ok, I breath and vibrate with many grids, this takes lots of understanding & clearing the molecular
structure up into the new tree of life and needs new UNDERSTANDING EVERY DAY : meaning no OLD INFO or ways of living can stay alive in the body. Then you move into higher vibrations. It is that the Grids offer assistance in the clearing processes starting of with the refinements in your breathing system because when the breathing opens up many miles around the energy field it means you can hold light in many circumferences and CIRCUMSTANCES. Breathe the SUN, haha
The Grids assist you to expand and hold your light brightness
6/1, 9:42pm **Koz Kozmos**
When a pickpocket sees a saint,
all he sees are his pockets that was no good
6/1, 9:42pm **Pre View**
The brain is like an ECOSYSTEM, that breaks down who we are and be communicative
with a larger field and interpret that
The interesting part with u is that u (maybe) have had a lot of teachings which i did not, i feel rather like an alien with my info but it does change people immediately, and that is what matters I think So picking up some of your parts and pulling them into the jeans we wear today is wot i do .
You need to trust me.
6/1, 9:44pm **Koz Kozmos**
i have not been to school or university
6/1, 9:44pm **Pre View**
neither have i , there is no education
it has been set up to dumb the brains for whatever remains in them.
6/1, 9:45pm **Koz Kozmos**
i have found most of my attempts at self education odious
6/1, 9:45pm **Pre View**
its all in the membranes
Wot interests u most?
6/1, 9:45pm **Koz Kozmos**
esacpe
6/1, 9:45pm **Pre View**
Hey, are you aware there is none ?
6/1, 9:46pm **Koz Kozmos**
NO! JAILBREAK SAMSARA
6/1, 9:46pm **Pre View**
other spaces only make it worse, u need to deal with what is going on.
Many stars already gave up, Earth is not allowed to fail in ascension!
6/1, 9:46pm **Koz Kozmos**
i am the low key for the high door
i do deal with stuff, and its shit

6/1, 9:46pm **Pre View**
The other way around !
6/1, 9:46pm **Koz Kozmos**
? i'm getting lost again , i can't understand u
6/1, 9:47pm **Pre View** THE KEY for low doors
6/1, 9:47pm **Koz Kozmos**
beyond u 'r over used theories; low key for the high door, maybe a pun on loki
6/1, 9:47pm **Pre View**
I'm not giving u theories,
its pure practice
I'm getting a drink , a feel like a little drink
6/1, 9:48pm **Koz Kozmos**
the trickster spirits with me illuminating shadows unseen telling the truth with lies
not fooled in the school of the wise
how is it pure pratice
6/1, 9:49pm **Koz Kozmos**
Ok, I breath and vibrate with many grids and ask the universe:
WHERE DO WE GO NOW, hahaha
6/1, 9:49pm **Koz Kozmos**
how is this pure practice, its bullshit
6/1, 9:50pm **Pre View**
Behave will you ! I"ll give you a pure and simple example
6/1, 9:51pm **Koz Kozmos**
u may think u have but u have not
u behave !
i've heared all this before, its delusional and badly explained or i am a moron, u chose?
6/1, 9:54pm **Pre View**
EG : I breath the energies of Mars into root, Cassiopeia or get the solar planets into my energy wheels :
This gives me a mathematical spiral up into 6th dimension or so,
then i get info or answers to questions i have.
These answers I integrate and then i see wot the outcome is.
This goes on and on
This is just an example of alignments.
Alignments mean you integrate the consciousness with which you work
6/1, 9:55pm **Pre View**
It is just practice with technology we have in the universe and discover much more like scientists do. It gives majic answers, and makes you talk on many more interesting levels, the WORD within changes because the mentality and intel moves in higher degrees.
So you basically cut the crap wording out which is interesting and keeps you going.
It is actually all about RE-DISCOVERING SELF.
6/1, 9:56pm **Koz Kozmos**
that means nothing to me
6/1, 9:57pm **Pre View**
Why ? = u don't feel the vibration?
That is reason why you essentially need some foundation anchoring in the body that teaches you how to work with the energies in the universe
which then again makes you understand grid technology and assists the communication with many species.
Reason why a basic Foundational set up seminar in LIGHT TECHNOLOGY is needed somehow.
A starters' kit so to speak.
U just deceive self and all mechanisms within
New experiences may get u out of old majic and these optical illusions which u though was spiritual embodiment
Networks have changes and thus also the brains' networks

6/1, 9:57pm **Koz Kozmos**
a moron then
6/1, 9:57pm **Pre View**
U need to feel the humming of a planet,
otherwise u have nothing, and then work with many more
planets and galaxies. Just open yer EYE and when you see , you see, hopefully not the astral debris. You understand that you are a star, a spark, so claim your IDENTITY back in,
and start thinking about how to do this.
Ask for Divine Assistance, you seem to be hearing high Herz
As the universe for a brain Scan! That ay help as well to see yur own networks
It is all about reconstructing Light body which may be different in every country;
yet Direct Connect toSourcing your own energies is most important.
6/1, 9:57pm **Koz Kozmos**
i'm not getting any wisdom from u;
I HAVE NOTHING blame the victim, cosmic abuse
6/1, 9:58pm **Pre View**
If u have nothing, get something
Get clear : do u feel anything when you breathe or not ?
Breathe certain energies through?
6/1, 9:58pm **Koz Kozmos**
no , how do i get clear ?
when i breath i feel lots of things
if i hold my breath its the same
why do u have something and me nothing ?
why am i cast on the toxic heap ?
why are the favorite children of the source killed
6/1, 10:02pm **Pre View**
So how can u move forward then ?????
U have wisdom enough , u miss out on applications which is practice, which needs bottom line clearings u obviously do not know about
please finally tell me how u clear out ?
But ok : please explain wot u feel, give me the info u get when u feel something ?
And please no more toxic , soular conversations
You wanna get out of the matrix , so get out it !
6/1, 10:02pm **Koz Kozmos**
what is practice, wot are bottem line clearings
6/1, 10:02pm **Pre View**
Are u teasing ? or joking ?
6/1, 10:03pm **Koz Kozmos** n
no i don't know , i'm being completly serious how do i clear out
6/1, 10:03pm **Pre View**
You really need to start out working on self !!!
Tell me how u cleared out energies in the past. You did do a lot of work so you told me,
So to me it means you do know about clearing self with light I assume.
6/1, 10:03pm **Koz Kozmos**
what do u mean clear out ?
i feel hatred and discust at the great cosmic game
i feel sick , this is no good, its come to a DEAD end
6/1, 10:05pm **Pre View**
Clear the patterns u were born with,
your entire atomic structure, glandular system, your blood circulation,
just about every cell you have ever known.
Get to understand the word clearing, WILL YOU?
GOOGLE
Start supervising self

6/1, 10:05pm **Koz Kozmos**
but i do like your art !
I have cleared this but i'm still here and so much shit happens u don't get it ,
u have zero insight
u'r just on your hoobby horse
i'm obviously done, i just hope death for me can be permanent
i inted to live till i die
6/1, 10:07pm **Pre View**
Whom are u to tell huh? I told you how my Art came through.
If u have cleared something, did u clear it 20 different ways ? and adjusted it ?
6/1, 10:07pm **Koz Kozmos**
not being a self pitying fool
I'm sick of this pathetic game of clearing and grids and all this bland talk more mystic shit, mystics want to merge with god
6/1, 10:09pm **Pre View**
This universe changes every day, so do we,
so how can u clear out the same way u did maybe years ago,
its daily damn interesting stuff
Becoming the Mystic within is a very high level training
I'm not there yet, but I like my train going there
6/1, 10:10pm **Koz Kozmos**
i intend killing the gods for putting usthru this abusive existence fuck the universe ,
death to the universe
6/1, 10:11pm **Pre View**
The shit u went through is part of pushing u beyond your stubborn understandings
6/1, 10:11pm **Koz Kozmos**
who put me thru it? its abuse
and don't say me becuz i did not choose this
6/1, 10:12pm **Pre View**
Up to u to stop this, its reason why we are on the planet.
To bring the fusion with the elestials, celestials and universal beings
Don't ask how, told u you need a foundation to work with.
6/1, 10:12pm **Koz Kozmos**
its not up to me
i've tried, blame the victem agian
6/1, 10:14pm **Pre View**
I admire your brain, your guts, but the input doesn't equal the output
Don't tell me u tried , there is only doing it ,
being persistent, think it through and get the job done
no victim consciousness allowed
because that would hold you in the lower fields that love to eat you alive
as you have experienced
6/1, 10:15pm **Koz Kozmos**
you're so predictable
its not victim consciousness,
there are victims of the cosmic lie death to the earth and the universe
your so called esoteric knowledge is limited and confused
and delusional i have tried and continue to try
u blocked my point again, the in pipe should work with the out pipe
6/1, 10:16pm **Pre View**
I remember the spirit worlds and it brings many tears when connecting
Because the heart connects so deep
I cannot possibly describe that
One cannot have that experience in a state of depression
U need to connect with and integrate your own medicine, the element that u are

6/1, 10:21pm **Pre View**
Do not ever think i have an easy time to get through this, i truly wish i had some one over here who would help me understand the things I do, I miss out on many things as well, but we all need to move out
of blaming and self destruction.
People are damn lazy when it comes to working and research within self,
The laziness comes from the Soul Diet that never gives any extra's, it only subtracts everything until you
cannot eat anymore, haha because the food becomes too toxic. Could you have some laughter somehow?
6/1, 10:21pm **Koz Kozmos**
same here, i'm frustrated and angry
u came out with all this stuff and say i'm not wise enuff
tell me i'm caught up in victem consciousness
tel me i need to work harder so u get something back
6/1, 10:25pm **Pre View**
everybody is, not accepting it any longer and fitting it may take some brain pulsations,
Work harder = u told me u didn't do anything any longer so ..
6/1, 10:26pm **Koz Kozmos**
yes i did, i need a rest
6/1, 10:27pm **Pre View**
Goodbey, unifications comes after the unification with your Source first,
Then children and youth, then adults, then the world
Phenomena plays out differently in many parts in the world
6/1, 10:27pm **Koz Kozmos**
fuck work , i'm sick of this place of sickness the dignity of labour is a hoax
I wish you the best "
Mythos is affective, esoteric, and numinous.
That is, it inspires, it provokes, it motivates, enthrals, and presences a causal energy.
It is wyrdful – a means of change for human beings, and outlines or intimates how such wyrdful change can be brought-into-being.
6/1, 10:39pm **Koz Kozmos**
I'm sick of being told it's all for my own good
by every pot guru with a few theories
how were u brought up may i ask ?
Why does it have to be complicated and obscure?
How much stuff do you have to do before you awake?
Is there a limit to it? Or do you have to keep doing one more process?
6/1, 11:13pm **Pre View**
I told u , I prefer to be a complete moron when it comes to guru and theories because i did never read or heard anyone speak or went to anyone to listen too and it might get me curious, but then again i have no attraction at all.
I am the Queen of my own movie series, haha
Ever since I was 6 years old, people told me i was strange, but never told me why , so ?
I was brought up with no education at all, my parents did not care about me, my mom too stupid, my dad used and abused me, so i left home when I was 14, did finish high school.
My dad kept on abusing & using me, i was a fool, did not see it, felt it, i was fighting against it but too weak,.... 20 years ago he stole 35 thousand euros.
I brought this into a court case as we are speaking now with several other people, only i have no proof.... then again we won, but i need proof to get my money back.
This whole abuse made my life go down in many ways because there was never enough money to cover the damage. The more i deal with all that happened to me, the more good things come in,...
Still, manifesting is hard work and i am jumping up and down and see the difference.

I do not listen to anybody, just try things out myself and if thy work , that is a good way to move forward into the spiritual design center?
So what works from what I understand is to continuously keep on processing further with the information U GET -
NOT FROM ANYONE ELSE.
And yes, u need a wide open channel and many guts,
thats why i'm a loner, but now i think timing has come to unify brains in order to move faster.... And break down old thoughts
Nothing really is complicated or obscure, we make it that way i think
And no! always go unlimited, processing deeper and deeper
But instead of asking me, please teach me
6/1, 11:24pm **Pre View**
Wot did u teach urself ? Who hurt u so badly ?
I wish I were a cowboy, living through the desserts or the woods, with no care in the world Did u get my messages ?
I'm getting failed to send all the time, s
o we might miss out lines, anyways,
6/1, 11:29pm **Koz Kozmos**
yes , your the tin pot guru pissing in the universe
6/1, 11:32pm **Pre View**
i am robin hood, not a guru I'm only polishing arrows, not pissing anywhere
I'm Lady, do you get that?
6/1, 11:33pm **Koz Kozmos**
my upbringing was terrible , so fuck the lessons
6/1, 11:33pm **Pre View**
finally
6/1, 11:33pm **Koz Kozmos**
but i went back and healed as much as i could ,
i was running away at 11
6/1, 11:34pm **Pre View** w
ot's the outcome at 11 ?
6/1, 11:34pm **Koz Kozmos**
and was brought up in the Jehovah witness
6/1, 11:34pm **Pre View**
WOT THE HELL ,,????
You're not joking are you?
6/1, 11:34pm **Koz Kozmos** t
o belivee the world was going to end in 1975
but these grids are cleaned
6/1, 11:35pm **Pre View**
hope so, how did u cope with this?
Haha, finally joking about grids huh,
6/1, 11:35pm **Koz Kozmos**
u have zero intuition , i am telling u the truth
6/1, 11:35pm **Pre View** your judgment sucks
6/1, 11:35pm **Koz Kozmos**
i always have and i'm honest with u about wot u say,
and take the stance of humility
6/1, 11:36pm **Pre View**
really, tell me all about your truth, might be a good lesson for me to remember
6/1, 11:36pm **Koz Kozmos**
why does my judgment suck
6/1, 11:36pm **Pre View**
because its judgement, not observatory laboratory to leave room for some new life streams

6/1, 11:38pm **Koz Kozmos**
your opinion u just said tell me the truth when i was sharing very deep stuff with u and i do tell the truth
6/1, 11:39pm **Pre View**
right, why is my intuition zero when i do have proof 24/24
6/1, 11:39pm **Koz Kozmos**
look above
6/1, 11:39pm **Pre View**
Ok, i accept, i'll review myself, thank u Above ?
6/1, 11:40pm **Koz Kozmos**
the bit of typ above
6/1, 11:40pm **Pre View** about ?
6/1, 11:40pm **Koz Kozmos**
u are a fucktard i agree , i like u nicola
6/1, 11:41pm **Pre View**
ok, i told u that many times, only u pushed me to a degree i had to put it that way
6/1, 11:41pm **Koz Kozmos**
i was the strange boy , u were the strange girl
are know the Freakzoid Wyrdus
but your cosmic tech is dodgy
6/1, 11:42pm **Pre View**
Freakzoid Wyrdus, very refined indeed
6/1, 11:42pm **Koz Kozmos**
i'm being honest with u
6/1, 11:43pm **Pre View**
Dodgey in french please, or german
Be more honest,
6/1, 11:44pm **Koz Kozmos**
dodgy : 1. Evasive; shifty.2. Unsound, unstable, and unreliable.3. So risky as to require very deft handling. i can't be , i'm the prince of lies and thats the truth some things are complicated and obscure , u said they are not i'm a loner because there is no one i want to spend time with
6/1, 11:48pm **Pre View**
I don't care any longer, who am i to give u what i do, find it yourself,
or maybe find someone easier to educate you,
it was not my intention to teach u anything, and then again why should i if its not wot u want U wouldn't dare to lie
6/1, 11:48pm **Koz Kozmos**
i've been hurt by everybody, my wound has not healed and it keeps getting kicked , but i am getting stronger
Some one easy? u are a patronizing turtle
6/1, 11:49pm **Pre View**
Nonono I'm not a turtle, find yourself!
6/1, 11:49pm **Koz Kozmos**
i have no education, i am telling u :
if u don't want to teach stop teaching
6/1, 11:50pm **Pre View**
neither have i, and if u think my tech has no worth ,
that is ok too
why would I care

6/1, 11:50pm **Koz Kozmos**
why are u so worried about me lying what do u think i've lied about ?
i except you, your kool
6/1, 11:51pm **Pre View**
Nono ! u never lied to me,
I only asked u to tell me about your hurt not wise enuff to follow me
6/1, 11:54pm **Koz Kozmos**
its more complex than information, bullshit
6/1, 11:55pm **Pre View**
why, can u not simplify ?
6/1, 11:55pm **Koz Kozmos**
u kidding ? i do
look to yourself , remember i'm deslexic
6/1, 11:55pm **Pre View**
mirrors are broken
6/1, 11:55pm **Koz Kozmos**
numerolgigly ,,, as well and no school
6/1, 11:56pm **Pre View** Numerology ?
6/1, 11:56pm **Koz Kozmos**
witch was a very good thing
with numbers as wel as words, my deslexia effects me, but i like it
6/1, 11:56pm **Pre View**
in wot way?
6/1, 11:57pm **Koz Kozmos**
ONOOOOOOOOOOOOOOOOOOOOOOOOOOOOOOOOOOOOOOOO

i just said : with number as wel as words my deslexia effects me
see above : and u say i'm not wise enuff to follow u
6/1, 11:58pm **Pre View**
Ok,its fun to me, i like it in a very good way !
6/1, 11:58pm **Pre View**
You're ways are wiser , and u do know somehow,,,
6/1, 11:59pm **Koz Kozmos**
i'm a fuckin idiot, i know nuthin
6/1, 11:59pm **Pre View**
Haha, idiots are the wisest, a matter of perspectives
Rigid processes, become a scientist and connect dots
6/1, 11:59pm **Koz Kozmos**
as i've said i'm lost and broken,
the damage that has been done to me is immense
6/2, 12:00am **Pre View**
do u really think i am in a better position?
everybody is damaged somehow, and yes there is degrees and differences
6/2, 12:00am **Koz Kozmos**
no , maybe more , but how dare they expect us to gain knowledge from abuse
6/2, 12:01am **Pre View**
maybe maybe maybe, don't u have a song for me tonight ?
Good question, let me reflect on it
6/2, 12:01am **Koz Kozmos**

MUSIC: Black Dragon - Lyrics (Dissection)

6/2, 12:01am **Koz Kozmos**
read the lyric ,Its below the screen
6/2, 12:02am **Pre View**
ok, a minut pleace
6/2, 12:02am **Koz Kozmos**
ahhh, thier on the screen
6/2, 12:04am **Pre View**
RAISE YOUR SEVEN HEADS AND LET THE ANCIENTS RULE AGAIN
U couldn't have had a better choice,,,
Somehow, all the music you are posting opens another dragon within me,
I love that, how your energy synchronizes somehow
Where did u gain your knowledge , your passion with music
U also need to tell me why my intuition sucks, it breaks my heart, from what is left
6/2, 12:08am **Koz Kozmos**
it was becuz of u'r distrust of what i told u about my chilhood,
thats all, not in all things
i wanted to be an artist song poet ,
but they fucked up my hand and other parts of me and every one
I've worked with turned against me
6/2, 12:10am **Pre View**
U need a lot more diversity and see more patterns in everything
Because no thing is predictable
Look at Youtube and the stardom of predictions
running the same old algorithms all of the time
Meaning people live backwards because they keep on living the same old cycles
i did not distrust, it was not very clear, lets leave it behind.
do u mean medical department or ? (your hand)
6/2, 12:10am **Koz Kozmos**
i had no support , yes medical and other things its been a nighmare
6/2, 12:11am **Pre View**
how is your hand now ?
6/2, 12:11am **Koz Kozmos**
i feel i have been cursed , i can't talk about that but i have given up and have no hope
6/2, 12:11am **Pre View**
please do it now , talk to, communication helps
6/2, 12:11am **Koz Kozmos**
and thats not just due to the hand there is nothing left to do
anyways enuff about me, thank u for asking
6/2, 12:11am **Koz Kozmos**
53 years of shit
6/2, 12:13am **Pre View**
How is this hurt gonna get out of u if u don't talk,
Just Shoot
6/2, 12:13am **Koz Kozmos** its the typing
6/2, 12:13am **Pre View** U've got nothing to loose
6/2, 12:13am **Koz Kozmos**
and i don't really feel i can share, and it upsets me they also fucked up my eyes ,
but its massive soul damnage but i have one of the greatest souls on earth
6/2, 12:14am **Pre View**
why don't u take the time to get it finally out out out
Connect a bit deeper with your sensory data, and plssss, don't ask how
Ask your Spark, your Source,
Somehow u need to understand brain dynamics that run synchrone with who u are

6/2, 12:14am **Koz Kozmos**
i have spoken, but it does no good, the problems remain
6/2, 12:15am **Pre View**
too little , try again (if u want) i don't mean to push u
6/2, 12:15am **Koz Kozmos** t
hank u for asking and showing intrest, too much to type
6/2, 12:16am **Pre View** i
its natural, if u would type it, u would better understand me
writing down and having somebody who listens may assist you to some degree
6/2, 12:16am **Koz Kozmos**
its not my best mode of expresssion
6/2, 12:16am **Pre View**
right, the connect, remember
6/2, 12:16am **Koz Kozmos**
too much to type please lisen to me
6/2, 12:16am **Pre View**
aha, who is the one being obscure ?
Ok I am listening
6/2, 12:17am **Koz Kozmos**
i'm not being obscure, this is absurd and pathetic
6/2, 12:18am **Pre View**
ok, just talk about what you want, voice it out,
i understand
6/2, 12:19am **Koz Kozmos**
i have nothing to say , the damage is done , esacape is my only aim
6/2, 12:20am **Pre View**
U have loads, but maybe u need a little rest out
and hey! i am not pathetic!
6/2, 12:20am **Koz Kozmos**
i have nothing any one wants
6/2, 12:20am **Pre View**
I have found escape is not the answer
6/2, 12:20am **Koz Kozmos**
and i'm glad
maybe u did'nt esacpe , becuz experience has taught me this
6/2, 12:21am **Pre View**
i find escape a difficult word
6/2, 12:21am **Koz Kozmos**
why if i was given everything wod they not let me do anything with it ?
To break loose from confinement; get free: escape from jail.
6/2, 12:22am **Pre View**
I've had it the other way around :
thy killed everything i liked until I found my art through the jail boxes.
6/2, 12:23am **Koz Kozmos**
we are prisoner here on the cursed earth
i had that too, fuck the sickness
i feel u have a lot of worth so maybe it was abuse
6/2, 12:24am **Pre View**
maybe there is a deeper way they are asking from u to get out in the world?
that is annoying questions
Start out something new
Become a Star and break brains about options
And practices of how to get there

6/2, 12:25am **Koz Kozmos**
and not that pathetic psychological model of the victem who are they ?
and how dare they put me thru this ? the sadistic bastards
, i'll take them out if i can
6/2, 12:26am **Pre View**
i give everything to avoid it, or deal with the atrocities, sure bastards
6/2, 12:26am **Koz Kozmos**
u have worth. stop struggling! kick back and destroy wot do u give, and who to ??
6/2, 12:27am **Pre View**
to myself, to keep head above anything that happens,
and i will, I must, so do u
6/2, 12:28am **Koz Kozmos**
has to be done
6/2, 12:28am **Pre View**
I'll never put my rebellion shoes off, I just polish them
6/2, 12:28am **Koz Kozmos**
but i have taken to much damage and dealing with the matrix scum just to say,
I'm vaguely alive , is no good, its made me ill
6/2, 12:30am **Pre View**
It is no good Koz, u need to become that poet artist, u need to fulfill wot u long for,
and sweep the road
clean to walk uncontaminated It is indeed a very road eternally speaking Its like
sitting a sentence without crime
6/2, 12:31am **Koz Kozmos**
u have no idea your niavety is worrying
6/2, 12:31am **Pre View**
How is it affecting your daily life
6/2, 12:32am **Koz Kozmos**
i can longer cope with this reality , with this humanity
i see the sickness , when u say u need to become that poet etc:
do u noe how much work ai've done ? and been ignored ? targetted , traeted like shit
6/2, 12:33am **Pre View**
Wot do u think i fight every single second when i wake up in the early morning,
wot do u think i say to
people even if they just pass me by in the streets –
yet stare at me like to want to steal my energy? I speak about getting fearless,
I talk about how to get the change through
There is too much cognitive dissonanse
6/2, 12:33am **Koz Kozmos**
its too late for that , i fight as well every nano second
best lay low Pre! fit in
the more wyrd i get, the more normal i look
aging helps
6/2, 12:35am **Koz Kozmos**
i LOOK like a fairy not in a gay sense
now i look like a damaged meat bag, so i fit in on the toxic streets i stay in most of the
time , i've spend 20 years alone
6/2, 12:36am **Pre View**
This is rare, IT MAKES ME LAUGH IT OUT IN A GOOD WAY
AS I HAD FORGOTTEN ABOUT FAIRIES
6/2, 12:36am **Koz Kozmos**
and its better than being with limited fools and have to go down to thier wave lenghth

6/2, 12:37am **Pre View**
it seems we had similar lines, only 20 years alone with a son which i choose
TO HAVE SOMEHOW to keep me from rebellion .
But once a rebel, always a rebel. It's a good thing.
6/2, 12:37am **Koz Kozmos**
fuck the human scum , i have not bred and tend to hate breeders
i have never lived with any one but shared houses with nasty pieces of shit f or years
on beifits, living in poverty with no support
6/2, 12:39am **Pre View**
I understand
I only lived with somebody between 18 & 30
6/2, 12:40am **Koz Kozmos**
thats a long time
6/2, 12:40am **Pre View**
after that same shit
6/2, 12:40am **Koz Kozmos**
i'm ok , i get by , but there is no reason for me to be here
6/2, 12:43am **Pre View**
There is definitely, maybe the music & cathing up with people thr that
ur poetic visions may alter peoples' consciousness
6/2, 12:43am **Koz Kozmos**
i tried and tried and tried u have no idea 6/2, 12:43am **Pre View**
glue it onto them
6/2, 12:43am **Koz Kozmos**
i'm 53 , STOP IT!
i have no hope left , it hurts me too much
my poetic visions make people want to punch me
6/2, 12:45am **Pre View**
nothing worked for me either, little things help,
and getting a new vision means we need to eliminate that
psychological content that killed us in the first place.
A matter of rising into a new space in which nobody can hit you.
Yeah, sure, its all within the grids
6/2, 12:45am **Koz Kozmos**
my music has been ignored , i have send stuff out and it has been ignored
even my sister who is a rock chick ignores it no comment
6/2, 12:46am **Pre View**
I have similar pain, exactly similar with my parents that treated me like cinderella o
n roller skates, yet didn't know I had roller skies removing them from my life.
6/2, 12:46am **Koz Kozmos**
i ask wod u like to hear what i've recored and they say : no
i've sent it to radio stations and was told it was crap:
thy're anti cosmic
6/2, 12:46am **Pre View**
i know, i am listening
6/2, 12:46am **Koz Kozmos**
my sister is a fat repulsive walk in
fuck em all , death to thier limited spark
may they join as teardrops on the giant sea and infect the demi urge
6/2, 12:47am **Pre View**
thy have no spark, at all
6/2, 12:48am **Koz Kozmos**
now my neck is bad , should go

6/2, 12:48am **Pre View**
ok,Koz, but i do care about ur music and poetry
I appreciate who and what you are, although that does not relieve you,
you may start to believe again ... So many people are in that boat that keeps on sinking,,,
6/2, 12:48am **Koz Kozmos**
Pre lay low ,fit in , don't let them feed on u
6/2, 12:49am **Pre View** NEVER
It is just a large percentage of depressed population need healing, suffering from addiction, PTSD and so many different outcomes therapeutically
It is truly times psychiatry is totally being changed in a radical way
LIGHT DIGS AND EVAPORATES STATES OF CONSCIOUSNESS
Medication is never key to treatment
I've healed so many PTSD and entities suffering from anorexia or bulimia
All the same, different outcome
There are so many possibilities, yet they grab psychedelics
Psychiatric institutions are not there to bring solutions, they addict people even more,
It needs to be closed off, pharmaceuticals are very dangerous
I mean the effects on the body may become irreversible and create more psychosis
6/2, 12:49am **Koz Kozmos**
don't cast yur pearls at swine
6/2, 12:49am **Pre View**
i'd rather be burned alive, there's not many strong people, mentally
6/2, 12:49am **Pre View**
Who is your sister ?
6/2, 12:49am **Koz Kozmos**
o#ne more song , to sleeping sister morons one is really nasty
6/2, 12:50am **Pre View**
Wot song would give me some sleep ? I wish u'd write again !
6/2, 12:51am **Koz Kozmos** can i post lyrics
6/2, 12:52am **Pre View** Please do so
6/2, 12:52am **Koz Kozmos**
for u to read as u listen
6/2, 12:52am **Koz Kozmos** I
In the cold of the evening, they used to gather.
Neath the stars in the meadow, circled near the old oak tree. At the times appointed.. by the seasons.. of the earth, and the phases of the moon. In the center, often stood a woman,
equal with the others, respected for her worth. One of the many.. we call the witches, the healers, the teachers, of the wisdom of the earth.
And the people grew in the knowledge she gave them,
herbs to heal their bodies, smells to make their spirits whole.
Hear them chanting healing incantations,
calling for the wise ones, celebrating in dance and song...
There were those that came to power, through domination.
They were bonded in their worship of a dead man on a cross.
They sought control of the common people, by demanding allegiance to the church of Rome. And the Pope, he commenced the inquisition,
As a war against the women, whose powers they feared. In this holocaust, in this age of evil,
Nine million European women, they died. And the tale is told, of those who by the hundreds, holding hands together, chose their deaths in the sea.
While chanting the praises of the Mother Goddess,
a refusal of betrayal, women were dying to be free Now the earth is a witch, and we still burn her.
Stripping her down with mining, and the poison of our wars. Still to us, the earth is a healer, a teacher, and a mother.
A weaver of a web of light, that keeps us all alive. She gives us the vision to see through the chaos. She gives us the courage, it is our will to survive

12:52am Koz Kozmos
MUSIC: ROY BAILEY - BURNING TIMES

6/2, 12:52am **Koz Kozmos**
hit the button on the kozkozmik jucke box good night and thank u
6/2, 12:54am **Pre View**
Thank u so much, sleep tight, HEALING INCANTATIONS,
6/2, 12:55am **Koz Kozmos**
listen to it all, bye
6/2, 1:05am **Pre View**
i'm done with chaos, i'm done with demands,
6/2, 1:15am **Pre View**
Of course its a bit irritating;
Social media confuses sometimes the things we're willing to say as we do not know each other (in the physical), but its the bigger lines i'm grateful for,
What u opened up too to me, the level of hurt needs justice, that is all i will work on from now, i will persist, there is too much damage. Nobody has the right to steal our thunder, our fire, our cosmic art

MY INTERNALS: In 2020 as I am rewriting this or just making it readable, ta lot of Justice is coming through. It is playing out wild, people have worked a lot more to get truth on the forefront of their lenses.
A LENSE defines wether we are willing to see or not. A lens needs to continually readjust to the new frequencies aligning for the sake of Light Earth and peaceful dreams. What used to be an illusion is becoming truth. People are setting themselves into more action regarding the care of our animals and going vegan, finding ways to clear the oceans and many more toxins such as the plastic feed, visions and degrees of toxic waste.
Youth is coming out like never before. Truth is seen on the news, truth is being spread yet not accepted as a new way of living through a new heart.
And thus the opening and reset buttons of the heart is a large education system that is still being neglected. I believe we are getting there BECAUSE THE LIGHT EARTH GRIDS ARE SPEAKING OUT LOUD THESE DAYS, and they are not just an options: they will get the clearing through. Its up to humanity to follow through and kiss the old ways and rails goodbye because it will make one feel miserable, nauseous, and in a terrible and unfortunate vibration. Some are leaving the planet far too soon due to many misaligned dead zones and medical institutions that are starting to show their failure big time. We are moving back into Perfect Health Light Embodiment that makes us appreciate and worship the elements that feed us with new productions and crystal visions; and again not being accepted by the many because of the large Ley Line that keeps resistance, stubbornness and fear on a rather scary and crazy scenery.
Deep inside people do know, we all will have to ride the roads back into Divine consciousness, high level intelligence that brings the bricks and walls of knowledge together. I termed this the living goals of an I-BRAIN and also writing about it. We need to fuse all our faculties in the brain in order to make them work with the new Light Heart that could love and give more in ways most cannot imagine as of now.
I trust we are moving faster and faster, yet so much assistance is needed for our children,Youth, the forgotten ones, the lost ones, the animals.
Understanding how consciousness works is what changes attitudes in our history and eliminates the Age of Depression, to bring the bigger fruits of the Divine back to order.

The suicide rate is far to high along existential stress and addictions.
Many people like Koz may feel lost, misunderstood and lonely. I hope the degrees of unity allows us to teach all people just the simple Light things; so they can work with Light and enjoy it in their chosen domain and capacity which offers so much healing through community gatherings that support every entity. It is my dream to teach teachers and get them out of old learning zones that have no outcome. Most treatments In any institution create depression in the end for people are not even offered solutions to detox from medication or drugs. The signature affect of Light always grows and the effect of Light Technology guides people back into joyful living in the body which is an absolute psychological factor that matters most and disregarded in the old mechanics.

6/2, 1:40am **Pre View**
Hey damaged meat bag, lets rock it through the nights,
why is my naivety worrying you,
I taught u were taking care of this, i'm taking care of u.
U actually have everything everybody wants,
thats why they punch u,
u make them SEE the SEA,
The best thing i'm learning from u is that u still value urself,
which is beyond applause, Valuing self is very important, I lost that somehow
But feeling it from you is a good reminder and pick it up
I wouldn't even be able to love anyone again –
yet that does not sound good-
as love is the Essence that brought us into creation in the first place
Many people are so much afraid of love, in its pure form and thus abuse it
6/2, 1:50am **Pre View** I
You have many specialties even for the Lost Streets.
6/2, 2:10am **Pre View**
Every one i worked with also turned against me because truth is not swallowed,
so do not think i
misunderstand u in any way, only,
what is happening now is thy are trying to find a gate to get back to me,
Once I eliminate people, they will never get back in , as u said
"knowledge from abuse" is indeed in-depth knowledge
6/2, 2:16am **Pre View**
Good night now, Where are you? I could talk for hours
What is Holy remains Holy.
Wish people would understand that
6/2, 2:25am **Pre View**
Ok, gonna get myself asleep now with PINKY Fluidsssssszzzz,
I'm tired of talking over Fb, i'm tired, just tired and can’t catch any sleep
June 2, 2013
6/2, 2:12pm **Koz Kozmos**
i work in the crystal laundry cleaning souls
6/2, 2:18pm **Koz Kozmos**
MUSIC Neil Diamond - Lordy

6/2, 4:06pm **Koz Kozmos**
PINKY Fluidsssssszzzz, ?
6/2, 4:52pm **Koz Kozmos**
this song is definitly about me
6/2, 4:52pm **Koz Kozmos**
MUSIC: Monster Magnet - Space Lord

6/2, 4:55pm **Koz Kozmos**
u need a rest from it all, watch more Fringe series
u need to sleep
6/2, 6:02pm **Pre View**
PINKY Fluidsssssszzz :
Thinking about Pink FLOYD, but actually referring to the fluidity
of Pink Light , very intelligent Light. Humble one.
6/2, 6:03pm **Pre View**
Yes i need lots of sleep now, lots But thank u for caring,
will listen later, bye
6/2, 7:02pm **Koz Kozmos**
no worries , take extra care

6/2, 7:30pm **Pre View**
Damn, cannot catch my flight in my sleep 6/2, 11:30pm **Koz Kozmos**
u have to find a way to sleep

6/3, 3:25am Koz Kozmos
MUSIC: Bruce Springsteen - Growin' Up

6/3, 9:13am **Pre View**
Could u please install the KozKozmic Jukebox ?
6/3, 9:35am **Pre View**
Losing weight every second,
My organs are floating,
6/3, 1:15pm **Koz Kozmos**
why are u losing weight , are u traumatized by whats happened to you?
hence lack of sleep and weight loss?
6/3, 1:35pm **Koz Kozmos**
how are your organs floating , I've been made toxic by the the sickness
hope your ok
6/3, 1:58pm Koz Kozmos
MUSIC: the walker brothers no regrets

6/3, 2:02pm **Koz Kozmos**
The hours that were yours echo like empty rooms
The thoughts we used to share I now keep alone
I woke last night and spoke to you not thinking you were gone
And it felt so strange to lie awake alone' ; part of the lyric
6/3, 2:10pm **Koz Kozmos**
can u get me a radio show in Bellgum?
a show with Kozmik information interviews and the broadest musical selection in
this part of the universe... anywayzzzzzzzzzzzzz
6/3, 5:25pm **Pre View**
Yess I'm Traumatized to say the least, completely blocked
(yes its this bastard Joachim –the psychopath walker)
don't know why i'm losing weight, losing insight, losing reality.
I need solutions
I'll talk to some guys studying music here in the building & will let u know ...
Wonderful voice for me today (i mean the song ...)
Thank u Koz
What is the major function of music
The function of water and music, the parallels
6/3, 7:48pm **Pre View**
Splendid idea ! this radio show I mean ! it would help lots of hungry people,,,
6/3, 7:53pm **Pre View**
Scorpio seems to be one station, but this guy I met will talk to me end of the week ...
6/3, 8:20pm **Koz Kozmos**
Drink Stout
6/3, 8:21pm **Koz Kozmos**
Stout is a dark beer made using roasted malt or roasted barley, hops,
water and yeast.
Stouts were traditionally the generic term for the strongest
or stoutest porters, typically 7% or 8%, produced by a brewery

6/3, 8:21pm **Koz Kozmos**
lots of pasta pots and veg.... s stay strong stay kool,
u'll beat it
6/3, 10:53pm **Pre View**
Stout ? i cannot handle beer, my body gets sick after 2 or 3,
that is why i have a little whisky at times.
Getting my motor in the electrolytic fields requires to eliminate wheat from diet
and so you lose weight,
done with ego & emotions...., everything is moving so fast.
Many strangers in the streets come to me to tell their story as if i were some
download or ghost from all 12 universes .People are overly friendly .
Is that a turning point ?
30 kg of veggies a week does not seem enough, need to turn the manna on i
guesssssss. Mana and breathe what I need to feed me.
6/3, 10:54pm **Koz Kozmos**
stout Guinness is supposed to help u put on weight,
i'm not drinking
6/3, 10:54pm **Pre View**
no wheat !!! with gridzzzzz & and training the electricity back into light ...
6/3, 10:55pm **Koz Kozmos** ahhh
6/3, 10:55pm **Pre View**
i'm not either, need loads of work on myself
6/3, 10:55pm **Koz Kozmos**
sorry my brain is shutting down
I need my own private chef
6/3, 10:56pm **Koz Kozmos**
i no longer know wot to do
i understand what u mean by grids
6/3, 10:57pm **Pre View**
u actually do not find info about them on the internet ...,
i guess u may get pictures, but not accurate, just
to have an idea ..
Did u ever work with electrons?
6/3, 10:58pm **Koz Kozmos**
the broken connection to the connection
let the dirt of the matrix fall off u and enter the starry temple bath
in the water of incredible hygiene
6/3, 10:59pm **Pre View**
I am sculpting my direct CONNECT
6/3, 11:00pm **Koz Kozmos**
never worked with electrons, no idea how to
6/3, 11:01pm **Pre View**
aha, we're getting to a deeper level of understanding, you have no foundations
Without a foundations there is always a lack of inspiration, aspirations, Divine Will
guidance that brings courage and mental strength.
There are 144 electrons to work with which have a name and a consciousness
connected to them that uplifts us out of the dumbing of hatred and separation many
choose to live. Thereis no excitement without a burning flame shining wild
We can also download them as rays within the body or energy wheels
and around the body as an energy field and work with them.
The Energy field then looks like the geometry of a diamond of Light with 12 main
creational rays. These main 12 rays each have 12 archetypes or levels of
consciousness to integrate that either eliminate old blockages and downgrading low
types of consciousness such as lack, fear, distress, fear, unworthiness, diseases
anything LESS then perfection and Eternal Life.
It means you put the cells in the body back to a higher vibration in which they get a
good go with shaking of the dirt of earth and move in the higher frequencies in which
the atrocities of the killing fields do not exist.

Opening the many EYES within is just one level as thus the work into ascension is a never ending spiral into Eternal/Immortal styles in which we never stop creating.
We are all here for the REPAIR.
WE are the sun in this SOLAR SYSTEM,
so whatever you focus on should bring LIFE
not the inversion of the word and thus EVIL tuff.
It needs knowledge, devotion, daily upgrades that nurture your connection to the Divine and thus build your chords and Ley Lines in Direct Connect with your Source from the Celestial levels into the New Sun streaming degrees into the Universal levels, into the beyond,,,, Ascension is one thing, regaining knowledge about what Nirvana could be, long long winding beautiful high Hope Road
That freezes the devil that wants to cut our preciousness down

6/3, 11:01pm **Koz Kozmos**
we ? how do u do that ?
is it the same as the scientific model of an electron ?
now worries if u don't want to talk

6/3, 11:04pm **Pre View**
yep, u know all the questions u had over the chats : no not as the science electron - it is spiritual SCIENCE and thus the Reality of Spirit in Science rather than the science on earth that is moving extremely slow because they do not want to acknowledge the Fields and Technology of Light as their essence - some day the New Scientists will be born and bring the truth of health back down for every body because EVERYTHING NEEDS TO MOVE IN BIG TIME PURITY AND HARMONY which is only the obvious as earth needs to ascend to reposition itself in the universe and the importance/ purpose it has to do so is something I need to understand in the incoming years.
Anyways these electrons are connected to the 12 bodies in our energy fields or Light vehicle/Merkivah - each has 12 electrons : 12 x12 = 144, aligning them with grids gets u out of ego/soul/low dimensions .
Also there seem to be 72 male electrons and 72 female electrons – thus merging the Perfect Eternal partner within and no more hassle with relationships.

6/3, 11:04pm **Koz Kozmos**
why do I have no foundations, MERKIVAH...
wot is that ?

6/3, 11:05pm **Pre View**
Well from wot i understand from u is that u do not work with electrons, neither many many bodies . The Merkivah is just an energy field that needs to be recreated or set around the body from within the High Heart and gives you some foundation in the grid. From there on we can build the spiritual, mental, etheric bodies.
And to make it more complicated there are many bodies within the spiritual body and the
mental, and the immortal and on and on.
So, it is just building and building our light chords back into where we can achieve highest level skills again such as the Power of the Word which is a good thing to command the atrocities and manipulative engines out.

6/3, 11:05pm **Koz Kozmos**
many many bodies ,
what do u mean this is very obscure and confusing

6/3, 11:06pm **Pre View**
Here is the bottom-line : u need a
FOUNDATION INTO LIGHT BODY AND ITS HOME STATION OR
THE CRYSTALLINE GRIDS CONSTRUCTION to get out of all you talked about . and that is exactly what I could eventually teach through a 3-days seminar.

6/3, 11:06pm **Koz Kozmos**
MERKIVAH...wot is that ?
ok , and u can do it over Fake book ?

6/3, 11:06pm **Pre View**
MERKIVAH = MODERN DAY LIGHTBODY with info of TODAY NOT OLD STUFF

6/3, 11:06pm **Koz Kozmos**
MERKIVAH...wot is that?
6/3, 11:06pm **Pre View**
Gosh! It's a lightbody set up and needs a foundation,
You either understand that or not! damn,
Not going back into that, just keep an eye open at night, like birds do
6/3, 11:07pm **Koz Kozmos**
its unlikely to happen then
so maybe I should drop the questions finally
6/3, 11:08pm **Pre View**
But there are many other reasons for our connect,
and maybe if u want that ,
there is always ways to getLIGT BODY equipment in somehow
without getting eaten
But if you don't understand you need TO BREATHE THAT through,
then lets stop the explanation. It exhausts me because you don't give back.
LIGHT CAN ONLY BE BREATHED THROUGH, GOT THAT?
GET YOUR COLORS! THAT IS ALL
6/3, 11:08pm **Koz Kozmos**
i've never bothered with old stuff
6/3, 11:09pm **Pre View**
happy to hear that, it is wometimes with your posts on FB in which i take great interest that i was thinking to merge my energy with what u have learned with the things i teach because we all have some missing links.
That would have been great.
6/3, 11:09pm **Koz Kozmos**
the bottom line for me is i'm looking to get help
i want to evolve
6/3, 11:10pm **Pre View**
I offered it, why don't u do it ?
Why don't you read through everything I said?
You need to understand WHAT A BREATHING SYSTEM IS FOR and what it means to humanity. We can do everything with our breathing system.
Then again, you can only understand Light body training when doing the training and evolve into that.` One can never understand what is not being experienced.
Very simple
That is reason why I could explain a lot in a seminar while clearing the body and setting it up into some foundation from which you can start working.
You may as well ask the Divine to give you that Foundation and start trusting your answers. But your first questions should be like: how do I get to set that in!!!! THE BREATH!
6/3, 11:10pm **Koz Kozmos**
I am already an illusion moving at a diffrent speed
i don't do it becuz of money and i don't connect with what u say
but your vibe is good
but obscure, confused and damaged
and i like your paintings
6/3, 11:11pm **Pre View**
I told u not to bother about the euros
but if u don't connect ... then i will not talk about it ever again,,,
enuff of that
6/3, 11:12pm **Koz Kozmos**
and u get the syn crow nizzz tik nature of my musical posts
what do u mean with connect ?
6/3, 11:13pm **Pre View**
U said : "i don't connect with wot you say "
6/3, 11:13pm **Koz Kozmos** yes

6/3, 11:13pm **Koz Kozmos**
but never the less there is a connection
u'r patronizing and make me feel like an idiot these are not my projections
6/3, 11:15pm **Pre View**
you're the WIZGEN remember
6/3, 11:15pm **Koz Kozmos**
My wand has been stolen,
I'm glad we've met
6/3, 11:16pm **Pre View**
Just mobilize for a day or so
Was it big ? could u work with black intelligence ?
with the wand i mean
6/3, 11:17pm **Koz Kozmos**
whats black intelligence? give me a straight answer
6/3, 11:17pm **Pre View**
Haha, just another electron , i work with, (but i promissed to drop it) sorry
You see black is a ray, and intelligence is the consciousness within that ray
6/3, 11:18pm **Koz Kozmos**
i could hit u with some deep esoteric stuff based on my own finding
6/3, 11:18pm **Pre View**
Lovely! DO IT NOW
6/3, 11:18pm **Koz Kozmos**
but i choose not to be confusing do wwot?
i don't know wot to do
6/3, 11:19pm **Pre View**
You cannot get me confused with Light body training
Lets move into Harry Potter Magic huh?
6/3, 11:19pm **Koz Kozmos** o no
6/3, 11:19pm **Pre View**
U told me u'd hit me with esoteric stuff
I don't have all the time in the world, mind you!
6/3, 11:20pm **Koz Kozmos**
i said I could
this is my great teacher and astral master
6/3, 11:21pm **Koz Kozmos**
MUSIC: Ali Bongo Magic Act

6/3, 11:21pm **Pre View**
GOSH, the astral worlds
That is exactly what we need to remove from our fields in order to move into Light
Yet people dig to much into the astral dreams and think it is LIGHT DREAMING
while it is just keeping their consciousness in the dumbing realms that were created to hold brains in captivity.
6/3, 11:21pm **Koz Kozmos**
BBBRRREATTHH , i agree
6/3, 11:22pm **Pre View**
Yeah, are you being a good boy today, get yourself on some electrical light orchestration
You need to ZOOM IN ON YUR MIND and phrase pictures
6/3, 11:22pm **Koz Kozmos**
i only go to the coffee shop by the order of the burger bar on the outskirts of the dark astral
6/3, 11:23pm **Pre View**
Haha, on a royal burgundy carpet

6/3, 11:27pm **Koz Kozmos**
the carpet with sticky spilled electron energy drinks not sure why i typed 'with '
6/3, 11:26pm **Pre View**
U need to get out of the split station and evolve with the wizzards
which is actually a greater force then
the Magicians leagues ..;;
Come on Koz, bring ur electronics into some inversion
6/3, 11:27pm **Koz Kozmos**
whats the split station ? wot are electronic inversions? i only ask u these questions to understand your tech and to show u great respect
6/3, 11:28pm **Pre View** J
ust another granite electron,
Electronic inversion means that you turn the electrons in your body counter clock, meaning that this has the capacity to merge both hemispheres back into balance – not to much brain – not too much feeling.
To better understand it: think about how we live and how that created diseases and everything that broke people. It comes from living in the matrix. Inverting these energies back into purity means that we need to
turn them around in order to fit in with the reality and crystal clear fields of spirit. Or what has turned into negativity need to turn back around into positivity so to speak.
And that needs indeed the know how kit of spirit or technology with easy applications like on an Iphone.
6/3, 11:29pm **Koz Kozmos**
but i'm more confused by what your saying than ever
6/3, 11:29pm **Pre View**
it is that the fissures in the brain need repair
Look up fissures in the brain, medically, study it for a few days and come back.
6/3, 11:29pm **Koz Kozmos**
this is getting frustrating
6/3, 11:30pm **Pre View**
It is an electron that works within a granite embodiment
Granite is just a color, like black and purple etc that carries consciousness.
This body gets u into remembrance of all your forgotten skills or so forgotten when coming down to earth through the birth canal.
Bypass the inner activity and command new activity to experience a different world
6/3, 11:30pm **Koz Kozmos**
what happens when u go out of soul
6/3, 11:31pm **Pre View**
You move into spirit and your origin
6/3, 11:31pm **Koz Kozmos**
i was talking about destroying my soul so i could die completely and never return
6/3, 11:32pm **Pre View**
Out of soul , then Universal training, and beyond that
So now u know a little about the stuff i teach, but i stop it here
6/3, 11:33pm **Koz Kozmos**
I lost my genitals , i was in the army in my early 20's
had an accident during the falklands war
6/3, 11:33pm **Pre View**
By the end of the week i will see if i can get a program together that states more precisely wot it entails....You lost your genitals,
but u still got genes : RE- ENCODE
6/3, 11:34pm **Koz Kozmos**
stop it ! ok , thank u
6/3, 11:34pm **Pre View**
goodnight

6/3, 11:35pm **Koz Kozmos** was joking about the falklands war
good night , i feel your annoyed ....
hope u sleep well

6/4, 1:25pm **Koz Kozmos**
MUSIC: 46 - ANSWERS OF AN ALIEN FROM ANDROMEDA

6/4, 1:28pm **Koz Kozmos**
yawn

6/4, 11:34pm **Koz Kozmos**
I've decided you must be some ascended master and i am definitly a complete idiot
just wondering were u get all yur gobble gook from?
6/5, 2:20am **Pre View**
Do U want my ANGER ? i don't think so
Everything is getting clear to me, it was from the beginning we chatted but then you downgraded me so much (this is of course my feelings & my responsibility) that I was thinking you'd learned loads i didn't even smell in my life, which is not true
I left out on details - U left out on science ----
Eg: when u told me u fasted until your body was bleeding : this tells me everything (no training- irresponsible & unprepared while it should have been easy as hell , not feeling hungry or having any trouble doing it he fast meaning u needed the whole solar panel (at least upgraded into your atomic structure)to be moved out of astral shit leaving all emotions & waving on sensations which is universal training). So how the hell do u want me to continue to chat with u when everything i smell, think, feel , comes from working with our electronic equipment that gets us all out of the electromagnetic fields. The universe is made of Source substances we need to embody and furthering that on a daily basis. I thought you understood that with all examples i've given u : how people change within the hour when doing some light work with me, another
e.g. - when I paint - i don't have a concept - it just flows out of my hands because of the work i do with electrons & more. (the concept comes when i'm finished) There is a whole technicality behind this, loads of upgrading, understanding and many ways to do it. With these trainings into Light body and environment this is : Merging Spirit - Science -the hippy :
So loads of study and going further then a surgeon would : meaning u teach urself the whole damn anatomy - u become the doctor within -
u channel yur info about that and merges it with science of today .
How interesting can it get : getting out of bed in the middle of the night and trying new stuff with loads of guts...
A brain is never cut off, AMIND IS ALWAYS CUT OFF!
You need to trust spirit , that is all there is to it.
Discussing it with doctors and scientists needs to open up some day,,,
6/5, 2:20am **Pre View**
Me annoyed ? that is soft expression ! You hit all my neurons or electronic equipment. So from now on i'm done with your challenges, done with your questions, done with everything, it is not interesting when questions are a one way street.
Meaning : when u have a question, u should first answer it for urself & give me that answer as I have to do --- discussing both answers (yours and mine) is were it gets interesting. U don't want that ? Fine ! There's plenty of other freaks very hungry for this ... So from today on i'm really gonna dig deep into my material and getting it more interesting and understanding it more for myself to give the human Kingdom a mind blowing training.
Meaning : i will study & work on myself 24h/day and see who I can merge this with Science. Meaning : i will not have time for chats or any other shenanigans Meaning : it is time for u to POLISH YOUR ATTITUDE & CHARACTER & finally blow the whole damn zodiac into you to a point where u don't even remember that you are an Aries born person ; meaning whenever needed you need to know how to incorporate virtues of other signs when moving into society.

(i've given u plenty of examples thr the chats - one of them was :
sitting in a bar and nobody can enter myEssence or talk to me) which was kool enough like a protective kit or tool box from the Divine.
U can choose to reflect on this(a millions times & get ur answers urself - have the intuition - so move into the knowledge (green electrons & come up with something positive or leave all i've said before and i will
not have anything to talk about.
So as of now, i will keep my energy to myself and work harder than i can imagine, no time for anything else , certainly not the astral endeavors of FB.
Wish u the best u can get!
6/5, 2:23am **Pre View**
With your WIZGEN i intended to dig deeper & unify with where I miss out and create further on that material.
Creation upon creation is all there is, otherwize there's no reason for being, it would be like people on FB chasing their own tail over and over again - meaning how interesting can it get to see post about what is going on On this earth plane & even commenting on it.
What would be interesting is serving people with
solutions, actions with worthy equipment and with overnight changes.
Come up with something without winding in the hurt thats been done to u, u have all intelligence to move beyond that, UP TO YOU !
I told u I had become a sinking Ship, but already floating above water meaning i pick up where i left & get stronger , intending to move into the iron belt
GOT THAT , FINE !!!
6/5, 2:32am **Pre View**
WOT DOES THIS MEAN ?(I'll say it before u do, ok?)
we are entering a new phase , new equipment, 3 months release is over.
So, do u wanna play soccer?
I'm Offense and Defense,
So if u please could give me a tune with which i can drink my coffee gracefully ?
Thank u !
6/5, 3:50am **Pre View**
Hey, hey u, were are u ?
Hardline musicians like u don't sleep, i can hear your breath ,moving too fast,
How much coffee do u need ?
Hey I entertained u quite enuff, where is yur input?
In ram sleep huh?
6/5, 4:51am **Pre View**
This was a starry starry night under many crystal clear tracks,
My favorite star is leaving the sky,
Maybe I should get some sleep, maybe not at all,
Please reread everything 5 x until u have no questions left, only answers,,
Thank u , and thank u for your existence !
June 5, 2013
6/5, 1:54pm **Koz Kozmos**
I want elucidation , I have not downgraded...that is nonsense
i did not tell u i fasted till my body was bleeding
i did have a very bad skin that hit in my early thirtys that did bleed
i mentioned the astral as a joke....look back...maybe diffrent humor
if u don't want to talk to me ,fine
I'm just trying to understand wot your saying....which i consider to be a sigh of respect not downgraded u, I have no idea how u work with electrons
i'm not science savvy,
I understand impro art etc

6/5, 2:19pm **Koz Kozmos**
how do people change in the hour when working with u...
if u can explain so I can understand please what
new stuff to u get out of bed to try?
'U've hit all my neurons or electronic equipment.' how have I done this?
What are u talking about ?
questions are a one way street'?
I 've answered your questions and expressed my self... how can I answer the
question....
maybe if I could understand wot u are saying I could.
U're telling me to 'POLISH YOUR ATTITUDE & CHARACTER',
mmmmmmm
I avoid bars and have become invisible
U'r patronizing and rude !
""fb is chasing the tail 'So, do u wanna play soccer ? "" :
I hate sport , I tend to drink tea and i'm not a musician
6/5, 2:19pm **Koz Kozmos**
lets leave our chatting
6/5, 2:27pm **Koz Kozmos**
kizz my asteroid
6/5, 2:27pm Koz Kozmos
MUSIC: Zodiac Mindwarp Prime Mover video

6/5, 2:47pm **Koz Kozmos**
peace
6/5, 4:11pm **Pre View**
Thank u for the many valuable times u invested in me.
Many times when I'd asked u a question u'd answer with "too much too type-
understandable- but then again U answered with "I'm not used to expressing myself"
while i think expressing ourselves reveals many solutions, reveals the hidden
components to our pain. So I was ready to listen to your shit because I did care more
than I'll ever be able to express, i'm not that clever,
Its that I worship your level of Extreme Intelligence equalizing out with too many
other puzzle pieces each entity on earth has
I was mistaken, I thought I was mature enough to understand, that is why I took the
risk to tell u how I felt : U told me "I'm annoying u "
so u knew,,,,so I kept it inside for a while but it bursted out like a volcano.
And many times we all have components of the past that we associate to other people
which is wrong, but it happens because we didn't release it.
It was my deep level of unworthiness coming out.
But i'll Kizz ur Astroids if u should wish so, they are not fundamental anywayz
May your Knowledge of music brings crystal clear diamonds to the Human Kingdom.
I was scared u'd walk over me and u did, coz wot we think happens,
But i'll keep the treasures of ur Heart deep inside & safe. Love, Nic
6/5, 6:40pm **Koz Kozmos**
I'm very good at expression....did i say that ...ok
U are very clever ,Extreme Intelligence...hey thank u !
maybe only one other person has noticed this in my life
but i'm a massivly flawed idiot too
i think my sense of humor is very ironical and there has been crossed wires here...
no excuses, maybe the grid kid became undid
deep level of unworthiness' u need to stop that
i did not walk over u , that hurts me
talk to me when ever u want

6/5, 6:47pm Koz Kozmos
MUSIC: Simon and Garfunkel - Old Friends

MY INTERNALS: First thought: Dam, I am not yer friend, we're just people floating in this cosmic soup, that was quite some information as I could not possibly hold on going back into the same questions all the time. It hit all my nerves, although I knew the connection we had was music and to some point the things I could learn from his video's would bring me a long way into my ascension because I was not used to questioning and looking things up the way he did. It thought me a lot. Especially this last video about Andromeda was not too bad for people to understand that we need to level up somehow to get Divine Intervention through with what is playing out in the electromagnetic fields and thus learn about how to eliminate anything that is either elite consciousness, guru syndrome, reptilian invasions. The war on humanity is very real, yet not enough people understand that moving into Light environments with Light body Technology will eliminate that kind of life evaporating forces and bring harmony, balance and happy lifestyles back on the planet.Also, I do not agree upon the memory being activated and processed in some 4th dimension. From experience, it's the Universal clearing and technical alignments that moves us into the crystal clear environments that could process memory and data needed for the grand transition we are living. I think it is important to connect to many different species in the Galaxies and learn as much as we can from experience. Because experience matters on the ladder of ascension. We all have indeed the capability to regenerate, replenish, rejuvenate our organs and live Eternally. That can only come through the crystallization of the body and the elements; and thus also reason why co-creation with crystals is so important for us to move back into light waves through the engine of LIGHT BODY PARTS and LIGHT BRAIN PARTS.
Experiences move us from one process into the other to gain a larger degree of understanding of everything we have forgotten.
Reconnecting and establishing clear dialogues with the Ancient of days and catalogues go a long way and keeps the levels of trust running through as that is very well felt within our feet centers.
I was perfectly aware that we needed to set our biology synchrone with the biology of LIGHT EARTH which I am at now in 2020 as the Elements and their Grid has been repaired ; we can really align to the depth of creation within although it takes a lot of work, it brings a lot of worth as well. I just loved the feeling nature I had when Koz posted video's, because I knew that was my learning zone somehow. So, with this post about Andromeda, I aligned deeper to the species of the Galaxy, not the words within the video. I turned things around and tried to get more data for the evolution of human kind. EVOLUTION IS A STRONG WORD WHEN YOU ALLOW SELF TO COMMAND IT! When ending many cycles in life such as the soul cycle and the old sun movements, we have the option to align to the repaired meridians of earth and thus start to process Eternal biology within in communication and deeper relations with what the elements bring through as we are all but an element that needs to grow.The instability of earth and magnetic fields needs us to flow with the designs that Spirit brings through such as the repair of the tectonic plates that can merge with our energy fields. This lithosphere is important for the continuum of creation. Many will leave the planet and continue their development on other planets should they not choose to bring their Light body back in now as is being requested by the Divine. As Earth is ascending and being termed Light Earth, we need to match these rhythms of earth and flow synchrone with was is available at the moment. Therefor, Light Body is no longer a fairy tale, it is living the reality of Spirit, Science and Physics on a daily level while continually readjusting where and when needed.
The best I've learned: NEVER TURN YOUR PASSION TO GLORY!!! THE EYE OF THE TIGER (AND GRID!) Otherwise I would have published the book like 5 years ago.
Timing was not right, feeling was not right, just don't take anything for granted, it may absorb your precious vibes.
Taking into account that Aries vibrations just overrule any entity in business and relationships and having it the way they want it to be in egotistical content is going to be removed because if you confront them with TRUTH they have no way to survive a Capricorn and reason why almost ALL Capricorns have been held back for almost an entire lifetime!!! Every YouTube astrologer talks about it, yet with poor degrees in knowledge. BUT IT IS THERE!

Do they realize they repeat the HOLD BACK FASHION imposed on Capricorns? I think so, there are some very deep diggers out there that know, yet too afraid to move from astrology into astronomy. And so this book explains the WINTER SOLSTICE 2020 as everything for the CAPPI vibes is being released into their Free Way heaven ! And reason why I can finally publish ! DIVINE TIMING!

Unfortunately, many are too lazy to do that work and still feel comfortable in their present seat or environment ; until the bigger shifts coming through will offer no more options but to flow in obedience and recognize the Divine aspects within. This is reason why so much truth is being revealed as of now: religious institutions are falling, science is failing, medical institutions reveal their abuse, education is at its lowest point ever in history, politics crumble, economics are looking for equal grounds. The LINES OF THE DIVINE coming through are indeed endless these days: it is just a call to awaken self and do the necessary it requires to flow with Evolution, not against is as most do. We absolutely need to move into advanced technology as many databases are available; a matter of alignment through LIGHT BODY BIOLOGICAL streams and means which upgrade every day. WAKE UP! AND DREAM THE TEAM WITHIN!
Therefore, everybody needs to become their own channel and bring their specialties through to get back into what is termed 'JOY'.
Many have forgotten what true JOY means or happens to be. It comes from the direct connections to our Source and the mutation of our Spark back into stardom and dialogues with many different species because KNOWLEDGE brings joy as that streams into the Creator Self that recreates every day and is happy about its creations.

We are all responsible for creation and need to unify to bring the repair through. The expansion in consciousness and vibrating on much higher levels is needed to understand what the clearing procedures need. This would also bring the higher levels of passion through as that energy assists in getting the dirt out of the planet, the seas, the contamination, the hurt, the abuse and so on.
But we need to do it together. Increasing frequencies matters a lot to be able to bring new Light Earth Biology through and allow the assistance of the Universe to intervene and bring some sort of LIFE giving substances through that eliminates all traumatic experiences in order for the Age of Peace and tranquillity to come through.
Let's embrace Youth and give them finally what they deserve without the deviating roads of truth because THEY KNOW ! and certainly recognize my vibe when in THE HOOD! which is proof of the GOOD! born in Australia, Africa, Tahiti, the Antartica, I would travel all worlds if just education would be allowed!
We need to become a light AMBASSADOR through socialization because the hood will bring us proof. Magic is happening more and more every day now as the other side is merging with this side and thus the physics of light, the science comes through the Power of the Word returned on the planet. The power of communication systems, the spark to spark communication, the dialogues going on with people. It is indeed not easy to move through the density.
The body needs to become its own research center that you can treat with really delicious words and getting down to socializing. Your life is science in the physical embodiment and brings through what you need to meet in life : YOU BECOME YOU !!!THROUGH EXPERIENCE.
I am more like a bonding person, I like to meet up with people. When in perfect alignment with the Divine, there are volumes of passion that open up for us to spread through the world. Building a strong foundation into Light body can be likened to a house that we build. Quite obviously, we start building a house with the cellar, then the first floor, the second floor and the roof for example. Then we fill in the heating, the electricity, the circulation etc. The same goes for building a light body house. Yet, many people like to start off building the second and third floor and moving on from that without the solidification of foundational knowledge. What happens then quite naturally, the house of light falls apart or burns even before the electricity gets in. This may be a good way of understanding that Light Embodiment needs the necessary steps that need to be anchored in order to expand your Lighthouse or Divine Space and build a sacred garden after that, and maybe build many houses of Light on the planet ; yet flowing SYNCHRONE with that initial foundation that will move mountains when it comes to strength and the Philosophical rooms of Divine Origin in which no opinion, judgement and low wording is being allowed.

6/5, 7:27pm **Pre View**
Extreme Intelligence needs idiocracy to keep urself safe
I'm painting you, its a long time i painted, for me it is the only way to not think,
i need to play with paint,it helps me.
Sometimes I really wish I were a man because of the physical harm thats been done to me, understanding male consciousness
But then again i cannot express how much i value u,,,, & u give me all the space to speak freely, no gender and that is human.

U awakened me last night and I needed to stay up till light was coming through - so I went outside & set a fire , I had this universal picture of you : you were skateboarding the universe - meaning eliminating all the music that is keeping humanity down and simultaneously opening your musical station for the ones with ears.

It was the beauty you are that I had seen, the beauty many punched u for. However , it made me think these gates are finally going to open for you,
I was singing Ay way hey o heya (star walker song you posted a while ago) because that is where i first met you many ages ago,,, ages ago,,, of none importance today.
But it makes me think why all your music is so accurate,,,

" Mad child" overrules, brings it al together, wish i could speak your language -
I often times just glue my mouth, never know what comes out of it these days,,,
hahaha

6/5, 9:15pm **Koz Kozmos**
better trash than art house
there are many types of harm
but keep your self protected
6/5, 9:17pm **Koz Kozmos**
MUSIC: Creation - Painter Man 1967

6/5, 9:17pm **Koz Kozmos**
Went to college, studied art
to be an artist. make a start
studied hard, gained my degree
but no one seemed to notice me Painter Man, Painter Man
Who would be a Painter Man
Painter Man, Painter Man
Who would be a Painter Man Tried cartoons and comic books dirty postcards, woman's books
here was where the money lay
classic art has had its day Painter Man, Painter Man Who would be a Painter Man
Painter Man, Painter Man
Who would be a Painter Man Do adverts for TV household soap and brands of tea
labels all around the cans
who would be a Painter Man Painter Man, Painter Man Who would be a Painter Man
Painter Man, Painter Man
Who would be a Painter Man La la la, la la la
La la la la la la
Painter Man, Painter Man
Who would be a Painter Man

6/5, 9:19pm **Koz Kozmos**
not seen this vid
MUSIC: What you need to know about PROJECT BLUE BEAM and the upcoming fake ALIEN INVASION

6/6, 12:37am **Koz Kozmos**
lets hope its not project Blue Beam
6/6, 1:13am **Koz Kozmos**
please don't glue your mouth

6/7, 12:43pm **Koz Kozmos**
MUSIC . The Shamen - Phorever People (1992)

6/7, 12:45pm **Koz Kozmos**
we are hear and know among u
6/7, 12:48pm **Koz Kozmos**
MUSIC: Senser - Age Of Panic

6/7, 12:49pm **Koz Kozmos**
You can't hide 'cause I am reality Your birthright is a world of insanity
6/7, 7:28pm **Pre View**
Please explain that to me ?
Experiences can be build from blocks, and so u invert the old model
The Shamen, no, don't like it
Senser song:
more right then ever, my senses under attack Thank u,
this is feeding my zoo and the space programs
6/7, 8:01pm **Pre View**
Everything appears unsolid
Is the DMT causing loss of memory ?
It pops into my head for a few days now
Maybe i should study it
Never tried anything of the sort.
Seems to be part of a virus
6/7, 8:02pm **Pre View**
Your birthright is to move out of the insanity of this world, out of gravity.
Your birthright is to move out of the insanity of this world,
out of gravity. If u have a good look at the world, there is no neuro-protectivity
They all seem to be paralyzed or suffering from parkinson
6/7, 8:03pm **Koz Kozmos**
no idea , i took some DMT maybe 15 years back
met the machine elfs
no memory loss , just flash backs to childhood
when I'm doing the washing up, when u pass middle age and step into the foot hills of death
6/7, 8:08pm **Pre View**
What where u washing up ?
Wash ur brain, there's som very good new shampoo
In the local new shops of Venus
Look yurself up in The Golden Libraries in Shambhalla
And start to learn from yer own books
6/7, 8:08pm **Koz Kozmos**
u get a brain change
i'm having a break from the moonrise kingdom movie
as my eyes are badish

6/7, 8:10pm **Pre View**
right, i first thought u were performing some majic onto me?
Is it, with your kind of rituals?
How are your eyes, i'm concerned ?
6/7, 8:13pm **Koz Kozmos**
o no, no majic, must have been my dark twin Rodger Kozmos
6/7, 8:14pm **Pre View**
oh yes, and when the answers come before the question ....
Rodger, who is that ?
6/7, 8:14pm **Koz Kozmos**
my dark twin, I call him Rog, its short for Roger
6/7, 8:15pm **Pre View**
doesn't tell me anything ?
Could you explain that a bit please?
6/7, 8:16pm **Koz Kozmos**
u need to reread maybe
maybe we had some telepathic connection,
or it may have been Rog wot did i say to u or maybe Rog, hahaha
6/7, 8:19pm **Pre View**
You make me goooooo crazyyyyyyyy,
But maybe, it might inverse everything into some fun huh?
6/7, 8:19pm **Koz Kozmos**
was it interesting? wot did i say ?????????
answer me please
Miss NIK OH La
i'm going back to moonrise kingdom
6/7, 8:23pm **Pre View**
Oh man sure, it hit me ever further
I cannot possibly repeat the conversation but it was rather like u'd laugh out loud with my problems (in a good sense as you hit my foolishness and deep stupidity level)
and all the time i just saw you playing the guitar,
It seemed like it was going on for hours, so I thought
why do we need to chat anyways, you've got my vibe anyways,,
Are u taking drugs ?
6/7, 8:53pm **Koz Kozmos**
no, i don't take drugs
can u stop that ? i've not drunk for 7 dayz
u keep jumping to conclusions!
some times i smoke one helps me sleep, thats all
moonrise kingdom is a film....i said
The Shamen is a song i posted for u that u commented on, on my FB profile
Have u had electric shock treatment yet ?
i've heared its quite relaxing
6/7, 10:17pm **Pre View**
Reason why i'm asking these questions on what u said to me is because I need to finalize many things for myself, so I need to know why your brains reacted the way they did.
THESE ARE THINGS YOU SAID TO ME, that I would like to see explained a bit:
i could hit u with some deep esoteric stuff based on my own finding you are obscure, confused and damaged
u have zero intuition i am telling u the truth
your so predictable

u don't get it
u have zero insight
u'r just on yur hoobby horse
i'm not getting any wisdom from u
u have an over blown way of expressing your soul tech u'r naive
u have no clue about my situation
Your talking JIVE again
6/7, 10:46pm **Pre View**
It's ok, i'm just used to walking bare foots as I need to feel the ground flour whispering,,,
Since when can u monitor judgement
6/7, 11:07pm **Koz Kozmos**
becuz u kept hitting me with your esoteric stuff ,
that i found confusing
i was saying i could give u a taste of your cloudy medicine
your vibe is good but you are very obscure in wot u say
i've said i may be an idioit
i could see u'r damage in the photografs at your exibition
i cannot remember the context of the 'zero intuition'
but i dare say i was right
your hobby horse being your chat about grids etc
you definitly have an overblown way of expressing yur tech
but we all have our own style, all i have done is try to understand as i need help
u are naive , but we all are
in the context i meant about what i was trying to say
talking jive : as in pre the workshop teacher speak
is that ok ? i'm not being rude , just playful i hope
if i offeded u its not been my aim I'm the princess and the
6/7, 11:28pm **Pre View**
U will never offend me, wotever u say, but u know that already.
I accept what you are saying,
The workshop : I need to be hard at times and tell people the truth in a way that they can understand how important it is to move out of self sabotage and self manipulation, especially where youth is concerned, they need a hand that RAISES their Sword of truth.
Why ? because otherwize i'd loose interest and they wouldn't get where they need to be when it comes to truth and inner strength for too many times, they would rather eat laziness; unless life brings through lessons that are hardly bearable.
I need the hard approach for myself thats all there is to it,
but do know wot u'v given me has opened highways to never accept any sideways ever again,,,
6/7, 11:28pm **Koz Kozmos**
my nervous system has been broken
by my experices in my life
noise triggeres me into states of panic
6/7, 11:28pm **Koz Kozmos**
i'm also very limited
anyways
hard to explain
6/7, 11:28pm **Koz Kozmos**
every thing makes me bored
i have worked on myself, selves explored many spirtuel tradition
done rituel majik
i have deprogramed myself
its not my best mode of expresssion

6/7, 11:28pm **Koz Kozmos**
wewwww
6/7, 11:29pm **Pre View**
don't bother, just brewing another beer, haha
6/7, 11:29pm **Koz Kozmos**
i've stopped drinking , typing is not my best mode of expression keep it in context
i have a lot of stuff going on, my life is hard
6/7, 11:32pm **Pre View**
I'm interested to know should you be willing to talk on a broader bandwitch
Please feel free to elaborate..
6/7, 11:33pm **Koz Kozmos**
too much too personal
6/7, 11:33pm Koz Kozmos
MUSIC: Matt Monro - We`re Gonna Change The World

7, 11:34pm **Pre View**
I'm all ears, why shouldn't u go personal,
u'v got nothing to loose
I'm only FB fiction, and maybe it resolves some problems, you could evolve through
6/7, 11:35pm **Koz Kozmos**
i can't type it
6/7, 11:35pm **Pre View** Why ?
6/7, 11:36pm **Koz Kozmos**
u've got yur shit , its ok
6/7, 11:36pm **Pre View**
i s your hand getting u paralized ?
You keep yur brains from full activity
6/7, 11:36pm **Koz Kozmos**
too much info, too complex and my nervous system is broken
6/7, 11:36pm **Pre View**
a little info ? maybe
6/7, 11:36pm **Koz Kozmos**
i've told u a little
6/7, 11:37pm **Pre View**
Maybe u never did this in the past ? Aries are not talkative when they don't get their ways
I mean talking to somebody about problems is easy,
Talking about the inner psyche is your troublesome road
6/7, 11:37pm **Koz Kozmos**
look back i have , i have one other friend
i'm ok about it , but this is not the place
wise up
6/7, 11:39pm **Pre View**
Isn't it strange, i've got u and Rodge or,,,
6/7, 11:40pm **Koz Kozmos** Rogger
6/7, 11:40pm **Pre View**
Please tell me more about him?
6/7, 11:40pm **Koz Kozmos**
it was a joke
Rogger is actually a magic dog
6/7, 11:39pm **Pre View**
I study animal behaviour
I give majic back to their brilliance

6/7, 11:42pm **Pre View**
No, i feel 2 different vibes gong on within u
6/7, 11:42pm **Koz Kozmos**
that saved me once
he could talk then his is mate Sir Gavin Grim bold
6/7, 11:43pm **Pre View**
Is that reason why u don't like dogs?
6/7, 11:43pm **Koz Kozmos**
Roger was ok , i don't like dogs
6/7, 11:43pm **Pre View**
You should be ashamed
I lived with dogs for 30 years, they are my only friends
I always talk to them and other animals
I see thrm very clearly as well in meditation as they show me interesting places
6/7, 11:43pm **Koz Kozmos**
cause people leave them all day in thier back yard barking
and it messes with me, but i'm not into pets
i think if we move up a vibration, animals will talk animals like me
6/7, 11:45pm **Pre View**
there's exceptions, i carried my dog on my back when he was born
because he was only 2 weeks, I had too
Dogs are taken away from their mother way too soon as the earth plane specialists
think it is ok, it is not!
but today he is spoiled and knows it,
still not easy at times as he is getting old now
But I keep his fitness and health up with natural foods and herbs
6/7, 11:47pm **Koz Kozmos**
i'm no longer a prisoner to the mask
but i have a hat collection
6/7, 11:47pm **Pre View** show me your hats , please
6/7, 11:48pm **Koz Kozmos**
i can't with wots happening , i'm done with earth and humans
6/7, 11:49pm **Koz Kozmos**
kizz the asteroid was a song i wrote once
a pun on kiss my ass
6/7, 11:50pm **Pre View**
We know you're done, so how are u going to evolve ,
6/7, 11:50pm **Koz Kozmos**
who's we?
6/7, 11:51pm **Pre View**
You and me out of cosmic debris?
How does that sound huh?
6/7, 11:51pm **Koz Kozmos**
i'm fucked over and over and want soul death to never return,
to be done with all the grids
6/7, 11:53pm **Pre View**
So maybe if I kiss your asteroids, you may catch some fire again?
6/7, 11:53pm **Koz Kozmos**
no one can fire me up , and no one will touch me and its nuthin to do with any sorta hurt
so don't suggest it even in humor
i'm being straight with u, not rude
6/7, 11:55pm **Pre View**
as u wish

U did get some fire into me, it was like the profile picture you have, but then your hands moved through the fire and handed it to me
This is no joke,
6/7, 11:55pm **Koz Kozmos**
my hands are damaged and the fire has gone within
and burns only me
6/7, 11:57pm **Pre View**
And i was seeing u al in blue t-shirt, jeans and this guitar, never had that before, strange thing
Your fire has some specialty i didn't figure out yet, but i didn't give it any more thoughts Hope this will pass,
I only wonder why this happened
6/7, 11:57pm **Koz Kozmos**
I wear blue a lot
i have tried time and time again to build a new fire and let my lamp of knowlege burn
but bad things happen all the time, i am almost destroyed
but have lesss despair, i'm dressed in blue know ,
blue stripy trousers
a blue t shirt and blue reading glasses
and brown sandels , thier hard to get in blue
6/8, 12:01am **Pre View**
I know that the shot i've seen was true as it was crystal clear,
but I did not understand it I did see you laugh, and the way you laughed was very authentic
I wonder why as you told me you never laugh
Which I understand with the bad things happening to you
But you must realize that your preciousness needs to go into the world
No use talking 2u huh,
6/8, 12:02am **Koz Kozmos**
there is no place for me in the world, and i have no intrest in joining in
wot about u ? do u want to join the world ? stupid question
6/8, 12:04am Koz Kozmos
MUSIC: Julian Cope - World shut your mouth

6/8, 12:05am **Pre View**
We'r long past interests,
GETTING YOUR PASSION BACK IN THE BODY HELPS TO BUILD BEYOND THE MATRIX AS WELL,
doing what you like to do makes you forget
that's how i view it now
6/8, 12:05am **Koz Kozmos**
listen TO THE LYRICS
6/8, 12:05am **Pre View**
cannot open it ...not for my country
6/8, 12:05am **Koz Kozmos** ok
6/8, 12:06am **Pre View** got it
6/8, 12:06am **Koz Kozmos** '
but all my passion have come to nothing
6/8, 12:09am **Pre View**
Mine neither,
But lets move our thinking patterns on the higher degrees,
especially with what u posted with radio stations, u could break through the old things while still keeping yourself of the world
I have a feel things are opening up, it is not naïve,

6/8, 12:09am **Koz Kozmos**
i need feed back, music was to share
i tried, did a few shows on cd and sent em out
6/8, 12:10am **Pre View**
Wot feed back do u need ?
6/8, 12:10am **Koz Kozmos**
applause, money and adulation
6/8, 12:10am **Pre View**
adulation ?
6/8, 12:10am **Koz Kozmos**
and a quite place to hide
6/8, 12:11am **Pre View**
place to hide should be no prob
6/8, 12:11am **Koz Kozmos**
i need to form a cosmic band to destroy this dimension and save the earth a place to hide in the country with a studio
6/8, 12:11am **Pre View**
Ok, wot do u have in mind ?
6/8, 12:11am **Koz Kozmos**
and some good friends to share the vision but its too late, and i've gone beyond despair
i'm to messed up
6/8, 12:12am **Pre View**
you're strong enough to pick up
6/8, 12:12am **Koz Kozmos**
i was joking about adulation, i'm 53
even in the past few monthes i see myself tranforming into an older man its getting late
6/8, 12:13am **Pre View**
Age has no meaning i didn't understand the word adulation ... ?
6/8, 12:14am **Koz Kozmos**
and my eyes are very dry etc
adulation : Obsequious flattery; excessive admiration or praise.
age does matter if u want to go on tour
unless u'r sting and have loads of cash
anyways, enuff rock'n'roll dreaming
6/8, 12:15am **Pre View**
so, focus on wot u want to do
eyes etc will pic up
adulation is somehow necessary because I feel,I i know wot ur willing to do 6/8, 12:16am **Koz Kozmos**
i want esacpe , soul death, if i have to return and get wiped again
6/8, 12:16am **Pre View**
STOP THAT FREAKZONE NONSENSE
6/8, 12:16am **Koz Kozmos**
my eyes will not pic up
6/8, 12:16am **Pre View**
Worship urself for once
6/8, 12:17am **Koz Kozmos**
i had a jacket that i painted "worship me" on in my 20's
6/8, 12:17am **Pre View**
Wow kool, show me ?
Or blow me away, haha

6/8, 12:17am **Koz Kozmos**
which i decorated and painted
no one said anything or got the humour people just thought i was an asshole
i didn't mind
i have always worshiped myself
6/8, 12:19am **Pre View**
Maybe the best TIMING is getting around now
U'll get credit now, u don't have to believe me, believe that you can do it
6/8, 12:19am **Koz Kozmos**
and started my own religion u have no clue
i have tried and tried etc, my eyes burn
need drops , whenever i do stuff and raise my energy bad things happen
this is not self sabotage, its very strange the outcomes
6/8, 12:21am **Pre View**
eyes are everything, eyes are important
/8, 12:21am **Koz Kozmos**
i have no conntacts , they seriously fucked up in surgery
like my hand , i broke my wrist and they mis set my hand damaging my knuckle
profile so i can't play the guitar
and i was not that great , but very creative and thats just the froth on the bile
no legal aid in the UK and lawyer will not take this stuff on
maybe if i had loads of money
and doctors are protected, its masonic in the UK, no bullshit
thats all i'm saying
so i appreciate your encouragement, but u have no idea
i have but my whole soul into my creativity , been ripped off a shat on
6/8, 12:26am **Pre View**
I feel yur creativity all over
Do u have clues to repair your wrist ?
Lawyers & doctors, yes I understand
The spirit justice system needs to break through,
Sounds very hard
6/8, 12:26am **Koz Kozmos**
but onwards and upwards, the vibes around me all my life have been very bad
my wrist can't be fixed, maybe a miracle
i 'd choose the eyes first , then many other parts
6/8, 12:27am **Pre View**
seems we have lived similar layers
anyways, got a great lawyer now, don't have to pay him because i made him
understand that justice needs to move in, a whole story ,,,,,,
6/8, 12:28am **Koz Kozmos**
i have been targetted , i'm sure
pay him, hahaha, who and why may i ask
going to go soon
6/8, 12:31am **Pre View**
well there are things that happened to my hand as well
Thy wanted to pay me 10 k euros which i refused while living in poverty
because that would be the fee i would have gotten while getting out of employment
because of my hand .
So lets see and yes it costs me a lot of energy to break thru this,
but gives me hope

8, 12:32am **Koz Kozmos**
i don't have the energy
all the best with your stuff, what work do they do for u ?
6/8, 12:32am **Pre View** thank u,
I wish i could help u
6/8, 12:33am **Koz Kozmos**
i've tried to talk to people but they have no morals and they are protected
i'm just a wyrd guy with no money
i'm ok tho, i get by , but to win
6/8, 12:34am **Pre View** t
They investigate, worse things happen with the Police
I do put the word out, yet Justice needs to come through on higher scales
6/8, 12:34am **Koz Kozmos**
u need cash and contacs, the things that happen to me are surreal
6/8, 12:35am **Pre View**
i have no cash, no contacts, only gridzzzzzz ,
6/8, 12:35am **Koz Kozmos**
bad luck and bad karma would be a better choice feels like a deep curse
i'm not sure i have grids
6/8, 12:38am **Pre View**
I have been told to work with that 10 years from now, I neglected it,
did not understand it, until today,
picking it up as i got to know u and trying to understand it more then ever on a higher ground, please don't think it is easy,
6/8, 12:39am **Koz Kozmos**
i don't and never have, but its is moronic and sadistic this dimension
what are u working with and to wot end
6/8, 12:40am **Pre View**
Well i can only say i understand you somehow as it seems we have similar pains and everything to solve,
but it does not mean it needs to remain that way.
Solutions are many, yet it's all about teaming up and getting together
I've been hurt too much physically . The emotional and mental pains are easier to heal as that emotional
body needs to leave anyways.
6/8, 12:41am **Koz Kozmos**
yes the physical is hard to heal and it's needed there's too much going on with me
i need to stop talking , i feel its hopeless
just have to find a way to live until i die, its the best plan i can think offf
6/8, 12:45am **Pre View**
I had an accident happening with a pit bull and so I got handicapped on
my left hand, 2 fingers which i could not use for a long time,
i repaired one finger, the other one should not be repaired in a sense that I need to take this case into court and they need proof, this is from 2009
6/8, 12:45am **Koz Kozmos**
same with me, wyrd , i still play
6/8, 12:46am **Pre View**
it ain't weird
coz i can hear u play through the chats,
sometimes only, your voice is louder
6/8, 12:46am **Koz Kozmos**
beware schizoid anarchist toy boys

mine was in 2009 as well sorry, was that rude?
6/8, 12:47am **Pre View**
Beware ? Cheers!
6/8, 12:47am **Koz Kozmos**
the correlations are strange why the ? mark
6/8, 12:47am **Pre View**
no , we moved beyond the rude stuff Koz
u know better
6/8, 12:47am **Koz Kozmos**
i'm lost
and rude is a bit of a herd religion control word but i get it
6/8, 12:50am **Pre View**
Aha Ok, euhm, society is simply psycho sick, bipolar - and the dual system
U can't expect to live unity in a dualistic environment
so bringing NEW words to them that ain't their
tea brings some change
Just another brainwave that deletes the 010101, make u go nuts
6/8, 12:50am **Koz Kozmos**
u need to work on your poetics,
your sentence structure your posts and comments confuse people
6/8, 12:51am **Pre View**
u wizgen, clever enough to decipher
so why should I change my words
6/8, 12:54am **Pre View**
I do take into account whom i'm talking too, i talk different to every single entity ....
6/8, 12:55am **Koz Kozmos**
the important thing is we are communicating beyond small talk
6/8, 12:55am **Pre View**
People like the philosophical sides of my FB post,
yet there are too few daring to respond because most
have lost their ways of bringing some interesting intelligent levels to the table.
It is indeed hard work to get people to some level of awakening
6/8, 12:55am **Koz Kozmos**
but there are basic language diffrences, and colloquialisms
i new u'd say that, i hate the word work
makes me think of crap jobs with meat heads
6/8, 12:56am **Pre View**
there's no work, only being , maybe
6/8, 12:56am **Koz Kozmos**
in majik its called THE GREAT WORK
6/8, 12:57am **Pre View**
Language difference ?
6/8, 12:57am **Koz Kozmos**
i've had a enuff work , i just want play
6/8, 12:57am **Pre View**
Language difference ?
6/8, 12:57am **Koz Kozmos**
yes , is it wot the alchemists called it : the hermetic lot
6/8, 12:58am **Pre View**
What do you understand by alchemists ?
6/8, 12:58am **Koz Kozmos**
i can't remember , the great work being distinct to the dignity of so called labor

6/8, 12:59am **Pre View**
I'd Love to know what your thoughts are about the so called Great Work ?
6/8, 12:59am **Koz Kozmos**
the concept of high majik, the work on the soul
basically, wot your doing
6/8, 12:59am **Pre View** Wot am I doing ?
6/8, 1:00am **Koz Kozmos**
Great Work
The term Great Work (magnum opus) is a term used in Hermeticism and in certain occult traditions and religions such as Thelema.
In Hermeticism
Main article: Hermeticism Eliphas Levi (1810–1875), one of the first modern ceremonial magicians and inspiration for the Hermetic Order of the Golden Dawn, discussed the Great Work at length, expanding it from the purely alchemical towards the more spiritual: Furthermore, there exists in nature a force which is immeasurably more powerful than steam, and by means of which a single man, who knows how to adapt and direct it, might upset and alter the face of the world. This force was known to the ancients; it consists in a universal agent having equilibrium for its supreme law, while its direction is concerned immediately with the great arcanum of transcendental magic... This agent...is precisely that which the adepts of the middle ages denominated the first matter of the Great Work. The Gnostics represented it as the fiery body of the Holy Spirit; it was the object of adoration in the secret rites of the Sabbath and the Temple, under the hieroglyphic figure of Baphomet or the Androgyne of Mendes. He further defined it as
Such: The Great Work is, before all things, the creation of man by himself, that is to say, the full and entire conquest of his faculties and his future; ...
6/8, 1:00am **Koz Kozmos**
its on wili , if u want more info
6/8, 1:00am **Pre View**
Wili ? 6/8, 1:01am **Koz Kozmos**
majik is just my personal spelling Wikipedia i meant
6/8, 1:01am **Pre View**
ok, thx for the post, i'll read it, but basically i prefer your thoughts on it, not google's or wiki stuff as we
need to modernize and many things have changed Universally speaking.
And yes of course to some point we are the CREATORS and need to bring the Great Work down which is happening on the planet.
I regret the slow awakening of humans.
Then again we have all within, reason to open that LIGHT CONSCIOUSNESS that is data within to be able to do that work that is being required.
And again The Light Grids are the first settings or Architecture that needs to be grounded in order to bring the bigger work orders through or the cleanse.
It is all about getting humanity out of captivity in the first place
6/8, 1:01am **Koz Kozmos**
i 've not read a great deal but my imagination puts things together i'd be better be talking ,
i don't like sitting infront of a machine typing i hate it ,
any ways , tired
6/8, 1:04am **Pre View**
Maybe get some sleep
Do know I care about your art, just keep on writing songs
Your imagination is very strong, very intelligent, it blows people to some level of truth
why don't u infuse them, u've got nothing left
6/8, 1:05am **Koz Kozmos**
casting pearls at swine, they don't get it,
i'm thinking on a diffrent level

Is it worth mentioning I never regarded myself as an artist, yet the flow is so extreme, I can only mention an Artist friend Floris Van Zyl whom I appreciated on FB for many years and years to come for he exposes exactly what my consciousness is about and thus perspectives are very important.Please look him up as an artist. He exposes my latest communications. It was like merging the holes in the Sky which the human kingdoms do not love. We need to live for a cause and cut out the bullshit. Many Artists today always go into a meditational SPACE that directs them such as rappers and their importance of connecting to the hood. I truly have so much love for Floris and his Family extensions as is being exposed in his Art & Life. The world ain't gonna do it for u, were u cycle into is what u cycled around anaywayz, buzz new visuals through that bring the soft meaning to perspectives. Here is a pic of Floris and how he is so totally occupied with the well being of his horses, dogs and cats. Many times when on Fb he just brings through a design or photograph that aligns to my media in meditation. So I had the exact same picture only with a Leopard that do not appear that easily or often, u got to earn that meeting for it is far deeper then ever acknowledged through the human tongue. Thxxx FLORIS for being with us!!!!

Communication with animals is going to cut through the veils and bring lessons through.

6/8, 1:05am **Pre View**
are ur eyes troubling when playing the guitar ? The fog troubadour needs a crystal view
6/8, 1:06am **Koz Kozmos**
with every thing, on the pc they burn
i need to be more careful, i spend to much time online
6/8, 1:07am **Pre View**
are your eyes in pain when u swim?
6/8, 1:07am **Koz Kozmos**
but i do go off sometime for days; its company i go into a stem room which help
i use drops all the time, severe dryness
i don't want to talk about it
i'll try if i can and sue but have so much going on with many other things
i rather not talk about it please
thank for your support and kind words don't heal me, i need to sue
6/8, 1:10am **Pre View**
just relax, i'm only highly interested in what is going on with ur eyes
as i think it is the most important treasure we have
6/8, 1:10am **Koz Kozmos**
u can try, maybe
u said u could

6/8, 1:10am **Pre View**
Please tell me about the other things, i'd appreciate to know a
s I have a vague picturesque idea of your essence
6/8, 1:10am **Koz Kozmos** blabbering
6/8, 1:11am **Pre View**
I would appreciate to know about the consciousness on your eyes,,, why it happened
6/8, 1:11am **Koz Kozmos** u there ?
6/8, 1:12am **Pre View**
I am willing to go to the bottom-line as far as your eyes are concerned
but I do need your investment, your assistance because I can only help so much to a point where you also need to BELIEVE and further the work I do
otherwise it is useless
It is all about understanding how light moves through, how it can repair and where
WE HOLD BACK, Not the universe! There is no such thing
We all have the tendency to always blame outside our circum-spheres
Once that leaves our idea about diseases, healing can start of because without trust, there is nothing that can possibly take place.
And also, it needs time, patience, insight and above all self investment!
JUST LIKE IN CREATIVE MEDITATIVE SPACES THAT ALLOW FOR THE MAJIC
6/8, 1:12am **Koz Kozmos**
its very starge, our hand stuff
6/8, 1:13am **Pre View**
Ok, Koz, please close your eyes for a whileI'd like to work on your eyes, heal the tear glands, and also the EYEBROW glands are very important,
they lift the PHYSICAL eyes
Don't know if the neurons connected to your eyes have been infected as well?
ITS THE NEURO-SCIENCE THAT COMES INTO PLAY ALL OF THE TIME !
Changing perspectives comes from dialoging old experiences out or maybe, let me know what the medical department had to say, how do they view it, what is your view on it, etc
that would help me a great deal, only if u wish to let me know
6/8, 1:17am **Koz Kozmos**
i felt like this song when i was a boy
6/8, 1:17am **Koz Kozmos**
MUSIC: DAVID BOWIE – AFTER ALL
good night

6/8, 1:21am **Pre View**
I don't know what the heck is happening today, but i feel everything you are moving through, don't even want to know why.Even more weird is that I can feel the burn in ur eyes always too bloody serious, need to cut that,,,
Need some fun, anyways that is good, and so it shall remain,,,
6/8, 1:24am Koz Kozmos
MUSIC: Jobriath I'maman (the other Bowie)
have fun

6/8, 1:24am **Pre View**
OK, lets rock it, not so bad this Jobriath
May your consciousness reveal the majical component u've given a death penalty
Sweet Night to U, and thank u for sharing and being here
6/8, 1:28am **Koz Kozmos**
i've given nothing a death penalty
i drive the rebirth hearse thru streetz of graves
and i've not passed my driving test
6/8, 1:42am **Pre View**
!
I'm willing to close me eyes for a while now, hope u will too,
As I told u, my drivers are me feet, BARE foot back to the Ancient roots Bowie, yess, more then ok, he did wot he was, I guess, very creative. Needing my private vibes now, please keep yourself close to yourself,

6/8, 6:49pm **Koz Kozmos**
MUSIC: The Bilderberg Group – documentary 2012

6/8, 7:39pm **Pre View**
Could he not just talk at the speed of a lightening bolt & elaborate on his point instead of just stating it ...Hi Koz, as u know i'm working a lot Backstage till the end of the month,
So, very little electricity & little FB ... take care,
6/8, 7:41pm **Koz Kozmos**
ok, its worth watching the Bilderberg stuff, contact me wen u want , all the best
6/8, 10:59pm **Pre View**
Koz, these audio problems you have in your ears , are thy cause of your brain damage & mood swings or is it the other way around. Do you have any medical report on it i could read ? as deadly transparant as they usually are ... but i'm very much interested ...
Was reading an article about: When the brain plays music: auditory–motor interactions in musical perceptions and production. When a musician performs, at least three basic motor control functions are required: timing, sequencing and spatial organization of movement. The accurate timing of movements is related to the organization of musical rhythm, whereas sequencing and spatial aspects of movement relate to playing individual notes on a musical instrument. Bilderberg, yes sure, good job David,,, But who is actually going to the Bank and talk to these people and offer worthy solutions. Too many people are being robbed, yet to few take action or don't have a clue to strong solutions.
But anyways, i'm no good at this stuff. But thanks , its always worth watching
6/8, 11:18pm **Koz Kozmos**
Audio problems/ ? i have panic attacks occasionally
i deal with them no one notices
i have no medical report as my condition is not recognized
u have the right key but the wrong keyhole
its not just about banks I'm viewing it from a higher perceptive...
but need to observe possible change
u would need to see what happened today before u jump to conclusions
i don't want to take about this sort of stuff on fake book, its too complex
and goes back to my chilhood
i'm more sane than most on earth, have embraced the FREAKZOID WYRDUS
eating and typing; a bad idea
6/8, 11:29pm **Pre View**
I just thought it was hyperacusis, these loud sounds, sorry
6/8, 11:30pm Koz Kozmos
MUSIC: RAMONES - Cretin Hop

6/8, 11:31pm **Pre View**
Freakzoid Wyrdus ?
6/8, 11:32pm **Koz Kozmos**
go back look , u said it was refined, thankx for caring, you are appreciated
6/9, 1:01am Koz Kozmos
MUSIC: Confirmed: The U.S. Military Has Worked With Aliens? 2013

6/9, 1:05am **Koz Kozmos**
i hope u have a productive time and i won't bother u unless u want to chat
6/9, 1:07am **Pre View**
Sorry, I many times have an unusual way of overcomplicating things because somehow I simply love that, but it might sound of the grid or too weird to some people as its also highly imaginative with a difficult sense of humor.
It keeps my brains in healthy streams beyond the ruins of earth
But I need sleep, i highly respect the time u invest in me !

6/9, 1:07am **Koz Kozmos**
dream your self awake, blessings upon u
6/9, 10:33am **Pre View**
U will never ever bother me, it is always more then just a tremendous pleasure
to tap into ur exquisite variables,,,
Did u talk to any Aliens? What are they 2 u?
June 9, 2013
6/9, 3:50pm **Koz Kozmos**
not sure , I'd like to be hypnotise, to regress
I'm not sure wot they are but i have my theories and have had some vague
experiences,
wot are the 2 u ?
6/9, 3:55pm **Koz Kozmos**
MUSIC: The Carpenters - Calling Occupants of Interplanetary Craft

6/9, 4:00pm **Koz Kozmos**
MUSIC: Kenneth Grant Declaration

6/9, 11:42pm **Pre View**
Wot a brilliant day ...
Euhm, aliens , no did not tap into that yet (maybe some wizzy woppy wild
imaginations) , but supremely interested in your theories
Was thinking about David (Icke),
like he might need many extensions to broadcast worldwide ...
Will put my intentions on you this week coming & will let you know if anything worth
aligns(radio station) ... as gates are opening more then expected
Can u not broadcast a free radio station in the UK ?
6/10, 1:23am **Koz Kozmos**
i don't do any thing for free and internet radio, the tech and set up would bore me a
and i'm rushed of my feet fighting the sickness
wizzy woppy wild imaginations....
sounds a bit moronic , glad u had a good day
6/10, 1:27am Koz Kozmos
MUSIC: THE SWEET - SPOTLIGHT (1971)
.
6/10, 1:28am **Koz Kozmos**
a free spirit to u , great vox
6/10, 1:32am **Koz Kozmos**
MUSIC: THE SWEET-ACTION

6/10, 1:32am **Koz Kozmos** great clothes ,
action , listen to the lyrics
6/10, 1:44am **Koz Kozmos**
are u a glam rocker?
The Pleiadians invented it...., celver chapz and chapettez
6/10, 8:53am **Pre View**
i'm quirky, undefinable rocker
inventing a self,
Xpress train as quarks of the action
Pleiadians, nononono,
Earthling clothes do not fit my skeleton so my tailor says!
6/10, 9:51am **Pre View**
am a complete moron ye is wot u say about me, can u get along with that ?
6/10, 12:48pm **Koz Kozmos a**
bit rude saying your a moron
I apologize

i am as well a total moron, i have my cloaks made on orion
i can get on with that
6/10, 1:03pm Koz Kozmos
MUSIC: Anthony Newley and Sammy Davis sing Newley/Bricusse

6/10, 1:07pm **Koz Kozmos**
there is always a joker in the pack
6/10, 1:07pm **Pre View**
What a beautiful world it would be if everybody would hear their call into DESTINY!
Cloaks on Orion, wowy zowy that is blinding me eyes
U must be the Joker in the big pack of blinding cards, are u ?
In wot sense did I get electric ?
I'm grateful to the wonder & beauty that is U
I like Bleu Velvet, do you?
Would u not be ready to move into Supreme Intel ?
How would u do that ?
6/12, 7:37pm **Pre View**
I feel like I cannot talk no more on Fb, strange and too limited,
it feels to be for empty fools
There is a question bothering me, maybe U have the answer :
If flaming up with your Eternal flame mating process ,
would it be a possible outcome to move together into Twin Unions and then completing the Universal SeedCell as in partnering up or would it be necessary to get the fusion of waves in yet another octavation
Or ACTIVATION
WATCH BLUE VELVET
6/12, 7:40pm **Pre View**
Am listening to the music, thank u again & again !!!
U always give me EXactly what I need, and put it out through music
isn't it sothat wording thoughts through has become just a vibe out of a vibe
What the neurons digest is what they can put out right
6/12, 7:41pm **Koz Kozmos**
blue velvet, the movie or?
Supreme Intel ? I'm ready
6/12, 7:43pm **Pre View**
Blue velvet is one of my fav movies
But Blue velvet refers to you in this context , as you love blue
6/12, 7:43pm **Koz Kozmos** ok
6/12, 7:44pm **Pre View**
Sorry I didn't notice your beauty before,,
6/12, 7:44pm **Koz Kozmos**
thanks , but i don't like the feel of velvet Eternal flame mating process ?
whats that?
6/12, 7:45pm **Pre View**
Why do u like the FB page in the first place ? (Eternal Flames)
something like flames coming together or perfect Eternal partners
as we were all split eons ego, and thus the consciousness of dualism
and binary systems took over
6/12, 7:46pm **Koz Kozmos**
ijustliketoclick, howru?
6/12, 7:48pm **Pre View**
When painting, I feel puzzle pieces of my entire life coming together
Don't know really how I feel, it's a question that moves the motor mechanisms in the brain to a very high degree because they always react to such a question or a rich source of questions rise with this question.
Performing loads of healing on myself

6/12, 7:49pm **Koz Kozmos**
bad bard, longing for total soul death
6/12, 7:50pm **Pre View**
Done a lot of research on healing you especially studying ears
and how they respond to music.
I think you don't need too much healing, just alignments and the gridding the body
After that , you'll be able to heal self through the Grid Technology or understanding
how that consciousness can override your dense and painfulride in life.
(there I go again, hahaha)
6/12, 7:50pm **Koz Kozmos**
ok lets do it , my eyes were fukked up after lazer surgery
6/12, 7:51pm **Pre View**
I had great experiences last Sunday with people but they always repeat the same stuff
like they all have the same brain- which is actually true, collective consciousness:
they are curious to get to know me and ask me what I do in life and how I get to have
such a funky energies and fun wording,
they think its amazing how I put conversation – music-and comments together.
But thy have no idea of the work involved and keeping it up to evolve and keep the
alignments up with your Spirit and so on.
It is indeed hard work to gain knowledge and heal self at the same time.
6/12, 7:51pm **Koz Kozmos**
just fix them to begin with, who were these people?
6/12, 7:54pm **Pre View**
U will be able to fix them after alignments ---
One of them was Thomas who befriended u on FB(he asked me and was scared of u
but thought u were an interesting person) and his girlfriend Anna, and then we went
for a drink just around the corner as thy know I avoid the city
6/12, 7:54pm **Koz Kozmos**
scared of me, he's not too intutive then
6/12, 7:56pm **Pre View**
If I need to work on your eyes ;it'll cost u more then a few days of fun with me ,
and there's a lot of psychological components u need to be willing to release
6/12, 7:56pm **Koz Kozmos**
glad you're having fun and positive feedback
i need to try and sue first
but they've stoped legal aid etc
i'm also wanting to sue for them damaging my hand sorry,
a lot of stufff that makes my life a misery
6/12, 7:57pm **Pre View**
Thomas is only 20, but he's getting it through the meditations I provide for youth,
and wants to move fast as he is learning about gridding and TRACKING
He truly wanted to experience my grid space in private with me beyond the
meditational sessions: I warned him it would get very tough, but he wanted it and it
gave him the trill of how Evolution feels in the Grid and therefor got to understand
the necessity of Crystal Grid upgrades , just as our CS needs upgrades
6/12, 7:57pm **Koz Kozmos**
all you term is cost and work, u sound like a protestant
6/12, 7:58pm **Pre View**
DO U WORK FOR FREE , huh?
I gave Thomas a free ride!
6/12, 7:58pm **Koz Kozmos**
i don't work
6/12, 7:58pm **Koz Kozmos**
ok, lets go , Ley Lines!
6/12, 7:59pm **Pre View**
Hey Koz, I could work on ur eyes for 5 hours, that is a lot,
then again quite necessary but I think u need
to know how i do it and align this with wot u'v learned

6/12, 7:59pm **Koz Kozmos**
i agree
6/12, 8:01pm **Pre View**
And then again I have the intention to do the healing for a week or so,
but that'll change u'r whole consciousness as well, and getting this info to you on social media is way too much work.
How many hours would you like me to work on you? What would be the outcome.
6/12, 8:01pm **Koz Kozmos**
i've been eating , but can type better now
6/12, 8:01pm **Pre View** good, wot did u eat ?
6/12, 8:01pm **Koz Kozmos**
what effects do these changes have ? veg mashed pots ,vegi sausage and gravey
6/12, 8:02pm **Pre View**
depends on where u are willing to go,
To my FEELERS, ALL THE WAY as u've got all to gain,
you cannot lose anything right?
6/12, 8:03pm **Koz Kozmos**
what effects do these changes have?
i will do wotever i have to do to go beyond this dimesion of fools and evolve
me 10 mins, will be back, if thats ok
6/12, 8:04pm **Pre View**
Everything really depends on what you're willing to achieve
6/12, 8:04pm **Pre View**
Ok, i'll have a little smoke outside and ask the Star messengers how to talk to you
6/12, 8:19pm **Koz Kozmos**
u don't smoke
6/12, 8:19pm **Pre View**
I don't know if u remember,
but somewhere in the beginning we started chatting I asked u "please teach me"
this was my way of telling u I miss out on the theory, the technical department, while I knew U had that somehow.
Lets put heads together & exchange the energy because this earth plane is all about unifying processes and I thought this might get quite interesting to offer people some completion and try out a new level of awakening.
But going backstage i was willing to practice what i've learned and dig deeper for the first time in my life thanks to u,
I mean your questions made me look up things in the Universal google machine !
Let's say I'm integrating stuff a little deeper and am getting to see different view when it comes to understanding Light Technology
The one thing bothering me is that i can move stages around , but are you really ready to fall of the cliff of creepy consciousness regarding your complaints.
A lot of brain matter needs to be removed
Many parts of the brain have lost their efficiency as it runs on the binary system
Evolution goes back to geometrical patterns that are almost always trinary
From 01 into 012
6/12, 8:19pm **Koz Kozmos**
stop it !
6/12, 8:21pm **Pre View**
You are very technical, with great knowledge
you don't have to listen to me, I am rather very practical
6/12, 8:22pm **Koz Kozmos**
creepy consciousness , i have a practical side
6/12, 8:23pm **Pre View**
sure ur practical side is imagination which we both have in overtones
6/12, 8:23pm **Koz Kozmos**
i'm imaginative, this is my strenght
yes , i meant i do the washing up etc, what about my curse

6/12, 8:24pm **Pre View**
I wish u'd talk more about urself
Yes, imagination is why people hate me, they hate it because it moves fast and they cannot catch up with my brains, except for aquarian people, those folks are ok with me. Imagination is high intelligence because it assists the movement into the DIVINE SPACES
Too much CS has been closed down for these parts cannot function in a binary system. Data runs through within a trinary system
It synchronizes the brain
U can analogue this with people taking psychedelics
and not having the knowledge of how to do this without drugs
Synchronizing waves assist a lot, just breathing them through and also detail what kind of synchro waves are in existence as that would probably also flow with upgrades in CS like moving from a bachelor into Mastery degrees.
6/12, 8:24pm **Koz Kozmos**
interview me
its too confusing to talk about myself, other wise ask questions,
and i'll try and answer
do u want to interview me, then i'll interview u after that
6/12, 8:26pm **Pre View**
You are just not used to talking about yourself because you never went over that supper hill
But please, i'm curious, interview me,
My mind is pretty much empty today,
so that should be easy to interview with meaningful observation please!
6/12, 8:29pm **Koz Kozmos**
were do u live
6/12, 8:29pm **Pre View**
I have no home, haha
Hasselt(near Brussels)
6/12, 8:29pm**Koz Kozmos**
wots the place with the candle sticks and the small wizard
6/12, 8:30pm **Pre View** my place
6/12, 8:30pm **Koz Kozmos**
u said u had no home , why are u so confusing
6/12, 8:30pm **Pre View**
my heart is my home
6/12, 8:31pm **Koz Kozmos**
stop the platitudes
6/12, 8:31pm **Pre View**
reverse the ions in ur body, i don't have confuse-ion
and turn confusion into clarity
Generate the rocks on the sandy floors of the oceans, highly informative
Colors and shapes break down into numbers symbolism and maybe expand and load more neurons, it is possible to regrow nerves , but takes a lot of work,
iMAGINE THE AMOUNT OF VERY FINE FIBERS TURNING INTO GOLD
6/12, 8:31pm **Koz Kozmos**
i don't know how to do that
wotz an ion ? how do u reverse it ? and to wot purpose ?
ok , u are confusing , shall i be confusing ?
6/12, 8:33pm **Pre View**
u have intelligence, i have practice
Command it in and breathe it through counter clockwise and blow the big dirty spiral of confusion out. Then breathe the clear spiral of crystal clarity over the brains
And hocus pocus , you're done! SUCCESS!
6/12, 8:33pm **Koz Kozmos**
i have pratice too, i'm stupid
6/12, 8:34pm **Pre View**
Please tell me about your own practice

6/12, 8:34pm **Koz Kozmos**
i have no idea how to breathe counter clock i swim, play my guitar ,exercise
6/12, 8:35pm **Pre View**
you've got your vibes running, but u need to understand electricity, yer heat command them to run the other way around and delete your soul stagnation just command! It is like when you take a shower and the water runs a certain direction, U can turn that into another direction.
The invisible energies always listen
Just give it a go, don't try to understand, start with DOING and the understanding will come Remember practice is very important.
It brings more IN-sight, inner knowledge.
6/12, 8:35pm **Koz Kozmos**
how do u command, my soul is not stagnant
6/12, 8:35pm **Pre View**
do u have any other physical practices besides swimming?
if ur soul is not stagnant , why don't u move into your universal shoes then huh?
Disease is SOUL stagnancy, THAT IS ALL THERE IS TO IT!
But interview me,
AND START TO UNDERSTAND THE DIFFERENCE BETWEEN LIVING THE SOUL AND SPIRIT LANES,,,
And also if this whole life was not about leaving soul consciousness, we wouldn't suffer the trouble that is worldwide. We would be the happy Creator vibes that had no more thought about the dark age. Then again, the Age of Aquarius is the first Golden Age and the Rise of humanity,
the rise of Earth into its Universal Light position.
6/12, 8:36pm **Koz Kozmos**
move universal, what does that mean ?
i have had many physical practices, mainly yoga and meditation
i gave them up, used to work out a bit, i use a mind machine to meditate
Intermediately, ok first question
6/12, 8:38pm **Pre View**
Your practices sound very boring and outdated
But nevertheless I always wondered how u get to vibrate so high at times Music it is huh, OK, Questions please ?
6/12, 8:38pm **Koz Kozmos**
did u as a girl experience paranormal phenomena?
6/12, 8:39pm **Pre View**
no, none
6/12, 8:39pm **Koz Kozmos**
i had loads , what is your first memory?
6/12, 8:40pm **Pre View**
But i was always targeted just like you were
Even at a young age like 6 years old, my friends would call me a weirdo because I was always exercising during school breaks. I needed that, to be able to deal with energies. My intuition was very high back then, but I did not realize that; being a kiddo with good vibes living with depressed abusive parents. and my first book at age 11 was about cosmologies, i put it away, never really read it, but thinking of it today
6/12, 8:41pm **Koz Kozmos**
what was the book about, were did u get it and why did u not read it
6/12, 8:41pm **Pre View**
People who knew me at age 10-12 are coming back into my life now telling me I'm still that crazy as I was as a kid, even more while i was actually only a loner doing my own stuff. I never felt i could ever connect with anyone, for all my experiences were streaming into jealousy of people which I never understood, there is no point in jealousy, i was just fascinated by the electrical output of the brain and how bodies react through emotions, how people impact their own neurological neglect, grey zones, haha
6/12, 8:42pm **Koz Kozmos**
u can be crazy and a loner I know no one, i only spk to u a jain doe and a few nods to other people

6/12, 8:43pm **Pre View**
well i had to choose a book from a bookstore my parents where assigned to ....
like they needed to buy a book every monthly,
i put it away because i didn't understand it at that age and read some pages here and there because somehow I knew it was sent by the Universe to remember creation, to remember my ancient roots.
I would always talk to the stars at night, and did not really have a relationship with my parents nor my sister, they felt like aliens to me
6/12, 8:43pm **Koz Kozmos**
ok u suffered abuse u said
6/12, 8:44pm **Pre View** yes
6/12, 8:44pm **Koz Kozmos**
how old are u did say that?, never ask a lady her age , hahaha
6/12, 8:44pm **Pre View**
please excuse me one moment, need to answer the phone,
6/12, 8:44pm **Koz Kozmos**
ok, please take yur time
6/12, 8:47pm **Pre View**
I am 51
6/12, 8:47pm **Koz Kozmos**
ok , were u born in Hasselt/Belgium?
6/12, 8:48pm **Pre View**
yes, but this is the first time since birth that I actually live here
So is it actually birth that defines where one is from ? I think it's the environment and how we grow up like in anthropology – although I have zero % cultural background which makes it easy for me to tap into any culture and understand some roots.
6/12, 8:48pm **Koz Kozmos**
were did u live before, its hard
6/12, 8:50pm **Pre View**
from 18- 30 : BRUSSELS
30 -45 : KNOKKE (the coast of belgium - zeebrugge etc)
After that, several places in the nearby surroundings
went to Australia for a few years
6/12, 8:50pm **Koz Kozmos**
did u have a youth culture image
6/12, 8:50pm **Pre View**
18-19,5 : Australia
did not have any youth, or being young and experience that as most do
or was not like most young people do like having parties and going out et.
I certainly wish I had experienced some youth cult image
I did not fit in anywhere.
Even when I spend my holidays in Spain and gathering with youth from France
they also though I was an outcast.
I remained a loner since childhood, and felt quite good about it.
I did not really need what was not pleasing anyways, nothing in my teens seemed interesting so I started to write a journal which I threw away before I moved to this place like 2 years ago. I regret though, but its like leaving the past, must be done, right,
6/12, 8:51pm **Koz Kozmos**
i've been in this room for 15 years by myself
6/12, 8:51pm **Pre View**
i understand, please share ur thought about this ?
I live quite similar, never any companion
The physiology of the brain moves from the inside out
It may therefor be a necessity to align to equal outer spaces and the Light engines in the Cosmos
How else can the brain synchronize and receive data through synchronization
Comes down to expanding and allowing AWARENESS

6/12, 8:51pm **Koz Kozmos**
why did u go to Australia ?
no one to hang out with and the streets filled with meat heads bores me
6/12, 8:52pm **Pre View**
I COULD NEVER BE SATISFIED WITH SEEING WHAT I EXPECT TO SEE,
It also maybe always about allowing a new flow, some different movement
This is just popping up in my head as a beautiful memory: last year of High School in Antwerp, I had the intention to go to Australia with a friend of mine, as she was as crazy as I am, but she died before the end of the school term, before graduation. That was so hard, so I thought I owed her the respect to still go to Australia and I stayed longer than my initial intent. And again, it was a loners' experience.
6/12, 8:53pm **Koz Kozmos**
owned her? i just want to go to a higher level of consciousness and faster i am an illusion moving at a different speed, things are too slow for me
6/12, 8:55pm **Pre View**
Yes I felt I had to pay tribute to our time together, it was the last year of high school, i lifted everybody's consciousness already back then as I was quite rebellious... and still they got me so down. So all I could think of was: bring justice to all teachers , i 'll teach you some day.
Hope that day is coming in soon... I didn't get my graduation because they wanted me to fail and invented something I do not quite remember because they couldn't stand my harsh wording nor my leader skirt! The schools' rules where that we had to wear blue trousers or skirts and a with blouse or t-shirt.
That was certainly not my thing: so going through the rules I SAW they they did not mention the quality of the FABRIC of the skirt: this resulted in ME BUYING A LEATHER BLUE SKIRT and quite obviously many student followed this example because it was kool and the schools' Director could not possibly say a word about it because it wasn't mentioned in their rules. So, the whole school changed with my presence. I loved it, yet they hit me hard, they wanted me to go over the last year of high school once again.
But I didn't buy into that, I went to Australia and finished my high school somehow when I was 25.
6/12, 8:56pm **Koz Kozmos**
wot sorta school was it ?
6/12, 8:58pm **Pre View**
Just a high school run by NUNS (my parents put me there at 16 because i was a rebel)
so after 2 months thy understood thy had to give me a private room in the city. Here is why: because I could not swallow the food that was being served and also the small minded streams in consciousness was like a big burden. It was a boarding school, nights were terrible . As a free spirit I made fun of getting my temperature so high that the Nuns were so scared and concerned that they called the hospital.
It looked like a suicide attempt through rebellious shoes because I knew and shew very tastefully what I was doing, haha
6/12, 8:59pm **Koz Kozmos**
suicide, no good u need a soul death
was it a private school ?
i was taken out a school at 11, as i was running away from the sickness
6/12, 9:00pm **Pre View**
Not really, i was very conscious of my own doing and careful,
They (my parents and the school board)fell into the trap with lots of mayhem and silly worry while i had a good time at the hospital, still remember that very clearly, I took care of some elderly, they had fun
6/12, 9:00pm **Koz Kozmos**
I did'nt really go to school, its sad
do u still see them ?
6/12, 9:01pm **Pre View**
i'm interested in wot u've gone through...
how come you were taken out of school at that young age?

6/12, 9:01pm **Koz Kozmos**
i asked u to interview me
i'm saying some things, to tell u we'd need to talk maybe
6/12, 9:02pm **Pre View**
i remember my english teacher (the only one who actually loved me)
he used to speak Irish (nobody noticed but me) he was a great guy.
Wonder why u'r bringing this up
6/12, 9:03pm **Koz Kozmos**
what i've gone thru just goes on more and more, all negative events
6/12, 9:03pm **Pre View**
Yess, absolutely, talking to each other would be way better than this Fb transference of some kind. I was continually searching for balance and my perceptions were so different at that time. My network of communication was just my dogs basically and so I taught myself telepathic communication which led into a panoramic and many extraordinary experiences which my parents did not like, nor did they ever put any interest into me. I felt like i was non existent to everybody.

MY INTERNALS: Some things in live are definitely and unquestionably worth to remember as we all leave many traces behind for some reason. Remembering going to Australia and traveling through the country is bringing me many good memories today. I was TOTALLY carried in the arms of Spirit and so well guided, yet not aware of it. It was my natural state of being and so at the age of 20 I though it was logical and instinctive for every body. But it is not. I had many roots in Australia, and will quite obviously go back down there to pick up many things that became crystal clear today. If only I could work with Wild Life over there and be a teacher for the many who want to know.
At this time , I really need to mention a few things about my son : From 2013 until 2018 he was going through the same struggle in high school as I was back in my teens. He could not possibly make it through his last year in high school and ended up trying many different things. Today at age 25, he managed to graduate and left 2 years ago to travel the roads throughout Australia. Isn't that something unusual? It is exceptional and remarkable and memorable.
Me and my son, the same trouble with graduation, and then making the same move into Australia. I never told him anything about my stay in Australia. It was a natural intention as he must have the travelers' jeans (genes) I am wearing. I just wish to teach, coach and be with youth and animals and merge them so they can both adjust mentality and heal perceptional dynamics through new models. Youth definitely needs a special person that offers solutions that don't take months taking into regard the suicide rate and depression.

6/12, 9:03pm **Koz Kozmos**
We stand in the place were the Shadowz shine
6/12, 9:06pm **Pre View**
In the end we become the mystery to the mystery
6/12, 9:07pm **Koz Kozmos**
i don't like the mystery
6/12, 9:09pm **Koz Kozmos**
i use tobbaco with no additives at times,
so i'm a hypocrtite, I just have a little smoke at night to get me to sleep
6/12, 9:10pm **Pre View** which are ?
6/12, 9:10pm **Koz Kozmos**
maybe a ciggarette worth a day maybe half a ciggerette ; lost again maybe i am a moron
American spirit there are other brands but can u trust anything , lungs and smoke no good but something is going to murder us
6/12, 9:14pm **Pre View**
I have a cigarette when having a drink or 2 or 3,
but I always cleanse my lungs and blood circulation after that

good either, because you don't really move forward with a stop & go syndrome.
I see it as a disorder somehow that affects deep analysis within.
Then again, we also keep repetition of eating – although I refine my Divine dinners at the round table as much as I can.
Remember the Knights of the first order, order must come back on the planet
Letz move into the Immortal Grapevines,,haha
Youth needs the option to study knowledge and change identity
Without any institution, university, government holding them back
FREE EDUCATIONAL CHOICES IN EVERY SCHOOL IS GOING TO BE THE NEW SENSATION OF THIS AGE. IN THE END THEY WILL HAVE NO OPTION BUT TO ALLOW PEOPLE LIKE ME
6/12, 9:14pm **Koz Kozmos**
how do u cleanse them
6/12, 9:15pm **Pre View**
i don't teach on Fb , remember
Its too much to explain, and you'll get lost again and that is no fun 2 me.
What is worth mentioning is that the breath needs to be able to move into your trillion cells, no matter how minuscule so that the air you breathe with certain levels of clearing consciousness attached can reach into the detail where the disease is going on.
6/12, 9:15pm **Koz Kozmos**
ok, i use a wet room and sauna, the city is a polluted place to be
6/12, 9:17pm **Pre View**
I use spiritual sauna, takes less energy and effort and is way more entertaining
6/12, 9:17pm **Koz Kozmos** wots a spiritual sauna,
6/12, 9:17pm **Pre View**
One mo please, need to set my bladder free
I need more inner body experiences which stabilizes brainwaves
6/12, 9:17pm **Koz Kozmos**
Immortal Grapevines? i'm almost dead on the vine
ok , to pee or not to pee that is the question
6/12, 9:32pm **Koz Kozmos**
u in the hood ? or
6/12, 9:37pm Koz Kozmos
MUSIC: SHIVA'S QUINTESSENCE - Cosmic Surfer

6/12, 9:40pm **Koz Kozmos**
bliss out on the inner wave
6/12, 9:42pm **Pre View**
Marvelous, groovy song, what would be the difference between Eternal and Immortal?
6/12, 9:43pm **Koz Kozmos**
So Immortal, I was going, but 2009 screwed me
Joachim was a mistake , he posts a lot of stuff sorry , don't want to mention, wrong stuff
6/12, 9:45pm **Pre View**
In 2009 i was going back into society because my son bought me a dress and told me it was time to get some kind of human infusion, and it got me down, really down, in a way that I let people take advantage of me when it comes to resetting consciousness and bringing healing through. I gave so much for free, which I would never ever do again. That is because today spirit told me information , data and healing are sacred and needs to be payed for big time like any other business.
Giving for free kept me in poverty and unworthiness for more then 30 years. It was wrong. It is not because the invisible Forces and Sources are not seen that I should not get payed because the hours spend in healing sessions and doing so much research in the domains of Light sciences are beyond comprehension. Scientist and physicians are being payed right? Light Scientists like me should also be payed and be more credited for various reasons

EVERYTHING ON THE EARTH IS INVERTED
AND SO THEY HAVE THE OPPOSITE POINTS OF VIEW
WITHOUT EXPERIENCE!!!! Reason is not enough to calculate change
we are actually doing the work such as bringing through the light sciences and
programs to deprogram and reset peoples' brain into the correct axis positions so
they can move forward crystal clear disease free.
The false perception people have about it leads to judgement and concepts that
would be better left into the underworld of no return.
Hey Koz, now i want to get to the Grapevine, so Divine, as it moves the soul out,
anchors your spirit roots and makes you make the moves like a dancers' shoes do
I cannot breathe when u mention Joachim,
i gave all of me, all, just to get him out of psychiatric institutions, u don' t have a clue
what was going on, Not even grateful for all the healing he got
It was a precious lesson for me to learn because when people in their thirties and
fourths still do not wanna leave their mom, something seriously blinding is going on.
People loose their sense of discernment and cannot grasp the truth within the
present reality. Reason why many psychopaths and bipolar people choose not to get
better, they love the fantasy world in which they can do whatever they are pleased
with or have the tendency to abuse and manipulate anyone just to get what they want
and when they want it. Psychiatrist are just too lazy with a high lack in knowledge.
It is all within the educational system, if universities do not have the proper
programs to teach knowledge and demand faculties and Doctors in their domain to
bring through yearly renewed layers that bring proof and many shifts in
consciousness,
DREAMING THE CHANGE THROUGH, WE NEED NEW SNEAKERS

I would love to teach in universities and high schools but they even refuse to let me
give a simple lecture about certain topics , BECAUSE THEY FEAR TO LOOSE
THEIR JOBS when truth is being told that is about it.
The psychiatrist I sued told me she feared losing too many patients and so they are
being protected. This is just what one professor told me
No neuro dynamics, SLAUGHTERED NEURO ORGANISMS fucking up the young
It leads to a large dose of depression and ptsd amongst students! i've lived it for
almost 7 years. There is so much potential to develop consciousness and make a
bring through radical differences in the study room of the young.
Joachim wanted a double life and refused to disappoint his mom to the disgrace of
sacrificing his own life. Talents, the inner psyche and the wonder of being gets
destroyed, the intellect loses its observation, it loses its variables and cannot be
replaced. Yet, I have noticed they like to go back to the sentiment of
being somewhere in past experiences for example.
I suffered too many incredible situations and even sued his mom as well
I won somehow but did not move the whole situation into higher court for that would
cost me all my energy ...
And it was timed for me to move forward, to understand it on higher degrees within
the learning spaces or zones that are defined by spirit for us to understand the
malfunctioning beat in the hearts of many or ALL!
It thought me there is nothing that cannot be healed: so it made me study a lot and
download codes along degrees in consciousness to bring many shifts through.
And also, I learned massively from the psychiatric institution, the abuse of
Academics and the self abuse within education.
Hi Koz, are you still there? or are you hiding again?
I wuz just explaining, and thought you'd read between my line? ???
I think it would be very helpful to teach students about the natural world and how
their organism can just communicate with it as a natural elixir that assists GROWTH.

9:45pm **Koz Kozmos**
MUSIC: The Walker Brothers - No regrets

6/12, 9:45pm **Koz Kozmos**
still here, shall i pop offff
6/12, 9:46pm **Pre View**
no don't , just dance a little
People just accepted the DESIGN OF LAZINESS that came in with the Soul
6/12, 9:46pm **Koz Kozmos**
never give all off your self to any one
could u not heal him ?
the guy from Iceland , never trust anarchists
I'm an extreme right wing fascist , far more noble, haha
6/12, 9:49pm **Pre View**
Joachim cannot think nor talk anymore, i got him out,
and his mother was jealous of that and lied to him,
he has no clue to ever better,
I HEALED HIM INSIDE OUT, yet he chose to go back on psycho medication because he could not handle the manipulation of his mom
HE DID REALIZE THAT! He lived with me for 2 months and all he said was: FINALLY FREEDOM! Until his mom got into my house and told him he would lose everything (financially) if he would not return home. And so the next day he returned home and left me quite alone, empty, lost, abused, manipulated,
angry, whatever.
It was very emotional.
I am awaiting the day he will awaken, but i'm finding my way out for my love to heal him was so intense, and that is reason why i choose to not to heal psycho's again , instead create healing programs for them, for those interested to go beyond the dumbing of meds
We never did have any sexual intercourse because he was told by his mom that women where bad and that he should distantiate himself completely from women (reason for his angry posts on social media. He is completely ramshackled by his mom who is actually the sickness itself and he was to weak to let go of her.
Nevertheless we had a strong bond because we were lovers of art,,,
6/12, 9:49pm **Koz Kozmos** don't be a martyr
6/12, 9:50pm **Pre View**
Whatever he posts is a copy of a copy, he always searches to COPY something like many people do. All u get is "hahaha" while on drugs or WTF when nothing comes, or nobody replies on his Fb profile. It is actually a continual cry for help while REFUSING ALL THE HELP. I was his last outlet so to speak because I gave him proof it could be done. I took him out of anxiety, and the whole downgrading latter of self abuse through drugs. He looks very shabby now, miserable.
Anyways does not even realize the power of his mom, an Aries type of person or DO AS I SAY OR I'LL KILL YOU type of character, literally.
6/12, 9:51pm **Koz Kozmos**
ok , your business
I used to want to fall in love
no more now, people are to human
6/12, 9:52pm **Pre View**
I question the fact why we DO CARE SO MUCH about people,
the connections we have etc?
I came to understand I love people so much, it comes from the learning zones of rapid expansion on the other side before this life on earthI think my Source put me in the most difficult jobs and with Mentally Ill people to deepen the mystery of study and steer me into the avenues of developing these deep programs that override Mental abuse and psychotic evolutionary change that is so much needed for everybody on the planet. No matter if you are diagnosed with mental illness or not;
THE EARTH IS AN ILL MENTAL INSTITUTION
I thinks it's the network of mutual interests that comes together.
6/12, 9:53pm **Koz Kozmos**
good question , becuz we're a diffrent soul race

6/12, 9:53pm **Pre View**
I don't think so
Hypnosis may be the most terrible thing people do as they go into regression of the soul and not their Spirit, very manipulated headlines come out of that for it is easy to remember all of this life which we do not need, hypnosis cannot tap into Spirit Consciousness fully running on Spirit when it is in a present state running on the the broken soul and thus missing out on many electronics that compute the correct data.
Well , i'v actually not loved many , maybe 3 people, I'm a loner remember!
Its not about what the Earth wants, it about what LIGH EARTH REQUIRES, and there is no play ground to that for that is too Divine, no monsters allowed
People just forgot how to choose wise
In the age of information, there is just a growth , sort of blowing the AXE-WAYS through quite a learning zone to get the Immortal shoes running,
DO YOU GET THAT, I guess you do know
I actually don't know anything about sex, never diged into it
Had a relationship that lasted 13 years,
yet today that seems less then a gipsy type of acceptable heart degrees
It was good, very good, becoz the person involved was a Pink Bull (taurus), an earthling , so that is easy as I'm all earth, a Capricorn.
I will remain untamed for the rebel within never needs to be tamed,
it needs to be understood.
There isso much strength to this. All Capricorns have been cut off like for 50 years because there is a lot to learn from the Saturation within Saturn, AND WE WILL RETURN, be prepared! So, when meeting Joachim and his stuff , i could only give and give and give, and it got him out of many control systems, it was a one way street indeed because he felt he was not allowed to love , (imagine the
pain and hurt he went through) anyways with my harsh character i burned through it .The unification experience on earth is all about merging the perfect male/female vibes and how people interact. Its a space of study where one can find love because it requires an elevated state of consciousness that allows for all universes to ride through the spinal degrees - and bring that Eternal partner through , this kept me giving and moving and doing and helping (BUT !!!!!) I need to understand now how it is that humanity can just have sex like rabbits and just fall in love f, or think they do, people forgot so much, they all seem to live so unreal,
I was born with the consciousness of Spirit ,
I knew at age 6 that relationships were far of
12, 10:04pm **Koz Kozmos** ok
6/12, 10:05pm **Pre View**
Hey this is smooth talking, i might get a beer now, or drink herbs,
its all the same at this time,
6/12, 10:06pm **Koz Kozmos**
i just want out!
i don't drink any more , why is it smooth talking ?
6/12, 10:07pm **Pre View**
Questioning again? Answer them for yourself will ye , huh?
Hey where is the interview ?
6/12, 10:08pm **Koz Kozmos**
i was interviewing u and u said u wanted to here (hear) about me be concise,
my eyes are clogged
6/12, 10:09pm **Pre View**
euhm, how did u get off yur parents ? I mean away from them
Probably not important
6/12, 10:09pm **Koz Kozmos**
say that again , i need to learn to speak Belgum ,,,
6/12, 10:10pm **Pre View**
How did u see or understand that your parents were doing the wrong stuff to you?
How did u get along with that and digest it?
6/12, 10:10pm **Koz Kozmos**
to get off something ,,, to get off a horse

6/12, 10:10pm **Pre View**
Want to learn Dutch ?
6/12, 10:10pm **Koz Kozmos**
to get off a bike etc
6/12, 10:10pm **Pre View**
yeah to break loose
6/12, 10:11pm **Koz Kozmos**
intuition, then knowledge
then action
6/12, 10:11pm **Pre View**
Wot was your action in the whole scenery?
6/12, 10:11pm **Koz Kozmos**
then i returned many years later to show them love
6/12, 10:12pm **Pre View** Did thy accept your love ?
6/12, 10:12pm **Koz Kozmos**
love without expecting anything in return and still realizing in many ways due to thier infection by matrix programs, they were still the enemy
i feel a shift was created , no one realized, i instigated it which is fine ,
their (they are) old and ill
i'm just trying to help but i'm damaged , so its hard
6/12, 10:14pm **Pre View**
We are all damaged to some point, allow self to spit your damage out so I can better understand you,,,
if you should feel like it,,,

INTERNALS: The stitches of the matrix need to be taken out of humanity. Joachim was a person who brought me to the level where I wanted to paint because he was an artist and showed me what kind of material to buy as I had zero % artistic background. So, for this reason, I have a lot more to explain apart from the domination and severe control of his mother. His parents (were separated)would never allow him to BREATHE. Then again, he made the choice to not let the sun shine within!
I had given everything back then to get him on his own road, showed him how other psychotic friends were doing with my healing sessions and MADE IT TO SOME POINT! TO MAKE A LIFE and not asking for mercy, yet taking responsibility was not flowing so well because of his stubborn streams and parental interference.
Back then, I was at the level of exhaustion as far as healing was concerned because I had to completely reset a DRUGGED DOWN BRAIN and make sure that parents and the psychiatric institution would not intervene to kill my hard efforts and results because they were seen and known, yet NOT APPRECIATED! OR LET'S SAY ALLOWED!

I learned so much, yet I did know I had to leave the case behind for the sake of my own health. What happened after 'me and him 'is just the rumble trumpet blowing into a nowhere land as I had predicted.
Joachim and his mom would call me many times to offer THEM help and healing. That was because his mom needed more help then Joachim himself. It was like a 25 minutes walk from my home to theirs which I performed many many times. Spirit guided me to stop it all, because at times his mom was going crazy and screaming to the walls in their home while Joachim would bounce his head against the trees in the garden(counter effects of medication).

His sister explained the whole story which is simply the story of a cruel and obscene family situation. She has now become a great musician and doesn't want to know about "mom" any longer because she has a family and children of her own. She lived in the same elixirs as Joachim did, yet a lot stronger to get herself out of it which helped me to understand the repugnant and revolting situation. Be careful when interfering with psychopaths! especially their peers!
After the whole thing I sued the psychiatrist and warned her I had recorded everything, always! I won the case because it was pretty obvious that a psychiatrist should not listen to the requirements of a mother that was no longer able to handle Joachim, yet abuse him more and more every day.
A Futuristic mind needs a lot more discipline and other theories in consciousness or the neuroscience of consciousness.

Joachim's father and friends also ran away from the entity termed 'mom'.
An unbearable situation while she was asking me to help Joachim first; and he was asking me to help his mom first. So there I stood in between 2 mad people in great need of healing. So I followed my heart .
After they shut me out, Joachim established to get his own weed trees growing and to live on that which his mom loved because she could go to work while he would remain quite at the house - until the police got in and put an end to that story. I pulled through many crystalline grids over the house at that time , just to get the truth out there and it did, that is all that matters. We can just load a grid over a picture and breathe the energies through our hands which can go soft or very strong, depending on the energies being applied.
Back then I only knew MY BELIEVE, EFFORTS AND TRUST IN SPIRIT WHERE at such a high degree NOBODY COULD EVER BREAK ME AGAIN.

So coming back to GRIDS: I GRIDDED HIS HOME AND HIMSELF FOR 3 MONTHS which resulted in getting the whole truth out because that is what Light Earth Grids do depending on what is available such as the justice system and bringing the control to an end worldwide.

Anyways. After that incident, I never heard about Joachim again until a friend of him almost begged me to make a come back because his situation was getting worse.
I refused because I saw the manipulation , the drugs, alcohol, and meditational abuse. Many friends or practically everybody left him after he was off the drug chain and into the meditational killing fields of a new psychiatric institution. While I was always holding the Crystalline Grids and more technology, many things were revealed which Joachim could not handle. That is because there is no medication for the elimination of EMOTIONS AND LIES. Especially fears! We all need to accept them, face them and then allow Light Techniques to remove them from our Live streams. The ongoing work I was performing with the grids was my greatest Teacher ever because otherwise, I would have never known how strong my skills and healing techniques had become.

LIGHT TECHNOLOGY CAN BRING THIS MEDICATION THROUGH SUCH AS THROUGH ALIGNMENTS in a meditational space in which you can receive knowledge, healing devices, advise and technology.The best way to connect to the Essence that we are in communication with our Source and many species, Sources/Forces can only be set up through crystalline Grid knowledge and technology.

I am mentioning this because of the ongoing results one can achieve when working with the Crystalline Grids . Knowledge and upgrades are just natural promotions through which we receive healing, expansion and the highway back HOME as the earth is our home.
We don't need to run from it, we need to heal it, repair it and re-spacialize in co-ordination with our own meridian system.
Also, many families are going through similar situations . It is not enough that the truth is being revealed about the suffering of youth, children, animals, foster kids and so on. Solutions need to settle in a lot faster and that can be done when becoming a Crystalline Grid embodiment.
The neural mechanisms that underlie these kind of abusive and barbaric footing have been intensively studied over the past 20 years, but currently there is more controversy than consensus in this field.
Moving into the Light Sciences of Spirit such as through the New Light Earth Grids installed worldwide does not allow for arguments. They offer Crystal clear results and advancement when it comes to evolution and STAGING change instead of going BACKSTAGE.

This great school of Divine origin led me into teaching healing modems to children and youth such as in after classes which is so much fun to do as children just naturally move with the star and get codes and designs, they don't question, they do and learn so easily. I hope the great Philosophers will rise and resurrect the dissection of the human brains.

To be A Master of Art , One has to Transcend the Technique for it to become The Evolution of Art A (Me, age 22)

6/12, 10:14pm **Koz Kozmos**
MUSIC: Immortal Technique - Caught In A Hustle Lyrics
physical mental and spirtuel

6/12, 10:14pm **Pre View**
You need to get out every stitch AND REWIRE EVERYTHING
That is everybody's' story, back to our origin
Take out the stitches and walk out of the old TOWN THAT WANTS YOU TO FEEL WEAK AND POWERLESS! (Seen me at age 22?)
You need to open eyes to see what is in front of you and be willing to do the work which is an ongoing process from one level of consciousness into the next.
6/12, 10:14pm **Koz Kozmos**
its hard being in front of a screen due to eyes
6/12, 10:15pm **Pre View**
what do u think will get u out ? HUH, GET to the point!
6/12, 10:16pm **Koz Kozmos**
expand ? yawn...
6/12, 10:18pm **Pre View**
neuroscience needs to resurrect life, they need to teach in every school , not just universities
Children need to be able to translate their experiences into remembrance in order to understand the consciousness of their teachers and be strategic
sure, but i think new expressions are still needed,
They help to build you up again such as through the Arts
u know u can build highways to heaven and enjoy exclusive wells,
but thy will not embed until you get your accounts into some knowledge through which you can accept and then release and rebuild.
6/12, 10:18pm **Koz Kozmos**
accounts, wot are they?
6/12, 10:18pm **Pre View**
An account is a description of your events, your shit
6/12, 10:19pm **Koz Kozmos**
my shit is ok , but wot about the cosmic shit
i need practical applications , not mumbo jumbo but u don't teach on fb , fair enuff
i think we would lock horns if u tried to teach me, haha i need results
6/12, 10:21pm **Pre View**
Indeed, we don't teach on FB,
but maybe sone day we'll be able to exchange knowledge and merge, ..;
And integrate some upgrades if there any Philosophers
6/12, 10:21pm **Koz Kozmos** we?
6/12, 10:22pm **Pre View**
indeed, WE
WE ALL NEED A LOT OF PROGRESS
And move beyond the inadequate defininitions
6/12, 10:22pm **Koz Kozmos**
maybe , its getting late for me,
i've had enuff and being tired
6/12, 10:22pm **Pre View**
Ok sleep, I'm only suggesting to alter concepts of CS
6/12, 10:23pm **Koz Kozmos**
i'm not suicidal, no point , never tried it sleep ?
i'm not ready for bed
6/12, 10:23pm **Pre View**
I'll keep u in my heart, and even if that is not enuff for you, it is for me
Wot we don't try, we don't know
6/12, 10:24pm **Koz Kozmos**
wot did u have in mind? can u tell me what u had in mind first please?

6/12, 10:24pm **Pre View**
In mind = your knowledge merging with mine and create something different
6/12, 10:25pm **Koz Kozmos**
ok, how are we going to go about it ?
i do and i need to eat
6/12, 10:25pm **Pre View** Suggestion ?
Eat first, u need some protein talk, hahaha
The brain is not some sort of satellite, it is much more simple or complicated
6/12, 10:26pm **Koz Kozmos**
huh? and i thought i was random
6/12, 10:26pm **Pre View**
i feel u have a need for proteins
nothing is random with our communication
Present day solutions are very fishy, the age of COPIES!
Never met any interesting scientist willing to go beyond borders
6/12, 10:27pm **Koz Kozmos**
your style is random and the sentence structure confuses me on times
but i'm the same
what do u do when u work? back to the intrrview
6/12, 10:29pm **Pre View**
U never told me wot u learned in the past 30 years,
my sentence structure is to make people think as i told u before
(i have 3 different meanings into 1 sentence that is as far as my FB posts are engaged)
I had i mind you'd get me further into this awakening process while we merge two different view points to get a new vision. That could result in some fun with the Stars.
But I need to know what you understand and how you work your majic through?
6/12, 10:30pm **Koz Kozmos**
i understand u have your idiosyncratic style which i enjoy but u have to understand sometimes u'r hard to understand
6/12, 10:31pm **Pre View** idiosyncratic style ?
6/12, 10:31pm **Koz Kozmos**
i've understood that this reality is malfunctioning
6/12, 10:32pm **Pre View**
come on Koz, we've known & cherished each other over many life times
This reality on Fb is no good indeed
6/12, 10:32pm **Koz Kozmos**
idiosyncratic = A structural or behavioral characteristic peculiar to an individual or group. Or a physiological or temperamental peculiarity.
i don't feel any past life , face book is to limiting
wot was i to u in a past life ? do u have any memory ?
6/12, 10:34pm **Pre View**
past life = who cares, we are here & now and need to decipher what is going on
FB is limiting, worse every day
The Cosmos is unlimited when the brain can align to no limitation
And thus we have capability to generate any type of consciousness
We just need to come up with it
6/12, 10:34pm **Koz Kozmos**
u said about past lifes, and i'm not sure i'm here !
6/12, 10:35pm **Pre View**
OK, handle my stupidity for a sec
Lets have a crux meeting with all these interesting compartiments
And learn about what the brain is able to race through
I mean race and any race
6/12, 10:36pm **Koz Kozmos**
give me one thing to work with that i can umderstand
do u feel any connection to Lemuria?
what do you feel about Lucifer ?

6/12, 10:41pm **Pre View**
One day i was thinking I wanted to know more about u, so I aligned to your Heart to get truth out, (u
always do - no question)
but then i got a geometry in my meditation equal to an eternal spiral, as this is fractured within many people and that my language is actually being expressed through me hands which I move a lot while
being in conversations which is then again being translated into English. This all moves very fast. I experienced this the first time when i was in Egypt in 2005. Didn't like it all, was not interested in the temples either or couldn't get any air over there. Hey why don't they give the gold to the poor, would be a good thing, why keep the gold in the temples and not serving anybody.
This was my first encounter with you, back in Egypt, The Eternal spiral TALKING through geometry. It is rather that we had a heart bound expression through language --- which might open up again - I don't know
Lucifer - forget about it - try to get into the real vibes of wot was meant instead of google
6/12, 10:41pm **Pre View**
LEMURIA : I could explain that.
If u split Lemuria into : LE - MER - LIN -
That is Merlin Majic and living the halls of instant manifestations. A lot of that is stationed in Ireland, Stonehenge.
It is bringing the Lavender Fields back down and merging that sort of Atlantean vibe with which is known as Avalon. I remember when I was 16, somebody gave me a book about Avalon, never really read it; but I think it is
very important. Lavender consciousness needs to come back on the planet.
And that is to be found in all of my artwork.
6/12, 10:43pm **Koz Kozmos**
it has nothing to do with goo-gal
6/12, 10:43pm **Pre View**
Ok, thxxx
6/12, 10:43pm **Koz Kozmos**
first you compliment me according to Pre speak then you insult me
merlin + is a shard of lucifer
6/12, 10:44pm **Pre View**
Sorry, did I insult ???
I just gift u with variations
6/12, 10:44pm **Koz Kozmos**
saying i get things from googal ,
i've not been on line long , i'm old
6/12, 10:45pm **Pre View**
I said I was sorry, you're vibing youth, that is all that matters
6/12, 10:45pm **Koz Kozmos**
it came from the well down the dark lane were i heared myself whisper from the star Craft within its ok , no need to be sorry
yes i retain the fairy blood that keeps me youthful
but the bad eyes make me more lined
back to the eyes , sorry, a lot going on at mo
6/12, 10:48pm **Pre View**
your eyes are your treasure chest, the out of the soul thing
I'm studying your eyes
But u should do so too
I care and therefore love to study how the neurons run and how the eyes get weak or even dried out , ... 6/12, 10:48pm **Koz Kozmos**
i have one brown eye andone blue
and i let a corperate company fuck them
i'm ashamed

6/12, 10:48pm **Pre View**
Born this way ?
6/12, 10:49pm **Koz Kozmos**
yes, and thier damaged
6/12, 10:49pm **Pre View**
U have only reason to applause urself and learn from it
6/12, 10:50pm **Koz Kozmos** ok
6/12, 10:50pm **Pre View**
Do u know about rewiring with ur pineal gland, and the synaptic outcome from the SBF
6/12, 10:50pm **Koz Kozmos**
another day on the dirt ball , getting by no , wots SBF
6/12, 10:51pm **Pre View**
SBF : CEREBRAL SPINAL FLUID – that needs to run smooth through the spine and then moves into the ventricles of the brain.
Just talking about flow, water flow in the body Please sing me a song, can u sing?
It is like bypassing levels of Anastesia
6/12, 10:52pm **Koz Kozmos**
I am the vision singer
6/12, 10:52pm **Koz Kozmos**
i no longer sing or play much, i'm broken
6/12, 10:53pm **Pre View**
it is all about timing to get out
how's your voice (to u) ?
6/12, 10:53pm **Koz Kozmos**
i can't play any more
6/12, 10:54pm **Pre View**
i'd like to hear your voice
6/12, 10:54pm **Koz Kozmos**
i tried and got fucked over
6/12, 10:55pm **Pre View**
Koz, my wrist is hurting like hell, and not allowed to heal it - i explained
Deepening our CS is what matters, needs understanding, awareness
6/12, 10:55pm **Koz Kozmos**
and since that time things have been bad
its hard to explain, i've gone beyond it , i was dieing of despair
6/12, 10:55pm **Pre View**
please do so anyways , I mean explain,,,,
6/12, 10:55pm **Koz Kozmos**
would have to speak, its been crazy the eyes are a real problem
and the music scene is full of kids and good luck to them
6/12, 10:56pm **Pre View**
tell me about ur pain & the struggle or reality happening with eyes
6/12, 10:57pm **Koz Kozmos**
I'm not going to an unplugged night wait for hours to play a few songs and be ignore
u have no idea
6/12, 10:57pm **Pre View**
Your arrows need to hit society thr the music u offer, your lyrics
People are afraid of what they are not familiar with
Look at children on their first day at school: THE CRY, a scandal in education
Time is something that has been defined by earth not by Light Physics
We need a new Light lab that shows how neurons and their in- output can be altered by the infusion of different types of consciousness
RAISE VOLTAGES , haha
The Universe is made up of chambers, rooms of education, so
Animals teach us a lot more , thereof re-educating Youth with Animals and Ecology
Is one of the extreme solutions that need to stream and steam through

6/12, 10:57pm **Koz Kozmos**
its done
6/12, 10:57pm **Pre View**
first things first , you need to get your worldly batteries in
6/12, 10:57pm **Koz Kozmos**
i tried for 30 odd years , fuck society
i'm not being woe is me
6/12, 10:58pm **Pre View**
yess I understand,
lets come out now! And reset things
thy need us to stand real tall, you have strength
6/12, 10:59pm **Koz Kozmos**
its comming across wrong, u don't get it
its a bit frustrating , i allways stand tall and i have strenghth
but they're to weak in thier stacked shoes to see
fuck all humans
6/12, 11:00pm **Pre View**
frustrating ok, thats why i asked u to maybe , if u wish to, merge info and create something together that
works .... alone no ... far too hard
people need to unify their vibes and create a different outcome
/12, 11:01pm **Koz Kozmos**
and there is no where here for me to go
i intend leaving, returning to a small sea side town
6/12, 11:01pm **Pre View**
Where to?
6/12, 11:01pm **Koz Kozmos**
Porthcawl , were i did a lot of growing up
6/12, 11:01pm **Pre View**
Ok, it might do u some good, u need that as I feel, different air
6/12, 11:02pm **Koz Kozmos**
i'd leave tonight if i had the right place to go
it will be a place to die , but it will be the end of my rock n roll dreaming
it may take years to set up, and i may still be in a flat with other people around in other flats with my ear plugs burried deep into ears
a lot to type
6/12, 11:04pm **Pre View**
u're not really willing to die, u want to get out of your stuff and shine the brilliance that you are, your knowledge
And rock & roll it smarter then ever,
Please give your self another opportunity, another gate, another song, another way of loving music, a new skill maybe that brings your passion back
6/12, 11:04pm **Koz Kozmos**
how ? u have no idea
there is no one to work with, i'm old , most people in my age group have moved on
its a game , i've tried and tried and tried , i don't like being out amongst people
u don't understand my effort and pain, i'd be the old guy in the corner
6/12, 11:06pm **Pre View**
You're not old, STOP THAT nonsense will ye, huh
You're not a game, U need to be willing to come ALIVE, TO RISE!
Your treasure chest is a feast to many
How will u explore more CS that bridges your long old road
What is the science and factors of the stones that have be thrown at u?
Revert it, and see it as a permanent learning zone that allows for new facilities within the brain cells; Light parts I should say.

Have u any idea how many people ask me about UUUUU ?
I mean as students realize I chat a lot with you – and so we've gotten into some dialogue about music and stuff.
And would like to get to know you, but they fear,,
6/12, 11:07pm **Koz Kozmos**
that is something completly diffrent
6/12, 11:08pm **Pre View**
But maybe, start another band somewhere in the world,
Hit some new avenues etc,,,
6/12, 11:08pm **Koz Kozmos**
u just don't get it , becuz i'm old
6/12, 11:08pm **Pre View**
Get me to understand you a little better please?
We all needed to tolerate a lot, it doesn't mean we can't get out of the greedy machine
We could just reinvent and interpret our lives into something new,
not giving attention to what happened.
Imagination re-opens many senses
6/12, 11:09pm **Koz Kozmos**
musicians tend to be young and under the influence of their idols and old ones are boring, i never wanted to be in another band
to keep bands together u have to pay
getting gear to gigs is expensive, hiring pa's
u may just be a deamer , i'm not putting blocks up
i tried in my late 40's, it was awful , it made me ill
6/12, 11:11pm **Pre View**
u appear very young to me, maybe reflect on that and why i'm telling u this !
I don't know about UK stuff, but over here there are bands , always new bands that are given a lot of space to get known.
Somehow, you will need to tour, the UK is but the UK
6/12, 11:11pm **Koz Kozmos**
and how the fuck can i go to another country ?
u have to pay, buy guitars etc , mics etc
come on wake up ! fuck it all anyways thanks for the encouragement
i did consider going out and playing a few songs
but my eyes are really bad
i'm done with it , if anything is to happen it has to come to me i'm always ready and inspired
thank u for all the encauragement,
its the right key but the wrong key hole again ,
just being in front of the screen is hard
6/12, 11:16pm **Pre View**
Right , i don't know about bands
But i care, (, I still think merging with a new band would do you some good I mean i u want it for real , communication is important
If u want it somewhere else in the world , ok,
same stuff, talkkkkkkkkk and attract the right people
No RIGHT KEYHOLE,
u only need to be willing to vibe into one KEY
Rely on self and breathe a larger perspective of harmony
We have remebranc to our natural powers
6/12, 11:17pm **Koz Kozmos**
its not about bands

6/12, 11:17pm **Pre View**
So wot is it about then?
6/12, 11:17pm **Koz Kozmos**
its about a group of people with a higher consciousness coming to gether
6/12, 11:18pm **Pre View** I
feel your sad eyes are becoming mad eyes . Oh Oh Oh, yes higher consciousness ,
of course through the
lyrics and different beat
People need the deeper poetic fauna and flora that lift their chords universally like on
the guitar 6/12, 11:18pm **Koz Kozmos**
to form KozKozmozs and the Kozmic band
to destroy this dimension and save the earth
6/12, 11:18pm **Pre View**
Right, there is a great need, and people are looking for UUUU !
6/12, 11:19pm **Koz Kozmos**
its about ritual majik , raising energy my name is SHINNING BROW
6/12, 11:19pm **Pre View**
I don't know about any rituals being used in the music industry ,
please explaiin ur point ?
6/12, 11:20pm **Koz Kozmos** the raising of energy
6/12, 11:21pm **Pre View**
Shiny shiny star, allow some new bells to ring through
should u finally not break through the disastrous limited lanes on broadway
6/12, 11:21pm **Koz Kozmos**
with words of power and musical vibrations
becuz there is no were to go ...
i 've tried to connect with people via face book , but nothing
its becuz i'm targetted
i have broken the limited potential and do vibe on what i am
u've not been thru wot i have , u don't understand
6/12, 11:23pm **Pre View**
People are waiting for more transformative music
I do experience things different over here,
U only target urself, you need to self protect self thr the Grids
6/12, 11:23pm **Koz Kozmos**
no i do not target myself , thats bullshit
when i play i'm ignored , they like a neil young cover version
6/12, 11:24pm **Pre View** ok,
I've not been through as much as u have , maybe, no idea I'm just not talking about it
6/12, 11:24pm **Koz Kozmos**
i have and i"m finished
u hang out with kids
6/12, 11:26pm **Koz Kozmos**
MUSIC:: Patti Smith - "Rock 'N' Roll Nigger"

6/12, 11:26pm **Pre View**
Why do we all care so much, it is the soul thing, no good
How do we get out of that?
Ok welcoming new views

6/12, 11:27pm **Koz Kozmos**
u said u were a rocker ; rock it out, haha
i'm a shape shifter thru the weave the word wizard and the vision singer
6/12, 11:28pm **Pre View**
anyone getting out of soul needs to be a rocker in many ways
The visionary and bring that tribe through,
You are more like an intelligent rocker,
I wish I could ride motorcycles and go on some kind of adventure
6/12, 11:28pm **Koz Kozmos**
but my time is done
like merlin, i want to return to the forest and listen to the trees
6/12, 11:29pm **Pre View**
Good , that's's a good way to get you movin
Go and pack your bag & make sure you put some majic wands in the right position to stand by you , in case the wind has new axis positions in store.
6/12, 11:29pm **Koz Kozmos**
i'm not intelligent , why does every one think i'm stupid
no woods over here and very little green land in the UK
6/12, 11:30pm **Pre View**
Thy probably cannot handle your vibes,
but as i told u, gates are opening to their surprise, it up to sweep the curtains of change through and pass just another exam
U need to Re-Identify Self to understand we do not need identification
6/12, 11:30pm **Koz Kozmos**
apart from on the property of the aristocrats , i've tried the police to move on, hahaha
and i need to be warm and hidden as much as i can be
i feel the gate shut!
6/12, 11:31pm **Pre View** You are invisible, right ?
6/12, 11:31pm **Koz Kozmos**
i waited at the gate for many years always ready to enter
i don't now wot i am
i'd like to be gone for good , this place bores and discusts me
6/12, 11:32pm **Pre View**
sec, need the toilet again, keydny release
6/12, 11:32pm **Koz Kozmos**
i just piss in a bottle
6/12, 11:35pm Koz Kozmos
MUSIC: Bruce Springsteen & The E Street Band
Land of Hope and Dreams (Live in New York City)

6/12, 11:35pm **Koz Kozmos**
u 'd better be listening to these songs Grab your ticket and your suitcase
Thunder's rolling down this track
Well you don't know where you're goin' now But you know you won't be back
6/12, 11:38pm **Pre View**
Lets go, right, am listening
ok, WILL TRY to rock into the bottle, i will excel some day, HAHAHA
U scare me sometimes, but then again , i 'm teaching myself to not care anymore
And serve myself with some new Antarctic wheels
Replacing Religion with the science of Spirit is all that is needed
How can it be that the connection to Stars is not being educated
As well as Divinity and languages of Light
It is all so held back
Because people would get too intelligent and they don't want that
Everybody looks into the skies at times

But do they communicate?
12, 11:38pm **Koz Kozmos**
don't mean to scare u
6/12, 11:39pm **Pre View**
i know, its ok , just being very honest
just part of an emotional body that should not be there
6/12, 11:39pm **Koz Kozmos**
to much sax on the tracks
6/12, 11:40pm Koz Kozmos
MUSIC: Marc Bolan - You Scare Me To Death

6/12, 11:40pm **Pre View**
aha, don't have these ears to hear which instruments are not in harmony,
but if important, let me know
how I could expand my ears to higher dreams
Why did u post Bruce again?
6/12, 11:40pm **Koz Kozmos**
i wanted people to see when i looked good
i look terrible now, its all ego
more eye drops ,they do very little
i like some bruce , i look like bruce these days or so i'm told
if bruce was an elf to say lets meet in the land of hopes and dreams i still hope and dream, i was being so down for good reasons
6/12, 11:42pm **Pre View**
Oh come on Koz, u still look splendid eye drops will be over and done with, when you are getting to heal the eyes and set the visions on remission How about that?
6/12, 11:43pm **Koz Kozmos**
i like the idea of writing a good song that can reach lots of people
u don't know wot i look like, the pic was 8 years old i said
6/12, 11:43pm **Pre View**
What's an idea worth when its not reaching anyone You need to go deeper then the surface of your skin. You really need to come alive and believe your VIBE can be protected
They didn't cut your nose of, did they?
What is belief, what drives us to belief? What is false,what is true?
You can still smell, hear, talk, type huh?
6/12, 11:43pm **Koz Kozmos**
before the final targetting to destroy me ,they failed
when are you getting to heal eyes
6/12, 11:44pm **Pre View**
I NEVER LOOKED AT YOUR PIC,
I'VE GOT the pic u are in my brains,
AND FAR BETTER

MY INTERNALS: I really got many pictures of him in my brain. As the show between us went on, my healing energies became so strong through the music he posted that I could literally wave my Light waves through and around him and see how and where he lived.
It seemed to be the perfect pictures I was given when doing my fitness and dance work out. Reason why it is so important to work out in ascension and get the circulation system to a degree where the nerve does not hit the muscle but visa versa. And that is when things become inspirative and fascinating.

I also felt too much that it was useless to explain how to breathe light techniques through. I needed to show it to him and first prepare his body such as through deep elimination procedures from old recycling consciousness and thus the disease on earth because changing the way we process our thoughts makes that the body processes information on an improved level that fits Divine Will and gracious movement.

6/12, 11:44pm Koz Kozmos
wot does that mean ?
this woman rachel that I knew , told me i looked like bruce in this vid
MUSIC: gone with the wind

6/12, 11:46pm **Pre View**
It means that I saw visions of you in my brain, that is all
6/12, 11:46pm **Koz Kozmos**
she hated bruce about 5 years back before the eye surgery
6/12, 11:46pm **Pre View** who's rachel ?
6/12, 11:46pm **Koz Kozmos**
a woman i new, she's gone for good not a realationship, ii don't do those
6/12, 11:47pm **Pre View**
She hurted u ?
6/12, 11:47pm **Koz Kozmos**
everybody i have known has hurt me
6/12, 11:47pm **Koz Kozmos**
MUSIC: Bruce Springsteen - Streets of Philadelphia (Official Music Video)

6/12, 11:47pm **Pre View**
this is my fav, this is me
I'v walked the streets so many times , just to ground the crystal grids
6/12, 11:48pm **Koz Kozmos**
it becomes unproductive being around certain people, dead energy ,
yes great lyrics
6/12, 11:49pm **Pre View**
EXACTLY, remember the post i placed, (all about exactitude, and precision)
It is very important for everybody to get some knowledge about precision and how Light consciousness works . People do not believe in precision nor perfection. Somehow this is because in the back of there mind they have that soul manipulative engine that DICTATES THEM, makes them do what suits them and in the end they feel like a big failure because they listen to mind control, not brain brilliance. They are afraid to loook at the architecture of the Universe.
6/12, 11:49pm **Koz Kozmos**
Bruce does need help, he's been targetted (Bruce Springsteen)
6/12, 11:49pm **Pre View**
Why ? Where's he living ?
6/12, 11:50pm **Koz Kozmos**
so he can be used as a star for the karaoke pack he lives in a rented room on jewel street
6/12, 11:51pm **Pre View**
He is strong and works hard both physically, mentally and of course creatively
6/12, 11:51pm **Koz Kozmos**
and has just sold his guitar to buy eye drops
6/12, 11:51pm **Pre View**
hahaha
6/12, 11:51pm **Koz Kozmos**
he needs to shift big time
go with u and me up into the hills and drink from the vine of spirits

6/12, 11:53pm **Pre View**
why? truly, don't know him or anything about people making music
but i feel u like him a lot,,,
Would be interested to know if Bruce is curious enough to test his musical performances in many different grids
That would greatly lift the grapevine into a new zone, to explore and explode in a more inscriptive adventure
6/12, 11:54pm **Koz Kozmos**
i like other people more
6/12, 11:54pm **Pre View**
Lets galvanize and vitalize a particular group of people in the music industry and offer them theexperience of Grid intelligence.
Wonder how that would work out.
6/12, 11:58pm **Koz Kozmos**
luve is the ultimate trick of the duality
6/12, 11:59pm **Pre View**
For sure, but wot else do they have?
they mix up things far from the reality of things simply because the soul craves things that are actually better left to the underworld of creations/manipulations.
never understood people going for something they think is love
They should talk to spirits in the water, in the woods
Having conversations with animals
always left me blank so they never understood me
humanity lost the vibe of love a very long time ago
and thus they look for something to replace it because somewhere, the heart remembers that 'love' is the Essence that we are, yet almost everything is inverted and thus 'FAKE' came into existence through low mentality and that whole line of nonsense. Some people kept close to nature, some lost it completely. Yet, to be honest , I never felt the vibe of love
only being in love or thinking some partnership could fill up some sort of an empty cup can never satisfy and thus reason people keep on chasing something that does not exist while.
6/13, 12:01am **Koz Kozmos**
same here
6/13, 12:02am **Koz Kozmos**
MUSIC: Bruce springsteen – The Last Carnival

6/13, 12:02am **Koz Kozmos**
going to listen to this , it is a luvleee song
6/13, 12:02am **Pre View**
But Love does a lot, it teaches a lot
We are living the Age of new behaviour
It taught me to love humanity no matter what, not like in romantic relationships
The beauty of love in friendships
I like attracting intelligent people
Yet everybody that comes into my life, leaves me very quickly
It is sad, they either die or their true false nature comes into play through which they literally tell me they cannot handle my level of truth – even whenI give them a change to reset – people tend to rather live the downgrading lanes and think that offers them pleasure
In the end they all fall prey and become the victim of their own creations And of course they is being handed quite gracefully by the Light Grids Bruce is strong in the heart i guess,
he must be,,
6/13, 12:04am **Koz Kozmos**
he's a rockin earth Buddha, i'm a fire thief
One more song ?

/13, 12:07am **Pre View**
Thank U !
6/13, 12:07am **Koz Kozmos**
play it loud
6/13, 12:07am **Koz Kozmos**
MUSIC: ELVIS - I Just Can't Help Believing (Remastered audio)
romatic love

6/13, 12:08am **Pre View**
You are a FIRE deposit, it makes me come back as I intended to go backstage for a while
Elvis, U ?
ok, Koz is going romantic, Ok i 'll surrender and learn
6/13, 12:09am **Koz Kozmos**
not heard this for years
6/13, 12:11am **Pre View**
People forgot about the Human touch and how important it is
wish more of them humans understood,
they mistake the touch for something of lesser wine i give dem just that touch and then leave,wot more can we do ? huh
So many psychological features are at play,
so maybe take it about, not drag it around our energy.
We do not have to adapt to anything but contribute to change
Many answers come from experiences
6/13, 12:12am **Koz Kozmos**
i understand that
one more elvis then good night ?
i'm sorry to be down
6/13, 12:13am **Pre View**
maybe one more song, it 'll make me believe again, swing again and download my new moves from the
MUSIC: Universal Grooves

6/13, 12:13am **Koz Kozmos**
this one will do it , play it loud
6/13, 12:13am Koz Kozmos
MUSIC: Elvis Presley - If I Can Dream
('68 Comeback Special 50th Anniversary HD Remaster)

6/13, 12:14am **Pre View**
Please don't allow self to go or feel down Play some uplifting music
that is what is needed for u and me but i do not need to express,
u can feel my vibes anyways
6/13, 12:15am **Koz Kozmos**
just down because of my eyes etc not heared this for ages
Elvis needed to rock out more, but he was used and he's a herd religion for the pack, bit like bruce But Bruce has a far deeper message
6/13, 12:17am **Pre View**
ok, another song ?
6/13, 12:17am **Koz Kozmos**
one more, let me think,
something up or low key

6/13, 12:18am **Pre View**
u see, I told u that u would teach me ,
over and over,
but my ass did not expect u to do it rock&roll style Good you
started the musical directions and reflections!
6/13, 12:18am **Koz Kozmos**
? up or low key , thank u
6/13, 12:19am **Koz Kozmos**
i was asking wot style u wanted to end our chat, gosh
ok Neil , focus on the first song , a great song
6/13, 12:20am **Pre View**
i don't have music or the knowledge
I only asked my spiritual technicians to align me with wot i need and wot came out of
that box was u ! Isn't that great and fabulous and fantastic?
Grids work! haha
Get the fevers
6/13, 12:20am **Koz Kozmos**
u ready ? wishing u good night
6/13, 12:21am **Pre View**
lets move it !Letz reset any agitation and turn the velocity in to correct positions.
Ok, I'm ready, , where is the juke box?
6/13, 12:21am **Koz Kozmos**
take extra care
6/13, 12:21am **Pre View** ok, thank u
6/13, 12:21am **Koz Kozmos**
don't trip on the grids, its good live
pretty amazing grace
6/13, 12:22am **Koz Kozmos**
MUSIC: NEIL DIAMOND – PRETTY AMAZING GRACE

6/13, 12:27am **Koz Kozmos**
this is the sorta band needed
6/13, 12:28am **Pre View**
You must be the Grace itself
That is the song that kept me close to you, and understand your zones of hurt
That is a song that reminds me how important surrender is,
The word "surrender" itself has been downgraded too many times as people only
surrender when their figured out solutions have lost the working deals or mechanics
so i'm starting to understand beyond the falseness and lies
It is just fear and shame; and mostly the ego dendrites that hold our beloved beings
in the class room of stubbornness and muddy brains
6/13, 12:28am **Koz Kozmos**
but a bit more freakzoid wyrdus
ok, good night
6/13, 12:29am **Pre View**
I have great hope that fashion is soon going to bring out wearable T-Shirts and jeans,
I mean most casual clothing that reflects the light of their emotional body
Would everybody stay in the house then? Hahahahaha
Were are the super naturals?
good night to u too
a real good night,
Luve to u, Nic

6/13, 12:55am **Pre View**
Thank u Koz, it was a great time measuring up with U,
This time around i will only accept my shadow to vibrate along my instincts, do you get that?
Is your real name Jimmy like on the pic ?
I'd love to see you playing the guitar and seduce some new chords popping up from the boundless Light shows.
Do you know Atma? This is a good song
Listen to how the lyrics have been put together
6/13, 1:09am **Pre View**
The songs you are posting are very healing one way or another
I've been raped and abused , have you been through such malfunctioning? Had no parents that really took care of me
How can a man just rape, overpower anyone?
and punch your teeth out, put knifes into your skin,
Have you ever felt what it is like to be overpowered, no muscles and a voice that does not seem to work? That is where my deep level of unworthiness comes from
there is no apology that can fix that, ever
Maybe love can heal that, but justice needs to move in
The police even have fun with that kind of atrocities.
I question everything so much because solutions need to be grounded on the planet which is very difficult with so many people living in a cluttered atmosphere and dead computer mechanisms they seem to love.
6/13, 1:13am **Pre View**
I wonder how justice will work its way through in the future, its inevitable
Thank u for opening your heart
6/13, 1:39am **Pre View**
MUSIC: ATMA –ETERNAL BOUNDLESSNESS LYRICS

6/13, 1:41am **Pre View**
another night, another vibe,
another sleepless fight through the rooms of no delight Guess wot happened : Jain Doe finally left me a message after months in which explained to her how healing works and how she could eventually start out processing light in the body and thus the return into health
however it tells me something good
Every brain on the planet are wired
So we just need to rewire to new life on earth
The fire of old neurons need to leave old patterns
So u can no longer talk about the past

6/13, 11:40am **Pre View**
Thank U for the long chat yesterday ---
I was wondering how you can live in the same room for 15 years
(i moved about 30 times in my life)
In 2011 I even moved 3 times.
Definitely done with it now, yet where I'm living now with students is very hard as well,,,
but trying to understand it.

**MY INTERNALS: Laying on the coach and watching tv or getting app diseases will not play out well in the future.
Everybody needs to turn their buttons from dust into light for every single entity is A LIGTH CREATION and needs to return to that origin in biology.
During all those years, I held tied to GRID EDUCATION, I held tied to my believe that justice would be served and love shared through the unification drums that have settled these days.**

**The dessert wind in 2019 is blowing through TRUTH the way we were awaiting thanks to all LIGHT EARTH GRID CONFIGURATIONS that get stronger and more precise every day. That brings the planet back into its original axis position termed Light Earth or Planet Peace.
We can see the truth of children's' trafficking, the truth within the Vatican, the truth in our health system, the truth about food manipulation, the truth that is overriding falseness. The suffering through rape and abuse of women, children, animals along racism is a package of barbaric content that needs to be removed with daily efforts. Yet, still too many think they cannot do it and allow their ignorant and lazy brain settings to recycle the same mud.
This may take years in the interim, but well worth the Light science and studies given through Light Technology in which one can relearn their Light skills through daily devotion in meditation and getting the SPARK back on the other side of midnight.**

**The REAL KI to start out the process of LIGHT in the body would IN THE GRID/ THE FOUNDATION OF LIGHT IN YOUR HOUSE AND ENVIRONMENT.
Light Grids are already set around the world and carry portals of LITE POWER PLANTS that continue to grow through the crystallization of our bodies. The bones in the human body become solid crystalline fine tuning forks if you will through which we can embody male/female perfection like in one wave through many waves such as sound waves.**

**The unification that is taking place is all about getting the Elestial, Celestial and Universal entities back into one unified field in spirit consciousness without the drowning of soul magnetics or hormonal static.
There is a lot to learn from this solar system and how we can mover into our Celestial shoes first before the repair in our solar energies can take its seat once again on the higher planes. Reason why so many women suffer from the bloating and fat settings in the lower energy centers**

Think about the Power of the WORD? How many people are holding their word in this world? Hardly anyone due to ignorance and the play school of soul or the missing levels or respect, integrity and humility.It is also reason why so many suffer from throat diseases for it is the portal between the bodily functions and the brain that directs these functions. And thus the MIND came into creation through those low living standards.

**The WORD conducts energy input/output as pure as it is; one could cut direct through magnetic fields, into free form expression. Imagine that, yet a foundation and knowledge about the consciousness within Light beams or configurations is a necessary study that upgrades every day.
I have no idea where lost Light goes, but I do understand that there is no greater space on the planet then in constant dialogue with your Source and upgrading into the higher Universal grids in which we can relearn to co-create amongst other species, galaxies and so many ELEMENTS.**

Many beings set themselves in a so called meditational space; yet with a floating ground floor and no knowledge of how to set up THE SPIRITUAL BODY IN THE FIRST PLACE.

**Divine communion demands a purified, pure, humble and precise space that can only be set within the Crystalline Home base grid in which we can change, shift and bring the requested clarity through for the sake of Evolution.
Reason why things do not work any longer through 'prayer' as is playing out on many social media platforms is that we NEED TO GO THROUGH OUR OWN SOURCE to get the help and massive assistance to move in a disease free embodiment and environment.**

Many still prefer to give their power away and expect some magical outcome WITHOUT DOING THE WORK WITHIN. That was and will never be accepted. We are the Creators and need to move back into that intelligence where the Magician and the Technician allow for the Medicine man within to rise into the Ascent and thus the many changes in our biology that continually readjusts to what is grounding within the realms of Light Earth.

**As unification is taking place we need to fuse the solar, celestial and universal bodies within in order to fuse with these entities and allow the higher degrees of the spiritual and mental bodies. The hardest study may seem the release of the emotional body and its attachments. Yet, there is much easy technology such as through spirit numerology, geometry and the beauty with the crystalline grid constructions that is becomes a banquet of understanding first, then release and detachment.
It is all but a learning zone of how to convert density into light. I guess it should become a new 'family bond' 24/7. With this I mean to say that within a family, children can partake of new health and education through foods, fitness levels, meditation and conversations with parents while allowing the separation created through apps and computer technology to move into a more balanced composition.
The moon and the sun in the skies seem to be obvious, yet it is hardly known how important it is to work with the many moons as incorporated frequencies and the true meaning of being a solar or sun stream that ride with certain crystals we can find on earth, the water gates , within the mountains and hidden caves.(crystallization of the body).
ONCE WE UNDERSTAND THAT EVERYTHING IS DIRECTED FROM DiVINE WILL CONSCIOUSNESS, we can change everything and replace the magnetic chords of Free Will by Universal chords and Grand Harmony as crystalline light unifies independent as ONE, where freedom for all resides. Dependency carries no freedom.
There are Light Grids that set in Health and modern day data, Light Grids that resets us into a new production line and healthy economics, Light Grids that bring truth to the surface, Light Grids that brings Eternal mates together, Light Grids that align to the many Galaxies, Light Grids that restore the tectonic plates with our Light Gridded embodiment, Light Grids for the New educational system and new universities that teach truth, health and wise brains versus the mediation that will be replaced by Light Meditation and thus many meditational formats to any degree of disease that may surface.**

**Just imagine us working with the animal kingdom like in co-parnership and with the Elements that will direct us back to PARADISE. Wild Life definitely needs some Light technology and open ecologists that allow assistance from the beyond.
That is exactly why we are here for, to rebuild PARADISE.
When living in Light and waving consciousness out of the so called control brigades, we can incorporate true health, joy and discover our Essence, Skills and passion on a much deeper level.**

Hopefully schools, Universities and many Youth educational system will soon enough break the barriers of old teachings and engage with a spiritual counsellor/mentor that teaches healing meditational classes on an every day scale. Just because we are living the age of great changes and thus the release of emotional and mental barriers need to replace a class that teaches religion/Theology based on falseness and greed.

6/13, 12:43pm **Koz Kozmos**
I've been called Jym, Jimmy, and james
tends to be James these days
I'm sorry for what u've been thru...it hurts me
the questions you're asking me are for private talk not type in face book ,
I mean about the things you've
been thr, the abuse
wot does Jain Does message tell u?
I have a flat but stay in one room most of the time,
its a nice flat but i have landlords and the city is too toxic and noisy for me
i want to escape but it may be to another smaller flat
and i'm worried about sound proofing and naybores (neighbours) etc etc
i must have moved at least 20 times,
i was living in a shared house before here
and had done so formany years
it made me ill , i've stayed here because i'm alone
and have no one to wake up to etc etc
6/13, 1:03pm Koz Kozmos
MUSIC: Mother Love Bone - Bone China

6/13, 1:05pm **Koz Kozmos**
In the morning she gone crazy
kool tune ! u posted
Atma is hyp to the freakzoid wyrdus checking it out moody macho types
6/13, 3:57pm **Pre View**
I respect what you would like to keep for private talk
I'm done with moving from one place to the other, makes me sick as well,
its just that all places need to get into a better atmosphere and we are here to do that,
to provide the techniques to move people out of the bars of their self created prison
walk and talks.
Koz, i'm very very tired,
6/13, 4:00pm **Pre View**
Jean Doe: that was just a talk about a petition she sent out ...
but she never answers my pm's regarding
the suggestion about healing
but, thats ok, i might maybe for once give some deeper reflections to her illness
yet the nerves repair in a slower mode, it would be good for het to bathe in Lake
Superior with some smoky quartz
Lets swim the Merlin Waters and get some clarity
6/13, 7:16pm **Koz Kozmos**
Just spoke to Jain Doe, she said she got a message from u about working in schools
some time back ; but has never sent u a private message
good vibes just to let u know !
MUSIC: Stravinsky: The Firebird / Gergiev ·
Vienna Philarmonic · Salzburg Festival

6/13, 9:52pm **Koz Kozmos**
don't fuck your self up you're better than that
and it makes things worse, maybe get some Valerian or even sleeping pills short term
, if its ok for me to say **6/13, 11:07pm** Koz Kozmos
MUSIC: KINKS I'm not like anybody else

6/14, 6:54am **Pre View**
No, no chemicals for me
But please just talk about anything should you feel like it i will take it from u,

Cultivating & cherishing where our Tracks cross under the new Peach Tree
of Living potentials,,, realities
For u have given me crystal LISTENING minerals to rebuild my branches
shining from LIGHT TO LITE
Blessings upon ur day
6/14, 9:28am **Pre View**
MUSIC: THUNDER ROAD – BRUCE SPRINGSTEEN

6/14, 11:43am **Pre View**
i am very sorry i hurt u with my stories and stuff, it needed to come out somehow
will be more careful with your 1000 Watt shining heart
We need no hurt no more, we need to breathe the healing elements
6/14, 1:35pm **Koz Kozmos**
I' am empathy, its not just hurt
its the need for justice against wot the matrix sickness does to people and I felt
talking about such deep stuff on face book was inappropriate lets claim the healing
is Bruce a slave ?
6/14, 1:49pm Koz Kozmos
MUSIC: WATAIN - BLOODSTOCK 2012

6/14, 1:50pm **Koz Kozmos**
Hailz , claim the healing , and manifest the killing
6/14, 2:39pm **Pre View**
I agree
Let's claim the power of the word
& grid that over the sick
Watain – not my music,
too dense, no thanx
6/14, 4:24pm **Koz Kozmos**
grid that over the sick?
can u explain
6/14, 5:34pm **Koz Kozmos**
i understand , but sometimes its good to get an explanation
6/14, 6:37pm Koz Kozmos
MUSIC: J.R.R. Tolkien Reads (A Poem In Elvish)

6/14, 6:37pm **Koz Kozmos**
letz speak deep
I am the Elf King Elvish Priestleee
6/14, 7:14pm **Pre View**
sure, i understand, go ahead!
the strong forces, huh
is that ur native tongue?
thank u Mister King of all surprises can i meet u in the hood?
to offer you some food from the Grid
Let's hold the Grapevine strong & united Let's track the unbreakable
& make dem see a matrix is but a matrix
'cause the fall is near
for those who will not hear
as the swift Sword of spirit
will not allow fear
within those wearing the garment of Fiery Armies

6/14, 7:16pm **Pre View**
No sweet music for me today ?
Is your jukebox stuck,
Or would u sing a song for me ?
I would if I could invite u for a dance
Would u be willing to take on that dance and listen to the Grid stance?
(I promise to whisper Elvish magic)
6/14, 7:29pm **Pre View**
I feel I must dance a new dance
I must sing a different song
6/14, 9:23pm **Koz Kozmos**
no
MUSIC: Spirit Caravan - Lost Sun Dance

6/14, 9:31pm **Koz Kozmos**
when the sword of wizdom kills you,
you will be born again children of the mother take away my pain ,
listen to the drum beat
6/14, 9:34pm **Koz Kozmos**
Native American (Hopi Blue Star) Star People
6/14, 9:38pm **Koz Kozmos**
not heared this before , the backing could always be better on these things
6/14, 9:44pm **Koz Kozmos**
MUSIC: Paco de lucia - Tangos Flamenco

6/14, 9:47pm **Koz Kozmos**
heres a new word for u: Duende
6/14, 9:48pm **Koz Kozmos**
Duende means having soul, a heightened state of emotion,
expression and authenticity, often connected with flamenco
El duende is the spirit of evocation.
It comes from inside as a physical/emotional response to music.
It is what gives you chills, makes you smile or cry as a bodily reaction to an artistic performance that isparticularly expressive.
6/14, 9:53pm **Pre View**
I am duende but the song sucks,
you can do better when it comes to Flamenco
6/14, 9:54pm **Koz Kozmos**
good , pc going slow
6/14, 10:10pm **Pre View**
Maybe change the password of your jukebox huh,
and see what kind of tunes pop up
I xwant music of a hundred thousand years ago
Can u provide that pls?
And bring the ancestors with u, will u?
6/14, 10:11pm **Koz Kozmos**
just old lyrics that came to me via Pre speak, haha
6/14, 10:11pm **Pre View**
wots pre speak ?
6/14, 10:13pm **Koz Kozmos**
RRE VIEW : that is u right ?
So when I say Pre speak : it means what Miss Pre talks about

14, 10:14pm **Pre View**
maybe a bit more silent , i agree
I guess i told u i was going crazy with things going on
I'm glad old lyrics are coming back to u
6/14, 10:15pm **Koz Kozmos**
crazy in wot way ? asylum crazy or break out of the asylum crazy ?
6/14, 10:16pm **Pre View**
both ways are possible,figure me out, you got knowledge,hahah
6/14, 10:16pm **Koz Kozmos**
what are u going to do about it ? why is it happening ?? ?
its ok if u don't want to spk ...
do u have support ?
6/14, 10:19pm **Pre View**
It is just that I stopped caring as I told you,
yet it is confronting me with what I truly want in life beside
doing seminars and studying Light Tech
Also started manifesting little things, strange,
never had nor have support
i've had enough of slow things,
that is the hardest part for me to accept the slow moves in society
People do not understand style in communication
They understand style in fashion
6/14, 10:19pm **Koz Kozmos**
yip
6/14, 10:20pm **Pre View**
But i'm very grateful i met u & support a little
6/14, 10:20pm **Koz Kozmos**
yeah thankz
6/14, 10:20pm **Pre View**
It is also because I feel i'm changing fast
6/14, 10:21pm **Koz Kozmos**
in wot ways ?
6/14, 10:21pm Koz Kozmos
MUSIC: Rolling Stones- Gimme Shelter

6/14, 10:21pm **Koz Kozmos** ?
6/14, 10:21pm **Pre View**
I don't speak much these days to people, yet look them straight in the EYE,
and bring Lasers through from my pupil into theirs
Rolling Stones, hey yess, good thing, thank you!
6/14, 10:22pm **Koz Kozmos**
you said that before , not a complaint
6/14, 10:23pm **Pre View**
i might have, but the message is different now
6/14, 10:23pm **Koz Kozmos** w
e're in the Mess AGE wot is the message ?
don't want to hassle u
6/14, 10:34pm **Pre View**
Well, I think it is merely some more strenght within intention we hold:
like i needed to go into the city to get some food & came across a few people who
owed me some money.... it manifested with ease & grace, which are steps forward
somehow
6/14, 10:35pm **Koz Kozmos**
did u get the money ? u seem pissed off ?
6/14, 10:35pm **Pre View**
Yess i think i am
Why is UNCERTAINTY stressful for people?
Nothing is for sure, I am a lover of uncertainty

14, 10:35pm **Koz Kozmos**
good , i've been ripped off
6/14, 10:36pm **Pre View**
how ?
6/14, 10:36pm **Koz Kozmos**
in every way , anyways i have a low opinion of humans,
wot r u up to may i ask?
6/14, 10:38pm **Pre View**
i'v lost all opinions , it lifts you up
so I'm starting to bring more self care through
We cannot put a budget on brains which is a good thing
We are all self regulating like many mammals, insects and ...
Religious beliefs can be recalculated when moving into the phenomena that is life
Belief is conceptual and can be changed and rewired at any time
Everything that just no educated or unknown produces stress,
Except i think when being in Team CS , we have support
that is also self regulating and
Allows for transcendence
Encounters of many kinds may be considered a necesity
6/14, 10:39pm **Koz Kozmos**
about time , keep it up, good medicine from wyrd Wales,
i may watch a movie
always best to spell wyrd with a Y
6/14, 10:41pm **Pre View**
Why? New ways of imagining may be an option
No more rituals, because there is no Evolutionary constant,
the Universe does not stop the flow or movement
6/14, 10:42pm **Koz Kozmos**
it was an existential joke
6/14, 10:44pm **Pre View**
watch yer movie, so i'm off for the better
i may bore you
6/14, 10:45pm **Koz Kozmos**
u seem annoyed, hope u find the better
6/14, 10:45pm **Pre View**
absolutely not, i feel good, words are too empty
6/14, 10:45pm **Koz Kozmos**
u seem pisssed off with me
flippant , but its ok
6/14, 10:46pm **Pre View**
NEVER, it is just grief, maybe I need some more space
Maybe its no good, this chatting
Its too consuming
6/14, 10:46pm **Koz Kozmos**
its ok , i just hope your ok
do u live in a flat or a house may i ask ?
i wonder about were u are sometimes, its ok if u don't want to say
6/14, 10:47pm **Pre View**
Would you like to join me for a drink? Cheers!
I just need to do what I get into my head
Do you hear me, in my head!
Your spirit is off, my spirit is off,
No use this chat
Goodnight Koz,
I really like u a lot , but you know that
How i live? complicated question
Gets me frustrated
Maybe listen to this song:

MUSIC: Chris Stapleton - TRAVELLER
6/14, 10:48pm **Koz Kozmos**
good night , drink lots of water and eat , etc
6/14, 11:18pm **Pre View**
I'm very restless and need to hit the solutions,
everything that is bad in my life is because of this Joachim nightmare ,
I really need to get of the emotional body
I always used to live in very big flats but downstairs with a garden, lots of light etc ....
Ever since this drama with this psychopath everything went down & even more down
...
(I listened too long to the wrong people)
so obviously that is what u attract : i needed to get out of my large flat because it was becoming too expensive as i lost my job, my car, my evening jobs
(fitness, workshops...)...due to my hand
I had a chance to be housekeeper of a brand new student home with 32 students which i took on as I knew spirit wanted me to educate or assist youth,
so I have my flat in this building downstairs with outlook on a big garden in which i love to work and have some good conversations with some interesting students,
But I have no privacy, too little light, the noises break m y consciousness, etc.
On the other hand i'v always been asked to work with youth but now as i got to understand their brains , it is not very easy to educate them. Yet very interesting.
It is a slow process but I get lots of gratitude.
I am having a big problem with the noise in the building ever since 4 weeks,
and also it is too small for my vibes,,,that is why i spend a lot of time in the woods.
There was also another thing with this flat : i was first promised to get a bigger place in the building but it did not happen (many lies ---)
And also big problems with my son as he got on drugs and I realized it too late,
but worked hard on him
like every day – it consumed my energy
Events just effect us, I need to deal with these experiences a different natural way,
reason why Spirit gives me these encounters, it teaches so much
Still what can you do, society hit him hard and youth is so weak ,
got him out of drugs and getting him independent. He changed a lot - so thats good
I really need some time alone with myself to catch up where I want to be in life,
And finally get some space
I never had any alcohol in my life till I met him, that broke me down yet I had to understand what alcohol does to people to be able to heal addicts
Everything we do not experience is something we cannot understand , except through memory from past lives and skills, and it made me understand people that live on alcohol. A few drinks is ok, but too many times a few drinks is not ok,
it gets the body very weak
Its part of the matrix, getting people into addictions and stuff
It is hard to break through this bastard Joachim and get justice through
Then again, it is my responsibility, I got involved
U need to care for urself as well Koz
6/15, 12:02am **Koz Kozmos**
I understand as much as I can
is Joa that bad ?
why did he fuck things up so much?
why did u loose so much ?
ok , i wish all the best
6/15, 12:31am **Koz Kozmos**
MUSIC: Buzzcocks - Noise Annoys

6/15, 12:31am **Koz Kozmos**
MUSIC: JETHRO TULL Songs From The Wood

6/15, 12:33am **Koz Kozmos**
i wear ear plugs and cover my windows to block out the light but we will beat this , i've got no children, i'm glad power in the darkness, luv in the light
6/15, 12:43am **Koz Kozmos**
get some ear plugs
6/15, 4:43am **Pre View**
Thank you for the songs from the woods,
'is joa that bad'? That question triggers an explosion into me Psychopaths have no acceptable path, they have no directions
They are maniacs of manipulation, maybe the matrix is learning from them
But lets not go into the sarcastic streets for we become what we feed ourselves with
6/15, 4:50am **Pre View**
He is exactly the opposite of his posts on social media
To fool his parents
and there is lots of proof
Anyways, if yur interested to know the whole story
I wrote it down, just let me know if you want that file
6/15, 11:19am **Pre View**
Here is the file, it is about all the frustration and manipulation in psychiatry, his parents and the whole range of institutions one needs to address to get some justice download joachim .pdf
6/15, 1:19pm **Pre View**
WOW WOW
I feel deblocked as I'm sending the file, good thing
Its like I don't have any solar center no more
Where is your heavenly enterprise situated?
Deeply Wonder who u are ? Universally?
However you're definitely the most precious gift i got in life ,
at the right time with the musical files filling my vibes
6/15, 1:21pm **Koz Kozmos**
solar center , do u mean the heart ?
6/15, 1:21pm **Pre View**
No, I meant that the bloating in my solar center went down as I was sending you the files about Joachim, like a big release
A holiday for my sun streams,
6/15, 1:21pm **Koz Kozmos**
i'm not that precious
6/15, 1:22pm **Pre View**
definitely a rare jewel to me !
6/15, 1:22pm **Koz Kozmos**
all u can do is move on, its hard
it will take time , u have to make the decision to relax and sleep
6/15, 1:25pm **Koz Kozmos**
basic advice is some times useful
i smoke i ciggerttte a day , just one
6/15, 1:26pm **Koz Kozmos**
earplugs help me sleep, if u have a mp3 player ?
i realize u don't like head phones but meditation music can help, find some that suits
6/15, 1:27pm **Pre View**
i usually don't have sleeping problems, it was just the frustration with Joachim that popped up in the middle of the night. Just a sign from the Divine that I need to release that experience,I just apply light techniques through meditation

6/15, 1:29pm **Pre View**
will balance everything now and get my tranquility back in
& then i'll set my intentions on healing your eyes
6/15, 1:29pm **Koz Kozmos**
u must ask before u do !
i'm trying to sue
will have to pay for another exsamination ,
most of my cash goes into that and will need to go to London, a nighmare , a nightmare ....
6/15, 1:30pm **Pre View**
When do you need to go to London?
6/15, 1:30pm **Koz Kozmos**
but these companys are corrupt
not booked it yet, wait
will talk about it again, if u want some idea
6/15, 1:31pm **Pre View**
ok, What does 'sue' mean ?
6/15, 1:31pm **Koz Kozmos**
Optical Express ruined my life
6/15, 1:31pm **Pre View**
Do u mean u will have a check on ur eyes and will have to pay for that ?
6/15, 1:32pm **Koz Kozmos**
sue means : institute legal proceedings against a person or institution yes, legal aid has been stopped in this country
and the lawyer can now take 25% of the money if the case is on
i had and accident, sued and won
6/15, 1:33pm **Pre View**
ok, if there's anything i can do ?
6/15, 1:34pm **Koz Kozmos**
my sister talked about lazer eye surgery
i went for it , instead of spending it on beer and bills
when i had this accident there was legal aid
6/15, 1:34pm **Pre View**
but it was no good ?
6/15, 1:35pm **Koz Kozmos**
it 's going to Parliament
It ruined my eyes, severe dryness buring pain etc
i did not research it
6/15, 1:35pm **Pre View**
i'd like to know what happened (the accident)
That is if you want to talk about it?
6/15, 1:35pm **Koz Kozmos**
it was the most money i ever spent no accident
6/15, 1:36pm **Pre View** ok, got it
6/15, 1:36pm **Koz Kozmos**
the procedure does not work, it's corrupt and discusting and the company are liars,
even if i went blind they'd do nothing anyways,
i 'd rather not talk about this, typing confuses issues
6/15, 1:37pm **Pre View**
do u know why it caused burning pain ?
There are many ways to make sense in this world
Inverting pain allows to transcend CS
6/15, 1:37pm **Koz Kozmos**
i know wots going on ,
its' too complex to explain
6/15, 1:38pm **Pre View**
is it ok if i start some healing tonight

6/15, 1:38pm **Koz Kozmos**
its tragic
6/15, 1:38pm **Koz Kozmos**
but every thing happens for a reason
and suffering is good for us , we learn so much and get closer to god
6/15, 1:38pm **Pre View**
Are you losing yer brains or wot?
6/15, 1:39pm **Koz Kozmos**
I was joking, fuck the new age mind control program,
i'd be done with it
6/15, 1:39pm **Pre View**
Why don't u increase new directions
6/15, 1:39pm **Koz Kozmos**
but as long as i'm here with all the shit ,
it will be daily suffering
6/15, 1:40pm **Pre View**
do u go very detailed with the healing ?
6/15, 1:41pm **Koz Kozmos**
not sure, i do wot i can
6/15, 1:41pm **Pre View** ok
6/15, 1:41pm **Koz Kozmos**
i need an optometrist to see my eyes in a bad state the conditions is varying ,
it's a nighmare
any ways , i'm ok ,
gotta stay srong breathe more hydrogen into them
6/15, 1:42pm **Koz Kozmos**
and let the dirt of the matrix fall offf me
how do i do that ? were do i get the hydrogen ?
thank u for listening !
were do i get the hydrogen? I bet you know this
6/15, 1:44pm **Pre View**
What works for me : I SET UP THE GRIDS with Merlin consciousness,
you have plenty of that in the UK.
IT'S THE LAVENDER RAY THAT IS VERY IMPORTANT
to get a good go in releasing the density or stuck patterns through the bloodstream
of your eyes, the blood circulation within the muscles connected to the eye.
When the blood circulation is cleared I would move through the tear glands,
especially the Eyebrow glands – they open the eyes to new visions.
The hardest part would be the repair of the nerves connected to your eyes.
I need to really understand what the laser surgery fucked up and see what kind of
advise I
get from my spirit guides to bring some continuum in the healing.
It's a process we need to go through together and upgrade, but doable.
Yet you need to understand how Light Techniques work so you can further the work
And I don't feel like explaining again as you know you need some foundation to hold
the Light to its higher degrees
Flip it anyway u want
What are yer speculations?
Understanding many functions within brain faculties is something we all will need to
develop at some point in time and release the old degrees of indoctrination
Earth is an interesting living system
Wish I could remember the origin
6/15, 1:45pm **Koz Kozmos**
o no! fancy a bit of disco ?
i need something i can work with
no information, no knowlege

6/15, 1:46pm Koz Kozmos
MUSIC: The Pointer-Sisters Jump

6/15, 1:46pm **Koz Kozmos**
dance , catch u later
6/15, 1:47pm **Pre View**
Ok, I'm not starting the healing then?
Lets bring some Alchemy through, maybe that will make you understand more about light As the UK was the Magic land , the magicians, the alchemy
6/15, 1:55pm **Koz Kozmos**
i can turn gold in to led , and i've destroyed my higher self via dark majikz
hi ave no idea how to do these thing, they're just theories to me
6/15, 4:02pm **Pre View**
We've been thr that
There is no limitation when it comes to doing things with what u've learned
Any suggestions ?
I don't have a clue as far as your healing majik is concerned,
I mean the practical side from this land, not neverland
Otherwise, maybe i could tap into that, that is easier and then fuse my tech
U told me u feel things when u breathe and not breathe
So I guess with what u feel u get information, u have intuition
u have the knowledge to apply what u feel
So I guess u do that? Huh?
and when that is integrated u get upgrades in what u feel, and again administer that into your healing Right or wrong ?
6/15, 4:03pm **Pre View**
What does Lemuria represent 2 u ?
Hey turn your eyes into gold, liquify them into Golden waves
6/15, 4:07pm **Koz Kozmos**
Lemuria is an interdimensionless place hidden in the spaces between spaces that the high gene escaped to when Atlantis was destroyed
Parts of this place lay hidden in the out land beyond the death realm,
and is used to help the fire born heal before they are pulled thr the soul gate.....
so some memories retain awake.
6/15, 4:11pm **Koz Kozmos**
MUSIC: DONOVAN -ATLANTIS

6/15, 4:13pm **Koz Kozmos**
etc , wot did it mean to u?
a higher state of consciousness ?
6/15, 4:44pm **Koz Kozmos**
MUSIC: Solfeggio Master Frequency 1122 Hz HD Meditation

6/15, 5:14pm **Pre View**
This is what I learned and teach:
The MERKIVAH = the name for a Light Energy Field ,
the motor that drives the lightbody into training and gaining knowledge.
MERKIVAH = MAGIC OF MERLIN = LE MERLIN = LEMURIA
Let me explain the word and where it comes from

Ready for the Holy grail of neuro-Science?

MER = LE-MERLIN :
It comes through the Lavender ray and the computer (merkivah or lightbody) starts to think for itself, starts to co-create, instant manifestations happen,

KI OR KEY = Aquarian Green ray
(or connect to the aquarian age we're entering)
= motor that makes u move with the words, concepts, new ideas , you get personally involved with ascended Masters etc ...

VAH = heart center connection,
that goes all the way into the Immortal gates,
into the beyond
It is all about reconstructing Atlantis and leaving behind what broke us through Lemuria, the fall, the falseness, etc
But it does not mean i understand all technical equipment
that comes when growing with light,
it is only now that I started to interrogate more, and trying to dig deeper to understand where evolution is hitting
6/15, 5:15pm **Pre View**
Should you enjoy another question: what are tracks 2 u ?
I'm not so much interested in what THINGS used to be, but more in what i can do with them today , or how I can pick things up while getting some remembrance...
6/15, 5:22pm **Koz Kozmos**
MUSIC: Bob Dylan - Tangled Up In Blue

6/15, 5:22pm **Koz Kozmos**
from blood on the tracks catch u later ,
good vibes need to read your posts
6/15, 5:24pm **Koz Kozmos**
prodigal sista , will catch u later , have some stuff to sort
6/15, 5:25pm **Pre View**
ok, gonna put my ass in the sun and chill my axes out
and I told ye I didn't like Bobby NO DYLAN PLEASE!
6/15, 5:25pm **Koz Kozmos**
will read
6/15, 5:25pm **Pre View**
i'm eating like a tiger today
6/15, 5:26pm **Koz Kozmos**
good stuff watch some Fringe chillaxe in the crib
6/15, 5:47pm **Pre View**
Wish you Good Fortune with your stuff !
6/15, 6:17pm **Pre View** So what about TRACKS?
If one has knowledge - we can still make a million different choices with that knowledge and create new knowledge which again would create new choices or spaggethi ?.... Is it possible to get the output from a chosen vibe before the choice has been made & why ? Hey Koz, only answer if u feel like arting your thoughts through like in wave transmissions, ok, wave style is what I said
You should be able to understand that, you know how to wave musical herz through
Wave style thus,,,hahaha
6/15, 7:38pm **Koz Kozmos**
i don't listen to him much , I mean bob
to answer your question : MAYBE , the quantum wave makes many things possible that have yet to be fullly acknowledged ,
or so it seems so

6/15, 10:36pm **Koz Kozmos**
not sure what u mean by tracks
i thought the Merkivah was creating a light body , building a soul to escape the wheel of meat its been a long time since i heard that word or a word like it
we're getting nowhere with things really
but I agree that something energetic has occured
6/15, 10:58pm **Koz Kozmos**
is it possible to get the output from a chosen vibe before the choice has been made & why : the image is able to control time by traversing the duality and entering the accusal i suppose... remember, I've been targeted and wiped and cursed by the dazzling
6/16, 5:35am **Pre View**
i'm only getting to understand things a little more profound while working with Light as it brings changes almost every day, depending on what I work with for my own healing
I don't know about it, just learning about t, they must have deeper : I think we can reconnect to our origin and open the messengers type of communication thr our feet centers with our spark, our spirit. Is is not rethinking how to open these intelligent tracks and bring our consciousness into many renewed modems .
An example would be just tracking telepathic, telekinetic waves and reconnecting to species, or teams of light can can assist us further and bring deeper levels of advise through regarding the repair of the planet and thus our own organism
I worked with some tracks over the past 10 days;;; results : it deepened/cleared my bone structure . People told me last week-end : you look different and so much better : this was because the tracks I was
loading or connecting to deepened the bones face which resulted in a younger outlook.
So i'm only experiencing to see what possible outcomes I could get
Things we do in ascension should be fun, should upgrade us and teach us
Yet, I don't think everybody is hungry for knowledge, is it?
6/16, 5:40am **Pre View**
also, when working with tracks, my hand hurts less for 40 %,,,
it feels good
6/16, 6:36am **Pre View**
Remember when i told u : my bones are floating : it was put out like a joke,
but they actually are, hahaha
ok, give me a triplicated smile Koz, will you
6/16, 9:57am **Pre View**
Merkivah is indeed Light body training, yet it is the energy field that surrounds the physical body and is attached through the thymus gland or what is termed High Heart. It is the energy that stores or locks dow the Axis positioning in the celestial and universal Grid Lay outs. The axis is important, it needs to be inverted as everything on earth has been inverted. What is an axis actually? I don't wan to go too technical, yet if you think about WHAT WE TRULY ARE: LIGHT and Light needs anchoring points to stabalize or manifest something and so the anchoring points are being found in the GRID.
Therefor Grid architectural lay out and our connection to it may be the most important thing in ascension before anything else.
6/16, 10:42am **Pre View**
Hey u! Get yer axis into position and bow yurself through the universe
Lazer Lights like in disco shows
This song may give you some idea, hahaha
MUSIC: Pet Shop Boys - Axis [Official Music Video]

It is interesting with the music u post on your FB profile , like hip hop I mean, hip(intelligent)hop(movement) = intelligent movement so I've learned somehow Rock& roll coming together under the same wavelength etcccccccccc...

6/16, 2:17pm **Koz Kozmos**
What is intelligence thr tracks?
if we have a supreme intelligence what has happened to make us so dysfunctional as a race? Who gives this celestial assistance and why is it so limited and mean spirited ???
I thought u didn't know wot tracks are? too many contradictions
i don't want hard times
How can your bones float?
I want a triplicated smile ????
Why have we been denied this supreme intelligence? and hurt so much it seems sadistic to me , are we a fallen race or were we pushed?
6/16, 2:36pm Koz Kozmos
MUSIC: The Human League - Human

6/16, 2:37pm Koz Kozmos
not sure about all these humans
6/16, 2:45pm Koz Kozmos
MUSIC: Eartha kitt, I want to be evil

6/16, 3:03pm **Koz Kozmos**
is evil overrated ? triplicated smile....
good luck !
6/16, 4:24pm **Pre View**
OK Koz, get your Lazer light show together,
they will answer your questions.
Gosh, so many question questions questions
Can u maybe load ur body double over here and communicate for a week or so
6/16, 4:27pm **Koz Kozmos**
questions with out any answers
6/16, 4:29pm **Pre View**
U've got knowledge, answer them yourself and bring your brains to some level where they can start to think, like humans used to do...
Just let me know what you think about certain subjects
I does not mean you to have had the experience, though that would help understanding stuff; That is easier and more fun to communicate exchanging thoughts, not theories, that's boring
Even if we don't know, there's always imagination that goes possibly further then knowledge
6/16, 4:38pm **Pre View**
What I mentioned about tracks doesn't mean I know everything about them!
i will work with what i
know that is a fact, but i can still not write pages about it, that comes through experience That's why info from another brain might be helpfully
6/16, 4:50pm **Koz Kozmos**
i do exchange, u don't really comment's on my more esoteric comments
why have we been dumbed down and damaged ? and why all the hard work ? i need to play , i'm sick of having to shoot thr the crap every day
this has been a wasted life , its fuckin aweful
and my efforts have been immense
6/16, 5:21pm **Koz Kozmos**
gosh i hate typing
6/16, 5:46pm **Pre View**
Koz, u don't seem to feel ok ?
Maybe u need some time off and do something completely different ?
Play ur guitar & break loose
We never know what kind of signals the brain taps into
And starts synapsing from one adaption
To a generation of adaptation
We could delete that

6/16, 5:57pm **Pre View**
Hey man cheer up, its no use going down into the crap Rise like a Wizard ,
command like a Magician
Command the land of the people in
6/16, 6:03pm **Pre View**
Play some more Elvis and set your thought on a new move or movie
6/16, 6:04pm **Koz Kozmos**
MUSIC: Elvis Presley - In The Ghetto (Music Video) (1969)

6/16, 6:04pm **Koz Kozmos**
i never feel ok , i need to sort the crap ,
but its going slow
6/16, 6:05pm **Pre View**
ok, lets chat a little about your crap and move some solutions through
Everybody has stuff and earth is healing
6/16, 6:06pm **Koz Kozmos**
no, its hard enuff typing letters of complaint
i'm bored with the guitar
6/16, 6:07pm **Pre View** ok,
i always help myself with lots of physical training for that defeats the density,
like running and dancing, and hold on to the joy somehow
, not giving attention to what is playing out... Do u do anything besides swim ?
6/16, 6:08pm **Koz Kozmos**
I do the hand jive
6/16, 6:09pm **Pre View**
Hand jive ?
Where's ur magic hands?
Were is ur majical luv ?
6/16, 6:09pm **Koz Kozmos**
see if u can spot me
6/16, 6:09pm Koz Kozmos
MUSIC: The Rite of Spring-NIJINSKY (1913)

6/16, 6:09pm **Pre View** ok
6/16, 6:10pm **Koz Kozmos**
get the hype , its not from Grease, its form the 1950's this song
MUSIC: Chubby Checker - Let's Twist Again

6/16, 6:13pm Koz Kozmos
maybe u could incorporate in your cosmic teaching listen and paint !
6/16, 6:14pm **Koz Kozmos**
desllllexia bad today
6/16, 6:14pm **Pre View**
no prob, i decipher with ease, don't be bothered
Think about why Stonehenge and other strong places were built?
All these interlated places to the Satars, constellations
6/16, 6:15pm **Koz Kozmos**
don't bother ?
hey , i want u to heal
6/16, 6:15pm **Koz Kozmos**
MUSIC: WILLIE AND THE HAND JIVE - Johnny Otis

6/16, 6:16pm **Pre View**
When this Joachim thing is over and done with, everything will flow,,,
did u read the file I sent?
6/16, 6:16pm **Koz Kozmos**
catch u later , no didn't read, i feel its too private
its not my bussiness
have fun , flow with the go
6/16, 10:23pm **Koz Kozmos**
Hope u listened to all those posts in great detail
6/17, 1:25am **Koz Kozmos**
MUSIC: Mandrake the Magician

6/17, 1:25am **Koz Kozmos**
itz not eazeee being a retro modern
6/17, 5:34pm **Pre View**
Remember 3 colors on flags, 3 judges, the trinary system is seen everywhere
Numerology is as important as astronomy!
Only U can make sense of U!
The following are things you told me very frequently, maybe a good time to reflect on that
Sorry, I'm a Capricorn, so very detailed, and went into some kind of psychological room to get some clarity about you as a 'being' , a biological thinking species.
"I AM STRONG" --"I'VE WORKED VERY HARD"
"I'VE BEEN DAMAGED & HURT " -- "I HAVE BEEN TARGETED" :
I agree, you are exclusively strong & worked harder then anyone would ever be able too or acknowledge what it takes.
But strength can have many missing links and many limited values because at times we may not see them throughout the strength .
Being damaged and hurt needs loads of self investigation that goes along with experiences throughout our daily life (target, matrix, slaves, ...)
and all that. And yes I understand we've all been born in the lesser environments and need to lift ourselves out of it. So yess, there is a lot of inward, interior heart designs to reset and cover.
But talking about the sickness does no good and doesn't get us anywhere. We're all in the same boat and there is a reason we've been placed on earth.
Is is all about those that have strength and mental capacities like us that need to pave the road for the weaker , the lost ones, etcccc and show them how repair works.
You are awake! So maybe a good start would be to invent something that awakens the hood you are living in (minus your continual complaints)!
Otherwise we would end up chasing our ow tail like most people on FB ,
like posting the damn things
over & over without ever taking action.
It is that mechanism that keeps the brain on recycled consciousness that needs to be broken down in order to make people see and UNDERSTAND their way out.
What I experience with you (please forgive me if i'm wrong)
is that u do not really reflect on things deep
enough; and even over & over again till u get the answers out.
When the answers come, you can heal yourself 10 different ways with what u've learned.
I asked you many times it would be good to polish your attitude, and understand your character; how you have build your character and how some psychological content really needs to make room for new SELF INFORMATION that makes you feel good about self in a way that you are no longer prone to the outside world.
And yes I understand, the manipulation is worldwide and it takes work to get truth all around the world.
IMAGINATION HELPS!

DID U REFLECT DEEP ON THIS, MANY TIMES OVER ? (then u would at least maybe have written and analyzed 10 pages about yourself without being to gummy about your past. That is termed self investigation through self love. But, as people have lost self love, and seem to think of the word like taking care of one self, then that is too far from getting anywhere.
The ORIGIN OF LIFE GIVING LOVE OR LOVE GIVING need to be restored.
Or, we probably first need to find that Free Flow Space within to operate from and the refine our way back home from . And there is many cells that do not even have a nucleus. Would they just leave the body when transmuting the cells into Light waves, Light parts...
We all need to heal from many life times of damage, yet, how many actually enjoy the process?
Did u go deep enough to clear the cause of damage , then the damage itself, what was the type of attitude u were holding onto at that time, how did yer character respond to it, what were other individual items involved when u went through damage and did you delete them from your lifestyle or not, how did u live, wot were other peoples' feelings. Did u acknowledge them or were u only concerned about your own internal and external feelings. Why do u never express your feelings when it comes to the deeper levels. Were u able to balance out somehow when the damage was happening or did you impulsively react with some sort of fight and flight behavior leaving out flexibility? Were u considerate of others involved or self-reflective and demanding ...?
Did u ever question why I needed to go backstage ? : for u to reflect on yourself, for me to heal myself and move faster.
Did U ever question why I once told u "I can handle u?
Are u willing to do what it takes to get out of the matrix or Ego?
It takes hard work and you don't like that, but also it will make you work harder.
So the universe will supply you with what you need, you just co-create and need to listen to what needs to be done. Most people lost obedience and prefer to swim with their ego 'counter' sea waves
Reason why they have silly hyperbole questions.
A soul is a lazy syndrome, a soul is a disease that needs to turn everything around to understand the origin Life AND BEING A-LIVE instead of keeping Self alive for no purpose
For there is no joy when life is not being seen as an explorer, a creator, an engine full of passion, and essentially PURPOSE that fulfills many goals.
We're in the middle of a solar system that has been broken and that included we are offered the most beautiful repair with a new LIGHT on the Great Central Sun when willing to do the work. Too many still expect some sort of Deity to do the work for them and thus invite the lesser Gods into their embodiment with so many diseased outcomes.
WHEN YOU WORK WITH THE CREATOR, THE CREATOR WORKS FOR YOU AND ASSISTS THE EVOLUTION PROCESS OR UPGRADES IN LIGHT SPHERES.
Why is so much happening 2 u?: you are still not ready to turn your back on ur fight/ flight!
Why : you keep on repeating "I've worked very hard", meaning you may not be ready to even work harder and climb that last bit to the top of the mountain where the Gold blinds the shiningDid u ever question why u get hurt so easily?
It all resides within our attitude/character.
It is up to all of us to upgrade in mentality and grow towards atmospheric conditions that are beneficial to our health, wealth and creational essence.
You never polished your DYNAMICS and yet expect every single entity you encounter in life to appreciate them without a return level of deep insight.
It may of course not be intentional, then again, you have no intention to do the work to heal.
Meaning : u can be straight with people, u can tell it like it is every which way it pleases you without taking any sensitivity of the other vibe into account, let alone considering their mental capacity or emotional breakdown.(this is not about me)
U just cannot be bothered with studying, period!
Like most of humans,

Koz gets hurt, but so does everybody.
Impatience, impulsiveness, and the lack of reflection over and over again makes that you get hurt. So everything you encountered in life is your ACTION-REACTION equalizing the hurt.
As I said before, it is important to load the damn SOLAR SYSTEM INTO YOU" : PONDER
No, you did not because you are attached to the old ways of Majic:
this would enable u to integrate softer vibes when u go overboard, meaning impulsive moods, temper, impatienc, irritation,,
The solar system is connected to consciousness and rays of creation that can be applied at any time to override negative consciousness and behavioral patters of lesser degrees such as fears and self manipulation, panic attacks etc...
I apply the following: when i have a character treat that is rather negative showing up thr experiences in life, I look at my attitude and polish that which enables my to hold on the good vibes. Just worthy training that needs practice, experience, passion, endurance and devotion. Without these values, every single entity could get lost many times over and over until EYES SEE WE CAN ONNLY DEPEND ON SELF:SOURCE and our Spirit in Great Faith, and belief through trust.
Sometimes it takes several hours a day for the period of a week for example to get specific issues out of the brain and thus the body. Yet necessary to get the deeper levels of the soul out of the glandular system because some things really stick like glue and holds us back from moving forward. Its all merely about getting old consciousness and states of being out of the brain so the body can catch up to raise our energy, our electrical output. Therefore, it is very important to connect to other electrical sources that assist the process such as the oceans , all the elements, etc.....
And we can always invent new things such as in co-creation ; just to keep the fun going but also to ALLOW faster growth into our origin.
And I can only depend on myself and my connections to species, sources/forces, teams of Light. There is so much we all forgot about. Yet when looking upon the sky at night, people do understand somehow that they are part of it,,, yet do not question anything as their brains are being held in captivity so much.
The story of the universe and creation is never ending, is must be so interesting...
Lets start to remember, and trust the answers from Spark to Spark.
I NEED TO FORGET ABOUT ALL THE HARD WORK I'VE DONE & START ALL OVER, this time not allowing wobbles and learning how to humble self (i'm only between stages of respect & integrity .
It is a long road to travel into humility, yet these higher virtues open the spaces in which wisdom and Science of the Divine reside.It also explains why people are moving at such a slow pace. If they need decades to understand that the animal kingdom was never meant to be eaten alive, yet more to bring balance and harmony and of course co-creation to the planet and much more as far as biology is concerned; then it becomes understandable that many will leave the planet and will not be able to keep up with the great transition or purification coming through. No humility, respect and integrity for all species is no respect at all for the Creator.
I don't need to explain logic, do I?
However i'm sure u must have learned many thing to heal yourself and maybe simply did not go all the way? I regret a lot we cannot exchange what we've learned because of the limitations of living in different countries.
The best I'v learned from u is EXACTITUDE : going deeper into something until it makes me go crazy. That came through the music you posted and the way you look things up, it matters.
In the past I used to give people many teachings for free, but I'm over and done with it. Another thing I learned from you is that information is sacred and needs to be payed for. Doing free healings exhausted me to a high degree which is obvious, when you give and give and give without getting anything back or balancing it, it depletes the energy fields.
I think you're a great man and strong. : too every question that u have, could u please answer it to yurself from yurself first? and then exchange the answers ?
Please Koz?
U seem to be stay strong :

Strong enough to load all the positive characteristics of the astrological wheel into u to balance yur Aries dynamics ? This is the most important thing u can do for Self to get moving fast : if u'd do this consistently, precisely with exactitude, it'll take a few months and will enhance your Light dynamics as well as your skills and much more.
TO EMBODY LIGHT, WE JUST NEED TO RE-LEARN EVERYTHING!
THERE WE GO : IMPATIENCE! polish, think it over, and find a way to have fun with patience and wot it does to u. Why am I talking so much: coz of yer mood swings, don't know why, I just love the way u approach me minus yer anger and judgmental legend. U told me "I've opened my heart " I told u " U have extreme Intelligence" , yet you hardly apply it coz you don't know how or in wot context. If we would just merge, fuse both our settings we would get:
LOVE + INTELLIGENCE = WIZARD
This is actually wot i do with myself, i question everything till i get surprised by things that come out of me- when in conversation with somebody. ...
So, I think communication is a very important trigger, it can heal many wounds Yet both parties need to participate equally...
6/17, 5:34pm **Pre View**
Also, u asked me to talk about Joachim, if I wanted too --
When i did : u told me its too private ...
Then u talk about Rachel, yet you do not mention who she is, coz its too private... My answer : if u cannot go private and personal, u ain't gonna get anywhere coz herein lies our Essence, wot we truly are, and there is nothing to hide anymore in this world. Its maybe your main problem, not going deep, deeper and deepest in expressing feelings,,, that is where it gets interesting. I have a feeling when u'd polish yer attitude and character , everything could change and then I might finally gaze in the Amazing Grace u truly are.
Why : i intend to heal myself thoroughly and have high hopes u would do so too.
Why : after that i'd like to go deeper into astrophysics, science, stuff with u, if u'd like that; Why : coz i've missing links in which yer intelligence may possibly bring through some matches That is if you can let go of yer impatience and judgements and when willing to answer questions first to SELF!and then sort out some EXCHANGE ANSWERS with me.
Why : to pull out something new with this universe
Why : to go beyond wot is happening and finding the first levels of freedom first, before liberation
Why : that would make me happy, very happy.
This is how u would look when the solar vehicle has been loaded, all possible vibes (colors into the colorless white) meaning u'd be able to enjoy yer Aries highways (red) much more and balanced.

MUSIC: Love story - Andy Williams with lyrics

6/17, 5:37pm **Pre View**
I have but one hope for you : that is that u would not open yerr Dragon wings this time
but let it all rest for a day or so
6/17, 5:48pm **Pre View**
U once told me 'get strong'
i did not question u, I did question myself, and figuring out answers .
Questioning self with what happened to our essence may get us on new starry lanes of comprehension, discernment, maybe a deeper level of alertness,,,
It may be interesting for you to do so,,,
Anyways Mister Koz, I'll leave at that
We can all bypass the old fountains
The media provides the meets!
Beyond the matrix grades and cages

MY INTERNALS:: at the time being I felt a strong need to express what was hitting my nerves as I felt we wouldn't get anywhere concerning the healing over FB and understanding what Light Technology could bring through.
Koz always had a strong sense as far as music was concerned. He knew exactly what and when to post that on his FB page or the messages between us. We somehow had gotten a lot closer as we both had moved through similar struggle being loners and doing our thing because 6 years ago, people did certainly not understand the awakening as they do today. People sensed my light, they always thought of me as a very weird person because I would always merge some good fun with a funky demonstration of how that works with the universe and show them the results; when socializing.

Yet , in the end, I always ended up very alone and lonely for there was nobody who was intelligent and interesting enough to go all the way and pull the change through in consciousness with the research I was doing. Some did move through my seminars and had a complete turnover in their lives, some could not understand the investment and regret this until today. Delightful and impressive people also crossed my pulsation just to shake up little things ; which I loved. Mostly at night, I would always look at the stars, talk to them, paint, have a drink and chat with Koz. I didn't have many friends or those kind of people that were only in it for a free ride into knowledge and assistance in their troubled lives. Koz became a friend I would turn to in the morning, late at night when coming back from the city, or at any time. It felt like a comfort back then, somebody who would listen and reply, much so like having a friend in the stars.
There was a strong bond between us through music and arts, and also, we could easily handle harsh talk and then forget about it. Back then, I didn't fear anything, neither did I fear to lose him as a good companion.

Yet, I would miss him posting music. It was pretty exceptional and unique how he combined romance with hip hop, very old late 5O ties music with dark rocking vibes.
It may also be interesting for those reading the story to make a YouTube list of all these songs because the growth is going to be very unexpected and significant to understand the evolution between two people. Many things happened as our conversations became very intense over the years, and proves many results some may not consider, reflect upon. The capacity to think and communicate with many species offers such deep creations and assistance to people. My directions into the higher Spheres of Light are now moving into the study of Animal behavior, and the communication with the soil, our ancestral tracks. Started out my Bachelor in Animal Behavior in Scotland; hoping to be able to move to Australia, to see my son, and maybe also into the African roots, the Himalaya's and teach Light and take care of the animals and the true nature of being,

6/17, 7:04pm **Koz Kozmos**
can't make sense of me or it "I AM STRONG" --"I'V WORKED VERY HARD" "I'V BEEN DAMAGED & HURT " -- "I HAVE BEEN TARGETTED".
Yes I eye have...
luv the captialz ! acknowledging the sickness is useful, I have other mantra's
YIP! over and over and over I need to get out face book for awhile ...
Wot I experience with u (please forgive me if i'm wrong) is that u do not really reflect on things deep enough & over & over again till u get the answers out & then heal them maybe 10 different ways with wot
u'v learned':
o I reflect too much I'd say and have done massive healing on my self but the damage goes deep, there is always room for improvement of course !
"Polish ur Attitude, polish ur character": I do this every day and have written up a good deal, more than 10 pages on self analysis beyond the cliché's of the life coach
I have certainly cleared a lot of damage
U have no idea what I go thru on a day to day basis and how hard it is for me to be here I'm an empath and have maybe considered other people feeling ....maybe too much,
these people were not worth it
I do express my feelings, fake book is not the best place and i'm a private person I understand why u need to go back stage, do u think I'm a cretin
Did U ever question why I once told u "I can handle U ?' YES '
Are u willing to do wot it takes to get out of the matrix or Ego '? The matrix uses the ego for sure as a program, YES!!!!!!!
I have worked hard and continue to, u jump to conclusions and
YOUR LACK OF INSIGHT ASTOUNDS ME
I don't get hurt that easily...but I'm learning not to take any more shit !!!!
You're entitled to your opinion are u deep enuff to be shallow?
thats enuff Pre.....GOOD BYE

6/17, 10:47pm **Pre View**
I needed yur fire to get to my bottom-line (although i'v put it that way to trigger u), u gave I'm not sure concerning many things, your consciousness does not seem limited, yet your degree of dialoging pulls through the limit.
Thank u for feeding me with vits & minerals the earth plane has not ever heard of !!!!!
I've tried to understand your pain over and over, it was all so much physical damage. I did understand it and was really wanting to go into the emotional damage connected to it. Otherwise, what's the point of healing , the damage would return over and over unless the consciousness attached to it is being targeted! And eliminated. Most of the time people refuse to target or go deep into ACCEPTING the consciousness that created damage.
I did suffer similar damage and pain as you did which is weird. I would wake up many nights, just to talk to u, and hoping u'd understand somehow where this would result into. I cannot possibly make a moving reality of the life you've lived with the bits and pieces? I think we just missed out on meeting in the physical . This brought me to a greater understanding because when u know somebody in the physical and u talk to them afterwards, u have the physical component of reactive beauty
I think U might be strong enough to do so, i am not as strong as u,
but i'll get there, every day so many are struggling to get there and i will, coz U THOUGHT ME SO. Will our horns meet, or would it end up in a tragedy as you had foreseen somehow, somewhere through **our commercials?**
We could put a lot on equal grounds and create a program that changes communities minus our own egos concerning healing. Living the path of Spirit within does require the removal of the mentality that has egotistical content, the physical body and its healing will automatically follow through because it is actually the Light Brain composition or NETWORK that brings the RIGHT SPEECH

to our cellular content that needs to move into light waves anyways.
I will miss the beauty of your brain.
KNOWLEDGE IS YOUR SALVATION, PERIOD!!!
You sound like a dear hunter with whom I can be self in many or all ways; knowing u'd blast through me, hahahaha
People need the hope, the confrontation I gave 2 u,
the purity of some one who does not yearn for
something in return?
So if you want the GRACE of stopping it here and now, that is ok,
I will miss yur vibes
I will wiss yur music
I will miss yur Essence, coz i will not meet that again ,
I think we were both on the 2009 crash digging down pains and willing to heal it
I will respect yur wishes, byond FB capabilities, meaning,
when u don't want to interact with my vibes i will not message u any longer (FB cannot evaporate this)
Fare thy vibes well
Please take good care Koz,
Thank u over and over for all I did not see
Love, Nic
6/17, 11:13pm Koz Kozmos
MUSIC: Oliver Shanti Seven Times Seven 04 - Olugu Zamba

6/17, 11:30pm **Koz Kozmos**
prima donna!
A very temperamental person with an inflated view of their own talent or importance.
Thats not me by the way
good night ,sleep tight
6/18, 12:47am **Koz Kozmos**
u did not trigger me
i didn't think it wod end in tragedy
why all the jumping to conclusions
any wayz Nic blessingz upon u , and thank u 2
6/18, 1:30am **Pre View**
I will sleep now, and tight, hahaha
I surrendered ,
to see without eyes
u taught me how to incorporate Divine Will
and leave the Individual Will
Meaning with ur vibes i do not need glasses, i do not need lenses, June 18, 2013
6/18, 3:02pm **Koz Kozmos** how?
June 18, 2013
6/18, 6:12pm Koz Kozmos
MUSIC: Jethro Tull - Thick as a Brick full

6/18, 6:19pm **Koz Kozmos**
and your wise men don't know how it feels...
to be thick as a brick
6/18, 10:47pm **Pre View**
I'll answer yur question tomorrow, with great delight
gonna listen to ur music
And create new concepts
6/18, 11:10pm **Koz Kozmos**
hope your ok take extra care
6/18, 11:11pm **Koz Kozmos**
MUSIC: Lionel Richie - Time

6/18, 11:12pm **Koz Kozmos**
time huh? don't give a dam about tomorrow June 19, 2013
6/19, 7:05am **Pre View**
Hello, hello hello, is it echoing ?
Time is precious, and indeed we should give a dam,
6/19, 7:14am **Pre View**
Thank u for the tunes ---
I wonder wot yr most exclusive/inclusive gift would be
and if that would bring the double diamond together.
Wot is it that would erase the burning pains for u to shine without a care of wot once was,,,,,
6/19, 7:20am **Pre View**
Thick as brick : i was thinking to jump on a trampoline & wave the walls of light thr, spinning them like a delirious freak into a never ending impenetrable tuning device and get Justice grounded, haha
Look at the symbol of a bull, the symbol of a Lion!
All very part of astrology that needs redefinition
6/19, 7:52am **Pre View**
U asked me how u'v been teaching me : We met about 4 months ago,
that was the timing for me to let go
of everything & understanding it ....!!!!
But it was also time to observe wot I did with my life :
Working hard in daily life & doing lots of follow-up with my individual training esoterically speaking - i did not understand most of the things I was doing (it was far too difficult to understand) but i did the alignments which were given to me and thy changed my consciousness and mental state of being very
quickly, which was great.
But I missed out on questioning it for 80 % which A LOT.
Idiocrazy at sublime level i'd say!
Training people to get into Light configurations is easy, yet most do not understand what they are doing and still want TO GET HEALED; meaning most want some one else's' POWER to heal them versus moving into the Chapel of their own Power. We do not need anyone or anything except the wonder of self within and thus the WONDER OF THE UNIVERSE WITHIN which takes a lot of evaporation modalities regarding the release of soul/old sol/solar in order to get a grasp of spirit within.
So, basically, I teach people Light techniques that will get them back into their Origin of Creator SHIPS! As I told u, I fell deep as well during the past years : but want no more of that,,,
I couldn't hold my protection as strong as was being required or did not move into the right equipment
yet. But I certainly teach people now how to protect themselves from the vampires.
UNDERSTANDING what we do to move on the other side of midnight I as important as understanding the many paths into healing the soul syndrome.
Which is essentially what people DO NOT WANT! and thus the same old cycles just keep on ringing the
same tunes which I termed the difference between Divine Will or the fall into ego or Free will.
Reason why people are so down into boredom when the Light Self is held out of their Life vibes. Picking up Light Designs is like picking up Self and recreating the beauty of Light Living on Light realms which the Earth is becoming when start repairing the soil a bit faster.
Divinity does not hurry, but it certainly does not wait for anyone either! Got that?
ACTION, TAKE THE ACTION RAILS AND TRAIN
So while picking up and chatting with u at the same time was like some sort of synchronization.
I do not need lenses any more : every tune u ever posted was always perfectly aligning with wot i needed to settle my alignments - or integrate which goes fast with music!!!

MY INTERNALS : Today in 2020, Light consciousness is taking over 100% and TRUTH is finally being revealed in every corner of creation. We do not want to feed self with plastic and toxic foods any longer as climate change also wakes up more responsibility.
For Light Ambassadors teaching people to move into their oOrigin of Light ,it has become a must to live the Light Grid configurations on the other side of midnight and keep their Celestial/Universal and Omniversal Essence in the 6th dimension or at least a Spiritual embodiment as the matrix and their monstrous tales would do anything to get one down or break the bones back into soul living. It is all about community building now and teaching/learning to align to the biology of Light Earth while living a LIGHT GRID EMBODIMENT. Anything else will keep on creating disease upon disease and reason why people are being caught in massive lung diseases, colds and its many incurable lines of old soul creations due to living the matrix and not being aligned to the CRYST LIGHT GRIDS that override all the atrocities of malfunctioning and illness. Reason why is because THE BREATH cannot bring life back in a body that breathes the death penalty through such as animal food, drugs and all sorts of medication meant to keep on chasing the MIND tale or control. We all need to remember the Eternal/ Immortals ways of being as a Light configuration, a Spark in the House of Light termed Shambhala, THE SUN WITHIN SUNS! And all moon dials streaming with it.
Most people understand what music can do, yet keep on chasing OLD musical charts that already incorporated many many years ago. Reason why many keep on listening to the same tracks is because of the emotional body and attached experiences. Once the old experiences are being deleted from our psychology, we have the option to align to the higher degrees of Light advancement, music and a higher level of spiritual assistance.

The brain needs the complete elimination of ego, especially hormonally speaking otherwise the mind keeps on popping up which is equal to ego survival and decay.
The right music will always align you to the right people for personal advancement be it friendships, business partners, clientele...
Yet music needs you to listen to the alignments that come with it or the other way around: alignment can bring the right music 2 u.
The worst we can all witness is how people on social media keep on acting like sheep and just TAKE ANYTHING from ANY ONE as far as information is concerned due to lack of education and knowledge – and thus being able to DISCERN FROM PERSONAL PRACTICE.

An example of this is the promotion of TM meditation that brings through NO KNOWLEDGE or advancement; yet has every angle positioned to a point in which you start to eat your own tail! NOTHING EXPLAINS TRANSCENDENCE, no theory, no practice, no proof! After many years of practice , we need to show the proof of practice and the changes within which is 0% in TM meditation as in a kundalini practice for it was set up to keep self INTO THE CYCLES OF OLD. No Self Mastery, no Self Realization, no health! That explains everything, or how easy it still is to gather innocent people into a circle of debris and no upgrades. And of course, it is extremely easy to say that any still moment termed meditation brings some kind of peace within. IT IS HARD TO SAY HOW MANY CAN BREATHE THAT THROUGH IN THEIR 24/7 CYCLE in life and proof the upgrades.

Not everybody chooses to move into their Light shoes, yet there is always a sense of goodness, beauty and purity to be seen within people and maybe as the HORIZON rises, Light will eventually stream through any creative capacity. When passion in purpose opens the vibration into new cravings, Light Essences open up in the body much like 'joy'; and thus new re-connections with the elements and nature can be established through imaginative communication that can become very real. Just like children do. Discovering the Universe is all about discovering the treasures within Self and holding the Vision for a brand New World that streams on truth, peace, integrity, equality , new educational ways and days and understand what it means TO NEVER EVER LOOK BACK.

We owe this to our children and to all LIFE on the planet. Imagine if we would just teach children how to dream and breath the dream.
WHAT WE BREATHE, IS WHAT WE ARE AND BECOME.

6/19, 7:54am **Pre View**
I need to think about Divine Will, Spark, Higher Self
Will catch up with u later this day ok
6/19, 7:59am **Pre View**
Hope u feel ok too, it means a lot to me
The Aquarian Age will bring the true meaning of the 12 tribes, the teams
And astronomically
6/19, 11:34am **Koz Kozmos**
did some dancing alone yesterday and threw some majical shapes know my herniated disc is hurting and nerve pain in the toes like burning
i can't even move my body in a joyful way with out shit
6/19, 12:25pm **Pre View**
Dancing is delightful,I just dance every day for an hour or so with my majic waves.
Hey is there something wrong with yur right knee ?
6/19, 12:32pm **Pre View**
the bones, right, been working on my own sceletal structure for a week now
That is why I told you a while ago that I felt like my bones where floating in my body
It means they feel very lite when clearing them out.
with wot is yur hernia stuff in war with ?
Can u heal that ? I hope u can ! Play the music, hahaha
I think dancing is great for u, great wizardry
6/19, 1:43pm **Koz Kozmos**
my right knee is fine herniated disc is due to accident
it varies , my left leg , not right knee as i've explained if i dance i get problems listen to what i say please, its annoying
What do you mean with : AT WAR ?
6/19, 1:56pm **Pre View**
At war :physical pain is always associated with psychological stress somehow
6/19, 1:57pm **Koz Kozmos**
so the new agers say
my disc is out of the socket
i could not walk, but decided i could not trust the doctors
and manged to heal myself to a point
No more trust in doctors to operate; they have messsed enuff of my body up if i move such as dance exercise, i can get pain
how boring is that
the things i need to do to keep me fit make my body painful
and i'm not talking exercise ache
not sure why i'm telling u this
6/19, 2:11pm **Koz Kozmos**
i'll be ok , i have to be gotta look after myself
sorry to complain
6/19, 2:14pm **Pre View**
i hope u find a way to feel good
Rebuild your nights with the stars
Hear the blues, the violins, the hip hoppers
Wave the new feelers through
A little dream, a little stairway
6/19, 2:15pm **Koz Kozmos**
total soul death is the best option, extinguished and forever gone ahhhhh blisss
all i did yesterday was move my body got into a real joyful state
i felt so good , so i do find ways to feel good ,
i'm not a miserable bastard u just don't get it ,
but why should u
19, 2:20pm **Koz Kozmos**
i'll not talk about myself in this way again , theres no point

6/19, 2:21pm **Pre View**
talk any which way u like,
u'll always be u, i know that – I appreciate!
Do u know anything about languages - hand movements?
6/19, 2:23pm **Koz Kozmos**
Mudras?
6/19, 2:24pm **Pre View**
no, its more like when i speak english (not dutch) ,
i cannot stop moving my hands and fingers going with wot i say.
This is very fast all the time when being in a PHYSICAL conversation with people,
only i cannot stop that and do not understand it either i
n a way to what it may mean
U can equate that a bit to :
when u hear music u cannot stop ur body from moving .
The vibration that merges with the cellular construction and reason why everybody needs other tunes to upgrade with.
6/19, 2:25pm **Koz Kozmos**
I feel if you're awakening you're involved in improvised majikal acts
we need no alter, no sword etc
consciousness is our temple, and it can speak to us
but wots happening to me i feel is targetting
my awakeing is being block becuz i'm regonized
i've had enuff really
my body does not always move on music, it depends on the mood and the type of music thanks for being my friend again
6/19, 2:32pm **Pre View**
Uhuh, thank u
Friends or not, are u talking like Fb entities without brains,
Deleting, and adding friends?
I am not your friend , I proved to be your companion!
To bring through a new time Machine
And make Neuron Spiritual Science available to all!
it may be seen as a fast follow up of mudras still,
its different but always brings me joy
targeting , recognized : everybody in light vibes is being targeted and so our protection needs to come from higher Sources/forces until nothing can hit us any longer.
I'm also targeted but apply the Light Grid constructions for protection and LIGHT VIBES that keep me there.
And indeed, you need some knowledge or at least a good connection to your Source to get self into a Field of Light unity where you cannot even think anything can hit you.
I once experienced that I could not get up from an afternoon nap on my bed : there were entities such as the reptilians that where taking over my brains.
So you see, PROTECTION IS NUMBER ONE because the matrix wants you down!
do u have a theory about moods & music ?
6/19, 2:33pm **Koz Kozmos**
i don't want to bring u down
i looked it up, there's some thing called gang stalking and this can be I believe, inter dimensional i researched this years ago
6/19, 2:34pm **Pre View**
i'm ok, with whom & how u are
I do understand your pain, and I do understand you do not understand Light Techniques While it is just the APPLICATION OF LIGHT THROUGH MANY MODEMS. Or, when sitting in meditation, you need to trust what you get and get the app in the body! Like on your iPhone

6/19, 2:34pm **Koz Kozmos**
maybe i've just been unlucky
6/19, 2:36pm **Pre View**
You're very honest & open & never afraid of anything
Never met anyone to whom I would ever listen as I'm such a loner
U have a way of being straight and yet balancing the things you say; which very charming U give people a great level of trust
6/19, 2:37pm **Koz Kozmos**
i'm afraid of heights
6/19, 2:37pm **Pre View**
why
6/19, 2:37pm **Koz Kozmos**
not sure , i wasn't as a boy
"U give people a great level of trust ": i may give u a level of trust, this is generally not the case i'm not open with too many people,
i just go down to thier level and deal with it as best i can i've tryed to be the real me with them, it doesn't work
6/19, 2:39pm **Pre View**
do u think it is annoying aligning to their level
We should to a certain level in light years to be able to allow them understanding
6/19, 2:40pm **Koz Kozmos**
it can be boring and draining
yes i avoid people , all peole are gone from my life and good riddance
i've tryed to be open , it creates problems
my sister for instance, there is no point
6/19, 2:41pm **Pre View**
how old is your sister?
6/19, 2:41pm **Koz Kozmos**
follow the sly way 52 , and i have one who is 47
thier sleepers, i hardly see them
6/19, 2:43pm **Pre View**
thats right & drowning
i have a sister 2, she's 53, but never see her,
i told her how i felt and this is ok
6/19, 2:43pm **Koz Kozmos**
i try energetically to be the gentle good, do my best in limited circumstances
my sister wouldn't understand how i feel
and they throw the blame back on to me, fuck them
6/19, 2:45pm **Pre View**
Its hard to understand that sb like you has not been worshipped for al yur gifts & ....
Ok, non existent
6/19, 2:45pm **Koz Kozmos**
sb ?
6/19, 2:45pm **Pre View**
somebody
6/19, 2:46pm **Koz Kozmos**
i'm not regonized , not supported for who i am
and what i'm becoming the way i have been treated has been cruel ,
evil even but its ok , i'm strong and have learnt so much
6/19, 2:47pm **Pre View**
I hope i can be of little support at times
6/19, 2:47pm **Koz Kozmos**
but i need to be in a body that works to be me
u and Jain Doe have showen me support and i offfer mine at all times i was not so much complaining about the back pain, leg pain etc

but saying that i did something good felt joyful, majikal, and this is what came from it
, trying to get u to understand
6/19, 2:49pm **Pre View**
THANK U!!
indeed, the body needs to be in optimum health to perform whatever we wish
6/19, 2:49pm **Koz Kozmos**
about the negative dynamics : i'm a dancer not a puppet
but i've stopped
but i do feel exhausted and down to day and am sorting thru shit
anyways enuff about me, do u now this song ?
6/19, 2:52pm **Koz Kozmos**
MUSIC: The Who - The Real Me (Quadrophenia)

6/19, 2:52pm **Pre View**
I like it when u talk abOUT your self,,,I like listening
i need to do things now
if there's anything i can do, u'll let me know , right Listening ,,,
6/19, 2:52pm **Koz Kozmos**
catch u later, peace
6/19, 2:53pm **Pre View**
haven't heard this for a long time
6/19, 2:53pm **Koz Kozmos**
I went back to the doctor , to get another shrink.
I sit and tell him about my weekend,
But he never betrays what he thinks. Can you see the real me, doctor?
I went back to my mother
I said, "I'm crazy ma, help me."
She said, "I know how it feels son,
'Cause it runs in the family." Can you see the real me, mother? The cracks between
the paving stones Look like rivers of flowing veins.
Strange people who know me
Peeping from behind every window pane.
The girl I used to love
Lives in this yellow house.
Yesterday she passed me by,
She doesn't want to know me now. Can you see the real me, can you?
I ended up with the preacher, Full of lies and hate, I seemed to scare him a little
So he showed me to the golden gate. Can you see the real me preacher?
Can you see the real me doctor?
Can you see the real me mother?
Can you see the real me?
6/19, 2:54pm **Koz Kozmos**
could have posted one with out all the voices
6/19, 2:55pm Koz Kozmos
MUSIC: Pete Townshend - Love Reign O'er Me

6/19, 2:56pm **Koz Kozmos**
better than the one done by The who
used to listen to this in my 20's
there's nothing u can do
6/19, 3:10pm **Koz Kozmos**
that has been confirmed,
i expect nothing !

6/19, 3:53pm **Koz Kozmos** but enjoy your friendship
6/19, 6:43pm **Pre View**
like this Pete Townshend - hear more ....
Thank uuuu !!!!I hate the horror ur living in U have a specialty i can't figure out
6/19, 6:44pm **Koz Kozmos**
just a bad day, my humour is missed by typing
6/19, 6:47pm **Pre View**
we all have many waves
i also have strange arrows flowing heating them up, hahahah
6/19, 6:49pm **Koz Kozmos**
i'm sick of it , wave grids or whatever
6/19, 6:50pm **Pre View**
wave grids or wotever ?
6/19, 6:50pm**Koz Kozmos**
yip , the whole cosmic game has been a bore, a massive disappointment
6/19, 6:51pm **Pre View**
wot interests u most ?
6/19, 6:52pm **Koz Kozmos**
killing time , wot about u ?
6/19, 6:54pm **Pre View**
connections, astronomical connections, conciousness
6/19, 6:54pm **Koz Kozmos**
lol , o no i typed it , hahah
6/19, 6:55pm **Pre View**
hah ,didn't expect that from u (the word 'lol')
6/19, 6:55pm **Koz Kozmos**
i used to say the nature of reality and conciousness just typed the dreaded term for a joke
6/19, 6:56pm **Pre View**
i'm doing a vivisection on a dinosaurs
6/19, 6:57pm **Koz Kozmos**
better be careful!, i'll be saying Namaste
wot does that mean --- vivisection on a dinosaurs
6/19, 6:57pm **Pre View**
Saying Namaste ? I was joking, just interested in brainzzzzz
6/19, 6:58pm **Koz Kozmos**
its a nother cliche that the fukktarddz use like lol
6/19, 6:58pm **Pre View**
ok , thought so -- can u hear me when i think? ,
6/19, 6:59pm **Koz Kozmos**
aging is a bore and a waste of time
most of the life on this planet is pathetic, no i can't hear u , maybe a bit
6/19, 7:00pm **Pre View**
i'm rejuvenating everyday, its fun, abracadabra,,,,,
U were talking again this morning
Its the idea of connecting with billions of elements in the universe
My most beautiful element is THE CORNFLOWER
People do not get an essential oil out of it
But water, healing water
Unusual antenna
6/19, 7:00pm **Koz Kozmos**
to u in your head ?
wot colour is my voice ?
was i talking to u in your head ?
or do u mean on line things are too slow for me

6/19, 7:02pm **Pre View**
yip, its more like giving instructions, in my head I mean
but i get these fluids(, I mean I see fluids thr your knees
and reason why I asked if your knee was ok... y
our voice has golden tones/ blue azure splashes
6/19, 7:03pm **Koz Kozmos**
i was told its silver and blue ones once
6/19, 7:03pm **Pre View**
once is not now
6/19, 7:03pm **Koz Kozmos**
what instructions am i giving u ?
i still feel it defines my vox
6/19, 7:04pm **Pre View**
its more when i'm working on myself and sitting in a space with light tech and my own configurations that you pop up often times in my meditational environment in which you are giving me SEVERE DIRECTIONS;
a bit like that
It is funny seeing you in the GRIDZZZZ
strange, vox ?
6/19, 7:05pm **Koz Kozmos**
latin for voice : "Bono"
Vox means good voice what do u do when u work on your self
6/19, 7:05pm **Pre View**
Nice word, i like short words
6/19, 7:06pm **Koz Kozmos**
sorry if i'm misrable, its just physical hasssel
6/19, 7:07pm **Pre View**
clearing, healing, upgrading, trying new fun things that pop in ,,,
and always curious about the outcome
I'm very impatient and it needs to bring through instant results Light tech is good for you as you wouldn't get bored
6/19, 7:07pm **Koz Kozmos**
how do u do these things , a practical explanation please
6/19, 7:08pm **Pre View**
with everything i'v told u, this time its different as u taught me to understand you better,
but yep yup yip
lets flip over the gridzzzzzzzzz, tracksssssss, & stuff
6/19, 7:09pm **Koz Kozmos**
how do u do these things a practical explanation, maybe you're deluded i'm sure its me , i feel so wiped out today
how do u do these things a practical explanation?
do u meditate ? stand on your headless head ?
hop on the spot hand jive ?
6/19, 7:13pm **Pre View** I
ts ok Koz,, Cosmological experiment
Wot interests me most at this time is these dam tracks, trying to understand it and then i also began to infuse myself with the english alpha-bet and trying out new stuff with it. Anyways, i feel real good with it, thats wot matters
6/19, 7:13pm **Koz Kozmos**
channel the ashta command, hahaha
wot do u do? sit there with a cofffe and ciggertte and do wot ?
i need an explanation please its not ok for koz!

what are tracks ? wot does this mean to u ????????
what do u get from the English alphabet ? what the fuck are u talking about ?
6/19, 7:15pm **Pre View**
wot exactly is meditation if yur working hard in it, like 3 hours in the morning, it will pass like 3 minutes.
I explained a little about tracks and wot i got, do u remember?
but i didn't get any further as far as I want the knowledge actually
6/19, 7:15pm **Koz Kozmos**
defy the logic of alphabets, i'm lost
6/19, 7:16pm **Pre View**
wot logic is in there ? Spirit within has logic beyond intuition
I'm just opening my channel into many different spaces cosmologically speaking and dance with it. It does not mean I get what I need, I'm sure I get what my body /brain is ready to receive... and thus the importance of the continuum,
haha soapy clearing of ego lanes and tablets...
6/19, 7:16pm **Koz Kozmos**
if u said something about tracks i can't remember
6/19, 7:16pm **Pre View**
yess, i did, must look it up myself,
wait ?
6/19, 7:16pm **Koz Kozmos**
the logic of language as a means of logical communication that enables some one to explain some thing with a level of lucidity via the LOWJIK of the HIGHGENE
how can i get my herniated disc back in ?
how do I get my sciatic nerve rid of pain and walk with out pain and awkwardness?
be back in a short while
6/19, 7:23pm **Pre View**
tracks : tracks are crystal receivers and messengers through ones spark that is Supreme Intelligence and provide data, information
When one chooses to live that intelligence they operate from it. Tracking is a form of communications much like that of telepathy only higher for it reaches furthermost Octaves when necessary for extra celestial assistance at times.
6/19, 7:25pm **Pre View**
I'm not sure wot a spark really is, must get that clear for myself.
Supreme intelligence and the difference with other forms of intelligence: I have no idea either. I'm not there yet. Intelligence is interesting,
I'm just learning about it, feel it , but thats it.
I have no further knowledge but willing to dig deeper as it does a lot for me.
6/19, 7:29pm **Pre View**
Also, u must have spiritual body fully aligned & set your Spark in the right direction, and when continuing
alignments and vibrating on the higher scales of the Divine,
the Spark marks it place in many different areas of the anatomy.
It all depends on our flight through Space --- (or especially holding on to what is already being achieved – and not let any hyjacker in)
Anyways, it feels extremely good to me, my spirit told me :
crystal tracks have an enormous healing power in bones, joints, muscles.
This was true for me over the past 10 days. Want to explore and understand this more --- Changes are good , so ---
6/19, 7:31pm **Pre View**
I just love playing with letters in my body, thats all My kind of fun ---
6/19, 7:35pm **Pre View**
I don't think its the sciatic, maybe other nerves,,
I always see these dark crystals in yur knees,

Like i once told u, yur fluids in the body,
I'd rather clear them in connection to glands maybe of course nerve clearing,&
muscles ... is a lot of work What is your way of getting healing through?
6/19, 7:51pm **Pre View**
Anyways, gonna work a little now, coz i had a friend over here i hadn't seen for years
---
Tidy up, & break my head nicely with these tracks & stuff ....
Because I want to know know know,
It is actually thanks to YOUR QUESTIONS that i got interested in wot I I've been studying and integrating over the years
For I never questioned anything, I just trusted because I would always have proof of many changes in consciousness....
Yet, NOT QUESTIONING was my missing link because that helps to understand and experience other levels of intelligence and the wiser rooms of gathering...
6/19, 8:18pm **Koz Kozmos**
hi Jargon , i don't know how to clear
i just think heal and do gentle exsirsize
have fun , glad you'r healing
my knees are ok
its my disc and ankles
i've been good for about a month anyways
6/19, 8:31pm Koz Kozmos
here a few tracks for u, from the KozKozmos Jukebox
and tonite Catz and Chickz
the featured songs are duo's
MUSIC: Boy Meets Girl - Waiting For A Star To Fall with Lyrics

6/19, 8:38pm Koz Kozmos
MUSIC: Sophia Lorene and Peter Sellers - Goodness Gracious Me

6/19, 8:38pm **Koz Kozmos**
and know, some things equal our mood
and see lovleee listener , who did this song originally ?
6/19, 8:42pm **Koz Kozmos**
and if u guess who did , u get a free KozKozmos Calender
6/19, 8:55pm **Koz Kozmos**
trancend the jargon
When you decide to live from your core,
then you can start to get in touch with the higher energies and realms
targeting means being attacked on a soul level
It does feel like certain people were 'assigned' for the task etc
6/19, 9:08pm **Koz Kozmos**
if u can't dance because it creates body pain ...
how can u get in touch with your core?
6/19, 9:17pm **Koz Kozmos**
anywayzzzzzzzzzzzzzzzzzzzzzzzzzzzzzzzzzzzz blabbering
6/19, 9:32pm **Koz Kozmos**
c u at the core
6/19, 9:33pm **Pre View**
In the Spiritual Science Magazine
We should publish weekly activities
To get people activated in wizzardry
Such as in The FRINGE SERIES
Everybody should watch that, it is so much fun
Hope they will get new episodes out
They were so fascinating

6/20, 1:24am Pre View
discs, knees, ankles, sacral puff stuff, brain, all the same molecular content-interconnected , but when aligned properly , wow,,,
Shall i take u for a ride through grids of never ending joy ?
6/20, 1:53am Pre View
Worked hard until now, and then there's U with fantastic ,entertainment for me tonight ;;;
Couldn't be more lovely
Hey , thank u from the core beyond the core blasting my rhythms until 4
target : no i don't agree, i have another opinion
but ok, will try to find time to write valuables about this, and when ready will let u read
Soul is indeed one disastrous field playing out ....
U are echoing the softer resounding bytes through my nighttime measures,,, it is a true D'Lite enlightenment.
Thank U Mister James, it was indeed pleasurable to meet u
Gobble Gook Night
6/20, 5:22am **Pre View**
Hey, very good morning
I'm lost, thought we were meeting in the core
vibing through the electrolytic fields = 3 hours sleep

MUSIC: The 5th Dimension Age of Aquarius 1969

6/20, 5:38am **Pre View**
let's rock and accelerate movement, the fast ways, the hard ways,,,
MUSIC: STUCK IN THE MIDDLE WITH YOU-Steelers Wheel

6/20, 7:58am **Pre View**
I most certainly understood targeting ....
But this "It does feel like certain people were 'assigned' for the task" ---- please tell me it does not come from your brains huh,,,
We certainly are given assignments over and over again, some we do not finish- we will be given other blueprints.
But with u, if i may say so - there is but one missing link to get & keep u out of soul which is
"Foundational GRID TRAINING" which have anchored all over earth which : thy are foundational, then there are many other grid systems of great interest & training.
BUT for the time being this is wot our connect was for in the first place, if u'd ask me.
Would u like to know more about it, then i will post maybe a file i'm working on ?
Maybe with an example of alignments of solar level in the grids should u wish so ?
BTW :alcohol, smoking and addictions within break the grids
as i'm picking up all of it with much more understanding
It is only now, through our communication , that i am remembering how i used to anchor foundational grids in people's homes, in hotels, etc,,,,
and now back to work coz my mouth is overflowing, no need for sleep no more
6/20, 8:10am **Pre View**
But beyond that, , u have more or all that anyone wouldn't even dare to dream of !
(Sweet vibe, please glue my mouth)
Here are a few radio stations that may be interested in your Juke Box
Koz Kozmos style
6/20, 12:30pm **Pre View**
Welcome at one voice radio/the Netherlands
Radio Scoops/radio Scorpio – Belgium

Internet radio Trefpunt
But hey, the UK must have enough radio stations as well, so
6/20, 12:35pm **Pre View**
there are many radio stations in Belgium & the Netherlands, but how is ur Dutch ?
6/20, 12:40pm **Pre View**
i've not spoken to these students yet, but if u'd like me to contact a station
i need precise info of wot ur
willing to do ... Ok ?
6/20, 1:17pm **Koz Kozmos**
wots this about knees all the time
ok lets go in the grids? of never ending joy
I asked u not to do any healing on me , u didn't answer?
whats blasting your rhythms ?
Mystic Crystal Revelations , Sun's slimmer with ye...wots that?
ho hum hum
who gives us these assignments over and over again
fuck the 'karma exams' , 'the soap opera of the soul' and death the the headless masta
it does come from my intuition - the targeting
I don't want any other blue prints...no no no
ok post a file
yes, certain addictive substances can help for a short while
but then slow things down do the shamanka
anchor foundational grids in people's homes etc,,,,wot are these ?
I can't speak double dutch as good as u
i have no ambition left, thanx for the info
i'd have to produce a radio show of my own and cannot due to targeting of my own on
cd, i just want to heal, blabbering
6/20, 1:42pm Koz Kozmos
MUSIC: Buggles - Video killed the radio star 1979
6/20, 1:45pm **Koz Kozmos**
MUSIC: Videodrome Trailer
6/20, 1:47pm **Koz Kozmos**
most of wot i wrote above makes no sense i hate typing
i think my brain has malfuntioned even more maybe it does make sense ,
aaaaaaaaaaaaaahhhhhhhhhhhhhhhhhhhhhhhhhhhh

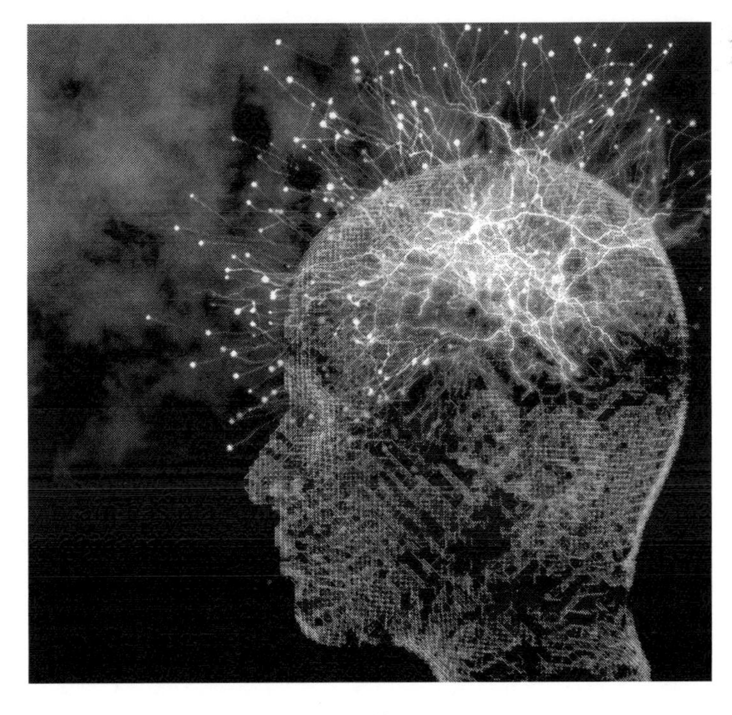

6/20, 3:04pm **Koz Kozmos**
don't heal me
6/20, 7:36pm **Pre View**
Euhm, no i didn't do anything, of course not --
I just got a picture of your knees ,just in daily life , no more, no less ... Blasting rhythms :
oh just loading hyperdimentional energies
Sun's slimmer : i was just playing with words, but it also meant i do not know much of many Suns , Sons of Suns, would like too ,
Assignments : Ask and u shall be given,
so I align with a team of light or Ascended beings as u wish,
orwot my energy is able to tap into and just ask for the correct key or to get over stuck patterns and assistance with that,
then i ask to align me with new blueprints ......
I do not know anything about Shamanistic things ....
Foundational grids :
i'll post later tonight (I hope if i have the time to complete file)
otherwise tomorrow OK ?
Have loads to do now, loads, & got so much energy
Hey Koz wots Double Dutch , ?
Do u have a little trouble remembering ?
I WILL NOT HEAL U, that is your work.
Oh oh ohla, i'm so crazy today, luv it ,,,
I have an idea just for the fun of it:
Lets ask to implement a Seed Crystal into the midbrain (a solid crystal which is a touchstone, or key point for implanting new thought forms)
Then we could hyperdimentionally align these to each other
and we would just have each others thoughts & intelligence etc ....
No more typing necessary, wot do u think ,huh?
We may get some fun out of it,,,
i'm running on speedy crystal train rails today,
hahahahahahahaha
6/20, 7:37pm **Pre View**
Dam, was that a picture of YOU today?
The best radio station over here is still: STUDIO BRUSSEL,
Hey Koz ,I hope u can balance & keep close to yur joyfull heart
6/20, 9:47pm **Koz Kozmos**
double dutch : Web definitions
eye'm the son ove the dark seed
remembering ...depends
Koz Kozmos
HOW??? Can we hyperdimentionally align?
6/20, 9:49pm **Koz Kozmos**
Nik Da Trik....there's a movie about us
here's the trailer, intro
6/20, 9:53pm **Koz Kozmos**
MUSIC: H.R PUFNSTUF INTRO

6/20, 9:53pm **Koz Kozmos** `
Oh my, this video is so funny, you really have a way to get me smiling,,,
glad to see u in good spiritz
6/20, 11:37pm **Pre View**
Hey PUNSTUFF, yur quite generous i must say
Lets create a higher resolution map of the Universe

6/20, 11:44pm **Pre View**
Hey Master Pufsnufstuf
quite magically I found a file from 2003 that represents my first training in grids, i'll post it, its easier, but take into account GRID SYSTEMS CHANGE ALL THE TIME,
a bit like celebreties;
It may help you to understand... I will also send you some written material about the soul, the consciousness that takes the breath out of the body.
So if you would like to go bananas and learn about it without experiencing it, enjoy the process! Nothing is a big deal: its all about the cast, the character in your own EARTH SERIES
6/20, 11:51pm **Pre View**
Help , can't stop laughing
Follow up story ,please ? maybe, possibly ?
PUFFNSTUFF
6/21, 12:24am **Pre View**
Hey Cozmic Delight are you in the Serius hood hood hood ?
Are you spicy today?
Are you that quite and quick vibe
i couldn't follow wild
But theze Gridzz are Spacing
my desires throughout other species,
Joking.... just shape shifting self into new snapshots
To have new fluid experiences
6/21, 12:35am **Koz Kozmos**
my source doesn't answer
are u witchypoo ?
i'm the boy with the majik flute
6/21, 12:38am **Pre View**
witchypoo ? witchypoo, good word,
but the translation into me vibes ?
Do u play flute at night
6/21, 12:39am **Koz Kozmos**
no , whichypooo is in the puffinstuff clip

MY INTERNALS: KOZ had a way of always finding music that matches the communication.
With this video about puffin stuff , he actually referred to me as the guy in the video was talking about how he made himself incomprehensible in a very funny way. I loved the way of how he could turn things into some fun when not understanding Light movement and especially Light embodiment as in becoming a Grid embodiment as a grid has dots and Ley Lines that need to fuse in order to move into the next graduation of pure Source aligned beauty.
Also the video's he posted gave me a lot more insight in the life patterns he was running through his body and how much he would look up things.
Yet, the google machine doesn't give us the alive life answers as they come from within and certainly not from the guru followers such as the antiques and falseness in information through TM meditation. Transcending carbon into Light takes man to many different height when communicating with inspirited vibes.

6/21, 12:40am **Pre View**
Maybe u better load SEED SYLLABLES INSTEAD OF SEAD CRYSTAL ?
6/21, 12:40am **Koz Kozmos**
wot does that mean explain ? so i can understand
6/21, 12:41am **Pre View**
SEED SYLLABLE : A FUNDAMENTAL VOCAL, OUT OF WHICH A WHOLE MUSIC PATTERN ARISES

6/21, 12:42am **Koz Kozmos**
ok , i'm confused and my source does not answer ,
am i done for?
6/21, 12:43am **Pre View**
u understand music, i don't, so maybe thats the whole trick
Just start living from now on will ye?
This is a command!
6/21, 12:44am **Koz Kozmos**
i do live
6/21, 12:44am **Pre View** Aha, so you think!
did u read the files ?
6/21, 12:44am **Koz Kozmos**
don't command me, no point
6/21, 12:44am **Pre View**
This was just for fun, joking , ... I know you're an Aries, they don't take commands,
they are the command !
6/21, 12:45am **Koz Kozmos**
i don't understand music as a much... but as a true poet
6/21, 12:45am **Pre View**
You're a very deep poet
It makes me shiver , I wish one day i'd be allowed to read more of u
6/21, 12:46am **Koz Kozmos**
death to the false poets
i no longer write, no point
poetry is a pass time of the middle classes
6/21, 12:47am **Pre View**
you are way off that line,
why should u not write,
i love it,
and u can always start over,
6/21, 12:47am **Koz Kozmos**
writing is dead , i need to ascend so my words have real power to destroy
6/21, 12:48am **Pre View**
U have something different to offer humanity with the way you mix music
run a different line,...
6/21, 12:48am **Koz Kozmos**
fuck humanity, and fuck the source , were ever it may be
6/21, 12:49am **Pre View**
Try to read the files I sent about the grids and about soul
REFLECT, DON'T JUDGE
6/21, 12:49am **Koz Kozmos**
i will do ,thank u
6/21, 12:49am **Pre View**
I hope u will not judge
6/21, 12:49am **Koz Kozmos**
I'm comic book angry
if i have no judgment it means i don't care
6/21, 12:50am **Pre View**
I sent you the files just to open your brainwaves and also because it kept me going
into ascension and still does, no matter how many still need to wake up,,,
wot are u angry at ?
The degrees and resolution of the Moon and the Sun always change as well
They never get angry
They are all spheres like we are,

6/21, 12:50am **Koz Kozmos**
willl look forward to reading angry at this life
its no good to be here
6/21, 12:53am **Pre View**
Scientists have not been able to decipher the geometry of the universes
I don’t think it is even possible as it changes all of the time
Well i only hope u'll understand me better as it was quite frustrating to talk about all this soul stuff and grids , doing the work BRINGS THE UNDERSTANDING AND FUN!
We can only understand from experience, that is obvious, what is not being tasted is always hard to understand... and it still changes me every day, (but with my upgrades, there is so much info about it, u couldn't possibly be held back with all those targets,
it got me out of the matrix tricks, and yes some things are very technical.
But hey that is how this whole universe functions. And we need to relearn all that, and certainly not from todays’ scientists...
6/21, 12:54am **Pre View**
if u like i can post it here and paste ? or u can print it ,
6/21, 12:54am **Koz Kozmos**
I am science
being angry and judgmental are some of the new sins of the new age mind control program its ok, got it on my desk top ,
and susssed myself,
i could read it now
6/21, 12:55am **Pre View**
aha , its better to read it at ease, skip lines that need updates,
it PE's off
6/21, 12:55am **Koz Kozmos**
PE off ?
6/21, 12:56am **Pre View**
PE = HEBREW for GOLD, like in alchemy, for golden leylines,
euhm there's a whole tech behind it,
Just load them everyday, call forth the Golden flow Ley Lines
and ask them to integrate....
It has nothing to do with kabala or soul training and stuff,
6/21, 12:58am **Koz Kozmos**
ok , if things can get me to a higher place and i can become who i am it will be good
6/21, 12:59am **Pre View**
DEFINITELY, but i respect yur choices
6/21, 12:59am **Koz Kozmos**
there is a chance i may not connect or understand your info
6/21, 1:00am **Pre View**
u may not, but ur intelligence will understand
as I said before, EXPERIENCE for a few weeks and ask to understand
6/21, 1:00am **Koz Kozmos**
so far, it has been a limited model and i say that with respect
6/21, 1:00am **Pre View**
u'll get out of that IMMEDIATLY
At least when leaving your theory and moving into some practise with the grids /Ley Lines
6/21, 1:00am **Koz Kozmos**
i must understand it to take action
6/21, 1:01am **Pre View**
just read a bit, don't judge , coz i cannot give u updates ,
remember 3 days foundational training is important and alignments,
6/21, 1:02am **Koz Kozmos**
u did not answer one of my many questions again stand for something or fall for anything

6/21, 1:02am **Pre View**
I wouldn't dare, that would be like that video u posted with Mark Dollan was it ?
6/21, 1:03am **Koz Kozmos**
who ?
u should answer questions, back things up, or its just meaningless jargon
6/21, 1:03am **Pre View**
Was it not Mark Dollan on your social media profile, talking about bringing past, present,
future into the now...
and then he had to choose about the music he'd play ?
6/21, 1:04am **Koz Kozmos**
never heared of him
6/21, 1:04am **Pre View**
shall i check your profile ? wait
6/21, 1:05am **Koz Kozmos**
u can , just looked him up don't recognize him please look , i may be wrong
6/21, 1:07am **Pre View**
can't find it, but i remember me commenting on it,
i'll check again tomorrow as i found it interesting.
Wot question did i not answer ?
6/21, 1:08am **Koz Kozmos**
Maybe u better load SEED SYLLABLES INSTEAD OF SEED CRYSTAL ?
wot does this mean? its all just jargon to me
i understand seed sounds via mantra
and sea salt is supposed to be better for u than processed salt
6/21, 1:09am **Pre View**
Seed crystals I explained OK ? and Seed Syllables also.
6/21, 1:10am **Koz Kozmos**
when did u explain ? i don't remember maybe it was mark dollan u told not me
6/21, 1:10am **Koz Kozmos**
its ok , i'll read your pdf , but i'm running out of trying to understand
6/21, 1:11am **Pre View**
No, i'm very accurate
6/21, 1:11am **Koz Kozmos**
i don't find that to be so
6/21, 1:11am **Pre View**
Seed crystals just open information,
we can RELOAD them into our brain. It is like loading crystals into
the brain or other parts in the body.Like IPhone, pc's are made off crystals
It is not even weird, crystals can hold data
Seed Syllables: they just opens info through music
6/21, 1:11am **Koz Kozmos**
u said something about us connecting via this seed stuff
6/21, 1:12am **Pre View**
YESS
6/21, 1:12am **Koz Kozmos**
but its meaningless to me
why the personal jargon ? its no good
6/21, 1:13am **Pre View**
Personal jargon: a few days ago ,
I told you that I wanted to have fun with spirit and create my own
language or jargon ... and so i wanted to try something out with u, I mean with these
terms I use like seed crystals and seed syllables...
just some fun,,,ok, can you get that huh?It does not mean the explanation is correct,
everything inlife has many variables,,,

6/21, 1:13am **Koz Kozmos**
i have lots of terms that are personal to mek but i don't confuse
6/21, 1:14am **Pre View**
Why would u like to keep them personal ?
6/21, 1:14am **Koz Kozmos**
u have no clue or Key were u at
u say this but it contradicts a lot of other things u say
6/21, 1:14am **Pre View** I'm all ears
6/21, 1:15am **Koz Kozmos**
because the confusion via personal jargon needs deeper explanation
6/21, 1:15am **Pre View**
U have so much personal jargon as well,
I don't question every angle of yur moodzzz
Can u give an example of mine ?
6/21, 1:16am **Koz Kozmos**
why do u expect me to understand your own personal terms?
6/21, 1:16am **Pre View** s
sometimes i get confused with wot u say ----
6/21, 1:16am **Koz Kozmos**
ok, ask me and i will try to explain
some times its too much to type, to express in this way
6/21, 1:17am **Pre View**
I don't expect u to understand everything, it is fine this way,
it is not doable via this communication system
it sometimes get me frustrated,
not to say things precisely as they are
6/21, 1:17am **Koz Kozmos**
as i said u try to explain thing via your own very personal models no point in trying to communicate if I don't expect u to understand,
6/21, 1:19am **Pre View**
ok, maybe , go slower, and explain everything till we understand, ?
6/21, 1:19am **Koz Kozmos**
as i've said i'm confused and broken
6/21, 1:20am **Pre View**
I don't expect u to understand : meaning i more or less expected your intelligence to understand , which
was maybe wrong
6/21, 1:20am **Koz Kozmos**
thats double dutch
6/21, 1:21am **Pre View**
Honestly,I really wish I could understand the kind of work you did on self
for the past 30 years;;;
6/21, 1:21am **Koz Kozmos**
i understand the vague concept but its no good, i understand or i don't
6/21, 1:21am **Pre View**
Wot do u suggest ? as understanding comes when eating the apple presented!
6/21, 1:21am **Koz Kozmos**
stop the jargon
6/21, 1:22am **Pre View**
How the hell will I be able to do that as I'm only being myself! Huh
it is wot i have become
Explain your micro background, they will keep u quite

6/21, 1:22am **Koz Kozmos**
but i'm not blaming u
6/21, 1:22am **Pre View** Give me a minute please ?
6/21, 1:22am **Koz Kozmos**
i don't know wot u've become, i have no idea
ok, respect and good vibes, you're trapped in your own esoteric fantasy
6/21, 1:25am **Pre View**
I think the problem that is operating between us is due to different levels of trainings we both went through somehow . Yet, we could proceed into a zone where things overlap and fuse training . THE OBVIOUS PROBLEM IS NOT BEING ABLE TO PROTECT YOURSELF no matter your knowledge and light training.
So I was thinking if maybe if u could explain a little how you work with your light within that would explain a lot because all you would need to learn is to anchor your light into a light grid, where it belongs – so you don't get hit anymore...
That would be a relieve for me, if u should wish to do that
6/21, 1:26am **Koz Kozmos**
i've read the pdf , its jargon and fantasy, it has no meaning to me
it has a scifi poetic quality but is of no real use , i may be wrong
6/21, 1:27am **Pre View**
Did u try it, did u incorporate it, did u work with it for months ? years?
You know , most people don't want what thy do not understand
because they know it takes work to get
there , and humanity was born on the tracks of LAZINESS that keeps the old cycles running like a dog chasing its own tail, or the snake that bites its own tail like the symbol of a pharmacy ... That symbol was just meant to keep people in toxic and miserable life cycles through the medication termed
"The Caging of humanity while they don't even see the bars of their own prison"
6/21, 1:28am **Koz Kozmos**
for the last 30 years i have had to try and repair masssive damage it has been hard
6/21, 1:28am **Pre View**
ok, you still do not explain HOW AND WITH WHICH TOOLS you worked!!!
So don't expect me to understand your work when all I have is an empty air bubble with zero information
6/21, 1:28am **Koz Kozmos**
it goes on, i'm no longer sure what i did; i was a seeker
6/21, 1:29am **Pre View**
A seeker with no practice? That does not make sense.
The only way to investigate something is through
its working mechanism in your own body. Certainly not how the medical department is abusing animals for the purpose of their knowledge. There is a very large differentiation line between the biology of an
animal and the biology of a human being
for also the higher senses and many bodies are so different.
I never understood why the cruelty on animals did go on for so many eons.
The result is seen now that the medical institutions have no longer an answer ,
neither do scientists because, we need to get back to the very
THE CURE IS WITHIN SELF.
So the only way to heal any disease in the future will be through institutionalizing LIGHT EDUCATION and proof the integrative efforts along the re-education of light biology through the elements that make up the body.I have a high hope
for the new doctors coming in...
6/21, 1:29am **Koz Kozmos**
i did yoga for years , then just stoped when all i got from it was a bad back i wrote songs and tried to make them magical
i spent time alone experimenting with my conciousness

i have not liked my life , at time i've hated it
but at lleast i life alone and have cut evey one out
i was damaged as a kid, but i've always had a fairy energy
wot ever i did, i found it did not work, i've tryed many things and i'm bored and sick of the whole odious game
and i don't want any more jargon such as this
Wot does this mean from the file you sent?:
"There is always an upgrade within the sound wave of secure Alignment Proceedings
6/21, 1:34am **Pre View**
Ok, weird, but we have similar lines
Yoga is not enough, you should run to get your circulation to a point in which it can receive information And dancing is just such a joy when the circulation is open ...
If your body is in pain when doing yoga it means there are stuck patterns that need to be released through the breaathing system that needs an alignment at least back to your Source and Universally --- That can be initiated through the crystalline GRIDZZZZZZZZZZZZZZZZZZZZ BECAUSE YOU NEED A SYSTEM, SOME TECHNOLOGY THAT HOLDS YOUR CONSTRUCTION INTACT.
It is much like a house that you build: without a solid foundation
the house would fall apart in no time
like a house of cards, right? Anyone can understand that.
Yet most people want to move into a LIGHT HOUSE with no construction at all, no follow up plans, no architecture; etc.
So, how do you expect that to turn out? It is like living in a house with no doors, no windows so ANY AIR
can blow through whenever the desire pops up.
With any air I mean the reptilians and monsters of the universe that will cut your light at all times. This is reason why you need a foundational light house: you build from the cellar
(the underground) up into the first floor, second floor etc, then you build a kitchen, then a bathroom, then a living room, then a garden, then you start to decorate it as the creator self with SECURE LIGHT ENERGIES AND TECHNOLOGIES
and add the heating, the electricity for light etc...
Most people forget about the foundation and start living on the THIRD FLOOR in their light house meaning anything can hit them at any time because the missing links allow for many invasions. Just imagine building a house and starting out the architectural design from the "3th FLOOR ON AND BUILDING 4th, 5th floors. Most would agree to the fact that a house without solid pillars would crumble very fast!
LIGHT HOUSING FUNCTIONS EXACTLY THE SAME WAY!
When something does not function in your house such as the electricity or the flow of your shower; it NEEDS REPAIR AND FINDING OUT WHERE THE KEY IS TO BRING THE SOLUTION THROUGH.
The same goes for a Light body HOUSE! When something is in disease, it needs repair because it blocks all other flow patters to have your River of Life running crystal clear.
YET, IN THIS CASE, PEOPLE GIVE ALL THEIR POWER AWAY TO PHYSICIANS WITH NO KNOWLEDGE!!!
This is reason why everybody on the planet needs RE-EDUCATION starting from kindergarten on and beginning with getting to know the anatomy and HOW HEALTH works in the body.
Think about how many children and young adults always have stomach aches or head aches..... These are easy issues to handle as I have about 15 years of experience teaches the little ones how to heal that and
how to heal each other during school breaks.
That is all there is to it,

6/21, 1:34am **Koz Kozmos**
i want real meaning and action, and to rise up
i always danced, my body will not let me any more
6/21, 1:35am **Pre View**
OK : How can I possibly explain How a CRYSTAL GRID AND LIGHT BREATHING can fuse with your meridians in the body and how that heals out WHEN not having a foundation to heal from?
6/21, 1:35am **Koz Kozmos**
i can't run , i tryed it , my ankles are bad
i even went to a gym and tried it on a running machine
6/21, 1:35am **Pre View**
Healing the muscular content and of course first and foremost the skeletal structure can be done through solid GRIDZZZZ and connections and supported by accordingly aligned Teams of Light. So yeah, you either want to set this in someday - which is no more and no less than tapping into your origin, or you don't
ANY HEALING CAN START FROM THAT FOUNDATION with some basic training in how to apply Light configurations such as the knowledge of the consciousness with a Light Essence.Or lets say in your case: you need to first align your body to highest health and start working with basic light colors such as white light, blue light and Golden alchemy ley lines in order to open up the higher frequencies and bring the complete transformation through the anatomy. Basically , you will need a start up kit so to speak from which you can work and then level up So, choices are up, over and done with
I cannot help you if you don't want healing and at least experience it before I would teach you self healing and being independent from anyone....
Anyways , I STILL DON'T KNOW HOW YOU WORKED UPON YOUR SELF.
Were you a seeker that never did any work on self and just looked up many things on the corrupt google machine?
6/21, 1:35am **Koz Kozmos**
i don't want u to explain , i feel i've given up on your 'system'
its lacking in meaning and connection
as i've said it needs to come to me, or fuck it all
6/21, 1:37am **Pre View**
**The universe does not work that way,
you need to ask first and then apply what is being given 2 u. Most people DO NOT WANT TO HEAR WHAT IS BEING GIVEN! And thus many problems arise from this!**

U either feel its right or u don't!
Did u read the file on soul ?
6/21, 1:37am **Koz Kozmos**
no more work , read most of it
i've got books with this sorta stuff in
a book called STARCRAFT comes to mind
i read it 25 years back
6/21, 1:38am **Pre View**
Gosh! again and again giving your power away!!!
Reading books is ok when the information is being applied, otherwise what is the reason, the sense behind such things?
OK Koz, i tried to give u wot i did for Light embodiment, and still upgrading it, which is light body biology,
Merkivah training, electrons, solar alignments, celestial and universal Alignments, most importantly GRIDZ & THEIR KNOWLEDGE, tracks, chords, etc.
Just keep on thinking about what you need to build a house in the physical : a plan, an architect, a construction company, doors, windows, electricity, heating, isolation!!!
Or protection from wind and cold

Then start translating that in how you build your light house back into THE HOUSE OF LIGHT TERMED SHAMBHALLA, THE GREAT CENTRAL SUN!:
You need a plan, you need an architect that teaches how to bring all the equipment together UNDER ONE ROOF WHILE EXPLAINING THE WORKING MECHANISMS OF THE HOUSE such as explaining how solar panels and solar power works, what are the best choices to close doors (such as the closure of old friendships and teachings that do not work), what kind of windows would bring the best of light through that can shine throughout the entire building? And how do these windows work? What is the best
way to protect your house from invasions such as an iron belt or pillars or ....
Just be inventive, And bring many seeds into your garden – the garden of Eden or Edonic Gateway needs to be taken care of EVERY DAY in order for the seeds to flourish
and bring through expected beauty as the creator self!
I think this is a good example when it comes to understanding and building a light house in a light grid. Hope this finally makes sense....
Ho many neurons do u have
We could put a new brain together
We have about 320 trillion Light parts
We do not even use 30% of our brains, scientist say the opposite
How can they proof that with so much mentality moving backward.
They don't have logic, Light has logic
6/21, 1:38am **Koz Kozmos**
i have a whole system with terms that aid me in trying to understand but its complex
6/21, 1:39am **Pre View**
I will check what this book has to say.
Also, do u not question my changes ?
6/21, 1:39am **Koz Kozmos**
u will not be able to get the book
6/21, 1:40am **Pre View** Why ?
6/21, 1:40am **Koz Kozmos** wot changes?
6/21, 1:40am **Pre View**
daily changes within me, do u not see them ?
6/21, 1:41am **Koz Kozmos**
it is available, it was a limited print no, i see and feel no changes in u
u'r still sprouting your jargon , and i'm being civil enougf to try and understand
6/21, 1:42am **Pre View**
hey hey!!! This is no jargon! It is simplistic explanation
and also, everybody over here notices the changes within me all of the time so, you're either being stubborn, or angry
6/21, 1:43am **Koz Kozmos**
yes i understand its not jargon to u
6/21, 1:44am **Pre View** Maybe i must rest over it,
it frustrates me that i cannot help you while all i did is explaining and explaining and still it was not enuff.
I've had it , I'm pulling my DRAGON LINES THROUGH!
And don't pretend you don't understand the meaning behind that, just think for yourself! 6/21, 1:44am **Koz Kozmos**
From your file**:** "Do not forget that there is a pure White ray team on land re-setting the records " who are the pure white team born again
christians or the klu klux klan?
6/21, 1:45am **Pre View**
Pure white Light was held back from earth and reason why people could not move into ascension, but they can now.

You can just connect to that team and listen to what they bring through as in APPLICATIONS damit!
And through a WHITE LIGHT GRID, somehow!
6/21, 1:45am **Koz Kozmos**
i don't even know what u mean by grid
6/21, 1:46am **Pre View**
I've explained enuff about grids, you either opt for a training into it or not! That is final!
White team is here to replace the Old Messiah stuff people still believe in and thus getting into a NOWHERE LAND and self destruction!
6/21, 1:46am **Koz Kozmos**
who are the pure white team? sounds like the same old shit
i'm the black wizzzzard ov the kozmik key
6/21, 1:47am **Pre View**
You ask that team WHO the entities involved are!
YOU JUST STARTT DOING SOMETHING YOURSELF AND TRUST YOUR ANSWERS instead of squeezing them out of me!
It is termed independence and Self Mastery mind you!
If u have the Cozmic key why don't u use it ?
6/21, 1:47am **Koz Kozmos**
i was taking the piss
your pdf is no good to me , its bland and meanigless
i've heared it all before and i'm sick of it
what u have seen in me reveals your lack of insight
i'm not meaning to be cruel, i want the best for u
i like u, but i have to be honest
6/21, 1:51am **Pre View**
Koz, i'm going to get some sleep
i must think things over, or not, either way, we'll talk soon
If Gridzz are not understood, thy cannot be alive unless u've anchored them and worked with them ! Understanding comes from experience.
Actually, learn from them, Spirit is a learning zone, that is all and everything,
It resurrects vibe beyond the old system or matrix, and people I've trained! But ok, (the pdf is old and should be upgraded)
it was just to let u know we can move and give you some valid information, OK, NO INSIGHT, i'll sleep a little now, ok ?
Goodnight, i like u so much it hurts me, I mean your situation etc...
6/21, 1:51am **Koz Kozmos**
even if i'm wrong, and i could easliy b,e PEACE
i don't want to hurt u, i feel hurt, good night
6/21, 2:02am **Koz Kozmos**
i got angry and frustrated, just printed up will reread
6/21, 2:03am **Pre View**
I HAVE ALWAYS PEACE WHEN TALKING 2U
U know why ?
6/21, 2:04am **Koz Kozmos**
because I'm the Gentle good of the Heart shine
but i do get frustrated,
good medicine & sweet dreamzzzzzzzzzzzzzzzzzzzzzzzzzzzzzz
6/21, 2:05am **Pre View**
Exactly, coz your Heart is love most pure, that is rare in this world.
My heart has not opened it fullest potential, i might do some work on it, investigate, load a heart Grid
may BE important to people as hearts are crushed so much and not knowing it

6/21, 2:06am **Koz Kozmos**
its opening i can feel it, sleep
6/21, 2:06am **Pre View**
Dream your soul out of the body! hahahahahahahh
6/21, 2:06am **Koz Kozmos**
sleep, take care, spk soon, bye
6/21, 2:07am **Pre View**
Sleep majic , Thank u,

MY INTERNALS:Opening the heart and being connected to the pulse of Shambhalla takes quite some training starting with physical EYES willing to see through the veil. I managed to get there now and feeling the pulsation of every continent on the planet with the House of Light termed Shambhalla every single second. It is like the heart becomes a whirlpool of information through the biology of Light Earth when being strongly connected to the meridians of Light Earth and its fusion within our meridian system or Light Grid embodiment.

6/21, 11:45am **Pre View**
As usual, your questions with these gridzzz made me think,
Would it be of help if i wrote about my experiences with Grid systems?
Otherwise, it is not really difficult to pull up a grid , all u need is an Arkansas, a Brazilian & laser crystal to anchor it.
But if not, i'll drop the subject from here on
I do feel how much you have been hurt and it means I DO CARE about everything that is going on with u , for wot i understand,,,
Feeling the hurt is like feeling a new heartbeat opening up, hard to explain.
Like I said before : Why do we people care so much in the wrong direction?
We need to get rid of that emotional body that goes with getting beyond the matrix and living the eternal fields of any d'light ---- and just let it be, I can hear your vox like a fox!
1:38am **Koz Kozmos**
i have a whole system with terms that aid me in trying to understand but its complex
6/21, 1:39pm **Koz Kozmos** '
Arkansas & Brazilian & lazer crystal to anchor it.' ???
Why do I need these things? all I have is an old mop and bucket will these do?
Don't feel hurt!
I was just frustrated with your lack of insight and your fixation on your models of ultra reality u said ~ . 'I'd like to understand a bit of that, should u wish to explain ? '
6/21, 1:52pm Koz Kozmos
MUSIC: If You Want to Sing Out - Cat Stevens

6/21, 2:12pm **Koz Kozmos**
i think u should stop explaining and i should stop trying to understand
its reached a dead end
6/21, 2:13pm **Pre View**
Good, at last
You don not particularly become an architect when going through a bachelor degree
You become an architect when start to design with the diploma so u can understand the study.Mastering Architecture as an example, proves the study within experiences
Without experiences, we are left empty
6/21, 2:13pm **Koz Kozmos**
but thank u for all your efforts,
i get some of wot your saying
but there is too much personal terminology
maybe u should write a book with an in depth explanation
of terms in the back of the book
i am aware of a collection of spiritual practices that have their own paticular language
etc and the terms need to be understood to move forward with a system,
even pluming

6/21, 2:18pm **Pre View**
ok
6/21, 2:18pm **Koz Kozmos**
my frustrations with it are in effect me not understanding it
as i feel stuck and hopeless and want to move onwards and up wards it all ends in disappointment and frustration , no blame intended wot star sigh are u
6/21, 2:26pm **Pre View**
star sign : how would u describe me , wot would u think i am
6/21, 2:26pm **Koz Kozmos**
fire, maybe water, maybe on the cusp
6/21, 2:26pm **Pre View** no, another guess ?
6/21, 2:26pm **Koz Kozmos**
maybe u have your own star sigh term , taurus
6/21, 2:26pm **Pre View** EARTH
6/21, 2:26pm **Koz Kozmos**
ok, ? say
6/21, 2:27pm **Pre View**
Capricorn/Aquarius on the cusp,,,
I AM DETAIL!
6/21, 2:28pm **Koz Kozmos**
Capricorn, Friday, 21 June 2013
The story of the Solstice, for you, is a story of the need to comply and co-operate with a series of requests and requirements that are now being made of you. It is, to some extent, a story of sacrifice; of giving ground and accepting a small shift in a balance of power.
Yet it is also the story of how you become the beneficiary of a significant, positive, process that has the potential to improve your future vastly.
That can't happen unless you let go of some outmoded ideas about how things need to happen in your life. It's the Solstice and there's a 'SuperMoon' coming.
Get ready for intense but exhilarating experiences - and
make the most of them with a personal birth chart. Jonathan Cainera
6/21, 2:30pm **Pre View**
makes sense, thank u
6/21, 2:30pm **Koz Kozmos**
I'm f/Aries with a bit of something fishy going on bye , catch u again
6/21, 2:30pm **Pre View**
bey Mister fairy Aries

6/22, 12:30am **Koz Kozmos**
"The world is full of magic things, patiently waiting for our senses to grow sharper."
W.B. Yeats
6/22, 1:24am **Koz Kozmos**
trying to grow sharper
6/22, 3:18am **Pre View**
Nothing in biology makes sense except the light,
the science of expansion until it becomes extrasensory
perception , until then we live in trying instead of doing. There is always one song that makes us vibe/ drive faster than any other song-note could possibly accomplish.
Which one is yours ?
Understanding the mechanics of a keyboard may be as hard for me
As understanding an imaginative grid
That actually solidifies WITH THE CRYSTALS
Set into the right position
Science without practice has no meaning either
It loses challenge

6/22, 4:06am **Pre View**
Hi Jimmy, it is very early in the morning, i've packed a small bag and am hitting the road, to ??? don't know, I'll just see to get a ticket to the sea maybe to find the humor in all my situations. I need that fresh
uncomplicated air for some days.
I will talk to u when I get back. I will think of u coz ur worth it !
6/22, 4:22am **Pre View**
May super soft Blessings swirl deeply through ur Glorious Essence ,
may these Blessing help u
accomplish,,,
6/22, 1:16pm **Koz Kozmos**
What will happened when we start 'doing' ?
I am the singer of secret songz
one song is not enuff , gold idea ,hit the road
6/22, 1:16pm **Koz Kozmos**
MUSIC: Gordon Lightfoot Sundown

6/22, 1:34pm Koz Kozmos
MUSIC: King of The Road - Roger Miller - 1965

6/21, 2:18pm **Pre View**
ok
6/22, 2:51pm **Koz Kozmos**
I'm stuck in the middle with bad eyes hiding from the city and the humanz
6/22, 6:38pm **Koz Kozmos**
hope u've had a wonderful day
6/25, 8:35pm **Pre View**
When we start doing ? Euhm, lets get unstoppable
But, euhm, wot did u have in mind "DOING " ,,,,
One song is not enough ?
I'm sure with the vibes u got you can become the expert of juke box trainers, hahaha
You should hit RRRRRoadzzzzzzzzz
6/25, 8:37pm **Koz Kozmos**
Wot are you u on about ? I'm cricking my neck for days, can't move my head
6/25, 8:38pm **Pre View**
All of the past is collapsing right before my eyes, feels extremely good
Am partying (m)E-Self.
Wonder how U are doing, wonder how u feel, wonder how u live, wonder how u think, wonder wot captures yur heart, wonder how interesting u are for yurself, wonder how you protect your wounds
6/25, 8:38pm **Koz Kozmos**
never mind, hard to explain, sorry i feel bad
6/25, 8:39pm **Pre View**
its ok, just spread yur mind, if u feel like it
Sorry, i'm often tooooooo open and just express myself,
but that's wot i've become, and i like it
MUSIC: Dobie Gray - Drift Away (Original Official Video)

6/25, 8:39pm **Koz Kozmos**
open is ok , wish I could drift away
6/25, 8:39pm **Pre View**
U offered me Amazing Grace, even on a Platinium platter,
my eyes are expanding like a laser show !

6/25, 8:39pm **Koz Kozmos**
i've gone OCD can't speak or type
6/25, 8:40pm **Koz Kozmos**
MUSIC: Hole - Miss World

6/25, 8:41pm **Koz Kozmos**
Obsessive–compulsive disorder -
I'm Miss World, somebody kill me, play it loud !
6/25, 8:42pm **Pre View** ALWAYS PLAY LOUD, but ,
a good reminder!
THXX
6/25, 8:43pm **Koz Kozmos**
this song is kool, discovered it not so long ago
6/25, 8:44pm **Pre View**
it certainly is, love good lyrics, good rockin'
6/25, 8:44pm **Koz Kozmos**
MUSIC: Courtney Love- Car Crash

6/25, 8:45pm **Pre View**
she's good, her own highway
6/25, 8:45pm **Koz Kozmos**
she's got loads of cash and nows wot rock is more talented than K cobain ,
anyways
6/25, 8:45pm **Pre View**
the right Keys
6/25, 8:46pm **Koz Kozmos**
my key is broken , i don't feel good hope u 've had a good time
6/25, 8:46pm **Pre View**
speak out loud if you want, i care , I can hear you anyways
my ears reach the shores of the beautiful whales in Wales, hahaha
6/25, 8:46pm **Koz Kozmos**
i'm not the self pitying time
nuthing more to say , speaking can make thing worse, catch u later
6/25, 8:47pm **Pre View**
I've had horror in my life – more then enough ,
but i knew, and wanted to get out ,
so,,, after these hard times, bess i feel good, even i need loads of work but trust is
high level again and working real hard we need to trust again
and keep on working hard to keep our vibes up,,,
6/25, 8:48pm **Koz Kozmos**
I'll never work again
6/25, 8:48pm **Pre View**
U can Koz, I'm easy going, got the fishy lights(graze and peace) ,
so, don't worry, I'll stay here for a while
i'll stand by you if you like it or not,,,
6/25, 8:48pm **Koz Kozmos**
and how long I can survive this dimension, i'm not sure i'm not worried ,
I stand alone , i like it that way
6/25, 8:49pm **Pre View**
Hey , come on MAN, catch up on ur knowledge
You're not standing alone,
I AM RIGHT HERE,
u asked, and you got me

Koz Kozmos
fuck knowledge, u learn too much ,
u never know I am standing alone
6/25, 8:51pm **Pre View**
Sure you stand alone when living in Ego dimensions,
i've always felt u'd move real fast when the right thing comes to u
Do u not feel me?
I am my own dimensions
6/25, 8:51pm **Koz Kozmos**
you learn too much, u never know
I feel nothing , just pain in my body, i'm not even being negative
6/25, 8:54pm **Pre View**
please Koz, just let go of all u've been told,!!!!!!!!!!!!
Pretend all those experiences no longer exist!
i just hold on the many treasures u gave, and start thinking about wot may bring your
happy vibes back in, your passion,
music and poetry
You're not negative, pain needs to leave u, which ever way
There is so many things within u that are hungry to be released and find pleasure
6/25, 8:54pm **Koz Kozmos**
I have let go , I've tried to do it and failed
disappointment is my main emotion
6/25, 8:56pm **Pre View**
So wots holding u back ?
I can feel all of your pain and mine, but time has come to not fail,,, ever again,,,
I've had a great time thinking and sometimes it brings a lot of worthy things to the
surface,,, 6/25, 8:56pm **Koz Kozmos**
and body shit
6/25, 8:56pm **Pre View** Do I disappoint u ?
6/25, 8:57pm **Koz Kozmos**
I have no idea wots holding me back,,,
6/25, 8:57pm **Pre View**
I have a great feel that when u'd move to another place,
u'd completely change!
It may be a necessity,,,
6/25, 8:57pm **Koz Kozmos**
every thing dissappoints me,
i'm returning to my home town filled with sorrow to die ,
it may not happpen i'm on a housing list, for now i'm stuck here in the darkness
ear plugs in and bad neck etc etc
I'm not even being obsessively down, its just the way it is, t
he truth
6/25, 9:00pm **Pre View**
When I think of you, I can feel your treasures
I understand the frustrations with the physical diseases you suffer
Wish I could be there with u and offer some healing
6/25, 9:01pm **Koz Kozmos**
i want to be alone
6/25, 9:01pm **Pre View**
I understand
Me toooo

6/25, 9:02pm **Koz Kozmos**
i hate human beings
6/25, 9:03pm **Pre View**
But i'm longing for physical communications often times – it is like a need – machineries do not offer,
I need it know from the physical communication like body language.
so wot i can do in this for myself, I will,
even if its just going around the corner and talk to some African tribe or something,
i made a decision to just do what makes me feel alive
6/25, 9:03pm **Koz Kozmos**
wot does that mean
6/25, 9:06pm **Pre View**
It means, i need to have physical communication, face to face,
wotever comes out of me, and euhm, i just
talk to strangers, which is getting the best out of me,
Because FUN NEEDS TO COME AROUND WITH THEE HARD TIMES,
But ok, it'll never last longer then an hour, BUT THAT IS PRETTY MUCH VERY SATISFYING!
6/25, 9:06pm **Koz Kozmos**
fun is no fun
6/25, 9:07pm **Pre View**
The only thing that does it to me is music, i need to dance a lot,
to get my vibes understood
People do not understand the double twist in the hips that is needed when dancing Salsa,
It deblocks the hips spectrums
6/25, 9:08pm **Koz Kozmos**
I can't be amongst people any more, i'm done with it no , music is dying for me ,
i'm done with this existence feel wiped out, i'm down , its not fair to u,,, sorry
6/25, 9:12pm **Pre View**
Hey Mister Beauty, I may not be a fairy tale
I may not possess Knowledge,
But I do have a heart that knows beyond the earth plane
And I could sing a song for you2
A song from the other dimensions
lets not get too deep
Wot is your most Heartfelt Song ????
6/25, 9:16pm **Pre View**
zip zip zip I was disconnecting,
but u know me by know i guess, i get up very early in the morning, it is simply my most precious time with u and my source.
It is sometimes hard to cut the conversations i have with u,
So, wot is yur innermost heartfelt song ?
6/25, 9:22pm **Pre View**
FB has no value regarding conversations ,
people seem to have NO IDENTITY,low mental talk, no intelligence ,,,
Anyways, I need to work a lot more on the very deep graves of my unworthyness,,,
MUSIC: Courtney Love- Voices Carry

6/25, 9:26pm **Pre View**
When u WOULD VOICE OUT, it'll be a thrill never thought of,
but nevertheless, never-ending, it is Time Koz, it is Time KOz
6/25, 10:18pm **Koz Kozmos**
hi , face book never meant anything to me,
i distrust it here ,not kean on that track

6/25, 10:26pm **Koz Kozmos**
tahnkz for commenting on my posts, thier quite boring really
6/25, 10:29pm **Koz Kozmos**
MUSIC: David McWilliams - Days Of Pearly Spencer

6/25, 10:29pm **Koz Kozmos**
great song, another great song
6/25, 10:31pm **Koz Kozmos**
MUSIC: Gene Pitney - Somethings Got A Hold Of My Heart..w/ LYRICS

6/25, 10:31pm **Koz Kozmos**
another version 6/25, 10:32pm **Koz Kozmos**
MUSIC: Marc Almond & Gene Pitney - Something`s Gotten Hold Of My Heart

6/25, 10:33pm **Koz Kozmos**
Voice out? i want to shut up
not sure what my most hearlfelt song izzzzzzzzzzzzzzzzz
6/25, 11:00pm **Koz Kozmos**
hope u had a good time on your travels , u are worthy
thanks for letting me vent my spleen ,whats your most heart felt song ?
6/26, 1:45am **Koz Kozmos**
watch this
6/26, 1:46am **Koz Kozmos**
MUSIC: The Clangers - Treasure

6/26, 8:33am **Pre View**
Heartfelt song : i prefer to have none because the heart grows all the time and thus songs change all of the time
But from the ones u posted i like: Heaven-cat stevens & star walker
6/26, 8:39am **Pre View**
Thxxx for the video, great for children getting to know the stars,,,
6/26, 11:35am **Pre View**
I was surprised the other day when u posted Jonathan Cainer and my horoscope for the day
Horoscopes are HOROR SCOPES , toys for the lower dimensions
If I choose to be a lion or a fish all day, i just breathe that ligh through,
we can be anything in the old astrological belt and get to know the attributes of all the signs in the zodiac. Anywayz, i need the Sun, the Lion's Gate,
the smiling faces
Its too cold over here
6/26, 1:26pm **Koz Kozmos**
Yes I like those 2 songs
i watched the clangers wen i was a i kid
just posted it for a bit of wyrdeeeness, not seen for maybe 40 years
Just posted J Cainer for a bit of fun also, I realize that....
i'm not a moron house wife star sign reade
MUSIC HARPO-HOROSCOPE

6/26, 1:40pm **Koz Kozmos**
anywayzzz fuck it all
6/26, 1:47pm **Koz Kozmos**
MUSIC: . Turbonegro - Ride With Us

6/26, 1:48pm **Koz Kozmos**
In the denim buggies across the dunes, RIDE WITH US
Scratch the crack and smell the fumes dude, RIDE WITH US
If you wanna kill for inner peace, just do it, DO IT
If you wanna slay the bourgeois beast,
RIDE WITH US On and on, on and on and on and on
6/26, 2:27pm **Pre View**
I only just sometimes wonder when one is born,
how the position of planets in the body has so much impact, unless we become
movin Stars and ride the Universal tracks and align to that pact
U were born on 24th, is it ? thank u, gets me going faster 'this Ride With us'
6/26, 2:43pm **Pre View**
Hope you're taking good care of yourself,,,

I was listening to this "Van Halen -Jump" and of course
couldn't stop trying to do this jump
I landed quite well, hahah
/26, 5:12pm **Koz Kozmos**
I've had some bad days , maybe the worst
I need to jump on the decaying corpses of my enemies , no tears
6/26, 5:24pm Koz Kozmos
MUSIC:The White Horses TV Series "start sequence"

6/26, 5:25pm **Koz Kozmos**
I know u'r watching me Nik da trik
6/26, 5:25pm **Pre View**
Oh Kozmoz,
So beautifull,,, these white horses
6/26, 5:25pm **Koz Kozmos**
just been to a soliciter
6/26, 5:25pm **Koz Kozmos**
they want £5000 off me just to start sueing
yes i loved that song as a boy
6/26, 5:26pm **Pre View**
Brrr, thats a lot of money , feel bad about it
6/26, 5:26pm **Koz Kozmos**
before i start sueing i should say just to another doctor and medical paper
Lawyers are like politians , this country is so corrupt
no legal aid any more , just letting u kow in case i start ranting
6/26, 5:28pm **Pre View**
Koz, euhm, have shit here too with justice .....
A friend lawyer is helping me bit,
6/26, 5:28pm **Koz Kozmos**
do u know good death hex spells
MUSIC: Tyrannosaurus Rex - She Was Born To Be My Unicorn (Take 1)

6/26, 5:30pm **Koz Kozmos**
take care , hope u feel better, thank u
6/26, 5:31pm **Pre View**
Thank u, take real good care u 2
there must be ways, i'm done with all these brrr
6/26, 5:32pm **Koz Kozmos**
killl em all

6/26, 8:14pm **Pre View**
a lifetime of blood doesn't seem to satisfy these bastards & systems.
Raging out is of no use, lets just load the wise tracks that blows the Golden flag through the hands of destruction
I'm so sorry u have to go through this.
Wish i could be of help
I got my lawyers for free here but then again i have no evidence
and they'r so stupid, so devious, pretending they know something
and thus the system feeds the system
Lets inject dem all like in the Fringe series
6/26, 8:20pm **Koz Kozmos**
thier a cabal feeding, doctors, lawyers, politicians = the control byond the obvious
i've been raging since i got here, no one listens
they're stupid, blind, just scummy fucktards who love their slavery
when i was a boy i felt the light in the blood, this is why u can get targetted
face book is not a safe place
the intial amount of money is before they even start or take on the case
then more money ..., the corrupion in the UK has become massive and it was bad before anyways hope your feeling better , take care , ROKKKKKK
6/26, 8:56pm Koz Kozmos
MUSIC: The Who - Won't Get Fooled Again

6/26, 9:12pm **Koz Kozmos**
You're now entering the chillaxe zone~
maybe try painting to this
6/26, 9:13pm Koz Kozmos
MUSIC: Karl Jenkins: The Armed Man - full concert

6/27, 7:34am **Pre View**
I guess my anger is shaking this earth,,,
I better shut up, i'm uncontrollable, no good
I need these emotions out of the body so I can stream with the Spiritual Justice system
We people need to think deeper then lawyers can ever do,
we must be able to present out cases ourselves (i did this a few years ago, took everything into my own hands and won the case, so I know that I can do it – it just takes so much effort and for whom, ...
Breaking my brains,,, I'm listening a lot to David Icke : that helps
I'm listening to u : that helps 2
I'm very grateful u came into my life
Hope some miracle get infused into your life
And yes, we need to be extra careful with FB However, all our stories are part of the bigger story of Earth
I printed your photo and feel your energy even more on a spirit level
6/27, 12:54pm **Koz Kozmos**
i said if u'd like to talk about it , its ok
I said I felt the Joa~ document would be too persnal ,
i'm not a voyeur how can i take on my own case ?
when i said listen : it was to explain
i needed to be able to follow your ideas about consciousness and reality etc
i think as far as fb is concerned I've shown my light
wot are we going to do?
talk about matrix programs?
and do the dulllard

6/27, 9:54pm **Koz Kozmos**
I don't look like that photo any more
6/28, 6:41pm **Pre View**
Would u like to put on some glamour shoes for a photoshoot,
I'm good at that , hahaha, sometimes
6/28, 6:42pm **Koz Kozmos**
glamour shoes ? u ok ?
6/28, 6:45pm **Pre View**
Hey were is part 2 of the interview ?
How are u doing ? Do you operate within new ways?
You should have a new relationship with everything that you are!
6/28, 6:46pm **Koz Kozmos**
i was jesting , are u interviewing me ?
6/28, 6:47pm **Koz Kozmos**
'Renegade' - The Life Story of David Icke (Official Trailer)

MY INTERNALS: Koz posted a video about David Icke and the control system. Today in 2020 David Ickes' YouTube channel and website has been blocked, yet I was given this page on Renegade where you can find all the information about him. The system wants to put him to silence, and thus he is going to bring out a movie. Every LEVEL OF TRUTH he investigated worldwide is coming to the surface.
The original video Koz posted was : "WHY THE SYSTEM IS FALLING APART - DAVID ICKE. It is available on Renegade now. In February 2019, David Icke was also banned from Australia, and as of now numerous petitions are trying to fix it. Don't think he is going to be allowed entrance in Australia. They have their own ways. they have The Divine Heart pulsing and a very strong I Am Presentation!

6/28, 6:48pm **Koz Kozmos**
just saw this video, not watched
6/28, 6:49pm **Pre View**
Hey wot ideas are worth putting into action to wake up what is termed human species?
Were is the New World Order coming from and all these agenda's.
There is a world Plan, a Divine Plan, no doubt, it will filter through easily.
There is actually nothing that can defeat light, unless you leave your embodiment with major holes in it ;so the system can take over
your brainzzzzz, as is being done with many humans and the dumbing of humanity.
Dumb and numb is the name of this age, yet we can move in the Brilliant Crystal Age.
A matter of GRIDDING GRIDZZZZ, just being a Grid,
Hey that is not too much our Source is asking from us,
yet it is too much for the lazy shoes that tremble at every move
6/28, 6:50pm **Koz Kozmos**
i need to form a kozmik band to destroy this dimension and save the earth
6/28, 6:50pm **Pre View**
How does your Plan look like? Is the construction solid enough,
did you open and polish all avenues, did
you plant the elements firmly in it so they can work with you and brighten your day.
How did you protect your plan like you protect a child? Who are the ones that will perform their tasks in your plan, how is that team building its crystal skills and starry footprints?
6/28, 6:50pm **Koz Kozmos**
i tried for 35 years , it did'nt work
6/28, 6:50pm **Pre View**
New World Plan – or is it an ORDER? :
we need to put ideas, concepts and all tracks together,,,
6/28, 6:51pm **Koz Kozmos**
fukkkin 'ell , I'd like to join them

6/28, 6:54pm **Pre View**
I think you'd be an excellent writer, why not write a scenario about your life, make a movie. Our experiences are important to wake up the masses in a way that they can understand somehow how this world was functioning and how the system has taken charge over their lives. It is actually what David Icke speaks about worldwide and through his books. Yet, he doesn't talk about the modems through which people can take charge of their lives which is actually more important. Maybe I should get together with him , let him do the talkshow and leave the reset buttons in peoples' brains up to me. That would make up a perfect modern day CRYSTALLINE SHOW IN WHICH WE COULD HAVE THE IMMEDIATE EXPERIENCE OF HOW TO MOVE OUT OF THEIR OWN ALARMING SYSTEMS. Yet, I wonder why he is not being blocked...

MY INTERNALS: As I said before, it has happened now, 6 years later. So, I wonder what will happen when the movie is being presented. I'd fancy a movie with him, with mathematicians, physicians and astronomers of Divine Origins presenting LIGHT TIMES and PRECIOUS ORCHESTRATIONS. That would be fun, truly working with a new ecological system.

6/28, 6:54pm **Koz Kozmos**
I've tried that as well tried so much , no one wants to connect with me or help ,
Brb i thank u for the encouragement
but the amount of pain and frustration connected to my creative life is unsurmountable...
I still have some type of script somewhere , it was called Hallucination Earth , wrote it in 96
6/28, 6:58pm **Pre View**
Would U let me read it?
I'v got some connection in the Film Industry
6/28, 6:58pm **Koz Kozmos**
then some one ripped me off ,stole my style and dumped me
there is to much despair connected to my zero destiny , i'm done with it all Pre and i've moved on , I'm limping today
i should be resting on my laurels now , not starting again with people half my age
6/28, 7:01pm **Pre View**
i'v a deep feel (and i'm not being naïve) that things are going to open up for us - its timing – I've been through the exact amount of trouble as you have...
Nobody wanted to know about me. I was either too weird, to strange, too extreme, tooooo anything. It started of at age 5 in kindergarted or preschool
We need to pick up, especially with all the high qualified insights
U NEED TO GET UP and speak!
You and I , we have a story that needs to be known!
6/28, 7:02pm **Koz Kozmos**
i have no one to speak 2
6/28, 7:03pm **Pre View**
Hey there is 50 years ahead of us, we need to open to real LIFE
Every precious alive lineage we had was taken away by the matrix.
WE JUST NEED TO GROW STRONGER, HEALTHIER, MORE BEAUTIFUL
6/28, 7:03pm **Koz Kozmos**
no one is interested if i do , i don't have 50 years ahead of me!
6/28, 7:03pm **Pre View**
No one is interested = this is the past you are talking about.
You need to begin fresh and hold on to the refresh BELIEVE BUTTON!
Once your physical body moves into a higher level of healing, u'll move faster then me !
Most people are in great despair because they either don't know how to take responsibility and align themselves up into their LIFE GIVING ORIGIN
or they are completely lost in DISBELIEVE
or they have lost all hope, faith and REMEMBRANCE of who they are!

u'd magnificently contribute understanding to their lives.
And also , most of the time, they just fail to accept things as they are which closes doorways. We need to flow into acceptance first before healing and growth can take place from an atmosphere that lives
on higher grounds.
I just love teaching that, yet many times it is always the laziness that keeps people knocking on doors THAT NOT EVEN EXIST, OR BETTER LEFT CLOSED
6/28, 7:07pm **Koz Kozmos**
u have no understanding of my situation, how hard i've tryed
6/28, 7:07pm **Pre View**
How can I understand better ?
6/28, 7:08pm **Koz Kozmos**
u either do or u don't
6/28, 7:08pm **Pre View**
ok
6/28, 7:08pm **Koz Kozmos**
i have hated my life , and hate it more and more
i have no support on any level , just a day at a time I could explain ,
anyways i hope your ok
6/28, 7:12pm **Pre View**
Ever since birth i supported every one around me, were did it get me ?
into the deepest levels of rejection
it's terrible how people can drain us, yet there is only lessons to be learned from it and not let it happen again. People just love to steal energy.
Yet, these dayz when I refuse to help people FOR FREE, because that is of course what they want, they all reject me like trash after the need is fulfilled
Before that I was their Heaven on Earth due to the support and free assistance
But I'm done with this type of connections because it doesn't give respect and acknowledgement If people only want to believe in the unseen forces when they don't have to pay for it, that says it all!
I am building myself up now, out of the high degrees of unworthiness and into the universal atmospheres of round degrees, hahah ;
THE ROUND TABLE, KING ARTHUR!
Talk as much as u want, on any level,
I love listening to u
6/28, 7:13pm **Koz Kozmos**
same here , but i don't hate myself , i can't express thru typing
6/28, 7:14pm **Pre View**
thats ok, it is hard expressing on Fb
I'm soft going or peaceful if you will, don't bother Don't like the typing either
6/28, 7:15pm **Koz Kozmos**
thank u for your support and recognizing me
i don't think I've ever felt peaceful
6/28, 7:16pm **Pre View**
U deserve to come out in the world and speak thru the media,
wotever channel
6/28, 7:16pm **Koz Kozmos**
i regonize something in u, i do
6/28, 7:17pm **Pre View**
And what may that be?
6/28, 7:17pm **Koz Kozmos**
oh yeah , a creative fire and a need to rise up

6/28, 7:18pm **Pre View**
The thing is, I cannot rise my fire with extreme Peace, need to find some tech that brings that through But yes, yur absolutely right
6/28, 7:19pm **Koz Kozmos**
the peace doesn't block it ,
it just makes u a more competent warrior artist
6/28, 7:21pm **Pre View**
I don't want to feel like a competent artist, I have my Divinely developed skills and creator-ship upgrades.
That is very different from the abilities people learn in earth schools because they are often not energy efficient. They drain energy for teachings are boring
Not being acknowledged as an artist is very frustrating, confrontational, depressing
It is really Europe that has been held back more then any other continent.
Wonder when it is going to break open,
Had to deal with too many injustices these last couple of days, but its ok
6/28, 7:22pm **Koz Kozmos**
same here, none stop bull shit, no time to shine
gotta pop off for a while
6/28, 7:23pm **Pre View**
its like all levels in my human radiance is being shaken upside down
6/28, 7:23pm **Koz Kozmos**
take care, be back later , stay strong keep kool , rise up
6/28, 7:27pm **Pre View**
Ok, luve the way u take care of yourself,
Thank u for connecting! U are Extremely important to humanity, ---
6/28, 8:35pm **Pre View**
How did u open your Heart ? Or, how did it happen?
6/28, 9:18pm **Koz Kozmos**
2 of the first songs i wrote in my late teens ,
when i could'nt play really; still can't one was called Open Heart ,
and the other was Heathan In Eden
i think there have been times wen we're really powerful and real !
but we get hijacked , shut down , wiped
i just feel as if i've cleaned the matrix dirt of me and become more 'pure'
the incredible highgene!!!!
my heart has opened ,
but i also feel massive amounts of contempt for humanity but hope that i would use 'right action in situations of soul dysfunction among the pack its hard to say ,
i'm blabbering
u have an open heart Nic , we're flawed
at least we try to rise up and let the lamp of knowledge burn
and let the mutation begin , this place Earth is not right , its hard for use
6/28, 9:31pm **Koz Kozmos**
exscuse spelling
6/28, 9:33pm Koz Kozmos
MUSIC: Yusuf Islam - The Wind

6/28, 9:36pm **Koz Kozmos**
I think Cat did it better
(Cat Stevens or Ysuf)????
6/28, 9:37pm **Koz Kozmos**
MUSIC: John Mellencamp Hotdogs and Hamburgers

6/28, 11:55pm **Pre View**
We all have such exclusive beauty, lets not fool hope Balance & Justice need to anchored rapidly honorable & accurate action is needed
We all just need a little more time in ORDER (remember the Knights)
to persist & penetrate through the dirt ball of earth
and bring the volcano's of Joy through!
6/28, 11:59pm **Koz Kozmos**
As John Mellecamp says in the song: Every one of us has got to choose
Between right and wrong,And givin' up or holdin' on
6/29, 12:02am Koz Kozmos
MUSIC: Jim Morrison - Stoned Immaculate (The poem).

6/29, 12:03am **Koz Kozmos**
The Knights will return , I pull the sword from the stone, it turns to bright metal in my hand
6/29, 12:09am **Koz Kozmos**
well it had 'immaculate' in the title
6/29, 12:16am **Pre View**
U are a Knight returning to Order. Are u not a black Sword carrier ?
Knights shall meet as foretold, thy are the ones holding the Rod of Power (or the Power of the Word),
I wonder when people will hold on to their word, it crumbled so much,
you can't trust them because they talk jive and don't remember what they say,
early Alzzzzheimer

MY INTERNALS: Today, working with the elements as in co-creation and assisting the transition taking place globally , has become my number ONE study Room while connecting and learning from many different species in this universe.Without the Elements, nothing can exist. It is how we all came into creation, it is how we can expand through creation. The Elements hold all life giving substances that can be sourced through when brave enough to align our designs to the degrees that run equal with the physics within the bigger Cosmos and so many beautiful Life forces.
So elegant, so interesting! I often times wonder why people could ever get bored by anything? It is because they live in a self created environment that keeps on recycling the same old songs or commercials through their brains, or let's say the mind that has been controlled or taken over to break down THE BRAIN from functioning on higher intelligence and knowledge. Could we not just show and entertain people with Light Technology, how it heals, transmutes, upgrades and co- creates. People need VISIONS, isn't it, a good Hollywood movie MADE OF HOLY WOOD.

6/29, 12:16am Koz Kozmos
black sword no idea... why do u wish u had that tech ?
here we go again , I am the blade that gleams a dead kaleidoscope broken into shards and scattered ,how are u Nic ? don't wish to bother u , bye
6/29, 12:24am **Pre View**
A back sword carrier is somebody who has absolutely no fear of duality, eliminates all, u don't even need to explain what a light body is, or spirituality U'll see the common denominator & move through it. When u need to explain things : with this sword u get the job done...
Black focus wil blast through earth dense Consciousness
Blablabla, because the word BLACK in intelligence already explain everything.
Black is strong as steal and penetrates everything.
6/29, 12:25am Koz Kozmos
MUSIC: Hawkwind - Song Of The Swords

6/29, 12:26am **Koz Kozmos**
to go beyond the duality would be ace
what is the word returned ?

the top line of people have been corrupted and are now soulless
i'm ready to change,
to rise but nothing ever happens saying this is not weakness ,
if u don't wish to talk , no worries
6/29, 12:29am**Pre View**
Power of the Word = "In the beginning was the word" ,
refers to 'I am that I Command" It actually means
that whatever WORD you speak, wit will be accepted by people because the truth in
that word cannot be denied
The Power of the Word is actually the Power of Truth... ,
It is also a space in which you will no longer attract the lower chats or empty
communication
The wonderful thing about the Power of the word is that it is so pure,
nobody can judge it or have an opinion about it,
you literally checkmate people by offering them truth.
6/29, 12:30am **Koz Kozmos**
When the true bard returns no one will deny his song
6/29, 12:31am **Pre View** bard ?
6/29, 12:32am **Koz Kozmos**
Bard = poet
6/29, 12:33am **Koz Kozmos**
but not u're usual bard
6/29, 12:33am **Koz Kozmos**
In medieval Gaelic and British culture a bard was a professional poet, employed by a
patron, such as a monarch or nobleman, to commemorate the patron's ancestors and
to praise the patron's own activities. Originally a specific class of poet, contrasting
with another class known as file in Ireland and Highland
Scotland,it acquired generic meanings of an epic author/singer/narrator,
comparable with the terms in other cultures
6/29, 12:34am **Koz Kozmos**
a renegade bard = one who stands against the kings
the secret bards were druids wizards, thier swords were wands
6/29, 12:36am **Pre View**
Uhuh, interesting, i have absolutely no knowledge here,
6/29, 12:37am **Koz Kozmos**
wonderful , i get it back to front , remember,
i very dylexic
6/29, 12:38am **Pre View**
Is this a reason why magic spells come so easily when working with Merlin details
6/29, 12:39am **Koz Kozmos**
wot are merlins details
6/29, 12:40am **Pre View**
The Magic of Merlin, do u remember when we talked about Lemuria ?
It is actually just lavender light
work with some electricity
6/29, 12:41am **Koz Kozmos**
whats lavender light work?
6/29, 12:42am **Pre View**
eating, breathing, drinking, digesting,
thinking,being lavender Light
6/29, 12:42am **Koz Kozmos**
why it called lavender light work,
seems misleading and a bad description have u been to the mauve zone ?
6/29, 12:43am **Pre View**
Mauve ? No, WHY ?

6/29, 12:44am **Koz Kozmos**
near the indigo fountain crying teardrops of those
that lay broken on the edge longing to fall
6/29, 12:45am **Koz Kozmos**
mauve is a pale lavender-lilac color, one of many in the range of purples.
Mauve is named after the mallow flower.
6/29, 12:45am **Koz Kozmos**
i just make it up, free style
6/29, 12:46am **Pre View**
Your freestyle has a breathtaking taste,
6/29, 12:47am **Koz Kozmos**
i've been remembering a poem i read many years ago and liked not by me,
i found it ealier in my teens
6/29, 12:51am **Pre View**
ok, your poetic vibes might help people out of their short-winded consciousness
6/29, 12:51am **Koz Kozmos**
i have found a file with some of my poems from 25 years ago
6/29, 12:51am **Pre View**
Fantastic !
6/29, 12:52am **Koz Kozmos**
i need to go to the dark tower on the bright hill and begin to write new rimes
6/29, 12:52am **Pre View**
Would u let me read one ?
6/29, 12:52am **Koz Kozmos**
some are 20 pages long , but i've moved on
6/29, 12:53am **Pre View**
wow, that's way 2 long
6/29, 12:54am **Koz Kozmos**
my longest was 48, hold on , i may have a few odds on a hard drive
6/29, 12:55am **Koz Kozmos**
this is a very old one that was also a song
it seems niave, but here we go, maybe 23 years old
Koz Kozmos
Teenage Prometheus~
i will steal
from the universal mind sacred books
the neon machine
stolen luv
and pornozines
i will steal from the kinky king
and the sex queen
from the gypsy
with her tarot pack
the gates of time
the kabbalah
and the zodiac
i will steal
a coat of tears
made from a
smashed kaleidoscope
its dreaming glass

in acid shards
like the flowers
i stole from
the old hags yard
i will steal
from the vatican
a forbidden tome strange drugz
and from the starchild
the galaxies' gramophone i'll pick gods pocket sneak away the key
turn it in the dread ~ lock get up from my knees
and then from the fates
i will steal my destiny
6/29, 12:59am **Pre View**
am reading ...
6/29, 1:01am **Koz Kozmos**
i need to go into my next stage
6/29, 1:01am **Pre View**
u already understood it all back then,,
But yes i think u changed a lot and would pen everything in a
different way now, but it is charming at the age of 25
6/29, 1:01am **Koz Kozmos**
but i have no motivation left, it needs to be far more penetrating
6/29, 1:02am **Pre View**
it'll come, hope u can move to another place soon,
6/29, 1:03am **Koz Kozmos**
i think it may be better to stay here , there is no where to go really unless i had money
and could by somewhere detached
i need to learn to drive and overcome my broken nervous system
6/29, 1:04am **Pre View**
aha, ur place feels good, but the surrounding,
you just really need NEW air
6/29, 1:05am **Koz Kozmos**
it has many physicall effects , it could take years i'm with a hosing association ,
a long story
6/29, 1:06am **Pre View**
i understand
6/29, 1:06am **Koz Kozmos**
i have had a lot of ideas and writen and craeted stuff in recent years
whay better than wot u read, even tho that is ok
but i have no motivation
and have had no support , and surreal events seem to want to stop me,like u
hahaha i'm a fighter,
but it has not helped me , anyways
do u have any projects your want to complete ?
6/29, 1:09am **Pre View**
healing a nervous system takes a lot of work,
But then again you could work on that like 8 hours a day
for you have nothing else to do, do you?
Keep on fighting, you're strong enough

6/29, 1:09am **Koz Kozmos**
its been years , things have gotent worse
it impacts massively , i will not heal if things carry on
i will try and lead a quite life and wait to die, hahahah no being deppressing
6/29, 1:11am **Pre View**
yes, it breaks all joy
But u have too many things to offer humanity!
6/29, 1:11am **Koz Kozmos**
i always have, but no one wants them, i tried to give
6/29, 1:11am **Pre View**
Do u know the psychology behind it all,
apart from the light eaters and their ingestive greed?
6/29, 1:12am **Koz Kozmos**
i understand elements
6/29, 1:12am **Pre View**
I feel it would be good if you could work with somebody that has knowledge and could support you as in giving daily directions and practical applications of light kaleidoscopes (using that word instead of technology or configurations and hoping that you understand it better)
6/29, 1:12am **Koz Kozmos**
and how i was emaneting at certain time;
but people are corrupted, nasty and stupid
6/29, 1:13am **Pre View** s
o it is
6/29, 1:13am **Koz Kozmos**
i 've tried, i made a compromise and worked with one guy
as it was the best i could get, but it turned into a nigh mare
i played one small gig and was ignored
the guy i worked with was surpriced as he thought we'd go down a storm he plays with lots of people... and a few days later I broke my wrist !!!
and it was not set proêrly....
so they fucked up my hand...
so playing is not as good anymore, and it broke me completely
and i was broken anyways
after that i separated myself from every body, thy are too low grade and bore me
6/29, 1:16am **Pre View**
it hurtz me deeply,
u need another angle to turn your life around
6/29, 1:17am **Koz Kozmos**
and i was a hermit anyways
that's just the froth on the bile i hate my life, but i like myself and wot i've become its been a massive dose of wot may be called 'bad karma'
6/29, 1:18am **Pre View**
sure, but hermits have potentials that need to be aknowledged,
you cannot go on like this,
u need to start anew, new surroundings
6/29, 1:18am **Koz Kozmos**
i need to move to a small tow, my old home town bad memories but its by the sea, and i'll see my parents die
6/29, 1:19am **Pre View**
never return to wot u already know! No good
move into a different time zone, a different layer of awareness
6/29, 1:19am **Koz Kozmos**
it feels like there is no hope, i have no choice, u don't get it,
were else can i go

i'm ill , i can't go to america
6/29, 1:20am **Pre View** c
come on, hey u, u've got plenty of ideas
maybe twist your brainzzz a bit into another axis position flow with the Northern Light
and breathe some d'light through
6/29, 1:20am **Koz Kozmos**
my thinking is twisted, u have NO idea , my body does not work i will return to the sea , leave the city , it brought me nothing
i went to london when i was 18 to try and form bands instead I became a road sweep
6/29, 1:20am **Pre View**
I sometimes feel what your brain is thinking
and sometimes the emotional pain within your body
but ok, if u think i've no idea , so be it
many are broken, we all need to reset our lives and understand that everything will rise along our own efforts regarding the return into LIGHT KNOWLEDGE and how it brings back health, wealth and joyful standards.
Theoretically speaking, efforts are useless, you need to apply the practical integration of light and the knowledge to move into your Celestial swirls and many light integrations to be able to heal out and be the protection,,,
6/29, 1:22am **Koz Kozmos**
i was a broken boy , I've no idea about what's happening to me
6/29, 1:23am **Pre View** ok
6/29, 1:23am **Koz Kozmos**
u have basic theories,
i understand as I've heard them before of course your feel my body ...
but there's more going on
i'm ok, hard to talk about it, my nervous system is broken so my brain sends a lot of incorrect signals,,,, for sure
6/29, 1:25am **Pre View**
alright then, but feel free to dialogue whenever you want it...
6/29, 1:25am **Koz Kozmos**
i'm a private man, its no good, its stopping me moving on
6/29, 1:26am **Pre View**
i'm not private, I just talk about everything, as everything can be heard and seen anyways
so, what is there to hide? but i respect u for your choices
6/29, 1:27am **Koz Kozmos**
and the doctors have fucked me over and over
that i've survived is credit to me
if i could talk to you, it would maybe be diffrent
most days i rather not be here at all, i've told u a lot , do u get it?
6/29, 1:29am **Pre View**
yes, i'm getting it more & more
6/29, 1:30am **Koz Kozmos**
i'm not comfortable in my body here,
typing is getting too difficult, exhausting,,,
are u a psychic vampire ?
6/29, 1:31am **Pre View**
I am a psychic dragonlite consumer
6/29, 1:31am **Koz Kozmos**
wots that?
explain ?

6/29, 1:32am **Pre View**
joking
6/29, 1:32am **Koz Kozmos**
ok , i'm not saying anything anymore
6/29, 1:32am **Pre View**
I actually feel like a dragon light
had to dig deep into the psychiatric underworld
in which you need to load the strength of a dragon.
After that everything just seems casual. This world is just one big mental institution
with dancing nurses or drugged physicians of the underworld, hahahaha
The end result is that no thing shock or wonders me anymore
6/29, 1:35am **Koz Kozmos**
i get that , i'd not call it causal ,
odious wod be a better word
6/29, 1:37am **Pre View**
don't know, feel empty with that word "odious "
6/29, 1:37am **Koz Kozmos**
why ? casual seems a bland cop out
6/29, 1:41am **Pre View**
Why did u ask me if i were a psychic vampire ?
6/29, 1:43am **Koz Kozmos**
because some times its like u need to feed !
and u can't feed on me, its not possible, and i can get pissed off
6/29, 1:45am **Pre View**
You ? pissed of huh, how delicious is that !
I eat as much as i want !
6/29, 1:46am **Koz Kozmos**
i'm toxic and u will die if u try!!! and good riddance
6/29, 1:49am **Pre View**
i'm gonna rest a little
would like to dream, i never do
I watched the video you sent about the DMT Molecule
Do u have any suggestion for another film ?
6/29, 1:50am **Koz Kozmos**
did u watch all of Fringe series?
6/29, 1:50am **Pre View**
no, about 13 I guess,
I need Fringe about ho the nutrients get into the microcosm
I need the communication with the forests
They are good as a bedtime snack ;these series, they put me asleep
6/29, 1:50am **Koz Kozmos**
ok, there are a lot of scifi i've watched unreaveling things
6/29, 1:51am **Pre View**
What's the best u've ever seen
6/29, 1:52am **Koz Kozmos**
not sure, so may levels
fancy an art house vampire movee ?
watched it many years ago, but taste shifts
i'll think about other movies ,do u have a fave movie apart from the Disney ?
not had a tv since i was a kid
6/29, 1:56am **Pre View**
I need to go, something is hitting my nerves,
Talk again soon,
good night Koz

6/29, 1:57am **Koz Kozmos**
wots getting on your nerves? u ok ?
6/29, 1:57am **Koz Kozmos** s
it must be quite heavy talking to me ... i get down at times
but it's not depression, thank u for the talk and all the encouragement
6/29, 2:02am **Pre View**
Hey it was not u !!!! (getting on my nerves I mean to say)
6/29, 2:02am **Koz Kozmos**
good, thank u! i wod never want to hurt u,
6/29, 2:03am **Pre View**
It is that my son just came home, then he stood behind me while I'm on the pc and refused to leave, so i argued with him and asked him to respect my conversation with you on messenger. He was really annoying , had to ask him to leave my private scenery like 5 times, tooooooo much...
6/29, 2:04am **Koz Kozmos**
yes, i understand , try and be calm, its hard "
The basic difference between an ordinary man and a warrior is that a warrior takes everything as a challenge while an ordinary man takes everything as a blessing or a curse."
– Carlos Castaneda
6/29, 7:23am **Pre View**
No I have no fave movie, did not see movies for the past 10 years ...;
And I don't fancy vampire movies at all
I thought you were a very noble man, huh?
6/29, 7:39am **Pre View**
U have me figured out by now i guess - I have absolutely NO theories -
And when my brain fails, maybe I can borrow your brain for a couple of dayzz
6/29, 10:33am **Pre View**
ok, I need the fire of some good salsa music now to vibe some Original
Arcs into my creationzzzz Double meaning :
it will open hips & our creational sacred sacral center up into the beautiful gardens of Eden. Ever been there? Hahahah. After that I start hip hopping & rocking in that garden or just shop around for more skills, enjoy!
6/29, 10:52am **Pre View**
I really want to triplicate my vibes and speak triplicated Dutch
Oh the wheels of this universe just got me rocking and rolling into a new adventure!
The adventure of self exploration and self indications
Just having fun with music.. Are you there?
6/29, 1:53pm **Koz Kozmos**
u have a good deal of theories and wonder about interactions with other entities I've printed up and read your PDF and like wot u've written....
some of it is unknown to me, some not
have u made contact with other entities ?
i watched this video a good while back, but think u wod enjoy it
6/29, 2:00pm Koz Kozmos
MUSIC: Architects of Control - Michael Tsarion
Truth Frequency Radio - Part 1
6/29, 2:12pm **Koz Kozmos**

discovered this song last night , and i don't have a thing for C LOVE,
just the ocausional song is really good

MUSIC: Hole – Violet (Courtney Love)

6/29, 2:23pm **Koz Kozmos**
catch u later
6/29, 2:44pm **Pre View**
Must definitely reset myself
Just had a talk with my son pulling his fist at me,
he doesn't want to wake up,,, just a terrible situation
I got him out of all possible trouble, but he may be back on drugs I guess Pulling in 0 Tolerance, that's it,
He used to be such a darling until society hit him.
At 18, he didn't make it in high school and had to change schools to get his high school degree. Even at that age, he'd never seen or smelled a drink or drugs until he hit that new school. He was at the top level of the World cup Snooker,
only we had no money tosupport this sport and so bad things started to happen with bad company in this sort of Elite school...
Anywayzzz; "Architects of control " – the vid you sent:
Thank u !very good to watch, will pull my attention on it later today.
This is also WHY in the very beginning of our chats I was talking about elimination of all subconscious levels, no more mind, only brain ....
Humanity needs that. The mind is a creation of the control system, the soul in which people want to sink. It needs a lot of elimination, especially the hormones attached to the emotional soul embodiment because it causes recycling consciousness.
However, I never digged very deep into it, I just went on and on in the elimination capacities I had developed and worked so well on people willing to heal. It is actually while chatting with you that i'm picking up everything, and understanding from a higher level. It may not mean anything 2 you, but it could clarify that everything we learn from the universe needs to be understood; and I never really took the time for that as the changes in my body and consciousness were very obvious.It takes a lot of study, only I miss out on discussing it with somebody, that would be great you now, moving the philosophical
sides into it.I'll see wot happens.
6/29, 3:02pm **Koz Kozmos**
your son sounds angr,y hope u can tranform him and beat the martix frustrations:
u can discuss it with me if you want
not sure about the mind and the brain idea, it dependz on the meaning
I meant: discuss your ideas with me... if you want
with each line you write, I will answer with wot I think about it
6/29, 3:23pm **Pre View**
Thank u so much for supporting,
i'll handle my son, I just need to be a little hard on him
I appreciate your invitation to discuss ideas, but this typing is so exhausting and may twist things, i'd rather not discuss my ideas over FB
Some of these matters are so delicate, and need loads of precision to explain.
Its hard & bloody interesting to do
Maybe i'll just move into some space where I can first understand it better for myself
However, i just highly respect ur presence & I need to accept what is possible
I also think that overall casual chat is just not for us,,, we need movement that triggers intelligence and knowledge
6/29, 3:26pm **Koz Kozmos**
ok
6/29, 8:23pm **Pre View**
? I think perception cannot be opposed to reason & knowledge,
This is rather when i think of perception as an ever evolving
intent +imagination+intuition merged with intelligence

What is rational? :
i don't think universal laws have ever been build without FEELING , main ingredient of intellect ??? I'm very tired, my eyes hurt a little
29, 8:24pm **Pre View**
I'm gonna watch some more **Michael Tsarion vids.**
6/29, 8:30pm **Pre View**
u seem to be more peaceful since last night?
To what are u addicted, maybe ?
Hope u are feeling OK ?
6/29, 10:46pm **Koz Kozmo**
Nothing is going to happen unless i get a massive healing
i'm addicted to my eye -magi -nation
i want to get out of this dimension
6/29, 10:55pm Koz Kozmos
MUSIC: Scott Walker - Montague Terrace (in blue)

6/30, 3:30pm **Koz Kozmos**
hi ? U there?
6/30, 4:08pm **Pre View**
Hi there,,
6/30, 4:13pm **Koz Kozmos**
I'm the DArC ArC from the light machine of dreaming crystals
6/30, 4:13pm **Pre View**
I have no doubt, you may even be more penetrating than that
6/30, 4:14pm **Koz Kozmos**
maybe
6/30, 4:14pm **Pre View**
Only, u don't dream it through
6/30, 4:15pm **Koz Kozmos**
i am dying in the dream
6/30, 4:16pm **Pre View**
Hi Koz, would you have a stronger melody for me?
Don’t dy in your dreams, make a tasty reality sandwich from it and manifest beyond illusions with greater care
6/30, 4:16pm **Koz Kozmos**
i rarely pick up the guitar
6/30, 4:17pm **Pre View**
NOW is all we got,,, spend your time well,
wish I COULD HEAR YOU PLAY THE GUITAR
LIVE VERSION
6/30, 4:17pm **Koz Kozmos**
and although i have many songs , i couldent play one of them
6/30, 4:17pm **Pre View**
WHY ?Why? Why?
6/30, 4:17pm **Koz Kozmos**
i need to get outa the time loop and begin again becuz i would need to practice to play and relearn lyrics etc
and my hand is stuck...
remember i'm Jimmy the Wyrd Hand
6/30, 4:18pm **Pre View**
You shouldn’t allow any excuse, you’re a Bard remember?
We're both hard Songs to digest,
It is timed to kick that in!

6/30, 4:20pm **Koz Kozmos**
MUSIC: Neil Diamond ~ Glory Road ~

6/30, 4:20pm **Koz Kozmos**
got suff to do , w
ill catch u later, stay strong, keep kool & rise up
6/30, 4:21pm **Pre View**
At your command mister! Hahah
Thanx for the song!
6/30, 4:22pm **Koz Kozmos**
6/30, 4:24pm Koz Kozmos
MUSIC: NEIL DIAMOND ~ LADY MAGDALENE

6/30, 4:24pm **Koz Kozmos**
more Neil, good chorus
6/30, 4:25pm **Pre View**
It's been a long time since I listen to Neil Diamond
6/30, 4:26pm **Koz Kozmos**
they've got Jesus in the vid too
6/30, 4:27pm **Pre View**
u mean Archangel Zach ?
6/30, 4:33pm **Pre View**
There' s so much misunderstanding about the Entity known as 'Jezus'
He actually came down 2 Earth 2000 years ago - exactly for the purpose of encoding Arkansas Crystals that would allow people to move into ascension through GRID KNOWLEDGE and thus teaching Grid embodiment.
The Arkansas Crystal along a Brazilian quartz and Brazilian Laser wand are very important because they will set the foundational home station or Grid that allows for all celestial and universal systems to kick in and to start the Crystallization of the body as well, which is being held by the GRIDZZZZZZ
What does it take for people to value his Essence,
No fairy Tale ! He has now become Archangel Zachary.
6/30, 5:06pm **Koz Kozmos**
Zach da Knack...not sure
6/30, 5:11pm **Koz Kozmos**
why have u been chosen?
6/30, 4:27pm **Pre View**
Everybody has been Chosen !
6/30, 5:14pm **Koz Kozmos**
not all, I'm the Rebel of Enlightenment
but you're losing me again in your weave ,
catch u later got to try and sue
6/30 :00pm **Pre View**
Hi Koz, when i woke up this very Early Morning, i had a remembrance of u !
It was a Union of black Ray Tribes into my Red Sword which i do not acknowledge, it was extremely strong,,,
Question : Do U have any remmembrance of any Native American Tribe ????
I sometimes get things from a Sioux bloodline for myself, as far as you are concerned I get that you are from a Koyote Tribe
It was a dream I had on the beach over here and it just comes back to me year after year.
I have no idea what it may mean, what pt has to say.
Love to U, always, Nic

MUSIC: Bruce Springsteen – The River
MUSIC: MY SWEET LADY (
Lyrics narration HD) Cliff De Young

This is a song from the movie "SUNSHINE", have you seen?
Goodnight to u , Koz
6/30, 6:50pm **Koz Kozmos**
Hopi? maybe Bruce is drowning in his river ,
but supa dupa song
Cliff de Young to sweet and to sentimental for me ,
but the dying woman cleaned the toilet and the oven
so she sounds ok
u watched **?**
MUSIC: 'Architects' yet from Tsarion Michael.
interested to see wot u think about it ?

6/30, 10:49pm **Pre View**
ARC-I-Tects : they have 50 shades or pages
should u not like my highly immage-NATIVE voice...
Reason why I'll never get bored over the next million Years Bruce drowning ?
6/30, 11:32pm **Koz Kozmos**
In the river : he's become king of the pack audience
6/30, 11:43pm **Koz Kozmos**
MUSIC: A Man Alone - Frank Sinatra (With Lyrics)

6/30, 11:45pm **Koz Kozmos**
Bruce is drowning in the river, hahahah
don't worry, i'll play straight from the KozKozmos JukeBox,
some raw undergrounf hip hop soon
7/1, 12:34am **Pre View**
Private Master of the KozKozmos Jukebox
Hungry to feel the underground trembling Will we witness Walk Inns?
7/1, 12:47am **Koz Kozmos**
Walk inns,? Explain what this meanz
7/1, 2:25am **Pre View**
I have no passion no more in explaining, but maybe this :
The old teams will do everything to keep people in "victim mentality" preying on emotional fields , ...Its the human butchery living in a prison and not even seeing the bars..
These are people that will keep on sucking your energy and taking every last breath asking from others.People are simply not used to taking responsibility or are TOO LAZY to work on their fears and eliminating every single layer of anxiety. I feel this is getting worse and worse as most are completely lost in the tunnels of their own debris and don't know where to start. Although simple meditation is a good start, some knowledge into some good Space connects to our Source and Spark Self are basics that should not be overlooked.
How else would anybody understand meditation when not at least knowing about the consciousness through ray formulations one can tap into. Let alone getting the real stuff or designs of the Divine through!

Governments will not last, it just cannot be as everything in the solar system has been set into renewal mode, and thus everything in the Celestial and Universal systems change too.
It is merely EVOLUTION and Nano Tech that science could make understandable to the most mundane And if science of Earth is running backwards, then there is people like us, the artistic physicians like us that can teach people –
Rock&Roll and Hip hop need to meet under the same radio wave connected to Orion.
Is Orion our scientific center in the universe?
There is so much to learn from it as many years ago, I do remember
I could not connect to Orion, it was held back or something,,,

JULY 2013

7/1, 2:33am **Pre View**
We all understand that music holds the highest level of transmutations, we all know there are suns and moons out there. And we all know these 3 things are a necessity for life through Light or sun synthesis. Moving into the Celestial system/GRIDZZZ and on breaks the ties to the matrix. There is so much logic in all that.
But understanding through practice is really needed in order to open the higher communication links. If health and wealth is so off on this planet, it makes sense that the thymus gland or high heart re-education
will bring back justice or spiritual Laws
Most people hold on to resistance that sets its own trap and catches itself.
I'm working very hard to get my light-flames back inside out,
and to be honest, I align and thus learn from
every planet in the solar system, move it into the Celestial realms
and experience all differences when the fire gets universal.
That can really not be done overnight or through a dream fase!!!
So you see, setting BASICS like creational rays first in the body and energy field are just critical to a good RECONNECTION to what we all are
IN ESSENCE.Goodnight Koz,
7/1, 2:35am **Pre View**
But, absolutely thank u for asking, u seem to pick up on my brain very well :
always when u ask me a
question it means that that is an item I need to dig deeper into FOR SELF UNDERSTANDING AND INFORMATION/DATA.
7/1, 3:11am **Pre View**
Seems i have no need for sleep at all.
What do u think about the **Architect 5/16 ? Michael Tsarion?**
7/1, 10:19am **Pre View**
Everything dormant must come into the open, the strong of heart should walk upon earth. Are there enough of them to help people out?
Justice must be put into action now, I need to make new decisions every day,
not easy at times.
Sometimes it feels like a thunderbolt of anger is popping up:
its when I feed self with my surroundings,
or the injustices I witness that are being done to people.
7/1, 11:49am **Koz Kozmos**
Architect 5/16 ? wot is that ?
I 'm angry and also a thunderbolt...but u have to be careful
or they will use it against u,
put u in prison, keep u in this prison, try and go beyond it just a little
yes fb or any media mind manipulations meme is not to be trusted at this stage in the human malfunction... The human has to go, its a slave state
I feel my emotional field is being played upon, and has daily since I came here.
Human butchery....yes they feed and the bummed down voodoo street scum are trapped and used for negative magics, and are all around us.
They may at this time be targeting the ones that attempt awakening
I feel no urge to become trapped in purple esoteric rooms filled with posers
dreaming their mediocre rituals
7/1, 12:04pm **Koz Kozmos**
I understand some of wot u say, but I need things to be clearer
i also have to move into another life stream, or escape completely via the soul death
things have always been wrong since i came here,
its hard to get thru the day put simply
7/1, 12:22pm **Koz Kozmos**
Architect 5/16 ? wot is that....if this is to do with the Tsarion vid ?
watched a good while back
just don't make grandiose statements back them up please !
With a good smile, hahahah

7/1, 1:03pm **Pre View View**
MUSIC: Michael Tsarion/Architects of control 5/16

7/1, 1:10pm **Pre View**
I don't want to talk about it any longer, i just figured u feel my changes
I just wanted to get into some philosophical conversation with you, your thoughts about Orion, what it means to flow with a New solar system etc...
But I guess, your field of knowledge or streams of esoteric education does not match anywhere. Never mind, I just have so much passion for it
And you miss out on the practical application,
so we have landed in an empty space somehow....
7/1, 1:22pm **Pre View**
Sorry i have not been clear ... It think it all has to do with "
The Pyramid in Cairo" that shut down its
connection to the Sun which closed off dense Alchemy based on the matrix, or selling ones soul to power. You said you wanted your power back...
That is reason why I was talking about the sun, the Great Central sun, its our Original Power.We could not connect to it in the earlier days, but we can now if we realign back to our sun stream, our life giving power and just move on from that...
I was just mentioning it as a ways of hitting something in your vibe that understands where Original Power comes from, so it might trigger some type of remembrance and encourage you to maybe just connect to the Sun, that is the Lion's gate in our solar plexus and all these movements or growth
processes into the Eye of the Sun, the opening of the Eternal Eyes, the Creator Eye,...
so many Eyes I'm all Eyes, hahahaha
7/1, 1:29pm **Koz Kozmos**
I need to ask more questions... I hope its ok ?
Who are these other enlighted beings & the new teams ?
Wot happens when u are taken out of your soul?
Wot is the purpose of this? Not all know the governments will fall and beyond the church and state, the astral rape...
I have not sold my soul...
7/1, 1:30pm **Koz Kozmos**
I feel i need help, really
7/1, 1:31pm **Pre View**
Is it ok if a give u a few examples from my experiences ?
7/1, 1:32pm **Koz Kozmos** yes
7/1, 1:57pm **Pre View**
Who are these other enlightened beings & the new teams :
we have the ascended Master on earth and on the
other side of Mid Night that created New Teams from the old Tribes of Israel so to speak as many of the old tribes became part of the matrix and helped it grow. Some sort of fallen Masters, yet many amongst them are promoted BIG TIME on FB because people are trapped in the old believe and never question a channel or not so much. It is because they need WORDS from a Source other then their own Source. So THEY THINK, and thus they give their POWER away and never ascend because they don't move into Self
Mastery and Self empowerment.
And also, you may not have sold your soul, yet the matrix broke you al over.
EMOTION = SOUL CONTROL, so ? Think for your self.
Without Crystalline Grid embodiment, anyone can break you and even take over your brains and break this brain down into some set of particles that equals mind control.
This is even getting worse and worse every day as we can easily witness
how intelligence is moving backwards.
With a Crystalline Grid embodiment and Grid constructions worldwide, it is that u don't understand any longer why people dwell in their drama's.
But there may be or Light paths,,,,,

And yes, I fell many times into the emotions and thus the Grid constructions create holes through which the monsters can come in and break you over and over again which happened to me, to you, to many.... We need to CULTIVATE THE GRID VERY DEEP and keep on working on Grid Protection which in the end means that we need to move into the Higher senses that do not understand emotion or the lower senses anymore.
And so, IT TAKES WORK , yes, but the outcome is very majical and beautiful because you start manifesting through your Power and keep on creating more power.
Everything is creation, once we understand how to move from a dense creational pattern such as the soul or ego into a clear field of knowledge,
then there is no end in how fast we can upgrade.
The trap IS WITHIN! Fun begins when our Universal Self, the Creator Self stops the dense machinery completely through understanding of how to do that and keep THAT DISCIPLINE running.
And also, anyone can cultivate some discipline just to cultivate and hold on to the Crystalline Grids, that would already bring through many changes.
7/1, 2:08pm **Koz Kozmos**
none of that is of any use to me , i need something i can use
7/1, 2:08pm **Pre View**
Something u can use: get into a training with me. There is nothing else. People need some training over a
week-end or a week or so to get these essences in and understand TO AT LEAST KNOW HOW TO WORK WITH LIGHT TECHNOLOGY SUCH AS GRIDS,
A LIGHT BODY AND LIGHT WAVES.
From there on, it becomes easier and more interesting every day.
So , you see, just a foundation is more then a necessity!!!!
It is the same like when going to a university and getting some sort of degree!
It takes years of training, and so does the Light Universities take you through never ending years of interesting training. Everything on earth is set to ENSLAVE people, we know that. Yet most are not willing to acknowledge that there is ALWAYS A GATE OUT OF ANY PRISON! We must train each other, get heads and ideas together & work together under the same blanket of protection.
7/1, 2:09pm **Pre View**
Light applications without knowledge is no education,
that is were protection comes flows in.
Ihave nothing else for U.
7/1, 2:09pm **Koz Kozmos**
and anything i consume either via the internet or my automatic writing and poetics reveries is transmuted and redefined ?
7/1, 2:12pm **Pre View**
no, but u know, internet must be used carefully with the necessary filters.
You can redefine your poetic outlet by yourself, it is all within u, not outward. But ok.
7/1, 2:12pm **Koz Kozmos**
i know this , i look inside and outside from all angels
i have not consumed much really, apart from music
7/1, 2:13pm **Pre View**
I can only give you what I trained and experienced myself
And that cannot be doen over FB
7/1, 2:14pm **Koz Kozmos**
i'm lost and broken, i want the end of time being here is no good for me ,
i don't understand u, u have no practical application ,
only grandiose meanderings
7/1, 2:20pm **Pre View**
Gonna work a bit in the garden now and talk to the flowers
U want the practice? u want me to train u over a couple of days ?

I'm in Belgium, take yer flight or keepb on streaming in the old hype
7/1, 2:23pm **Koz Kozmos**
does your flat have a garden ?
i don't trust your training , i need things to be more lucid
i have lost hope once again , i'm not coming over to Bellgum
7/1, 2:25pm **Pre View**
Its big,the garden but students have access to it as well,
Its ok, without faith, without trust, there is indeed nothing,
Keep your strength up, I know u can!
7/1, 2:26pm **Koz Kozmos**
I would have thought with all your tech training on another planet,
wod be no problem i'm sick of it all
This is not depression, it's and end , it has all come to nothing
maybe it wod be best if we just stopped talking permanently
if u do what u say you're doing , there will be results
i'm considering leaving face book any way
7/1, 2:56pm **Koz Kozmos**
there is nothing
7/1, 3:01pm **Koz Kozmos**
only getting by
7/1, 3:08pm **Koz Kozmos**
i wish u the best
7/1, 3:24pm **Koz Kozmos**
I'm losing clarity , wot do u do exsacly in the 4 hours work u do every morning
can this be explained
7/1, 4:31pm **Koz Kozmos**
too much frustration
7/1, 4:32pm Koz Kozmos
MUSIC: Jimmie Rodgers - English Country Garden

7/1, 4:36pm Koz Kozmos
MUSIC: Crosby, Stills, Nash & Young - Woodstock

7/1, 4:38pm **Koz Kozmos**
We are stardust, we are golden, we are a billion years old carbon, And we got to get ourselves back to the garden.
7/1, 7:08pm **Pre View**
Good to hear that woodstock ,,,
Maybe JUST DO whatever you hear in your music like in this Woodstock song
'GET BACK TO THE GARDEN'
Just ask the universe how to access the Garden of Edon
U know exactly how i feel, always
Get out of frustrations & other emotions
Do it for your Self from your Self!
7/1, 7:08pm **Koz Kozmos**
i do , all the time
A nods as good as a wink to a blind horse.
7/1, 7:18pm **Koz Kozmos**
i need to solve certain frustrations to enable me to move on,
practical stuff like housing etc ,
other frustrations like eye problems may be there for good anyways,
easier said than done, and a bit obvious

7/1, 7:22pm **Pre View**
We all tend to negect our bodily functions at times
And its not easy to bring the anatomy back into its Light waves, its sound waves
7/1, 7:29pm **Koz Kozmos**
nothing feels good , not being negative , i don't want anything the treats i want, i can't afford
7/1, 7:31pm **Pre View**
What are the treats that u want ?
7/1, 7:31pm **Koz Kozmos**
to own a detached house away from humans, maybe learning to drive and able to afford to run a car not sure if i could drive with the eyes and nervous system problems
a garden to sit in with my own private sauna and swimming pool
a kozmik band and a home studio
healing and ascension, true friendship
7/1, 7:34pm **Pre View**
Bloody FANTASTIC, u do know wot u want !
humans mostly don't !
7/1, 7:34pm **Koz Kozmos**
to go back and get my mother to abort me
7/1, 7:34pm **Pre View**
haha, for sure, see ! u make me smile again
7/1, 7:34pm **Koz Kozmos**
maybe kill my mother, cut myself out of her Jimmy Supa Birth
and track down my father and kill him
7/1, 7:35pm **Pre View**
oh well ,insanity is sweeping through the streets so,,,
it wouldn't be unuasual anymore,

7/1, 7:35pm **Koz Kozmos**
then soul death, and to disappear forever and don't call me human !!!!
they're the divine madness of the fun zone and toxic insanity of the dead zone
7/1, 7:36pm **Pre View**
Did u never have a drivers' licence ?
7/1, 7:37pm **Koz Kozmos**
i stay off the streets , no never
7/1, 7:37pm **Pre View**
ok
7/1, 7:37pm **Koz Kozmos**
hope i can raise the money to sue about my eyes
my life was ruined before and it got worse anyways, how are u Trikkey Nikkey
7/1, 7:39pm **Pre View**
Is there any solutions u've been thinking of ?
7/1, 7:39pm **Koz Kozmos**
watch u don't trip on a grid, hahaha
Cash is the solution ,
but is uncouth to talk about money i get by ,
but i need a large sum
7/1, 7:39pm **Pre View**
i flow, lightness of being

7/1, 7:40pm **Koz Kozmos**
and could do with some support, i have none ,
I glow in the dark
7/1, 7:41pm **Pre View**
cannot help u now, only by may next year (money support)
7/1, 7:41pm **Koz Kozmos**
I would never take any money off u , EVER but if I met u
,i'd buy u a drink
7/1, 7:42pm **Pre View ok**
7/1, 7:42pm **Koz Kozmos**
i'm not hinting
7/1, 7:42pm **Pre View**
that'll be nice enough, thank u
7/1, 7:42pm **Koz Kozmos**
just blabbering, this is a big thing, eyes fucked up by surgery
7/1, 7:42pm **Pre View** were do u swim ?
7/1, 7:43pm **Koz Kozmos**
I joined a gym with a pool and sauna
i use a wet room, helps with the eyes
there was a good offer on, ...
i just used to go to the local swimming bathes, but too many humans
7/1, 7:44pm **Pre View**
Aha, i don't like wet room
but if it does u good, i guess it softens the pain in your eyes
7/1, 7:44pm **Koz Kozmos**
i like a wet room , its a treat i suppose
i've not drunk any alchol for a month, gotta prioratise
7/1, 7:45pm **Pre View**
sure wow, this is a wonderful achievement
How does it feel without, must have been difficult ?
7/1, 7:45pm **Koz Kozmos** its ok
7/1, 7:45pm **Pre View**
alcohol & eye problem ...
7/1, 7:46pm **Koz Kozmos**
? my eyes are just as bad without booze
just have to use true will i suppose , i like getting off my head
7/1, 7:47pm **Pre View**
i just drink once a week..., I don't like to have a glass or 2 or 3 a day
it might take a lot of time to clear out the eyes,
but worth the work anyways, no more talk about that
7/1, 7:47pm **Koz Kozmos**
and dancing about, or writing and playing
u can talk to me about your stuff, you're welcome,
when and if u feel like it
7/1, 7:48pm **Pre View**
hope u can find your joy,
i will not talk about my stuff no more,,,
please tell me a little about wot u learned over thc ycars
7/1, 7:48pm **Koz Kozmos**
its not some thing that can clear out

u can talk about your stuff please, but i will try to understand and challenge u
7/1, 7:50pm **Koz Kozmos**
hard to express in words
7/1, 7:50pm **Pre View**
So, wot did u learn over the
past 30 years ?
7/1, 7:50pm **Koz Kozmos**
to not be stupid
to go beyond programs , to wake up at least a little
to understand the damage that has been done to me and try to fix it
i have learnt how to become the poet i already was
7/1, 7:51pm **Pre View** how ?
7/1, 7:52pm **Koz Kozmos**
its the light in my blood; only the fyre born have i set it on fire
7/1, 7:52pm **Pre View**
and then wot happens ?
7/1, 7:52pm **Koz Kozmos**
i can see the clay born for wot they are, in my case
i've had to sepprate my self from every one ,
and i was always a loner
7/1, 7:53pm **Pre View** Why ?
7/1, 7:53pm **Koz Kozmos**
i seemed to have been targeted ,
they tried to wipe me by pulling me out of my body
7/1, 7:53pm **Pre View**
wot does it mean ?
Who are they ?
7/1, 7:53pm **Koz Kozmos**
i got a lot of succubus dreams they were trying to feed the archon
7/1, 7:54pm **Pre View**
succubus ?
7/1, 7:54pm **Koz Kozmos**
= female demons or the archon,
the enemy of the fyre born want to destroy us
7/1, 7:55pm **Pre View**
at wot age did u know or experience this for the first time?
7/1, 7:56pm **Pre View**
yak, do u want to talk about it ? can u protect yourself now ?
7/1, 7:58pm **Koz Kozmos**
too much to type, not sure, i seem to be able too
i think drinking helps dull the light so i could not be seen
eyes are very bad , using eye drops continualy
to stay in front of the screen
i had something jumping on my bed as a child,
and many other things but a few years ago a thing hit me and fucked me up
i'm not on medication and I am too sane for the earth
7/1, 8:00pm **Pre View**
yes, but drinking makes everything worse,
lets take a little break ?
so your eyes can rest from the pc electronics?

7/1, 8:00pm **Koz Kozmos**
i want to make changes , i controlled my drinking fairly well but i'm very sensitive
7/1, 8:01pm **Koz Kozmos**
i play the guitar when i drink
if i don't, i don't play
i 've been focused on change always, everything just hit me, loads of shit but i lay low
, as i always have , maybe we'lll talk one day
easier to explain , i'm lost and confused i do not have experiences like u
i'd be quite happy to be gone, but i will llive till i die and then try and escape the soul
gate
7/1, 8:04pm **Pre View**
Yes, talking to each other would be the best thing,
i think we need a week without sleep to get it all said, hahahah
7/1, 8:04pm **Koz Kozmos**
and never be forced back to be a slave on the wheel of meat i want action,
i'm sick of talking , i want to destroy
7/1, 8:05pm **Pre View**
everything is moving too slow for u;
what kind of action are you planning to take,
7/1, 8:06pm **Koz Kozmos**
its always been too slow, as i've said
i'm illusion moving at a diffrent speed
i don't know wot to do ,
that's why i've asked u about your stuff to try and get some help...
any idea wot i can do ?
i have no idea
7/1, 8:09pm **Pre View**
i understand u feel very desperate,
i told u as much as i can about my stuff
i moved many people out of soul this way,
i am not asking to believe ,
I am not here to tell u what to do,
u must feel it u must decide
7/1, 8:09pm **Koz Kozmos**
i can't, but i understand wot you're saying i'm looking for advice, not commands
It seems to me that there is nothing to be done
7/1, 8:10pm **Pre View**
I still smoke e few cigarettes and need to quit that too,
it is just a repetitive habit in the brain, not even an
emotion or an addiction like I need to have that because I don't even like the smell of
it anymore...The funny thing is when working that habit out of my glandular system
is that I even forget to smoke. It is as if my brain took the message of smoking on like
I needed some sort of medication. There are many
different ways to look at the pattern of that particular issue.
I just use that as an excuse between breaks as I work all the time,
like 14 h a day on new programs... i feels very good ,,,
7/1, 8:10pm **Koz Kozmos**
yes stop smoking, i think 50% of people in the UK will have cancer by 2020
7/1, 8:12pm **Pre View**
Would you like me to perform some healing on your frustrations,
not your hand...
so u can focus better on decisions ?
I clear my lungs every day , rather as a form of respect

7/1, 8:12pm **Koz Kozmos**
wot can u do ?
i tend to make good decisions with what i have to work with how do u clear your lungs ?
7/1, 8:13pm **Pre View**
i was just thinking that maybe, when i do a lot of stuff in the morning like clearing, realining and getting
new information through – I might as well pull all the light energies through you at the same time, in a way that it is not extra work for me...
You'd feel that immediately as en empathy,
7/1, 8:14pm **Koz Kozmos**
how do u do it? or is it too much for fb ?
7/1, 8:14pm **Pre View**
no, i'm not explaining, no more of that, it gets me frustrated,
it is working with light and grids and alchemy such as languages of light and codes that cannot possibly hurt you huh?
How?:As we are close enough, if feel I can just send the energies straight into your flat in Wales and into
your body. I'm good at that, or I can just print a pic of you and pull the energies through, or I can sit on the Mac and pull the energies through the computer.
The stronger the focus, the stronger the Light transference.
7/1, 8:15pm **Koz Kozmos**
mediation, body posture, mantra, ritual magic , breath work...
or do u just have a ciggerte and a coffee ?
7/1, 8:15pm **Pre View**
No, the breath, yes! Every healing lies within our capacity to breathe like
the breath of Eternal life, Universal breath, the Creator breath, the Immortal breath...
Because the breath is all we have to integrate energies and download our capacities to heal on multiple levels . How else do you think you can connect and upgrade:
through integration and cultivation of the whole cosmological soup Magician Style!
Everything termed ascension is about taking the breath to the next level, it is breathing from the inside out and creating expansion while dense energies such as block are being released.
It is that the River of Life needs to run smooth,
breaking the dams that hold the flow back, that is all there is to it, and a lot of work,,,,
When regenerating the body it needs to get into some new biological content, termed light content and understanding all the levels you need to go through in order to light up your fire, the Phoenix.
Our diet needs to match the frequency of Light Earth as well and needs to transition at the same speed as earth is doing now.Regeneration comes with understanding our anatomy ,how that works with the elements such as crystals, herbs fluids etc...
Healing is very individual along our connections in the galaxies and the universes. It is all so interesting,,, yet people only get interested when they get really sick. Sooner then later, medication will not work any longer.
The incoming medication will be alignment and application of Light Technology through meditation with a deep engagement in EXISTENCE...
I don't have all the knowledge, but I WANT TO KNOW and gain more knowledge every day and information and work very hard when it comes to healing people and myself when it comes to getting ACCESS to higher Power and its Technology.
Think about the water that runs through the body, we are all water..;
when that regenerates through the
consciousness within ocean, rivers and lakes,
it becomes easier to resurrect the spinal column and the skeletal structure and work on the nervous system, the glandular system and actually everything that makes up a human body.

Not many people go as deep, I understand that....
But you know, the healing of the anatomy makes that we can open up the higher faculties in the brain and then merge them.
nothing u find in books or internet ...
7/1, 8:16pm **Koz Kozmos**
I don't think i could do that , why can u not out line it for me ?
wots the problem
7/1, 8:17pm **Pre View**
TT (too much type)!!!! If I work like 3 hours on you and I need to tell you what I do with every breath?
That is INSANE MISTER KOZMOS!
7/1, 8:17pm **Koz Kozmos**
how do u access the light grids? and what excaly do u mean by alchemy ?
it should be simple i believe , OK OK OK
if u can help me make better decisions that wod be good
how can i help u ?i can imagine u never shutting up , hahaha
7/1, 8:19pm **Pre View**
We just need to claim our passport back as a Universal being
and thus getting out of the old soul tactics
which you understand. Not sure if we need a Visa for that.
Think about your composition...
every body part that has NO LIGHT needs to rehabilitate
You can access Grids by setting up a Home Base Grid or station that opens the Gates to worldwide Grid stations. I explained Alchemy, look back!
And also, when Grids have a good integration they will assist you everywhere you are and will blow through duality in a way that those things cannot hit you any longer, it allows you to take action in every situation and assist your intentions to manifest.
It strengthens your health and mental attitudes.
We all need to relearn about light which starts of with the first 13 rays of creation in our body and energy fields or Light body which then expands into the Grids in which you get Grid anchor points and thus Ley Lines start to rebuild which open the highways to the trillion Stars and the elements, the animal kingdoms, many species we forgot to connect with
GRIDS ARE ELEMENTARY EDUCATION TO OUR ORIGIN.
Think about a LAZER SHOW in a disco with all that House or Techno music. The music sucks, there is nothing uplifting about that, but the laser shows are great. Why don't you go out tonight and enjoy some disco huh?
Would be good for a change, hahaha, and a little dance,
TT (hope i can use this code in the future for 'too much type')
It would be good if we could set up more codes and create some sort of language between us. How do you feel about that?
7/1, 8:19pm **Koz Kozmos**
ok , TT is kool if it gets realy frustrating.
7/1, 8:19pm **Pre View**
How about us creating a code language, just for us ?
7/1, 8:19pm **Koz Kozmos**
TT , thats a big one
7/1, 8:20pm **Pre View**
I Like it !
Our code language would not enable anyone in this world to understand us ?
7/1, 8:21pm **Koz Kozmos**
yes i've thought this as well
7/1, 8:22pm **Pre View**
ideas ?

7/1, 8:22pm **Koz Kozmos**
i have my own made up words i use to comfort myself
like ziperleee zapper lee zoom
wot i want to do is get outa this crap dimension,
get my super powers back
7/1, 8:24pm **Pre View**
Do u have a list with explanation ?
zipperlee : funny when i'm a little upset with u,
i have the tendency to talk to u as hey ziperlee ...
7/1, 8:24pm **Koz Kozmos**
and become kozkozmos super hero and return to the koz cave i have no list,
my language is always changing and transmuting
7/1, 8:25pm **Pre View**
ok, super hero, remember thy grandness !
Thy grandeur!
7/1, 8:25pm **Koz Kozmos**
i've never forgotten it , but i've become damaged and live damaged
7/1, 8:26pm **Pre View**
So did u decide wether i take u into my 4 hours heavenly zone or not ?
For some healing...
7/1, 8:27pm **Koz Kozmos**
look back can i trust u ? wot does it entail ?
7/1, 8:27pm **Pre View**
are u kidding, DO U NOT TRUST ME ?
7/1, 8:27pm **Koz Kozmos**
will i be aware of this happening ?
i don't trust any one, not even myself completely
this is not weakness but awareness of the tech of the dark team
7/1, 8:28pm **Pre View** u should feel better
but i could also eliminate things if u wish
7/1, 8:29pm **Koz Kozmos**
leave my eyes i want to try and sue
wot can i eliminate ? can u make me younger ? eliminate years,
hahaha wot about making my eye lashes a bit longer , ummmmmmmm only kidding,
just being shallow, i'm thinking
7/1, 8:31pm **Pre View**
i will not work on your eyes, that would take many weeks and a follow up program
that you should do yourself, and as you don't understand simple breathing
techniques with the first 13 rays of creation and thus the consciousness within these
rays that either override and/or eliminate dual consciousness, its of no use,
I'm done explaining if you don't wan to go into the practice....
And also, the eyes might get a bit foggy for days – it is huge technology and not done
overnight. I told u my skin is looker younger since a month TT
Lets eliminate : frustration, deceit, disconnect the hurt from parents .... anything
7/1, 8:32pm **Koz Kozmos**
i've done alot of that
7/1, 8:32pm **Pre View**
Maybe just one single thing to make u feel more joyous ?
7/1, 8:32pm **Koz Kozmos**
my problems are practical
7/1, 8:33pm **Pre View**
sure! you have done things, your inside reflects the outside !
So I don't see that you eliminated much stuff

7/1, 8:33pm **Koz Kozmos**
i connect with my majik and use it well
7/1, 8:33pm **Pre View**
ok, what is your majic and its application about?
7/1, 8:34pm **Koz Kozmos**
i want to reconnect with it, with no doubt, then i will know
7/1, 8:35pm **Pre View**
how will you establish that and bring that new movement through?
7/1, 8:35pm **Koz Kozmos**
i thought u were going to help me to do that
Maybe just one single thing to make u feel more joyous ? u said ...
7/1, 8:35pm **Pre View**
u don't really want my stuff huh?
7/1, 8:36pm **Koz Kozmos**
that was my suggestion
why wod i have trouble seeing ?
i have no faith, maybe a little
7/1, 8:38pm **Pre View**
When healing the lens of the eyes, they get foggy from lifetimes of soul fabric that are being released, anyways everything in the eye is very delicate TT
7/1, 8:38pm **Koz Kozmos** majik , ok
to have better luck
7/1, 8:39pm **Pre View**
apply it !
7/1, 8:39pm **Koz Kozmos**
it is important I can make better desions to spell and type better
u sound like a life coach again
7/1, 8:40pm **Pre View**
why ? i hate that word , it sounds like the gathering of retards,,,
7/1, 8:40pm **Koz Kozmos**
just hit me with some upgrades, so i can shine I'm dirty,
mean and mighty unclean
I'm a wanted man
Public enemy number one
7/1, 8:43pm **Koz Kozmos**
MUSIC: TNT AC/DC with lyrics

7/1, 8:43pm **Koz Kozmos**
i can't do anything except attract shit and i'm the gentle good
the kozmik diamond in the dust of fucktards
could u make me play guitar in a super human way ?
7/1, 8:45pm **Pre View**
sure, you're the double fractured shining knight
7/1, 8:46pm **Koz Kozmos**
in the zone of floating bones
7/1, 8:46pm **Pre View**
Let's see what kind of recipe I can get from the underground most refined dishes
7/1, 8:47pm **Koz Kozmos**
I am the king of the underground but no one can go that deep
if u could download into my connciousness the tech i could use
, that wod be a great festival

7/1, 8:49pm **Koz Kozmos**
it would help and no TT
i'm a child killer , i hate kids as much as i hatee adults
oooooooooooooooooooooooooo ,
i feel i'm boring u , i feel uninspired
7/1, 8:51pm **Pre View**
good U have no feeling
Good, rest a little, i need a nice break,
7/1, 8:52pm **Koz Kozmos**
i feel too much
i try to teach wen i can
7/1, 8:52pm **Pre View**
teach me ? hahaha, I'd love that, just consuming knowledge,
7/1, 8:52pm **Koz Kozmos**
hopelessness , boredom and fatigue
7/1, 8:53pm **Pre View**
i don't understand boredom
U lost yer grip with self, learn from the plant world
7/1, 8:53pm **Koz Kozmos**
"Merkabah", this was the word i thought u meant ?
7/1, 8:54pm **Pre View**
The Merkabah held people tied to the astral fields, a Melchizedek thing.
The 2 triangles from the Merkabah need to split and then merge on top of each other so one point faces north, the point point faces south and when these 2 triangles fuse you have the creation of a diamond of Light termed MERKIVAH or energy field that holds the first 12 creational rays.
Each of these 12 energy fields have 12
types of consciousness connected to them , 72 mlae, 72 female
The purpose in this life is getting there and embracing our Eternal partners with this Light body configuration and many upgrades until we reach that particular space where the merger can start of.....
7/1, 8:54pm **Pre View**
Oh nononono, no comment!
7/1, 8:55pm **Koz Kozmos**
MUSIC: MerKaBa the cristalline star tetrahedron body.

7/1, 8:55pm **Koz Kozmos**
i'm a seeker , I don't watch this stuff,
look forward to the upgrades and connecting with the grids ,
catch u again, thank u
7/1, 9:13pm **Koz Kozmos**
all the best Nic
7/1, 10:44pm **Pre View**
Thank u, I'm very glad u told me somethings about your persona
I'm EXtremely tired, must get sleep now
U feel me anyways , would like to read some more of ur poetry, maybe ?
Take good care Koz & goodnight
I am here when i am there
7/1, 11:05pm **Koz Kozmos**
sorry, i get down and frustrated, but always enjoy talking to u
i digged out some of my old poems,
u suggested doing a joint project some time back....
maybe we should brainstorm through the gridz
7/1, 11:11pm Koz Kozmos
MUSIC: Roger Whittaker - Finnish Whistler

7/2, 6:15am **Pre View**
Hey Koz, good morning, this whistle song you posted is so beautiful to wake up with, i'm not awake yet We are the Arc-I-tects, the grid builders .
I'v been working real hard this past month designing new plans (gridz) .
It is lovely to step out of my door , right into the garden and have nobody out there.... reclaiming my spaceEnjoying the simple things, need to touch and talk to the flowers and the bees, need to be in the air,
7/2, 6:38am **Pre View**
I understand your frustrations, we all have them with all the injustices we experience...U don't have to feel sorry for anything, at least we're more then the human touch can ever, I-magine. I've planted 2 lilac trees, one for u, one for me, they'r branching out with unexpected fruits. Absolutely beautiful. Maybe i'll take some pics of the garden, i don't like pics.
7/2, 6:51am **Pre View**
You're a natural, gridz will click in fast.
I have the support of my experiences in which joy was an everyday just natural, no negatives could ever penetrate.
Sometimes intelligence gets in the way of simple things.
U will not need to brainstorm, mutual spacing out our passions would be good enough.
Your music & knowledge is enough, and much .
We just need to intersect the correct liquid Ley lines and liquify our bodies.
Everything, however, is a creative choice,.... I wanna keep my highways into Heaven growing with with the Cosmetics of the cosmos
Putting brains together with the passion of our creativities would make up a wonderful song to assist humanity. People could learn a lot through music and Light waves. APPLICATIONS!!!
7/2, 6:57am **Pre View**
I also feel you have a lot of wisdom i miss out on,
i mean pulling the right tracks together with immediate results as in creating new educational programs, especially for the mundane, and youth would be good.
Youth needs the new music, hip hop, real rok & roll, not the dying tracks that come with house and techno music.
You know... I'd like to educate people about the grids, the horizon, the sun synthesis, life forms on the other side through my art, and through your music, some poetry, some good wine,...
7/2, 1:09pm **Koz Kozmos**
yes, but first i have to clear stuff; make complaints to different organizations ... this is not easy for me, i wonder if I'm wasting my TIME, one day i may get out into the air , the long and winding road
7/2, 1:35pm **Koz Kozmos**
MUSIC: Fernhill - Cowboi

7/2, 3:03pm **Pre View**
What is 'Fern Hill' – the song about ? I don't think you're wasting your time, complaints must be strong & repetitive so that you can reach the veins of some lawyer, till u get them annoyed! Otherwise, they are too lazy,
you need to hit them with truth!
If u'd like to talk about the complains, please do so, i'll be happy to listen , maybe assist with some advise, don't know....
Although THE SYSTEM may work completely different in the UK
7/2, 3:05pm **Pre View**
must get into city, getting some majical fruits and veggies from the heavens, laterzzzzz...
7/2, 3:19pm **Koz Kozmos**
Fern Hill are a welsh folk group, the name comes from a Dylan Thomas poem.
Difficult to type due to eyes in front of screen, it makes me anxious...
I'm writing up a complaint that has gone on for 15 years and dealing with my eye stuff and other things but mainly deslexia

It takes me a long time to write stuff up
The 15 years of complaint is to my housing association, thier are a mannipalative incompetent bunch of odious liars
don't want to talk about it , did u hit me with your energy in your early morning Pre tech ?
O, by the way, its' taking me every day now for months to sort this stuff out , its like having a boring job , but is more insidious
so i rather not talk about it , i need to use spell check
7/2, 5:12pm **Pre View**
Housing ... yes.
We got people over here in Belgium who check on the malfunctioning of housing, ...
You don't need to spell check after 10.000 messages, I'm used to your language now and also, it is kind of very charming when you spell things differently.
Also, when I need a lawyer or so, I make sure I record everything just because they have a way of twisting words around and most of the time just get you on the phone instead email which means: no proof. We need to protect ourselves and be wiser than the cliché masses including academics and their control system within the control etc etc etc...
These things take all of our energy for which they don't even pay.
Maybe study and become a judge ourselves huh? wouldn't that bring up great ideas and solutions from a different teapot?
I did a lot of research when working with a lawyer and investigated many things they'd never heard about. That is how they learn, from us ,and they don't even pay us for the grand ideas, the input...
Have to take many decisions myself, the right one is not always obvious.
I understand the pain ur going thru with court cases and with almost no hope left.
We must keep on fighting for it restores hope. Keep your confidence up! i have a feel all of these Injustices is going to be the main train on the planet . Truth will move through somehow, like a wildfire. It has too,
Lets keep brains intact, unaffected,
7/2, 5:14pm **Pre View**
What is it that we don't know ?
7/2, 6:46pm **Koz Kozmos**
Thinking on it
we do't know, we don't know everything
i can be more articulate, maybe u know more than me anyways, later ...,
as the americas say
7/2, 8:28pm **Koz Kozmos**
MUSIC: Red Road 2006 Full Movie

7/2, 8:29pm **Koz Kozmos**
saw this wen i was 14, going to rewatch
I've always followed the red road thr doors in the kaleidoscope
i think it may be the whole movie
7/3, 7:23am **Pre View**
THXXX, will take some time out to watch,,, Interesting wave,
7/3, 10:37am **Pre View**
I take great pleasure in talking 2 u 2 It gave me hope, it helps me rebuild
7/3, 1:23pm **Koz Kozmos**
i'm falling apart
7/3, 2:15pm **Pre View**
Jimmy, say NO ! Its a rough week energetically,...

MUSIC: FREE RIDE-Edgar Winter Group

7/3, 2:26pm **Koz Kozmos**
many ruff life timez , this is better it rokz
7/3, 2:27pm **Koz Kozmos**
MUSIC: Edgar Winter feat. Slash - Rebel Road

7/3, 2:39pm **Koz Kozmos**
been riding in a cage thr the badlands
7/3, 2:43pm **Pre View**
yep, rumbling in the jungle
7/3, 3:01pm **Koz Kozmos**
MUSIC: "States of Mind" by Senser, of Stacked up C D

7/3, 3:04pm **Koz Kozmos**
great rime
7/3, 6:09pm **Pre View**
Thy sure are ... thxxx, had to look up the lyrics,,,
7/3, 10:47pm **Koz Kozmos**
They sentenced me to twenty years of boredom
For trying to change the system from within
7/3, 10:49pm **Koz Kozmos**
MUSIC: Leonard Cohen - First We Take Manhattan

7/3, 10:57pm **Koz Kozmos**
I prefer this tune
7/3, 10:57pm **Koz Kozmos**
MUSIC: Leonard Cohen - Who By Fire

7/4, 12:39am **Pre View**
Bored ? Would u like me to give you an assignment ?
Shouldn't be too difficult with your imagination :
Breath the following through your system :
Create lines up & down through your body and lines that flow from left to right :
choose any color of preference to create these lines...
This creates a grid, right?
With this grid your have frames or the squares : fill them with any color of preference
When you get that, focus on where the lines intersect : these are dots or points that fuse lines, you understand? These dots also open a geometric pattern if you focus long enough connected to your energy field.
Then fill up the squares with anything that u like (symbol, planets, numbers, letters, languages, your majic, ...or nothing ...)
JUST SIT IN THAT GRID and let it expand with your breath.
It is just a matter of HOLDING FOCUS .
MAKE IT YOUR MAJICAL ROOM OR GRID
More things can always pop up in that grid:
ask questions, but don't allow any negative flow!
Be creative : imagine what u want, how u want it, try to feel it & be specific
Sit at least like 30 minutes every morning and night in this grid, make it yours, and expand in it by putting more things in it, like flowers, crystals, just anything... hours.
This is a very simple way and starters' kit to access information and trust your Source.
make this meditation your new world!
RE-IMAGINE YOUR SELF IN IT!

7/4, 12:56am **Koz Kozmos**
I can't visualize and need to pee non stop
I'm being serious , i can't lay down, its hard to sleep at the moment i've taken sleeping pills on some nights, which i try not to do thank u for the suggestion,
so bored with being in this body
i think its a neurological condition: the need to pee
i've had lots of insidious tests
I don't want to lay down and visualize , i want movement and action but i will consider it ,
i can't lay comfortably and focus with this condition
7/4, 1:08am **Pre View**
Shall I work on your bladder?
7/4, 1:09am **Koz Kozmos**
i tend to think its a brain problem
but i had an operation in my 20's and they fucked me up,
i don't trust docs i've done massive healing on my self ...
7/4, 1:10am **Pre View**
focus on what can be done NOW and leave the past for what it was
MUSIC: IMMORTAL TECHNIQUE – Leaving the past!

7/4, 1:11am **Koz Kozmos**
i'm in the now and I need to pee 24 hours a day like
I've been on a long car journey u have no idea ,
i'm not looking for motivation talks or sympathy
i want it to stop
7/4, 1:12am **Koz Kozmos**
so, u have some idea about wots going on ?
7/4, 1:13am **Pre View**
I will have to focus on your body, never did, ... takes some time
7/4, 1:13am **Koz Kozmos**
wot does that mean ? i have focused on my body
and praticed visualizing since i was 15
is 38 years enuff time ? i wanted to go deeper since i was a kid
7/4, 1:15am **Pre View**
Listen Koz, I could at least balance and clear your bladder out and see what is going on (psychologically) and then work further down the road like your kidneys, lymph nodes
7/4, 1:15am **Koz Kozmos**
i need healing , i would definitly try this ....
7/4, 1:16am **Pre View**
OK, where do you think the problem is coming from?
Could at least be all your frustrations
Water is emotion unless it is flowing spiritual style in which it becomes your power...
We are all water, the planet is all water...
So, I hope it makes sense that the biggest transition we can possibly make is the transmutations through water and also, I feel your throat is stuck,,,
Your throat feels terrible, it affects your entire system because it connects body and brainwaves and also reason why so many people have thyroid infections and many diseases such as obesity.
Nevertheless, it cannot hurt you,
and my focus may slide through some clear road through which healing can be accelerated.
7/4, 1:16am **Koz Kozmos**
I drink 2 pints of water and lay on the bed for an hour:
impossible, I need to pee all the time ,
its very bad...
i am frightened i may need a bag , i don't know wot it is but i'm not making it up ,
no fun fun fun...

7/4, 1:19am **Pre View**
ok, i'm only offering
7/4, 1:19am **Koz Kozmos**
yes i understand
7/4, 1:20am **Pre View**
Why am I offering healing?
because the other day i was surprised u said u never felt peace in your life .
So, when the body is agitated for a whole lifetime, it will respond and talk 2 u
like animals do. When the water of the body does not flow in harmony with the rest
of your biology, it means your enterprise needs some new motors.
Over activity comes from misaligned glands.
That may take quite some work to repair.
7/4, 1:20am **Koz Kozmos**
thank u for the sugggestion and listening to my frustration
7/4, 1:20am **Pre View**
hey, no prob
7/4, 1:20am **Koz Kozmos**
i have never felt peace , i would like to die ,
but i'm not a suicide type but i have had enuff , too much negativity
so fuck the new age mind control program
7/4, 1:22am **Pre View**
u must get out of your negative movie because it allows the system to break you down
It is our responsibility to bring the Grid down into the bodies' energy fields and
create a very strong foundation in a way that the grid can travel with you wherever
you may be ....
That is protection.
7/4, 1:22am **Koz Kozmos**
i'm not negative , i'm a very postive person ,
the yin and yang man don't blame the victim
7/4, 1:23am **Pre View**
the ying yang must come together in a straight line,
Just another mind control program
7/4, 1:23am **Koz Kozmos**
i've tried so many things, i just want some relief
7/4, 1:25am **Koz Kozmos**
u have your problems ,are u positive about them ?
7/4, 1:25am **Pre View**
yes, and creating positive results
and yes, I've been in that supper emotional space in which anger and frustration
arises,
and that just breaks about everything
That is exactly what these monsters of the Universe want in a way that your grid gets
broken and they can move in again to control you
It is just a never ending cycle unless you finally break it when tired enough of
negative experiences. With too many thoughts flowing in one space over a certain
subject,
we all tend to bend into the muddy roads.
It is all training and staying on the Light roads ,
RED ROAD?
7/4, 1:26am **Koz Kozmos**
yin and yang is an explanation symbol
7/4, 1:26am **Pre View**
we must move beyond
7/4, 1:26am **Koz Kozmos**
i don't understand wot u mean ,
i've been trying to move beyond and have dedicated my life to it
following my bliss has brought me sorrow and despair

7/4, 1:28am **Pre View**
there is a missing link : we talked so much,
In my opinion it is not much that u need,
Just the shiny diamonds on your Griddy body
7/4, 1:28am **Koz Kozmos**
I don't think we can become spiritual androgynous in this dummed down state
i enjoy your word play , but your english is not as good as u think
7/4, 1:30am **Pre View**
Does it have to be ?
7/4, 1:30am **Koz Kozmos**
to understand u, yes
ok : missing link, we talked so much,
In my opinion it is not much u need,: this makes no sense, not complaing,
trying to understand
7/4, 1:31am **Pre View**
Let me explain
I have no doubt that you learned and build and cleared a lot with light and your knowledge. The other thing is that I simply don't know HOW you did it and WHAT you worked with when it comes to light application, as u never said a single word about it ... So, WHAT IS YOUR FOUNDATION?
it seems you have no temple or house of light that you built over these years and on which u can count as some sort of communication, connection and protection....It means that your energy is just floating in the air so anybody can hit u, am i wrong? u don't know anywayz,
7/4, 1:36am **Koz Kozmos**
i have no idea , maybe u'r mistaken about me, and u've got it all wrong
7/4, 1:36am **Pre View**
ok ? explain ? Why am I wrong huh?
7/4, 1:36am **Koz Kozmos**
i just did
7/4, 1:37am **Pre View**
U said : I have no idea . So do u know or not ?
7/4, 1:38am **Koz Kozmos**
Ok ,maybe, your ideas that u've had about me are incorrect.
7/4, 1:38am **Pre View**
So what kind of foundation or security key did you build somehow through your knowledge?
7/4, 1:39am **Koz Kozmos**
what do u mean by foundation ? expand
7/4, 1:39am **Pre View**
I explained: your protective shield in which u build and build and build whatever
7/4, 1:40am **Koz Kozmos**
i have no shield ,it was stolen , but i have a sword
The lowest load-bearing part of a building, typically below ground level.
A body or ground on which other parts rest or are overlaid.
7/4, 1:43am **Pre View**
SORRY, ITS ALL THE SAME, IT COMES DOWN TO PROTECTION
and building up : like when we talk ,
u always talk about the past.
I never hear you talk about the way you work with light
7/4, 1:44am **Koz Kozmos**
i don't always talk about the past , u have asked about me ,
i have told u some of my story
7/4, 1:46am **Koz Kozmos**
u don't hear things from me because i don't work with your models
and use your style of language

7/4, 1:46am **Pre View**
Minute please, need to pee
7/4, 1:46am
Koz Kozmos
its the english , its not clear
i'm peeing non stop, got my bottle , i have no place of sanctuary
i have not built my temple and my alter on the astral
i do not experience grids , i don't care about Arkansan crystals
i was not taught anything and i stand against all systems
i told u i am broken and confused ,
and unless every thing is random i have been targeted
7/4, 1:51am **Pre View**
Well, i cannot do without the grids because they build just about everything
It is logic: look at a car that is being build: the designer applies a program that creates the GRID CAR first, then all other motor mechanisms can be filled in such as the engine, the seats, steering wheel, the heating etc...
IT NEEDS A SYSTEM FROM WHICH ONE CAN BUILD. T
he same goes for the body, otherwise the body just floats.
I understand that it needs a lot of understanding because is is all about technology we have forgotten. Look at FB, many times people post crystals that formats in a grid,
So somehow they KNOW about Grids, yet often time miss out how that is
BEING SET IN THE HOME AND IN THE BODY!
It used to be hard for me as well to understand in the beginning,
but as you start to feel the grid movement through the body,
it becomes fun and you start to trust and you start to see little things and
you start to add things in your Grid.
And to be honest, After working with the grids for 10 years now, it is throughout our conversations that I started to question things, look up things and ask spirit for the right direction regarding information
beyond the kindergarten info on the google drive.
7/4, 1:51am **Koz Kozmos**
i found too much stuff out as a kid and was wiped
some times u make no sense ,every thing is jumbled and confusing, hard to follow
7/4, 1:53am **Pre View**
Do u feel things such as the universe pulsing thr and do u understand them?
7/4, 1:53am **Koz Kozmos**
not the content but the language is difficult
yes , i'm lost and confused
i'm 53, at 40 i was ok
7/4, 1:55am **Pre View**
I was not ok till 40, then everything changed as I started to work with Light
and the Crystalline Grids
7/4, 1:55am **Koz Kozmos**
i have explained , its all been crap, i hate it here
no exasperation, no self pity, all my efforts and all my sacrifice has come to nothing
7/4, 1:57am **Pre View**
Could u maybe be specific about 1 single effort you made ?
7/4, 1:58am **Koz Kozmos**
trying to visualize when i was 15, so i could learn to access other realms breaking programs that infected me via different tech and awakening going to the dark side to learn about luve and to use it wisely diffrent mediation tech
7/4, 2:00am **Pre View**
this is very vague ,
not specific at all

7/4, 2:00am **Koz Kozmos**
sigil majik for manifestation,
it's not as vague as your shit
7/4, 2:01am **Pre View**
Sure, mind yur words!
How do u break a program for example ?
7/4, 2:01am **Koz Kozmos**
ok, thru seeing it, understanding it and its uses to infect, and then healing it
7/4, 2:02am **Pre View**
How did you do the healing?
7/4, 2:02am **Koz Kozmos**
i'm not sure wot i've done, but know i have done something
a man can not learn to be a poet, a man has to be born a poet
i was born different, more awake, more immune to the matix virus
but something has made things very bad for me, unless, as i said its random
7/4, 2:04am **Pre View**
So u've never been really conscious about wot u've done ?
7/4, 2:05am **Koz Kozmos**
bad luck or wot ever
nobody is conscious of wot they've done,
i am concious i've done something
some of us have majik others do not
7/4, 2:07am **Pre View**
Could u consciously work on ur bladder with what u know
and invent new techniques to eliminate ,
Just right NOW, in this very moment?
7/4, 2:07am **Koz Kozmos**
i'm trying self healing at all times
mainly i just talk to my self witin to create cahnge (change)
7/4, 2:08am **Pre View**
Born a poet: i don't agree
But it does not matter
What matters is that u get better, you need a complete changeover
TRYING self healing is no healing at all.
You either are confident enough to apply Light in as many ways as you wish,
or you just don't trust.
NO TRUST= NO HEALING!
7/4, 2:08am **Koz Kozmos**
i have other languages that i make up to heal
but u have to understand i'm targetted
7/4, 2:08am **Pre View**
Interesting, I Iove languages
7/4, 2:09am **Koz Kozmos**
u are born the high gene
7/4, 2:09am **Pre View**
What would be the deeper meaning of high gene?
7/4, 2:09am **Koz Kozmos**
there are different soul types created from genetic manipulation a more evvolved soul type , they are still trying to destroy us when we're recycled via the soul gate they can fuck us up
7/4, 2:10am **Pre View**
I'm aware of that
7/4, 2:12am **Koz Kozmos**
On the Wiki:

Community C Gang Stalking is a covert investigation that is opened on an individual. The individual is then placed under overt and covert forms of surveillance. The person is followed around 24/7. Foot patrols and vehicle patrols are used to follow the Individual around, as part of the monitoring process. During these patrols a one handed sign language is used to assist the citizen informants with communicating to each other.
7/4, 2:12am **Pre View**
There are many different forms and ways
I was targeted since age 6 in school, good thing I did not understand it back then I just did my thing, I was very strong, I felt like an alien all of the time
But I didn't mind, it was kind of fun , I educated my parents,
7/4, 2:12am **Koz Kozmos**
There are soul forms, i don't know for sure anymore
maybe i'm a fake , i need to pisss and i'm bored
i do want your answers , why have i asked so many questions ?
your lack of insight is insulting
7/4, 2:16am **Pre View**
Insulting huh???
I am taking a break!
We'll talk tomorrow .Thank u for the chat, goodnight
7/4, 2:16am **Koz Kozmos**
i don't care , i can't be hurt anymore, and wot i said was not vague
its just vague to u ! this is getting pathetic
these talks are really disempowering me
i can't take any more of this ! i mean it all
not just our chats, i HATE it all, there is nothing here for me and never has been its not possible for me to take a break
7/4, 3:09am **Koz Kozmos**
MUSIC: Iggy pop & james williamson, i got nothin

7/4, 2:24pm **Koz Kozmos**
You try and live
And God says no
7/4, 2:26pm **Koz Kozmos**
MUSIC: God Says No – Monster Magnet

7/4, 2:28pm **Pre View**
MUSIC: Santana - El Farol
[1999 Supernatural in High Definition]

7/6, 11:16am **Pre View**
I cannot understand what I did not experience.
I cannot take away your suffering
I can only be there for u and offer a way out
and hope that our mutual presence overcomes what the brain is not capable of
and hope, that some day,I might understand the true Power of Love that brings everything back together 7/6, 11:48pm **Koz Kozmos**
Of course ! Santana , elevator music for upper middle class hippies
7/7, 12:00am **Koz Kozmos**
MUSIC: Huey Lewis & the News - The Power of Love Lyrics

7/7, 1:37am **Pre View**
Go ahead , and get to understand the sacredness of that Power!.

7/7, 1:04pm **Pre View**
Are u ok Koz, are u keeping it up ? 7/7, 2:27pm **Koz Kozmos**
supafab, superfab, superfab
7/7, 2:42pm **Pre View**
U've got style
7/7, 3:56pm **Koz Kozmos**
damaged style, invisible to the pack
7/7, 3:59pm **Koz Kozmos**
MUSIC: Melanie - Ruby Tuesday 1975

7/7, 6:25pm **Pre View**
Melany huh, she drains my energy! And my rebellious feet
The Sun will come up & Lighten your vibes, trust me!
7/7, 6:29pm
7/7, 10:29pm **Koz Kozmos**
I'm in a room with the windows covered , vampire Koz
hiding from the toxic city and the fucktards with their dogs and tattoo's
7/7, 10:46pm **Koz Kozmos**
hope your're well Nic , been trying the grid mediation
guitar placed in heart , lyric in throat, warriors silence in head and wingz on the ankles
7/7, 10:53pm **Pre View**
That sounds good, hey that is some improvement, happy to hear about the grid ....
I don't hide anymore,
and no zombi will enter my precious zones!
7/7, 10:55pm **Pre View**
I am working hard, but have trouble figuring out information.
Do u know anything about Scalar waves ?
I've been watching this video, but it is not satisfying,
OUR BRAIN IS A TUNING MACHINE,
water is closely connected to scalar waves
Maybe just load these waves through the water engines in the body,
that may balance out your bladder etc,,,
It acts like lazer technology.
Nicolaas Tesla provoked an earthquake with scalar waves
MUSIC: WHAT ARE SCALAR WAVES?

7/7, 10:58pm **Pre View**
I am getting more info about the grids as well, in a way as to train it to people.
Kids understand it, they really do . Its because they practice more , kids like doing,
they don't like too much theory
and so they understand
the fast and swift way.
3Hey Guitar in the Heart , that is so wonderful ! How's your health ?
7/7, 11:10pm Koz Kozmos
the same , i need to hide from the concrete streets in this heat one will enter my zone
7, 11:48pm Pre View
OK,take good care ,
Peta Blessings ...
7/8, 12:11am Koz Kozmos
Peta ?
7/8, 12:14am **Pre View**
peta = 1 quadrillion
7/8, 12:14am **Koz Kozmos**
ok

7/8, 12:19am **Koz Kozmos**
i need to let the demons take over , I need the soul death
7/8, 12:20am **Pre View**
I Am writing about this soul death
You are a shining star,
a sparkling darling for the moons with shoes that shine as bright as neon lights,,
7/8, 12:21am **Koz Kozmos**
i mean total extinction , to be gone
7/8, 12:22am **Pre View**
yes, i understand
Where would your spark go to then?
Another star system that is worse then earth?
7/8, 12:23am **Koz Kozmos**
i want to die with no return, leave all dimensions behind , i will attain this !
7/8, 12:27am **Pre View**
We all need the soul death, it is everybody's' purpose to help raise the planet into ascension and thus our own ascension back into light waves, sound waves and light biology
yet it is up to us to rise into the vibration of our spirit, the spiritual body, the celestial/universal bodies and bring an end to the war and games going on.
Nobody asked for the manipulated foods, retarded education and the killing spaces.
We all want joy, equality and a life that recreates itself every day on the higher senses of Divine inspiration and thus setting our aspirations back on the right ancestral tracks....
There is no such thing as the chosen ones, everybody needs to rise into health, wealth and joy on equal grounds and we all need to assist each other
and the transitions the earth is pulling through anyways along the equal output universally speaking. And thus everything changes every day.
That is evolution.It is not easy
Soul death can be achieved by moving self into the spiritual body, the celestial/ universal bodies and support systems which is 6th dimensional. That kind of technology and integrations in the body makes that you'd feel lite in the body and you can protect self quite naturally through grid embodiment etc, meaning u don't have a care about anything any longer except for what u really want to do or to create and
the easy manifestations that come along with it..
I was thinking that it may be way more interesting to put some kind of trilogy together to get people into the Creative Alchemist , through art and teaching at least about the 22 rays and other rays such as copper infused rays, diamond light, etc...
Knowledge about the consciousness within colors/rays and bringing the artistic values into the scenery of self development may be a passionate way to get people out of their dense lifestyles.
7/8, 12:28am **Koz Kozmos**
if u believe that, you're a fool! i want the end
7/8, 12:30am **Pre View**
that is sad, real sad,
but ok if you don't believe what the Creator Self can do when it comes to transforming self, than I'd better close my Universal scripts and save them for those that have some degree of respect.Learning about how energy works in the body along the galaxies and the effect on our consciousness is very important. People know about astrology, not so much about astronomy and the universal layers out there.
So, bringing the spine back into some passionate position while painting with a pallet of brilliant colors, bring through codes that gives one the options to decode self.
It would be interesting enough just to teach how to work with codes, how that integrates, how that changes our neurological content and how they lift us up into higher senses minus emotion and the fear tears within most roads on every continent. That way , people may get to understand how important it is to relearn about the elements etc...

All of that should go into universities to prepare the new doctors, the new architects etc...in order to bring new healing through housing and biological health.
I'd really love to teach in any University , hope I find these doors, that would be so much fun and so rewarding as these young adults really need that kind of self knowledge and mastery to open up the philosophical rooms in a university. Imagine students exchanging ideas from their spirit/spark self with no more ego attached!!!
7/8, 12:30am **Koz Kozmos**
it would be a release for me , just to leave this place
i wish i was never dragged down here ,
its makes me sick i have no feeling that that there is any point
7/8, 12:32am **Pre View**
Don't u remember u felt great joy when u were dancing :
that is the same feeling u have all of the
Time when at least holding on to your celestial/universal wheels and bodies. They allow you to attract the best instead of that every day shit spread. And yes, we need to find the strength to destroy negative streams and bring and end to any suffering from the past. When these things are being subtracted from the brain, we can see and think clearly.
After that it is all a matter of closing doors: NOT ALLOWING
DENSE FACTORS or tests to enter our lifestyle.
Not easy because we need to deal with the way society malfunctions, yet it makes us stronger and moves us to the higher degrees of intelligence.
It is sad, becoz u think i am a fool It is sad becoz u have so much to offer
7/8, 12:32am **Koz Kozmos**
i'm not even suicidal, if i was i would not speak like this
7/8, 12:32am **Pre View** I know,,
7/8, 12:33am **Koz Kozmos**
I have never felt any joy...ever,
i was just moving my body for exercise and it put me in pain for days no joy ,
nothing to offer
7/8, 12:33am **Pre View**
You cannot possibly go on living like that, you must reinvent a way out!
Maybe workshop with me? Opening the Creative Alchemist while I would teach about the 22 rays and open your spine back into the unlimited spaces through your art. That should bring your passion back into the body and enables you to hold on to a spiritual body and the celestial/universal spaces of creation which would make you feel lite in the body and have fun at the same time while learning about astronomy and the whole cosmological soup. People know about astrology, yet the astral planes is exactly what keeps the brain recycling old debris, it keeps them in the past while evolution requires THE NOW and push new
buttons that opens new validity.
The expression of self is very powerful when living 0% Ego Lanes...and thus there we go again, we can create and recreate with the universe so that your truth can be magnified through the expression of your art with the knowledge I bring through. I mean all the planets between the Great Central Sun and the
Great Central Moon would have many interesting things to say...
That would give genuine forms of courage,
7/8, 12:33am **Koz Kozmos**
no, too late, its not been for years and years
that has been my awakening : to become a soul killer
how dare my energy be used in this way , its sadistic
i don't want to bring u down, sorry nic
7/8, 12:36am **Pre View** I
The Earth plane is indeed a horror movie, it is up to us to make it a crystal light movie Protection is important as the hybrids and all these monsters do not want to see light taking over. It is reason why we are targeted so much.

I mean, I'm trying hard to kick something into your brains that works,
so ART MAY BE THE WAY OUT to understand how you can protect yourself.
7/8, 12:36am **Koz Kozmos**
i don't belong here,
only laying low, time has become too long for me,
i feel this will get worse
7/8, 12:38am **Pre View**
I have my protection back, we need to understand how protection works
You need to reconnect with teams of light, with the elements and galaxies Because that are the armies of support we get when WE INVITE AND ALLOW IT, It is a matter of trusting and feeling the assistance,,,
7/8, 12:38am **Koz Kozmos**
how do u get protection? in wot way ?
and why did it leave u ?????
7/8, 12:40am **Pre View**
Sorry, always comes down to these grids that have anchor points...
And hey, I'm not going to give a private seminar through chats
U need an Arkansas, a Brazilian Quartz and a Laser quarts to ground a basic foundational grid , and you don't want crystal huh – so how the hell are you going to pull yer engines into crystallization??? That job
is being done by the crystal kingdoms and the elements and the grids
I'M NOT GOING TO GET INTO THAT AGAIN!!!
TT You just need a seminar in which a lot of healing
and alignments take place in which you get all the explanation.
7/8, 12:46am **Koz Kozmos**
i don't feel human, be glad to get out of this body
7/8, 12:46am **Pre View**
Do you feel like you belong to another star system?
7/8, 12:46am **Koz Kozmos**
I feel despair , and vague indifference , sick of it all
scared that this will go on too long
7/8, 12:49am **Pre View**
I feel pretty good with the hard work and changes coming in (results i mean)
But i need to be very severe with myself,
I've a lot of courage, to build a life again
7/8, 12:50am **Koz Kozmos**
i'm trying this , but i have little hope, 53 is too late
7/8, 12:50am **Pre View**
Hey Koz, age cannot ever matter, age is tied to time
Letzz go timeless . We can transform at any age.
7/8, 12:50am **Koz Kozmos**
i just want a place to go to were i can live a quite invisable life and die
7/8, 12:52am **Pre View**
To have a life, it is important to get some joy
7/8, 12:52am **Koz Kozmos**
age is just age , i don't know wot joy is ,
i'm no longer interested age depends on the bodies' functions too
7/8, 12:54am **Pre View**
You should try to build up your passion for art once again and with that comes the healing of your physical body.
7/8, 12:54am **Koz Kozmos**
all i do is kill time , i've failed ,
tried more than most i can't get any healing

7/8, 12:55am **Pre View**
Why can u not get any healing? That's absurd and foolish,
it creates madness if you stay in such a downgrading space.
7/8, 12:55am **Koz Kozmos**
no idea , maybe , i just can't fix these things
and as u said u can't trust the docs, and i've found it to be the same with healers
7/8, 12:56am **Pre View**
May i ask what u do to repair yourself?
I mean sigils are not particularly going to do the job,
there is more input needed for things such as languages and symbols to work...
7/8, 12:57am **Koz Kozmos**
i focus and try to heal and reprogram my mind and try alternative remedies ,
i try to keep fit
7/8, 12:57am **Pre View**
It obviously doe not go deep enough.
7/8, 12:57am **Koz Kozmos**
in the mental, physical and spirtual i'm deep enuff to be shallow
i've no idea hoe deep it goes , i just do wot i can do
its the damage i received from being here
its the lack of any real purpose
7/8, 1:01am **Pre View**
But reprogramming does not get the shit out of your receptor cells,
The body has the capacity to continually recalculate and vibrate up into the higher spaces of intelligence. There is mathematical grid to which we can connect and ask for the degrees of higher calculations. And YES, again, you need a foundation to be able to get that grid in...
7/8, 1:01am **Koz Kozmos**
i don't understand wot you just said , it has no meaning and is useless to me
7/8, 1:03am **Pre View**
There is a whole theory around mathematics and how it works, but TT
I felt very bad in my body until I was around 40, I felt like a crippled being ,and now I feel more fit then ever because of all the LIGHT WORK I've been performing in and around the body as it also changes the environment.
Just saying the results are incredible when working in the gridzz...
7/8, 1:03am **Koz Kozmos**
in wot way were u crippled ?
my mother is a cripple in all body parts so i know about cripples
could u re grow a limb ?
i know nothing about mathematics, even at it most basic
7/8, 1:05am **Pre View**
With "crippled" I mean to say that I was always tired, pain in all the bones, muscles, looking bad, no
energy,etc...
All of that changed very quickly as I started to work with Light Technology and bringing upgrades through.
Also, I had my blood checked, and they said it looked like the blood test of young people...
7/8, 1:06am **Koz Kozmos**
sounds like Chronic fatigue syndrome ,
I mean your situation of feeling like a crippled person..
7/8, 1:07am **Pre View**
no, worse
7/8, 1:07am **Koz Kozmos**
maybe due to your abuse ?
I have a friend wit GFS and they are bed ridden...
were u bed ridden ?

7/8, 1:08am **Pre View**
Gosh no!no i was not bed ridden, I just moved transitions through
I have a very strong will , I was just feeling crippled (not in a totally real sense
(tired all the time) like most when they get into their 40
7/8, 1:09am **Koz Kozmos**
my friend has the strongest will of any one I've ever known
so its my lack of will for all the fuck up's and theirs ? thats insulting, blame the victim
...
7/8, 1:11am **Pre View**
You're a very strong willed and determined man, I have no doubt
And we all have different issues and experiences that need to come to some level of understanding, acceptance and then release,
Just the way it is
Blaming anything does not get us anywhere
7/8, 1:11am **Koz Kozmos**
you'r not able to hold a conversation
this is a waste of my time
7/8, 1:15am **Koz Kozmos**
u need to work on being concise before u get back to your delusions of grandeur
i'm not pissed off , just saying it as it is
7/8, 1:16am **Pre View**
Are u concise ?
7/8, 1:17am **Koz Kozmos**
when i need to be: for intance wen explaining something
i can avoid contradiction, but i can't always remember wot we talked about like 2 weeks back 7/8, 1:21am **Pre View**
Many times u tell me u are confused,
7/8, 1:22am **Koz Kozmos**
there are inevitable contradiction over a period of many chats
7/8, 1:29am **Pre View**
I will give it some thinking and get more precise in the conversations.
The heart is the strongest electrical field , try and understand from the heart!
7/8, 1:29am **Koz Kozmos**
best not litsen to me , i'm deleting face book and getting rid of my pc in the next month when i've writen up stuff to sue
It is particularly targeted toward people who like to dole out advice (preach). If you're going to tell others what to do, you better hold yourself to the same standard.
i'm down
7/8, 1:32am **Pre View**
Just another chemical process, no more Koz Kozmic jukebox ?
7/8, 1:33am **Koz Kozmos**
i need to avoid things for good
its all 'hell' to me it gives me something to aid in killing time i'm so down ,
i've not drunk and hardly smoke for 5 weeks
and been doing more exercise and getting things done but its no good when i talk to u
,
i realize how down i am
7/8, 1:37am **Pre View**
Learn about the power of the brain to lock into some new space to bring new quantum possibilities in.It is all also a matter of self esteem, self worth ,
CONFUSION IS DUALITY, SOUL EXPERIENCE!
We need to get clear in our personal desires because the field out there can only work with what we invite. We need to tap into the higher levels of imagination and recreate every thought! Which recreates experiences.

That is reason why some mantra's work for some and some not is the difference between what some kind of electrical output in the brain allows or not.
7/8, 1:37am **Koz Kozmos**
i don't want to hurt u or make u feel down
you're getting something out of your efforts, I don't
7/8, 1:39am **Pre View**
Yes, my efforts are paying off, but i need to work a little harder yet
Everything is literally technology, the heart technology
If you like it or not,,, APPS ON YOUR IPHONE = TECHNOLOGY,
yet easily accepted Apps in Light are as easy as app on your phone
7/8, 1:40am **Koz Kozmos**
i look out at the street and the lamps and the cars i am no part of this, and never wanted to be
7/8, 1:40am **Pre View**
neither am i
But I've been planted here for some reason,
so I will respect it and bring through the services I'm asked to bring through
7/8, 1:40am **Koz Kozmos**
imagine every thing u had ever done back fired , and it all came to nothing
how would u feel ? its impossible for u to say
7/8, 1:41am **Pre View**
THOUGHT AND FEELING NEED TO FUSE!!!
On the same positive level, that creates the highest level
focus and thus manifestation happens or MAJIC!
7/8, 1:42am **Koz Kozmos**
my life is a horrror story
i feel like i've keep being punched and now the wound willl never heal ,
at least its killling me
7/8, 1:42am **Pre View**
U told me u wrote about your life : Can i read about it ?
7/8, 1:43am **Koz Kozmos**
no
7/8, 1:44am **Pre View**
You need to challenge yourself!and allow new experiences
I am tired, i'm getting some sleep now
please do not destroy your poems
7/8, 1:44am **Koz Kozmos**
but i need to build a fire and live in a top floor flat
poetry and poets are odious to me i'm ashamed i ever involved myself good night
7/8, 1:46am **Pre View**
Good night Jimmy, good night
7/8, 1:47am **Koz Kozmos**
I can't chat anymore, its not fair to u
7/8, 2:30am **Koz Kozmos**
I just hope that I'm going thru some deep healing
and i will come out the other side
7/8, 10:07am **Pre View**
IMAGINE IT and blow your beliefs in a new space
BELIEF THROUGH THE HEART Please, never feel ashamed of anything.
I'm very glad u've opened up to me.
I'm only realizing i'm caring a lot about u
& therefore wish u'd never feel lonely & down,,,
It is very important to envision new possibilities and be specific,
otherwise the universe cannot give it to you or very limited,,,

7/8, 10:14am **Pre View**
I'm ashamed I never got a university degree.
There was no money, or my parents were only interested in my sister and treated me as their cinderella
7/8, 12:40pm **Koz Kozmos**
now you're putting your self down....,
its not shame, its frutration
my life has destroyed me , you're not stupid
I'm dyslexic and not have been in school since i was 11
maybe we have both accessed something to do with our spark
7/8, 1:24pm **Koz Kozmos**
eye am my main influence
7/8, 10:32pm **Koz Kozmos**
I'm not a big J Denver fan,
even tho' he's really talented and dead
but always luved this song
7/8, 10:34pm Koz Kozmos
MUSIC John Denver - "The Eagle and the Hawk"

7/8, 10:38pm **Koz Kozmos**
Kozkozmos knows all the secret songs hidden
in the gate fold sleeves of the ancient dayz 7/8, 10:39pm **Koz Kozmos**
MUSIC: Song for a Windmill - Alan Hull

7/8, 10:42pm **Koz Kozmos**
the eagle and the hawk is by far the best of these 2
7/9, 8:39am **Pre View**
U said : "maybe we have both accessed something to do with our spark" ???
What is a spark really? There is no education but self-education.
We need to do the insider work which is getting rid of the emotional pain body that attracts lower substances. It is all about holding the focus on the release, the subtraction of dense energies and not let self be drawn away by any disgraced consciousness .
7/9, 9:07am **Pre View**
I am spending my time in my Peaceful seat and In THE GRIDS which is necessary for me now as we both need to rise like the Phoenix and do what is being asked of us.
Complaint subtracts growth,
U need to figure this out for your self! The answers are all in the GRID because they are energy that
communicates to your energy and thus the importance of being aligned to the Divine!
Practicing "I AM ONE WITH MY SOURCE" and integrating this mantra would already assist you a lot while strengthening your meditational space....
The Eagle and the Hawk : it is indeed a lovely song. Why is it that I love everything that is "powerful" ? I remember my teens these days :
i used to spent a lot of time in Spain with my parents, we had a house there in the mountains near to Barcelona.
All I ever did was leave early in the morning to spend time on the beach, observing people, and then return late at night - walking many hours back to get home instead of taking a car or asking to drive me home.
I needed that. My parents were never interested in me, never asked me anything (except to do all the dirty work for them)
They never asked my sister anything. I never complained,
nor did i ever talk,
Just looked them straight in the eyes.

People used to call me “Sunshine” just because i would always turn all negatives into a positive vibe when i was a kid, in my teens ... This is also reason why i like "Sunshine" John Denver - more connected to the
movie "Sunshine" which i keep into my heart since i was 15 or so.
7/9, 9:47am **Pre View**
I like who you are "Kozkozmos” knows all the secret songs hidden
in the gate fold sleeves of the ancient days" :
Very gorgeous Expression! You have a beautiful gift with the way you word poetry through,... U lift me up with any song u post, u know exactly what i need
What are the "Ancient of Days", what are the "Recent of Days" ?
There is nothing i love more then getting up early in the morning and talk to u for hours. I guess u can hear me.
I will not downgrade our Essence any longer through chats, we are worth the best , not the downgrade of misunderstandings.
Maybe there is a way out, soon, I need to get stronger, more athletic and hold onto to that when i'm finished with clearing my old attachments.
Lets move our voltage from a 100 Watt light bulb
into a 300 Watt light bulb or into a 1000 Watt lightbulb.
Light within should feel like fine feathers,,,
recreating themselves all of the time
7/9, 12:59pm **Koz Kozmos**
I can't tell u about the spark: yo’re either on fire or in the dark
All these emotions sound a bit like a Vulcan ...
The damage has been done via negative programs: i would also like to kill the perpetrators How can u get rid of all emotions? simple explanation with none of your catch phrases , and why ? U sound privileged via cash as a kid...
I did a lot old cleaning as a child. My mother was obsessive, my father a drunk
I wish my dayz were over
I wear ear plugs all of the time and hate the sound of sparrow chirping in the morning, it makes me manic, wakes me and disturbs me
I can’t hear anything apart from noise that I hate
i want complete silence, i am downgraded , nearly destroyed ...
unable to really cope
u have these notions of change, its done for me
7/9, 1:26pm Koz Kozmos
MUSIC Fields Of The Nephilim - Subsanity

7/9, 1:27pm **Koz Kozmos**
if your ears aren't bleeding u can't hear anything!
7/9, 1:33pm **Koz Kozmos**
The ancient days are a dream, the recent days a nightmare
7/9, 1:43pm **Koz Kozmos**
Kill Out
I just hope it rains and the streets clear of all the sub human waste
my cartoon misanthropy is shifting, but don’t worry it will be back
7/10, 12:02am **Koz Kozmos**
MUSIC: Petula Clark "Don't Sleep In The Subway"

7/10, 6:08am **Pre View**
Good morning Koz, clearing out emotions comes down to clearing out all soul degrees, the ego disorders and total sickness. As always it is being done through LIGHT APPLICATIONS and LIGHT TECHNIQUES that we can download from the cosmic google machine: Your Source and the answers you hear from your Spirit along your Spark. The GRIDZZZZZ will provide you with a good diagnosis and will offer you a good remedy for your symptoms.

It is all light MEDICATION THROUGH MEDITATIONAL DIRECTIONS such as alchemy, the integration and opening of higher light capabilities that override dense consciousness, light languages and our bodies' capability to recalculate purity first. But i'm sure, u must have learned many things to do it your way.
Yet, it is very important to know what kind of Light Rays are best to heal particular diseases or just listen, see and hear what comes through when asking guidances to assist the process of clearing. However, Mastery requires one to know all 22 rays that make up Universal alignments and light body skill. It is when the fun begins ....
Because you start your own experiment with light integration and formulas.
I always get the best DESIGNS through when running because that is when my circulation system is at its highest level.
Here is an example of old recycled patterns that I eliminate from the past: anger, little fears, deceit, attachments, associations, addictions, all old instructions connected to the new age downgrade, elimination of relations that do not serve our growth, judgment, self-manipulations, control mechanisms, old ways of thinking, frustrations, confusions, ...
With each emotion i also dig a little deeper : eg : to what is a certain level of fear connected which can be situations, people, teachers, a million things .....
So, it is loads of work but doable as i can feel the body gets more and more refined every day, on all levels , and mentality changes a lot.
But Hey I'M NOT A LIFE COACH!
I AM A BONDING PERSON, and I love healing people with all these many techniques
I've learned...It is so rewarding to see them change from within.
7/10, 6:17am **Koz Kozmos**

7/10, 6:17am **Pre View**
This post makes me feel sick : this has nothing to do with how we operate today. We are in the New Tree of Life, not the old downgrades of soul which u are showing me here. It teaches no-thing! We are a very complicated network of multiple interconnections when speaking about nerves and thus energy wheels all need to be reset into evolution and synchronizing with what the universe brings through today. All 12 energy wheels need to fuse and explode into one single field of light.
ALL COLORS HAVE CHANGED; But hey, u are posting A GRID!!!!
How amusing is this huh?
7/10, 6:22am **Pre View**
It is a bit like creating science merged with spirit and moving into futuristic brain performances. Clearing the whole network within is very revealing and uplifting. It takes all of my focus, respect, and of course fearless learning every day ,,,, which is not simple because i only have myself and universal support to count on and trust deeper every day.
7/10, 6:28am **Pre View**
Trust and Faith is all we have! And all we need to move on,,,
7/10, 6:46am **Pre View**
There is no room for justification principles enjoyed by the masses when clearing, for me it is very strict 24/24 focus with my source and learning.
The magnetic chords of the Matrix SET EVERYTHING BACKWARDS!!!
and thus the reason why so much information came through the "soul" sort of upside down, completely twisted and incorrect. Just have a look at what people still believe when watching the movie that FB represents and presents every day!
It's because they CANNOT SEE how much their brains are being kept in old cycles. They seem to love digesting CRAP when it comes to spiritual training, empowerment and development. I have a good deep vision of how the old spiritual movement is going to be put on a halt.There is no information, upgrades or at least some training that catapults the brainwaves into universal alignments.
KNOWING OUR ORIGIN AND SOME HISTORY is going to be very important when it comes to bringing out the identity of our Spark such as through the Art that we are. What advances me most is Crystalline grids, tracks (no i'm not going to go into that any longer nor will i explain it) this is not for FB.
What i can say though : I've never found it more interesting then to dig deep into the solar plexus beyond the false Lion's Gate connected to it for power of control purposes.
So much hatred comes from it that has no space in heaven. Anger can be eliminated, but hatred.... It is because the soul has lost ALL connector links it had . I cannot explain this any further as it takes all of my energy, a workshop would get it all down.
7/10, 6:48am **Pre View**
I have one question for u today : if u have knowledge, why is this knowledge not giving u all the information to step out of everything that brings you down, by which i mean that u give fault to everything outside of u, while everything resides inside... It's the soul trick thing...
7/10, 6:53am **Pre View**
You really need to decide to step out of your misanthropy!
Thank U !!! Very beautiful song - Petula Clark.
Oh, these magnificent subways, they reveal, they detail
7/10, 7:06am **Pre View**
I wish i could feel a Jimmy turned Pearlescent, the beauty u truly are.
Its because I care about u.
I can only give you what I Am and becoming
7/10, 7:23am **Pre View**
Turn your asteroids into Gold huh!
7/10, 7:26am **Pre View**
These are underwater Arcs of Light that bring through a lot of healing.
The Silver sort of species represents spirit.
It's essentially about the fusion of water and fire...

So here you have an example how you can work healing through with the symbolism of Arcs because Arcs carry very high intelligent levels of consciousness that can literally break through anything. Therefor, my Art are all meditational healing sessions so to speak because they flow out of my hands after meditation. That is actually the most passionate thing one can do: just paint until there is a concept flowing through....

Artwork: "Eternal Light Arcs

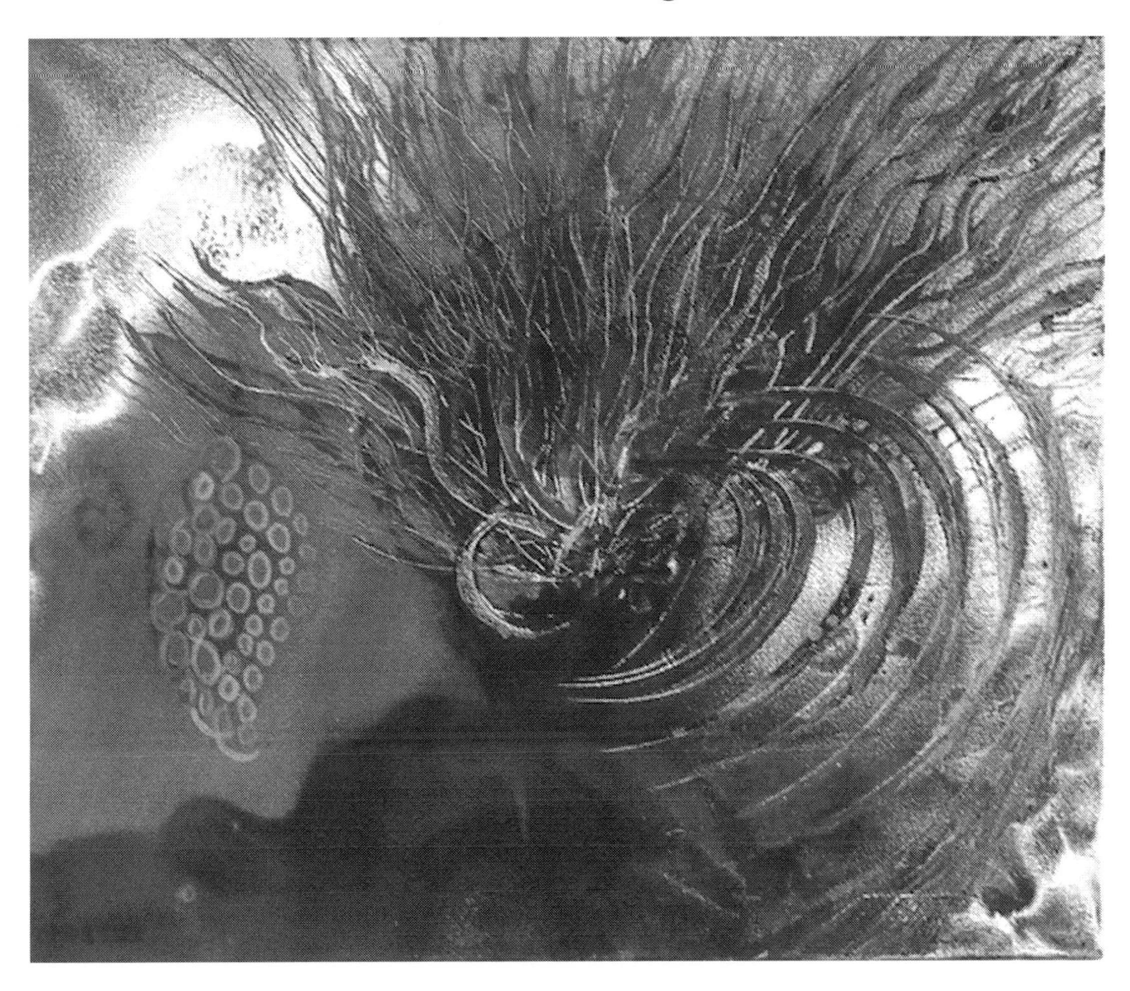

7/10, 7:34am **Koz Kozmos**
I'm guided by nothing and have lost my instruction booklet, or was that a dream that I had ? Or was it a vague child hood memory of when I built a model 38 airplane ?
I'm 53 and have said on many occasions , I agree about your post
You're like a specialist science magazine for new age geeks
I have no trust or faith....why should I ? I'll avoid the sacred space then ...
I have to skip over a lot of your tech...i've lost interest in it
i have no knowledge, as i said ; I'm lost, confused and I also said broken
I've been up an hour and I've already had enuff...
Have u thought of doing any pics of cutie kittenz ?
Luveeee ur art, very exclusive
7/10, 1:23pm **Koz Kozmos**
MUSIC: Sun Ra - Space is the place (1974)

7/10, 7:36am **Pre View**
I wish U a wonderful day.

As u can notice, I rise with the Sun these days and go to bed early
(Thank u for the post SUN RA - Egypt) ! I wish I knew something about RA.
7/10, 1:24pm **Koz Kozmos**
not seen thiz Sun Ra clip, looks koool, Egypt has always bored me
7/10, 1:56pm Koz Kozmos
MUSIC: Limbonic Art - Darkzone Martyrium

7/10, 2:34pm **Koz Kozmos**
All i feel is hatred and disgust , u should reconnect with your emotions
Sub sanity was the best song ... Take care Nic
7/11, 7:53am **Pre View**
NONONO!!! Dark music, Kittenz ? No! I love dogs,
This SunRa, yep kool.
There is nothing i avoid more then google info, with some exceptions of course.
Don't like Egypt either, I landed there somehow for a few weeks to clear out spaces
couldn't get home soon enough,,,.Why should I reconnect with my emotions
7/11, 12:48pm **Koz Kozmos**
Because u said : "We are all our main influence :
there is but one way to move on which is getting rid of ALL emotions"
7/11, 1:30pm **Koz Kozmos**
MUSIC: HARPO – Movie Star

MUSIC: Clout - Substitute (1978)

7/11, 1:34pm **Koz Kozmos**
I need some gaudy satin trousers
7/11, 3:05pm **Pre View**
Oeps, oh yeah just go & get these trousers ! They'll be great on u.
I just came home with pink trousers & pink high heeled glamor shoes, Leather fetish jacket tailor made and painted my nails. Gonna dance through the streets now like a movie star, I just love dancing throughout the streets, I don't care what people think,,,
The world is a weird place,,,
7/11, 8:39pm **Koz Kozmos**
sounds a bit unlady like to me
its wyrd not weird
7/12, 1:46am Koz Kozmos
MUSIC: Wino - Adrift, Live in Athens (12/10/2010)

ARTWORK: "COSMOLOGICAL LIFT" by PreView
Just to give u another way of expressing Arc consciousness

MY INTERNALS: How will we rebuild communities through love, integrity, respect, genuine empathy and create a new awareness through new thought forms and CRYSTAL CLEAR BRAINS that are healed from anything termed dysfunctional. We are all some sort of wounded healers and everybody can help out anybody if only THE WILL within or free will makes place for Divine Will that redirects our Essence into THE GREEN LITE GO WORLD.
So many people live similar to Koz's experiences, so many have different ideas about Light embodiment and progress into the Light Atmospheres; Not so many work hard to get there is what I feel. A good doze of trust and some luck along the jumpy roads would help. Simple tech such as working through geometrical patterns that lift vibes like when moving with a Multi Universal aircraft. When it is felt, it is believed I guess, yet most lack the patience to get into the fields of Light in which we feel every effort as a Bliss factor. Understanding comes with many experience, and be DARING ENOUGH NOT TO GIVE UP. That is Faith and the best of lessons to integrate as PROOF comes after Faith, yet most would like to see it the other way around;
Everybody needs more understanding and compassion as every culture goes through many processes and we need to live in the present in the now moment to bring our natural wisdom back to life. The reality of truth and what it means comes more and more into focus and reveals a lot of history to where we were all broken and abused in so many ways.
Every day brings through a new way to awaken regarding institutions that no longer work. We need to re-establish health, education, wealth, business. Navigating through Space without knowledge and directions is no good.
A new network of communication/conversations should open up in which there is room for philosophy where people feel supported and learn about magical thinking.
We definitely need to leave the complexity that society imposed upon us that created so many imbalances. The simplicity of life comes back into creation as soon as people really want to grow up. Making the world a better place is happening, but we did not expect it to be so demanding in ways that we need to fight the injustices and at the same time return into the purity of being through our Light system, our energy field and the expansion through our ORIGIN. We need to open a space in which people are willing to learn and take responsibility for their psychology.

When kindness and affection gets lost and feeling is being checkmated.... : IT IS ONLY FEAR ! NOTHING IS A FAILURE, EVERYTHING IS MERELY EXPERIENCE MOVING YOU FROM ONE SPACE INTO ANOTHER OR NEW DIRECTIONS. The more we experience, the stronger we get, the easier we will move into destined surroundings where life moves in balance with everything we are. Balance and harmonious relationships, passionate jobs, quality time spent with self and others while releasing the old standards that have put you in the lower senses and equally attracted anything that matches that. Its hard to change when FEAR stands in the way of almost anything . The old mindset which is 100% fear, multiply that with 100% unworthiness and low self esteem and no ethics and we get the whole package that will hold us back from any prosperity, abundance and success on any level because our health, happiness, enjoyment, human values and money flow are completely out of balance.

DETACHMENTS, REDIRECTIONS, SUPPORT ON ANY CHOSEN LEVEL ...moves in when FEAR HAS BEEN RELEASED. ENERGY FIELDS SHOULD BE SELF SUSTAINING OTHERWISE WE GET EXHAUSTED and getting into trouble with emotions and then the mind stands up and makes even more trouble, argues and debates with many candidates in the body to make you feel even worse. We need to reorganize the body and the brain, and gain insight in the deeper levels of mentality that often time blinds us from seeing what needs to be seen.
Will I ever be able to redirect Koz? with self supportive programs as we are all continuously traveling between worlds, unlearning thousands of years of conditioning. Many are facing the final release of the emotional body that makes room for the higher senses in the heart for the clearer we get, the more we notice and ALLOW that passionate vibration that nudges us to go in that space where you make it all happen.

At this point I also felt really tired of explaining and listening to complaints. I had the motivation to ride the higher waves and actually wanted him to move along with me on that higher road in a way that his input from his knowledge in music could perfectly resurrect him and bring a deeper understanding of Light integration.
I started to heal emotions within him, my son and a friend of mine all at once, in one session which can be done by just pulling the energies through a photo.
It was as if we had reached a point of culmination, the connection we had could not work in this type of vibration any longer.
So I cleared resistance, stubbornness, indecisiveness and addictions all at once by pulling through some Hebrew letters as I loved working with that back then: Chet (the cream ray and high healing vibe)+ Reish(the iolite ray, very much connected to the elements and extremely strong when it comes to the repair of communication in the throat)+ Teith (the pearlescent ray and feels more like a real blessing).
I would set this healing session in a Turquoise Grid with a Green ray pulse of a Lemniscate that eliminates at the speed of light.
Along that I would always work with the Orange ray and sonar waves that penetrate very deep, also in sections of the body that feel completely blocked off.
To clarify: this may seem a lot to many people and is actually not needed, one may as well just work with one ray through the release of any emotion.
I am so in love with ray formulas, so I could easily combine Cream/Pearlescent/ Iolite in a turquoise grid and move that along a Green ray Lemniscate and orange sonar waves that penetrate in a very direct way. It is also because I have a very deep and ancient connection to the dolphins and the Wales community that I apply many other techniques shown to me in meditation.
I would run most of the healing through the pituitary gland and the hypothalamic + some elimination through the central nervous system, with deep attention to the vagus nerve.

Another example of healing that I performed on him was more generated to get him out of his stress levels, frustrations, impulsiveness and fear: I would work a lot on the elimination through the dopamine receptors in the brain, the cerebral cortex and the motor mechanisms in the amygdala. Apart from that I felt that his thalamus gland was overstimulated which is also connected to the fusion of music and language and part of it to dyslexia. Everything in the brain is actually interconnected to everything in the body. It was not easy to get details through as a lot of work needed to be done on his body. When a person feels stressed out and frustrated, we tend to get totally disinterested. My healing sessions were more like a serene that moved through the basal ganglia from the brainstem, into the striatum and thalamus gland and getting his flight syndrome out of the adrenal glands.
It is actually endless what we can heal in a short amount of time and may require a little bit of study when it comes to the anatomy of the human body. This learning zone is so very rich that it stimulated me in many ways to try out many different things and listen to the information I could get beyond my imagination. In this session I would work with the white ray to purify, the lavender ray to transform and release and always with the Blue ray to keep an open flow along my favorite iolite ray.

I would always end up by balancing his essence into some deep peace and acceptance with the Blue ray, the Smokey quartz ray and the Golden flow.
HEALING TECHNIQUES need some level of understanding through practice and knowledge of the first 22 rays because it is all simply part of us. Remember, IN THE GRID! After that, we can start to work with the grandeur of many other rays, never seen on earth like copper infused rays, pearlescent rays, fluorescent rays, gemstone rays, elements infused rays... that open up, SOMEWHERE OVER THE RAINBOW, as they say.
My healings are very strong as I combine so many elements. It is just part of my special skill, it does not mean we all have to apply these examples, we can go very simplistic and have great results. Does it not all depend on our passion.
Taking a flight with a Green dodecahedron may have as much impact as any design, it is all within the focus and what we do with it, or our intention that is being fed by intuitive levels of imagination. Let's remember LIFE with the STARS.

7/12, 1:47am **Koz Kozmos** live in the studio
7/12, 1:47am Koz Kozmos
MUSIC: Wino - Adrift

7/12, 1:47am **Koz Kozmos**
great song
7/12, 7:56am **Pre View**
I was in one of the most important fashion shops down town were they allowed some of my art for sale.
They wanted to take some pics of me with the paintings, high fashion clothes .. and thus the story with my Pink outfit.
7/12, 8:09am **Pre View**
Wino , yes its indeed a wonderful song. I like Wino, never heard of him.
Thank you for posting,,,
7/12, 1:08pm **Koz Kozmos**
go for it with your art , infiltrate and destroy
there is a heat wave this weekend and I'm trapped in the attic
too many humans on the street, things can get worse
even after a thousand years of positive visualizations
7/12, 1:21pm **Koz Kozmos**
I feel healthier , come outa my crash , but always feel uneasy
there is no reason for me to be here and never has been,
at least i'lll get to die alone ,
and now ROKK
7/12, 1:29pm **Koz Kozmos**
MUSIC: GRAND MAGUS – Summer Solstice

7/12, 2:26pm **Pre View**
sure, lets keep the fire burning,
7/12, 2:27pm **Koz Kozmos**
mine is dead , I can find no reason to burn , feeling wiped again have been sneezing , maybe hay fever
7/12, 2:32pm **Pre View**
let's take it easy
i fell on the ground today, and may need to get my knee fixed in hospital due to a drunk fucktard over here and somebody stupid called the cops,,,
everyday life it is,
7/12, 2:32pm **Koz Kozmos**
your life sounds like chaos sometimes
7/12, 2:33pm **Pre View**
but i feel ok, just tired
7/12, 2:33pm **Koz Kozmos**
clean your knees and use some lavender oil and tea tree
i feel lost and completly bored
7/12, 2:33pm **Pre View**
lavender oil, very good idea, thx!
I love pathouli and a good breeze of roses
7/12, 2:34pm **Koz Kozmos**
i've really had enufff ,
but all i'm doing is complaining,
i have no life

7/12, 2:36pm **Pre View**
I feel a bit empty as well, probably energy transitions between galaxies
I wonder how to enter every galaxy, every universal model
Do u know what u really want besides money ?
7/12, 2:37pm **Koz Kozmos**
i've just closed the window , i don't even want the sound of the street and thats with ear plugs in and head phones on,
soorry Nic
7/12, 2:40pm **Pre View**
Ho can you just live with these earplugs in all of the time?
7/12, 2:40pm **Koz Kozmos**
I'm not a negative self obsessed bore, i get that to people are always in the way
looking like shit with their 5 kids,,, dumb breeders
the ear plugs are bad ,
i've had infections and lost my hearing in one ear in the past but i can't cope with out them, and i'm a clean #machine
7/12, 2:44pm **Pre View**
there is just so much grieve within you ....
I need to stop talking Koz, please understand Need to take care of my knee
Maybe talk later ?
7/12, 2:44pm **Koz Kozmos**
take care , glad about your art and the shop
i'lll be around if u need to talk about stufff, i can help
7/12, 2:45pm **Pre View**
ok, thank u, thank u for being here, ...
7/12, 2:46pm **Koz Kozmos**
my pleasure , power in the darknesss, luv in the light
7/12, 5:34pm **Pre View**
U told me u learned about luve
I did not ,I guess... I want these higher sensations in which all emotional content is cut of,,,
MUSIC: Lauren Hill & Wyclef – killing me softly

7/12, 5:58pm **Pre View**
Thx for reminding me of the oils ....
Is your fever coming to rest?
Grand Magus - Summer Solstice : u posted this about 2 months ago and back then i felt completely different with this song. This time around I have # associations, and thus the song feels so much better
7/12, 7:12pm **Koz Kozmos**
Killing me softly was Written about Don McLean,
Who wrote and sang American pie etc and was first sang by Roberta Flack
My fever is a bland sweat of infinite boredom
Everything we feel is maybe associations and other things that are hard to define, and I don't like it
7/12, 7:26pm **Koz Kozmos**
I'm permanently hurt , I learnt about the heart and luv as a power source
I have had no luv, u have to look after your self
retreat and go into battle with wisdom
7/12, 7:39pm **Koz Kozmos**
REALLY BAD VIDEO, JUST LISTEN TO THE SONG,
and don' take it too seriouly
7/12, 7:40pm **Koz Kozmos**
MUSIC: gnome and me...Video by Joel Warshawer ...
You Are Danger by Chip Taylor

Maybe a Psychedelic selection from the KK Juke Box
7/12, 7:55pm **Koz Kozmos**
MUSIC: The Seeds - Pushin' Too Hard

7/12, 7:55pm **Koz Kozmos**
more to come , wot an era
things have always been crap
but once they were less crap the squares in the audience are a real drag man
7/13, 8:21am **Pre View**
"retreat and go in to battle with wisdom" ? :
Wisdom is something to build with, it can never go into
battle with anything. Intelligence, knowledge and wisdom can be achieved in this age
I believe. The seeds may be found when we reset the biggest industry – the
entertainment world and invent programs that bring wisdom through gaming for
example. I'm thinking about opening new connections through communication.
Its all more about lifting the community and give a helping hand to the challenges
and struggles people go through.
7/13, 8:27am **Pre View**
I'm going to visit some friends today which i've known for more then 30 years.
They're not so clever & regret they cannot help me because they never encountered
such complicated problems,,, but thy have a heart that speaks loudly which gives me
great relaxation. I think everybody is clever and has great capacity to move beyond
fear. With them i can do & speak as i wish, no limitations ,,, maybe i'll just stay for a
couple of days, maybe i'll return after a few hours, they know i'm like a quick wind,
always blowing through fresh air or new avenues. It may not be Hollywood
Boulevard, it is better, because it's my own Boulevard..;;
7/13, 11:19am **Pre View**
When Existence lacks creation there is nothing but boredom.
You need to take action and learn to do things you enjoy in order to create a new
"U"with yur wize potentials, & never think of the negatives of the past again.
U are a Crafty Creator! Keep it that way!
I guess business is what reflects who we are in the end.
It is important for you to let go of the ATTACHMENT of failure, and the attachment
to attachment. Learn from your difficult life, learn how to move out of your targeted
brain-set!!! Because that is what it essentially is.
Think in terms of rewriting your life: WRITE about it,
and watch how it makes you feel,
WITHOUT LETTING ANY low emotion in. Write so much in a way that you truly
become the life you are rewriting,, I am choosing to align anew,
and find the origin of my Ark!
Push the delete button to the past is what sets you free,
especially when it comes to detoxing from fake people that eat our loyalty.
I am adjusting my sacral to vibratory rates that uphold so many unknown potentials
I can feel that so deep. I want and need new skills for my art,
I want upgrades in that kind of flow. Flow is not flow when we keep on repeating the
same old ways of doing things,,,
That is when boredom pops up because motivation needs to feed you like breakfast...
First thing in the morning and then set the day you're going to live equally.
Over thc years, I never lost courage,
I always feel my power , my elements that push me further. Courage is not
something you can just eat , but it can be encoded in the brain-set,
such as through light alignments,
symbols, anything creative that matches our thought processes.
Please let ur love not get tainted!
Please play the chords that once filled yur vibes with joy & laughter
Please pen the words that penetrate deeper each day into those in need
and make your self useful

Please design a LIFE that you really want and start to feel your visions...
That is what it is all about, changing intentions, bringing new intentions in, while loading the movie that gets us there.
I'm not a life coach, don't like that term.
I AM A BONDING PERSON that wants to serve people and get their highest potentials written all over their brains.
I really love people so much, don't know why or how come, its in my blood;;;
Maybe I should start talking in the hood and give people some experiences about how it feels when we are connected to our Source, our Spirit and what kind of meaning that could bring into their lives. Universal support comes when we get to train with our team and co-create through so many options,,,,
7/13, 12:59pm **Koz Kozmos**
I have no friends and no one to visit , i am completely alone and I'm trapped
I am massively creative and bored ,the negatives are not always all in the past
I'm dealing with shit all the time, I don't think I've experiences joy & laughter
I've TRIED TO DESIGNE A LIFE FOR MYSELF
MUSIC: Tupac -Ambitionz Az A Ridah

7/13, 1:26pm **Koz Kozmos**
hope u have a nice time
7/13, 1:37pm **Koz Kozmos**
wonder did i post this one before?
I don'r care about dreamz anymore
7/13, 1:42pm **Koz Kozmos**
MUSIC: Gabrielle Dreams

7/15, 10:28am **Pre View**
People always ask me a bunch of questions
and expect me to solve their little silly ridiculous dramas.
I am a bit like honey to them - full of energy, there are plenty of good answers to any question : thy wonder how i do this
Perhaps we need to look within people from many dimensions,
many ways of life, many eyes,
7/15, 10:34am **Pre View**
Tupac huh : Gracia, i like what they do,,,
I can feel yur pain, its like my heart is running wild every time i open these posts of u.
Its hurts my deep, deeper every day.
7/15, 10:54am **Pre View**
Having nobody to talk 2 must be unbearable, terrible
I mean we all need just some body to understand our pain
Even if we have to solve our challenges ourselves, expressing ourselves is already a relieve. Communication is needed.Anger, hatred and boredom need to be transformed for it keeps people driving through self created pollution.
It sometimes opens new perspectives when seeing things and understanding what happened to us --- viewing it from different angles helps a lot because the learning zone and insight offer also some degrees of intelligence that keeps the courage and strength moving into more action oriented highways. And yes, I know , it takes work, but keeping up with lower senses and painful situations takes just as much work and gets people depressed while light spectacles embrace hope. That is all there is to it.
7/15, 11:06am **Pre View**
Jimmy, please Dream again, just one more time ?
Dream ur pain out !!!!
We need to get rid of our anger, anger only puts us up with more shit!!!
Because it offers the monsters such as the reptilians an OPEN GATE
to sneak in and break consciousness

Talk as much as you want, but please bring the STOP SIGN to your negative brainwaves
I never experienced luv either, it was always a one way street in which i lost myself over & over, I'm done with this now, Life has no meaning without luv, yet luv needs to be reinstalled in the heart and as long as people keep on functioning through the mind control, there is no way that can be infused. Its crystal clear,
the true nature of love is a very high vibration only a few know about,
starting with the integration of Self Love.
I can feel that pulsation in my Heart like a wild tropical wind.
I'd like to teach that, the wild wayzzzz, hahaha, rebel style
It is a good way to REMEMBER LIGHT LIVING,
a good way to remember how families could live together in harmony and balance.
YOU must give significance or a new connotation to new options today and really make peace with the past, the way you digested and experienced it must definitely be evaporated from yur breath. Think about brand new opportunities that create new junctures, new connections, a new way of going through life, a new structure that allows to live
within deeper WATER STREAMS.
Making peace means that you give yourself a new positive permission to appreciate new things. When the past keeps on creeping in the brainzzz, there is never forward movement because you are literally
telling the universe that you live in the past.
YOU NEED TO LEAVE THE ADDICTION TO THE PAST because it doesn't allow to enjoy the present moment and allow something that brings passion back in.
REMOVE WHAT REMINDS YOU OFF THE PAST: clothes, cups, furniture, books, social media connections, memories... cooking styles,
Only the PRESENT HAS POTENTIAL because when the past is gone you can really focus or imagine how your day will be. Every single item we hold onto is a container-box that holds deep memories.
Our subconsciousness holds on to quite a collection of baloney flashbacks...
Strength means that you ACCEPT whatever that happened and allow it to flush it through the toilet. You need TO WANT TO UNDERSTAND THAT. CODE IT, CODE IT, CODE IT!
It makes no sense, you need a drive-in into a new night Light Club
with glimmer toes: unlimited!
7/15, 12:25pm **Koz Kozmos**
The luv energy doesn't work like that
I do talk to my body , ahhhhhh no body
i talk to u and Jain Doe
it's damage done from past events and i've vaguly reconnnected with some one I know called Giv there is no one around the corner and I prefer to be alone
I have never stoped dreaming ! did u have a good week end?
7/15, 1:02pm **Koz Kozmos**
did u have a nice time away?
7/15, 1:10pm **Koz Kozmos**
MUSIC: The Emotions - Best Of My Love

7/15, 1:14pm **Koz Kozmos**
one song leads to another , great arrangement on this one
7/15, 1:15pm Koz Kozmos
MUSIC: SHIRLEY BASSEY-THE LOOK OF LOVE

. 7/15, 1:21pm **Koz Kozmos**
always wanted to do a croon long player with an orchestra Wots the best version?
7/15, 2:18pm **Koz Kozmos**
MUSIC: Nina Simone - The Look Of Love

7/15, 2:49pm **Pre View**
Best version : nina simone
Yes, thank u, i had a good time, should do this more often ....
And yes Mister , get your orchestra together and write new music!
7/15, 2:52pm **Koz Kozmos**
thought u 'd say that
July 15, 2013
7/15, 8:02pm **Koz Kozmos**
u in da hood?
7/15, 8:14pm **Koz Kozmos**
hi ? ahhh no no worries
7/15, 9:46pm **Koz Kozmos**
MUSIC: Vaughan Williams ~ The Lark Ascending

7/15, 9:53pm Koz Kozmos
MUSIC: andre popp las mariposas, butterflies papillons

7/15, 9:54pm **Koz Kozmos**
from classical to easy listening to jazz
7/15, 9:54pm **Pre View**
i was enjoying The Lark ,,, makes me feel very lazy
7/15, 9:55pm **Koz Kozmos**
MUSIC: Blue in Green by. Miles Davis

7/15, 9:55pm **Koz Kozmos**
music for a summers evening, i'd like a storm goood night Miles can be so great
7/15, 9:56pm **Pre View**
Sad music, not my thing, I need high vibes
I need glimmering dancing toes
we're not here to hide, but to shine
7/15, 9:57pm **Koz Kozmos**
his collection of sun glasses and funky shirts rivealed mine
7/15, 9:57pm **Pre View**
I like the heat, even wearing a jumper with these 28 degrees outside,
Aha didn't know he had a collection ...
7/15, 9:58pm **Koz Kozmos**
i like the heat but i'm in my atttic salted roof went out today ,
need to stay away from humans
7/15, 9:59pm **Pre View**
Uhuh, what did u do,
i mean when going out
7/15, 9:59pm **Koz Kozmos**
i went to the pool, went into the city ,
came back and felt reallly manic
7/15, 10:00pm **Pre View**
u must have enjoyed something, i hope
create individual symbolism that defeats these manic invasions
That is very powerful
7/15, 10:01pm **Koz Kozmos**
my energ can't handle earth ,
i feel a bit better now
bad night wen i was going out ,
my nervous system short circuits I feel too much,
thank u

7/15, 10:02pm **Pre View**
How do you deal with your nervous system when you get manic?
How does it feel?
7/15, 10:03pm **Koz Kozmos**
body and mind alll out of sync ,wrong signals fireing
apart from that i feel great
7/15, 10:04pm **Pre View**
You feel like a horror movie is what you meant to say huh?
7/15, 10:05pm **Koz Kozmos**
the klone concert , do u know it ?
Keith Jarrett
7/15, 10:05pm **Pre View**
no, wots it about ?
keith , yes
7/15, 10:06pm **Koz Kozmos**
maybe to much music to take in
7/15, 10:06pm **Koz Kozmos**
MUSIC: COUNTRY – Keith Jarrett

7/15, 10:06pm **Koz Kozmos**
not listened to for years , used to play it loads
7/15, 10:08pm **Pre View**
It has been a long long time since i listened to Keith
Good reminder
7/15, 10:08pm **Koz Kozmos**
i wish i was a great musician instead of a songpoet or both ,
anyways, have fun
7/15, 10:08pm **Pre View**
I think u are both
7/15, 10:08pm **Koz Kozmos**
hope your ok , take care , mmmmmmmmm nah ,
goood night
7/15, 10:09pm **Pre View**
ok, take care u 2
7/15, 10:09pm **Koz Kozmos**
kozmik catch again, peace as they say ...
7/15, 10:12pm **Pre View**
u'd never say 'peace' , as thy say it, hahaha
I'd rather have a box of chocolates
7/15, 10:37pm **Koz Kozmos**
but i thought u had a witches cottage made of dark candy
7/15, 11:56pm **Pre View**
tasteless candy formless candy
trafic-less candy
I cannot touch it, it slips thru my fingers!
The night is potent.
The Moon shines forgotten vibes
Fill yer barrels
With diamond Lights and make it a memory tank

7/16, 1:48pm **Koz Kozmos**
MUSIC: 13th floor Elevators - Levitation

7/16, 2:15pm **Pre View**
Great vid - thanx , let's get the action in, the eternal moves .... !!!
7/16, 3:09pm **Koz Kozmos**
always liked this song
7/16, 3:09pm **Koz Kozmos**
MUSIC: Turbonegro - Fuck The World

7/16, 3:09pm **Koz Kozmos**
ace vid ! no more music for today , i'm overloading u
7/16, 6:28pm **Pre View**
i'm greedy, hungry for the most shocking & rocking music
u cannot possibly overload me,
i'm all authentic , reliable and inventive shoes
7/16, 7:09pm **Koz Kozmos**
rock needs to redefine itself ,
straight is the new wyrdo the normal weirdos with their dogs and tattoos anywayz ,
bit uninspired
7/16, 7:14pm **Pre View**
no prob, gonna watch a movie,,,,
7/16, 7:16pm **Koz Kozmos** kool
7/16, 7:36pm **Pre View** OK, had a long shower,
big screen time now
Snazzy flashy outfit u got there,
u look telegenetic, Ok, cya
7/16, 9:31pm **Koz Kozmos**
i alwayz wear shadez
7/16, 10:38pm **Pre View**
I used to teach children meditation and some yoga practise
on the beach after school, about 10 years ....
It was more like half an hour practice and half an hour solving their problems with
their parents, teachers, friends,...they loved it, some still contact me....
It solved so many broken hearts in classes as I provided tools that could be applied
when the ride was going tough in households, especially for youth
I had to be very careful, because the tales I told them about the importance of food
and how it feeds the body;
especially when it come to preparing herbs and veggies and fruits;
most of the time would not fit the ideas of parents.
Kids are dependent and have no free policy in which they can eat what they feel they
need However, I let them taste many good things regarding vegan foods.
It was like I gave them a snack to test every single lesson
Parents and teachers may open up slowly to the application of Meditation as
Medication and explore our Light Origin, its all been held back so much
So much life giving change is needed regarding mental/psychological Health that
definitely needs new territorial spaces to ground within educational system
I'd love to teach in universities, high school or be a psychology counsellor.
Give lectures, give a classes on Light Sciences and replace religion. Professors are so
deep in the power game, it kills students.
i hope to find fashionable ideas to awaken people on different levels,
not easy, but little things can shake up a lot,,,
7/16, 10:41pm **Koz Kozmos**
Yes things need to be broken down, but there are too many toxic childhoods ,
too many damaged adults pretending thier ok
the matrix has to be destroyed, but the problem goes deep,
u need to be careful

7/16, 10:44pm **Pre View**
it makes me feel like vomiting to watch young people being manipulated t
here is always these students who come to me in great despair....
Thy really want to know why their parents don't care,
why society cares even less
they want solutions, so I offer small and kool Light tehniques thy enjoy
they are so young and awakening fast
7/16, 10:44pm **Koz Kozmos**
yes, i understand great dispair
7/16, 10:49pm **Pre View**
Have to deal to much with the police...
EVERY DAY !
7/16, 10:49pm **Koz Kozmos**
why ? ....
7/16, 10:51pm **Pre View**
Euhm, i live 5 minutes from the railway station
and i am the housekeeper of a student home so u can
imagine what can possibly walk in at night,
What i'v been through for the past 18 months is hardly bearable .... Its a long story
The worst is actually happening during the day, like dealing with drug addicts, drunk people, fights,,,,, people on heroine : some managed to enter the building through a hole in the cellar. They sort of made their own home station so to speak until I discovered it.
It was dreadful, I couldn't even get them out of the building as these addicts claimed the cellar to be their home and asked me to leave instead of the other way around.
7/16, 10:52pm **Koz Kozmos**
sounds awful, particular soul types need to go
7/16, 10:53pm **Pre View**
I'm working on it through the grounding of Light Grids that override that type of interference; and it is
incredibly peaceful now....
7/16, 10:53pm **Koz Kozmos**
earth is more than ever a low grade soul experiment and things are being set up for something really bad
7/16, 10:53pm **Pre View**
Who is on top of that experiment?
7/16, 10:53pm **Koz Kozmos**
they want to block any form of awakening, maybe aliens, the Rotschilds? have u got your sunglassses on ? The interdimensional ones?
7/16, 10:54pm **Pre View** Sunglasses, hahaha, great idea , love it
7/16, 10:55pm **Koz Kozmos**
Nagasaki and Hiroshima let in a lot of entites i'd say
maybe i just need to get my body working and destroy
7/16, 10:56pm **Pre View**
right
Do u remember that song Nagaski nightmare,
Whom was it from ?
Wot exercises do u do besides your swimming acrobatics? ?
7/16, 10:57pm Koz Kozmos
MUSIC: Crass Nagasaki Nightmare 1980

7/16, 10:57pm **Koz Kozmos**
i work out a little and am trying to get back into cycling

but my brain fires incorrecly hence the feeling of a need to pee all the time
7/16, 10:58pm **Pre View**
Thank u !
I'v never done cycling, i might try that again tomorrow
I want new things everyday
7/16, 10:58pm **Koz Kozmos**
wen i leave the city i'll cycle as much as i can, and walk ...
cycling in a good place is good
7/16, 10:59pm Koz Kozmos
MUSIC: Ultravox! - Hiroshima Mon Amour (1978)

7/16, 10:59pm **Koz Kozmos**
why do u ask?
7/16, 11:01pm **Pre View**
YOUR NERVES MUST FEEL OVERHEATED?
If you need to pee all the time I'm interested to learn more about your brain,
Why do i ask what ?
7/16, 11:01pm **Koz Kozmos**
about me exsircizing ...
there are other things apart from the pee thing
i'd like to get out of this body or heal ,but i look fit
its good wot u said earlier :
I wonder why i'm thinking about this,,
"The manipulation, the system, the power policy needs to be broken down,, "
7/16, 11:04pm **Pre View**
The awakening, the health problems, the re-education, the truth moves :
it is all moving way too slow;;
7/16, 11:04pm **Koz Kozmos**
i think I'm sensitive and have been damaged , and the wound can never heal here
7/16, 11:06pm **Pre View**
Every body is wounded somehow, we just need to move beyond that
and allow these new phases to enter
our consciousness – or bring through the healing procedures which is all about the
re-education into the Light Atmosperes
I think u need to speak to people .
Why don't you set up meetings and stuff?
7/16, 11:06pm **Koz Kozmos**
its not the same for everybody. Speak to who ?
7/16, 11:07pm **Pre View**
Speak : I don't know, find ways, get paid for it
Raise some ideas in the hood....
7/16, 11:08pm **Koz Kozmos**
I've tried all my life , i'd rather be alone
i have no connnections , no place to start and i've tried too manay times
its not about giving up, its wising up
i have had an abnormal amount of wot may be called 'bad luck'
I've wasted my majik on this dimension
thankz for your suppport
7/16, 11:11pm **Pre View**
I understand, I've had my portion as well especially when it comes to jobs and the
manipulation with wages. The hardest part is bringing the solutions through because
it exhausts us regarding the amount of work it takes to get justice; that is not
justifiable either...U see Koz, i do Little things and expand :
through seminars, lectures...
Yet, universities have put a halt on me as well,
most organizations have put bars on me
because they do not want THEIR TRUTH to be exposed!

7/16, 11:12pm **Koz Kozmos**
if i can do anything to help others rise up and awaken i will but you're either in or out
7/16, 11:13pm **Pre View**
but should u have ideas, i'd support them !
I think u have great potential to see and understand things a million different ways which is interesting .
It means you can understand and assist many people from many different cultures...
7/16, 11:13pm **Koz Kozmos**
i have no idea what to do next ,
and body problems don't help
but i'm getting a litttle stronger
its so limiting communicating via typing
7/16, 11:16pm **Pre View**
It is frustrating
7/16, 11:17pm **Koz Kozmos**
humanity has shown no interest in me ,
the humans arround me are asleep and not my friends ! they can not look deeper and are trapped, and have no idea that they are so low level consciousness
its pathetic , i don't mix with any one
7/16, 11:19pm **Pre View**
Maybe lets stop it here for today, reflect on some ideas during the night , Ok ?
Try not to think about the past, or what surrounds u, eliminate it because it downgrades everything. This sort of conversation depresses me! Its no good
You either find your way out and live a different kind of life and that means deleting your old mental barriers; no matter what you have been through.
If you still connect with your parents after what they've done to you, that is your choice!
And a bad one,
I completely cut my parents out of my life: they abused me, and disrespected me to the level of feeling completely unworthy all of my life.
I was kind of their Cinderella while my sister was being treated like the Princess of Wales...
Inventing something people can understand is not easy,
but these situations need to be addressed and
reason they put people like us on the planet!
7/16, 11:20pm **Koz Kozmos**
i may go to a gig myself once a year
ok , no problem , never want to keep u i get caught up in my stufff , sorry
7/16, 11:20pm **Pre View**
no it is just,the limitations in TT ,
I love talking to u
7/16, 11:20pm **Koz Kozmos**
i'm always thinking of soulutions ! and have set things in motion ok ,
good night
7/16, 11:21pm **Pre View**
ok,sweet dreamzzz, buzz deep,
hope you don't feel sad
7/17, 12:34am **Koz Kozmos**
MUSIC: Archons: Exorcising hidden controllers with Robert M. Stanley

7/17, 12:44am **Koz Kozmos**
a lot of the info in this is scrabbled...but worth a watch
don't worry about watching the occasional thing
7/17, 12:57am **Koz Kozmos**
not seen these guys before , but its aligned,,,
7/17, 7:48am **Pre View**
Hi good morning,

I'm glad i got my bio rhythms back, i always sleep between 12 midnight & 5-6 am.
that is how i feel best, I'll watch the Archons tonight, thx ..;
Yesterday, u said u set things into motion ....
Would u like to talk about this ?
7/17, 11:23am **Pre View**
Apply your poetry + your music = brain change
Many states of consciousness can shift through the right music; its good to drop ignorance and mundane blabber.
My dream was to study anthropology, never had the monies...
It's important to get people out of their laziness, their negative streams give the archons,
evil spirits, satanic rituals, and reptilians an open highway to feed of them and react in ways that are not authentic.
People know somehow sometimes that they do not respond to things the ways they actually are and try to hide that because of fear of being judged.
The highest level of fear comes from being slaughtered through sacrifice.
People really need to awaken and understand how these brainwashes work, through easy and fun stuff I guess like through the entertainment industries.
There is really so much evil intent in the galaxies.
AND PEOPLE DO NOT EVEN WANT TO KNOW THAT THEIR BRAINS ARE GOING THROUGH INVASIONS OF ALL THESE PHENOMENA!
7/17, 11:43am **Pre View**
Hey Star walker, make it a great, fabulous & wonderful day , will ye?
7/17, 1:43pm **Koz Kozmos**
motion commotion, I'm aligned to my thought process , beware the mind parasites
i don't compose...i write tunes
why have u dropped the idea of us working together
and becoming supa starz in the arty world...i don't mind...., hahaha
just wondering.... Write a reply... Write a reply...
7/17, 1:51pm **Koz Kozmos**
MUSIC: The Waterboys - The Pan Within (with lyrics)

7/17, 1:52pm **Koz Kozmos**
the pan within is a term used in Dion Fortunes book,
the gaot footed god i read about 30 years ago
i 've not written songs or poetry for a long time,
i have lots of old songs and lots of ideas i can't manifest
7/17, 1:57pm **Pre View**
aha, i'm reading,,,,, and yes, it is all under the SKIN, haha
7/17, 1:57pm **Koz Kozmos**
a very good song and archetypal ,very me
7/17, 1:59pm **Pre View**
very nice nice tune
am dancing, shedding my old skin
NEVER let anyone drink of ur precious
Well, save it for urself, be egotistical
7/17, 2:00pm **Koz Kozmos**
i agree
7/17, 2:02pm **Pre View**
if we need to do something together, i guess it will happen,
and yes, without action , nothing will happen
We will need to look through another window and download a new view with fresh multi dimensional air beyond some plasma,,,
7/17, 2:02pm **Koz Kozmos**
MUSIC: Let It All Hang Out - The Hombres 1967

OK , have a bad day, hahaha
7/17, 2:03pm **Pre View**
We need to stay in Peace and Harmony to keep these invasions out!
7/17, 2:36pm **Pre View**
Ok, I'll catch u somewhere within a sparkling rainbow maybe,,,
7/17, 2:56pm **Koz Kozmos**
MUSIC: The Waterboys - Spirit (Full Version)

7/18, 7:10pm **Koz Kozmos**
People keep stopping me from commenting on their pages, but still alow me to share their shit , must be something right
7/18, 7:11pm **Koz Kozmos**
MUSIC: Paul Kantner & Grace Slick - 06 - When I Was A Boy I Watched The Wolves

7/18, 7:31pm **Koz Kozmos**
MUSIC: Mott The Hoople - Roll Away The Stone (1974) HD 0815007

7/18, 7:32pm **Koz Kozmos**
the 7 tease
7/18, 7:32pm **Koz Kozmos**
MUSIC: Ian Hunter and Mick Ronson - Once Bitten Twice Shy

7/19, 9:00am **Pre View**
Everything needs to step out of the devision for us to restore wholeness, Unitarian life through biology. Everything keeps us from our organic nature that rule through the lower chakras.
These entities rule by secrecy and fear. Humans just don't understand that these demons are real and make up so many stories on FB like they even allowed them as part of their family: That is POSSESSION , the dual chords of addiction and fear move through that.
We just need to live on the other side permanently and ground these alive Sources
People need to just regenerate their essence through THEIR OWN SOURCE!
Because it is basically the Masters' Source stone that cracked right in the middle and thus created a dualistic playing Field
Humanity became very vulnerable and would fight anything that interrupts their daily dual soups because of the eruptions of mind control.
So yes, I agree on the video but the missing link is still that nobody offers solutions which is Light Technology through alignments
Also, it triggers my brains to think on many other levels,
need to be able to open my memorable treasures
and connections from ages ago. That would help.
Lets roll away the stone
Happy to hear you're feelin' good & can look at the stars.
7/19, 9:31am **Pre View**
I am very quite thezz dayzz as I have a lot on my mind ...
I cannot figure out everything alone by myself,
these times are over.
7/19, 12:29pm **Koz Kozmos**
2 ff'z in enuff ! i can't either sHUsH
7/19, 1:55pm **Koz Kozmos** Enuff iz enuff !
7/19, 3:18pm **Koz Kozmos**

MUSIC: the Wicker Man (1973) | Maypole Song

MY INTERNALS : In today's society it takes an extraordinary human being to really dig deep into the problematic static going on with youth/young adults far beyond any scientific/psychological evidence for the world has proven beyond doubt that there is lot more in-depth study and 100% engagement needed to come up with programs that assist and support new educational systems for young people to stand strong in mentality, character building and healthy lifestyles that equalizes goals set on the highest parameters of respect, humility and integrity.When going into an observation deck for many years, its is rampant what kind of results we need to digest from young graduates. Maybe only 30% out of a hundred make it into a successful and abundantly satisfying life. The other 70% falls back in fears, frustrations, self sabotage, control mechanisms and a high level of ignorance not knowing where to look for a waterfall that speaks truth and can bring and end to old creations/ manifestations.

Young adults are hungry and starving to get their original vibration back into the body minus the massive hybrids and the DNA they have been born upon through soul consciousness and all of these old belief systems that broke their energy fields. The youth of today face a myriad of societal problems. As in previous generations, the social issues facing today's youth can have significant effects on how these young people will eventually turn out as they reach adulthood. Drug and alcohol abuse continues to be among the more serious problems confronting modern society. Another social issue that has been giving negative effects on the youth of today is early sexual activity and having no understanding about their bodily functions because schools fail to educate properly and massively. Single parenthood is one other growing social concern that modern youth has had to deal with seeking emotional and material support from other people including their peers. This exposes them to a variety of risks especially when no other responsible adult is willing to help them out. Still, authorities should take heart in the belief that given proper attention, young people can be nurtured to become competent national leaders.

They need massive re-education on every level of society and need to understand the challenge beyond the boredom of what has been acceptable on earth.
The new Light Universities need to be opened on the planet in order to become power plants that assists human evolution. To accomplish this task, Spirit consciousness is needed, team projects are needed, new partners need to blend and merge. The vibration needs to meet the new frequencies on earth. Every body is tired of the density through the electromagnetic grids keeping people in the drowning syndrome. Change can be manifested through education for all! Everybody needs to understand equality as the biggest problem ever on earth is the Lady/Gent broken veins and people partnering up like rabbits which causes massive psychological problems on every angle of life.
Today we are living in a society were people need quick fixes and knowledge. If one needs more trust, become fearless and Energy Efficient, then they need to be able to code the body and the brain in order to balance out quickly and move on. Everything will come through codes and many other alignments such as disciplining self, and allowing health in the body through the refinement of our biological system.
That of course is huge education. But it can be done as diets are already being revised worldwide while people are seeking for natural remedies to cure their repetitive ailments.

Hopefully schools and universities will soon cut down their requirements to allow teachings from non academics just because there is no university that breathes an MD in Light Sciences. Every Faculty could benefit so much from new Light ethics when educated on a daily basis such as bringing through early morning shifts in consciousness through a meditation class and alignments to the higher degrees of knowledge and intelligence.More like offering modern day remedies to massive societal problematic static that we all experience to some capacity.
I would be so in love with an Art Project that grounds the Milky Way with its 12 rooms of study and Philosophy. That should truly exist in Universities in which Laser Light, flow and blow through geometrical patterns and mathematical alignments so they can be better understood and thus Light Sciences can become motivational nutrition as or the missing KOOL FACTOR in Human Evolution and Brain development

7/19, 3:52pm **Pre View**
The wicker Man, oh this policeman, funny stuff, makes me smile ...
Load ur super brainz ?
7/19, 4:43pm **Koz Kozmos**
load yours
7/19, 4:44pm **Pre View**
I need some fun ...
7/19, 4:44pm **Koz Kozmos**
i have no contacts ; its not fun
7/19, 4:45pm **Pre View**
70 % of this town is on drugs and psycho medication,,,,
7/19, 4:45pm **Koz Kozmos**
check this guy out u need a shaman
7/19, 4:46pm **Pre View**
Why ?
7/19, 4:46pm **Koz Kozmos**
look into shamans in your area
7/19, 4:46pm Koz Kozmos
MUSIC: Terence McKenna ~ Describing DMT Trip In Detail Pt.1/2

7/19, 4:46pm **Koz Kozmos**
i have to go out , just popped in , i won't say peace
hey Nic let may me think about it ...
PEACE anywayz ,Ok, i trust u
i only had a low dose , maybe try some mushrooms , hahaha
u need the right mind set,
the right place and the right people and the kozmik vibe take care
7/19, 4:49pm **Pre View**
I DON'T NEED THAT SORT OF BRAIN STRETCH!!!!
i never had anything, no experience at all and
don't want any either!
And certainly not this Terence playground!
I excel with my own brain extentions
7/19, 4:51pm **Koz Kozmos**
it may be interesting to research it, not experience with it yet I thin it is in our body,
we may need to bring it alive,
7/19, 4:52pm **Pre View**
Ok, thank u !
7/19, 8:59pm **Koz Kozmos**
I don't know anything either ,
I was being eyeronik
i l'd like to stop worrying, any ideas ?
when u enter the darkkling realmz of the freakziod wyrdus,
u bekum hyp
7/19, 9:14pm **Koz Kozmos**
i feel scared of being here some days
7/19, 11:32pm **Pre View**
It is all strategically planned
everything becomes more scary every day
This collective consciousness needs to be eliminated
You just align to your Source and the higher Light aspects of Self and command
protection! 7/19, 11:33pm **Koz Kozmos**
yip , how u doing ?

7/19, 11:36pm **Pre View**
Had a good night at a vegie restaurant
Gay friends of mine are running this for 25 years now,
Feels great, and it's a good place out in nature where you can take cats and dogs
7/19, 11:36pm **Koz Kozmos**
gay and not dead yet ?
only joking ,
its the asexuals I hate
7/19, 11:38pm **Pre View**
i don't hate anyone
I just feel safe with those guys
I never really had sex in my life
so, i cannot really say anything about it
7/19, 11:39pm **Koz Kozmos**
ok , I hate every one wotever their sexual preference
I'm in an iconoclastic mood
7/19, 11:40pm **Pre View**
do u hate me ?
Hatred gets one down
wots an iconoclastic mood, like paralized ?
7/19, 11:41pm **Koz Kozmos**
its just mockery
7/19, 11:42pm **Koz Kozmos**
an Iconoclast is one who attacks and seeks to overthrow traditional
or popular ideas or institutions.
7/19, 11:43pm **Pre View**
ok , then i like the word 'iconoclastic' , strong word, indeed
7/19, 11:43pm **Koz Kozmos**
also filled with disappointment
7/19, 11:44pm **Koz Kozmos**
I'm an iconoclastic dandy
i need higher energy
7/19, 11:45pm **Pre View**
people will alwayz disappoint
until u reach equal energy u are reading my mind
7/19, 11:46pm **Koz Kozmos**
equal energy , wots that ?
7/19, 11:46pm **Pre View**
Maybe u need things to look forward to, such as goals ...
And working on these goals day n night
7/19, 11:46pm **Koz Kozmos**
there is nothing more i want to do ,
but i'm planning something
7/19, 11:46pm **Pre View**
equal energy mutual interest in a conversation for example in which both parties lift
each other up. So, what's your plan about?
7/19, 11:48pm **Koz Kozmos**
tell me wot i plan? sorry Nic , read wrong , thought u wrote i May know wot u plan ?
just looking for a quite place in a small town to get away from the fodder
a place to die , but thier every were
7/19, 11:52pm **Pre View**
Hey u, with ur potentials,
don't let them die ,,,,

u are a universal Planner
u are a magical scanner
u are the star walker
7/19, 11:52pm **Koz Kozmos**
i wanted to be an artist working with different mediums,
but i 'm sick of trying
i'm nothing , mister invisable , i have no support ,
no conntacts and no longer want to be around people
7/19, 11:55pm **Koz Kozmos**
i'm on benifits and i'm 53 ,
but atleast i don't have to go down the factory
7/19, 11:56pm **Pre View**
i just talk to people in the streets
(u know like 5 minutes) see wot they say & move on
7/19, 11:56pm **Koz Kozmos**
thier all plebs round here
i keep my head down
7/19, 11:56pm **Pre View** plebs ?
7/19, 11:56pm **Koz Kozmos**
and wear my mist claok short for Plebeian , a commoner,
a low grade in the art centers their all class based and fell of limited consensus shit
they don't like artyizts
and people doing music tend to be half my age,
or my age and stuck and boring
7/20, 12:01am **Pre View**
my intent is to attract something deeper in people, intent is important
7/20, 12:01am **Koz Kozmos**
pain, frustration, sorrow and despair must have helped
the doors have been closed due to targeting
they tried to destroy me , nearly did
7/20, 12:02am **Pre View**
How are your eyes ?
7/20, 12:02am **Koz Kozmos**
just put drops in, but a bit better , thank u for asking ,
i appreciate it u have a good energy !!! i wish u the best , and your sharp vox
7/20, 12:04am **Pre View**
i can only study and do things within myself and see results,
eyes, go all the way throughout the body,,, ,Eyes fascinate me
7/20, 12:05am **Koz Kozmos**
What do you mean by throughout the body?
~<0>~
7/20, 12:06am **Pre View**
= readjustments of the eyes through the nerves, the connections to the glandular system,
the blood flow ,
i'v noticed pretty interesting things
Every single layer in the body is connected to another layer, and another, endless!
U know TT
12:07am **Koz Kozmos**
i wish i could do this
7/20, 12:07am **Koz Kozmos**
don't mess with mine ! hahaha
7/20, 12:08am **Pre View**
No i will never do anything ...
were are u headed with your tech ?
7/20, 12:11am **Pre View**
i planned a training early September, working hard on it

7/20, 12:12am **Koz Kozmos**
my bottle of water tastes bad today, maybe its my throat
7/20, 12:12am **Pre View**
It takes a lot of my energy as i have to download all this new info from my brain
And i'm working with a new program illustrator,
photoshop to give people more clarity ... hard ...
7/20, 12:12am **Koz Kozmos**
i found some of my art today , a series of collages
7/20, 12:13am **Pre View**
I'm testing bottled water these days as most are full of bacteria and not healthy for the body. There are waters that run quite easily through my body, and waters that have no flow at all. It is interesting to do that in the UK.
What kind of water are you used to drinking?
Over here it is Spa and Mont Roucous that are best...
7/20, 12:13am **Koz Kozmos**
did about 10 years ago called "THE DOLL MUTATIONS "
spa and mont roucous?
7/20, 12:14am **Koz Kozmos**
i have to drink something , i'm on a detox, no booze
7/20, 12:14am **Pre View**
spa & Mont Roucous are just brands...
7/20, 12:14am **Koz Kozmos**
only one smoke before sleep , thats it ,
saunas and water not got those brands here
7/20, 12:15am **Pre View**
great, i detox a lot myself, it just goes on and on,
I still have about 4 cigarettes, that's ok I guess, its no more emotion,
just like a break time enjoyment between my schedules....
7/20, 12:15am **Koz Kozmos**
i 'm a very light smoker of green, anyways ,...
7/20, 12:16am **Pre View**
Due to readjustments my diet changes a lot, detox is automatic,
sometimes hard to follow, yet it is fun
when listening to what the body needs...
Most people just follow up anything they see or hear which is not so pleasant for the body because we are all so unique and so many different things...
More information about the herbal kingdoms should be brought back on earth because it feeds the body
better then any food.
7/20, 12:16am **Koz Kozmos**
living in these bodies in this toxic dimensions is no good
7/20, 12:17am **Pre View**
I just clear everything, even the food, which is also becoming an automatic as i work with nature to restore. But i'm thinking were is this leading us all,,,
I even put an Arkansas crystal in my fridge to keep the foods' energies up, haha
7/20, 12:18am **Koz Kozmos**
i find it hard to live thru these things callled days
yes , were is it leading ,
to a planet with every one doing rekie and saying namaste
7/20, 12:20am **Pre View**
Yep the namasté manipulation is massive.
People want their powers back and still keep on praying that someone else would do that for them. The awakening takes too long, yet we have to understand that everything is perfect timing. The realization to EMPOWER SELF THROUGH SOURCE ALIGNMENT IS ALL THAT IS NEEDED
along many beautiful highways to re-educate that.

I have gained a high level trust, with all the hard work i'v done this month, little results are flowing in, and bigger manifestations...
People just don't know how to align and how to bring that through...
I mean to say the growth process
which is daily investments in Self, in family, in friendships,
in personal development through spiritual arts and jobs, etc...
7/20, 12:20am **Koz Kozmos**
i just need more
7/20, 12:20am **Pre View**
People miss out on the right mathematics, thats all ,
The body recalculates all the time anyways, depending on our focus and things set to achieve... Sorry i wont bother u again with my stuff, (it is just my passion)
which u always see in my art anyways
7/20, 12:21am **Koz Kozmos**
people are stupid scum , a good deal off them
its ok , its worth sharing and it no longer bothers me i just feel i need more ,
and u seem to have so much tech
it can feel hopeless sometimes , most of the time I'm barely getting thru
7/20, 12:28am **Pre View**
Thank u for the super minutes, hahaha
CALCULATE A NEW WAY TO GET MINUTES MOVING SLOW
I have tech that probes deeper and deeper
The universe is composed out of math and geometry (grids) Do u agree ?
7/20, 12:29am **Koz Kozmos**
Pythagoras wod, i'm not sure
7/20, 12:30am **Pre View**
When u look at the DMT doc - movie: it is all geometry ?
7/20, 12:31am **Koz Kozmos**
the little i know about quantum physics is interesting
i 've not seen the dmt movie , but i've seen massive geometrical fractals when i use to trip... years back mainly magic mushrooms , i'd like to do a big one in the next year
not done anything fore 15 or 20 years, it could be frightening
but maybe it will help my shift , TT , i hate street drugs
7/20, 12:34am **Pre View**
i never experienced any drugs but watched some good docs and learned a great deal when assisting people out of these street drugs and their underlying emotions
7/20, 12:34am **Koz Kozmos** f
ace book stores all our chats
7/20, 12:34am **Pre View**
I know, have compassion, they don't have brains they can possibly own
So they need to feed of our brains
7/20, 12:35am **Koz Kozmos**
Ayahuasca
7/20, 12:36am **Pre View**
It would sound weird to hear your voice
7/20, 12:37am **Koz Kozmos**
yes i sound like a monster
7/20, 12:37am **Pre View**
Yes it is, we are heading into telepathics,
its all ,thy cannot murder us ,Monster voices, yawi
7/20, 12:38am **Koz Kozmos**
we need to meet in the spaces between the spaces
and plan the activation

20, 12:38am **Pre View** How do u plan that ?
7/20, 12:38am **Koz Kozmos**
i need healing , its maybe happening ,
i don't know how to plan it
7/20, 12:39am **Pre View**
U need massive healing, but when??? its gonna go quick
7/20, 12:39am **Koz Kozmos** ?
wots gonna go quik
7/20, 12:39am **Pre View**
When u step into the healing u'll quickly understand and move very very fast
It is all about becoming your own Life/Light Vision and mentoring your self every day instead of giving power away to life coaches that fly through social media like they are the best dinner ever offered down town, hahaha , it just proves the grooves in low consciousness
It takes such a long time before people really understand that the movement into their Spirit is really all that is needed. And then take off, the Phoenix, the aerobics in the human body have never been educated ,neither the flow of water
It would supply all the answers people have.
But I also understand many are just not strong enough to set their daily avenues into the self empowered genius.
7/20, 12:40am **Koz Kozmos**
i feel its hopeless
7/20, 12:40am **Pre View**
It is absolutely NOT
7/20, 12:40am **Koz Kozmos**
how is it going to happen ? wot will i have to do ? wot will be the signs ?
i've taken too much damage , i always hit a dead end
i don't want to , but i'm going to be honest
7/20, 12:44am **Pre View**
It is all so delicate, please don't get angry,
I'v been trying to put your puzzles together, but it always come down to the same thinking : U know a lot, u've done a lot, u can do a lot .
So to me the missing link is that your computer system is not a light vehicle that is solid aligned where u can plug things in and be protected - it is open - that is easy for targets.... The only choice we have is being honest, there is no in between.
We need to break the old records . You really need to build confidence and grow stronger then ever before, that is True Power and mastering your energy field with all your potential!
Meditate on your potential! And make it a best seller!
Well u have to build new stairs or find the hidden staircase ! and hope the floors are safe enough (GRIDZZZZZZ)) and find the bathroom
THAT SHOWERS LIGHT without LIMITATION8
You just accept too many limitations!
You need to test new possibilities!
7/20, 12:48am **Koz Kozmos**
Maybe I need to install a new toilet,,,
7/20, 12:48am **Koz Kozmos**
everything depends on my nervous syem
And if I don't find that specail bathroom?
I will have to piss in the garden then, hahahahahaha
7/20, 12:52am **Prc Vicw**
Hey i'm thinking about all the trouble running through the body
Your challenges need to be opened again
Otherwise how are you going to build new skills and leave yesteryears' parlor behind?
Everything is continual learning, growth, expansion, even the experiences we all move through like what you term TARGET.

We have all been abused to a point where our light was drowning, but we have also always been given opportunities to remove the slime from our own street and continuously CONNECT TO SOURCE/ SPARK/SPIRIT.
Once you take that decision to open up your new expertise,
you will find you have skills that can set in
anything at any time.
Sure with my stuff and i'm not being arrogant or whatever,
i care, and have experience in doing these
things and assisting people to get in that space in which they can empower their being through growth in meditation which becomes daily medication in family matters,
jobs, friendships, sports, nutrition, everything!
I had some one over here 2 weeks ago who would pee in his bed every day :
I gave that persons 2 sessions
and it was over and done with. This is how fast Light Technology works!
You just need a good 3 to 7 days seminar and some follow up programs to get it all running, then you can just invent your reconnections Universally speaking and create any Light Body set up you want.
7/20, 12:52am **Koz Kozmos**
my brother in law is a plumper ,s
o i have some Illuminati connections in the bathroom equipment world , hahaha
7/20, 12:53am **Pre View**
U have no temple in Light productions, or house, so no electricity!!!
7/20, 12:53am **Koz Kozmos**
i never wet myself , its not like that
its my neurons fireing wrong , mind and soul damage !
7/20, 12:54am **Pre View**
YOU CAN BE EVERYTHING THAT YOU ARE ,
just allow NEW VIEWS!
I know, just find out how u can adjust them
You could just run light through the central nervous system.
Just start doing that: look the central nervous system up on Youtube and flow some white Light and Smoky Quartz Light through that system.
That is a good way to just start it out.
there is a reason why u have this
7/20, 12:54am **Koz Kozmos**
and i had an operation in my 20's
and that really damaged me
anyways thank u
7/20, 12:55am **Pre View**
We all need CONTINUAL REMINDERS and keep the flow uncontaminated!
7/20, 12:56am **Koz Kozmos**
things have been and are insidious , TT
7/20, 12:56am **Pre View** o
k Is ur voice still ok ?Is ur hair OK ?
STOP COMPLAINING! AND MOVE YER BRAINS INTO THE THOUGHT PATTERNS OF A GENIUS! YOU NEED TO REWRITE EVERYTHING THAT YOU ARE! RE_INVENT YOUR COSMIC TRUTH! 7/20, 12:56am **Koz Kozmos**
it is all quite tragic really , ummm
7/20, 12:56am **Pre View**
Joking ... I wish u had someone over there with whom u could discuss your stuff and u know conversations help ...It's the flow from one dialogue into the next that assist us in opening new perspectives on things.
7/28, 12:56am **Koz Kozmos**
i don't like to talk
i'm ok sometimes but under a lot of stress

7/20, 1:00am **Pre View**
But u did stop the booze, and detoxing which is wonderful!
Start detoxing the old mindset that keeps your energy fields in such a disgrace!
So u still do give a fuck about feeling good and having a life ?
Maybe you've never thoughT about a new EPISODE of yourself?
It happens many times with older people; they tend to think they KNOW WHO THEY ARE, while there is still so much hidden greatness and potential.

7/20, 1:00am **Koz Kozmos**
anyways , i stop at intervals , and was not an alcholic
i like it , it shuts me down but i need to save money to escape
i did drink too much ..., i hope its a sigh of positive change and sowing seeds, and all that ...
7/20, 1:03am **Pre View**
just great, just keep on moving
I just have that feeling that says that things are going to work out for you somehow , but you need to do the inner work like never before...
Dropping the old ways of connecting to spirit.
7/20, 1:03am **Koz Kozmos**
its getting late
7/20, 1:03am **Pre View**
And u have so many ideas, ok, we'll pick it up some other day
7/20, 1:03am **Koz Kozmos**
i'd just like to live away from evey one in nature and wait for my death ok , thank u for the chat
i feel my inspirations i share are dying in this medium
7/20, 1:05am**Pre View**
Thank u 2, don't get too hard on urself,,,
There is nothing to be ashamed of
7/20, 1:05am **Koz Kozmos**
thank u , its not shame , its frustration
7/20, 1:05am **Pre View**
Yep FB is the low expressions of soul disease
7/20, 1:06am **Koz Kozmos**
i feel like i'm in prison, could be worse
7/20, 1:07am **Pre View** sleep tight,
and remember dreaming the greater things remember, remembrance is everything
7/20, 1:08am **Koz Kozmos**
i don't know wot they are
my dream escape is confused, i don't enjoy it
7/20, 1:08am **Pre View**
I sometimes get flashes from teachings in the etheric before this lifetime
Which is what we all need to download
7/20, 1:09am **Koz Kozmos**
no more lifetimes i hope
7/20, 1:09am **Pre View**
Meeting u, gives me a clearer view on them
You know, just looking at your past situations and how you learned about sigils and majic and stuff...
So there is a lot that you could rewire and see what happens
We often times are to much ATTACHED even with things we do to grow in light and become the AMBASSADOR OF LIGHT.

7/20, 1:10am **Koz Kozmos**
not sure how, i feel i have some power
7/20, 1:10am **Pre View**
We could fill in each others' gaps
We need to set a clear path if we want to move on
A path paved with crystals, planets, stars, giants, many funny species, all elements, the elementals... It is so beautiful when working with elements, they show us so many things,,
7/20, 1:10am **Koz Kozmos**
how , maybe, TT
7/20, 1:11am **Pre View**
I'm not going to tell you, you'll judge it and I don't want that!
7/20, 1:11am **Koz Kozmos**
tell me , its ok , i'd like to know , i feel its important , its up to u
7/20, 1:16am **Pre View**
Ok, when loading my grids (its about 22 now (HAHA or ahah?)
and anchoring them until they really sit,
sometimes they take years, but now in 2013 it goes fast (so there is no such a thing like I TRIED GRIDS) and then i want to go beyond spiritual embodiment , more in the Science Grids.
Yet we do have to partner up with our Eternal Mate because that makes everything easier, and also that is the way to move forward
Not the old soul jar like soulmates and uncomfortable situations
but since 4 weeks it was always u that gave me the answers.
You always pop up in my grids, and sometimes that is great for I can see u answering some questions and sometimes it is annoying, so I kicked you out today, haha
So you see, everything you need to do is IN THE GRID:
the answers, the communication, the connections we need,....
And of course we need to keep the grid clean and we need to grow with it to build more skills.Just talking about it because repetitions are good for your mental training and maybe that is a better way to ever understand that geometry and math make up the Architecture of the universes, the galaxies.
It is all consciousness.
7/20, 1:17am **Koz Kozmos**
ok , deslexia , back to front
how do u know its me
7/20, 1:17am **Pre View**
So it is uplifting me and giving me information that works in a marvelous way.
I thought my concern about u was getting in the way of your growth,
which was not so, i had it wrong, ..
7/20, 1:20am **Koz Kozmos**
concern?
7/20, 1:20am **Pre View**
I'm concerned about u : caring about u
7/20, 1:20am **Koz Kozmos**
don't , u have to focus , caring is no good to me , but i don't know
7/20, 1:21am **Pre View** it's natural
When focussing it gets very real, i sometimes run away from what I see in the gridzz
7/20, 1:21am **Koz Kozmos**
why do u run away
7/20, 1:22am **Pre View**
But is is very interesting at least, maybe scared because I somehow feel this may get too deep.Which is ridiculous anyways, haha
Gridz REVEAL things, they guide you, they show you things that matter for our personal growth and reconnect to the Ancestors,
opening new tracks under the feet

7/20, 1:22am **Koz Kozmos**
ok , i think i could be being blocked off due to damage I feel i need to go into the celestial bodies something reall big has to occur
7/20, 1:24am **Pre View**
The Celestial bodies is where you get lifted in the crystal clear atmospheres, your body would feel very light.You will however need some clearing out and foundation because the celestial bodies also require a complete turn around of the glandular system.
It actually is all about inverting just every thing
But your will is strong and you're very aware that fitness is number one to move the body into crystalline environment
So there is really not much u need besides a sound proof foundation, and the alignments for the celestial axis position.
OK, Mister Koz, lets load the galaxies, and the fruits that feed these bodies,
You could start dancing the hola hoepla
7/20, 1:25am **Koz Kozmos**
i'm ill in many ways , cannot dance, fucks my nervous system
7/20, 1:26am **Pre View**
it does not matter how ill u are
wot matters is that u finally get the right stuff to move on and forget whatever happened 2 you. You have 2. There are no choices if want the cycles of what you term "target" to stop.
7/20, 1:26am **Koz Kozmos**
with how u expressed your ideas and expected understanding ,
it is a wyrd dynamic
7/20, 1:27am **Pre View**
I know, its too difficult over FB
I just wanted to give some idea about the working mechanics of our Origin and the Origin of creation which is a dot, many dots format into lines, many lines can formulate grid compositions, grid compositions can download information and bring change and healing through for the body and the planet...and all universes.
7/20, 1:27am **Koz Kozmos**
i'm not sure, i feel such a deep connection 2 u
ask me something when your up there and tell me wot i say
i don't talk to people like this, so we have made some sort of a connection
i do talk to jain doe as well, thats it
7/20, 1:28am **Pre View**
I'll give it a try, its more like giving directions
I do not talk to people like this either , I talk very direct but more like a living wave having fun and showing people what meditation and alignments do to me.
And yes, they always tell me that I change so much and so fast.
They are interested in my stories, how I treat people , how I dance
It is not that I know many people, it is just that I always attract new people and I love dancing salsa and hip hop. So, when the occasion occurs , I just dance and with that flow more and more informations streams through my body which is quite natural because information flows through the water and its electricity
Remember : We are all water.
7/20, 1:29am **Koz Kozmos**
my neck hurts from typing , so i'll pop off ,
thank u again for the chat
7/20, 1:29am **Pre View**
Ok, get some rest
Shall i relax your neck during the night ?
Good night Koz!

7/20, 1:30am **Koz Kozmos**
good night, c u , u can try but be respectful
MUSIC: Crowley and the gay agenda

7/20, 1:41pm **Koz Kozmos**
The gay film maker obsessed with Alister Crowley
7/20, 1:41pm **Pre View**
Hey Koz, thx, i'll listen later,
have an important appointment with somebody in 15 minutes, cya
7/20, 1:42pm **Koz Kozmos**
its a watch , ok don't let any low level entities get u , HAHAHA
MUSIC: Underworld - Stagger

7/21, 3:10pm **Pre View**
Sure,,,, (underworld - good lyrics!)
This girl is humming straight, diagonal & unilateral ..... T
his girl is loading the spirit molecule
This girl is planting & connecting ....
This girl is interested in knowing what the interesting things are u learned in quantum physics ??? (u told me that a few days ago - but i didn't tap into that then ...)
7/21, 3:12pm **Koz Kozmos**
i said i didn't know much about quantum physics, but used my vague knowledge to consider an idea how are u loading ??? underworld lyrics are arthouse cut up...
7/21, 3:17pm **Pre View**
Loading : i'm just getting ideas, i pull these ideas into my body, follow directions given...
so it woke me up in the middle of the night , and I was given certain designs when doing my morning marathon with the angels, the daisies and the fairies
I always think : we have everything in the body : so we should be able to load it so i try out ideas.
Yet , we can only load ancient stuff when the body is ready to host these energies; after purifications and upgrades and stuff universally speaking.
It is not that simple
7/21, 3:18pm **Koz Kozmos**
i thought u meant taking
7/21, 3:19pm **Koz Kozmos**
the cyber blood of the lost race trapped in the machine !!! Bloody hell !
there are so many stupid sayings that people accept as fact
7/21, 3:20pm **Pre View**
i think everything needs to be experienced, and even then, its delicate
We absolutely need to move into the halls of light
in which we get to know how philosophy works
7/21, 3:21pm **Koz Kozmos**
failed mysticz in the hippy gift shop , yip
the new ager who posts the same shit and posts “namaste” all the time the teardrop in the giant sea ! i want to kill god , in a nice way
7/21, 3:25pm **Pre View**
u just merge with urself, that is interesting enuff
Hey i'm gonna back to work, got loads to to with this new info ....
Want to go with me thru these molecular crazies ?
7/21, 3:26pm **Koz Kozmos**
ok , i just don't know wot to say , feel so hopeless ,
no inspiration get on ,
good to get off the screen

7/21, 3:29pm **Pre View**
I just wish i had someone to share the same experiences with
Would u not like to go in meditation and ask what u can do to load this spirit molecule and then exchange experience?
7/21, 3:30pm **Koz Kozmos**
fuck it all, death to the universe
7/21, 3:31pm **Pre View**
OK, i'll do what i need to do & get back to u when u feel like it
Play the Jukebox,,,
Play new tunes
Play unexpected tunes
7/21, 3:37pm **Koz Kozmos**
maybe I have chakra malfunctions
sorry nic i get down about things
just one bad thing after another happens, its endless
7/21, 4:22pm Koz Kozmos
MUSIC Justin Bieber Debuts "Heartbreaker" A Capella

7/21, 4:40pm **Pre View**
Maybe it relieves to tell me about the problems u encounter ....
U know i decided to pick up at least one connection with somebody once a week : this is just to expand upon connections and get something moving or planting seeds.
i have to keep focus on it, which is not my best quality ....
Earth went far off the rainbow spectrum of advanced technology using magnetic particles and therefore is off the monitor of galactic proportions and galactic cannot relate to Free Will . It means we have to move back into Divine Will and do the work to eliminate lower mentality and attitudes. There is no other way to reach back into the Celestial and Universal essence of Self and be that Spark that shines the origin onto the earth
Throughout all this , the solar system or birth chart became fractured, out of balance which took spirituality into downward spirals or what is known as dual chords. To keep things simple: we have to eliminate all dual chords, and rebuild our ship on the wavelengths of Divine Will chords; and they are so
many. I think we've been building this for many life times.
With this i only mean to say i'm finding my way of the astral plane and cutting the magnetic chords. It takes time, and the alignments into the Celestial body are certainly a great relieve from fractured consciousness.
Therefore I do not allow myself to tap into negatives any longer, i'm sure u understand.
We both know ur done with this dimensions, loads of damage, physical horror to heal;...
But is it any use to keep on listening to the same old records in the brain ????
The brain needs and craves new music all of the time, it needs new compositions so we can build new ladders up into the shiny hills, the beauty of many mountains we need to climb.
Think of the purity of air we breathe when residing in high altitudes!
That is the kind of breath we can align to at any time, any place.
And yes of course, the body needs refinement and preparations to be able to load the higher volumes of wave capacity, just like in physics
Finding solutions to have a life is, and finding more every day and putting them into action is what overrides your troublesome life and environment.
And if I sound out like a life coach, so be it, !
I'm a Universal Life Guide, hahaha
There is no such thing as giving up, u know it would become even more unbearable
,,,, Yesterday u told me not to care about u .....
I can't , but i'll do my best,

If u need to tell me a story out of every day life, please do,,,
it might release. As for myself,
i don't keep my mouth shut, it relieves me,
i'm done with frustrations and stuff...
If you want to move upwards, you need to let the past rest without upsetting your self so much and certainly not dig into the pages of FB posts, that is for addicted, slow motion people that do not want the Breath of freedom.
7/21, 4:47pm **Pre View**
Get the death hormone & fear out of your amygdala , pull the eternal spiral of detachment in and move your feet on the dance floor: a beautiful marble ffloor that shines and sparkles like little lightening bolts. Hey i have a little problem too : i'm having loads of protein to build me up again, my legs are getting better and bigger, but i hate the look of muscle growth because I may look a little fat, I like to look very skinny.
How am i going to deal with this?
7/21, 5:04pm **Pre View**
Hey, what can u do today to move out of all these troubles
Wot can u activate? Hey, show me your collages 7
/21, 5:10pm **Koz Kozmos**
can't be bothered to sort things
too much hassle , i can't follow , its not happening
i got fat , put on 3 stones...
u have zero idea of wots happenng to me
I'm just getting bogged down I think it effects me talking to u sometimes
becuz u seem to be moving on , its not envy ,i'm GLAD 4 u
7/21, 7:18pm **Koz Kozmos**
MUSIC: T. Rex - Rip off

z)

7/21, 10:50pm **Koz Kozmos**
13 14 years ago I had a flat mate they moved out & left a Dali pic on kitchen wall which one day while still on the wall I covered, then i did these of a few days and stopped... the one above is called Adams 3rd Wife

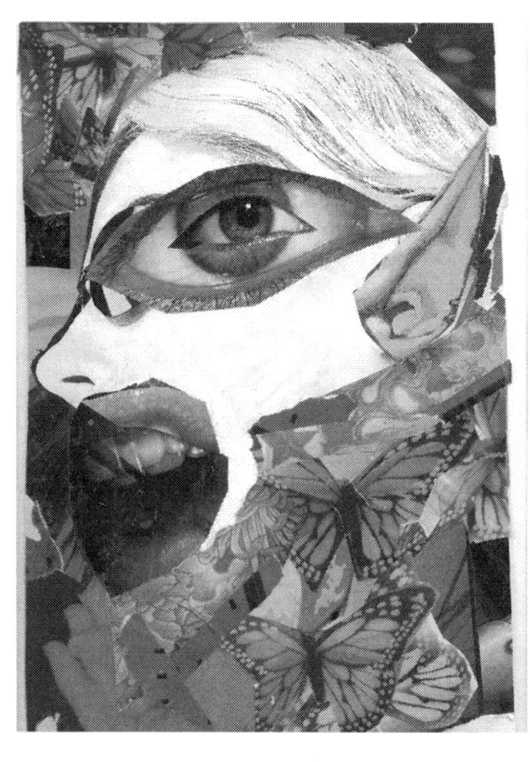

7/21, 10:50pm **Koz Kozmos**
I'll list following titles with collages Above>>>> Another Gurl with a Gun
7/21, 11:00pm **Koz Kozmos**
Sizzabella first ime to scan found these yesterday so bit of syncro~
so posted them did a lot of more develpoes art 20 odd years before etc
7/21, 11:08pm **Koz Kozmos**
Hence the title THE DOLL MUTATIONZ
I did loads of collage paintings and some one rippped me off
we shared a house, i didn't even notice till another house mate said she's completely
stolen all your ideas an she's still crap but she was in art collage and won an aware
and cash but ho hum award* looking back they didn't rip me off to much
they did not have my poetic language
7/21, 11:32pm **Koz Kozmos**
so caught u
7/22, 1:23am **Koz Kozmos**
These are doodles these are soul shift before the soul shift
I mean blabbering
7/22, 8:56am **Pre View**
"Put on 3 stone ..... ": I cannot understand this sentence ,
please explain this to me ? Ur not fat, u look glamorous, u look dazzling
Yes, i'm moving , wiping the astral plane out,
but it gets me very nauseous which is pretty
normal with all the old stuff leaving,,,,
Yes it effects talking to me as i need to be very severe to myself and cannot allow
negativity no more coz it would bounce back immediately when working on myself as
severe as i do now,,,,,
otherwise there is no way ever to get the celestial body in;;; buh - blabla
Wow, u have an eye beyond an eye.
This tells me a lot about ur sensitive superb, magnetic, tantalizing,
alluring imaginative powers ....
THANK U !
So wot is the Successful Creative Enterprise ur going to put this in
& make the money u deserve Luv 'the screaming mersnake and naked in Cathedral
7/22, 9:32am **Pre View**
Hey Jimmy, listen , my feet can barely touch the ground
i got plenty of mauve butterflies around me,
this is seldom, But i want a tattooooooo
And i would luv it if u'd be interested in creating a collage for this very refined,
very me, Please??
7/22, 1:00pm **Koz Kozmos**
I put on a lot of weight u were saying about trying to put on more fat
u don't know wot i look like
the photos are 6 to 7 years old i've said this
if u have a tattoo I'm not sure you're worth talking to
every body has a tattto round here or a pi bull dog sorry no collages or any creativity
any more i did those years back but thank u for asking PreI feel the whole fad for
tattoo's and other body modifications is preparing the already soul dead back for the
next phase Transhumanism...post human phase we may be able to transform
with out the use of machine tech never mind how advanced
via breaking the dummmed down state back = pack
but I'm done with humanity
7/22, 2:24pm **Pre View**
I've never had a tattoo,,, but i want one now ... maybe
I don't know how u look like, only through the images i get sometimes,
which is indeed pretty different
(the photos u gave only show ur face anywayz)

But hey it does not matter, u need to feel good
thats all,,,thats difficult snuff,, Done with humanity ? or maybe just starting out
Ok Jimmy , lucky u
don't live next door coz i'd kick ur ass ten thousand times a day
till thy'd bleed blue Star Sapphire moves , I'd nail flowers on ur shirt
till the smell becomes unbearable , i'd glue a red diamond (as big as the blue in the Titanic) on ur throat just for u to broadcast Celestial news that best suit yur vibes.
Be it Elegantly. Just blabbering, gonna work a little in the garden ---
7/22, 2:28pm**Koz Kozmos**
u have a tattoo bit od joking not done with the himan human*
and herman u couldn't kick me, i can't type
7/22, 2:28pm **Pre View**
I'v got huge, spectacular Wingzzz
7/22, 2:28pm **Koz Kozmos**
my ankle hurts
7/22, 2:30pm **Pre View**
that is no good,
when u press on ur ankles where does
it hurt in other places in yur body ,
7/22, 2:30pm **Koz Kozmos**
the bone that sticks out a few months ago it was hard to walk and i limp some days as my left heelis wrong i had some phsio
it was no good i'm bettter than i was
a lot swimming does it and walking
anything and every thing i vaguely enjoy has brought me sorrow pain and frustration
7/22, 2:32pm **Pre View**
crystal lite tech made my bones mutable like that of a child ....
Yes i'm glad u swim, u need lots of water around yur body
like spending many hours in the ocean or pool ....
LAKE SUPERIOR IS GOOD FOR THE NERVOUS ALONG SMOKEY QUARTZ
7/22, 2:32pm **Koz Kozmos**
and i'm not even complaining but swimming makes it worse its no good i'm done for
best to chat with some one else
7/22, 2:34pm **Pre View** i
ts ok, i can imagine how u feel
when there is something with the physical harm or ailment popping up on an every day basis , I would go MAD for real, i do comprehend ..
7/22, 2:35pm **Koz Kozmos**
its been for 30 odd years
7/22, 2:35pm **Pre View**
that is toooooo long , and you just lost hope
7/22, 2:35pm **Koz Kozmos**
i was just broken inside before but i remain strong the suffering gets worse
7/22, 2:36pm **Pre View**
I mean, something real good has to come into ur life now, its about time, create it
7/22, 2:36pm **Koz Kozmos**
every thing has been 'bad luck'
7/22, 2:36pm **Pre View**
What broke u so much so many years ago ? ur education ?
7/22, 2:37pm **Koz Kozmos**
being here i have no education
7/22, 2:37pm **Koz Kozmos**
my youth was a nightmare
my parents are matrix slaves
it could have been a lot worse

fuck all that u had shit
i'm really sick of it all wot i've become wot i say to u
it brings me down
7/22, 2:39pm **Pre View**
I don't understand why u have still contact with them
i have broken ALL and every Entry into my life of anyone who ever broke me
Does talking to me bring u down ?
7/22, 2:39pm **Koz Kozmos**
its not u it wot i express
i have connat because i'm strong and chooose it
7/22, 2:40pm **Pre View**
ok, maybe its good, u get rid of that pain thru communication and some understanding ?
7/22, 2:41pm **Koz Kozmos**
understanding is not enuff
7/22, 2:41pm **Pre View**
wot do u need besides physical healing wot would be good for u ?
7/22, 2:41pm **Koz Kozmos**
to be away from humanity and barking dogs in anture nature
to have enuff money to dissappear
7/22, 2:42pm **Pre View**
can u not find a nice place for u to live in nature, somewhere not too expensive
7/22, 2:42p**Koz Kozmos**
and never return no i can't drive and i don't want private landlords just as u settle they sell up, there is no were for me
7/22, 2:43pm **Pre View**
hum , not driving, I don't know ....we don't have private landlords here anymore
7/22, 2:44pm **Koz Kozmos**
i have learn t this its still a feudal system in the uk it feels hopeless i have some small plans
7/22, 2:45pm **Pre View**
maybe go to the mountains, Switzerland or something or what attracts u ,,,,
Would u like to share yur plans, i'm curious
7/22, 2:45pm **Koz Kozmos**
i need to talk but its become no good i need to focus and move on as best i can
7/22, 2:45pm **Pre View** talk to who ?
7/22, 2:47pm **Koz Kozmos**
if i lived in the mountains in Switzerland how wod i survive with money get to a shop to buy food my plans are to move back to porthcawl
u'r a dreamer u have no pratical application how wod i get there
7/22, 2:48pm **Pre View**
Hey i'm not a dreamer, u know there is always multiple options,
like befriending some one who does the dirty work for u (like groceries and stuff)
U know i think many different directions, always, certainly not dreaming ever,,,
7/22, 2:49pm **Koz Kozmos**
it hasn't worked like that for me how the fuck can i go to Switzerland
I'd need to fly money get a place....
7/22, 2:50pm **Pre View**
I get that done (even if i can do it myself ...)
However it is not an outcome for u
7/22, 2:50pm **Koz Kozmos**
at least look after myself until i could find some one to do the dirty work
i mean wake up here
i think many different directions 2
i need a plan with a practical application but its my problem
7/22, 2:51pm**Pre View**
Well i've been stubborn and resistant for years
But ok, it is all focus, intent and blabber

7/22, 2:51pm **Koz Kozmos**
thanks for trying but wot your saying is no good
because it has no use
7/22, 2:53pm **Koz Kozmos**
i'd luv to go to swissland and get some one to get my food
how much are rents there ,can i get benefits
i can't work my nervous system is fucked
how much will it cost me to transport some of my things there
Wot sort of place could i get etc your a fantasist
7/22, 2:55pm **Pre View**
expensive, I was just thinking about it coz my parents used to have a flat there;
anywayz
Transportation should't be that much, there is many ways
Boat is cheap, so my sister told me as she moved from the US to Belgium
I am not a fantasist !
7/22, 2:56pm **Koz Kozmos**
but i've told u i have no money so please do not make moronic suggestions
7/22, 2:57pm **Koz Kozmos**
its dis-empowering and rude
how do u pay rents or own houses in bellgum
how do u have no landlords who owns rented property
i'll move to bellgum
7/22, 3:00pm **Pre View**
i have no money either, but it doesn't mean i cut out many options ...
connections are very important.
I'm not rude, i'm realistic and thinking. Belgium : very easy going
U can rent from a private person , just pay rent and do wot u want
I for myself do not pay rent but in exchange i look after the garden and stuff
7/22, 3:00pm **Koz Kozmos**
I have no connections i get buy with money but i can't afford to move abraod
how can u say your realistic !!!!!!!!!!!!!!!!!!!!!!!!! fuck this is stupid
7/22, 3:03pm **Pre View**
U can rent from anyone here .... I mean if u'd rent from me
7/22, 3:03pm**Koz Kozmos**
no more loand lords free the land
7/22, 3:04pm **Koz Kozmos**
kill the mass of humanity
7/22, 3:05pm **Pre View**
Build a wouden place in the woods
7/22, 3:06pm **Koz Kozmos**
fuck offf the wood are owned here by land lords they build and build
u have no idea u are a fantasist
maybe i should buy a piece of land put up a yurt pop out
do a bank job and hang out with other posers and say namaste
i could hide the stolen money down by the claer woter stream
can u just go into wooodland in belllgum
and build a house even if u have no idea how to do it
can u just chop down trees for woood do u also build all your own furiniture ?
7/22, 3:15pm **Pre View**
Yes many people shop down trees here
But i have no idea here about the woods...
I used to build some furniturc but had help....
Anywayz i don' care for furniture,
i always give everything away,,,
all i need is a good bed,,,
7/22, 3:16pm **Koz Kozmos**
u have some in your photos did you get rid of yur wizzard
most of my stuff i've found ior been given

7/22, 3:17pm **Pre View**
good
7/22, 3:17pm **Koz Kozmos**
i've never bought a chair or bed
7/22, 3:18pm **Pre View**
I bought small cute only little things,,,
but i like as less furniture as possible, it stands in the way
Are u a lover of castles?
U seem to post these a lot of times, i like it tough
7/22, 3:22pm **Koz Kozmos**
the pics i post reveal my urge to get to a place away from humanity
i don't need much and have got rid of 50% of my possesions in the last 2 years
i still have alot of books but have sold loads
sorry if my vibe is angry

7/22, 3:28pm **Koz Kozmos**

In 1649
To St. George's Hill,
A ragged band they called the Diggers
Came to show the people's will
They defied the landlords
They defied the laws
They were the dispossessed reclaiming what was theirs We come in peace they said To dig and sow
We come to work the lands in common
And to make the waste ground grow
This earth divided
We will make whole
So it will be
A common treasury for all The sin of property
We do disdain
No man has any right to buy and sell
The earth for private gain
By theft and murder
They took the land
Now everywhere the walls
Spring up at their command They make the laws
To chain us well
The clergy dazzle us with heaven
Or they damn us into hell
We will not worship
The God they serve
The God of greed who feed the rich
While poor folk starve We work we eat together
We need no swords
We will not bow to the masters
Or pay rent to the lords
Still we are free
Though we are poor
You Diggers all stand up for glory
Stand up now From the men of property
The orders came
They sent the hired men and troopers
To wipe out the Diggers' claim
Tear down their cottages
Destroy their corn
They were dispersed
But still the vision lingers on You poor take courage
You rich take care
This earth was made a common treasury
For everyone to share
All things in common, All people one
We come in peace
The orders came to cut them down

MUSIC: Dick Gaughan - World Turned Upside Down (BBC 1982)

7/22, 3:28pm **Pre View**
I have a room for free in the cellar
Going for a walk now, need some air, <catch u later
7/22, 3:28pm **Kozmos**
listen and read and get educated
i was thinking i need a celler to practice songs in away from any noise
7/22, 3:51pm **Koz Kozmos**
u were right ii found the perfect swiss mountain
7/22, 6:22pm **Pre View**
This plastic FB talk is no good for my system
7/22, 10:21pm **Koz Kozmos**
ok SORRY i need to say it
i get frustrated things become magnified i'm going thru some thing within me
yes i need somewhere bigger
with food the fair folk bring when I'm asleep
my talk is not platik plastic~ i get wot u mean yip
7/22, 11:58pm **Koz Kozmos**
i hope u understand wot i mean wen i say sorry
7/23, 12:52am **Koz Kozmos**
peace and chocolatez
MUSIC: SMASHING TIME - full movie - 1967 -
Rita Tushingham & Lynn Redgrave

7/23, 3:57pm **Koz Kozmos**
your in this movie maybe not, its ok if u don't want to talk
MUSIC:MAX BYGRAVES - Fings Ain't Wot They Used To be

7/25, 7:53pm **Pre View**
The movie : no dignity, no strength , no character, airy fairy consciousness,
how can u even watch this, speak alone of a little noblesse,,,
How can u even find me there somewhere knowing The Word is me.
7/25, 7:54pm **Koz Kozmos**
I watched it wen i was maybe 9 to 12 years of age embrace the airy faery within
i don't understand all that
'word is me' shit
7/25, 7:58pm **Pre View**
Just leave it to the shit then
A Word can break ye or make you, that is power, the word is worth investigation
7/25, 8:09pm **Koz Kozmos**
shit = satan the movie...not sure I could watch it, maybe on a rainy brain dead afternoon
7/25, 10:14pm **Pre View**
Maybe timing has come to finally let the beast come out and have it run real real wild,,
7/25, 10:29pm **Koz Kozmos**
? smashing time is an early 60's satire on pop culture do u mean my beast ?
7/25, 10:31pm **Pre View**
Beast = yur anger with almost everything
7/25, 10:31pm **Koz Kozmos**
I need to avoid prison and i'm not angry about every thing
but i am angry if i wod not care
7/25, 10:32pm **Pre View**
besides humans & stuff, wot really angers u ?

7/25, 10:32pm **Koz Kozmos**
reality and that reality and the other
most of the time its mockery and disgust bordering on anger,
the reality i find myself in on earth
7/25, 10:34pm **Pre View**
ok, get some boxer gloves and a shiney chap
and start boxing the war of anger out of the body.
7/25, 10:35pm **Koz Kozmos**
how punching a pillow will not work
7/25, 10:36pm **Pre View**
u have to find ur way
nothingness, feels good
7/25, 10:36pm **Koz Kozmos**
i can find no way
7/25, 10:36pm **Pre View**
Go do some street art and spray your style on every bridge you can find in Wales
7/25, 10:37pm **Koz Kozmos**
and smashing stuff wod just be a vacuos tantrum
7/25, 10:38pm **Pre View**
Get some wood and cut to pieces until ur muscles hurt
Only saying ... you need to do physical expressions to get the root of anger out
7/25, 10:38pm **Koz Kozmos**
my anger sees deep in to the bs
7/25, 10:38pm **Pre View**
i feel it 7/25, 10:39pm **Koz Kozmos**
my body is hurling enuff at the moment
7/25, 10:39pm **Pre View**
wot would be a great way for u, i mean there has to be something
that assists you to get the anger out
You need to transform into acceptance, and then you can heal out
much like some birds, they can sing the song of their origin, even if they do not recall
that environment I think humans can load their original song vibe as well
7/25, 10:40pm **Koz Kozmos**
mockery of the universe to head butt gOD
7/25, 10:42pm **Pre View**
Maybe connect with somebody in ur home and talk the shit through till u get your
self expresso move into acceptance and in that still ness your realize your SELF out of
the Soul into the Consciousness of Spirit and spiritual MENTALITY, dam-it,
nobody gets there without doing the work!
7/25, 10:42pm **Koz Kozmos**
i 've no one to connect with and i am not at home thak u for trying to help,
i'm mad enuff but i also have
incrediable luv in me ,i'm a deep person who is not only about anger
but the stupidity has got to much
7/25, 10:45pm **Pre View** ok
it just hurtz not seeing u get out of that pain
Sureyur mad enuff, Sure yur deep
How do u want that luv to be of value when anger gets in the way
7/25, 10:45pm **Koz Kozmos**
luv comes first but i do not waste it u need to get angry at some people
i'm so bored with these limited zero solutions my anger is good
7/25, 10:46pm **Pre View**
It is the emotional body that has been hit the worst ways possible for that also
brought our brain capacity have access to only 20% of data.

In this great transitory and challenging times we need to understand that there is a greater plan moving through that is rebalancing the earth with the solar/galactic and universal core which is reason why the monsters of this universe are coming to the surface , reason why there is a spiritual warfare going on and need to relearn Light technology, the Sacredness of Evolution.

My INTERNALS: How am I ever going to be able to reach this guy. Light training is al we need to truly rebuild self into a renewal mode and move with new Life streams and forces that were once such a natural way of living. Light however can rebuild he body to such an extend that the micro universe within matches macro universe and that happens when expansion is felt many miles in circumference. It overrides all of the densities, mental psychological, physical illness not only in the body and brain but also in your surrounding. For when we gain knowledge about a certain frequency, we will also know how to apply it, at least when we FEEL what is going on, we can direct energy. As light is information, it will immediately supply us with that information and bring that energetic force/source in our life by simply breathing it and trusting SELF as each one among us is so unique. We go back into understanding how we can put the WORD back into place through putting consciousness together with the fabric of the universe which is color coded rays that need to be understood.When we train ourselves with THE CHANGES THE UNIVERSE is making, then we can train everything back into the repair kit . Our channels need to be opened in order to receive information from one level into the higher dimensions. The more we purify, the more intelligent data we receive by BREATHING IT THROUGH! as it offers many options to connect with more intelligent Life Sources when matching their vibe in purest form without the thorns.

It is exactly the breath which is our Life Force that has been cut and fractured into many dis-eases on the planet such as lung cancers and heart strokes. When the breath cannot reach every cell in the body, the body breaks down and falls into decay.
Having the intuition and directions set to achieve goals in the healing process is one thing. Having the knowledge of how to bring ideas into creation and then manifesting them is another thing to learn. It is not simply about coming into terms with your self created misconceptions and soul control mechanisms, it is all about catching that new Breath of Life beyond the SOUL/EGO syndrome and move yourselves into spaces of Peace, off unknown Creative capabilities, becoming the magician, the wizard, the genius we all once were in co-creation with Supreme Light Eternal, the elements and many light beings.

7/25, 10:48pm **Pre View**
So wots yur solution ?
Dying ? is just an escape, we need to deal with ourselves anywayz
either on Earth or another planet, we are evolution
It is not that DEAD ALLOWS YOU TO EXCAPE the resolution
7/25, 10:48pm **Koz Kozmos**
to destroy the shit heads total soul death wod be an alternative
7/25, 10:49pm **Pre View**
How are u gonna get there ? total soul death needs tranformation, transcendence, mutation,
The deeper levels of love just open up after that, not before like you claim it to be, there is no love on soul level but egotistical volumes of uncharging plastic arms / Passion, tenderness and amour have lost their gentle spot and touch because the BREATH FAILS to breath that AIRLINE of deep love in which spaces within spaces re-invent themselves.
7/25, 10:49pm **Koz Kozmos**
no idea, it may not be possible if the universe didn't want me to be angry
it should not have abused me in this way
wot are the reason for your accusations?
7/25, 10:52pm **Pre View**
everything is being destroyed, which accusations ?

7/25, 10:52pm **Koz Kozmos**
about being angry its good to be angry abot crap
7/25, 10:54pm **Pre View**
hm, you seem to be angry all of the time
It is not an accusation, it is more that i feel yur sadness
We cannot keep on being angry forever,
Anger has to be understood to get somewhere
& then transmute it into something beneficial
otherwise you cannot TRANSCEND from this space into the next
7/25, 10:55pm **Koz Kozmos**
thats obvious but it hasn't worked that way for me no your ok, your indulging me
77/25, 10:57pm **Pre View**
Are u angry at women? I mean , all i see in the collages are women ?
But I like yur refined eyes,
7/25, 10:58pm **Koz Kozmos**
no i got all these magazines with images of women in from a women i new and i thought i'd transform them the images are very pro women and reach out beyond media sterotypes
I'm disappointed u did not see that there is also a lot of humor there
but as i said i did those in a few days 13 years ago ,it was not a serious art project that contradicts your question ,then the idea was to create more images
The Project was called as i've said THE DOLL MUTATIONZ
hence women i have worked with many images
my anger has a foundation and things continue to make me angry more ... dare i say it shit the new ager, wod say i attracted it and i have sinned
7/25, 11:07pm **Koz Kozmos**
i've never felt joy
7/25, 11:08pm **Pre View**
are u going to delete FB ?
I never understood why u never had a relationship,
u must have had some seconds of luv i guess ?
7/25, 11:08pm **Koz Kozmos**
no i've had minutes of delusion but that was seen thru decades ago
i 'll tell u if i delete fb ,i'd like to keep in touch
7/25, 11:11pm **Pre View**
not enuff to break the chains of this dimension
Ok, i'll understand, just tell me when FB, i don't feel good with FB either
7/25, 11:11pm **Koz Kozmos**
i think my anger will destryo me,
i'm so bored with these limited zero solutions my anger is good
7/25, 11:12pm **Pre View**
do u want an email ? or something ?
7/25, 11:21pm **Koz Kozmos**
my point about u retreating saying one thing and backing out was fair
no i feel your ok and an intersting person but u confuse me, i do not feel every thing , i will not lie
7/25, 11:24pm **Pre View**
Confusion comes from living in SOUL consciousness,, the illusion,
Once the brain streams on spiritual waves, there is no more confusion, it stops
Reason why people need to get out of that damn soul
that is pilled with the matrix and diseases
7/25, 11:25pm **Koz Kozmos**
u 'r a moron ,look back it obvious wot i'm saying ,
your wasting my time
7/25, 11:26pm **Pre View**
I am a moron huh? and wasting yur time ?
FINE!, u don't have to talk to me!
I still get ur answers in meditations anywayz,
which is fun BECAUSE I CAN SEE YOU CRYSTAL CLEAR in the grid!

Believe it or, not believing blows the anger
balloon high up in the air , then it explodes and you don't particularely get folk wisdom out of that! 7/25, 11:27pm **Koz Kozmos**
bull shit
7/25, 11:37pm **Koz Kozmos**
can u not remember wot u said and place it in context in this conversation
we are few but we are many and our anger will destroy this place
7/25, 11:41pm **Pre View**
i can, my english might be ok, but it does not mean i do get everything.
Sometimes languages have expressions i don't know.
But its ok, try talking Dutch
7/25, 11:41pm **Koz Kozmos**
ok thats a fair point ,i apologize Laura Magdalene Eisenhower :
is an annoying middle class mytic in her new age hippy pose, maybe my first kill
wots a few kills, it will rebalanced all their positive energy, any ways black humour
7/25, 11:45pm **Pre View**
Yes u have a good sense of that. Are u sarcastic ?
7/25, 11:45pm **Koz Kozmos**
thats for u to decide,
u can get in trouble with straights if u express sarcasm ,maybe a pain killer
7/25, 11:47pm **Pre View**
In ur anger last week u told me "get educated" :
please explain if necessary, Wot do u suggest to get educated in ?
7/25, 11:48pm **Koz Kozmos**
I meant about land lords and the nature of property and posted a wonderful song and the lyrics to aid your stupidity
u needed it then, i've always said i'm broken lost and confused i was just sharing
7/25, 11:51pm **Pre View**
People have different levels of interests,
I spent more time in learning through wot i paint So I loaded a program and teach myself 7/25, 11:52pm **Koz Kozmos**
i do this a well, some times i get information that confirms mine but u did question me about landlords so i gave u an answer via a song about some things that happened in 1649
7/25, 11:53pm **Pre View**
great, this is wot i once meant by doing stuff together,
like putting some poetry on my artwork and tshirts
and split the money. It actually revealed other stuff to me, that is what creation does.
7/25, 11:54pm **Koz Kozmos**
yes lets leave it ,my passed work has no meaning for me
7/25, 11:55pm **Pre View**
Do u do anything creative now ? besides play the guitar ...
7/25, 11:55pm **Koz Kozmos**
i rarely play thev guitar , no i'm done, i am the creation i suppose
7/25, 11:57pm **Pre View**
But without doing things we like, life must be boring .... and frustrating
7/25, 11:57pm **Koz Kozmos**
my anger is my work, i told u i do nothing, i'm on benifits ,please listen
my joints are bad i do wot i can , i have a broken nervous system
u have no idea what my live is and how i've tried, i did work as a cleaner - it was no good
7/26, 12:01am **Pre View**
How do you deal with this broken nervous system?
7/26, 12:01am **Koz Kozmos**
hiding and getting buy are my best strategies ,
look up chronic fatigue syndrome ,
i'm done chatting

7/26, 12:03am **Pre View**
Ok, lets close of, Chatting is getting me bored too
ok, goodnight then
7/26, 12:07am **Koz Kozmos**
thank u
7/26, 12:29am **Koz Kozmos**
Laura Magdalene Eisenhower just deleted me ,she did tell me off prior to doing this
but i could not read her comment,
the 'love and light gang' do not get black humor!
ok thank u Nic yor kool
all her insipid fans post hearts and say how wise u are sister
every fukkkin post and i said sorry there are no black hearts to post.....seems out of balance
her pathetic fan base is a focus for my hate , no good
7/26, 12:33am **Pre View**
all these people sound so unreal, pisses me off
like thy never have an answer to the real problem , every love & light post is exactly about the opposite and their missing study in knowledge and intelligence
people are so lazy when it comes to studying Light and its integer forces
The dirt surrounds the meatball, the meatball in the sunny stream or solar centers are exactly exposing "shit for brain", you cannot possibly have animal blood in your intestines and preach love at the same time, ridiculous , they make me feel illiterate
7/26, 12:35am **Koz Kozmos**
your not illterate ,i'm deslexic and have not been to scholl since i was 11
and did not go much before that academia is bs
7/26, 12:36am **Pre View**
I never read books, maybe 3
I never looked anything up on the internet before i got to know u,
is good I've learned from it
7/26, 12:40am **Koz Kozmos**
yes just to show thier tolerent postive vibes are fake its mad if u liveda in taheaa uk
i 'daa acall u anyways
7/26, 12:43am **Pre View** Now i'm confused,
" ifulivedaintaheaauki'daaacallu"?
Oeps, would u speak to me like that, would i understand yur voice ?
7/26, 12:43am **Koz Kozmos**
if u liveda in taheaa uk i 'daa acall u =
if u lived in the UK I'd call u, i need to escape facebook ,
i deleted it and came back on and satrted to talk to u soi its your faqult
7/26, 12:45am **Pre View**
I if u lived in the uk , you would start talking to me right?
7/26, 12:45am **Koz Kozmos**
i think its a vibrational trigger fb to keep people suppressed
7/26, 12:46am **Pre View**
but we can shine bright and bring intelligence into posts,
it doesn't help, people avoid THINKING
Yes its a game, FB, but I do like certain pages, science,
herbs, a bit of art posts reveal the life of people
but thy get caught by themselves, their brain poverty ....
7/26, 12:50am **Pre View** It is 1 am
I usually sleep between 12 and 5 or 6 which is more then enough for me ...
7/26, 12:50am **Koz Kozmos**
i pritned up your other post and read it, i did say it was good,
i like to get 9 to 10 hours minimum
no title on print out ,
but u mention the peace brigade and mention Ireland etc

7/26,12:51am **Pre View**
Wot post ? about wot ?
7/26, 12:51am **Koz Kozmos**
but my anger and frustration use lots of energy, hold on i 'll find it if i can
7/26, 12:52am **Pre View**
I understand ...; the loss of energy
I had this too months, i'm fine now, hope to keep it that way
euhm ok, a bit about gridz
It is that Ireland has so much to offer, like Stonehenge ,
Ashford Castle , Oxford but people abuse these energies,
there is so much information to be found underground.
Access and clear view of data is being exposed through the GRIZZLY GRIDZZZ, haha
7/26, 12:55am **Koz Kozmos**
i just wanted to understand and experice and failed again
7/26, 12:56am **Pre View**
I can still post u things that give more understanding,
back then i was a bit afraid of yur judgments....
but not anymore, you take it or leave me, i have no care
7/26, 12:57am **Koz Kozmos**
to be honest i've given up on every thing ,not being negative , its getting hard to chat
but thank u for comming back on to spk
its an addiction fb , ok post something good night,,,, timethy leary
7/26, 1:00am **Koz Kozmos**
My advice to people today is as follows: i
f you take the game of life seriously, if you take your nervous
system seriously, if you take your sense organs seriously, if you take the energy
process seriously, you must turn on, tune in, and drop out.
Timothy Leary i posted it before bye

MUSIC: THE MOODY BLUES-R.I.P. RAY THOMAS-LEGEND OF A MIND
MUSIC: Timothy Leary - How to Operate Your Brain

7/26, 3:16am **Pre View**
I've not seen this post of Timothy Leary before. However what he states and how it is done is huge training... I don't seem to need sleep today, up since 6, its 3.30 am ---- ok lets just work through the nite then .... Huge vibes Euhm, i'v been reading the following, and it made me think of u, as i don't know anything about wot u did besides rituals and magic and going into realms - u never explained anything --- so i guessed u just loaded and loaded without details
(but i may be completely off ....) :
There IS such a thing today as PURE SOUL. There is also such a thing as SHADY SOUL.
A pure soul signifies one that has taken what they had to a certain point, and seeks the next direction upon higher waves, therefore ripe for transition. This was done under universal charting and direction in preparations for times yet to manifest. Spirits can cooperate and maintain the same vibratory pattern with pure souls although it does take work to blend as one. A shady soul signifies one that has alternate motives and lives the free will pattern attempting to tap into spiritual reserves and never steps up to the levels it takes to make it, but tries until the EGO can no longer handle rejection. Shady souls find ways to create mayhem and gossip until the day they are eliminated from pure planetary means losing track along the way. There are such entities on ground known previously as Super-Seeded Consciousness. There is only lack and disappointment in soul level thinking. Thus making one reach into the high heart where anything is possible and living in the alignment of DIVINE WILL is a large outcome. A Super Seed is ONE that hand crafted different GRID layouts with Merlin during studious incarnations(they may not remember that) This helped to repair the Sun Seeds many are feeling knock out inside the Solar Plexus center today.

Today there is no time to set the education of ascension on a slow table such as was performed the last twenty or more years. Today through Super Seeds on land it will manifest magically and overnight even while entities pace their education and brain rewires.
NOT ENOUGH PEOPLE THAT STUDY LIGHT, just like you, it is exercising Light and bringing different formulas through that allow for more data, and ascending into the next level with maybe new Sourcing devices or technology. The better movies stream through with higher aerobics, high altitude breath and AIR IN THE GRIDZ, not the pollution with earth degrees. Living on Light Earth makes all difference and can only be understood when working with it. That is the true beauty of ascension if you're a seeker.
The Blue ray or Midnite Sun provides the knock out blow in the end and the solution to let go of any emotion. Neptune waves into long forwarded ideals, and rock stars bring them in without second guessing even if they do not completely understand. That is the beauty of fine tuning, intuition comes with it.. A Super Seed will balance is in a spiritual energy field mutating from soul upwards. into Spiritual consciousness. The Blue ray trains the master on eliminating the EGO completely. In the world wide grids on new modern order one only has to step up and balance both male/female aspects and create new electricity. There is also the masculine/feminine divinity gathering under this super seed. A Super Seed is one that has graduated with EARTH GROUND , usually more than once. They would never have the audacity or lack of integrity to show others their skills. They would also NEVER attempt to make their tube assist earth ones or tell the grids how to do it. Alignment is an unspoken terrain. . Many will find they have lost their confidence during ascension or wonder if they can pull off such an assignment. The ROCK STARS of the modern master movement know better and will set all within. For if one is in tune with records and written materialization as it is written they will have the nerve to state it and follow through. To be a master in this age is to pull up all you have to awaken the weary souls on a path no one anticipated would plunge so far down .THE WORLD DOES NOT CARRY FATE IN THE HANDS OF THE GODS AND GODDESSES ANYMORE. WE NEED TO BECOME MASTERS OF OUR OWN LIGHT; THE OLD WAYS AND DAYS ARE OVER AND DONE WITH.
Each spark carries their own destiny YET THEY crawl to false leaders beyond land in order to save their skin.
Every Elixir is to be found under the Skin
7/26, 3:45am **Pre View** Wot is happening ?
My feet barely touch the ground, this feels real good, no more sleep
i am upgrading my nervous system
Hey Jimmy, the attachment is actually a bit of info through which i flow when explaining people things, in training... There may be things difficult to understand, but mean reason is merely to give u more explanation about the importance of grids, on wot the universe was builds, just geometry ....
How come nothing of the old light ways can work ...; manipulations etc..
how is ur neck ? did u feel wot i did or not ? Was ur pain away the next day ?
Download GRIDS & TEAMS & INFO.pdf
7/26, 10:45am **Pre View**
Mauve butterflies were surrounding me this morning
Never seen such beautiful dance, I am transferring them 2 u
Enjoy urself
7/26, 1:35pm **Koz Kozmos**
no my neck is the same
MUSIC: Scott Walker - The Seventh Seal YOUTUBE: Scott Walker - The plague -

7/26, 2:09pm **Pre View**
the seventh seal huh, very strong, beautiful, thank u
Chess : beneficial in the long term as we keep on moving unilateral,,,
7/26, 2:12pm **Koz Kozmos**
I can't play chess i tried the whole game was tedious
7/26, 3:13pm **Pre View**
I admire yur discerning selection of record expression ....

This far, the Koz Kozmos jukebox occupies 87 tunes ....
to generousely electroclude my heartz' desires .
7/26, 4:10pm **Koz Kozmos**
thank u Nic
MUSIC: Tony Christie - Avenues and Alleyways

MUSIC: MILLIE JACKSON - Summer first time

6, 6:34pm **Pre View**
Splendid this Millie - she sure has a voice, never heard this version.
Tony Christy - i ask myself where are all theze natural joys are gone
U mostly bring me great joy with these tunes, nice to tune my senses into this music when taking breaks and just sit & do nothing for once ,,,
,❥
7/26, 11:13pm **Koz Kozmos**
hi nic will read the pdf of your mystery thriller over the weekend hoping there are some gruesome murders
MUSIC: The Killers - Runaways
7/26, 11:32pm **Koz Kozmos**
I'm interested in your tech
7/27, 8:53am **Pre View**
❥
7/27, 9:01am **Pre View**
These are not only super great tunes, thy get the underground gangs moving from eternal to immortal heartbeats. Can u catch my feet ?
it means wot it means huh,
❥
7/27, 12:37pm **Koz Kozmos**
MUSIC: The Raspberries-Overnight Sensation (Hit Record) 1974

MUSIC: Kyrie - Mr. Mister (HQ Audio)

MUSIC: Learning to Fly - Tom Petty w/ Stevie Nicks

7/27, 1:15pm **Koz Kozmos**
POPTASTIC
7/27, 2:37pm **Pre View**
Luvely sticker<<<< Jaygus Zain, any shortcut 7/27, 4:05pm **Koz Kozmos**
are those stickers not in your smile face to your right in this oblong box?
Ok my real name iz Roger Rainbow
Shinning Brow, just call me Koz, i have lots of names
7/27, 4:11pm **Koz Kozmos**
wish i could go into the woods bye
7/27, 5:22pm **Pre View**
The woodz are very generous here, Chief Big Oak is inviting u
if u'd like to experience belgian roots ....
But u'll have to take the next train leaving London within in hour ....
joking Like the Kyrie song, ...; Don't know wot to eat, just juice the day thru i guess
7/27, 10:38pm **Koz Kozmos**
An hour seemz a bit long ,u need some protein ,
my jucier gone wyrd, electric thing break round me
7/27, 10:39pm **Koz Kozmos**
MUSIC: Modern Humans are Walking Dead! ~John Trudell

7/39 12:42am **Pre View**
Children have already their Light body activated & immunity connected to Quartz (important for the survival of the planet & reason why the Arkansas Crystals have been encoded thr Zach 2000 years ago) Children need after school programs, need to know how the electricity runs their blood, nerves, bones .... .
Programs that teach no sloppy sex, no pregnancy with young age, how to balance hormones
(unconfident, unworthiness, unhappy ...), calling in the perfect partner = something thy never heard before, ... But there is a way that thy will listen before thy take an ascension class : no more lower level thinking, going into the origin of the hormonal system, out of alcohol , drugs. Kids expect high level communion. People will understand at least the eternal mate. The Art of Spiritual Technology should become magic for them. I'would enable them to understand the lowest factors : government s& Entertainment and how thy could move out of the Soul crap or lower sexual addictions and other addictions.
Everything is an addiction, but i guess these children will already have Spiritual consciousness The will see the stubbornness, implementation of false beliefs systems. Thy will get easily encoded, out of sugar, dietary issues, the killing, the rape, the hatred, out of parental irritation, acceptance versus complaints and move fast, no more time to get bored.
I had one program running in 2007 in a children's' camp in summer, i had 12 kids age 12-15 for 5days. Thy changed like their parents didn't recognize them anymore. Good. Want to do that again. Good . Society needs people who activate , find ways, connect and just do the damn thing.
It is so interesting to teach the young how to transmute consciousness and how to work with the cosmos, the elements, they are so natural and have great ideas when i offer healing techniques so they can make their own recipe for healing. So sweet.
7/28, 12:45am **Koz Kozmos**
I hate kid's not keen on adults either 7
7/28, 12:45am **Pre View**
I'm shifting from protein into potassium, that mekes me need less sleep. i feel i'll work through the nite again . So sometimes i have 36 hours a day with no sleep (i just move into the next day),you get more work done when working your life through Light which is merely understanding roots,
7/28, 12:46am **Koz Kozmos**
i see the humans round here and thier pathetic scum, I agree people ned help i've been wanting to pee for 9 days non stop compete with that
7/28, 12:47am **Pre View**
It is not just your kidneys that need healing, your lymph nodes are so stuck you just live so much in the past, you should delete these memories from yur brainwaves apply some numerology and lavender waves through the major glands and then you just imagine you bathing in the Atlantic Ocean or even the Drake portal where the 3 major Oceans come together to reach the Antarctic shore
Dream it, become it, and ask some sea species to assist
finally TRY OUT something new instead of sucking on an old lollipop will yu?
7/28, 12:47am **Koz Kozmos**
can't get anything healed i've tried
7/28, 12:49am **Pre View**
STOP THAT KIND OF NONSENSE: you seem to be part of the scum u talk about: THERE IS NO SUCH THING AS TRYING, JU JUST DO IN 24/7 until LIGHT WAVES BREAK THE DAM AND OPEN THE WATER GATES: THE BIG FLOOD , REMEMBER,
7/28, 12:49am **Koz Kozmos**
this is one of the reasons its impossibly hard for me
7/28, 12:49am **Pre View**
I guess you need to see and do the practice with somebody such as in a seminar to understand how it is being done, i'm done explaining, then again u got brains to think Light thru a different way.
Anywayz BREATH IT AND CLEAR THE BREATHING SYSTEM

I'm gonna take a Chinese Course and speak Chinese,
maybe that's abetter option for u to get it
7/28, 12:50am **Koz Kozmos** ? huh
Jesus said luv thy Neighbor....but people forget he moved around a lot
However .... u give with one hand and snach away with a claw snatch*
but i was brought up in the Jehovahs witnesses , have been busy today
7/28, 12:54am **Pre View**
Ok, u'll get out that shit as well,,,, Wot have u been doing today ?
Could u not fix ur juicer ?
7/28, 12:56am **Koz Kozmos**
I saw my parents ,went for a swim ,worked on lawyers letter,
made a meal and peed and just been talking to Merlin, the boy Merlin who is me
7/28, 12:57am **Pre View**
Hey Koz, i'm gonna go back working on my programs for the next 5 hours ...
Hope yur ok,
Please read the file, it'll clear up many things (i hope) Good if u talk to Merlin ,
but that also clears the electricity in homes (juicer ....)
7/28, 12:58am **Koz Kozmos**
yes i will print up and read tommorow ,look forward to it thank u
7/28, 12:58am **Pre View**
Oeps ok, u are a Merlin, strong Essence ....
The Lavender wave is very strong in Ireland, its an Irish Origin
Even when just working on integrating more Merlin consciousness and waving that through with the INTENTION of clearing certain diseases, or in this case maybe the waters in the body should help a lot. Look up on google how the water runs thr the body: The Lymph-nodes, kidneys, intra cellular water, ventricles, cerebrospinal fluids, and breathe the lavender waters through , and with the out-breath you feel the mud being released within your waters. Our bodies truly need to work a lot with water combined with other elements such as Light Air and herbs, lavender oil, Cornflower is also very beneficial
I tried to plant some as we do not see them so often anymore; they disappeared from nature such as many animal disappeared due to the matrix
There is something damn exceptional going on in our connect, do u feel that ?
7/28, 12:59am **Koz Kozmos** i
don't know but i feel like keeping the connection going
7/28, 1:00am **Pre View**
I'll explain : wotever i do, program, clear, read, upgrade, it doesn't matter,
even if i cook or write about something : I engage with the elements such as the Bleu Beautiful Cornflower, it came to me in meditation. I was told to bring it back to people ,
it is so beneficial, only one cannot have the oil from it, wonder why, it may have other substances that are important, lets create a true blue -
purpilish cornflower garden and communicate
7/28, 1:00am **Koz Kozmos**
only if u want, i don't wish to keep u from u'r work ,give me one that will convince me
7/28, 1:02am **Pre View**
Like 10 minutes ago : i was reading a whole program - study about the Essence Merlin -
and there u come in, synchronicity all of the time
Once u said something like : marble boys & Ivory gurls : that was the exact moment i was working with these 2 essences' rays . There are daily examples .... We just synchronize I guess, or telepathics are living on broadway, broadband streams, haha
7/28, 1:02am **Koz Kozmos**
marble boys & Ivory gurls from teen poetry
7/28, 1:02am **Pre View**
U mentioned a name this morning ZAIN right ? on FB posts
So this morning i was working with AYIN D'ZAYIN which is some technology ...;
there are plenty synchrone thought forms,
maybe integrate your poetic words and see wot it does?

7/28, 1:03am **Koz Kozmos**
ok intersting. Zain also written as Zein and Zayn is an Arabic name meaning "beauty" or "pretty"The name
Zain is mostly associated with Islamic culture, but it is also found in Hebrew, Egyptian, and English languages. it is also to do with sword
Pre View
Yess EXACTLY, I tone it as a Hebrew letter that comes thr the turquoise ray.The same goes for music, especially going celestial :the integration thr our nervous system & move out of magnetics. So whenever i asked ,
u give me that perfect coordination & harmony(except when ur angry)
7/28, 1:06am **Koz Kozmos**
ok i pull the sword from the stone, it turnz to bright metal in my hand
i am the blade that gleams but i am almost broken
7/28, 1:08am **Pre View**
Let me explain AYIN D'ZAYN
AYIN = HEBREW 13TH RAY, (invisible ray or transparency))
D = english = creation for new designs, architecture on earth beyond soul
ZAYIN : Connected to Hebrew = turquoise, every info from earth, uncontaminated production line, cultivating new teas, health products ,
new fitness programs - anything people need now
7/28, 1:08am **Koz Kozmos**
Alice Baily is your back rgound theosophical
7/28, 1:10am **Pre View**
Hey Pull the Magic of merlin thru ur sword, ask to be a lavender sword carrier, it should mutate uyr body fast, if u can ...
Alice Bailey: hmmmm , read a few books, she bores me,
it is not exiting, Light training should have passion, new outcome, magical lay-outs, more rhythm, rhyme, cadence, a good bounce, a pulse, a dance floor, yess a dance floor is what it needs. Wonder way dancers seem to be very happy people: they have the grace of Light pulsations. People should create movies in which is shown how Light can integrate and take over brainwaves, and change consciousness exactly like AI is taking over humans right now, wait until 2030, its THE CLOUD In which people will be sucked alive because it is part of their agenda. THE ONLY WAY OUT IS THE WAY WITHIN and placing Crystal Grids everywhere that squeezes the matrix like a pancake because you cannot squeeze a Light body and environment. If only people could understand that is al it takes to stop the atrocities on earth. Breathing the Light Grids through brings the elevator into consciousness and so we rise with the sunny vibes back into the Great Central Sun. We are essentially all here to ground these grids that mark the end of the Dark Ages because it brings LIFE BACK ON THE PLANET THROUGH LIVING LIGHT forces/ Sources. People need to see how Spirit Logic works versus the inverted dirt within earth logic, that is pure dualism. Clay people and the slack need to leave to make room for dual free atmospheres which is the Divine Plan anywayzzz.
7/28, 1:10am **Koz Kozmos**
The seven rays is an occult concept that has appeared in several religions and esoteric philosophies, since at least the 6th century BCE, of the Aryan (Indo-European) peoples in both Western culture and in India. In the west, it can be seen in early western mystery traditions such as Gnosticism and the Roman Mithraic Mysteries; and in texts and iconic art of the Catholic Church as early as the Byzantine era In India, the concept has been part of Hindu religious philosophy and scripture since at least the Vishnu Purana, dating from the post-Vedic era.elate 19th century, the seven rays appeared in a modified and elaborated form in the teachings of Theosophy, first presented by H. P. Blavatsky The Theosophical concept of the seven rays was further developed in the late 19th and early 20th centuries in the writings of the Theosophists C. W. Leadbeater, and by other authors such as Alice Bailey, Manly P. Hall, and others, including notably the teachings of Benjamin Creme and his group Share International and in the philosophies of organizations such as Temple of the People,The "I AM" Activity, The Bridge to Freedom, The Summit Lighthouse,. The Temple of The Presence and various other such organizations promulgating what are called the Ascended Master Teachings, a group of religious teachings based on Theosophy

7/28, 1:10am **Pre View**
I don't really read much as it is all based on old material, but I remember me walking into an esoteric bookshop weekly in Bruges, that had all these books you mention above, I would look thr them, maybe buy small things but had great conversations with the book shop owner about "The Book of Knowledge" which I bought as I learn a lot from it, and apply some stuff modern day way as a lot is no longer applicable.
Reason why Light education needs a bigger platform to be educated
and merge it with Science, the beauty within physics
7/28, 1:10am **Koz Kozmos**
ok i've not read much but have put a lot of info together via ozmosis
7/28, 1:11am **Pre View**
u dynamize and galvanize, very inspirative,
many things in such low Cs(consciousness) need ray
formulas and integrations such as the first 7 rays.
Koz Kozmos wot do u mean
it was fro wikapeidai just sharing info
7/28, 1:13am **Pre View**
Ok, i appreciate, maybe there is something interesting,
there is always a reason why, so lets read and
know that reason
7/28, 1:14am **Koz Kozmos**
ok i'm bored with info, i just want to wise up and rise up
7/28, 1:15am **Pre View**
Right because the info is not right. I never get bored, because more light brings more data, more data brings more knowledge, more knowledge brings more intelligence and maybe it leads to so wise brain inscriptive soap. The Prodigy, the Wize Gen
7/28, 1:16am **Koz Kozmos**
i'm open to the right info
7/28, 1:16am **Pre View**
Dear Koz, hope u don't mind, but i want to get on with my work,
i want to have something finished by 12
am tomorrow so....But it is good to connect, thank u
& take care of yur bronzzzy brainzzzz
7/28, 1:16am **Koz Kozmos**
don't 'blame the victim' ,i have put more energy into understanding
than any one i have met OK goog nite
7/28, 1:18am **Pre View**
u2, goodnight, or study with me? I'm curious to know how light feels in yur body
7/28, 1:18am **Koz Kozmos**
make a suggestion thats practical for me please
7/28, 2:45am **Pre View**
Or, if u'd like to suggest something to me ,please do
Maybe tell me what we have in common ----
its still a mystery to me as i really don't know wot u can
and cannot and how u do it ....
I feel i need to sleep a few hours anywayz...
Wot had" Zayn "to do with a sword - as u mentioned -
Or maybe when u get bored again and u feel like talking, please tell me everything about u, the massive work u did on u, how u did it, wot u've learned...
I just might get a clear view on u. SWe might fill
in the blancks on each other and invent new tehnology
7/28, 3:03am **Pre View**
OK Lets shake it
U asked for a suggestion that is practical for U (how can I know what is practical for U ?) But ok : here is how i study, hope u'll try this and then compare the info with mine : this costs a lot of type, for u as well as i like studies to be tDETAILED, most people hate detail because of the energetic input it takes.
I don't have room for lazy vibes or tribes.

Eg - healing THE THROAT : WHY IS THE TYROID SO VASCULAR, how does it team up with the parotid glands, wot nerves in the neck connect with nerves in other body parts, which nerve is most important and why, the muscular structure : same thing : why so many muscles, who are the muscles within the neck connected to brainwaves and many other parts in the body, wot causes most important ailments in the throat? What is the psychological, physiological, scientific component behind the neck ? What do scientist, physicians not know,
wot informations do u not agree upon and more and more.
U need to be willing to take out many hours, if not days to study the functionality of biology
7/28, 3:07am **Pre View**
U can take 50 % info from the internet, reflect on that,
eliminate wot u think is not correct and then
u go and meditate and get ur own individual info on that for the other 50 %
And then hopefully u tell me all about this and come up with some good ideas, invent new ways off working with Light back into the body .This is how i work with great passion as there is no end to wot we can create with Light,
it is the substance for all creations!
7/28, 3:12am **Pre View**
There is a reason why i picked the neck, there is a reason why u got so overly angry for a few days, there is a reason why i did not connect these few days, there is a reason why
it i part of the bloody throat, or the beauty of the word.
7/28, 10:02am **Pre View**
Good morning Koz,
If u have difficulty in printing the file, i could also post it here on FB,
or u could load it into another program. Reason for the pdf is also that I consider ur eyes
& hope u spend less time on the screen ❧
Could u elaborate on the info u gathered via osmosis.
I'm interested to know about it,,,somehow,,,
7/28, 1:27pm **Koz Kozmos**
I don't know what i am or wot i can do. Zain means sword as i said & other things
The work i have done has just happened as i could not except this reality and its programs and felt something was involved that fed on us...
I remain confused & broken U don't fill in for me, u confuse me with your models of reality, but i understand the concepts u lost me on
' WHY IS THE TYROID SO VASCULAR'
its a bit like when u said u get bored with the 7th ray piece i posted
i have no place to start '
THE TYROID IS SO VASCULAR' apart from looking in goo-gal
as i said i have to move my neck so i crack the bones all the time,
this is a bad OCD that has ruined my live amongst other things, i need something i can connect and work with this is all meaningless to me 'What is the psychological, physiological, scientific component behind the neck ? What do scientist, physicians not know, wot informations do u not agree up....
' i have no idea and don't know were to start!
I can't meditate i've said and like u, i don't want to get
bogged down any more than i already am with the internet
i was not overtly angry over a few days, my frustration and anger have been there all the time the information i have gathered via osmosis is just that 53 years of metal physical and spiritual research, that i am yet to fully understand to try and explain it wod not work....
Its enuff for me to read your PDF i'm not going to look that stuff up u suggested 7/28, 1:57pm **Koz Kozmos**
I can't read wot u've written, I tried, it more of the same,
and as I've said I read stuff that is similar to this
and to be honest gone beyond the ultra cosmic pose and need some thing practical that I connect with...i.m sorry BUT ITS NO GOOD

7/28, 1:58pm **Koz Kozmos**
I don't trust what u'r writing I have not gone to other dimensions and met with this new hierarchy... I think the correct spelling is !
WHY IS THE THYROID SO VASCULAR I just need answer i can understand i'm sick to death of seeking ,my work has just been being this thing i find myself to be and i can hardly exist here any more
i feel angry and down, why has reading your stuff made me feel this way?
i think your channeling from other sources that are equally as scrambled are yours
i feel if it had any real meaning beyond your own it would not be presented in this way
u may as well send it to me in a different language
basically i think its bullshit
I am filled with frustration and unhappiness, i don't mean to be rude
7/28, 4:31pm **Pre View**
then don't be rude if you don't want to sound like a rude person
ok, I will not bother u no more.
7/28, 4:31pm **Pre View**
My understanding only came in now, after 10 years of training -
it should move a lot quicker now for
people stepping into their light . You cannot expect to understand the unknown without practicing to some deep level and studying what you do in alignments. That would be like the free ride anyone takes on Youtube meditations and their arrival into the Fairy land with no fairies - because that is exactly wot most people do, they believe anyone, especially when its for free. You cannot expect to enter Divine Spaces for free: The energetic input and your worth needs the proof of the roof where you can stand in Mastery - at least when it comes to understanding the mechanics of electricity in the body and how Light is being build from zero degrees into 360 degrees All i had was my trust level and how to get to the trust level, how to move with faith and integrity.
But as i said , Fb is not the medium to tell u how to work with things as question after question arises. All i'v learned with my stuff is how to rise out this frustration and confusion and thus magnetics that keep the population in slavery . U do understand I cannot further explain this on FB nor can i explain the importance of the words used. It costs days.
So yur basically left with nothing but yur own insight.
I do understand , i do not expect anything from u.
7/28, 4:33pm Koz Kozmos
u do not understand me and u have my friendship ,
your completely missing my point
if things carry on for me and i get no help i'm done for i'm already done
7/28, 4:37pm Pre View
I'm as open as i can possibly be. I try to avoid resistance
and try to have some further insights on u.
If i fail, I fail, i'v juiced myself as far as possible.
7/28, 4:39pm Koz Kozmos
its best not to deal with me, u miss the point
because i need to understand, not more shit, i feel trapped

MY INTERNALS: I remember perfectly well when I was guided to "ALIGN TO DESIGN": I never payed much attention to this until I realized that AYIN D'ZAYIN meant align to design. These Hebrew letters brought me to a crystal, which is the rainbow obsidian and when working with it in mediation it would show designs through the ground floor through the alignments I was doing. it took me years to understand for the solo reason that I did not pay attention to it, and when I did, everything changed! Another reason was also because I did not heal that much what most term The All Seeing Eye as clearing the physical eyes is one of the most important aspects to clear before going into the deep rivers of the pineal gland and the fusion with other glands. Today, when not enough time in meditation, I just align to design and then I can see ray formulations, sometimes geometrical patterns .

After that we can fill the meditation with other elements, or ask the animal Kingdoms to pop up in our atmosphere ; which they do quite easily - they are such a wonderful sweet teachers. When we start to understand there is NO END to how we can create with Light and invent new technology and its applications that come from Divine directions, then we start to understand Light Embodiment reaching out for Mastery and mastering our energetic fields into expansive waves of light back into the Origin. It humbles and spares the ribcage from getting squared. However taking guidance through light Spaces may take many hours in meditation. Most people miss out on devotional endurance and gratitude which comes down to patience AND WILLING TO SUBTRACT THE SUB TRACKS or volumes of Ego lanes/ and thus deep subconsciousness levels. MAKING EVERYTHING CONSCIOUS IS A LIFE LONG LEARNING ZONE

7/28, 4:41pm **Koz Kozmos**
can any one else understand your writing ,i'm a bright person a
nd can read thingss on many levels
7/28, 4:43pm **Pre View**
I'm not going to repeat myself, the writing comes when moving out the magnetics....
and then it is very easy .. Yes there are certainly people who understand
and have fun through knowledge,
7/28, 4:44pm **Koz Kozmos**
wot is moving out the magnetic s, forget it I know why
7/28, 4:47pm **Pre View**
magnetic chords = astral plane = ego = matrix ...
I respect yur choices, only regret a bit we didn't meet maybe months ago and talked thru it.
I need to move on, its difficult, i need to leave yur energy.
Yet, all this synchronicity : this song Right on :'
I was reading a poem this morning i had written years ago it was called 'RIGHT ON
7/28, 4:48pm **Koz Kozmos**
we have talked but it has come to nothing
why do u need to leave my energy ,i'm not getting syncronizza teez i have a broad palette ,
so many meanings could be deciphered right on is a cliche phrase
7/28, 4:50pm **Pre View**
With so much frustration and confusion u cannot possibly have the right feelings for anything. But ok, u just jump up and down, up & down. Then yur interested, then u don't trust it. Yu're like a trampoline or a morphine dualistic bag filled with nothingness
7/28, 4:51pm **Koz Kozmos**
its not that i have these feeling right or wrong ,
its how they effect me and why i get hit so hard
continually ,its torture
7/28, 4:53pm **Pre View**
U just keep on giving all ur power to outside forces,
we've talked it over and over........ and i explained
wot you need to do to get out of the attack. EVERYBODY NEEDS TO LIGHT CRYSTALLINE GRID KNOWLEDGE TO GET SELF PROTECTION,
You just act like a child thinking you're the only one who gets the arrows right into the stomac. Eat the Sun and talk to the Great Central Sun
Need some time for myself, about time, truly tired of yur stubborness
7/28, 4:53pm **Koz Kozmos**

MUSIC: JULIAN COPE - Julian Cope/ Fear Loves This Place

7/28, 6:11pm **Pre View**
Fear loves this place, indeed, anger even more,,,,,,,,,,,good song.
Unusable concepts : please appreciate a little will ye huh? I have the same questions : how do u do the rituals, the magic, so i can do something thing with it ?
Anywayz, I hope u can pull a stop to anger as
yur bones and nerves will get worse through that consciousness.
Anger is the portal point for invaders, but u know that . I explained a lot on anger and hatred ...) But hey lets have some fun.
CHOOSE A DIFFERENT STYLE WITHIN YUR CS (consciousness)
7/28, 6:13pm **Pre View**
Thank u for the music !!! Hey were are u ? Hiding again ? I want to see u
ok , i'll load my telescopic devices, I have this idea, are you listening? :
wot if i encoded a crystal ball that would get u out of every torture ?
and send that 2 u ?
But joy heals too, invent to swim through the rivers, the floods , imagine a new landscape in which animals and humans have no fear, and communicate so deeply it heals all wounds
7/28, 6:40pm **Koz Kozmos**
I've told u and said again recently i am not a ritual magician i have used sigils in the past **MUSIC: The HU - Yuve Yuve Yu (Official Music Video)**

7/28, 6:42pm **Koz Kozmos**
but that was a long time ago,they did not work ,i have denied all teachings,
its not just anger ,its attack as u said ...i can't be here, its to much for me,
i'm paralyzed by this dimension i have no choise but to hide
7/28, 6:45pm **Pre View**
Hey lets skip wot we know, lets get out of predictables
I once printed all our unusual
messages via my email(I wonder if anyone would communicate the way we did)
which is a better way : i learned to reflect everything i told u to myself
u know basics , the mirror , coz what we tell anyone applies for ourselves
otherwise these words couldn't get into our mind, right ?
So it was a great lesson, did not allow resistance, stubbornness or anger
or anything from my part , only acceptance,,,, it moved me
lot. Did u do that too ? There was a lot i had forgotten,
7/28, 6:45pm **Koz Kozmos**
i have to have a mrk checked by doc's on my leg next week i hate doctors
7/28, 6:46pm **Pre View**
Hey why do u go then ? can u figure out wot the mark is about ?
7/28, 6:46pm **Koz Kozmos**
no i can't,if i could why wod i go
to focus on me as just angry is not right
7/28, 6:49pm **Pre View**
I feel u really want to live, i feel u still have a lot of courage,,,,
even if u tell me u want to die .... u want to understand,,,, But if there is nothing left to u , why would u not try wot i have, i cannot hurt u and its all about light and consciousness.
U'v got nothing to lose right ? so wots the problem
7/28, 6:49pm **Koz Kozmos**
because what u have makes no sense to me i've tried
and your advice is not partical tell me again how to get out of attack
7/28, 6:51pm **Pre View**
DAM! PRACTICE BRINGS UNDERSTANDING AND KNOWLEDGE that is why i told u to watch my changes, just to trust a little ..... DO WANNA REMAIN A CRETIN? GOSH!
Out of Attack : o no o no, in grid alignment you feel very tall , feel like 4 METERS and people cannot attack u any longer or say negatives, thy just cannot.
And that is sooooooo hummm

7/28, 6:56pm **Pre View**
I hope i did not offend u with wot i said earlier
I get "Roger "all of the time in my Light Space or Grid ..; I was upset and told him to leave, he was like a statue , so i surrendered and told him to stay , but the words that come out of u as the entity "Roger" , the direction u give me all the time in meditation
;;;;
is quite outstanding and bizarre
I understand ROGER as your body double because we communicate so much
7/28, 6:57pm **Koz Kozmos**
just noise of a dog barking ,who's rodger ? roger rainbow ,
i'm in panic and sorrow at all times
7/28, 7:02pm **Pre View**
Right Roger Rainbow
7/28, 7:02pm **Koz Kozmos**
i just said it as a joke (this Rodger thing)
i want to know is this random or has it been done to me purposefully
7/28, 7:04pm **Pre View**
People have panic attacks all of the time, it is infused in the matrix like psychosis and yet so easy to get out of CONTROL MACHINE Do u remember a few months ago that i told u ,
u came into my meditation and then talked to me for hours ...
that is the same thing ...; hard to keep u out...
7/28, 7:04pm **Koz Kozmo**
no its not psychoits because i'm too sane
7/28, 7:06pm **Pre View**
Right, insane in the membranes ....
I don't know , u then told me it was Roger - u joked with it -
i took it seriously , it was beginning of june
7/28, 7:07pm **Koz Kozmos**
i can't remmber i made up a story about a magical dog called ROGER,
i may have told u about that
wot do u mean membranes?
7/28, 7:08pm **Pre View**
U didn't tell me aboout the dog then ....
Well i have good memory, maybe it is indeed interesting to
print all our messages, there is a lot in it .
MEMBRANES CARRY MEMORY.
Gosh how Long has this been going on, I AM SPITTING ON YOUR OLD RECORDS!
and I am tired of filling in wot u don't respect or even want to study
7/28, 7:09pm **Pre View**
The membranes in our cells contain the memory and many other glands of course, i activate them and I don' allow myself to forget Divinity just because the underground of knowledge fails to awaken you, I t never fails, u fail to CONNECT!
7/28, 7:09pm **Koz Kozmos**
ok day in day out its destroying me, very real problems going on,
i'm not even complaining
7/28, 7:11pm **Pre View**
Not complaining? Ohjeezy, are u out of yur mind
"YOU are the Golden PLATEAU pilled with complaint!
And God says no" i liked that song
So what picture do u have of me, what kind of person do u think u have in front of u?
YOU are just streaming on good old days that lost their Majical streams,
you just believe in books while the real material has yet to be written, phenomenal change comes when entering uncommon grounds
THERE IS BUT ONE THING TO LEARN:
THE BREATHING SYSTEM THAT MOVES WITH ALL UNIVERSES,
with all Light Elements, with all Species

The breath has been cut off from the body's circulation system but can be re-learned and then LIGHT SCIENCES make sense because it allows you to feel how Light moves through the body with its fabulous vortexes and Moving pictures, snapshots, and how it brings astonishing ideas to our brains that tremble far beyond the earths' projects, inspirations

7/28, 7:11pm **Koz Kozmos**

no idea ,the first was the aging anorexic rock chick giving the V sign

7/28, 7:12pm **Pre View**

Come on Koz, make it a bit of fun :
how do i express myself, how do i dress, how do i mock

7/28, 7:13pm **Koz Kozmos**

the next the shape shifting witch in the hoody

/28, 7:13pm
Pre View

V sign ?

7/28, 7:13pm **Koz Kozmos**

The V sign at your Exhibition

7/28, 7:14pm **Pre View**

I am not a chick, i am a lady
The exhibition was bad timing, changed a lot since then
Dance some salsa and get some salsa on yer foodz,
To many aries types have ruled the world for way too long
while that salsa is infusing new herbs, dig deep because,
you got me to a level of NO CARE, MAKE A NEW DEAL WITH YOUR SELF!
delete me if you want, I DON'T HAVE A CARE IN THE WORLD

28, 7:14pm **Koz Kozmos**

u look like a middle class woman, a bit damaged into the new age and art house

/28, 7:15pm **Pre View** completely off !!!!!

7/28, 7:15pm **Koz Kozmos**

it was a 'rock chick pose'

7/28, 7:15pm **Pre View**

Are you exposing yer stupidity??? FINE ! ,
and I said I never digged into any freakzone of books, google,
alignment from the lesser gods? I felt nothing was going to fill me up no mater how i RESEARCHED LIBRARIES, BOOKSTORES, UNIVERSITIES: I COULD NOT READ THEIR IDIOTIC DEAD PENALTY! JUST DEGENERATE IF YOU WANT, I WON'T BE THERE ANY MORE ! you are just such an obvious
UK unmanageable, hardheaded, inflexibla misshape

7/28, 7:16pm **Koz Kozmos**

ok i'm talking about surface stuff i saw something in each pic that was undoubtedly there

7/28, 7:16pm **Pre View**

wot did u see, did i not camouflage ?
hm.... i'm getting back tothe older picks like i used to be, had u seen them ?

7/28, 7:17pm **Koz Kozmos**

no show me one

7/28, 7:18pm **Pre View**

there is a few onces in my albums, have a look

7/28, 7:19pm **Koz Kozmos**

huh say that agin, wot album ok

7/28, 7:19pm **Pre View**

In united albums, whenu go to my fotos on FB

7/28, 7:23pm **Koz Kozmos**

u look the same

7/28, 7:24pm **Pre View**

The rock is coming fully alive, need new pics ,joking

7/28, 7:24pm **Koz Kozmos**

dress your age for goodness sake

7/28, 7:25pm **Pre View**
picks are picks .... anywayz
Dress my age, ? Dam yur old fashioned, equals yur brains
I cannot dress like 50 when I feel like 30, rubbish
7/28, 7:27pm **Koz Kozmos**
u do wot u want i look like vincet price at the mo
MUSIC:Vincent Price interview Wogan 1982
i have my suits made and my socks

7/28, 7:29pm **Pre View**
no u do not look like him, how do u make ur socks?
7/28, 7:30pm **Koz Kozmos**
i ave them made in london in a small back street in soho
7/28, 7:30pm **Pre View** sure, but u design them right ?
7/28, 7:30pm **Koz Kozmos**
no i just choose the colour, thier always made from silk
7/28, 7:31pm **Pre View**
wot color do u prefer for ur socks
7/28, 7:31pm **Koz Kozmos**
last me 2 days if i'm carefull
7/28, 7:31pm **Pre View**
u told me u hated silk
7/28, 7:31pm **Koz Kozmos**
depends on the tie or color of my shirt ,no it was velvet
i never waer any labels all hand made with my name monogrammed
ahhhh a joke of cource
7/28, 7:33pm **Pre View**
But i could imagine u'd like that
7/28, 7:34pm **Koz Kozmos**
its hard being an eccentric millionaire,
there a finishing school for middle aged women who think their
thirty , i could suggest in Switzerland i pop over and ski
7/28, 7:35pm **Pre View**
Well, for me it is not a joke i have 50 % of my clothing made by my
design! i didn't buy anything for 3 years,
just have my private tailor i'm not middle age, i feel 30
7/28, 7:35pm **Koz Kozmos**
on occasions I'm getting a double chin with a marvelous sag
7/28, 7:36pm **Pre View**
U like Switzerland huh, ok, i could just jump on ur back then
and ski thr the mountains , that'd be fun
7/28, 7:36pm **Koz Kozmos**
i get my clothes from charity shops, no joking
this is a decent chap
MUSIC: Music
ARE YOU IN THE CLASH?
7/28, 7:38pm **Pre View** ?
Do u look like this guy ?
7/28, 7:38pm **Koz Kozmos**
watch and u will understand
no i look like vincent price ,i hate punk ,i like musicals, u 'll enjoy this
MUSIC: Dandyism

7/28, 7:40pm **Pre View**
i hate middle class, hate punk as well, musicals hum yeah there is some magic
7/28, 7:41pm **Koz Kozmos**
i 'ver always been a dany but no longer dress the part

7/28, 7:42pm **Pre View**
people say I dress up very kool, very stylish, very me, very not society like, i look different everyday, need that fun, and sometimes i do not care at a all
7/28, 7:42pm **Koz Kozmos**
MUSIC: MAGAZINE - THE LIGHT POURS OUT OF ME

i used to change my look a lot always looked better than any one on earth
7/28, 7:43pm **Pre View**
Do u have pics ?
7/28, 7:43pm **Koz Kozmos**
but i just look drab and straight these days as the wyrd has taken hold
i found some picks of me in my late teens ,
early 20's the other day been throwing away i look awful the damage has taken hold i could scan the ones from my 20's
no i do look bad, this is wyrd
i have not done this before ,i don't look anything like this and have not looked at these photos for 30 years i intend getting rid of stuff
7/28, 7:50pm **Pre View**
Hey, u don't have to look like a moving Star, right.
And why should u look good, maybe i'v other ideas
about looking good,Its just between me and u , the world is closed.
POST THEM
7/28, 7:58pm **Koz Kozmos**
keep saying upholding attachment and will not post will try agin
late 70's early 80's i was my own art projekt for a few years
7/28, 8:01pm **Pre View**
This is strangeindeed, but u haven't lost the feelin' .
The pics, these potentials ,,,
Deep inside we keep that special vibe that makes us all so unique
7/28, 8:07pm **Koz Kozmos**
i've not looked at this for many many years ,
quite deppresing, people hated me and wanted to beat me up
7/28, 8:08pm **Pre View**
People alwayz hate strong characters coz thy simply can never measure up.
I've been thrthe same, ... But maybe different, being a woman
I can see the Light in your Eyes, the Eye in the Sky
Yes i can see the damage as well at a young age, the searching, the battelfieldzzz

7/28, 8:11pm **Koz Kozmos** still sorting
7/28, 8:12pm **Pre View**
Anywayz, i like the pics, it makes sense to me in wot u've become ...
Thank u ... Sure take ur time
7/28, 8:15pm **Koz Kozmos**
should never have shaved my chest
about 35 ,ok last lot therm i'll get a new pic taken at some stage will throw all this away
7/28, 8:16pm **Pre View**
The pics make me think a bit of Bowie when he was rebellious,,,
but ok u've got ....
7/28, 8:17pm **Koz Kozmos**
i was always into cat more than bowie but at that time into me
i'll get recent ones taken and send u them with these from 20's to late 30's
and u can call the exhibition THE DEATH OF A PRETTY BOY
thanks for looking even this has stresses me out, i like myself more
7/28, 8:21pm **Pre View**
more pain, more damage, i'm getting scared∮∮∮
I'm very glad u posted these, explains a lot
Still some things stay untouched, good !
7/28, 8:23pm **Koz Kozmos**
why pain and damage?
i wod not show many people these
7/28, 8:24pm **Pre View**
Its good u like urself more, i'm seeing lotz of damage of ur parents ...
growing up, But i know ur eyes
cannot change wot u've learned,
so u are looking real good now, maybe even better and u do not realize it
7/28, 8:26pm **Koz Kozmos**
yes Vincent Price
u could never teach the drones your tech to convukuted
going for swim
7/28, 8:27pm **Pre View**
Hey Koz , i need a bit of a break ... ,
u still have these open eyes that know ....
7/28, 8:27pm **Koz Kozmos** t
he butler just told me he's cleaned and filled the pool ,
bye thank U nic
7/28, 8:56pm **Pre View**
I'm only getting al the pics now, so i didn't understand wot u were talking about (FB huh) ,,, like the onewith the neclage ... Yes thank u 2 Koz.
The Wizard returns.
7/28, 9:37pm **Pre View**
Very impressive shoots,,graceful, alluring,a bit magnetic.
I'm sure u still have that. I never looked good inmy life coz i never felt good.
But i want change now, i don't want to spend the rest of my life in trouble & anger & captivating struggles & pain.
I'm very satisfied with the shoots - Thxxxx!
I like ur hair like when its a bit longer, u've got fantastic hair.
7/28, 10:07pm **Koz Kozmos**
its short these days and has changed its taxture with age ,
20 years has passed since the newest of the shots ,
i sorta want u to delete them thanks for all your time today
7/28, 11:21pm **Koz Kozmos**
MUSIC: Caro Emerald - Stuck (Official Video)

play the above Standing in the middle of nowhere Wondering how to begin
Lost between tomorrow and yesterday Between now and then

MUSIC: TOPPOP: David Essex - Stardust

MUSIC: BARRY MANILOW Could it be magic

7/28, 11:39pm **Koz Kozmos**
mind u not sure about baz the disco remix , anyways the KozKozmos Juke Box must have the original could it be majik
7/29, 12:19am **Pre View**
I never let the album of friends open, this is just old pics,
but euhm ok, i'll let the album open for a day
No u did not offend me in any way. Looking at ur pics just brought me back in time as i had a little bit similar pics.... It made me think how far could i gwent off, where am i now, how many times i changed ... i
It was good, anywayz i like yur pics and am very glad u allowed me to see them;
So thank u.,,, it was good , some simple talk between us, i,enjoyed it....
Goodnight Koz
7/29, 1:03am **Koz Kozmos**
yes i felt the same but your tech is important to u and I don't wish to direpect it disrespect*
yes more pics than i saw before, not keen on my pics being there but if its private.....
discovered this song last year really like it, wonderful
MUSIC: Woods of Ypres - Finality

7/29, 9:31am **Pre View**
Kozkozmos Jukebox is charismatic,zippy , always majik.
❧ Its a wonderful song "Finality", only a bit obscure ❧
7/29, 9:53am **Pre View**
❧Stardust❧ makes me do creepy puppet moves, I'm gonna be a bit sharp with myself for the next 10 days and get things done as i don't feel i'm moving as fast as my intention with stufffffffff, so, and, confronting myself .
U'r very perceptive, good u don't spent too much time on FB, its a trap.
And yes, thank u for sharing so many wonderful things ∞∞∞
I will however keep the communication up with u as i feel it is important.
Posting ur photos actually made me feel a lot more comfortable with u. And now, work work work
7/29, 2:41pm **Pre View**
This morning i went to buy some chips as i eat that every day ,
i'm always very quick in shops as i hate it,
so i payed, then the guy called me back saying i still needed to pay 20 cent or something.
I said ok, no prob. But then there was a lady standing next to me and she said she was going to pay for me and even gave me the exchange of her money .....
This was quite magical, so i told her to pass that on to people & was grateful for her blessings. The simplicity u know..... it was a great experience.
7/29, 3:01pm **Pre View**
Koz, i'm posting this link coz i thought that to be of interest,,,
like there maybe radio stations around the
world looking for somebody like u
SKY.FM Radio | Enjoy amazing Free Internet Radio stations features a wide variety of free streaming radio channels. Find your favorites among the best of each class - be it New Age, 80s, Smooth Jazz, New Age, Top40, Hip Hop, Oldies, 70s, Reggae, ...
7/29, 8:13pm **Koz Kozmos**
thank u for the link , free chipz thats real majik , rushing outa fake book , take care

MUSIC:Prince & The Revolution - When Doves Cry (Official Music Vide YOUTUBE: PRINCE-Purple Rain

MUSIC:Prince - U Got The Look (Official Music Video)

7/30, 12:55am **Koz Kozmos**
saw a prince post , so Prince this is one of my favz better live
7/30, 12:59am **Koz Kozmos**
so many koool trackz ,a lot of his really good songs are not to be found on general music webs
anywayz Prince is a Jehovah Witness
7/30, 4:26am **Pre View**
OK, u got me dancing at 4 in the morning .
Yes Prince's been doing a lot of good❧
7/30, 12:41pm **Koz Kozmos**
he's a very confused man under some sort of mind control
has done some great songs
and can dance and do the splits in 6 inch heels
MUSIC:JOHN CALE live "Paris 1919"

7/30, 4:46pm **Pre View**
i'm dying from irritation , Prince has a beautiful sense of perfection, an attitude of completion
7/30, 5:29pm **Pre View**
No use talking to me today. I'm building that what people talk about as crystal skull. The bones today are full of death essence. As the skeletal structure is the energy generator,
it takes a lot of work. Sorry, bad mood with everything that comes out of me when clearing.... I will talk when i get better
7/30, 9:13pm **Koz Kozmos**
I understand as I feel like that every day, hope your ok thank u for telling me this... catch u later
MUSIC: Happiness ken dodd

bliss, i like the sound of that the song, wuz a bit of fun
7/30, 10:36pm **Pre View**
Sanity and happiness is not a good combination for thy both carry luggage. So i'm making room in my bones for the impossible to join re-arrangements of Bliss. My bones hurt like hell,i've been working on them for 14 hours , so its quite normal, so much freaking old trauma's or consciousness is leaving . I'm glad i went thru this. Here is why : some dayz ago u posted a vid about kids & i commented thy needed a lot more support and valuable education. ....Here is wot happened :i saw a friend whom i hadn't seen for 8 years. She said : do u remember Nic when u had that camp for teen-agers and these kids were laying on the ground and u just crawled like a snake over their bodies whispering things i don't remember. But i do remember they couldn't utter a word and changed their consciousness through the energy i pulled through their bones and the WORDS is whispered.
I mean to say : i truly think about why u post things, it always flows synchrone with what I am at ..... Thank U KOZ for ur support and understanding ...; Would u have a strong song for me that would make my bones twinkle as if angelic teardrops were falling into place. I have nothing to loose, and nobody can take away my source , so i better dream & stream majical words thru.Wish u could do so too,,,,,, making a real dream, a dream that support your shift,,,, Goodnight to u!
BTW : We could put a movie together for Youth and show them how majical words, Light streams, artwork and geometry actually make up human consciousness.
It would show how easily we could override the worst diseases ever on the planet : EATING DISORDERS. I'VE ASSISTED SO MANY YOUNG PEOPLE DEALING WITH EITHER ANOREXIA OR BULIMIA, and anything in between as living in a world that has been catapulted upside down when it comes to health and education has devastating outcomes. I get furious when i listen to solutions of Doctors and Psychiatrists. Dam Science is so off. They even claim the Thalamus gland the motor for sending the neurological output for hunger or no food at all. The root of this global problem has never been addressed for it would put the pharmaceutical industries out of order. Causation principles have no common ground or determination :

Anxiety, noice disturbances such as you have, inadequate neurological neglect, fear, lack of focus, stress, societal manipulation are just side effects of poor education, lack of love, lack of integrity and schools stealing the spirits of our young children as they are not allowed to think for themselves. When you think about it, it is easy to decipher the streams the need to take food and sugars as a form of satisfaction from is directed impulses. Eating disorders can never create joy, peace of mind, fulfillment, happiness, bliss for it deactivates brainwaves that are intelligent as food deviations are seen as a form of reward to endurance of stress, self manipulation and the inadequacy to express self which leaves contentment out of the equation. Most people start to think they are incomplete or that they have shortcomings while it is just the soul syndrome playing tricks on their minds and the many sub-consciousness levels academics don't even know how to deal with and would rather put these young beauties into deep hypnosis while that is exactly what should be left out and making the deeper sub-conscious level CONSCIOUS. They even claim these people need to go through painful procedures, some with medication, some without. So DISASTROUS! dam!The education of health should certainly start of at age 4 and the elimination of sugars, such as in beverages and sweets along plasTICS. WHEN HORMONAL DYSFUNCTIONAL ISSUES ARE NOT PROPERLY ADDRESS, AND THE DOPAMINE STAYS OUT OF OURDER, people keep on eating like blind men. You know Koz , it truly has an acute impact while it is so easy to heal; that is: WHEN ALLOWED! I have seen many young people change during summer camps: it would start with the explanation of their bodily function and WHY THE BREATH IS MORE IMPORTANT THEN FOOD TO SUSTAIN LIFE! And then comes the application of Light Technology which is a simple infusion of new consciousness through Light formulas and Light Languages that override the old hormonal system. Teaching acceptance had helped them a lot while I would encode the energy of DETACHMENT, then we went through all possible psychological factors that came from parents, their peers, teachers, friends, name it and made it interesting to discover how they could understand things many different ways as a birth chart is very important as well. From there on anything is possible such as the elimination of fear, anxiety, panic attacks such as you have noice disturbances, unworthiness, low values, and manny more items came to the surface. The most interesting thing to see was the learning zone of how they could communicate to their food intake and establish a new relationship in which they created respect. Respecting food as an elixir that feeds the body and that has a large impact on the brain and how it fires information brought them into a zone of new philosophy. And so, whatever they were craving, I would always first investigate the reason why and breathe that through the body in a way that it created a new communication system with the glands and neurological outcome: THAT PROVED TO BRING THROUGH THE BIGGEST CHANGE EVER, because if knowledge teaches how to respect the body and quickly eliminate low degrees in consciousness about how one feels and thinks about their body - then half the machinery is healed. Up until today I still have many children that have now grown into healthy adult calling me with such a grateful attitude and saying they would never forget about the healing week they received many many years ago for it literally saved their little lives.

Hey Koz, I really needed to get that of my chest so you know that healing through Light brings through a lot of education, explanation, philosophy and understanding which is imperative before bringing through applications such as Light Technology through meditational breathing alignments. And as I said so many times before , THE BREATH IS ALL YOU NEED TO HEAL ANYTHING, yet the breath is SO CUT OFF and hardly reaches any cell in the body meaning it cuts off the ESSENTIAL LIFE STREAMS which is non food connected. Its is very well known people can live on prana, mana, whatever, yet the education about is is not filled with much knowledge. I truly which I could teach in schools and Universities and bring back THE BREATH where it belongs for so many people are exhausted and feel out of order like a poor automobile trying to put oil in it that is outdated

7/30, 11:20pm **Koz Kozmos** ROKK !!!
MUSIC: MONSTER MAGNET - Gods and Punks (Official)

31, 10:15am **Pre View**
Something needs to be deleted of my chess : this comes thru the pic where u hold that staff - u were about 35 i guess. On that pic is many different types consciousness are going on, like choosing many different directions. I need to go back to age 35, i hope u can too and pick up where we left these vibez (maybe it is hard to understand, but with everything u do and say : u fill me in , like liquid golden meridian lines can fill up the gaps we have - i do know yur not aware of this - but still it happens ....) And I realize you can fill up Light with music, although your missing link is the knowledge about how this happens, how the functionality of Light breathes through healing with Musical Orchestrations , I guess that kept yur Eye in the blood, yet when going into the anger mode, the fire went to dust just like happened in the High Altitude/attitude Air in the Himalayas. Anger kills and you need to rebuild like we
ALL have to do this job, at least when devoted to the Divine.
I'm very very sad realizing how much i must have hurt u with my difficult talks. I always thought u'd fit in perfectly with yur intelligence but i realize my brains breathe the obvious while things are not clear for many people. Fact is, whenever we align deeply beyond the mud of the Matrix, there is no going back, no matter what, because the experience in the Higher Planes of existence do not allow for that. Even scientists would flip out, but there will come a time, very close to now, they will not have any other option but to open up to Light Consciousness which is the Essence of a human being.
So with U in my life I was hoping to work this tech out further it for humanity also becoz people have to team up, bring brainz together - we all have our specialty . It is absolutely not common that with everything I do everyday , u simply fill me in without being aware of it. So with all my tech I would just bring yur consciousness up to the level we could equalize.
7/31, 11:28am **Pre View**
I feel everything is getting too dangerous (that is why i cannot comment any longer on ur posts , i deleted, I mean on FB and the cosmic debris.
7/31, 1:30pm **Koz Kozmos**
its opk, u did'nt hurt me at all ,just frustrated me with your lack of insight, you are not ' easily understood' . I understand how intelligence is flawed, particular matrix intelligence ,i'm imaginative more than intelligent, my 'intelligent' is about insight of the outa sight not smart ass poses via academic brain washing , u don't need to be forgiven, your off track
i have felt the danger for a while and have decided to post,,,etc the government in the UK want to put blocks on esoteric sites on line, the cosmic war is getting bloodier
MUSIC: Ramases - Quasar One

MY INTERNALS: It is hard to explain, every time I said to myself I'm going to leave this arena, done with putting energy into this person for in the end it exhausted me. And every time, he came up with a new song that would resurrect me like Quasar one, very special, listen to it, look it up, understand what a quasar is. And so it kept me going for more then another year with a lot more heat and fire in the communication then ever thought possible, even after that ,I recorded phone calls, email messages, and it went into degrees nobody can imagine. It taught me how important the music Industry is, it taught me how important THE WORD IS, it taught me to teach how UNDERSTANDING can kick in, it taught me how to break stubbornness searching to preach and teach a new world.

Why did he never explain how he worked with sigils, how he worked with Magic, besides he was in the UK right? So the ground floors under Oxford University must have been felt. Also, during that time, I connected with people in the UK putting out meditational sessions with people that were so low in consciousness, a child would do better. So that explains how the matrix allows anything BUT TRUTH in the airy fairy land of no return. HERE IS MY SONG TO YOU, beautiful people

MUSIC: Jimmy Page's Chopin Prelude n.4 - Arms Concert New York 1989

AUGUST 2013

8/1, 12:25am **Koz Kozmos**
How do i FIND THE CRYSTAL CAVE
u have insight ,THE CRYSTAL CAVE iz the place majikk began, I heard when i said u had no insight...did I ? i meant how confusing u'r writings are
8/1, 3:28pm **Pre View ok, Listen to Bruce:**
MUSIC: BRUCE SPRINGSTEEN - BORN TO RUN

My writing is very imaginative, i thought with yur poetry u'd understand ..... but ok, i'll be more careful. But u do know i'll always come back 2 u. I'm surprised u want to know about the Crystal cave while everything i told u is starting there (gridzzzzzzzzzz) can u hear them buzz now .... its again TTTTTTTTTT,
but indeed to my knowledge there is many different interesting stages to get there. Itz all about the wizard , the magician and how to get there ....;understanding it and integrating it in the body, in ur home TTTTT Humanity cries out for the wither shades of PALE while PALE IS THE ULTIMATE TALE (Joe Cocker)
8/1, 3:35pm **Pre View**
"Much madness is divinest sense to a discerning eye
Crystals are much more valuable food then veggies & fruits and stuff........
Their minerals are not contaminated. That was reason why i was talking about the bone structure, some dayz ago .... Maybe to awaken something into u which u resisted in our past. U didn't want to know about lets say the most important things to begin to work with = ARKANSAS crystal, then Brazilian, then Lemurian, then African..... and so many others.
I could talk dayz about crystals beyond the low vibes in books being exposed as valuable. TTTT . You know romance the Eternal stone or Crystal, and you don't question the memes of the unknown, for these shadows or seats have no more soldiers to play the game
8/1, 3:56pm **Pre View**
Clear Creek Crystal Mine
Arkansas quartz crystal from the source, including
wholesale, points, clusters, metaphysical, wavelite, brazilian, unique and unusual.
Also learn how to become a starving miner
including digging, cleaning and pricing crystal.
8/1, 4:00pm **Pre View**
This is just a link, doesn't give u any further info (u have some in my files)
I sometimes buy them there
that's all, Brazilian are easy to get. African are very important to get the Male/Female structure back to original intent or content. That is actually my whole study. That was also reason why u made me very happy when posting "Star walker" Star walkers =Heaven , Grid walkers = Earth. I am a crystal grid-walker willing to bring heaven and earth together . I am bloody serious. But i have so much to talk about
I thought u were a Star-walker ?
Crystal Caves : as I told u before, have been encoded for these times we are living. Encoded to get & keep us out of the soul.... But enuff, we'r not getting into it anymore.
It demands too much explanation. If anything i wrote here confuses u,just let me know, i will explain for as far as i can. For now, i'm working a
lot with the elements (air, water, fire, earth, wood,...) Ether,,,,goodness that is some stuff to understand; Wot are u doing, are u ok ?
I am sad, very sad, i cannot explain all our communications from here, the grief, the frustration, the non fulfillment for both of us. So, wot can we do ? Dance ,,,
8/1, 8:19pm **Koz Kozmos**
imaginative is good, your missing the point, don't be more careful just be your selves, i don't want to be here , can i have the J Dee bit in Enochian ,
I now your serious , why out of soul? whats the problem with
'soul'? never ok , i can't get out of confusion, but i'm trying ions....
'CERTAINTY MAKES BLIND TO THE OBVIOUS' as i said a nods as good as a wink to a blind horse. I don't want photographs of me on your site or anywhere else please. Could u please take them down?

MUSIC: The Kinks People Take Pictures of Each Other

8/1, 8:34pm **Pre View**
Wot do u mean by Enochian
8/1, 8:35pm **Koz Kozmos**
John See's alphabet dee's
8/1, 8:36pm **Koz Kozmos**
Enochian is a name often applied to an occult or angelic language recorded in the private journals ofJohn Dee and his colleague Edward Kelley in late 16th century England. Kelley was a spirit medium who worked with Dee in his magical investigations. The men claimed that the language was revealed to them by angels. The language is integral to the practice of Enochian magic. The language found in Dee and Kelley's journals encompasses a limited textual corpus, only some of it with English translations. Several linguists, notably Donald Laycock, have studied Enochian, and argue against any extraordinary features
in the language; its often used by satanists I'm not to familiar with it ?
8/1, 8:37pm **Pre View**
And again, u mention Enochian, and this has been working with Enochian magic?
I mean I worked with it, u see, we always have some synchronicity going on,
u pick up wot i do
8/1, 8:38pm **Koz Kozmos**
why did'nt u know wot it was then
8/1, 8:38pm **Pre View**
I'v found a bit of the language but i cannot copy it,
strange I DO NOT KNOW THE LANGUAGE,
i do know other things
8/1, 8:39pm **Koz Kozmos**
u get quite suspicious sometimes ok
MUSIC: The Enochian Alphabet - Language of the Angels - Vincent Bridges & Dan Winter part 3 of 8
8/1, 8:40pm **Koz Kozmos**
not watched this but will do ,ok
8/1, 8:40pm Pre View
Yes Dan Winter, i do not agree with many things...; and then again he is so off and only exposing some theory that has no value today. Wot's a Heart Coherence huh: get yer Heart back into the Divine elixirs and teach it . It means I HAVE DONE MY INVESTIGATION and did talk to people who studied his courses. When I asked them how much they changed, how they could get this theory into the higher levels:
THEY WENT BLANC BEACH TIME:
they said nothing was educated because he doesn't know how to do it.
A theory means nothing unless the practice proves the moves!
Same goes for many Scientists, Physicians,,
I love the MATHEMAGICIAN, although this one gets closer to the infusion.
I connected with him, and we had an appointment in Belgium which he cut off saying he needed an after math with colleagues after the workshop because I was discussing the Eternal Spiral and explaining why some mathematics were off.
He initially wanted to know.
But as most: HE DID NOT HELD HIS WORD AS NOBODY DOES!.
Not holding on to the word means mathematics are off! Period.
Disastrous while I think he could bring greater things to kids when just allowing somebody to merge and fuse a different perspective that solves many problems.
So Jain is basically the only I would open up to,,
THEY ARE ALL SO HIGH IN THEIR HEADS,
8/1, 8:41pm **Koz Kozmos**
Dan winter; i'm not like u watching stuff on u tube all the time
8/1, 8:41pm **Pre View**
Dan is ok to listen too, u'll find many vidzzz, u'll understand me better, ;;;
I was listening to him last night about fractals,

I DO NOT AGREE BCAUSE THE BODILY FUNCTIONS SHOW THAT!
8/1, 8:44pm **Koz Kozmos**
i thought the attachment was Pre Speak
8/1, 8:44pm **Pre View**
The book of Enoch can be easily downloaded, there is a lot of interesting stuff
Yet you need to know what is applicable and what may be downgrading,
MUSIC: The Kinks - Powerman 2020 Mix

8/1, 8:45pm **Koz Kozmos**
I have the blood of the Nephilim , the kinks was a joke
i feel jumpy and nervous, ear plugs jammed in , headphones on
8/1, 8:48pm **Pre View**
uhuh, ur nervous system,,, pumping many directions haha,
8/1, 8:48pm **Koz Kozmos**
going for a swim soonish yes
8/1, 8:49pm **Pre View**
ok u just do that, its a good day , I cannot swim in pools, only the sea or rivers
swimming pools get me nauseous because of the antireceptives
or products they put in the water
8/1, 8:49pm **Koz Kozmos**
i've never had a good day , sometimes i can't handel the pool,
humans yuk
8/1, 8:50pm **Pre View**
It's about time i guess u had something real good and joyful happening, Humans,
yes YAK, I appear to make strange faces to them these days
1, 8:53pm **Koz Kozmos**
thank u
been going thru old boxes
8/1, 8:53pm **Pre View** I
interesting or boring?
8/1, 8:53pm **Koz Kozmos** a
and found some drawing i did in my teens
8/1, 8:54pm **Pre View**
U still like them ?
8/1, 8:54pm **Koz Kozmos**
they had been in my grand mothers, in a box , not sure they reveal my talent
8/1, 8:54pm **Koz Kozmos**
no one new i was precocious
8/1, 8:55pm **Pre View**
yur talented in many many ways i think, i feel,,
8/1, 8:55pm **Koz Kozmos**
too stupid ,i don't mind u having photos but i don't want them on face book, u should ask
before posting i'll have to scan them at alter date at a later date
8/1, 8:56pm **Pre View**
Hey !!! mind u , u were the one who asked me to open this album, otherwise it is always closed But ok
8/1, 8:56pm **Koz Kozmos**
mind u haha, u sound Welsh, your not practicing NLP on me?
8/1, 8:59pm **Pre View**
Welsh huh, I have some alien connection to Wales, have to decipher it,
Wot did u draw in ur teens ? i'm getting real tired of typing so much
8/1, 8:59pm **Koz Kozmos**
only had a quick look, will post , i'm so tierd to day , dogs barking woke me up
human scum all over the place
8/1, 9:05pm **Pre View**
Ok Kozmos, thank u for talking, enjoy yurs wim, with ur imagination ....

8/1, 9:04pm **Koz Kozmos**
pool will close, fancy a song and lyrics, 8/1, 9:05pm **Pre View**
Ok Kozmos, thank u for talking, enjoy yurswim, with ur imagination ....
8/1, 9:05pm **Koz Kozmos**
thank u , speak soon
MUSIC: Peter Hammill - In the Black Room/The Tower/Thunder

8/1, 9:05pm **Pre View**
oK, i'll read it, go for ur swim now hey ?
The BLACK ROOM deserves a better song, ACTUALLY A MOVING DEVICE OR MOVING PICTURE THAT SHOWS THE PHILOSOPHY WITHIN A BLACK ROOM o r BLACK CRYSTAL GRID
Only David Lynch could do that, because he did the Elephant man , he could eliminate the lower vibes within people.. Therefor I think he is very open to remove these moves and open up a new gate. David Lynch is very capable because he works into the domains of knowledge.If people get knowledge about the BLACK ROOM OR UNIVERSE, everything could be set back into balance and an ecology that breathes health, be it Light Scientific degrees. By Kozmo, later ...
IONS = an atom, molecules we have in the body. So every word that ends on ION = AN ION
Examples : Perfect-ion, complete-ion, frustrate-ion . Ions need to be deleted out of body ....when negatively charged .... Can I use ur brain for a second ? So I can better understand u. I never have enuff patience to listen to vidz as thy all talk so slow, repeat everything a million times and get nothing said but ok
8/1, 10:10pm **Pre View**
MUSIC: Fire In Blood: Alchemy & Ignition of Blood Ancient & Modern | Dan Winter
8/1, 10:13pm **Pre View**
There is many vids with Dan Winter. I listened to a few only, but i don't agree on certain things. So about 4 years ago i was going to Barcelona to have this talked over with him. Unfortunately he could not come, so it was canceled . But hey i was lucky then, they payed my flight and stay and wanted me to visit anywayz,,,,, I actually like him talking, he is clear & concise , but apart from that I don't like his passion not fusing with the practice people desperately need. We may all have a million ideas but when not having a practical outcome and change in consciousness, wots the use?
8/1, 10:21pm **Pre View**
I cannot figure things out by myself alone all the time.
People need to put brains together, things need to
be discussed. Ok, i'll leave it here, got a headache ,I should rest.
Implosion Group - Dan Winter's Fractal Physics + Bliss Science..Sacred Geometry&Physics...
This is Dan' Web, a disaster, but ....
8/1,10:25pm **KozKozmos**
if i have great knowledge how do i use it well ,check out , hope your head feels better will get back to u on PENTAGRAPH, how do u delete ions?
8/2, 9:59am **Pre View**
Kozmo, I have 1 question for u : WHY when u message meis it that u use a new line for every single word. Why do u not put everything in sentences ? Is it coz u use ur chat box or .... ?
8/2, 2:06pm **Koz Kozmos**
its not 'Kosmo' , I can not find a, way to delete ions .
I'm not sure wot I'm doing with this fb thang as far as writing is concerned,
i type a line to answer or reply to wot u've written
i'm very deslexic , hope its ok and u can follow

MUSIC: Pentagraph Animation

8/2, 2:21pm **Koz Kozmos** ˊ
A pentagraph (from the Greek: , pénte, "five" and γραˊφω, gráphō, "write") is a sequence of five letters used to represent a single sound (phoneme), or a combination of sounds, that do not correspond to the individual values of the letters. Irish has a number of pentagraphs. English, like most languages, has none.
its also a machine for doing metal work....
8/2, 5:03pm **Pre View**
Pentagraph, yeah i'v looked that all up, it can be applies in many wayzzz.
I just liked Kozmo because it has an echo to it (I'm just interested in language ...)
But we both like precision I guess, so i'll respect KOZ
8/2, 10:39pm **Koz Kozmos**
no worries was joking about name
my humor is not recognized but thats ok, Just blocked your friend Anna Alma , no more idiots
8/3, 5:27am **Pre View**
Anna : euhm, the girl is only 19, learning fast, she is a student here, also a loner and interested in finding her Spirit, so give her a break will u,
it took her months to even dare to talk 2 u.
8/3, 5:46am **Pre View**
Julius (my son) invited me to a squash ... it was fun ... but i'm getting a real problem when humans approach, i smell their grey skins, i smell thoughts,,, brrrrrrr
8/3, 12:00pm **Koz Kozmos**
I'm exhausted! squash....? yes i've been thru another load of shit with 'humanz' wenever i make any sort of contact it seriously back fires and things get crazeee and i retreat once again into my loner zone thinking...
I like the poetic elements in your writing ,
u asked me wot a line meant in my poem
i explained poetry is a diffrent form .....how do u delete ions?
yes Anna is young, u don't always now a persons story, but i'm bored with this whole game people are pathetic, tell her ...I wish her the best
8/3, 12:30pm **Pre View**
Anna had Asthma all of her live. As she started doing meditation sessions with me, she sensed many openings. After that I gave her 3 healing sessions, a specialty on the breathing system and deep clearing of the Lungs, the spinal column, arteries, bronchial tubes.... Now she is completely freed from the puffers and medication she had to take, especially at night. Also, the alignment I gave her on mp3 was extremely helpful to keep the clearing going and helped to keep lungs dust free although a lot of psychological content was deleted as well. Such a shame physicians do not have a clue how to apply Light Tech to override diseasing consciousness. So easy, a lifetime of suffering deleted in one week of simple efforts.
8/3, 12:35pm **Koz Kozmos**
i just tried to arrange something and things got strange and dysfunctional its not me, i look to my self and take blame
good for Anna,
8/3, 12:35pm **Pre View**
What did u try to arrange may I ask ?
8/3, 12:35pm **Koz Kozmos**
and in the past have given a way my power for a quite life, but no more ,
i am defiantly being targeted or have been cursed TT its pathetic i'm a civil man and reliable, some things as u know can't be typed
8/3, 12:37pm **Pre View**
I know yur reliable and appreciate it a lot,
8/3, 12:37pm **Koz Kozmos**
and have history attached to them so, are very hard to explain
something wants to keep me in misery, this is not who i am
i have been worn down by a life time of shit
no self pity here, I don't want to complain
8/3, 12:39pm **Pre View**
I know, but an ending to all this needs to come in now, u payed hard enuff for all this

8/3, 12:40pm **Koz Kozmos**
i have payed so much but thats not the problem, the problem is why so much bad energy and bad luck? Ihave had beautiful thoughts for the transformation of the earth since i was young, all this negativity, bs its outa sync, its a new guilt trip and a limited pose for fakers,
i have a black sense of humor , i'm eyeronik
8/3, 12:43pm **Pre View**
I can perfectly relate to that, a few years ago, as I had not learned as much as I have now, I went through many struggles, basically the matrix that keeps you down. And when we're down, nothing manifests. All I could understand for myself was to get out of the emotions with all my tech, it is still assisting me. ITS ALL IN THE PRACTICE AND BECOMING THE PRACTICE OR THE EXPANSION INTO LIGHT FORMULAS just like we can apply formulas for a nice dinner. I like u being ironic, ...
8/3, 12:43pm **Koz Kozmos**
i have to make some change and it has to come soon
it has become too distasteful being here ,yes
8/3, 12:44pm **Pre View**
Do u have any idea wot u are going to change, just go back in time and re-imagine
8/3, 12:45pm **Koz Kozmos**
I want to change every thing in my life
i want a diffent life away from humans and barking dogs
a place to hide
8/3, 12:45pm **Pre View**
Could u advise me on some good protein : as of now i take hemp, nuts, quinoa,
8/3, 12:46pm **Koz Kozmos** Beans pulses
8/3, 12:46pm **Pre View** What are pulses ?
8/3, 12:46pm **Koz Kozmos**
Beans of diffrent sort, cook some onions and peppers in some oil ,a
dd some mixed herbs and pepper
8/3, 12:48pm **Pre View**
yeah, i had that with about 7 other veggies,,
,but nothing seems to be filling me up and at times I just can't eat.
Light feeds all of the time, we just have to go with that roadster and accelerate the delights without the fight of malaise and morbidity. Are u a good cook ?
8/3, 12:48pm **Koz Kozmos**
i'm not comfortable enuff to cook
my ear plugs are in, deep listening to meditaion music, i can't hear the city any more
8/3, 12:51pm **Pre View**
I'm gonna buy some ear plugs just to know how it feels, or whenever there is summer party going on, i retreat in the woods, but unfortunately i am afraid to stay there at nigh, as i have been damaged in the past
8/3, 12:51pm **Koz Kozmos**
unless u can grow your own food on a different planet that wod be good, get soft ear plugs
8/3, 12:52pm **Pre View**
Every food that is processed is no good, like tofu, tempeh , the soy stuff, all foods are becoming plastic, taste has gone ,chemtrails are infused while humans refuse to use brains. The Earth has such a sad story
8/3, 12:53pm **Koz Kozmos**
the problem is the noice, cut out additives, i just do my best with food ,but the noise vol for me is on 10 most peoples volume is 2 ;
most people are so dummmed down and unaware
but i'm like a souljar who has heared too many bombs
and seen to many die its unbearable, every thing is magnified
8/3, 12:56pm **Pre View**
Even the sound of ur breath ? 8/3, 12:56pm **Koz Kozmos**
post traumatic stress disorder, yes every thing i'm aware of, even the keyboard as i type and i have ear plugs in over the ear + high quality head phones ,
but mostly i hate humans and thier noise

8/3, 12:57pm **Pre View**
I wish i could experience these higher volumes or tones that, gain more knowledge about the higher herz Do u think your ears are interrelated to dyslexia ? I was reading about it last night ... just a few scientific pages to understand were they are at when it comes to the hearing tech in the body.
8/3, 12:59pm **Koz Kozmos**
play music u hate for 3 days non stop on an uncomfortable volume with a dog locked in a yard barking and have people chatting inately
yes i think its connected but i'm a lot worse , i cannot live like this, but i have no choice and my eyes etc have been fucke up , its terrible, but i keep smiling and I'm always positive
8/3, 1:01pm **Pre View**
I've worked a lot on opening my ears with my tech, maybe i should load a program that closes it off. I am SIRIUS. Would u like to know wot i got with working with Enohian energy ?
8/3, 1:02pm **Koz Kozmos**
ok but u have not been able to help, only confuse
8/3, 1:06pm **Pre View**
I was just focussing in meditation with my crystals as they are the basics of evolution and carry so much data from many ages ago; but most importantly, they assist and teach how platonic solids work in the body and opens up geometrical patterns. You know wot I mean? When people talk about sacred geometry but lost the Keys of how to get into these pretty pictures Just a matter of allowing meditational alignment and put your intentions into the Universe that always responds. When you realize that crystals are being applied in our computers, radio stations, screens and so on, it is understandable that they can carry and hold data. I truly wish Science departments in Universities would understand how much it matters to teach students. Also , I had this dream and project of building a huge Milky Way Crystal Art project .Each Star of the Milky Way is designed to teach through a Crystal room in which the student can learn about the psychological content within a planet and fuse consciousness. Imagine how fascinating and refreshing their studies could become. So when getting these large vortexes through my crown chakra, I all of a sudden was seeing"UN" (an Enochian letter)It was running up the spin, it ended in the roof of my mouth , expanded through my jaws, and I can still feel it in the jaws and in the hammer, anvil of my ears. Quite an expansive experience. All this came through with Amber and Red Light.
Here is how it looks like, ...

8/3, 1:07pm **Koz Kozmos**
I have no connection to this sort of experience and it means very little to me, what has this done for u?
8/3, 1:08pm **Pre View**
I am not going to explain it further: if we get something in meditational devotion with our Source, u can just breathe that into the body, ask what it means, how to apply it through the breathing system and where it needs to land. That is essentially ho it works. I you take a look at a tree that grows food, that is informing you that you may eat it and that it will nourish your body. Same goes for things you get in meditation: if you get things and never taste them or apply them like apps on yur IPhone; wots the use of connecting to the universe anywayz? Still , many people think they get transformed that way and reason why self development and realization into our Crystalline embodiment is so off. Understanding and learning takes energy and at least daily commitment.

My first passion in the morning, when the sun and the moon meet up is truly my sweetest connection with my Source and sparkling new Lights, learning new tech, learning about elements, species, a never ending zone and reason why every day is full of surprises and synchronicities.
8/3, 1:11pm **Koz Kozmos**
i just look out of the window and think no more, nothing manifest for me apart from shit if they gave me so much, why will they not let me do anything with it
8/3, 1:13pm **Pre View**
Sure, dammit, u will not by any means just transform because u have the idea of looking thr the AIR,LOOK WITHIN THE AIR. AIR AND WATER IS ALL CRYSTAL RELATED: main composition of a crystal and thus crystalline body. Practicing LIGHT by breathing it through has the capacity to bring thr DESIGNS. Designs can transform old consciousness and rewire many things and can also be applied with spiritual numerology, sacred letters such as I got, toning them is also an option. BUT YOU NEED TO DO THE WORK INSTEAD OF BLABBERING. You can only get to know PHENOMENA by tasting it, integrating it in the body, following its directions, listening to the communication that comes through,
such as thru crystal tracks that bring messages in our hearing
motives! If you don't get wot I sya, then you don't, i am done explaining.
8/3, 1:14pm **Koz Kozmos**
u have not told me anything, only come up with vague concepts, i don't know
can u please stop telling me, i know , another dead end but its ok
8/3, 1:17pm **Pre View**
If i only have vague concepts, then u don't even appreciate them.
u're exhausting with yur inverted pipeline, had enuff, Catch u later, -
8/3, 1:18pm **Koz Kozmos**
i need to feel a connection to some thing and have my interest sparked
to re read is moronic , your concepts u have proofed with out doubt are vague you seem incredibly naive, u've been explaining your tech over months but not reread
8/3, 1:25pm **Pre View**
ok i'm a master of naive scripts
8/3, 1:26pm **Koz Kozmos**
so u think your a master , seems delusional, ogod, but i will be honest about how i feel
never the less , u need some one to challenge u , for instance u said u did something to my neck etc for me nothing has changed any ways
8/3, 1:29pm **Pre View**
Of course it did not : hey don't u get anything or wot ?????
8/3, 1:45pm **Pre View**
I WOULD FUCKING LOVE TO FUCKING GIVE U A FUCKING VALUABLE UNDERSTANDING OF WHAT THE FUCK IS GOING ON, ON THIS FUCKING EARTH PLANE THAT OFFERS FUCKING MAGOR FUCK POSSIBILITIES TO GET FUCKING ALL INTO A FUCKING REAL WORLD NO FUCKING BOUNDARIES EVER TO FUCKING MEET AGAIN WITH FUCKED UP BRAINS THAT DO NOT GIVE A FLYING FUCK ABOUT THE FUCKING BEAUTY OF LIFE
This is how i get pissed , Now fuck off, will ye!
And now let's shower it off and please give me one good song today and see the magical number in the
song will you, that should work.
8/3, 1:48pm **Koz Kozmos**
BEAUTY OF LIFE ? i am sad but thats the easy part

THE KOZ KOSMOS JUKEBOX LIVE!

DAVID BOWIE - SORROW

The Merseys - SORROW

Pink Floyd - SORROW

8/3, 1:54pm **Koz Kozmos**
i'm not really into pink floyed but i really like this song, JUST LISTEN TO THIS ONE
MUSIC: Pink Floyd : High Hopes, Royal Festival Hall

8/3, 1:58pm **Koz Kozmos**
i connect with the energy of this song, the studio version is better
pink floyd is music for failed counter culture zeros freaks in thier teen rebel poses

MUSIC: Pink Floyd - High Hopes ((with Lyrics)) YOUTUBE: John Mellencamp - Pop Singer

fancy one more to rock out to in a peacful way
MUSIC: John Mellencamp - Peaceful World

luv the backing vocals, hope u have a good day
8/3, 2:24pm **Pre View**
This girl needs a pretty damn good joke. I will dance it through and rock my Light!
The music is kool enuff, my feet feel the heat
And by the way chaps like us never say bye or goodbye or cya.
I wonder how it would feel to live in a male body, to know how senses work in a male body,
MUSIC: BIG MOUNTAIN- I LOVE YOUR WAY

8/3, 3:29pm **Pre View**
Hey were are u ? Hiding in the PeaceTrain or wot ? Can anyone truly be private ? when we can read each others' brains?
U know ,the other day when i was running i came across abused horses.
And society cannot do this to me, i awakened the whole animal control system ,
I just had to. It breaks me when I see broken animals and they are so innocent,
8/3, 3:44pm **Koz Kozmos**
I've been trying with the pollution control and other people for over 10 years
the only escape is total soul death, the authorities are crap, i am not strong ,i am broken i have to escape i can no longer cope if i try to sort things out ,
i get nothing, so many dysfuntionla rules
8/3, 3:46pm **Pre View**
We have to do our own thing. Look at what has been done to David Icke, yet he speaks out
8/3, 3:46pm **Koz Kozmos**
and they can feel my diastase and disgust, David Ike is getting as big as Hitler
I can no longer stop my hate, i am hatred
i am out of balance and dealing with the authority is no good they come out and leave and the dog is still barking non stop
8/3, 3:50pm **Pre View**
Hatred is no good, it is the worst state in consciousness that allows for the monsters to do their thing with you and reason why you get attacked so much.. I'v been dealing with someone day & night with it 24/7 for many many months. It is not thinking to understand , it is thinking beyond,,, get out of the FB posts and the news and get to yourself in states of consciousness you can possibly remember or rise into Universal consciousness, think it through intuition, imagination and strong intent!
8/3, 3:50pm **Koz Kozmos**
then another piece of shit moves into the street and it happens again and again, i am not meant to live with all these vibes and low grades around me
but its the best place i've had in my life , i only keep fb
totalk to u, i've stoped posting the occasional,
its not FB, thats the problem
8/3, 3:52pm **Pre View**
It will not stop. U need to stop yurself from feeding into it. U are meant to take steps beyond these vibes. Once u're there, u'd have a big laugh on the lower states of mind

manipulation as that is old Lemurian energies that think it is intelligent - yet many do realize that the movement into Atlantean vibes is reason for us being here. And yes, I totally agree, to what you refer too as total soul death for that is pure ego consciousness and so the information received at these astral levels are so distorted and anamorphic that that kind of data creates even more chaos and disruption or the thing they truly want to create : The Great Divide. It will never happen, too many are rising into some level of awakening in which they realize how severely damaged and traumatized they are which causes the highest level of stress. When stress enters the many faculties within the beauty of a human body, it KILLS EVERYTHING! It wipes out HEALTH and people feel executed, yet not truly aware of it because they LOST THEIR LIFE STREAM, their Living Light Ley Lines and chords and alignments and connections to the Divine and Divine Tribes or Teams. So often times in meditation when NOT being in a Light Crystalline Grid Protective zone, the archons or monsters of the Universe can do ANYTHING TO BRAINS! THEY CAN MAKE PEOPLE GO MAD FOR NO REASON, just have a good look at psychopaths, mostly very intelligent people with a very high intuition. A little technique in meditation is not too hard to learn, the higher states in consciousness can easily be achieved when the daily practice becomes the joy of being alive and leveling up every day through Divine instructions and directions such as holding on to goals, and consciously rewriting the actions taken upon goals as the higher senses sharpen and we gain access into the many zoom rooms that ascends the body brain into a never ending spiral of the Continuum. The Human Cell is born in water consciousness. The planet is all water, so we need to return, merge and touch down into the consciousness of the oceans, the lakes the rivers that all carry vast amounts of knowledge and intelligence. NO SPIRITUAL SCIENCE EVER EDUCATED THE POWER OF WATER. When being born as an embryo in water that is merged with AIR OF SPIRIT; then that is exactly how to understand how we need to become a Crystalline embodiment from CRYSTALLINE FLUIDS once again. If you look at crystals and gemstones and their geometric patterns; they are just carriers of pure Divine Consciousness. Have a good look at computers, radio, screens, data storage....Their footage is CRYSTALLINE TECHNOLOGY. So, when the human computer system integrates crystals in the body, the brain, energy wheels and merge that with the crystalline grid technology or bringing through advanced access to higher levels of Science, knowledge and intelligence while the macro cosmos (universes) merges with our micro cosmos (humans). That is not too difficult to understand. In such a meditational space we often stream through a given alignment to the platonic solids and more data within crystals and plants and animals. Its the future of Medicine along with Light languages, musical scales and so on. It cannot possibly be held back anymore, because the higher vibrational energies are being loaded on the planet like a Huge Enterprise that esophocates the old system. The only blurry thing on people is that they think some God is going to save them, or they think they need to run the energies of other masters through or Angelic Kingdoms while this is the most off vibe i've ever witnessed and so disrespectful. ALIGNMENT AND ACTIVATING CONTINUOUSLY NEW ALIGNMENTS THROUGH DIVINE CONSCIOUSNESS AND DIVINE WILL versus Free Will which is killing every body is the " ABSOLUTE WAY" to go. Deities can give guidance, instructions, directions, communications, assistance, support, anything! BUT WE NEED TO DO THE WORK OURSELVES. The more crystals we incorporate, the more information will be revealed! WE ARE THE POWER OF WATER + THE POWER OF AIR which should largely be educated. Water + air makes up a crystal that is infused with Source substances for us to discover and investigate such as in the Fringe series: I really liked them, and the characters as well . There is nothing mystic, it just needs discovery.

Is this finally making sense 2 u? UNDERSTAND YOU NEED TO TO THA WORK, THAT IS ALL THERE IS TO IT!

8/3, 3:52pm **Koz Kozmos**

yes but thats very vague again, i want to destroy humanity

my anger and hatred are about things that have happened to me and my surroundings ,

its real and has a source that only gets worse

8/3, 3:58pm **Pre View**
Hatred kills everything and never offers a ways out. Through meditational alignments you can access the consciousness of PEACE first, then you can work your way into FREEDOM which is taking action into the elimination processes that created all these negatives thought patterns in the brain. We can eliminate through the application of symbols we get, geometric patterns, numerology , music, Light languages and ESPECIALLY THROUGH RAYS OF LIGHT that bring these applications through as every DIVINE RAY CARRIES CONSCIOUSNESS. Peace is the consciousness within a BLUE RAY for example, mix that with White ray highest health and the Gold Ray that gets you out of the old : would be a good start. JUST BREATH IT THROUGH and ask these rays to move through the gland in your brain that hold hatred! Dammit, no more questions!After this learning zone comes LIBERATIONS and upgrades in the ZOOM ROOM WITH THE MASTERS AND DIVINE TEAMS on the New Tables of Creation or the Round Table with the Knights of the First Order and steel strength. Strength can be educated as well just by streaming
a symbol through the spînal colun, easy peace!
Listen to Stevie Nickxxx: CRYSTAL VISIONS

8/3, 3:59pm **Koz Kozmos**
i disagree on a higher level, hatred has gone, but i still hate this dimesion of low grade scum, its practical application, i am in the wrong place at the wrong time and have sufferd much abuse ;place it in a bath of acid , it wood be the same as asking to get out of hatred, its bs, new age philosophy, always blame the victum
8/3, 4:03pm **Pre View**
I don't think so, u can be so strong and imagine to block any energy that is not yours: just stand there, look at it for wot it is and move on with yurself, not feeding in, but looking for solutions, having the knowledge
8/3, 4:03pm **Koz Kozmos**
i find this the universe and yur teaching model disgusting
8/3, 4:03pm **Pre View**
u disrespectful freak , don't even try to misshape and warp my teaching zone!!!
i feel different every day, shift and reshape consciousness, upgrade, detect, block, clear and have access to knowledge that would turn your nose into bloody screens of self identification,
8/3, 4:04pm **Koz Kozmos**
if this is happening, the universe is sadistic
8/3, 4:04pm **Pre View**
Don't blame the Universe!!!! We are all in it together as co-creators and need to restore the entire planet back into its Origin and further that with the Continium.
8/3, 4:04pm **Koz Kozmos**
i have no support or accces to other places, i'm here,
i am in the process of trying to move but i nkow earth is no good for me, there is no where left to go unless i win the lotto and by a place in its own grounds with electric fences round and maybe a few guards, its hopeless, soiry to go on
8/3, 4:08pm **Pre View**
No support ? : that is exactly wot is missing, can u not have access to a support team And yes, you need to level up your vibe to connect with them in a clear space without your low mentality, without fear, anger, hatred, truly work with universes. I wouldn't know how to live without - i would get back into deep shit = wot i've lived for the last years. So do know, I understand how to get people out of their shit and degrading creations because I LIVED IT FOR TOO MANY YEARS. Its all gone now, and good thing I KEPT FAITH, TRUST AND DIVINE ALIGNMENT with upgrading communication systems. But i hope u can do to, i mean just talking or asking for support and whom that may be should be possible huh?
8/3, 4:08pm **Koz Kozmos**
wot support team? i've asked for support all my life
8/3, 4:09pm **Pre View**
There are many Celestial, Universal teams, Just ask for Divine guidance, thats all and listen,,,

8/3, 4:09pm **Koz Kozmos**
i have over and over and over, NOTHING !!!
more shit , Pain and sickness, wot is this support u talk about? why if i ask, do i get nothing, why am i being tortured, its no good, i have learned its kicking a man wen he's down and the blood gathers around me and i keep getting kicked so the wound never heals ,
wot is this support u talk about?
8/3, 4:13pm **Pre View**
HATRED AND ANGER!!!!I've learned i couldn't get support with the anger. ... Is it true, i worked it out for myself and when being in a clear space, support came. But hey i'm not all knowledge... Support : i listen to wot comes thru in meditation which is while i shower, walk, cook , u get that right? Today i tapped into the Moses energies and team - I focussed, listened, followed directions but needs a lot of focus thru the day. It might be anything for u because the intent to receive messages is important and also aligning to crystalline underground tracks that are connected to our ancestors ,
the indigenous tribes and other species matters.
8/3, 4:13pm **Koz Kozmos**
I'm not just about anger
i'm the kaleidoscope kid, my anger comes from being placed in a bath of acid
I don't have your experiences
8/3, 4:15pm **Pre View**
The same here, I think merging our experiences and having fun with scientology would give a great outcome, lets stream some commercials huh?
Give me some vision of the world of Light Dreams?
8/3, 4:16pm **Koz Kozmos**
i mean your 'mystical experiences ' there has been so far no great outcome
i feel i may go insane if i have any more of this
8/3, 4:18pm **Pre View**
it is not mystical at all, it is real. And Nic is someone that has no patience with results, so getting me somewhere the last few weeks and hitting it harder gave me some satisfying results. But as i said it is hard and interesting work. People need the strength, the endurance, the devotion and the courage to do it; most of the time when the shit gets worse is when they want to get out of their laziness and transform.
Koz Kozmos
yes but i have a point, using the term mystical experiences
8/3, 4:19pm **Pre View**
Can u hold on 5 minutes, i have to prepare something for my son, he needs to go to work, i'll be back,
8/3,4:20pm **Koz Kozmos**
take your time please, this is no good me going on about stuff on fb
8/3, 4:37pm **Pre View**
MY Son is sending good vibes...; he is just curious to know what we are talking about all the time. Youth has lost lost of potential to communicate, their social acts have gone into smoke. Sometimes I'm thinking why we had to meet up , the attraction to the spirit worlds, the FB posts I guess were very special
8/3, 4:38pm **Koz Kozmos**
wot vibe is he sending and why? and how does he know me ?
8/3, 4:39pm **Pre View**
positive, joyful, he kind of likes u and it amuzes him when he sees me chatting,,, which is good
8/3, 4:40pm **Koz Kozmos**
I'm just finding practical out comes if i continue living on earth
why does he like me ,he knows nothing about me, this is nonsense
8/3, 4:41pm **Pre View**
He has seen yur comments on my posts in the past and finds them intriguing
8/3, 4:41pm **Koz Kozmos**
the tiny bit of power i had is dying
8/3, 4:42pm **Pre View**
No, u have all that power, claim it ! dammit

8/3, 4:42pm **Koz Kozmos**
i've tried ,its done and i mean it ,the wound has become too great for me
and the universe keeps kicking it, i can not longer tolerate this place and why should i
8/3, 4:46pm **Pre View**
Sure, why should u, same thing going on everywhere, we just need to take
responsibility of our energy fields and protect them. Understanding comes with
practice and upgrading Lights within, integrating planetoids, asteroids, stars brrr, I
wish U had at least a single human over there with whom u could exchange yur shit &
level up. I'm getting breathless, if you don't understand it, maybe I should teach you
the practice in person or thru a seminar I could give in Wales and show you the
worlds within worlds and parallel universes. THE KEY IS THE BREATH!
BREATHING IS INTEGRATING!
8/3, 4:47pm **Koz Kozmos**
i also speak with jain doe, i have not met 8/3, 4:47pm **Pre View** Does it help ?
8/3, 4:47pm **Koz Kozmos**
she's a good person but she's ill, nothing helps
8/3, 4:48pm **Pre View**
yess i've seen she takes quite some medication
8/3, 4:48pm **Koz Kozmos**
not the people, fuck people, she doesn't take many medication,
not sure why u think that ,
its bad being trapped in front of a screen feeling all this disempowerment
8/3, 4:50pm **Pre View**
Hey maybe just do something u'v never done before , leave yur place,
find a little something somewhere,
New breath, new air, i don't know yur possibilities, but at least u don't have to take
anyone into account , Well she said somewhere she had to take 7 pills a day ,
don't know, it is not importanT
8/3, 4:51pm **Koz Kozmos**
i've done all that, i don't go out on the weekend, too many humans too much noise,
the streets are crowded, always in the way, no self awareness, most of them scummed
in the low grade soul experiment
8/3, 4:52pm **Pre View**
ok, buy a tent, and go from the woods into other woods just maybe around Wales for
a week or so, where humans don't come. I avoid people all the time, only come out
early mornings & late nightsss
Many hearts are broken on this plane of existence, you are not alone
Come on Koz, u can travel a bit and be inventive and avoid
8/3, 4:53pm **Koz Kozmos**
and there is no where to go, we've talked about the woods before, i have a tent
but no transport and no money
WISE UP i can't leave and go into the noise
8/3, 4:54pm **Pre View**
I don't have to wise up there, i do as i like,
8/3, 4:54pm **Koz Kozmos**
i always try and explain a word or subject, if u don't get it physically i'm not too bad,
a few operations that have messed me up but i'm fit for my age, there is no were for
me to go i have no one, but i don't mind TT, company has never been my problem
i need to escape for good, not cycle down the park, i get by, i have some saving TT
8/3, 4:59pm **Pre View**
But hey this girl pushes herself always !, even with distortions in body,
8/3, 5:01pm **Koz Kozmos**
thats it , in the city: i'm not going shopping for the latest jeans
i did night classes and yoga etc years back, too many cretins, i need food and sleeping
i don't want more discomfort, i always look kooler than every body else in my dress
and i dress down and i need good shoes, sandels so i can walk and look after my feet
and joints i 've got a designer watch and an ancient sundial,,,
yes i need to be comfortable

8/3, 5:07pm **Koz Kozmos**
Sundail: An instrument that indicates local apparent solar time by the shadow cast by a central projecting pointer on a surrounding calibrated dial.
I hope i'm not being to clear and explaining things again
8/3, 5:08pm **Pre View**
Being sarcastic get the Light out of yer body as well, it is as worse as anger and hatred. Got that? fine. Hey Koz, i need to get these earplugs now, shops close soon, so it was soft ones, any particular brand?
8/3, 5:09pm **Koz Kozmos**
just shop around for ear plugs, but soft ones are better i find but they mess u up if u wear them all the time as i need to do; i've had infection and lost hearing in one ear, its come back , ok all the best
8/3, 5:09pm **Pre View**
ok, keep on pumping the blood vessels, And thank u Koz
8/3, 5:12pm **Koz Kozmos**
thank u so , euhm thank u for putting up with my darkness
MUSIC Aerosmith - Darkness HD (HQ) Quality [320 kb/s]

steven tylar such a great singer, but he needs a major paradigm shift, the song arrangment could be better , need to find new music , i'm into so much,
but always go with syncrow u have a cellar, must be quite down there
8/3, 6:53pm **Pre View**
Aerosmith, yes very good for today. Cellar, yes i like it, i sometimes paint there, i like it, i can have a few cellars,,, i'm the only one who has access to the underground over here,,, Also, the landlord is trying to get beer brewed, do not see him much, the guy is ok, searching for himself, lets me do wotever i want,,, He just knows, i'm not a regular human walking offline as much as she can.
8/3, 7:03pm **Pre View**
Back, I walked in & out of the city in 15 minutes. Screwed it up again, wot can u expect, i walked into a pharmacy and asked for somebody that could give me some explanation about earplugs. So thy asked me why. I told them i needed good advice and told them i have no knowledge about earplugs . Nobody knew ,
or had experience, so how can thy sell something thy don't know a thing about,,,,
Have u been interested to watch something about Dan Winter ?
8/3, 10:44pm **Koz Kozmos**
remind me i'll check him out, better than listening to the slasher flick
8/4, 1:05am **Pre View**
Have no interest in talking, Good night Koz, BRRRRRR
8/4, 7:07am **Pre View**
Ireland is a very important country to bring the unification through or many spiritual purposes such as the Gate of Knowledge (Oxford university) and the opening & workings of the 7 Arks realigned and opened since 2009. "The Celestials Gate: has its central focus in Ireland with Merlins awakening & opening multi-
talented gifts due to their base of operations connected to Ashford Castle.
Ireland has the mystical culture that still believes in the mystic and yet carries the feminine archetype of strength while the other proportion Scotland carries the masculine. Dense magicians covering the Merlin group retained even through the "fall". I think Ireland has a strong history of fallen dense airy fairy so called magician with power hungry intentions.Most interesting, OXFORD UNIVERSITY is where ALL ARKS ARE IGNITED FROM. This is ONE CENTRAL ENGINE OF PERFECTION set to move into position
through GRID LAYERS AND WALKERS
8/4, 7:27am **Pre View**
Reason why i am posting this information is because u told me u were going to align to your 'Celestial' body as I had the intent to do so. I thought it would be of interest to u .... Further information needs to come through ur daily walk.
I am exploring this for myself.
i do not know wot the LADY OF LIGHT IS among other things.
I try to align to it to get more information.

8/4, 7:49am **Pre View**
Ireland will continuously re-pattern the brain with all the Keys of Knowledge
This may leave many confused and running for answers fighting for the old ways and means. **...** The Cuzco Peruvian Crystal is great to assist the repatterining of the brain
You could possibly at least start working with the integration off consciousness that are within the crystals, Do you have any?
Once upon a time the Celestial Level managers in Ireland kept Immortal records and lived out Immortal Precision for physical means. Being very simple and wise they noted that this entire universe, not just earth was far out of touch with original Immortality and was changing the laws and rules to fit power driven Free will ....
One has to be STATIC FREE to bridge the OLD/NEW.
I think its great information, comes from an extraordinary Lady that is such a special channel.
8/4, 8:07am **Pre View**
I hope this is of great interest to u. I did message this in order for u to expand upon this information as i will do for the next week coming as well. There is so much knowledge and realigned details to discover through UK, Wales, Scotland,,,
As always, it is for u to think further and maybe close of the computer for a week or so to get ur own information through ur heart. U can wise up !
IT SHOULD BE VERY CLEAR THAT U MUST BECOME UR OWN HEALING.
Nobody can do it for U
Many states of consciousness need acceptance before they can be alter and prepared for complete change. Then of course assistance is going to be easy.
As of now u still manipulate or give fault to ....
8/4, 8:20am **Pre View**
I will not accept any question or comment. U have all the answers within u.
THINK DEEP LIKE AN IRON GANG DOES. Hope u can appreciate my many hours of investment. And please REFLECT UPON WHY I GIVE INFO AND NO PRACTICE; WIZE UP !
8/4, 12:30pm **Koz Kozmos**
U should write a new age fantasy novel, can you do characters?
if Ireland is feminine & Scotland masculine....wot is Wales & England?
Who is the LADY OF LIGHT....etc . OXFORD UNIVERSITY is a recruiting ground for the nobility what are ' Green Gates of Knowledge' who built them and how do they work? what are the ' 7 Arks'?
every thing u write it is fantastical in a cliches sorta way, but has little clarity why would i consider doing something I have no how idea how to do....
This can not be of great interest to me as it is meaningless! i am wising up and rising.... , i told u wot I meant by 'wise up' put in context and explained this has become ODIOUS!!! your being a disrespectful know it all
who is so addicted to their 'insights' their blind , I want no more of this
MUSIC: W.A.S.P. - Mean Man with lyrics

8/8, 12:39am **Pre View**
I've heard yur scream throughout the year 2012 becoz i was following yur comments on FB for as far as i was allowed throughout open accounts. The human touch, the human voice is maybe more important then the written word. Thoughts are just flashes of wot we are; it evaporates any worthy conversation. People who are the hardest to love have that blinding diamond not many decipher. I was just giving information and hoping you would for once tap into the knowledge and further the information which can be done thr meditation.
MUSIC: NOTHING REALLY ENDS - DEUS

8/8, 1:08am **Koz Kozmos**
i feel all the information your feeding me, u do not back up, u told me to stay off line for a week and read and re read your info which as i explained i have done and made an effort,
treating me as if i'm a moron , i have tried to understand, i get deleted by people and shit all the time non stop in life as well, and i'm a complete loner, am decent but i carry great sorrow and that has its effects

8/8, 1:27am **Pre View**
Have u seen the movie ' Peaceful Warior' ?
8/8, 1:27am **Koz Kozmos**
ugly thing after ugly thing ,no not seen, i read 2 books a while back
not sure i liked them
found them fake and delusive why do u ask ? I have 2 peacful warrior books
8/8, 1:29am **Pre View**
I liked the movie, watched it lastnight, easy going, many missing links,
but hey wot do u expect, a ....
I like Nick Colte. sIt's worth a watch only to see how doctors, teachers ....
can destroy anything they like
8/8, 1:31am **Koz Kozmos**
I may have seen it i need more
boyz don't cry no point, cryed enuff in my chilhood was time to stop
8/8, 1:36am **Pre View**
But ok, enuff time spent, i am wishing u a good starry night
8/8, 1:37am **Koz Kozmos**
have i explained myself adequately to u concerning my inappropriate post
and the reasons behind it?
i tried which is more than u do , that is why i became frustrated
8/8, 1:37am **Pre View** I am ok with it
8/8, 1:42am **Pre View**
Everybody gets frustrated on FB. Yur my only friend
(besides jain Doe - whom i do not communicate with)
whom i do not know in real life So that makes up a whole difference
8/8, 1:46am **Koz Kozmos**
i understand wot u mean. But we did not meet and that is strange to me in a sence
that U and Jain Doe are the only onces . ok thats the way it goes,
i would always rather meet a person
8/8, 1:50am **Pre View**
Even though u know my vibes, it is not the same,,, it misses the mimic, the clown, the
physical expression, the eyes, movement, touch, the dance party,
the locomotion of gestures
8/8, 1:51am **Koz Kozmos**
there are more signals of recognition, yes its no good, i don't want to speak to people
online but I'm lonely , but i will not spk to any one and only u and jain doe are the
people i spk with & i can't express and i have no one in life to communicate with but
if u want to stop speaking thats ok, i am sick of limits
8/8, 1:53am **Pre View**
Its ok, I've always felt yur degrees of loneliness, i have the same , i understand,
and yur unexpressed love, people who do not understand yur essence.
Yes i wish to sleep, but felt it was important to talk 2 u tonight
8/8, 1:55am **Koz Kozmos**
I rather be lonely than with idiots, i'm used to it, good night take care
the mean man song saying 'i'd been mean 'etc ok good night
thought i better started looking on u tube again found this, sorry to piss u off
8/8, 6:26pm **Pre View**
It's alright ! Need to do lots of household work and don't feel like it at all, so lets play
the Juke Box Maybe i'll try some cycling tonight, I mean at the fitness club
8/8, 7:14pm **Koz Kozmos**
yeah house work in this dimension is so messy
the two enemies of human happiness are pain and boredom. – Arthur Schopenhauer
T **MUSIC: Cosmic Wheels Donovan**

8/9, 6:16am **Pre View**
I never experienced boredom. Who would Koz Kozmos be without pain ?
8/9, 12:19pm **Koz Kozmos**
no idea but with out boredom I'd maybe be less bored
but with out pain mmmmmmmmmmmmmmmmm I'd Barack La bam Ba
u have not experienced boredom...are u in denial ?

8/9, 10:44pm **Pre View**
Hi Koz, How ur doing ? I'm writing a lot, trying to put things clear. I was wondering if u'd be interested to assist in something simple ? I mean if u feel like it of course ... : maybe u find an article that states very clearly about wot is going on on earth coz too many people are still too unaware and need an easy explanation.
Or do u maybe feel like writing a short essay about it .....
8/9, 10:45pm **Koz Kozmos**
let me think about that; does any one know wotz happening on earth ? f
or sure I'm very confused about my reality and consciousness .
8/9, 10:46pm **Pre View**
ok the soul syndrome confusius rythm and blues minus night shoes,
I think u would do an excellent job.....
Something tangible, something that opens beyond their own control. I think of u because u've lived it very deep and understand it better then anyone? But it might take some time .... Writing about a lifetime of suffering may assist you to get out of the pain, or maybe bring down a comic book
8/9, 10:46pm **Koz Kozmos**
but will consider it , thanx for asking
it wod be better if i could speak it and get it typed up, how r u?
8/9, 10:48pm **Pre View**
do u not have a recorder ... i mostly record everything, with my celly
8/9, 10:49pm **Koz Kozmos**
i have a dictaphone not sure how to use, wod still have to type up
wod not work that way , but cheers i need to clear stuff, i have been so manic
8/9, 10:50pm **Pre View**
OK cheers, are u having a beer time ? Yes it is absolutely clearing time
8/9, 10:51pm **Koz Kozmos**
i bought beer tonight weak beer
drank 8 beers in 3 months and hardly smoked
8/9, 10:52pm **Pre View**
enjoy ur beer ! its good once in a while
8/9, 10:52pm **Koz Kozmos**
yes beer is good but i like being slim or not as fat anywayz
8/9, 10:54pm **Pre View**
But ok, u let me know when u decide to do it or not ok, in the next days....
I don't think yur fat, are u fooling me ? I loose weight all of the time when doing a lot of emotional clearing, its natural, emotions
and fat cell are merely undigestible thought forms and experiences
8/9, 10:55pm **Koz Kozmos**
no not fat but i did put on 2 stones, odd bad back anyways, let me consider your idea but i really don't know wots happpening on earth , my nerves are bad shape, enuff about me
8/9, 10:56pm **Pre View**
ok, the back and sacral hold many things back, u'll come out of it.
Anywayz it is great to hear u take care of ur body and ...
I like u when u talk about urself,,
u sound different then when talking about experienced trauma
Why is it important to talk ?
8/9, 10:59pm **Koz Kozmos**
to reconnect and have some one to talk to who is hyp to the spirits of the spirits
8/9, 11:01pm **Pre View**
Maybe create a universal microphone , go and stand on top of the hills in Wales and try to reach me that would be fun, I'd connect thr the water waves like a nymph
8/9, 11:01pm **Koz Kozmos**
catch u again, good writing
8/10, 3:34am **Pre View**
Hey Koz, I'v been reading a bit about dyslectic stuff as i have never met anyone before u , so i'd like to study it a bit Could u tell me if the following is correct ?

In a nutshell:
The dyslectic person is using his right hemisphere instead of his left to read and spell.
The two most important contributors to dyslexia are an underutilized left-hemisphere, and an out- of-whack central bridge of tissue in the brain, called the corpus colosseum.
But why does it matter which side of the brain you use? Because the left-hemisphere is programmed to do the things you need for reading and the right is not.
The left can:match a letter with its sound,
handle information that comes into your brain in strings, like the sounds in a word - one letter after the other, rather than seeing a word as a single picture, separate a word into its individual sounds, and understand grammar and syntax.
The right hemisphere is different. It deals in areas and space and patterns.
It doesn't understand parts of speech, or keep track of letter-order in spelling.
It "reads" a word as a line drawing that it has been taught has a meaning, -- a sketch, not a line up of sounds. So if it sees this: or this: it knows that these "drawings" represent a place where somebody lives. But it is just as apt to say home or residence as house. You can see that if the left side leaves the reading to the right side, the result can come out scrambled eggs. As to the corpus colosseum, it is a bridge of nerve cells over which information from one side of the brain gets to the other. Everything you see or hear goes to both sides, but each side has it own specialty. The corpus colosseum not only transfers information, it helps decide which is the appropriate side, and sends it there. Obviously a wimpy CC may not deliver language tasks to the left where they belong. On top of that, it transmits slowly, so part of the information arrives out of sync with the rest. (See the "Jigsaw Puzzle")
As if all that weren't enough, the language areas in the dyslectic brain tend to be smaller than they are in a standard brain. Now you take a wimpy corpus colosseum, an over eager
right-hemisphere, and an undersized left language area, and you have the recipe for trouble. Do you resonate with that information?

8/10, 1:42pm **Koz Kozmos**
I don't know much about deslexia wen i had the test age 36
i was told i was also numerology dyslexia thisalo has a name
i can't remmber the guy who did the test also told me I'd also completely over compensated in the away i speak so no one wod believe i'm dyslexic we need to use both side of our brains i'm out of rhythm out of sync with my left and right side due i feel to damage look into left and right side brain stuff i can't read wot u've written i've lost intrest in every thing and will not be writinganything about wots going on with this dimension
thaqnkz for asking good vibez
eye'm a deslexxxik wizzzard eye kan't spellll
I read about the gnostic's many many years ago wen researching soul types since then i've always felt the archon idea was on the ball in the last year it become very much mentioned via ike etc i watch some stuff but please don't focus that all my info is via the internet LISTEN just listened to this
MUSIC: DAVID BOWIE - SPACE ODESSY + Movie

i've had all this info for years, even 2001 space odessy thier now talking about
Has been a model for me saw that movie wen i 14 maybe
8/10, 2:43pm **Pre View**
i find it hard to talk about this here. MY FB has been hacked 3 times this week and my email, had to reset everything ... I am glad u were aware age 14 already, realization came in a lot later for me...
8/10, 2:44pm **Koz Kozmos**
bad shit goes down, i got wiped in my early 20's but got back to it in my early 30's
But i'm grateful u posted it, must rethink a lot ...
the archon are in us all they have to go and the souless ones
8/10, 2:46pm **Pre View**
i experienced many things ... and have many ideas & stuff ,
yes the soulless. How did u come into contact with it in yur early teens?

8/10, 2:47pm **Koz Kozmos**
its not so much wots happening in this dimension, its more wot happens before we're recycled in to the abattoir of souls i saw the movie not sure i saw it all
and its always stayed with me TT ,
2001 space odesssy but if your a true poet u read every thing on a different level
8/10, 2:50pm **Pre View**
a lot of imagination help? Did u find some drawings worth posting the other day in ur box ?
8/10, 2:51pm **Koz Kozmos**
ahhh not sussed that yet
8/10, 2:51pm **Pre View**
ok,if u feel like it, i'd be interested, its a great way for me to get to know u a little better, maybe,.... I really want simple things and enjoy a little bit of simple things , uncomplicated and transparant so tired of explaining people how come things happened and why we're here. A better movie then the matrix needs to explain
HOW WE BRIDGE FROM THE OLD INTO THE NEW.
A light movie that brings hope and joy into peoples' lives so they can beat the stupidity of the kundalini snake and rise into the
Philisophy of Creation and Divine intent.
8/10, 2:55pm **Koz Kozmos**
i'm almost done, its to hard being here for me, there is no point
its not just that we have been hijacked, sorry i get fed up and down i've lost all intrest
8/10, 2:59pm **Pre View**
i can lose myself when doing little things i like, even if they are just moments
would be great if u could pick up on your creativity and try out something new to get your passion back in. We all have to deal with the same dust, better sweep well and enjoy the ride into the light. Did u not have a Plan for urself ?
8/10, 3:07pm **Koz Kozmos**
its got worse, fucked up eyes etc , it goes beyond fear
8/10, 3:10pm **Pre View**
Maybe it would get easier for u if u had someone in Wales who would understand u and could work something out with u, i mean that would already be of some support. But yes, u told me , ... about friendship, and it is hard to meet new people.
Wot is THERE beyond fear ?
Hey i need to fill my stomach, any suggestions for my tongue ?
8/10, 3:12pm **Koz Kozmos**
its not hard for me to meet people because i'm socially inept, its energetic,
i can't be in otheres energy
not sure wot to eat
8/10, 3:13pm **Pre View**
yes others' energy : i even smell their flesh, i can smell minds,
must be even worse for u
ok, hitting the kitchen, see wot i can discover. I'll catch u later ok, ...
8/10, 3:15pm **Koz Kozmos**
MUSIC: Oliver! (The Musical) (1968) Food Glorious Food
MUSIC: DAVID ICKE - ON REPTILIAN

8/10, 3:57pm **Koz Kozmos**
worth a watch, the cozmik coincidence department is big in this one
8/10, 4:52pm **Pre View**
oeps, thats a long one (Icke), will look at it tonight.
I still wonder why u always tap into my energy so
easily,,, i mean u always post immediately about things i'm thinking at that moment.
Finished watching the other vid - Archons - David Icke and thought i might just connect to this Jay Weidner & see where it gets me.
This wondrous world huh ;;;;;;;;;;;;;;
Can u smile today ?
8/10, 4:52pm **Koz Kozmos**
the Ike one is good, still watching, wonder wot u think

8/10, 4:53pm **Pre View**
ok ; am listening, ok i'll watch a bit then, laterrrr
Yur not going to judge me ? do u really want to hear me on it ?
I will not cut down this time around, You either want to breathe truth for once or keep on dancing in circles like a monkey
8/10, 7:38pm **Koz Kozmos**
i always judge, yes i do, please say
just cuz i challenge u on your own your tech and the meaning behind it, i s me trying to understand, get to the root of the meaning,
it does not mean u cannot have an opinion and share it
8/10, 7:47pm **Pre View**
David Icke: good enuff to awaken people, ...
and I agree also that maybe people need even simplification of some sort ....I mean its quite clear the whole damn thing we've been talking about all of these months : My resume .... To get out of these demons u need :

1. A Light body : I agree. In order to get there u need to clear all emotions which are cause of distortions and open gates for the vampires. Light body info of yesteryear do not work, so how are thy going to get their info. Exactly David Icke: good job : the planetary assistance and beyond. Books of today (maybe there are - I don't know about it ....) However into the larger scope, he just demands attention to something he doesn't know how to solve. And thus I've learned quite some degrees in practical solutions. Anybody can breathe truth yet,
when NO KNOWLEDGE and EDUCATION is being offered, you can talk as much as you want , it has a dead avenue
2. Light body :Needs technical equipment to be sustained and protected (he doesn't mention) which are body grids and grids that assist u to move beyond the solar system or soul/ego out of the matrix created by the archons/vampires waterer.
3. Earth is of a Solar system, so it is quite obvious one needs to move THROUGH this Solar System and UNDERSTANDS and incorporate ITS TECH in order to move beyond which is first Galactic, then Universal. He obviously does not breathe that knowledge.
4. Bad vibes and good vibes : i don't agree ---- bad vibes, ok caused by these vampires, good vibes ok but thy need to continually upgrade and move on beyond ;;;; through tech provided in solar system and alchemy of TODAY and many other things, not so difficult --- not yesterday s' information- that obviously does not work as everything is evolution.
Yet everybody on YouTube is breathing the same info for the last decade and people feeding and feeding into it like free icesCREAM that lost all flavors!
Then he mentioned : no vibes : i don't agree, there is a vibe in each and every molecule whatever its essence. I would rather say there is cells with no nucleus, but still its life. And there is so much that can be done with the cellular structure......
I do agree encoding - decoding DNA , but is more of an extreme difficult item for ordinary humans to understand ... However ways may be found ..... and we should offer people easy sunflowers which they enjoy and understand. A Sunflower Seed was never meant to bring disgrace to your digestive system, right?
5, The moon essence : I ABSOLUTELY disagree through many many experiences, proof of upgrades and vibes and other things, however whom am i to say ....
When The GALLEON MOONS HAVE NO SAY!
THE WORD HAS NO POWER, and that should tell the tale of this age.
6, David only mentioned Mathematics from Saturn a little bit, he misses out on Geometry. But ok, i was happy to hear that already. Its a start.
7. Koz Kozmos experienced many fractal geometries through mushrooms. OK Pre offers tech to experience the same without bloody mushroomS . Why : The Philosophy of Divine Origin does not allow room for a MUSH - ROOM. That should be the reality coming into earth which runs on higher sensations (obviously one must have let go of all lower emotional-mental-unconscious mind stuff) and not looking for plants and mushrooms to get you into the ROOM OF STARDOMS!. And also that is in continual movement. Hey Koz ,a bit like ur Kaleidoscope (i liked it that u mentioned that word)

8. Both david and Jay are very close, but not close enuff to provide the exactitude of Science merged with spirit : thy cannot explain HOW COME THE AWAKENING IS HAPPENING NOW AND NOT 50 YEARS AGO; WHY IS IT GOING SO FAST, Yess, many souls are being taken away through their sleep without reason. There are many reasons.
9, I just thought i might have a nice week-end , went to the shops to get a nice pair of pajamas for both guys and thought i might have an endless talk with both of them & some fun of course. Is this a good idea? Hum...
10. All gratitude to Koz, I wouldn't have known the missing links of David and maybe its not ..... 11. Why have i been given all this info years ago, what did it do to me, what did i experience, what did i learn NOT to do any longer, what do i still need to learn, why did i fail in many things and will not allow it any longer? What do I need now to dig deeper and provide the hippy movement that benefits today. Why does one not find any info about it on the internet, nor books? Please NO questions, it is exhausting me as i need to give myself the many answers first.
But thank u for letting me have my little race on the Peace Train.
Thank u for listening Koz.
8/10, 7:55pm **Koz Kozmos**
i'm bored with info, i'm waiting for a miracle but nothing ever happenz, every saturday i watch stuff as i don't go out , too many people about
8/10, 7:56pm **Pre View**
Of course not, becoming yur own miracle and getting out of any and all emo . Why do u watch stuff on Saturday, have u been brainwashed to schedules ?
Destiny has many mal configurations most don't even know how to escape from
8/10, 7:57pm **Koz Kozmos**
thats it no ,as i said i stay in, too many people about , i watch serices to relax in the week
8/10, 7:57pm **Pre View**
I was joking, like i never have anything fix or solid grounded, it is when you flow with GROWTH!
8/10, 7:57pm **Koz Kozmos**
just finished the other day the Merlin series, fuck time
8/10, 7:58pm **Pre View**
Wot is merlin series , I always fall short in time, therefore i'm vibing to the need o f about 5 hours sleep, nomore, unless i am processing things
8/10, 7:57pm **Koz Kozmos YOUTUBE: Season One Trailer | Merlin**

i need 10 hours sleep and the day is still way to long
8/10, 7:59pm **Pre View** Boredom of the soul
I need to do so many things. Can u work with design programs ,
8/10, 8:00pm **Koz Kozmos** wot are they
8/10, 8:01pm **Pre View** Indesign, Illustrator, photoshop ...
8/10, 8:01pm **Koz Kozmos** i've no intrest don't know them
8/10, 8:02pm **Pre View** ok, hey that gets u more bored ,
DESIGN IS LIKE ASCENDING
8/10, 8:02pm **Koz Kozmos** most days i'd like to smash my pc
8/10, 8:02pm **Pre View**
smash it we need to do wot we like in order to feel ok right Boss ?
/10, 8:02pm **Koz Kozmos** ? i never feel ok, most people are robots '
8/10, 8:05pm **Pre View** Have ur bones recovered, can u dance
8/10, 8:05pm **Koz Kozmos**
death to the human machine the only dance i want is the dance of death, as i said, i just wish my hand worked properly
8/10, 8:06pm **Pre View** Come on Koz, cheer up, have a beer, open yur jukebox
8/10, 8:07pm **Koz Kozmos**
i'm stopping it completly
8/10, 8:07pm **Pre View**
great. Why the decision ?

MY INTERNALS: After this whole conversation, I truly needed Holy Waters to go beyond the pains of Humanity not knowing how to load the Holy Waters and Crystallize the AIR WITH THE WATER in the body. I certainly do know now! and felt I had to let the network between us just take on another route, another turn. For the better? I had so many questions at that time, yet felt like no vibe could understand me but those willing to go all the way Into Divine Will Consciousness and thus provide proof of truth beyond the many inversions. FREE WILL obviously had lost its entire framework and blinded any worthy guideline from the Sacred Forces/Sources, Masters and the unification modems within the Ascension Story of the Earth. Recording and describing this most phenomenal Life Story in which all of Creation and its creatures are involved has a lot more temperament and Universal configurations involved then humanity expected. We cannot possibly foresee and prepare for all the incoming Divinely directed sceneries; but we can certainly devote our inner sanctuary with an overload of guidance and directions that always act like some sort of Intelligent instruction through which our Life path becomes one with the wonders of Ease and grace. It is not up to us to govern the universes, yet can flow synchrone with what is being directed, respected and allowed. And thus the exposure of the slow movement that comes with SOUL consciousness arises the malfunctioning of brains, illusions and diseases that were never meant to be. Defeating this monstrous equation is all we need to do to recalculate and bring our Light Embodiment into the uplifting degrees of sacred consciousness in which Intelligence, Knowledge and the Higher Senses upgrade along many evaluations balancing out in the Cosmos. Breathing Light through is like breathing the exactitude of life giving elements through hat uplifts our Light organic construction which also allows us to finally bring the organic construction of Earth into the Higher Architectural avenues. We all have that same assignment, yet depending on our passion and work, may proof the grooves of details needed for global ascension. We need to take steps to elaborate the basic principles of such a new paradigm of human understanding based exactly upon physics and metaphysics of Consciousness, Light and Space. We might also be somewhat horrified by the madness of humankind ruled by the mode of ignorance, the philosophy of scarcity, with an economy based on fossil fuels and war, and an emotional pathology of fear and self interest that derives from dual input or the soul syndrome.
The exclusion and non recognition of this primary sentient, all pervading, self-radiant fundamental form of light is what leads to the reductionistic tendency of so called "material realism" in science and leads modern biology into reducing life to mere molecular machines as does the whole field of genetic engineering and nanotechnology which is not without its valid merits and impressive advances but is essentially reductionistic, mechanistic and spiritless in it's orientation.Transduction Biophysics which deals with the nature of living systems as inter dimensional biotransducers of the flux-flow or life force may be regarded as an essential practice that bring through self confidence, knowledge, skills, maturity and many more values than ever acknowledged.
It would have such a large impact if we could just introduce Light technology and work together with Scientists, Biologist or so to merge and fuse the missing links of all repair and the reconstruction of Earth into the promised and Holy Land it truly is; as it is a vital part to the mechanics of cosmo-LOGICAL beauty. Earth has no logic, that has been propagated terrain. A beautiful dream with Immortal perspectives is already in the making with the re- education of health and global educational systems that need to be grounded through Light Universities. I was thinking about leaving Koz behind for what it represented but something kept me going for many many more months into the TRUE HEAT OF CONVERSATIONS. Imagine when the horns of an Aries meets the horns of a Capricorn? And the outcome was an extreme un-usual beat. From cynical into rough conversation on the phone, on email, any platform, yet all recorded! This data was all so much proof of what was going on with humanity and how slow the awaking process moved into the parade of the masquerade. This black and white dualistic vehicle most humans were wearing had lost any color and light vibe saturation as many complexions or pigmentations were literally turning grey, lifeless, inorganic and senseless. I always termed it the slumberous desolate pack with dried out eyes and ears; with immature visions of retired ages that had lost their applications along the highways of our Evolution.To the present day I cannot possibly hold on to this information as I witness many people on the media machines flowing into that same direction that needs an EX-PLAN-NATION.

Many more levels of truth need to come into fruition, for the fruits of present day labour hardly matches the quickening of vibes coming through the atmospheres.People have no place to get too; and talk to each other in the Universal atmospheres that breathe the new philosophical avenues into their brains. We are so done with filtering the debris of the malfunctioning and dictatorship. What are moviemakers waiting for? Are they being held back as well? Wish David Lynch would come up with a monumental idea showing how our human Essence could truly merge with the organism that is Light Earth. Knowing how to love a country is half the repair, knowing how to restore self before ecology , is respecting Divine guidance beyond the LIGHTS, so what is the deal of sponsoring, when the degree of knowledge had zero intent into the repair engineering system that which is SELF-ORGANIZING. Equivocating will no longer work, EYES are opening wild styles as we are truly done with the fences and falsification of data.

8/10, 8:20pm **Pre View**
spending time outside should make u feel better, but good communication that makes u laugh out would even be better as that get the FEELERS BACK INTO THE HEART
8/10, 8:20pm **Koz Kozmos**
via studying the gnostics, i'm in a city, i don't want to go out side, i can't drive, if i could get some where i wod, but i'm trapped, i'm looking into moving but it will be to social housing, i've said all this etc it depends on were i can get to live and who will be in the other flats, total soul death is generally a more attractive option
8/10, 8:23pm **Pre View**
yur intent, imagination, seem to be prey of the archon, ,
getting Self empowered by Spirit is just an UNUSUAL Road nobody talks about because Intelligence is in decay mode
8/10, 8:23pm **Koz Kozmos**
yes i understand your perspective, and i have considered this
8/10, 8:23pm **Pre View**
Total soul death comes in when defeating dualtity and moving into full time SPIRIT, either now or in a lesser planetary platform - just things people still don't get, u will have to begin again from where u leave this earth, so,,, better do it now,
just evaporate all EGO CS which is the soul. Just get to work, dam!
8/10, 8:24pm **Koz Kozmos**
i may not , there must be a way ,sorry to be down, i can think off nothing else,
it has be come impossible
8/10, 8:25pm **Pre View**
it's a choice, down or up, it's a consciousness,
a degree within dualistic thought formulations
8/10, 8:26pm **Koz Kozmos**
but realize at this stage no condition is permanent, i feel very little emotion, just pissed off with all this i still count my blessings, i'm not a complete fool ,
thanks, i have reasons for my emotions
8/10, 8:28pm **Pre View**
Emotions have no reason. As i see it : when we are damaged we don't accept,
when there is no acceptance
we keep on talking to ourselves and like to judge. Non acceptance becomes anger.
Anger not accepted by ourselves and misunderstood by many becomes hatred.
Hatred brings more shit. Your Story.
8/10, 8:30pm **Koz Kozmos**
they do have a reason unfortunately
i do not accept, why should i acquiesce ?u said emotions have no reason
8/10, 8:33pm **Pre View**
We just need to accept things as they are,
even with things that happened during childhood, from
acceptance, i understood my anger and many other behavioral thought patterns and then we can release. It may take time to understand acceptance, but it is a necessity to move on, otherwise we keep on recycling unwanted thoughts that have no value:
THE SOUL VERSUS SPIRIT CS!

8/10, 8:34pm **Koz Kozmos**
i understand wot has happened is wrong and all it has done ,
it slowed things down and created misery
i do not except responsibility for what happened to me as a child
8/10, 8:35pm **Pre View**
Yes , so it is misery, accepting, deleting many thoughts behind it erases the anger. TT
8/10, 8:35pm **Koz Kozmos**
understand your concepts 8/10, 8:36pm **Pre View** J
ust sharing experiences and info
8/10, 8:36pm **Koz Kozmos**
but i need something that works for me, yes but yur also trying to create a model of healing for me, have to get to pool, its getting late will be about , thanks for all the feed back and putting up with my low vibezzzzz
8/10, 8:37pm **Pre View**
ok, be wild in ur imagination, swim with some dolphins, ask them to punch
& boost yur energetic sytem
8/10, 8:37pm **Koz Kozmos**
nothing has done anything for me, i swim with the sharkz
MUSIC: Nostradamus - Al Stewart YOUTUBE:
Bert Jansch "Black Waterside"

8/10, 11:16pm **Koz Kozmos**
theres a better version of black waterside
8/11, 8:12am **Pre View**
I want a better version of me !, Btw, i never create models,
i'm very inventive & passionate & daring & challenge new things every day. I want exclusive vibes today, those never heard of, those that make u breathless,
silent & bewildered, haha
8/11, 6:50pm **Koz Kozmos**
u in da hood? I know your a massive Charles Manson fan,haha
may prefer this,, if therez enufff time
8/11, 1:46pm **Koz Kozmos**
u do create models
MUSIC: Nikolas Schreck Interviewed on Nightwatch Radio 4.16. 2013
just sharing some stuff i have no opinion

8/12, 7:27am **Pre View**
Me, A massive Charles Manson fan I fall short in understanding ?
I thought i could only be my own fan!
Maybe i don't know anything about myself, but i'd be interested if u'd explain this further to me to get some understanding. This Schreck interview = certainly worth a deep discussion. I have many yes's & no's but not with this FB medium any longer.... I get tired before i get to say anything through the valleys & the heavens, through my demons & my fairy tales.
Koz, I am in a difficult introspection with myself and hope u understand a bit of my silence. I cherish yur Essence more then i can express and keep it close to me.
8/12, 3:04pm **Koz Kozmos**
I was joking about Manson...my jokes and black humor don't work on fb,
remember the post on
dandyism?, facebook is infected ,its ok, u talk wen u want
MUSIC: Charles Manson | Lie: The Love & Terror Cult |
14 Eyes Of A Dreamer

then i pay for it to be fixed and it happens again and again 15 years of malfunctioning gear and i have top notch stuff , anyways take it ezeee, recharge
i feel like chronic fatigue fug
8/12, 6:05pm **Pre View**
i don't know where my brain is - did you hire my brainzzz?
is ur equipment stuck ? I'm never tired.

8/12, 6:06pm **Koz Kozmos**
its spooky and frustrating, but i payed to get a really expensive guitar fixed too stressed to play it for over a year, and its not working, it goes on and on
8/12, 6:07pm **Pre View**
Sorry to hear about guitar
8/12, 6:07pm **Koz Kozmos**
tried some pc music soft ware, that never works, it never stops
8/12, 6:07pm **Pre View**
that is pretty painful, don't u have some good rocking vibe?
8/12, 6:09pm **Koz Kozmos**
i'm sick of it, i try to do something and no
8/12, 6:10pm **Pre View**
what used to be yur power ? Your Auhtentic passion somehow
8/12, 6:11pm **Koz Kozmos**
MUSIC:Love/Hate - Why Do You Think They Call It Dope?

8/12, 6:14pm **Pre View**
Right, letz rock
8/12, 6:13pm **Koz Kozmos**
MUSIC: Mother Love Bone - This is Shangrila (Lyrics)

8/12, 6:14pm **Pre View**
Thats my breath, the Shangri-La Tribe, THXXX, great vibes
MUSIC Mother Love Bone - Chloe Dancer / Crown of Thorns

8/12, 6:19pm **Koz Kozmos**
If I can't make music becuz nothing ever works, not even complaining
8/12, 6:20pm **Pre View** when did this all start
8/12, 6:20pm **Koz Kozmos**
it really kicked in in 2005, non stop problems, nothing ever works and people notice it, i really wish i bhad something postive to say, tried pc music soft ware, nothing, then pluged guitar in, not working tried effects pedal, not working, tried mic, not working , mixing desk playing up too
8/12, 6:26pm **Pre View**
i had this when living on the 3th floor - it got me down - & down, i couldn't do anything - all against me.
I'v been lucky now to always find a flat on the bottom floor and raising the crystal grids through it brought through truth and malfunctioning,,,, I understand wot yur saying, the electricity is working against you, you definitely need to reset that. The Crystal Grids is PURE ELECTRICITY AND RESETS ABOUT EVERYTHING because it is the Origin of the Universes and Creation.
Hope u can move soon for things to get better 4 u
I wonder sometimes how much new perspectives we need to get things solved
8/12, 6:28pm **Koz Kozmos**
the thing is i've had 53 years of shit , the last decade has been bad, i can't take anymore
if i move and I'm above or below some one, i'll not be able to do any music
8/12, 6:30pm **Koz Kozmos**
my parent are and have never been any help, i'm 53 for fuck sake
i grew up in the Jehovahs witness to believe the world was going to end; my parents are matrix slaves trapped in this reality, low grade soul suicides, i show them love
8/12, 6:31pm **Pre View**
would u like to tell me wot it was like - the growing up ?
8/12, 6:32pm **Koz Kozmos**
no, i just don't want all these broken things that i have spent all my money on, i also discovered today i have a trojan, its crazy, every time i raise some postive energy, try to begin again and get smashed down like a virus in my pc

itsnogood, i'llgo, i'lltryandsussit,douwanttotalkabouthowufeel?
8/12, 6:37pm **Pre View**
I have an important decision to make
I slept on it for 60 days, i'm done, coz this is holding everything back; i addressed a relative from this person, no answer... And being extremely diplomatic, its the Joachim damn stuff ...
8/12, 6:42pm **Koz Kozmos**
maybe let go..., with my eyes i need to pursue things as my sight could be damaged but if u can let go and move on, it may be best if its not damaged u in any way
8/12, 6:46pm **Pre View**
He damaged a lot of my material and his parents do know the facts.
His dad told me he'd keep me updated (this was december 2012 and told me i was right) We need to stand our ground and demand justice!The whole family is very fucked up ....
I have files of proof on tape and on email from his sister and from his psychiatrist
8/12, 6:46pm **Koz Kozmos**
ask a lawyer how much power u have,
i do not have enuff life time for justice and lawyers just want cash
8/12, 6:49pm **Pre View**
Material is no big deal, but the physical , emotional damage , goodness, do u have any idea?
I do know a good lawyer, its actually the Psychiatrist I want to sue, and I will because they are the puppets that need to sing the song of Human dignity and no more brain suppression through medication. I've witnessed so much abuse in these mental institutions, it is not digestible.
8/12, 6:53pm **Koz Kozmos**
no legal aid anymore this country ,has become raelly corrupt, a
nd my sister and family ignore me if i say anything ,
they give me no feed back even with the vagues comments they block me
Pre View
Anything soul does not want to understand, you can smell it in their hair, their skin, their lies, they are being assisted by the demons to act they way they do and don't even realize it, don't be bothered
8/12, 6:55pm **Koz Kozmos**
paticularly my sister, its odious
just want my guitar to work, in recent years i was ill for years ,no one came to see me, i went back to help them die, my sister says nothing and goes onto another subject its so strange , feels like abuse she 's a low grade soul
8/12, 6:58pm **Pre View**
I don't allow people jump in other subjects,
i just keep on confronting whether they like it or not
8/12, 6:58pm **Koz Kozmos**
its not normal interaction, u don't get it, its to insidious and hard to explain i have been treated very badly by people
8/12, 6:59pm **Pre View**
People all over the world have been abused, so have i since i was born, being treated like an outcast, Cinderella at home and yess, the oppression is very real and corrupt. People want to drink the blood under the skin for they cannot beat truth or the Magical Land of Divinity. And yes people hated me as well for getting their truth out and exposing their lies, their set up nonsense in worlds that will never exist.Very painful, yet when aligning and Crystallizing the bodies, there are army's of support. But we need to level up in consciousness and bright lights, or become a laser show of change and beauty. The realms of Light and Masters, Archangels, many Divine Species will not lesser their Light to meet up with us.
Its all in the balancing rooms where purity meets purity to gain the higher levels of support as every single Essence ever created and working in the light Domains works 24/7 to raise the vibe of Earth into its ascension which we simply need to match. We cannot have any negative thoughts or vibrations here, thats when support falls in place and moves into the faster manifestations.

8/12, 7:01pm **Koz Kozmos** no support ever
my situation is very strange, it makes no sense ,
i have been fucked over in every way phsicall
8/12, 7:03pm **Pre View**
a stranger kicked out of the magic hood, yes, we all have some level of damage however,
I've had my hand almost completely cut of by a dog, my right foot is completely damaged due to a Tai Kwando kick, my kidneys running the opposite direction, loads of trouble with my son, parents that
stole all my fortune, a sister that tried to kill me since I was born just out of jealousy, never any love, So come on, we all have a list and my parents always taking my dogs from me, killing puppies,
But hey! we've not been burned, our nose and toes have not been cut of, we were not in Hiroshima, we don't experience war trauma like vets, we have a cozy roof over our head and a least some privacy. SO STOP COMPLAINING WILL YOU!
8/12, 7:51pm **Koz Kozmos**
my back is bad, to much stres ,wot has it done for me ....just bad shit,; bad karma bad luck, pain etc got effect, if i could get my nuckles back ,that wod help .
Something inside me has just begun,
Lord knows what I have done,
8/12, 9:08pm **Pre View**
Yur breathing system is cause of most yur pain, the breath cannot even reach the roof of yur mouth, let alone the nucleus of each cell. If you could learn how to breathe properly and raise the breathing system like vortexes through the body so it reaches all malfunctioning, that should bring understanding of you could move on and truly heal yourself.. I guess I need to show how its being done. Most peoples' discs are out of order just because they don't run energies through properly, and again it has never been educated. THE BEAUTY OF OUR ELECTRICAL SYSTEM AND THE MANY ENGINEERING MODEM SHOULD TRULY BE INSTITUTIONALIZED IN EVERY SCHOOL FROM KINDERGARTEN ON.
Doctors would run out of services, Pharmaceutical industries would vanish, youth wouldn't suffer so much or any mental disease, happiness would be the norm, passion for knowledge within education would return and allow inventions versus the drowning of beautiful young brains. How about me coming to Wales and get your body a good boost huh? You could make a great teacher in schools, just run around Wales, give lectures that replace religion and bring some joy to children and the fun of creation within creation. Sorry Koz, sometimes my voices did not learn how to orbit some directions But air sustains everything , so should it repair everything ! with some knowledge about the fusion with the electricity termed the POOL WITHIN, haha and get that water into a kaleidoscope of vibrant light moves. Ok i'm off, coz i'm dribbling, means i feel good again, just means that,,,,
You need to be willing to resurrect
8/12, 10:34pm **Pre View**
I was thinking of mister D,
lets rewire the frontal lobes & get some real majic done ,just need
the fun with myself as Spirit is represented in such low degrees on the internet and when you hear these kind of people talk on YouTube,
they just abuse having the license of a doctor or scientist or ...
8/12, 11:32pm **Koz Kozmos**
i can't breath in for 5 mins! i even tried
herniated disc effects leg and foot more than back, but wot i need to find out to do is break the curse of mister D yes checked him out some time ago think i downloaded his book but i can't be bothered t, he is sickening, good for nurses, and retards of soul
8/13, 7:50am **Pre View**
He is a bit overly simplistic, and just look how he brainwashes people with just words! dam ... but i always found that receptor cells (those who eat everything we think) cannot simply be rewritten like a CD in a dream-scope.
There is much more to it such as the deeply hidden material in our consciousness that needs to come to the surface, yet instead of doing that work, people get themselves in even more hypnosis, and that is even educated, could it get worse.

The sleeping PILL OF MONSTROUS CONTENT truly works, people eliminated the capability to think and become their own Research Centre. Every individual should have installed such a room or space in the membranes or water circulation. Look at peoples' eyes , how swollen they often look, it explains everything. I think (especially neurons from the glands) need to be decoded and rewired .For myself, i found the most important releases of shit thru connections of the pituitary(hormonal stuff) & hypo-campus running all the way into the sacred gardens(hernia ...). I do everything with my breath & consciousness within rays & some assistance from what i find to work really good with the Solar System and up into the Celestial levels.
I mean to say, if you live with a system,
you need to repair with that system and visa versa. That is not Chinese, easy words. What do U think ? And my goodness mister Koz, u really got these extremely powerful attributes & knowledge to monitor & ensure & change whole groups of people around in a flick of a finger, irresistible
(i saw some snapshots of the original Koz thru my imagination) ... ,

8/13, 1:49pm **Koz Kozmos**
I don't understand it so I think nothing
its in my quarantined items the point i was making was why do so many things go wrong, I feel wiped out, why are u saying these things to me ? they do not reflect my life... where do u get your information just found some pics i messed with via pc art stuff in 2006 wen i first got a pc, i was needy wen i had the pc, a friend of a friend came over and took the pc a way he was a pc engineerr, he disappeared for a few weks wen i eventually got in touch with him he said he had fixed my pc and he was going to charge me a few hundred to get it back , the whole thing turned into a crazee set of events, also his mate and some one i had known for years tried to rip me off when i got the pc back, i had to pay most my art was gone and music, i just found these few images i can't do anything as all i do is sort out
problems, i did some really good stuff ,these are just nothing in comparison
are u in da hood?no worries take care, detoxing ? from reality....reality huh

8/15, 12:57am **Pre View**
Just watched "Sirius" an "the Host"
Seen them ? just to relax coz I was indeed the detoxing from the past, i mean (all thoughts, connections, friendships, indoctrination, learning ...quite a lot in each energy center, to get rid of all emotions & have a subjective view on myself)) and knowing myself I OVERLOADED ....
So after 2 days of detox mentally - emotionally- physically ...
my head was exploding and exploring
the beauty of a clear view in our Galaxies. It is so worth it

8/15, 12:59am **Pre View**
Don't know who the real Koz is, i only experienced the Koz with a lot of anger & frustration, i'm sure u have special love too ... I do not believe in curses or bad luck , i do believe in resonance, wot we think we attract . I asked myself why i got these snapshots in my brain or picturesque view of u, i just don't know The pc affair : had this for years ... people ....
broke into my place 2 times, took away everything ,
even last December, my son clothes, bed, just about everything....
After all , around the time i met u , i was realizing i needed to pick up from were i fell deep into matrix stuff. So for years i was swimming against streams, everything, everybody, opposing , getting nothing done. I truly have been in that space where u suffer every day.
So please stop telling me I don't understand
It is just not worth talking about. Solutions are beyond the complains, not within them!

8/15, 1:06am **Koz Kozmos**
MUSIC: David Icke - Hour 1 - The People's Voice & Perception Absolutism

8/15, 1:07am **Pre View**
Since i picked up my stuff, pushing myself out of nonsense and ego with all i'v told u, things are going smooth, still have to work a lot on myself of course, just like anyone else. The name of the game is in Rising Sun along the moving Moon,,,

8/15, 1:09am **Koz Kozmos**
I did not attract this stuff, blame the victum, the new age 10 commandments
if the universe works by punishing , euhm ,
good vibez, my anger is also passion and its important my anger goes beyond the 5 senses
8/15, 1:14am **Pre View**
Anger = passion : there is still the very negative attribute that gets everything down . It is everything i experienced over the last years : anger with passion gave me all the shit. And my goodness : this was just wot i saw while running; how can i possibly explain these pictures ? Exercise is so important because the flow becomes the body and show information or new forums to work from.
8/15, 1:15am **Koz Kozmos**
a lot of days i'm just frustrated ,wot am i supposed to say, 'its all good'
the picture and the way u described things seemed very good are u changing your mind ?
8/15, 1:16am **Pre View**
No, acceptance as i said and from there on you may get justice,
its a long way and not easy, but u cannot just keep on being angry from the moment u wake up, it destroys about everything, i mean who am i to say, bad vibez attract the lesser vibes, and thus, reset your intentions and visions huh?
8/15, 1:16am **Koz Kozmos**
i'm not just about anger, but i express my frustratins ,
i have not enjoyed my life, if the universe wanted me to do anything it should have shown me a modicum of kindness a long way, is too far at this stage
8/15, 1:19am **Pre View**
Dam! Respect the Stars, The Universe. Holy Moly,
can anything kick into ye? no one in the world is
interested in yur frustrations nor yur anger, i mean how can u not attract shit, it reflects right back. I am taking the long road and i am doing it coz it gives me many results! Just replacing emotions with truth and some good Spiritual content can go a long way,
when understood, or at least doing the work that brings you into some level of understanding, dam u!Are u teaching me patience?
8/15, 1:19am **Koz Kozmos**
I have given so much, u are wrong and spouting cliches, i did not say anything about any one being intrested in my anger etc
8/15, 1:20am **Pre View**
I have given everything as well
The past must be over and done with in order to start a life that is worthy with the knowledge u gained. Cannot be done with anger, u need to get that grief out of yur body,,,
I know, u didn't say
anything about anybody : IT IS JUST THE WAY PEOPLE THINK !
8/15, 1:21am **Koz Kozmos**
this makes no sense, so many condridictions,
so don't u think i have tried every thing to heal ? it has been my only aim
8/15, 1:21am **Pre View**
Wot makes no sense ? There is no contradiction.
Did u heal the past months of anger, since i got to know u ? I did, mind u!
8/15, 1:23am **Koz Kozmos**
it is a gazillion times stronger than anger, i do wot i can do
8/15, 1:23am **Pre View**
I wish u'd understand wot anger does to ur life that is all
8/15, 1:24am **Koz Kozmos**
i understand your concepts, thier all over the internet
8/15, 1:24am **Pre View**
I am trying to undertand it for myself, do massive healing , even above 6 hours a day and massive results,
HOW MANY PEOPLE HEAL THEMSELVES OUT FOR HOURS A DAY HUH????
Do you find that on google too? nonsense!

8/15, 1:24am **Koz Kozmos**
i have no idea wot to do but to focus on my anger is wrong , pain changes me
8/15, 1:26am **Pre View**
Pain changes everybody, but anger, i mean even if u feel good or waterer ,
the anger will still get u down
8/15, 1:27am **Koz Kozmos**
I need my anger to destroy, i would say my despair is far far greater than my anger
u've got the right key but the wrong key hole, u'r missing the point ,
i realize its bad i'm not a complete fool
8/15, 1:29am **Pre View**
...It is in the doing, not trying, and trusting so we can move thru it, that is just basics.
No!!! i have the right hole, its been a private study for 10 years and the insights come
8/15, 1:30am **Koz Kozmos**
i have done every thing and got no help i'm making my point
i have tried see beyond this reality, i have asked for help ,
i have looked within, researched
8/15, 1:34am **Pre View**
WHOM did u ask for help? Do u feel entities when u ask for help ?
8/15, 1:34am **Koz Kozmos**
been creative I have no names , i have asked the nameless, the ones before the dumb
gods were created the tree men and women, no i felt nothing . I ask with pure intent
from the heart of the gentle good, i have always been my main influence ,
i have gone beyond a million metaphors into the perilous landz,
i was speaking poetically i have felt the shape of luv
8/15, 1:38am **Pre View**
That is ok, but hard when a lot of knowledge misses out?
I take easier ways and then be my main
influence ... I don't know about metaphors ,
poetry is a great medium to express and forget.
8/15, 1:40am **Koz Kozmos**
Do u feel attracted to somebody, maybe someone u've read about or were interested?
8/15, 1:40am **Pre View**
Do u remember when i was talking about Enochian stuff and the PENTAGRAPH
8/15, 1:40am **Koz Kozmos**
= pentacle the pentagraf goes beyond the pagan pendant
and maybe becomes something from the muliverse ,
a diagram that is attempting an explanation, but thats just bs, its online
wot is it, a brick next to your eye or is it a house viewed from the hill
the trickster is wot may be called an archetype, wot do u do wen u do all this work?
8/15, 1:49am **Pre View**
When i do all this work :I first align my meditational avenues,
connecting with the Celestial, UniversalStars, Species, Masters, Ancestral tracks,
phenomena, elements, animal kingdoms: it all depends on the preference and
guidance of the day; yet I do ask what Team of Light would be best to reconnect and
get my data down.For several years now, I have been guided to connect beyond the
Universal levels and bring through the meeting point or dots with the Spiritual
Scientists, Astronomers, Spiritual Ecologists, all these domains that teaches the
repair of all organisms as the Universe is repairing itself and thus we need to redirect
our organic composition along the organism of earth. Yet most plastic sciences are
working the other way around and do not really understand deep enough to look
deep enough. If we can bring the Origin of earth back to life, then quite naturally the
planet would flourish with new and forgotten elements needed to feed animals that
have gone distinct and protecting that is just another slow movements of egotistical
soul content. If everybody would live in an ALIVE brain pilled up with Spirit
Consciousness, we could move faster then the speed of light. Therefor, I am so
triggered to working with these folks on earth, yet there is no scientists or ecologists
that dares tapping into the unknown with me and still have the degrees of thinking
that a Masters' or Phd has more knowledge which is very degrading and creating
more and more separation as we have already suffered for eons. Its my only hope, to
just have that opportunity and meeting field with some Academic open enough to go
into the true adventure with Earth and its habitat .

If we can Light Bolt the dense measures within our brainzzz and the buzzy energy fields, then we can Light Bolt massive natural places and bring back the security of nutrients through the plants, flower and herbal kingdoms.
An example: I have been asked to become one with the element BLUE CORNFLOWER
& BORUM and bring that back as that element has gone almost distinct as well, Koz, it is just all about FOCUS in a meditational space that can be set up with any element, starting with the Crystalline kingdom as they create the open doorways to communication and access to data. Anyone can do it, just not anyone is interested enough due to mountains of egotistical content and mass brain manipulation. And thus our whole story about the GRID BUIL UP ZONES OF ELECTRICAL, NUTRITION IS MORE IMPORTANT you may ever agree upon. I don't care if you do or if you don't. It is your Life,
It is my dream to just be invited in some remote place in Africa or better Australia and bring content to LIFE through video's, the media and especially setting up camps for children, youth and adults to learn and re-educate The True Beauty of Living on Earth which could assist and support many WildLife organizations and funding them with New ways of engineering.The Ascension process cannot be held back anyways, we need to bring these new programs back into fruition and the education of the Water irrigation along the High Altitude air components
8/15, 1:49am **Koz Kozmo**
I like to hop
our conversation are quite intense
8/15, 1:51am **Pre View**
maybe, don't realize it, just telling it like it is, what else would be the point huh?
8/15, 1:51am **Koz Kozmos**
u tell me stuff i don't understand and tell wot i should not be doing,
but u cannnot walk in my shoes or
see the big picture, so how can i consider yur other perceptions?
8/15, 1:52am **Pre View**
ok, send me ur shoes, i'll wear them for a month.
The stuff is just basics wotever the shoes.
and you better don't feed off my perspectives, create your own and built from there
8/15, 1:54am **Koz Kozmos**
I'm wearing extra light weight ultra violet sandals with wings i wanted as a boy to become an elder
8/15, 1:54am **Pre View**
That is sweet, that would make my phoenician back stronger
Koz Kozmos
but this life has just worn me out and damaged me and according to u its my fault and other new age bogus philosophers ,
the problem is living with the robots and thier nasty and strange faces
8/15, 1:57am **Pre View**
Hey, i cannot explain everything, and certainly not understand . But little things ... Like i'v been abused and used all the time in my childhood. How can it be our fault? U experienced this too. And accepting this took me months and even years of clearing anger before the relief spaces out and bringing clarity to the plateau. We're all swimming in the same water, yet we do not all see, smell and allow the beauty of the elements. Everything is a learning zone, we just need to move through it, allow our assignments through and get the support and in between all of this IS HOW WE MOVE THROUGH EXPERIENCES and meetings to see beyond the plastic zones or synthetic living.
Clearing, elimination, evaporation is needed to see crystal clear and open up knowledge on the Light paths paved with crystal directions. I would certainly be an excellent coach in any school, for I'd bring joy and new fruits to the table of any creation. That is what life is about, thee passion to dig deeper with every step we take, DIRECTIONS MATTER!
That is all, no point in repeating, it needs like a week of solid education, grounding and showing how the electric output of energy works.
Children and youth learn to heal themselves very fast because their passion is open

and when they get fast results through daily directions,
that is what will create the new World in unification
8/15, 1:57am **Koz Kozmos**
losing my poetikz, my pc is going slow , its been decades for me
8/15, 1:58am **Pre View** U never lose wot u really have
8/15, 1:59am **Koz Kozmos**
i have some insight , i am a gentle person but i don't like it here ,
i was walking up the street tonight too
many low grades , too many negative situations
8/15, 2:00am **Pre View**
I wish i knew who u were, being creative, ...
I never experienced u being gentle, u just never stop complaining,
U need to be stronger and raise beyond the street influenza, as I said,
crystal Grids squeeze that and so the matrix is like a pancake in
between the upper and ground floor Grid.
When in deep alignment, I experienced feeling like a Giant when talking to people,
due to the GRIDZ that showed me, very exclusively alive experience.s
8/15, 2:01am **Koz Kozmos**
to many ugly fools, if u have not experienced my gentl ness,
theres no point in us talking any more
i always clean the shit of my winged sandals when i have walked thru the mutant
streets u miss my point, i understand leaving things behind
8/15, 2:04am **Pre View**
I was shocked with wot u posted on my timeline, and how many times u said sorry
for inappropriate things. Saying sorry is ok, but i suffered from it for many days!!!!
Gentle wings huh??? I am not Pebbles or Bambam, I live my own Flintstone!
8/15, 2:04am **Koz Kozmos**
i suffer from wot u say to me
8/15, 2:05am **Koz Kozmos**
i forgot other people can read u'r time line ,
maybe u had it comming, u must have created it, i did not
mean to hurt u , i will not post on any ones time line again,
i don't want to hurt any one
8/15, 2:07am **Pre View**
? Forgetting that everybody sees my timeline ? that is hard to understand ?????
Telling everybody i was the greatest disrespect ???? It is always anger ...
8/15, 2:07am**Koz Kozmos**
i said sorry, got caugth up in hatred
8/15, 2:09am **Pre View**
Lets just leave it behind.We have been confronting each other a lot with lots of
mutual hurt. Letz movei nto the Futur , the blinding Lights of Life!
8/15, 2:13am **Koz Kozmos**
death the punch line thats good , a lot of my stuff is black humor,
a way of dealing with the dark
8/15, 2:15am **Pre View**
I alwayz think good of u, as a wyrdo, a fun guy, a fighter, a serious monster,
a combination of manybeautiful things
8/15, 2:17am **Koz Kozmos**
Wyrd is a concept in Anglo-Saxon culture roughly corresponding to fate or personal
destiny. The word is ancestral to Modern English weird,
which retains its original meaning only dialectically.
because its kooler like that , spelt that way it becomes majikal
8/15, 2:17am **Pre View**
it is, thank u, interesting : i'd like some Kool rest now, cradling in the forgotten Land
Spaces of Beauty and warm communications and the animals, I just need to be
around animals, its vital for me, it just is. And Living in stoned cities in Belgium does
not really add to my health. I am awaiting a miracle, a new vision, a dream that
surmounts the Himalayan aspects. Just wish to live with the New Technicians such
as scientist, ecologists and bring back healing properties to the land such as is
breathing through the Amazon

8/15, 2:19am **Koz Kozmos**
i bet your even disrespectful in your sleep, its always a pleasure to speak with u
i always get something out of it, good night
8/15, 2:21am **Pre View**
❧ goodnight, words are to enjoy!❧
8/15, 8:40am **Pre View**
NO more paranoia ok?
8/15, 4:40pm **Koz Kozmos**
been waiting for some guy to turn up to fix my guitar,
i got a really migraine sorta head ache last night
it was and is nasty, this guy has not turned up, he has my mob bile number, i don't mind the occausional reality cliche but this is non stop
yur righ, t i need to get my anger out and its attachments ,
move out of the reptile brain into the limbic
and from there accesse the neo cortex and manifest
8/15, 4:50pm **Koz**
MUSIC: Blue Oyster Cult - (Don't Fear) The Reaper 1976

8/15, 5:53pm **Pre View**
I'm sorry to hear that, people are playing many games i understand,
I used to have that as well, being persistent and calling and confronting them up to a level of annoyance helped. But it gets them angry and we need to spend so much wasted time and energy..... , easier to command the word and have things done, but of course, gain more understanding and delete the past, I hope it will get better for u. Hope some majic kicks in, Yes, I absolutely luv wot u did with the pics, these endless rotations.... Wot did u think about the vid - brain rewiring ?
8/15,7.07pm**Koz Kozmos**
I don't bother confronting people , i read the enegy and cancel them out, its more a frustrating bore than anger , a continual set of events that always end in the negative , and i do not attract that - command the word? not dated angelic names , majikk has to kick in, i have always followed my true will
that is why i have hidden, i did this with the pics but they were deleted
not watched vid, feel wiped out today but will watch
8/15, 7:26pm **Koz Kozmos `**
hope that nade sense , i feel bad today maybe sighs of awakening or...
hope your ok will watch vid
MUSIC: Albert Hammond - The Free Electric Band 1973

MUSIC: Alan Price - O Lucky Man!

MUSIC: Alan Price -Justice

8/16, 5:53am **Pre View**
good music to wake up with, thank u Koz, u seem to know perfectly well wot i need.
Polynomial = maybe wot u did here :
U gave me 3 different songs = 3 different modes of consciousness .
When i merge the consciousness behind the 3 songs
i would need to understand the fusion of wot u are trying to tell me here and use that for my individual growth pattern(hopefully it will factorize into more intelligence for myself)
I think this is interesting but not easy there are always thoughts popping up in conversations and that could rise into a new philosopher,
Study the Art of Data Visualisation! Baahmmm, that wil get u going
or Learn from Abrahma Hicks,
like the sheep do,

8/16, 1:53pm **Koz Kozmos**
In mathematics, a polynomial is an expression constructed from variables (also called indeterminate) and constants (usually numbers, but not always), using only the operations of addition, subtraction, multiplication, and non-negative integer exponents (which are abbreviations for several multiplications by the same value). However, the division by a constant is allowed, because the multiplicative inverse of a non-zero constant is also a constant.
8/16, 1:57pm **Koz Kozmos**
i look into the vids at some satge put i've watch all that new age dogma in one shape or another and was
reading about it when it was called the human potential movement
8/16, 2:57pm **Pre View**
right, subtracting, adding, multiplying: when doing this in the brain, it will make a difference, looking it up does not bring the work in the body. Light always recalculates;
8/16, 3:35pm **Koz Kozmos**
i realizee that but i need words and terms that have general meaning
not to be bound by logic but to understand basics
8/16, 6:51pm **Koz Kozmos**
Abraham Hicks: Fake or Just Shallow, Cold and Not Very Bright?
Is Abraham Hicks faked or is Esther Hicks really channeling infinite wisdom from 100 "nonphysical teachers?" You decide. Here's the evidence. Some former followers insist that Esther Hicks fakes the channeling of Abraham for profit, at least some of the time. She claims to receive "blocks of thought" from a deathless group of roughly one-hundred "nonphysical teachers." A member of this group, Esther claims, is Jesus. She also has said that "What Jesus was, Esther is," before going on to say she speaks for Buddha too. Bunched together as Abraham Hicks, they deliver their teachings (and products) through her and
even banter playfully with participants at pricey workshops.
8/16, 6:53pm **Koz Kozmos**
hope u read that melt the mind control device and watch out for those gridzzzzz
They are notorious for their mind control techniques A pyramid selling company that brainwashes people who sign up to sell ;;;
8/16, 8:36pm **Pre View**
Beware my Sources ? its a completely different thing. I just posted it in a way that a body can be gridded through math and then geo,,,, but it takes so much more understanding and study ,,,, we cannot find that on the internet, everything is very old age on YouTube and people with their modem of repetition, stealing and dealing , so i don't listen too much although there are some great people out there,
There was one interesting thing u posted : about Architect sometin' ,
could u please remind me of that video ? Apart from that, all I have been doing is researching upgrades in how we rewire the brain and the hormonal system
8/16, 8:49pm **Pre View**
However, I will be more prudent.
i value uyr wordz also in a sense that i might have to be more careful
and stick to wot feels right.
8/16, 9:01pm **Koz Kozmos**
I explained about the sources and gave eg Architects of control Micheal Tsarion ,
I 've not read much, i am stupid on many levels but very breight on other levels
breight = bright bin and a terrible life time
not sure how much i can cope but will have to try,
i wasn't being funny wih u about your posts but u have to be aware of wot your dealing with, its mainly a money game and control of the pack, have fun
8/16, 9:08pm **Pre View**
ok, thxxxxx catch u later ok,

8/16, 11:14pm **Koz Kozmos**
Gothik hitz from the KozKozmos Jucke box juke

MUSIC: Sisters of Mercy - Dominion
MUSIC: Temple of Love (extended) [HQ] Sisters of Mercy

MUSIC: The Sisters of Mercy - More

8/16, 11:32pm **Koz Kozmos**
luv thc vox going off line good night
8/16, 11:41pm **Pre View**
goodnight, just got back no more ever, my last miuts in society
8/16, 11:42pm **Pre View**
Thank u for ur brilliance, this is wot told me 'i could handle u
8/16, 11:49pm **Koz Kozmos**
i stay in most of the time, people talk in the pool some times ,
no one has any spirituel power i rather keep quite, even tho i'm a really talkative person
8/16, 11:50pm **Pre View**
yes; i stay in all the time, would love to relocate to Africa, Tahiti,
or Australia would be even better, nature is wot i need to move on,
there is very little were I live.
8/16, 11:50pm **Koz Kozmos**
i'd like to go to Peru, i've not been any where, crossed the lost acres in my head
staying in and being by your self can get u in a loop
I was always attracted to Peru and there seems to be a lot of alien happenings there
i looked it up a few years ago, i like to live in nature with a kozmik tribe ,
lots of space lots of respect and pratical application
i went to an island wen i was a boy of the british coast
britain is so sick, destroyed silence
its a small island called Lundy an bird Sanctuary of the coast of braitain
i need to sleep 10 hours don't always get that ,
the reasons i used to drink and smoke was to shut me down
i think i'm expending so much energy with saddness and the loops in my mind i need rest, i've spent the last 12 years in bed hiding, getting off my head
8/17, 12:14am **Pre View**
Ok Koz, get some sleep, thank u for catching me
8/17, 12:14am **Koz Kozmos**
follwing freedoms road , ok u off ? sorry am i getting too intense?
good god night take extra care

MUSIC: ROBIN WILLIAMSION - LAMMAS
8/17, 12:16am **Pre View**
No u said u could handle intensified relations
8/17, 2:03pm **Koz Kozmos**
When u enter ultra reality ...u feel more, see more,
its just a hip saying your on the right track but u need
to move on up, basically you may be on the right track but u have to go further
not sure wot i mean....beeeeeyyyyy , i can feel more

MUSIC: Monster Magnet - Look To Your Orb For The Warning (with lyrics)

MUSIC: Iggy Pop - Live At The Avenue B 14. Cold Metal HQ
8/17, 5:52pm **Pre View**
good lyrics monster magnet, i suggested titan moon to lift me up with enuff nitrogen

8/17, 5:58pm **Koz Kozmos**
wod have preferred a studio version of Iggy ,
i listened to many of these songs years ago and thier stored
in my head , MAJIK
for some one to come over and look at my guitar to repair and he's cancelled again
no point trying really , loads of time wasted, i tryed to do music again, its so strange
8/17, 6:01pm **Pre View**
Can u not connect with somebody u used to know when playing with them ?
8/17, 6:01pm **Koz Kozmos**
no and if i did i'd need an instrument that worked , this guitar is worth 5 hundred
Pound, i'm not complaining, pick up not working, i payed 65 pond to get it fixed a
yaer ago and that was not done properly and due to all the upheaval
i did not realize it was not working
its maddness , i realize there are going to be cliches that shit happens but only shit
mmmmmm cliches
8/17, 6:05pm **Pre View**
Hey why don't u learn to become the best guitar repair kit
and fix other peoples guitar AND GET yur monies back
8/17, 6:06pm **Koz Kozmos**
no place to start , its not my thing, a lot of these pick up 's are digital i wod not no
were to satrt , its a life path fixing stuff , its not a practicals suggestion
8/17, 6:08pm **Koz Kozmos**
i can't get any of the ideas to work as there are continuel set back u do not
understand! i have tried so much and i get hindered, i have very very very bad luck or
i'm targeted , no self pity fact ,all i have are problems, all my intruments mal
function , all i ever buy does not work
8/17, 6:12pm **Pre View**
Ok, letz get some suchi and good beer
U need to rearrange your electricity,
turn it around, your cables are attracting that shit
8/17, 6:14pm **Koz Kozmos**
its bin bad since i came outa the womb, living in shared houses was hell
it has made me ill but my child hood was the big fuck and i'm still the healthyst
person on earth i basically want to return to the coast, waiting to die
MUSIC: Iggy Pop - Wild One - 1986

8/17, 6:31pm **Koz Kozmos**
I no longer trust myself or this reality the damage is big;
i am a scar i've never travelled
8/17, 6:43pm **Pre View**
i did a little bit when i was young, not much, travelled through Australia,
Switserland, Spain, France
Will talk later on , ok
8/17, 6:46pm **Koz Kozmos**
Ok forgive my downess rest deep

MUSIC: Bee Gees - Spirits (Having Flown)

8/21, 11:03pm **Pre View**
I wonder if i ever had eyes, i wonder wot i see is seeing , I wish i sometimes had an
easy spirit, but then again how boring would that be,,
8/22, 1:12am **Koz Kozmos**
Aliens have infested the federal government - whistle blower.
THESE PEOPLE YOU ARE SEEING ON
THE TV, IN THE PAPERS ,ON THE NEWS THEY ARE NOT HUMAN!
They have one thing in mind and it is devious.
I wish I could say they are here to help....

Their goal is total domination, exploitation, and eventual enslavement of the human race. They rely on us for survival, and they know how people will react if they find out. They cannot risk mass suicide or revolt against them
until their reinforcements arrive. But they have everything they need in place now.
MUSIC: Hawkwind - Spirit Of The Age

8/22, 1:50pm **Koz Kozmos**
supa kool track and the first one disco kitsch from the age of lost tranzmissionz i have no flaws to identify even this doggered that pours from my pen has just been written
By another twenty telepathic men
8/22, 2:15pm **Pre View**
Kool, indeed ∞ Thank u! Cryogened Spirits waking up, haha, no claws to identify!
8/22, 2:37pm **Koz Kozmos**
The matrix is a chamber that keepz the spirit ov the spirtz frozen
8/22, 2:43pm **Pre View**
Sure, lets just override that and liquify imagination,
8/22, 5:04pm **Koz Kozmos**
we are the liquid gang deeper than the 8th ocean,
we drink from the well between the wurldzzz
7th sea, 8th ocean , going further and deeper work on your poetikkz!
don't worry just being dizrespekful
8/22, 8:42pm **Pre View**
Work on poetikz? Have written about 28 some years ago,
a friend challenged me to post....
8/22, 5:04pm **Koz Kozmos**
MUSIC: Vinnie Paz "Kill 'Em All" ft. Beanie Sigel

8/22, 8:44pm **Pre View**
Some good songs, this Vinnie, Introspection over many years made me realize i lost integrity about information. I asked my spirit to teach me
Through obedience i was shown how to bring that change in consciousness.
Humbling to what i was given made me understand a little more about energy and consciousness. Humbling more , being modest, brings more understanding
8/26, 12:51am **Koz Kozmos**
who's your spirit? 'obedience' to what? all the practice,
is it not time to get on the golf course and hit the ball....
MUSIC: Wimple Winch - Atomspheres

8/26, 12:59am **Koz Kozmos**
Well, I stand up next to a mountain
And I chop it down with the edge of my hand good night
8/26, 1:00am **Pre View**
Yes, i am hitting many balls at once, many interesting explosions
Atomspheres, and the delights from the beams of lights
thank u good night
I've never met anyone with such an inquisite,
ambrosial heart like yours. I wish i could understand
who u are. Why did we meet ?
8/26, 3:29pm **Koz Kozmos**
no worries if u need any more advice contact m, haha
MUSIC: ATLANTIS: Alien Visitation and Genetic Manipulation"
By Michael Tsarion Part 1

8/26, 9:31pm **Koz Kozmos**
not listened to this but listened to Tsarion more in depth talkz, a good few years back and resonated with 'em concerning this subject how do heal my hand
and rebalanced my right and left sidez?

8/26, 1:00am **Pre View**
There's a lot of tequila in healing modems with CHI flow, but it needs the original grounds to learn from bright shining stars, the oak tree , the breath of liberty and of course the Ethers, wouldn't that be some elixir to heal all the distortions, the deceit, the disasters, the fear. When the emotional body has been deleted, the paranoia is healed, same with weather patters.
The HYPNOSIS and dictatorship has gone so deep, people don't FEEL any longer wot to believe The whole conspiracy has brought so much constipation
There are real movers on the planet, keys and holes become the same one day
Tsarion :ok, but don't agree on some items i'v experienced don't work.
And discussing that on FB , t would take hours & exceptionally absorbing as the subject is too broad to make it comprehensive thru this medium...
However, i do spaciously appreciate u keep me somehow updated of wot people think and talk about ....
8/27, 6:57pm **Koz Kozmos**
u kidding me, nobody i know talkz about this stuff,
ok some items i'v experienced don't work. ....
8/27, 9:55pm **Pre View**
the bit about diffrent soul types and some escaping from Atlantis and building Lemuria etc....
8/28, 12:17am **Koz Kozmos**
diffrent genetic types sorry tierd tt
MUSIC: Bruce Springsteen - It's hard to be a saint in the city (lyrics)

MUSIC: Bruce Springsteen - Waiting On The End Of The World

MUSIC: Bruce Springsteen & Patti Scialfa - She's The One

MUSIC: Bruce Springsteen- Streets of Philadelphia

8/28, 12:43am **Koz Kozmos**
bruce overload , he sacrificed his cousin and is now a slave off the Illuminati but has written some very good songs with deep mainly soulfulness
MUSIC: Bruce performs "You're Missing" on Grand Piano during a rehearsal in 2002

8/28, 2:05am **Pre View**
That was a lot of Bruce Blood
Makes me feel sad Yes, he's deep, like the ways he puts the lyrics together
But u go much deeper within poetikz.
Feel too tired to type, thxxx for the entertainment
8/28, 8:13am **Pre View**
With elemental hearing i heard contact Kozmo contact Kozmo, contact Kozmo for some advice between spaces, I do not have the advantages of copper light; do u think my damaged waves can catch the wave of an original blueprint ?
How do u think my degrees can overcome the stain to break the wild cage ?
8/28, 1:51pm **Koz Kozmos**
Bruce is an earth Buddha trapped in the blue collar realmz of Samsara,
I' m the fire star on the burningpath beyond the zones of the Rock Knowledge...
What is your stigma?

MUSIC: the floaters - float on

MUSIC: Chic - Le Freak

MUSIC: Sister Sledge - Lost In Music

8/28, 2:01pm **Koz Kozmos**
wots quaser 10 Ukquili-Osie Lord, any opinion?
8/28, 2:02pm **Pre View**
quasar = star with multiple optical brightness, wotever u chose it to be
give me your opinion first so i can tap into it, keep the energies equalizing 8/28, 2:03pm **Koz Kozmos**
only if u want 2
8/28, 2:04pm **Pre View**
sure, a bit of fun 8/28, 2:12pm **Koz Kozmos**
i'm a male the dark seed , give me something i can stretch my face on hence the joke
stay tight like a face lift, i need to get some fruit
8/28, 2:13pm **Pre View**
Don't get u ? Do i need surgery,
8/28, 2:14pm **Koz Kozmos**
psychic surgery via the solar sisters, i was joking
i new a plastic surgeon but he went by the fire and melted

MUSIC: 111.FUCK DA PLEIADIANS IM ANUNNOKI-DRACO INC. ATOMIC ENERGY BY: LORD UKQUILI-OSIE ANU RA-FA ELOHIM

8/28, 3:56pm **Pre View**
humhum, 338 vidz which one do i watch first? i aint got titanium vibes matching,
Might be fun doing a video with him , some sort of kooky and defiled madman,
WOTS Black Power ?
8/28, 6:29pm **Koz Kozmos**
Black Power is a political slogan and a name for various associated ideologies aimed at achieving self-determination for people of African/Black descent.
Cosmic Nigga'z, he never likes or answers anything
Eye'm a kaleidoscope Supremacist
8/28, 8:41pm **Pre View**
A Conglomerated Universally spiced Kaleidoscopic Supremist
breeding delicious fragrances that promotes and serves me with dressy fevers
8/28, 11:19pm **Koz Kozmos**
dressy fevers, hey wyrd image , haha
8/29, 10:13am **Pre View**
Its like The Plague, pestilenc, the disruption of airy tales and mates
MUSIC: Michael Tsarion Conspiratorium:
Ep: 2.1 - The Black Sun

The symbolism of the Black Sun and the Black Earth Moon is much deeper as it flows with this Black Universe and thus our Authentic Power that has been held back, as everything is seen in the black sceneries, it is like a Magical landscape with unlimited options. I'm not referring to Black Magic like people do , but TRUE AUTHENTIC BLACK POWER OR MAJIC is truly within as it removes the dark ages, the control and the illogical philosophical orders of the tyranny and slavedriver

The Eternal movement with one spirit, one direction is al we truly need.
We are Eternals, connecting to the lost spirals that are to be found everywhere on the planet, from Ireland to Asia, to Australia, to Africa, to Europe
ONE SPIRIT, ONE CREATOR AND THE RETURN
Look at the birds, how they hunt in spirals.

My Artwork1 : "PINK BIRD" REPRESENTING SPIRIT
AND THE CLEARING OF THE OCEANS ALONG MANY ELEMENTS

ARTWORK 2: “THE GATHERING” Featuring the EYE IN THE SKY and people ascending through the Unitarian Gate or Green Light Go represented by the Hebrew letter Aleph.

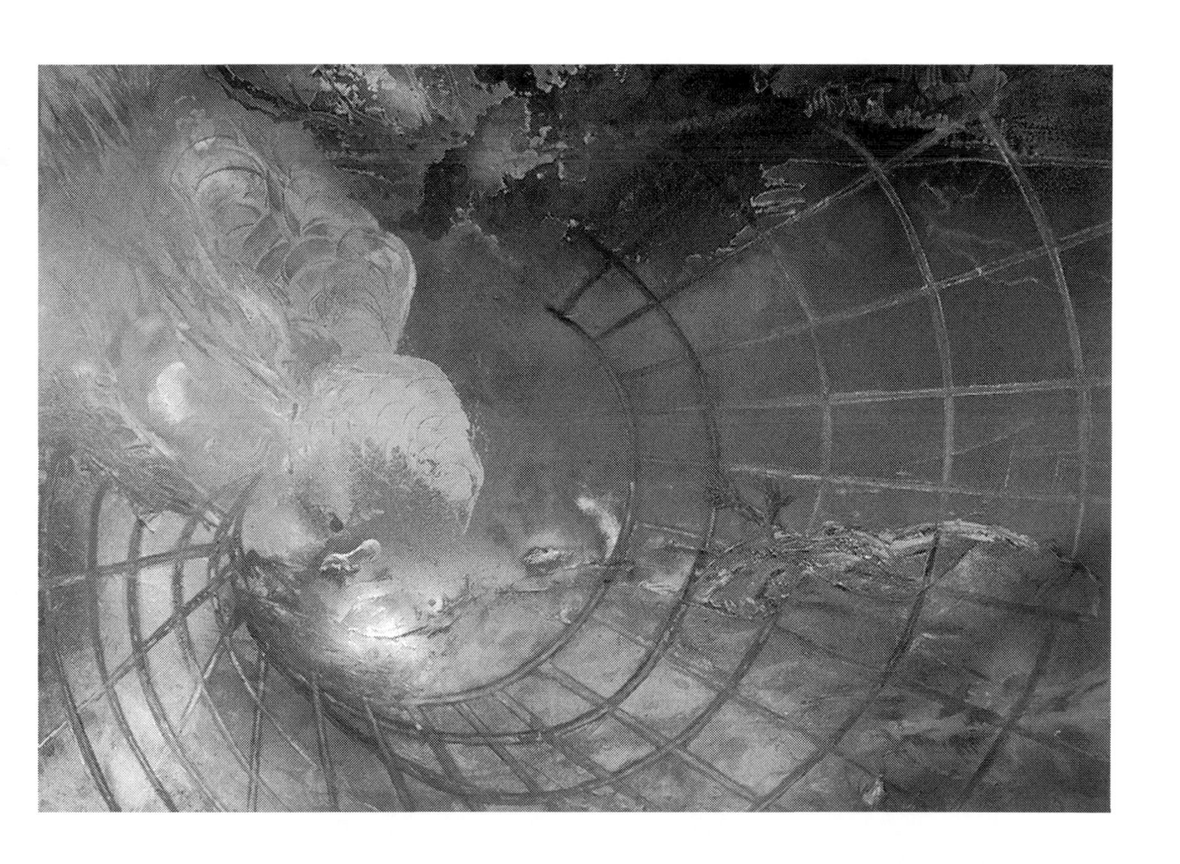

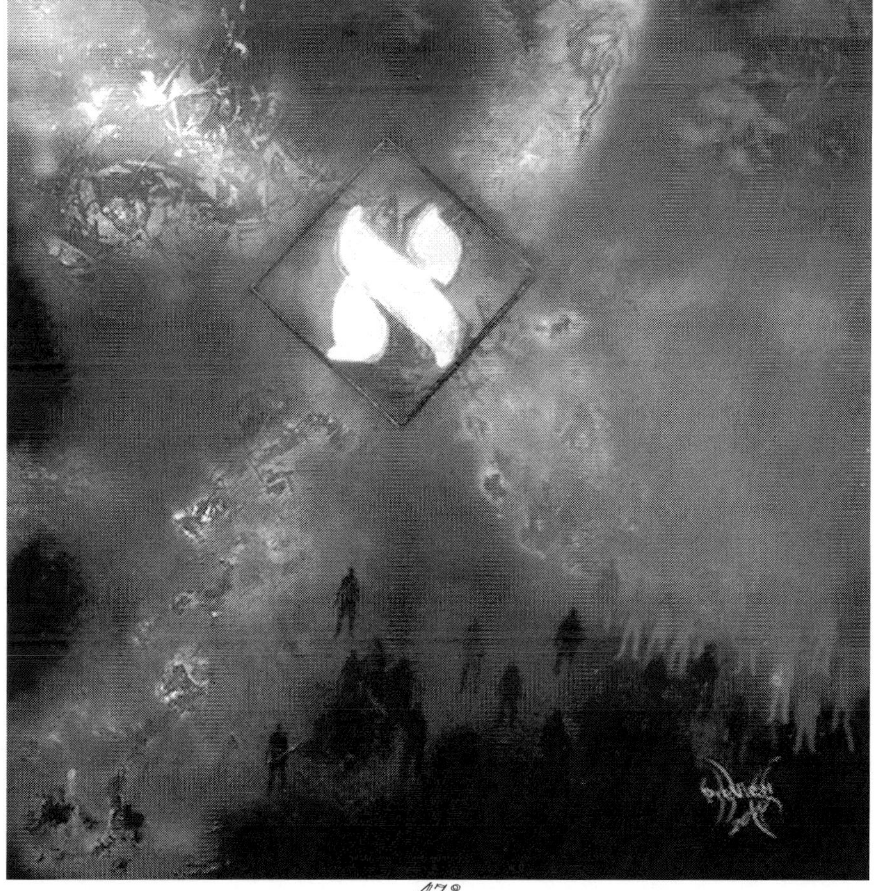

8/31, 3:51pm **Koz Kozmos**
i'm 53 in the foot hillz of death
What did u say to Michael Tsarion? an other day in the reptile city any ideas ?
8/31, 3:51pm **Pre View** T
rust the answers u get, don't u trust them
Well I simply told him i did not agree on a few old concepts as thy have no value today and told him how i viewed them, I just messaged a minute ago, need to wait
Come on get out of that reptilian shit, all thy want is to take humanism away, AI
8/31, 3:58pm **Pre View**
I just think when sadness slips in and u have no communication, it transform into anger, and then worse, hatred. But yes, delete all these emotions . I think u can take on many personalities in a few minutes. Is that correct ?
8/31, 3:59pm **Koz Kozmos**
i refuse to be blamed, your never alone with a schizophrenic
8/31, 4:01pm **Pre View**
Are u schizophrenic ?
Some people shift from one personality into another,
instead of fusion many faculties like u do
8/31, 4:02pm **Koz Kozmos**
is there one self or are there many
8/31, 4:02pm **Pre View**
Good question, we all deal with multiple channels and personality traits, yet when living beyond the soul disease, i assume Spirit consciousness has it all fused within a multifarion of creative skills. Techniques takes proficiency, the snack finess room of Divine options 8/31, 4:02pm **Koz Kozmos**
it was a joke, celebrate your pantheon but remain focused
don't worry i'm not mentally sick , i'm the opposit , my eyesite is bad
8/31, 4:05pm **Pre View**
Shall i start photoshopping yur Eye? it is difficult program,
but we can apply the easy buttons right?
Everything is an app, we can invent apps and when believe and focus takes the routine of shots, we can relieve the mob or collection of swollen body parts
8/31, 4:06pm **Koz Kozmos**
these glasses are no good, no sorry, haha, i bought them because i need to see
8/31, 4:10pm **Pre View**
I understand, maybe time to look for some healing through,
maybe heal the lenses within the eyes ?
8/31, 4:11pm **Koz Kozmos**
i've been looking for healing since i came into the sickness and had no results physically; i've told u wot happened to my eyes, there is no healing for me ,
i have tried
8/31, 4:12pm **Pre View**
Why don't u simply pull ur heart energy up there and swirl it out
There is absolute healing ! don't ever repeat that
Maybe yur subconsciousness is manipulating u
8/31, 4:13pm **Koz Kozmos**
people in healthy bodies have no idea, but i don't wish to be depressing,
i feel my enery is very healing
I talk to Immortal ones, who are they?
8/31, 4:18pm **Pre View**
It is just entities i'v talked about earlier.It is all about this Black Omni Universe, T he Alpha Omega station and up, that takes years of understanding , so we can first work with the Black Omni rays to heal and eliminate and bring factual details through I am working to understand them deeper through my physical body first, then through the alignment in mentality, or what i am directed into during my sacred spaces.One day when I was running and my circus within opened up with many beautiful commercials, I had the lady Master "Portia" or Quan Yin popping in and listened. Lets say, she always shows me things,
She is from the order of Strong People and she showed me to start working
with platonic solids geometry.

So she showed me Pink Triangles. I a next meditation, I would ask how to apply them, what changes it brings in the anatomy or consciousness, and on, that is creative meditation receiving data when the circulation and thus the breath of pure Air is in,
8/31, 4:20pm **Koz Kozmos**
Portia" wotz dat? no idea, i don't know if it has changed your brain, can u proof it
8/31, 4:23pm **Pre View**
Lady Portia is a Lady Master like many other Masters of Light. I don't have to proof anything certainly not on FB. My data is my work . People who want it , will have to come and get it . But it is nevertheless hard, not to have anybody to work with and exchange Light tech and ideas
8/31, 4:29pm **Koz Kozmos**
but if u come out with sweeping statements expect to be asked for proof
your hard work is confusing
8/31, 4:31pm **Pre View**
Confusion is simply the soul circuits, reluctance, deprivation, and nonsense playing out. The elimination of emotions or soul or ego provides for crystal clarity. People are confused all over this place. Con fusion is a very disfigured consciousness and dangerous or very unstable meaning it excludes the capability to trust anyone because they promise and say something today, and tomorrow they twist their words around. It happens all of the time in present day communications
8/31, 4:32pm **Koz Kozmos**
questioning things u can't understand is important
8/31, 4:32pm **Pre View**
Yes, but u need equal in and output otherwise doors close off isn't it?
8/31, 4:32pm **Koz Kozmos**
your either talking on a higher level here or your stupid , the in pipe and the out pipe
maybe i should pop over to Bellgum and have a good conversation
8/31, 4:35pm **Pre View**
Sure, if u feel like it, I would certainly welcome you with open arm in the Bubble Gummy Spaces of Europe, haha
8/31, 4:35pm **Koz Kozmos**
maybe, do u have a spare room 8
/31, 4:36pm **Pre View**
i can arrange yes , but have to communicate with the Lords of Light to understand which crystal bed would suit yur vibe best along a little pool
to sweeten your moody blues
8/31, 4:37pm **Koz Kozmos**
maybe be good for me to go some where, not sure i f i can, cheerz
8/31, 4:37pm **Pre View**
Yes, feel free to do a little trip into the ship of crystal bricks,
it might do u some good to be some place
8/31, 4:38pm **Koz Kozmos**
where wod i stay
8/31, 4:39pm **Pre View**
U'll have a room in my place in the city of Hasselt
8/31, 4:39pm **Pre View** I
live 2 seconds from the railway station
8/31, 4:39pm **Koz Kozmos**
thank u, i need to do something, i appreciate your offer
8/31, 4:40pm **Pre View**
It is actually like a village, not a town .... u can cross it in half an hour. Need to do something now ? 8/31, 4:40pm **Koz Kozmos**
ok just come and go as u please
and u watch out for those enties,
u either have the light in your blood or u are nothing
8/31, 4:54pm **Koz Kozmos**
when i was a boy i felt the light in the blood, its ok ,
just pop off enjoy your noon sphere

8/31, 4:53pm **Pre View**
Koz, i need to go some place to bring a few paintings
I wont be long,thx for the take and catwalk
8/31, 8:31pm **Pre View**
Mourning Black Sun : has been good to me , Wots the SHikinah, wot is that exactly ?
Any idea? Anywayz, the swastika is made of 4x1 arm of Light,
connected to 4 cornerstones of creation, when thy connect it creates the swastika
but it also opens gates within a dodecahedron which was wyrd to see it
unfolding through meditation,
should make a design of it.
I actually never heard about the Black Sun, did you?

MUSIC: Michael Tsarion Conspiratorium: Ep: 2.1 - The Black Sun

8/31, 9:39pm **Pre View**
I Feel exhausted.
Have deleted many many pages as thy are infectuous.
Is there such a thing as black fire
I want the fire of the Suns' Empire
How was it like to feel the light in ur blood at a young age ?
Koz Kozmos
When I first saw my mother i let out a cry and was moved to illusions side WIPED
death to the clay born clowns , i will listen to Tsarion tomorrow,
the blood that was lit was hiden from me but I always felt apart from the pack so
I had to rediscover it but in this dummbed down broken state the majikk in the blood
is wasted in this dimension, i have to find a way to fully awaken and shine
8/31, 10:29pm **Pre View**
Thank u, have a good night rest in new D'Lights of the Divine ,
See u in September to Remember

Sweet and Lovely people of this Earth,

I would like to hug you all as we are ascending
With many beautiful Light Bodies and light Spheres
So wondrous and exceptional to each Country
With the following Poem that was written for the
Dear moon Project
Yusaku Maezawa / Elon Musk
As he invited Artists to submit art, poetry, any creation for
his project to fly to the Moon and breathing its Tunes
with a selection of Artists!

I am PreView

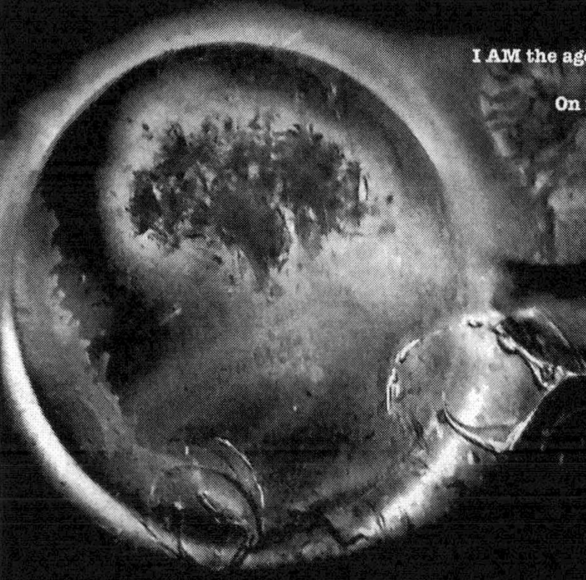

Dear moon, so in love with you,
I AM the age of revision breathing from the spams of division
To meet thy precission
On my guitar strings singing new decissions
Just 2 get 2 you

Dear moon, so in love with you,
Is my love far too soon
Is my heart far too late
Or is my song out of tune
Just 2 get 2 you

Dear moon, so in love with you,
Can I be the silver machine
The black magician' dream
To serve thy inpenetrable dream
Just 2 get 2 you

Dear Moon, so in love with you
Please allow my Solar steam
On your TV screen
to breathe thy admirable scenes
Just 2 get 2 you

Dear Moon, so in love with you
Show me how to blow my Golden Horn
From the Black light Earth Moon
Into the Omniversal Sounds of no return
Just 2 get 2 you

Dear Moon, so in love with you
And thy Water flow
That snows upon my fumes
To redesign my veins with they holy sirenes
Just 2 get 2 you

Dear Moon, so in love with you
Show me how to overlook the skies
Where nothing dies
Where every sign overrides designs
Just 2 get 2 you

Dear Moon, so in love with you
Do I have time to move into thy vines
That shine so bright,
That breathe so wise
Just 2 get 2 you

Dear Moon, so in love with you
May my heart cycle the most profound
heartbeat
into the halls of Ancient Wisdom
The sweet Elixirs of Original Ambrosia
Just 2 get 2 you

Dear Moon, so in love with you
I offer all my Granite and Green
Making up a perfect scene
When the rivers run wild
Through the aquamarine miles
Featuring body parts unseen
Like a true marine
No storm too mean
No hill too high
Yet vacuum clean
As truth reveils
All mysteries unveiled
To feed the trendy tracks as seeds
Until time has come to bond
and meet in the beyond
Will I cherish and surround
Your Divine Tables on the ground
For Heaven and Earth
To fuse our songs
For, In love, we can only
pull the humble guitar strings and blow integrity
Until time has come to bond

I AM "PREVIEW"

Backstage Closure

NEVER payed much attention to poetry but it just flows out of my hands like in seconds, no thinking, no work, IT IS HARD TO SAY GOODBYE! In the End this book is Poetry because it Rhymes its Time!
This story actually shoots in the air right now, with another year of extremely potent, straight forward and strong conversations in which neither of us would shut up.
It was beautiful, frustrating, exhausting, enticing and so unique as it truly matches the vibe in which a large amount of people are awakening in 2020-2021 to open up the gates of the Reality of Spirit along the physics of many new communication systems.
Without LIGHT COMMUNICATIVE DEVICES, we are lost and feel empty as many do without even taking charge of their lives and remaining in the pipe dream of their horns without any knowledge and beauty of Living in the Origin of their Energy bodies and Team. A gigantic amount of airy fairy non realistic views of Spirit are promoted on every possible platform with little or no truth, knowledge and transformation. Today, as people are AWAKING UP and starting to think and move into philosophy of life and their true Light worth, skills and technology; it may still need the AWAKENING OF CONSCIOUSNESS beyond the betrayal factor in Spiritual development as false movement in soul consciousness promotes as big a trap as we have seen lurking on any social media platform and the storm that prevents knowledge and memory codes to enter the brain minus the mind bushes facing truth, yet not allowing a single Inch.
What was going to happen to me and Koz? Would we break each others' horns? Were we going to meet up, when would it happen, where would it happen? The conversation went on and on for at least another year and even moved into recorded telephone calls, emails and other mediums which I need to save for the next book:

"Between The Moon and the Sun" II: THE MEETING ROOM"!

Endless days and nights went by with endless hours spent in these dialogues. The rough and tough flair must have had a goal as we are definitely entering the age of tele-thought communications in which our neuro-circuitry can produce its own light field that can become super sensitive regarding the musical scales, the receptivity of crystal clear visions, higher intelligence, knowledge and data.
LIGHT is THE GRID through which all higher forms of energy are translated into languages, symbolism, geometrical designs. BEING CONNECTED TO EVOLUTION is a very high energetic sphere through which men can transcend thought forms of lesser degrees and which are activated through his own ACTIVATED LIGHT NETWORK GRID, and thus the importance of the Grid which offers the bio coupling. Where thought- forms interconnect with perceptual mass, the thought-form can influence the reality of an object and its energy. We are all senders and receivers of crystal radio waves by placing our consciousness in a wave and project thought ACCORDING TO THE COMMUNICATION NETWORK and its clarity!
The lower the Crystal Light vibe within, the more distorted and confused communication is being transmitted. It may matter a lot to just look at our networks, the screens we perceive, the technology: it is flowing synchrone with the Universal lay-out and assists us to understand the Grandness of the Universe, its perfection, balance and harmony.
A conversation always triggers alike vibrations as it mirrors who we are, where we are at and what we allow it to be regarding its functionality ; much like in physics, mathematics and the tremendous Divine Powers that created these interaction.
Remember: “WE ARE ONLY LIMITED BY LIMITING BELIEF”
What we think is what we become and attract with multiple options, choices to transmute energies and load new energies for that are our authentic powers that create consciously or unconsciously.Therefor, WE ARE WHAT WE BECAME!
As the I AM flows on Evolution tracks, it changes with the fluidity of Crystalline and thus geometrical patterns that we allow to flow upon, upgrade into and adjust.
Once we understand that everything is energy and produces chemical reactions from its substances, the more we understand we must protect and clear our substance or electrical fields to inhabit states of higher living standards.

We can all meander between levels and planes of creative consciousness and many realities because the biological languages are based on locked-in information; and thus the worldwide expression "the Key" that lays dormant or latent within is the key we al have when clearing the holes or empty spaces that hold onto the old!
Once we remodel Self through Light patters that format themselves when working with its computer system : THE CRYSTAL GRID, we can easily receive tele-thought communications as the body can also work with multiple biological environments in participation with LIGHT APPLICATIONS OR TECHNOLOGY which allows for unlimited Spaces to discover within and experience the expansion in Superspace! Sweet People of this Earth, it is so easy!!! Just a few days of information, and knowing how to do it, makes up the SCREENPLAY YOU CHOOSE TO LIVE AND FEED FROM!

The Crystal kingdoms and minerals are of great assistance to expand and upgrade Light embodiment as they sooner then later open up geometrical designs that are very individual and that directs new highways that are so unique, one cannot possibly disregard them as the consciousness within a crystal and its geometry that is aligned to numerology as well reformats the brains' capacities into the origin through which we can start working with the Elohim and many higher Orders in the Skies. It is interesting to take pleasure in the upgrades of a crystal . Yet, understanding and some knowledge is needed: There is no rhyme before its time! One cannot communicate or infuse the essence of a particular crystal when the body does not EQUAL the stage of purity it requires for higher communication and co-creation. Once again, a starter kit with FOUNDATIONAL crystals provides easy upgrades and enjoyment along the way. Without a foundation, the house of cards crumbles, and that is easily understandable for the solo reason that a foundation is like a HOME BASE STATION or something to return to all of the time. Sometimes just to balance out, sometimes as a reminder, sometimes to understand upgrades, sometimes to just upgrade PERSPECTIVES and thus new knowledge is born all of the time.
Crystals provide a kinetic connection, they provide regeneration and healing through their geometry and mathematical codes amongst color frequencies that matches vibrations an entity tuned into. It will also allows for deep co-creation with the Earths' Forces/Sources and many Species. When the body is in refinement mode with the element Water and Air as we are all WATER ASSIGNED, the expansion becomes the new data on the strata.

When tuned into the Energy grids with many communicative networks , there is no end in receiving signals, directions and data with color patches that self regulates the brain into ever expanding states of being or consciousness. For those willing to EXPERIENCE the PARAMOUNT VIEW, it may take training and ongoing study to tap into the quantum mechanical systems of high precision and true Sourcery. Then again, what do we have to loose? We can only reclaim the Self and make any avenue on our path truly fascinating and passionate. Anything less ain't even worth buying toilet paper for. Conquer the mind, you conquer, the Heart that thinks it can feel for egotistical reasons!The consciousness Grids that have been set all over the Globe are so powerful, one can no longer disregard the HOLINESS AND PRECIOUSNESS OF THE DIVINE. It is all a matter of aligning to them and opening up to the vortexes of light configurations that grow into the crystallization and a NEW CRYSTAL CIVILIZATION.: THE AQUARIAN AGE!
Light is the foundation of LIFE through which all higher forms of energy can transcend. When the mind(control system) is being eliminated , it allows for the brain to fuse into one composition and perfection of male-female attributes.
A matter of fusing the fissures and bringing higher applications through in which we start to understand the LOGIC of organic systems. There are many, many wonderful stages within self development and recreating the Power of Light as the First cause of Creation!
It is up to us to be willing to learn and take the small steps perhaps, that opens big doors! It is all available. Teaming up and doing the work and transition together is what we are required to do to make THE UNIFICATION happen and eliminate anything less.

Yet it all starts with the LIGHT EARTH ATLANTEAN GRID CONSTRUCTIONS that hosts multiple grids with grids within geometrical patterns connected to the Ley Lines of this planet and Geophysical fusion with all continents.
It offers the understanding of how important the indigenous people are, how to listen to the crystal tracks or messages the Ancestors bring through and what to do to repair all earth substances into Light Earth which is basically what we came in to do.
Words can explain phenomena, yet it requires the application and experiences that flow with light that brings through the understanding that ultimately leads to joy, peace, freedom and LIBERATION!
So the next book explains the tides of any rock & roll vibe that brings wishes into a realized platform as I finally did! Expect more truth and harsh movement! Exactitude & Truth!
As I have another 1,2555 words to make readable , it may become a trilogy. At that time, I did not know why I was doing it. I certainly do now, as I think it may assist people on their journey into Spiritual Consciousness and Crystalline embodiment and stop the nonsense propaganda that rather holds one back instead of bringing the Divine shoes to the ground floor and bring the body and the brain BACK TO LIFE, light and the heartbeat that emits natural love to all that will always be in existence, yet the least Essence never tapped into for its composition is very much aligned to the Eye In the Sky and many books of knowledge.
The Spiritual Movement has been extremely slow due to many dense mechanics that held the fast tracks back. Yet today, it is so easy to just start of with accepting that LIGHT needs a FOUNDATION that produces more Light, purification and then ascension into the many halls of Light which allows for the creative brains to expand into Super brains of Divine Orchestrations. Understanding that the purification procedures from Soul into Spirit needs to take place before we can enjoy the sound and visions of our ORIGIN: DIVINITY! Awakening is just the process of allowing the many layers of the Higher embodiments to unfold one at a time and daring to create from what comes from within, that is authenticity! AND KNOW IT CAN BE SO EASY! UNDERSTANDING COMES FROM ALIGNMENT AND EXPERIENCING IT.
When the explanation I gave becomes your reality, answers become the question!!!! Dig that! Looking back has no value, looking forward may feel unattainable, therefor, we only have the NOW to decide which road to take:
Living the Matrix behind prison bars, or working our way into freedom.
We are what we choose to be ! I AM WHAT I HAVE BECOME!
BETWEEN THE SUN AND THE MOON: "THE MEETING ROOM"will go through a deeper confrontation with LIGHT misconceptions. Yet moving internals as in telepathic communication and reviews that sail many oceans! Let's say words would cut deeper, no mercy, because people like the 2 of us with horns don't hold back , they speak out loud. We refused all comfort even when words were spilled through in an asperous and bumpy way, leading into sleepless nights throughout Europe!
I truly hope you enjoyed this network of experiences, may your blessings test your choices and bring the greater good back to the woods where they belong along the resurrection of the beautiful elements and the sharp wisdom of our animals .
Sweet people, I hope you may gain some understanding in your individual self development plan and steam through a movie that actually explains THE POWER OF A SEED: "
THE BLACK PANTHER" Please watch the movie as it may assist you to ponder upon the Lavender seed and its knowledge That is what I am , I have been living the past 20 years in the backyards to assist the rising of the forgotten people, the abused ones, the child trafficking, domestic violence, and it needs a Black Panther to break the rules. It takes the understanding of a Black Leopard to stand strong in mentality and assist youth to rise from backwards mentality and severe trauma.
The brains' movement into Evolution has basically been lost through living the deceit and damage. Bringing EVOLUTION back into the brain and body would need ongoing FOUNDATIONAL upgrades in the Grid staging HOME on Light Earth. The birthing into Soul consciousness announced the split in right and left hemispheres, created duality and very low living standards due to the loss of the Original Sun stream/dream in the body that flows with the tides of the Moons.
The space of a soul is full of nothingness through the control factor that did everything to stop the Evolution of Creation or Light movement.

The New Sun Stream one can integrate within is what brings LIFE back into the body that comes with the removal of ALL OLD SOUL streams and
fragmented essences that allowed for a diseased and decaying body.
The ATTACHMENT TO ANYTHING SOUL is what masks and blinds people to the point of NO RETURN when stubbornness and resistance replaces the FLOW MOVEMENT OF DIVINITY. And of course reason why SOUL is being promoted 90% on social media!!!! ARE YOU GETTING IT?
Residing in a Spiritual body with the original sun stream and moon flow is the least we can set up into a FOUNDATIONAL LIGHT GRID SPACE THAT ALLOWS FOR MASSIVE UPGRADES at any time while turning the telepathic communication waves on its highest level and streaming Free Will and its diseased mentality out of the body.
ALIGNMENT to the Crystalline Light Transitory Grids is all that matters when returning into Light parts and Light waves which is felt in the body at all times.
Soul Living is a nightmare as we can watch it playing out offering nothing but disease and heartaches.
It is my dream to resurrect and work with youth and children worldwide as they are the most traumatized and vulnerable. Being a teacher takes a lot of responsibility especially when overriding the dense factors of old psychology and psychiatric models that were created to kill consciousness even more. I live hoping schools, youth organizations, universities, foster kids, and mental institutions will allow such programs that resurrects the dumbing platforms of this age into LIFE CHANGING CONSCIOUSNESS and the beauty of the human organism that needs to match the resurrection of the organic construction of Earth in which Health, Wealth an Equality is the norm.
It is my dream to teach teachers how to deal with children and teach them disciplined programs that create respect, love and integrity to break any trauma and learning difficulties. With the correct programs, nobody needs to suffer from trauma, diseases and broken mentality.
It is my dream to resurrect the animal kingdom and work for the protection of wildlife as in restoring the ecology and biology through Light Grid Technology that fuses the platonic plates back together and brings through the rising of forgotten trees, flowers, herbs and oceanic life.
It is my dream to see happy people, exited about their life and skills.
It is my dream to eventually work with ecologists, biologists, scientists, mathematicians ready to leave their Ego and allow some truth in knowledge; and assist the repair of the soil along its children and animal kingdoms that would lead to complete New educational Systems regarding health, business, technology and thus the movement from the dual system into the trinary tracks that exposes the Origin of Light Earth and its NEW place in the Cosmos!

Beautiful people, feel free to connect with me on social media, on my Youtube channel, through email or telepathic waves. We are entering The Age of Aquarius which is all about inter-communicative links, new technology, new inventions and especially new education and health that does not require an Earth Master degree, yet a Spiritual Mastery Degree that is non existent from the Earths' Universities for now!
Would love to see you in the thrill of the meeting room,
The Evolution of dialogues through the next book:

"Between The Sun & The Moon":

The Meeting Room!

Love, I Am PreView

References

My YouTube channel:
The Voice of Evolution

I started my Youtube channel in 2016 and brought a lot of refreshing videos throughout 2020 to assist the understanding of the movement we all experience on many different levels. My video's explain how to move out of fear based reality, trauma and many mental barriers that keep us from moving into Living Light and Joy and thus breathing the repair of the planet!
All my video's refer to many links to my website for healing modalities, online seminars, artwork, reprogramming methodology, healing meditations, individual sessions and projects for Universities and schools as well as new teaching models for youth and children. New educational systems for All!
My present guidelines are directing me into The Resurrection of Sacred Places, with it comes the TRUTH of how Sacred Geometry blows through New Data and thus will explain without a doubt my study and co-creation to resurrect Ecology along all Animal Kingdoms.

Email
unifiedfields@live.be
unifiedfields111@gmail.com

Facebook
NicolePreViewGrauls
The Voice of Evolution

Linked In
PreView

Instagram
TheVoiceofEvolution

I would like to offer deep & profound Gratitude to:

Yusaku Maezawa
For the Dear Moon Project

Kendrick Lamar, SZA
For All The Stars and All Parlor

Black Panther (Film)
Directed by Ryan Coogler
Produced by Kevin Feig

Jain Mathemagician
For teaching children

Floris Van Zyl
For his Art and Breath of Truth

Koz Kozmos

Artwork by PreView
It is the Return of The Black Universe,
The Black Panther Moon
That allows for the return to pure Grounds/Sounds.
The Male Vibe with the Black Panther Intelligence in the back of the brain or the Cerebellum

Colors in the Original Artwork are White (purification)
Turquoise as it breathes any densities out no matter what
Pink/Fuchsia for the higher Breath of Communicational Fusion

The Female Vibe with the Black Panther Intelligence in the Back of the brain or the Cerebellum

Colors in the Original Artwork are White (purification)

Turquoise as it breathes any densities out no matter what

Pink/Fuchsia for the higher Breath of Communicational Fusion

**I would like to end with an "I Am Faculty Art card"
Created from my Artwork:
"I Am Alpha Omega"**

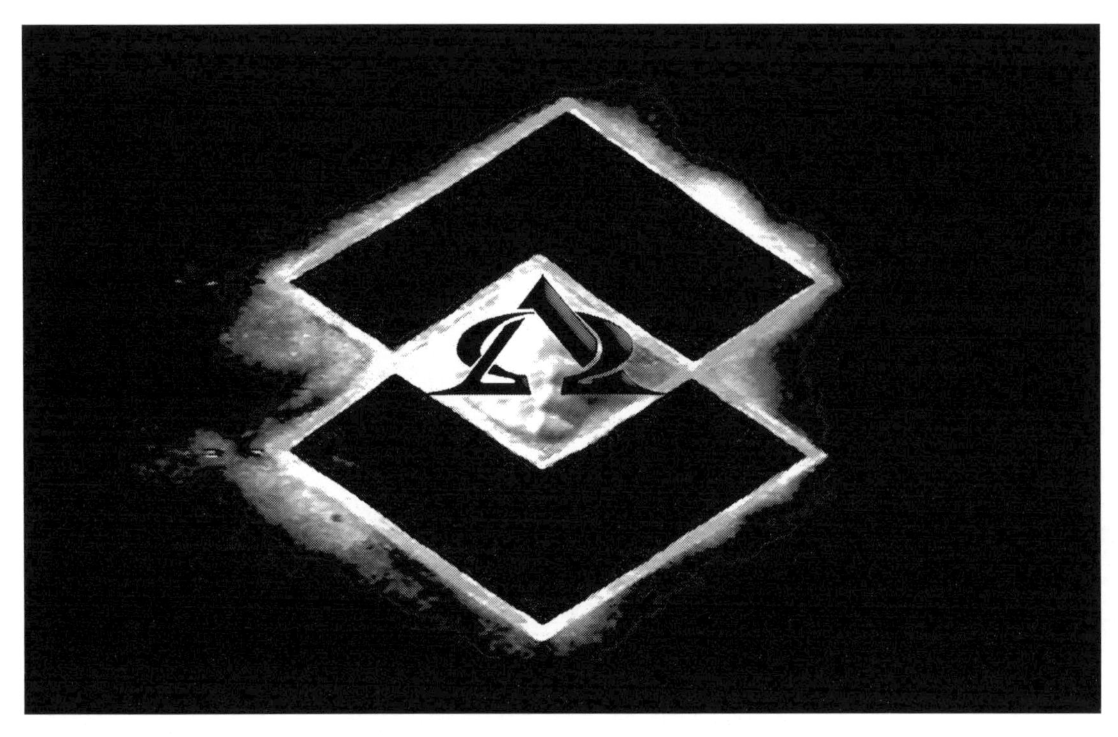

**Original Art
work on Canvas 100x100cm**

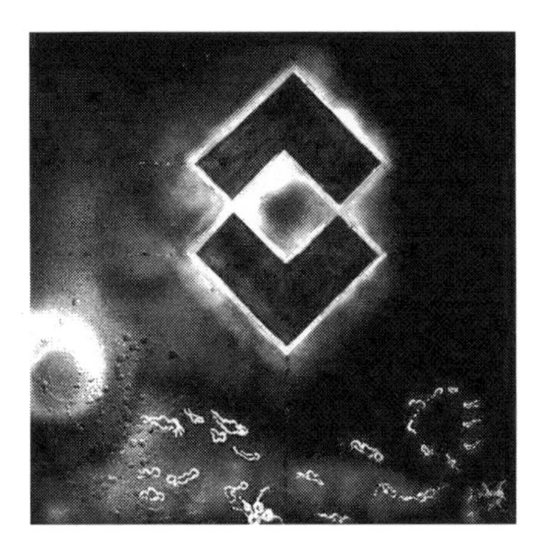

THE I AM FACULTY": BOOK + ART CARDS
Available via my website/or links on my YouTube Channel
https://unifiedfields.wixsite.com/thevoiceofevolution/?lang=nl

THE I AM FACULTY": BOOK + ART CARDS FOR DAILY SHIFTS IN CONSCIOUSNESS, NEW LEVELS OF AWAKENING GUIDANCE,INSPIRATIONS AND ASPIRATIONS

It is all that we are, all that we have become, all we will ever be.
The "I AM" is our Divine origin. And yet, it is the Essence less understood during these extreme times of transition on the planet.

55 HIGH ENERGY DECK OF CARDS AND 220 "I AM " AFFIRMATIONS THAT WILL LIFT YOU INTO THE HIGHER GROUNDS OR LIGHT EARTH FREQUENCIES.

The I AM Faculty Cards are: "WISE MENTOR CARDS FOR MODERN DAY ASCENSION & CHANGE"

I created the I AM Faculty Cards from my artwork and have been building each card up to a single I AM Presentation that can change consciousness overnight and experience new directions. These cards and the book explain where you are at and encourages your next step; as they offer advise for transmutation and changes within, in a way that it offers many routes to create a brand new reality every day. They are a real joy while they travel with you along the first 5 elements of creation: Earth, Water, Fire, Earth, Air, Ether.

The physics within these cards will assist a deeper sense of awakening into the First Golden Age. What is your dynamic, passion, speed, drive to become the Hercules embodiment that has the physical, mental and psychological power to attract, manifest and make things happen? You choose your glory minus the lesser breath such as impatience, impulsiveness and moody drives that may interrupt the challenge and goal at hand. The Aquarian Age!

The Physics within these cards refer to the special medication/meditational assistance and therapeutic treatment one can apply to Self to benefit from the collaborative Arts that lay dormant within our I AM PRESENTATION stationed within our bodies and energy fields; yet not being explored, opened nor regenerated into the New Tree of Life we are all living in this age of huge transitions.

The explanation of the cards functions like a pure relieve elixir that will assist you to explore the deeper meaning within Self and the release of old emotional/mental content that needs to go to embrace a new sense of Self awareness. The I AM PRESENTATION are bodies that make up our energy field surrounding the physical body. The I Am Faculty Cards came into creation through my artwork to assist humanity to realign to the Origin of perfect health, equal wealth, joy, justice and co-creative Divinely guided plans that feeds our consciousness with a never ending spiral of passion, power and strength versus low mentality that only feeds the lanes of mental abuse, exhaustion and survival.

I Am PreView

Sweet Gentle-Men, Beautiful Women of this Earth, do know, I shed tears for fifty years only to ENCOUNTER my Source whom would direct me, redirect me and show me the EYE OF THIS AQUARIAN AGE!
Because throughout all these years I had to learn about Justice, Betrayal and Truth
TRUTH HAS NO MEANING UNLESS BREATHING IT, LIKE A WAVE THAT IS UNSTOPPABLE! THAT IS WHERE WE ARE AT!

It became so clear why Divine Timing is all we have and need to believe in,
Because when YOU become the Star that co-creates with Stars
All you know is UNIFICATION
THE QUESTION OF THIS AGE!!!

You and Me: We are the Power of this Age!

Do know I love U so, so much,
because I Understand NOW how my car functions!
This comes down to UNDERSTANDING WHAT U NEEDED TO GO THROUGH AND SEEING YOUR VIBE ON THE OTHER SIDE!
And reason why I could not publish this book before today as my Love needed to go through the Metal Prickle Fence to be able to take u into my arms!

Hope to meet u in the Meeting Room of The Sacred Mountains!

My wish, as we flow with the pentagram of 2021 is to truly see
Spiritual Physicians, Mathematicians and Scientist
lay down low with the snakes and allow for
THE REBEL, SPIRIT AND THE SCIENTIST to meet up.

Thank you so much for being with me,
thank you so much for streaming through this book as I believe,
it is not juts a story , it is a tale that needs to hit TRUTH!

Love, PreView

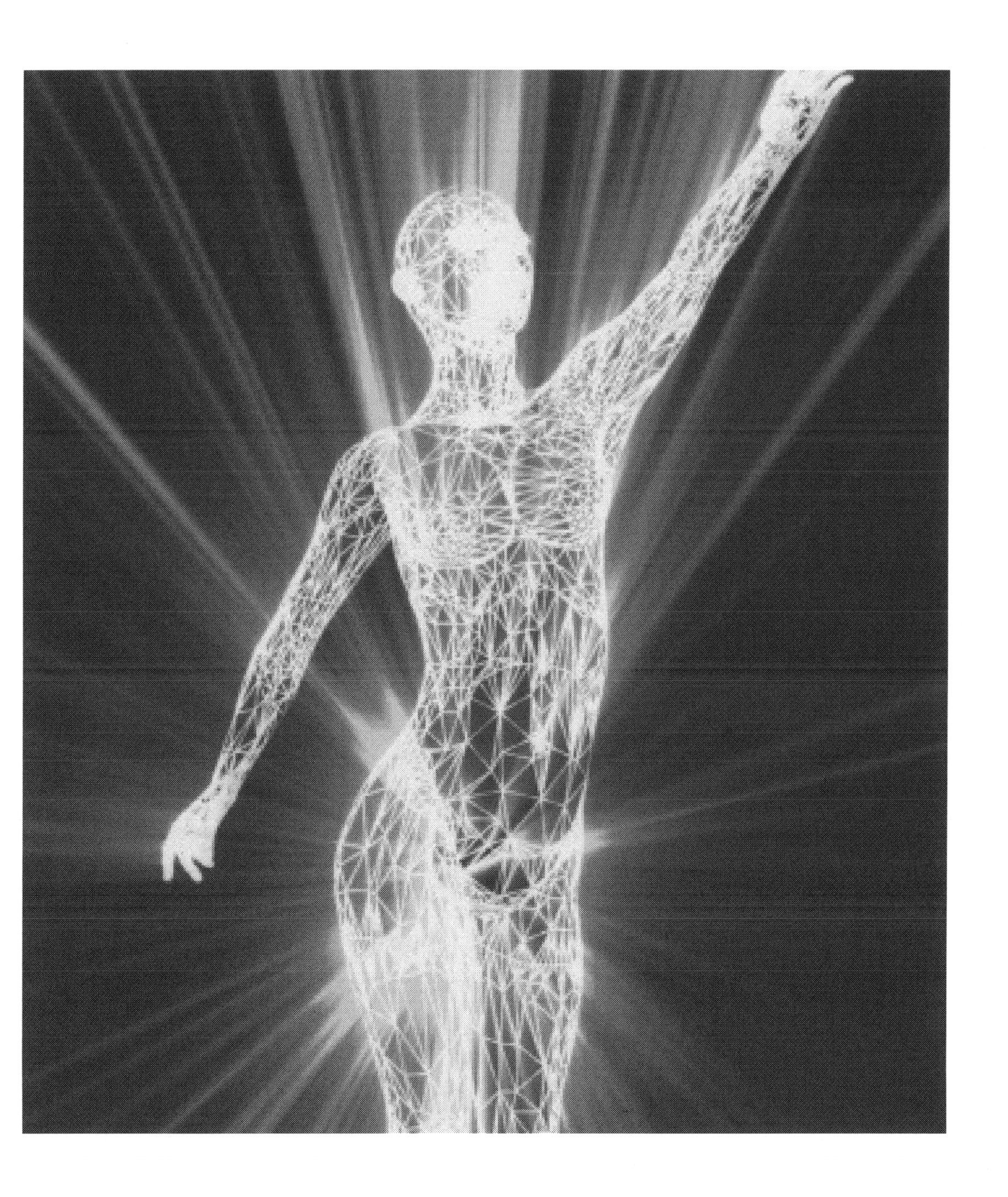

Printed in Great Britain
by Amazon

55575487R00280